D1035793

WITHDRAWN

1995
- 5

WITHDRAWN

The Claim of Reason

Other Books by Stanley Cavell

Must We Mean What We Say?
The Senses of Walden
The World Viewed

The Claim of Reason

WITTGENSTEIN, SKEPTICISM, MORALITY, AND TRAGEDY

STANLEY CAVELL

Truly speaking, it is not instruction, but provocation,
that I can receive from another soul.

> Ralph Waldo Emerson, "An Address Delivered
> before the Senior Class in Divinity College,
> Cambridge, Sunday evening, 15 July, 1838"

Clarendon Press · Oxford
Oxford University Press · New York
1979

Copyright © 1979 by Oxford University Press, Inc.

Library of Congress Cataloging in Publication Data
Cavell, Stanley, 1926–
The claim of reason.
Bibliography: p.   Includes index.
1. Knowledge, Theory of—Addresses, essays, lectures.
2. Skepticism—Addresses, essays, lectures.
3. Ethics—Addresses, essays, lectures.
4. Philosophy—Addresses, essays, lectures.   I. Title.
BD161.C355   121   78-26970   ISBN 0-19-502571-7

The author is grateful to Basil Blackwell of Mott Ltd.
for permission to quote from Wittgenstein's
Philosophical Investigations and *The Blue and Brown Books.*

Printed in the United States of America

121
C378c

Dedicated to Thompson Clarke
and to the memory of J. L. Austin

34165

34162

Contents

PART THREE
Knowledge and the Concept of Morality

PART FOUR
Skepticism and the Problem of Others

[Few of the following entries are meant as headings, as if each extends over the tracts of material to follow until another entry stops it, say like signs for city limits. They are better regarded as road signs: shifting numbers of them may simultaneously extend over one or more segments of the whole. Accordingly, these entries only accidentally coincide with the occasional large breaks left in the text between paragraphs. These breaks register convenient resting places, to let the mind clear, or a thought complete itself—matters which may or may not coincide with the introducing or the dropping of a theme.]

Foreword

The following pages contain writing of four distinct periods. The earliest is earlier (except for the title essay of *Must We Mean What We Say?*) than anything else I have published that I still use; the latest is later than everything else I have published. The present publication was supposed to be a revision of my Ph.D. dissertation, *The Claim to Rationality*, submitted to the Department of Philosophy at Harvard in 1961. But it is no more properly speaking a revision than its predecessor was properly speaking a dissertation.

I was on the road toward a proper dissertation (on the concept of human action) when, in 1955, J. L. Austin came to Harvard for a term, among other things to give as the William James Lectures his work on performative utterances (*How To Do Things with Words*, published posthumously in 1962). Austin also offered a graduate seminar on Excuses, the content of which is summarized in the essay of that title in his *Philosophical Papers*. This material, together with the procedures inspiring them — procedures some of us called ordinary language philosophy — knocked me off my horse.

Thus grounded, I came to the end of graduate studies, went to Berkeley to take up teaching, began some work that was incorporated into the early essays of *Must We Mean What We Say?**, and planned a new dissertation on the implications of Austin's procedures for moral philosophy — implications, let us say, of the sense that the human voice is being

* Unless separately listed in the bibliography, the essays of mine referred to individually are all collected in this volume.

xi

returned to moral assessments of itself. Some of that material remains here as the bulk of Part Three. These chapters on morality seem to me the most thesis-bound in this book. They were, in plans for the submitted dissertation which, for various reasons, fell through, to be followed by chapters which developed further certain of their guiding ideas. Some of those ideas still seem to me worth continuing. For example, that there are contrasting places in epistemological and in moral arguments in which one's "position" works itself out. Or again, that something of what we think goes into competence as a moral agent, the ability to excuse or justify or explain our actions (to elaborate them, as I come to say) is the same as something that goes into what we think of as competence at knowing oneself, a way of saying what one is doing, hence into what we think of as having a self (so that in such a way morality finds a foundation in knowledge). And again, that problems we summarize by speaking of weakness of the will can be studied by exploring the facts of games — especially of what it is which allows games to be forms of play, and to be practiced — which apparently allows games to sidestep these problems. And that moral discourse is not singly an order of public debate on issues known and taken to be of moment, but is a form of intimate examination, you might say private, by one soul of another. It teaches us to ask not alone, What is to be done?, but as well, What am I to do? And not just, Is what the other does acceptable?, but as well, How am I prepared to confront that other?

The shock for me in Austin's procedures was doubled by Thompson Clarke's ability to accept and absorb these procedures, almost completely, within rather than against the procedures of traditional epistemology. A certain readiness on my part to respond to Clarke's work was prepared, as he and I came early on to appreciate, by our having both accepted, in something like the same way, the genuineness of philosophical inspiration in the teaching of C. I. Lewis. I think I had not ever exactly thought that Austin's procedures simply repudiated traditional epistemology, but I know I had not thought, what Clarke's work seemed to me to show, that the dictates of ordinary language (doubtless including all the favorable things I had said about it in the essay "Must We Mean What We Say?") were as supportive as they were destructive of the enterprise of traditional epistemology. Since this discovery is as much about Austin's as it is about the tradition's procedures, I saw that, even saw where, I was going to have to take backward steps before moving onward again. This was borne out by my beginning serious study of *Philosophical Investigations*, in which the recurrence of skeptical voices, and answering voices, struck me as sometimes strangely casual and sometimes strangely conclusive, as sometimes devious and sometimes definitive. I knew reasonably soon thereafter and reasonably well that my fascination with the *Investigations* had to do with my response to it as a feat of writing. It was some years before I understood it as what I came to think of as a discovery for philosophy of the problem of the other; and further years before these issues looked to me like functions of one another. (Fascination with the *Investigations* had withheld itself from me for some six or seven years. I had looked at its first dozen dozen sections when it appeared in 1953, to prepare for a study group on the book conducted by Paul Ziff. In the course of what I remember as the three or four meetings of that group I found what Ziff was saying to be surprising and excellent, but the book itself I found boring. It appeared to me at best to be going over matters I had learned from pragmatism, especially from Dewey, but in a less trustworthy and less orderly fashion.)

Not confidently until around the center of Part Four, arrived at well over a decade after writing the submitted dissertation, would I feel that I was saying something fairly continuously at the right level for thinking usefully about the connection of writing and the problem of the other, and about the connection of both with my interest in a tradition, anyway an idea, of philosophizing opposed to the tradition in English, as that tradition is represented in the best English-speaking departments of philosophy. But I have made no effort to sophisticate my early, tentative, amateur efforts to link the English and the Continental traditions, because I want them to show that to realign these traditions, after their long mutual shunning, at any rate to write witnessing the loss in that separation, has been a formative aspiration of mine from the earliest of the work I refer to here. It remains an aspiration to define and to date a place of its overcoming. (My confidence in the reality of these issues, among others, is inextricably bound up in my mind with conversations over the past twenty years with Kurt Fischer.) In *The World Viewed,* and especially in *The Senses of Walden,* I found I had to, and felt that I could, write as though these paths had never divided. That is also sometimes the spirit of Part Four of the present book. But I should add that what makes this spirit possible for me has been, I think, that the philosophical pressure to comprehend this division or splitting between cultures has begun transforming itself for me into the pressure to comprehend the division between the writing of philosophy and the writing of literature, hence the splitting within (one) culture.

But the paths of philosophical traditions *have* divided, and the mutual

shunning, and doubtless the sometimes fatal attractions, have produced
further consequences since the time of my first desperation to rejoin them
(as if something inside myself had torn), particularly in developments in
French thought (you might epitomize them as a reception or appearance
of Freud) and their reception in turn in American literary studies (you
might see this as a displacement of Freud). I am not, not at any rate here
and now, prepared to speak to this. And of course there have been significant domestic alterations of the intellectual landscape since I began in
these pages to paint my way into and out of it. Naturally I have periodically felt that I should deliberately and systematically try to relate the
work of these pages to those alterations, as it were to keep bringing my
work up to date. In the end two thoughts prevailed against such an effort.
First, if the work presented here proves worth this relating, I am less well
placed to manage it than others will be. Second, my occasion, and a competing obligation, has seemed more specifically to me to be that of keeping lines open to the events within American academic philosophical life
that we can call the reception of ordinary language philosophy (sometimes called then Oxford philosophy, and represented here primarily by
some work of J. L. Austin's) together with that of Wittgenstein's *Investigations,* as if certain paths for philosophy, opened by those events, are
always in danger of falling into obscurity. If this reception comprises
events mainly of the fifties and early sixties, they are to be seen as one
significant reaction, the principal inner reaction, away from, or beyond,
the reception of logical positivism in the thirties and forties. The events
of the fifties and early sixties have not in turn, I believe, been reacted
against or outgrown so much as partially incorporated, producing, it
seems to me, a kind of immunized state. To keep lines open to them
would mean to show that philosophy can still be produced out of their
inspiration. Naturally I do not know whether I have been successful in
this demonstration, i.e., whether I have produced convincing philosophy
from that inspiration, but my ambition can be described as one in which
something in my work is, after all, being brought down to date.

 Of all the developments I have not tried to relate myself to systematically, or explicitly, one has seemed, to certain friends whose judgment
matters to me, to remain standing after my explanations and excuses have
done their level best, and that is the publication of other of Wittgenstein's later work subsequent to the appearance of *Philosophical Investigations.* Especially *On Certainty* seems to them to call for comment. I
find myself unable to agree to this. I cannot read Wittgenstein out of
curiosity, and why should I *force* myself to study him? I have found the

Investigations, I suppose more than any other work of this century, to be paradigmatic of philosophy for me, to be a dominating present of the history of philosophy for me. This has meant, as these things will, living with the sound of it, subjected to the sound. To find a certain freedom from that sound was therefore necessary if I was to feel I was finding my way to an investigation of my own preoccupations. This in practice meant discovering ways of writing which I could regard as philosophical and could recognize as sometimes extensions — hence sometimes denials — of Wittgenstein's, and of course also of those of any other writer from whom I make my way. I should say, accordingly, that as my book moves into its latest strata, and continuously after about the first fourth of Part Four, I no longer regard my citations of the *Investigations* as interpretations of it.

What appears here as the enclosed two Parts (Two and Three) constitutes the concluding two-thirds of the submitted dissertation. They have been more or less heavily edited, but the original structure and ideas and prose have in each case been kept intact. Had I not finally decided, after countless changes of heart, that they could be so kept, this book could not have appeared. Of the opening third of the submitted dissertation, just over one-quarter consists of an Introduction published separately as "The Availability of Wittgenstein's Later Philosophy"; it is sufficiently reprinted and is dropped from this occasion. What in it is necessary here has been specifically referred to; it is in effect replaced by the present Chapter I. The dropped Introduction together with the present Parts Two and Three account for all but about 100 pages of the original 440. An amount adding up to some half of that 100 was salvageable, in fragments running from individual sentences and paragraphs to two or three consecutive pages; these are interspersed among 100 newer pages to constitute Chapters II through V, i.e., the bulk of Part One. In sum, about three-fourths of the original material is preserved and constitutes about half of the present volume.

I go into these externals partly because I am not unaware that *The Claim to Rationality* has acquired a certain life of its own. Much of it circulated in mimeograph soon after its completion; a substantial idea of it is contained in Hannah Pitkin's *Wittgenstein and Justice* (1972); and the copies deposited in Widener Library at Harvard, I learned with pleasure and dismay when I went to its Archive to look at the original introduction, are regularly consulted and on loan. Such are of course significant reasons that my periodic decisions to let the matter rest in the Widener Archive have always been retracted. But partly I go into these externals because they are not externals. I remain, and no doubt must remain, imperfectly satisfied that work I would not, could not, write now should now appear. (Part Four is a different matter, to which I will come back.)

It may be of the nature of having something to say about Wittgenstein's later work that one is uncertain whether it is worth saying, or necessary to say, or whether it is common knowledge, perhaps already said, perhaps in his own words. (It seems to me that Rogers Albritton and Saul Kripke, in their remarks on the *Investigations* at the Wittgenstein Congress in London, Ontario, in the spring of 1976, were expressing similar opening sentiments before rehearsing ideas, many of which each of them said they had had for more than a decade.) I think one will the more strongly feel this uncertainty the more strongly one feels that the shape Wittgenstein's work takes is not arbitrary, that it was not willful of him not to have given it a more systematic cast (more truly: a differently systematic cast). For then one will feel both that Wittgenstein expressed himself as well as he can be expressed, and yet that there is something he did not or could not express.

To the extent that it is true of those who have sought to internalize Wittgenstein's teaching as part of the history or progression of philosophy that they are still living off their thoughts about that teaching at the time of their original conversion to it; and to the extent that they have not published those thoughts, or not expressed what made their reception most significant for themselves; to that extent it must seem that our philosophical culture has not had a use for these thoughts. Something similar is true of Austin's work. So it can seem that the reception of Wittgenstein and of Austin has yet to have its public or historical effect on this philosophical culture. I do not say that this is a bad thing. Wittgenstein's writing is not of a character that lends itself to professionalization (but just that should not distinguish it from Descartes's *Meditations:* how does the call to philosophy lend itself to professionalization?); and if Austin wished for professionalization, it was not to be as philosophy. Nor do I say that this lack of a certain reception is surprising. *Philosophical Investigations,* like the major modernist works of the past century at least, is, logically speaking, esoteric. That is, such works seek to split their audience into insiders and outsiders (and split each member of it); hence they create the particular unpleasantness of cults (at best as a specific against the particular unpleasantness of indifference or intellectual promiscuousness, combatting partialness by partiality); hence demand for their sincere reception the shock of conversion. If I say that the basis of the present publication is that Wittgenstein is still to be received, I mean to suggest that his work, and of course not his alone, is essentially and always *to be* received, as thoughts must be that would refuse professionalization.

I am reminded of a moment in a discussion some fifteen years ago at which a brilliant, successful, exasperated member of the philosophical profession said, "You know, it's possible that Wittgenstein was wrong about *something!*" Recalling the unpleasantness of cults, one must not ignore the sorts of behavior that can, in the most patient, justifiably produce such exclamations. But one must not make too much of such exclamations either. You could as helpfully say, "You know, it's possible that philosophy is wrong about something!" Without a doubt. — This should prompt us to consider that disciplines which live on criticism — call them philosophical disciplines — understand themselves as subject only to particular terms and forms of criticism, and at the same time as providing universal criticisms of other disciplines; and to consider that in a modern era intellectual works with designs upon the most serious attention of their culture must give themselves out as, or allow themselves to be appropriated as, philosophies. A consequence, or cause, of this situation, where no ground or direction of thought or of art is accepted as more fundamental than another (except by fundamentalists) is that criticism becomes incessant or totalized — sometimes it flies to the level of the reductive, sometimes it floats to the level of unmasking. — Wittgenstein confesses, or rather cloaks himself as subject to the accusation, that his work "seems only to destroy everything interesting, that is, all that is great and important" (*Investigations*, §118). His consolation is to reply that "What we are destroying is nothing but structures of air . . .". (I translate literally in order to let out the Zen sound.) But after such consolation, what consolation? — What feels like destruction, what expresses itself here in the idea of destruction, is really a shift in what we are asked to let interest us, in the tumbling of our ideas of the great and the important, as in conversion. Who knows what will cause such a shift and tumbling? Sometimes satire works; sometimes shame does not. Sometimes the loss of old interest is so scary that one seeks to convert anything but oneself — say philosophy into science, or language into logic, or film into language. Sometimes one is right. I have known some who have taken Wittgenstein, early or late, as the last word of philosophy, and who have thereupon left the field of philosophy, perhaps in favor of a field. And it seems to me that a certain motivation to philosophy — by no means the least ancient nor the least honorable motivation — leaves one subjected in one's work to doubts about whether one is in the right place, whether there is a workable field in this place at all, doubts about the character of one's talents, or conviction, or interest, or about one's taste, or lack of it, for arguments that forever seem on the wrong ground. — What follows may be thought of as the record of one who stayed.

The four periods of writing, or strata, in this book are as follows. (1) The submitted dissertation, put into consecutive prose in the six months preceding its submission in April 1961, was a culling from manuscripts composed over the three years since the writing of "Must We Mean What We Say?" in December 1957. I knew of two matters that required attention before I could honor the contract to have the dissertation published. I felt sure that something was wrong with what was for some who read it early its most notable feature, the understanding of Wittgenstein's notion of a criterion; and I knew that I had more or less suppressed, out of dissatisfaction, what thoughts I had had concerning the problem of other minds. By 1965 or so I arrived at a development of the notion of a criterion that continues to satisfy me, and within a year or two thereafter (during which the ideas incorporated in "Knowing and Acknowledging" were in play) I was also lecturing on the material on other minds that appears here as roughly the first fourth of Part Four, leading up to the proposal of the question of soul-blindness. Although I devoted my ensuing sabbatical term (fall 1967) to completing the final essays (including the introductory essay) of *Must We Mean What We Say?*, I felt confident enough with the work that was included there, and the work it implied, to announce in its opening Acknowledgments the imminent publication of *The Claim to Rationality*. (2) The full extent of my rashness in making this announcement only showed itself to me during 1970–71, when a year's leave of absence enabled me to accomplish the reworking of Part One and the writing out of the material on other minds mentioned as the first part of Part Four. For by then I had also completed the drafts of manuscripts to be published as *The World Viewed* (1971) and *The Senses of Walden* (1972), and the conclusions so far achieved in the dissertation revision seemed to me outstripped by those pieces, however much they all seemed to me parts of one another. (3) Soon after I began my next stretch of freedom, the successive fall terms of 1973 and 1974, I knew the direction the conclusion was hauling itself toward, and I knew that it would never leave the house apart from it. The conclusion had to do with the connection of the two concluding essays of *Must We Mean What We Say?* ("Knowing and Acknowledging" and "The Avoidance of Love: A Read-

ing of *King Lear*"), the reciprocation between the ideas of acknowledgment and of avoidance, for example as the thought that skepticism concerning other minds is not skepticism but is tragedy. How I might *arrive*
at such a conclusion was distinctly less clear. What emerged during those
autumns and winters, which is to say during the writing of most of Part
Four, was something I more and more came to regard, or to accept, even
to depend upon, as the keeping of a limited philosophical journal. Writing it was like the keeping of a journal in two main respects. First, the
autonomy of each span of writing is a more important goal than smooth,
or any, transitions between spans (where one span may join a number of
actual days, or occupy less than one full day). This ordering of goals tends
to push prose to the aphoristic. (For example, as I wrote I came upon a
number of formulas for relating skepticism and tragedy. If today I were
to be continuing from the place Part Four concludes, I might begin by
remarking that I am no more skeptical of the existence of others than I
am skeptical of the necessity of my own death. I know that I cannot doubt
it; yet I do not know that I know it.) Second, there would be no point, or
no hope, in showing the work to others until the life, or place, of which
it was the journal, was successfully, if temporarily, left behind, used up.
I felt progress toward that departure, but the question was always whether
it would happen in accordance with the academic calendar. (4) It almost
did; anyway, closely enough so that its public finish could wait until the
next time I could see several clear months ahead, which proved to be the
summer and early fall of 1977.

From beginning to end the writing of these pages has been more or less
bound up with talking, sometimes with lecturing, sometimes with conversations (sometimes imaginary) with friends, some of whom were colleagues, some students, some imaginary. Virtually all of the material of
the submitted dissertation was broached in lectures and seminars at Berkeley over the years 1957 to 1961. It seems to me that for those four years I
was engaged together with six or seven graduate students and with three
or four colleagues in all but continuous argument, sometimes consisting
of friendly exchange, sometimes of (temporarily, but you couldn't be sure)
estranging dispute, set generally in one of my classes, or perhaps in one
of Thompson Clarke's, or else it was in a corridor of Dwinelle Hall, or in
its minimal coffee shop, or in the large Teaching Assistant office, and
often Kurt Fischer was there, and there was Thomas Kuhn. I do not think
I exaggerate the continuity of the discussions over those years; I know I
cannot exaggerate the importance of that intellectual companionship. We
seemed at times almost in possession of something you might call an in-

tellectual community, and sometimes one or other of us said as much. It is an essential part of my indebtedness to the work of Austin and of Wittgenstein that it, for a time at least, helped make possible such a visible community, or the concrete hope of one. I hope that those whom I no longer see who participated in those times recognize some of them, and something of themselves, in what follows. Of that group of students I allow myself to single out the name of Philip Hugly, an exchange or two with whom at a critical time on the topic of other minds weighed strongly with me.

I have had occasion in previous books to mention some friends and students who have influenced me since I moved back to Harvard in the fall of 1963. Here in addition I must thank first Margaret Drach for having helped to show me what was off about what I had written, and how I was lecturing, about the relation of grammar and criteria, especially in relation to the passage from the *Blue Book* discussed in the present Chapter IV. In January of 1972 I presented what material I could in a series of five or six seminar discussions with the faculty and graduate students of the Department of Philosophy at the University of California at Santa Barbara, a period as immensely congenial as it was helpful. My notes for and from those discussions were of direct service to me in orienting the stretch of writing I began the following year.

In recent years I have counted on regular conversations with Norton Batkin and with William Rothman, not infrequently the three of us together, on just about any and every topic in this book. It seems to me that I have never left one of those conversations without taking encouragement and instruction with me. Peter Hylton's careful reading of the manuscript resulted in a number of corrections and clarifications I am glad to have entered. Late conversations with Jay Cantor and with Louis Goldring helped me find my way to formulations allowing me to insert pieces I had until then tried but failed to place. Still later, Arnold Davidson pointed to, and helped find ways to avert, several serious misunderstandings. And I now add the reading of the present book in manuscript to the other causes I have to be grateful to the collegial and the friendly offices of Burton Dreben and of Robert Nozick. The questions or reservations they have expressed to me go too far to be much taken into account in the few modifications I have made in response to them. They are matters to be pondered, and at a level which itself is encouraging to me.

My indebtedness to Thompson Clarke is so systematic and of such long standing that I want to give a little specification of it, particularly in view of his having to date published just two extracts from the work of his I have profited so much from. The whole idea of visualizing the Cartesian investigation through an Austinian format was his; so was the explicit emphasis on matters of the stage-setting of the investigation, matters I sometimes call "the rehearsal of beliefs" or "the skeptical recital"; and the way I expose the material concerning "the amount seen" in Chapter VIII, in the section entitled "The Philosopher's Projection . . .", is due directly to the work of his that later appeared in *Philosophy in America*, edited by Max Black. Contributions of mine were of such things as the concept of the generic object, of the differing "morals" of different failures of knowledge, of the description of the "non-claim" context, and of the interpretation of that context as one at once inevitable for the human being and a denial of the human. From the first, I contrasted such considerations, developed in responding to skepticism with respect to the external world, with their working out in the companion case, often contrary, of knowing other minds. One of my first expressions of my contrary intuitions about these cases was to say that at the conclusion of the material object case I was left sealed inside the circle of my own experiences, whereas at the end of the other minds case I was left sealed outside the circle of the other's experiences. The presence of such expressions in the present book reveals me as the, or one of the, "intuitive philosophers" cited in Clarke's "The Legacy of Skepticism". That paper of Clarke's was the starting point for a graduate seminar he and I offered for the term he visited Harvard (spring 1974). And that occasion inspired me to press as far as I could the symmetries and asymmetries that kept seeming to me to matter in thinking the relation between the material object and the other minds regions of skepticism; this turned out to free me for the fresh start I needed in order to get on with Part Four. As late as the late spring of 1977, in Berkeley, there were days of discussion with Clarke (some of which Barry Stroud notably contributed to) which would make their presence felt in the winding up of my manuscript.

The occasion of this Foreword would not be complete for me without the pleasure of thanking Bernard Williams for his encouragement and criticism of my work, most especially in conversations during an otherwise dismal period of my life, in the early months of 1963. Nor without the pleasure at least of listing the names of David Hilger, Vivian Kerman, Belle Randall, Mary Randall, Eugene Smith, Bob Thompson, and Nancy Watson, each of whom will know his and her contributions toward launching and docking this book. — Such a list is something whose personal significance to me is quite out of proportion to its essential insignificance to strangers, and is thus at deliberate odds with the bright side of the intention to write. But I include it, beyond its sentimental value for me, and beyond its signal that writing has its dark sides, to suggest an answer to those who have been curious whether my tendency toward elaborately detailed acknowledgments hasn't some resonance with my intellectual interest in the concept of acknowledgment generally. What it suggests is that an elaboration of acknowledgment may declare a sense that complete acknowledgment is impossible, perhaps forbidden for one reason or another; and perhaps that one senses oneself for one reason or another to be insufficiently acknowledged. — If someone does not find such thoughts properly prefatory, I might offer instead the idea of a democratic equivalent of the Epistle Dedicatory, together with an aimless revival of the Epistle to the Reader.

Yet again I express heartfelt gratitude to Wesleyan University's Center for the Humanities where, taking up my residence for the year 1970–71, I spent the first months on the revisions which produced what appears here as Part One. In the summer and fall of 1974 a Senior Fellowship from the National Endowment for the Humanities gave me the time for what I earlier called "arriving at the conclusion" in Part Four.

Not for the first time, and I hope not the last, I am indebted to Mrs. Peg Griffin, Administrative Assistant of the Department of Philosophy at Harvard, for organizing and participating in the preparation of pages of mine for publication. I have, in this regard, again to thank Norton Batkin for his meticulous care in sharing the chore of correcting galley proof. A number of improvements of style and of substance are due to his discernment.

My daughter Rachel appears in these pages recurrently, at greatest length in Chapter VII, where the topic is the learning and the teaching of a word, and the issue is explicitly whether generations are to come to talk together. She was about three years old when I wrote that material, and we have found, over the eighteen years intervening, that we, I think I may say, speak the same language.

My lawyer, Cathleen Cohen Cavell, to whom I am married, and our son Benjamin, a year younger than the Rachel of those early pages, took time I thought I did not have and converted it into energy I thought I had forgone.

Greetings to you all.

S.C.

Emerson Hall
Cambridge, Massachusetts,
Saturday, July 15, 1978

PART ONE

Wittgenstein and the Concept
of Human Knowledge

This philosophy does not rest on an Understanding *per se,* on an absolute, nameless understanding, belonging one knows not to whom, but on the understanding of man; — though not, I grant, on that of man enervated by speculation and dogma; — and it speaks the language of men, not an empty, unknown tongue.

LUDWIG FEUERBACH

I

Criteria and Judgment

If not at the beginning of Wittgenstein's later philosophy, since what starts philosophy is no more to be known at the outset than how to make an end of it; and if not at the opening of *Philosophical Investigations*, since its opening is not to be confused with the starting of the philosophy it expresses, and since the terms in which that opening might be understood can hardly be given along with the opening itself; and if we acknowledge from the commencement, anyway leave open at the opening, that the way this work is written is internal to what it teaches, which means that we cannot understand the manner (call it the method) before we understand its work; and if we do not look to our history, since placing this book historically can hardly happen earlier than placing it philosophically; nor look to Wittgenstein's past, since then we are likely to suppose that the *Investigations* is written in criticism of the *Tractatus*, which is not so much wrong as empty, both because to know what constitutes its criticism would be to know what constitutes its philosophy, and because it is more to the present point to see how the *Investigations* is written in criticism of itself; then where and how are we to approach this text? How shall we let this book teach us, this or anything?

I will say first, by way of introducing myself and saying why I insist, as I will throughout the following pages, upon the *Investigations* as a philosophical text, that I have wished to understand philosophy not as a set of problems but as a set of texts. This means to me that the contribution of a philosopher — anyway of a creative thinker — to the subject of philosophy is not to be understood as a contribution to, or of, a set of *given* problems, although both historians and non-historians of the subject are given to suppose otherwise. — And is the remark about texts and not problems itself to be taken as a philosophical text? It seems argumentative or empty enough, since obviously not all texts are philosophical ones, but only those that precisely contain problems of a certain sort! — The fact that the remark is short would be no bar to that status. Many philosophical texts are short, like the tattle tale told by a Cretan, or the story about the tree falling in the forest for no one to hear. Some philosophers are able to make about anything into a philosophical text, like a preacher improving upon the infant's first cry; while some people are not even able to start a quarrel with God. Some texts are as long as long books, but generally treated as though they are sets of given problems, something between conundrums and formal arguments, e.g., Hume's *Treatise*, which few seem actually to believe but which many feel compelled to try to outsmart; as if so *much* argument just oughn't to stand unanswered; as if to contribute a text were a kind of defacement; as if argumentative victory *consisted* in spoils. Some philosophical texts are as short as short books, e.g., Descartes's *Meditations*, which so refines our essential options for philosophical belief that thinkers have seemed, since its appearance, and whether invited or not, compelled to reply to it; as if so *little* argument just oughn't to stand unanswered. When its conclusions have seemed more or less disreputable its repliers have focussed on its "methods", hoping to head the conclusions off, or outnumber them. But I think one feels the knack of the methods (call it the arrogance) to be missed, which is no doubt something that perpetuates fascination with this text; as though its repliers find it incredible that one could, truly and legitimately, *use oneself* (clearly and distinctly) in arriving at conclusions so strange and so familiar. But in philosophy to find that position incredible may well amount to disbelieving that one could oneself contribute a philosophical text. Some philosophical texts are for practical purposes as unending as the writings of, for example, Kant or Hegel, where the problem resides largely in mastering the text itself, hence in commentary; as though if one could believe *all* of it there would from then on be no isolating problems of belief left. (So Kierkegaard condemned the system; so Nietzsche contemned it.) Here contribution consists in opting to be marginal (which is of course not the only way of *being* marginal). (You may think of these instances as beginning a budget of philosophical genres or paradigms. Then someone will think that I have been arrogantly neglectful of the genre of the academic paper, modest in its aims, content with its minor addition to a subject greater than itself. About the comparative greatness of the subject over its subjects I have no doubt. But I would be more convinced of academic modesty had I not seen many who are daily surprised that, for example, Descartes or Pascal or Rousseau, or the spirit of religion or of rationalism or of romanticism, has survived the criticism fashioned in their essays on the subject a few years back. I speak of professional lives, frightening matters.)

A measure of the quality of a new text is the quality of the texts it arouses. That a text may exist primarily in an oral tradition would not counter my thought here. Though the fact that it exists primarily in an oral tradition may determine the size or shape of its response, i.e., of an acceptable contribution to its text. I may say that while Wittgenstein's philosophizing is more completely attentive to the human voice than any other I think of, it strikes me that its teaching is essentially something written, that some things essential to its teaching cannot be spoken. This may mean that some things he says have lost, or have yet to find, the human circle in which they can usefully be said.

(If one asks: When *must* a work, or task, be written, or permanently marked?, one may start thinking what makes a work, or task, *memorable*. And of course the answer to this alone should not distinguish philosophy from, say, music or poetry or early astronomy or ruler and compass proofs in geometry (or, I wish I knew, what level of logic?). Poetry (some poetry) need not be written; novels must be. It seems to me that a thought I once expressed concerning the development of music relates to this. I said ("Music Discomposed", pp. 200, 201) that at some point in Beethoven's work you can no longer relate what you hear to a process of improvisation. Here I should like to add the thought that at that point music, such music, *must* be written. If one may speculate that at such a stage a musical work of art requires parts that are unpredictable from one another (though after the fact, upon analysis, you may say how one is derivable from the other), then one may speculate further that Beethoven's sketches were necessary both because not all ideas are ready for use upon their appearance (because not ready ever in any but their right company), and also because not all are usable in their initial appearance, but must first, as it were, grow outside the womb. What must be sketched must be written. If what is in a sketch book is jotted just for saving, just to await its company, with which it is then juxtaposed as it stands, you may say the juxtaposition, or composition, is that of the lyric. If it is sketched knowing that it must be, and gets in time, transformed in order to take its place, you may say that its juxtaposition, or composition, is essentially stratified and partitioned; that of the drama; the drama of the metaphysical, or of the sonata. Here are different tasks for criticism, or tasks for different criticisms.)

But I was supposed to be saying more, having said something first, by way of introducing myself, and concerning how we should approach Wittgenstein's text. Accordingly, I will say, second, that there is no approach to it, anyway I have none. Approach suggests moving nearer, getting closer; hence it suggests that we are not already near or close enough; hence suggests we know some orderly direction to it not already taken within it; that we sense some distance between us and it which useful criticism could close.

Leaving myself, I trust, without an approach, I find a blur or block from which to start, a turn in Wittgenstein's thought that I can report as having for a long time seemed to me both strange and familiar, far and near. It concerns his recurrent idea of a criterion. I would not wish, if I could, to dissipate this sense of far and near about it; on the contrary. But a superficial cause of its strangeness dawned on me only after some years of acquaintance with the *Investigations,* I mean the trivial fact that the notion of a criterion is an everyday one and the somewhat less trivial fact that Wittgenstein's account of it, while not exactly the same notion, is dependent upon the everyday one. And in the light of what I have read and heard on the topic, I believe that my difficulty in coming to this pair of facts may not be uncommon, and therefore still worth mentioning and assessing.

It is, of course, not hard to make out that the notion of a criterion is "important" in the *Investigations.* Wittgenstein characterizes his investigations as grammatical ones, and an essential feature of such investigations is the eliciting of what he calls criteria. His explicit characterizations of these notions are as obscure as any obscurity he permits himself (and he is, about that, quite tolerant): "Grammar tells what kind of object anything is" (§373); "Essence is expressed by grammar" (§371); "An 'inner process' stands in need of outward criteria" (§580). Such obscurity may be a fault in a philosopher. But the greater the attachment to a concept (as to a person, or to a god), the harder it may be to explain either the attachment or the concept; or perhaps it should be said that everything one does is, or could be, the only explanation of it.

Then let us ask: What are Wittgensteinian criteria supposed to do? On the part both of those who wish to defend Wittgenstein and those who wish to attack him, it is taken, roughly, that his criteria are supposed to be the means by which the existence of something is established with certainty — in perhaps the most famous case, that the criteria of pain (outward criteria of course) are the means by which we can know with certainty that another is in pain (that what we say is going on in the other really is now going on there). The two most forceful presentations of this view remain, for me, that of Norman Malcolm in his early and important review of the *Investigations,* and that of Rogers Albritton in his essay "On Wittgenstein's Use of the Term 'Criterion' ". The permanent value of this view lies in its awareness that Wittgenstein's teaching is everywhere controlled by a response to skepticism, or, as I will prefer to say, by a response to the threat of skepticism. The view takes Wittgenstein's motivation with respect to skepticism as that of showing it to be false. (I do not, as will come out, take Malcolm and Albritton as agreeing on all significant points; just on these points about skepticism.) I might put it as the first phase of my argument to show that criteria cannot do this and, on my reading of the *Investigations,* are not meant to. On the contrary, the fate of criteria, or their limitation, reveals, I should like to say, the truth of skepticism — though of course this may require a reinterpretation of what skepticism is, or threatens.

There is a companion reason for a defender of Wittgenstein to attempt to make out such a view of criteria as Malcolm and Albritton have done. If the presence of criteria settle as little as, on my reading, they evidently do, then it would seem on the face of it that they are not so much as serious contenders in the battle to turn aside skepticism. So before indicating, in Chapter II, why the Malcolm-Albritton view cannot be right, I want to say what this crucial little is that criteria are meant to settle; or why, on what representation, it appears so little.

The thought that Wittgenstein is counting on the ordinary notion of a criterion ought to seem an unpromising line for a beginning. There seems no prospect that the ordinary notion could do all the work he can appear to count on his appeals to criteria to do, whatever that work turns out to be; which is a very good explanation for the prospect's not being considered. Still, the force of the notion may depend on keeping it as simple as possible for as long as possible. And it is, once one heads into it, somewhat abashing to find that the bulk of Wittgenstein's rhetoric in manipulating the term "criterion" is just the rhetoric of the ordinary word: he speaks, for example, of criteria as possessed by certain persons or groups of persons (they are "mine" or "ours"); of their being "adopted" or "accepted"; of their forming a "kind of definition"; of there being various criteria for something or other "under certain circumstances"; of their association with "what we call" something; and of their showing what something "consists in" or what "counts as" something. But all this turns out to be just the ordinary rhetorical structure of the ordinary word "criterion". To show that this is a significant fact about Wittgenstein's usage, we need a more detailed view of this rhetorical structure.

The following are instances I have collected, at random, of ordinary uses of the word:

A. "American officials listed four criteria for judging a government here [in Saigon] as stable: ability to maintain law and order in the cities, the capacity to raise and support effective armed forces, an adequate degree of protection for vital American and Vietnamese installations, and the presence of responsible officials with whom their American counterparts can conduct useful discussion." [*New York Times,* Wednesday, November 25, 1964]

B. "The sole criterion for me is whether it [a poem] can sweep me with it into emotion . . ." [Hans Zinsser, quoted in W. K. Wimsatt, *The Verbal Icon*]

C. "In language, the African tradition aims at circumlocution rather than at exact definition. The direct statement is considered crude and unimaginative; the veiling of all contents in ever-changing paraphrase is considered the criterion of intelligence and personality. In music, the same tendency toward obliquity and ellipsis is noticeable . . ." [Ernest Borneman, in *Jazz,* eds. Hentoff and McCarthy]

D. "It is thus impracticable to use for the evaluation of an infantile neurosis the same criteria which we apply in the care of an adult." [Anna Freud, *The Psychoanalytic Treatment of Children*]

E. "Since the color and size of paper, ink, and handwriting, and the stationer's mark had led to the identification of one distinguishable group of leaves, I went on to see if differences in these points in the remaining leaves would identify other distinct groups. They did so. No single criterion was conclusive by itself in establishing further groups, but all the criteria taken together were generally decisive. The relations of the contents of the groups confirmed or corrected the reading of the physical signs." [J. Lyndon Shanley, *The Making of Walden*]

F. Official Register of Harvard — Information regarding Radcliffe for prospective students — 1968–69:

p. 107 — Freshman admissions —

   — Radcliffe assumes high degree of intelligence . . .
   — Other qualities considered of major importance in final choices:
         Personal integrity
         Sense of social responsibility
         Ability to work independently
         Stamina to carry out demanding work
                     ("Major factors in deciding a candidate's
                     eligibility for Radcliffe")

— Also other qualities, more difficult to define:
        Liveliness of mind
        Breadth of interests
        Flexibility of temperament
        Stability
        Maturity

"Beyond these criteria . . . Radcliffe hopes for diverse student body."

G. "Arguing against Kovalevsky's view that three of the four main criteria of Germano-Roman feudalism were to be found in India, which ought therefore to be regarded as feudal, Marx points out that Kovalevsky forgets among other things serfdom, which is not of substantial importance in India." [Eric J. Hobsbawm, Introduction to Marx, *Pre-Capitalist Economic Formations*]

H. "Society before the Great Depression and the Second World War was much less equalitarian than it has since become. Among the main criteria for distinguishing the strata from each other was their respectability, their diligence and dutifulness, their capacity and readiness to persist faithfully in a given task and their willingness to submit their performances to the assessment of authorities they regarded as legitimate." [Edward Shils, "Of Plentitude and Scarcity," *Encounter*, May 1969]

From such examples, I extract seven elements as functioning in the ordinary idea of a criterion:

1. Source of authority
2. Authority's mode of acceptance
3. Epistemic goal
4. Candidate object or phenomenon
5. Status concept
6. Epistemic means (specification of criteria)
7. Degree of satisfaction (standards or tests for applying #6)

      See table p. 10

On this lay-out, criteria are specifications a given person or group sets up on the basis of which (by means of, in terms of which) to judge (assess, settle) whether something has a particular status or value. Different formulations bring it closer to other regions of Wittgenstein's surface rhetoric: Certain specifications are what a person or group mean by (what they call, count as) a thing's having a certain status; the specifications define the status; the status consists in satisfying those specifications. (E.g., "American officials in this case define stability as . . ."; "Stability here consists in . . .".)

Granted the general similarity between this ordinary or official idea of a criterion and Wittgenstein's idea, it is illuminating to note a series of discrepancies or disanalogies between them.

	(A)	(B)	(C)	(D)	(E)	etc.
1. Source of authority	American officials	I	Africans	Anna Freud	Shanley	
2. Authority's mode of acceptance	set up, established	use, take, care about	consider	recommends	tried out	
3. Epistemic goal	to judge	to tell, evaluate	to prove	to evaluate	to identify conclusively	
4. Candidate object or phenomenon	government	poem	a person	children	leaf (of manuscript)	
5. Status concept	stable	valuable, successful	intelligent	neurotic	belonging to a group	
6. Epistemic means (specification of criteria)	law and order, raise and support, supply protection, etc.	can sweep me	ever-changing para-phrase	[different from adult]	color and size of paper, etc.	
7. Degree of satisfaction (standards or tests for applying #6)						

Begin by looking at the seventh element ("Degree of satisfaction"). While this is not mentioned explicitly in the examples I have cited, it seems clearly enough entailed in each. It introduces explicitly the idea of standards, the idea of a determination of the degree or grade at which a thing manifests or satisfies the specifications in question. Both criteria and standards are means by which or terms in which a given group judges or selects or assesses value or membership in some special status; but criteria, we might say, determine whether an object is (generally) of the right kind, whether it is a relevant candidate at all, whereas standards discriminate the degree to which a candidate satisfies those criteria. In varying contexts, one or other of these levels may be taken for granted, and one or other of them may be highly articulated. The cases raised by my examples indicate various reasons, in different contexts, for wishing or having to leave open the issue of standards. In the psychoanalytic instance, only an expert is able to assess the fit of the criteria with the individual case; in the instance of the African's view of intelligence, assuming the reporter is right about the criterion of inventiveness, only a member of the group will be able to say with authority how fully a given person manifests it; in the case of sorting manuscript leaves, once the criteria are defined, and supposing the collection of candidates are fairly gross in their differences, anyone would be able to sort them reliably, the issue of standards would in practice not arise; in the American assessment of Saigon governments, the issue of standards is at least as critical as the issue of criteria, so to leave the issue of standards open must be either deluded or devious. That general criteria or standards may require further specification (further criteria and standards) for their application is not intellectually vicious, but merely gives occasion for particular forms of moral and political noxiousness. In the case of Radcliffe admissions, who gets in is obviously going to be a matter of what standards or tests are used to determine the fit of the announced criteria in the individual case. In such contexts, social or political influence may get a given individual admitted who fails to meet the expected standards; but while the institution may in a given case feel this is justified for reasons of state, it also feels clearly enough that the intellectual issue is settled — to the extent it can be settled objectively — by the question of standards. (When, under the recent pressures upon institutions of higher education to correct social injustices that society at large is unwilling or unable to correct, an institution accedes to this demand in certain new ways, some will say that any adjustment from the results of the conventional tests, even within the announced range of criteria, is necessarily "lowering standards", whereas some others pressing the demand will say that justice requires a redefinition (a recasting of the criteria) of the institution as such. So "political" in some mouths refers to adjustments or eradications which make exceptions in individual cases; in others, it refers to adjustments or eradications of the system which is empowered to define the individual as central or exceptional.)

There are familiar practices — preëminently, contests — in which criteria are explicitly granted and emphasis falls wholly upon standards: for example, Kennel Club or Horse Shows, or diving competitions. It is essential to the conduct of such practices that the criteria in terms of which candidates are judged are sufficiently lucid to be known and understood and agreed upon exhaustively by those involved in the practice; it is what makes possible the civility in these forms of assertion. This is registered in the fact that the element of *judging* is isolable as a separate office within such institutions. The judge has a more or less clear area of discretion in the application of standards, but none whatever over the set of criteria he is obliged to apply. It is expected that judges will differ over how *well* the diver entered the water (such is the point of having judges), but not over whether excellence of entry into the water *is* a criterion of the excellence of a dive. (And judges who differ ought to be differing in their full judgment, not differing in some degree to which they hedge their judgments. The diving judge who writes "5" (on a scale of 10) beside the element "Water Entry" on his sheet, is not saying that there is a 50% probability that the diver satisfied this criterion. A 50% probability of rain is, one might say, a 50% probability that the criteria of rain will be satisfied; but not: a 50% satisfaction of the criteria of rain; which, if anything, suggests drizzle.) Some citizens wish judges of law to be understood on this model; others are glad they cannot be so restricted. Like judges in competitive games, the name itself implies that the office is incompetent to alter the criteria by which it decides the individual case; but it is expected that a given case in law may raise controversy over just which established criteria it satisfies or escapes. The work of the judge, in such instances, must be to decide the identity of the case in question, i.e., decide which established criteria, if any, apply to it, i.e., decide the question and the criteria of the question simultaneously. This situation has been described as one in which "judges make the law, not merely apply it", a condition some find incompatible with democratic rule of law and others find essential to it. There may be historical stretches in which judges habitually either "merely apply" or "make" law; but as a neutral description of the process of deciding cases and criteria together, it presents a false alternative, or a false picture. In reaching his decision, the judge is obliged, in faithfulness to his office, to be open to and to provide arguments of an institutionally recognizable character; and the point of such argument is to allow, if possible, a natural extension of the body of law, which is neither merely applying existent law nor simply making new law. The guiding myth must be that it is not the judge but the case itself which extends the law. Justice will depend upon this being true, and being seen to be true, more often than not. Umpires are more restricted even than judges in shows or meets. Their guiding myth is that they merely *see* whether the criteria and standards are met, and simply call what they see, i.e., call it out publicly. One of their explicit areas of discretion concerns the edges of plays in which intention is at issue (e.g., deciding whether a player went for a competing player or for the ball in that player's reach). Internal to the different restrictions and discretions of show judges, judges in law, and umpires are the direction and outcome of competition in the cases each must judge. Show judges and umpires have no authority to choose or alter or extend, however naturally, the criteria they are bound by; but umpires do not decide who wins, the score tells; and the divers (say) are not competing primarily against one another, but each against the perfect dive. Judges in law do decide the win and loss (leaving aside jury trials) and their extents, and the adversaries are in competition with one another; but what they are in competition for is exactly the favor of the law, so settlement is not determinable here by the score publicly amassed, but only by the favorable or unfavorable response of the law. This is why justice under law depends as essentially upon the obligation of the law to respond as upon its obligation to respond fairly; and hence upon the right and the power to ask for the law's response.

Now the disanalogy here with Wittgenstein's ideas I can put this way. In no case in which he appeals to the application of criteria is there a separate stage at which one might, explicitly or implicitly, appeal to the application of standards. To have criteria, in his sense, for something's being so is to know whether, in an individual case, the criteria do or do not apply. If there is doubt about the application, the case is in some way "non-standard". This means that we have no decisive criteria for it, as we haven't "for all eventualities". And this is itself informative about the case, as it is sometimes to answer a question by saying "Yes and No"; for example, Is Schoenberg's *Book of the Hanging Garden* a tonal work?;

Can you play chess without the queen?; some would say, Can machines think? is such a question. What would be the point of deciding upon a more definite answer — I mean, a shorter answer — to these questions?

The second disanalogy I note with Wittgenstein's ideas concerns the nature of the "objects" which are candidates for judgment (the fourth element) together with the concepts which assign to the objects a certain "status" (the fifth element). In official cases in which criteria are appealed to, the object in question is one which in some obvious way requires evaluation or assessment, one whose status or ranking needs determining or settling. The point of setting up or establishing criteria is to allow these evaluations and decisions to be as rational (consistent and coherent and impersonal and non-arbitrary) as possible. Wittgenstein's candidates for judgment are not of this kind; they neither raise nor permit an obvious question of evaluation or competitive status. Remember the sorts of things Wittgenstein appeals to criteria to determine: whether someone has a toothache, is sitting on a chair, is of an opinion, is expecting someone between 4 and 4:30, was able to go on but no longer is; is reading, thinking, believing, hoping, informing, following a rule; whether it's raining; whether someone is talking to himself, attending to a shape or a color, whether he means to be doing something, whether what he does is for him done as a matter of course, etc. Such "objects" and concepts seem quite unspecial; they are, we might say, just the ordinary objects and concepts of the world. If *these* concepts require special criteria for their application, then any concept we use in speaking about anything at all will call for criteria. And is this true?

Wittgenstein's insight, or implied claim, seems to be something like this, that all our knowledge, everything we assert or question (or doubt or wonder about . . .) is governed not merely by what we understand as "evidence" or "truth conditions", but by criteria. ("Not merely" suggests a misleading emphasis. Criteria are not alternatives or additions to evidence. Without the control of criteria in applying concepts, we would not know what counts as evidence for any claim, nor for what claims evidence is needed.) And that suggests, according to what has so far emerged, that every surmise and each tested conviction depend upon the same structure or background of necessities and agreements that judgments of value explicitly do. I do not say that, according to Wittgenstein, statements of fact *are* judgments of value. That would simply mean that there are no facts, that nothing can be established in the way statements of fact evidently can be. The case is rather that, as I wish to put it, both statements of fact and judgments of value rest upon the same capacities of human nature; that, so to speak, only a creature that *can* judge of value *can* state a fact. But doesn't that just come to saying that only a creature that has speech can make judgments and statements? And that is hardly surprising.

It is not surprising if what it means is that only a creature that can say something can say something in particular. But what motivates Wittgenstein to philosophize, what surprises him, is the plain fact that certain creatures have speech at all, that they can say things at all. No doubt it is not clear how one might go about becoming surprised by such a fact. It is like being surprised by the fact that there is such a thing as the world. But I do not say that Wittgenstein's thoughts demand that you grasp these surprises before you begin studying those thoughts. On the contrary, I believe that such experiences are part of the teaching which those thoughts are meant to produce. Whether the thoughts he produces should be called a "philosophy of language" depends on what it is one expects from a philosophy of language. Wittgenstein has some fairly definite ideas about meaning and understanding and signs and communication and propositions and uses of words; and these are topics a philosophy of language, on any account, is likely to discuss. But Wittgenstein's interest in them is no more nor less than his interest in the topics of intention and willing and thinking and belief and privacy and doubt and teaching and pain and pity and conviction and certainty. They are topics in which the soul interests and manifests itself, so the soul's investigation of itself, in person or in others, will have to investigate those topics and those interests as and where they ordinarily manifest themselves. And he is interested in language because philosophy is more or less obsessed by it. But if one is interested in providing a theory or science of language, Wittgenstein's remarks must seem very haphazard. And so far as a philosophy of language, on familiar views of philosophy, would or ought in part to consist in an interpretation or reconstruction or analysis of the language of science in particular, Wittgenstein has no philosophy of language at all. He can better be read as attacking philosophy's wish to provide theories of language — as one would attack a philosophy's resort to, or imitation of, physics, or psychology, as a way of understanding the problem of skepticism, i.e., as a way of avoiding it.

That criteria are object-specific is familiar enough: what makes a government stable is not what makes a table or a bridge or a relationship or a solution stable. (This is obviously a point at which, since criteria provide a "kind of definition", we may wonder whether, or in what sense, "stable" means the same throughout its various contexts.) Wittgenstein counts on this feature of object-specificity for a different, apparently for an opposite, purpose. In his cases we do not first know the object to which, by means of criteria, we assign a value; on the contrary, criteria are the means by which we learn what our concepts are, and hence "what kind of object anything is" (§373). Or rather, Wittgensteinian criteria are appealed to in the course of grammatical investigations, and it is grammar which tells what kind of object anything is. But until we have some grasp of what Wittgenstein intends by "grammar" it is not much help to say that in using ordinary or official criteria we *start out* with a known kind of object whereas in using Wittgensteinian criteria we *end up* knowing a kind of object.

But it is a little help; it helps uncover the area or level at which we should look for an understanding of Wittgenstein's notion. It is a notion obviously meant, at least in part, and at some level, to provide a line of answer both to the ordinary question, "How do you know?", and to the philosophical question, "What is knowledge?", an answer that competes with other philosophical lines of answer to such questions. Because of its obscurity, Wittgenstein's answer may be thought, so far as it means anything clear, to have the same force as the answers it is in competition with. His reiterated question, "But what criteria do we have for saying that?", may seem to be asking essentially for the verifiability of our claims to know; his insistence on the use (in apparent contrast to the meaning) of words and sentences, and on our having "set up" or "agreed" upon the criteria in terms of which we use them, may look like a claim that the meaning of our concepts goes only so far as we have defined operations in acquiring or testing knowledge; and his tendency to speak of criteria as what phenomena, especially mental phenomena, consist in, where that in turn is usually a matter of what we do in certain public contexts, will create the impression that he regards references to the "mind" as being, so far as justified or comprehensible, descriptions of behavior. That is, ideologies or paradigms of comprehensibility, at the moment and in the intellectual environment of Wittgenstein's writing, are Verificationism, Operationalism, and Logical Behaviorism. A way of stating Wittgenstein's originality is to say that, while his teaching absorbs these tendencies, it adopts none; as one might say, it dates them. Reading him in one or another of the familiar ways, as well as trying to read his originality, is a function of the way one understands his idea of a criterion.

When epistemology raises the question of knowledge, what it asks for are the grounds of our certainty. But we are reminded that what we call knowledge is also related to what we call getting to know, or learning, e.g., to our ability to identify or classify or discriminate different objects with and from one another. Criteria are criteria of judgment; the underlying idea is one of discriminating or separating cases, of identifying by means of differences. (This is reflected explicitly in the sense of "discrimination" as "prejudice".) All I want from these considerations so far is a prospective attention to Wittgenstein's emphasis upon the idea of judgment. In the modern history of epistemology, the idea of judgment is not generally distinguished from the idea of statement generally, or perhaps they are too completely distinguished. The problem is not that in focussing upon those forms of utterance which are characterized by their exclusive possession of truth or falsity a philosopher fails to attend to other "uses" of language. One may presumably study what one chooses. The problem is to see whether the study of human knowledge may as a whole be distorted, anyway dictated, by this focus. The focus upon statements takes knowledge to be the sum (or product) of true statements, and hence construes the limits of human knowledge as coinciding with the extent to which it has amassed true statements of the world. The philosophical task will be to provide an organon which will justify or improve and increase those statements. The focus upon judgment takes human knowledge to be the human capacity for applying the concepts of a language to the things of a world, for characterizing (categorizing) the world when and as it is humanly done, and hence construes the limits of human knowledge as coinciding with the limits of its concepts (in some historical period). The philosophical task in this case will be to provide an organon which will bring those limits to consciousness — not to show the confinement of our knowledge (as Locke more or less suggests and as Kant more or less implies) but to show what in a given period we cannot fail to know, or ways we cannot fail to know in. (We are, or until recently were, so drilled in the knowledge of the difference between ways of discovery and modes of proof, that it is hard for us to conceive what a logic of discovery or conviction could be: such things can have no logic, only a psychology. My describing Wittgenstein's criteria as necessary *before* the identification or knowledge of an object, and as prelude to that knowledge, is meant to remind one of a thesis of such a work as Dewey's *Logic*, a product of the Idealist tradition, according to which the subject of a judgment is not known prior to the knowledge of the predicates which are taken to hold of it.)

A third disanalogy between Wittgensteinian and everyday criteria indicates that, and why, although Wittgenstein's immediate audience was the empiricist tradition of philosophy, his views are going, or ought, to offend

an empiricist sensibility at *every* point — which is only to say that this
conflict is an intimate one. Go back to the first element of my lay-out, the
one I label "Source of Authority". There one finds "American officials",
"I", "Africans", "Anna Freud", "Shanley"; and one would include, from
the original samples, "Radcliffe", "Kovalevsky and Marx", "American
society before the Great Depression". Wittgenstein's source of authority
never varies in this way. It is, for him, always *we* who "establish" the
criteria under investigation. The criteria Wittgenstein appeals to — those
which are, for him, the data of philosophy — are always "ours", the
"group" which forms his "authority" is always, apparently, the human
group as such, the human being generally. When I voice them, I do so, or
take myself to do so, as a member of that group, a representative human.

Two questions are immediately to be expected: (1) How can I, what
gives me the right to, speak for the group of which I am a member? How
have I gained that remarkable privilege? What confidence am I to place
in a generalization from what I say to what everybody says?: the sample is
irresponsibly, preposterously small. (2) If I am supposed to have been
party to the criteria we have established, how can I fail to know what
these are; and why do I not recognize the fact that I have been engaged in
so extraordinary an enterprise?

1. If what I say about what we say is in fact a generalization, and all
I'm going on is the fact that I say it (and perhaps, but not necessarily,
that I've heard some others say it too), then the thing is preposterous.
Since I do not think the claim to speak for "us" is preposterous, I do not
think it is a generalization. But what else is it? For all Wittgenstein's
claims about what we say, he is always at the same time aware that others
might not agree, that a given person or group (a "tribe") might *not* share
our criteria. "One human being can be a complete enigma to another"
(*Investigations,* p. 223). Disagreement about our criteria, or the possibility
of disagreement, is as fundamental a topic in Wittgenstein as the eliciting
of criteria itself is.

This point may not fully alleviate the sense of Wittgenstein's dogmatism, but it might help raise the question of what he is being dogmatic
about. It may even turn out that he sometimes does not care at all
whether others would say what he says "we" say. — Well, evidently;
that's what his dogmatism is all about. — No, I mean he "does not care",
not in the sense that he will go on maintaining that he speaks for "us" no
matter what "you" say, but that he is content not to speak for us, should
it prove that he does not. This would make him not so much dogmatic

as egomaniacal. "If I have exhausted the justifications . . . then I am inclined to say, 'This is simply what I do' " (§217); "Explanations come to an end somewhere" (§1); "Well, how do I know [how to continue]? . . . If that means 'Have I reasons?' the answer is: my reasons will soon give out. And then I shall act, without reason" (§211).

Then I am inclined . . . ; somewhere . . . ; then I shall act. . . . But when and where is this? Who is to say when? — These are not my problems at the moment. Anyone has as much right or need to say as anyone else; and when one will or must admit the exhaustion of reasons is in each case an empirical question. My problem is rather to see what kind of crossroads this is.

When Wittgenstein, or at this stage any philosopher appealing to ordinary language, "says what we say", what he produces is not a generalization (though he may, later, generalize), but a (supposed) *instance* of what we say. We may think of it as a sample. The introduction of the sample by the words "We say . . ." is an invitation for you to see whether you have such a sample, or can accept mine as a sound one. One sample does not refute or disconfirm another; if two are in disagreement they vie with one another for the same confirmation. The only source of confirmation here is ourselves. And each of us is fully authoritative in this struggle. An initial disagreement may be overcome; it may turn out that we were producing samples of different things (e.g., imagining a situation differently) or that one of us had not looked carefully at the sample he produced and only imagined that he wished to produce it, and then retracts or exchanges it. But if the disagreement persists, there is no appeal beyond us, or if beyond us two, then not beyond some eventual us. There is such a thing as intellectual tragedy. It is not a matter of saying something false. Nor is it an inability or refusal to say something or to hear something, from which other tragedies may spring.

"I should like to say: 'I experience the because' " (§177). Suppose someone responded: "Well, I certainly shouldn't. It isn't even grammatical speech!" At such a crossroads we have to conclude that on this point we are simply different; that is, we cannot here speak for one another. But no claim has been made which has been disconfirmed; my authority has been restricted. Even if Wittgenstein had (and it is significant that he did not) introduced the ungrammatical wish by saying "We should like to say . . .", then when it turns out that I should not like to say that, he is not obliged to correct his statement in order to account for my difference; rather he retracts it in the face of my rebuke. He hasn't said something

false about "us"; he has learned that there is no us (yet, maybe never) to
say anything about. What is wrong with his statement is that he made it
to the wrong party.

The philosophical appeal to what we say, and the search for our criteria
on the basis of which we say what we say, are claims to community. And
the claim to community is always a search for the basis upon which it can
or has been established. I have nothing more to go on than my conviction,
my sense that I make sense. It may prove to be the case that I am wrong,
that my conviction isolates me, from all others, from myself. That will
not be the same as a discovery that I am dogmatic or egomaniacal. The
wish and search for community are the wish and search for reason.

Wittgenstein, in sampling what we say, goes beyond the mere occurrence of the words, in ways that make him unlike other philosophers who
proceed from ordinary language; unlike Austin, say. He proposes words
that he says force themselves upon us in a certain context, or words that
we wish or would like or are tempted to say, and he cites words he says
we do not mean or only have the illusion of meaning. How does he know
such things? I mean, apart from any philosophical claim into whose service he would press such findings, how can he so much as have the idea
that these fleets of his own consciousness, which is obviously all he's got
to go on, are accurate wakes of our own? But the fact is, he does have the
idea; and he is not the only one who does. And the fact is, so much of
what he shows to be true of his consciousness is true of ours (of mine).
This is perhaps the fact of his writing to be most impressed by; it may
be the fact he is most impressed by — that what he does can be done at all.

It can seem sometimes that Wittgenstein has undertaken to voice our
secrets, secrets we did not know were known, or did not know we shared.
And then, whether he is right or wrong in a given instance, the very intention, or presumption, will seem to some outrageous. I take that to be
a significant reaction to the book, an accurate registering of what it
claims. Others will find the intention, or presumption, stirring. And then
it is difficult to see how dangerously seductive, and self-seductive, such an
intention might be. What is the presumption which asks us to look to
ourselves to find whether we share another's secret consciousness? What
gives one the right? The direction, in any case, is all wrong for philosophy, which ought to point away from the self, not toward it. When I
found reason (in "The Availability of Wittgenstein's Later Philosophy")
to relate the *Investigations* to the genre of the Confession, I was not at
pains to guard against taking that to imply that Wittgenstein's writing
is, as certain of his readers had shrewdly suspected from the beginning,

beyond rational criticism. Guarding comes to an end somewhere. I hoped what the relation would imply is that while a confession and its truthfulness can come into question and be subject to criticism, while indeed it is often more urgent to question and criticize a confession than to question and criticize a piece of testimony or a proof, there is no good reason to suppose that the modes of question and criticism resemble one another more closely than a confession resembles a proof. (One difference is that while the making and checking of both confessions and proofs may require much experience, it is in general easier to check than to make a proof, whereas the reverse may be true in the case of confessions. A further difference is that this fact can be proven about proofs, by someone other than the one who found this proof.)

Of Wittgenstein's parables about the nature of philosophizing, one of the most puzzling is this:

> If I am inclined to suppose that a mouse has come into being by spontaneous generation out of grey rags and dust, I shall do well to examine those rags very closely to see how a mouse may have hidden in them, how it may have got there and so on. But if I am convinced that a mouse cannot come into being from these things, then this investigation will perhaps be superfluous.
> But first we must learn to understand what it is that opposes such an examination of details in philosophy. [§52]

"Such an examination." What kind is it? And what "opposes" it, i.e., opposes it in philosophy? It is an examination that exposes one's convictions, one's sense of what must and what cannot be the case; so it requires a breaking up of one's sense of necessity, to discover truer necessities. To do that I have to get into the state of mind in which I am "inclined to suppose" that something I take to be impossible may be happening. Which means that I have to experiment in believing what I take to be prejudices, and consider that my rationality may itself be a set of prejudices. This is bound to be a painful prospect. And it is likely to lead to ridiculous postures. But no more ridiculous than the posture of looking for an explanation in a region in which you have no inclination to suppose it may lie. (We might call such an activity "academic".) — So it is I, as I stand, who oppose such an examination of details in philosophy. It was always a mark of honor in a philosophy to be opposed. But it would miss the point to take reassurance from that; for that would mean that you conceive yourself to be exempt from the fear and pain which naturally oppose serious philosophy. "Psychophobia", I learn from a recent text in psychoanalysis, means both "fear of one's inner life" and "fear of ghosts" (Bertram Lewin, *The Image and the Past*, p. 25). It can motivate intellectuality as well as anti-intellectuality. And philosophy can be the fruit, or work in the root, of either. (I associate what I just now called the "breaking up of the sense of necessity" with what in "The Avoidance of Love" I call the "breaking up of our sense of the ordinary"; e.g., p. 316, p. 350.)

2. When I remarked that the philosophical search for our criteria is a search for community, I was in effect answering the second question I uncovered in the face of the claim to speak for "the group" — the question, namely, about how I could have been party to the establishing of criteria if I do not recognize that I have and do not know what they are. The answer, in terms of that remark, should best be to make out that there *are* (what Wittgenstein calls) criteria (i.e., to produce some), and to admit that nobody could have established them alone, and that of course whoever is party to them does know what they are (though he or she may not know how to elicit and state them, and not recognize his or her complicity under that description); and to emphasize that the claim is not that one can tell a priori who is implicated by me, because one point of the particular kind of investigation Wittgenstein calls grammatical is exactly to discover who. This is not much of an answer, but I do not mean it as much more than a further indication of the level at which I seek an answer.

The question it answers sounds like a familiar moment in the history of modern philosophy, the moment of Hume's attack upon the idea of a social contract, an attack which I believe many philosophers still find sufficient to show such an idea intellectually disreputable. I cite the moment to recall also that it is an old, if unestablished feeling, that the mutual meaningfulness of the words of a language must rest upon some kind of connection or compact among its users; and that the classical locus of philosophical investigations of this idea of a compact lies in the discussions of the social contract supposed to have established the political community. I want to go on here a bit with this idea; it will show a natural outcropping of concepts which will later come more centrally or thematically into play.

Remember Hume's raillery: "In vain are we asked in what records this charter of our liberties is registered. It was not written on parchment, nor yet on leaves or barks of trees." Philosophers who nevertheless retain a sense of accuracy in the idea of a social contract, or a need for it, have undertaken to justify it as of course not historical, but . . . what? An explanatory myth, perhaps. But what is the need of the myth; what is it supposed to explain? Something like why it is I should obey the government;

why I have, as Hume puts it, "an obligation to allegiance". To answer this by speaking of a contract is, he says, in effect to give the answer, "Because I have an obligation to fidelity (to my promise)"; and this is no answer, because both obligations rest upon the same foundation, viz., the advantage to men of the subsistence of society, and the overwhelming disadvantage of the dissolution of government. This objection is empty. First, because it merely reasserts that there is no contract. A contract is not just a promise; it is a conditional promise in view of some consideration, and the consideration is the "advantage". Second, while it may be true that society depends on the making and keeping of contracts, to give that as a reason for keeping a *given* contract is either devious or is a way of saying — an impatient way of saying — that whatever you may think, the contract is in effect, and there is no sufficient reason for breaking it. About the social contract, Hume's answer flatly begs the question; because the force of the idea of a social contract is to put the advantage of a society, as it stands, in question. What the contract says, as it were, is not merely that I will, so long as the government keeps its part of the bargain, obey it. I *will* in fact more than likely obey a usurper or tyrant, and mostly that is what there is for me to obey — facts which Hume insists on, taking them to show that consent has nothing to do with the question.

What I consent to, in consenting to the contract, is not mere obedience, but membership in a polis, which implies two things: First, that I recognize the principle of consent itself; which means that I recognize others to have consented with me, and hence that I consent to political *equality*. Second, that I recognize the society and its government, so constituted, as *mine;* which means that I am answerable not merely to it, but for it. So far, then, as I recognize myself to be exercising my responsibility for it, my obedience to it is obedience to my own laws; citizenship in that case is the same as my autonomy; the polis is the field within which I work out my personal identity and it is the creation of (political) *freedom*.

But if this were the way things are, the question "Why ought I to obey?" would be even rarer than it is: the advantages it would then put in question are those of society at best — of membership (i.e., fraternity), equality, and freedom as such. It is to Rousseau's credit as a grammarian of society to have insisted that the blessings of even the perfected polis will cost the precedence of other blessings — of God, of friendship, of family, of love. (Here I recognize an indebtedness to Professor Judith Shklar's *Men and Citizens: A Study of Rousseau's Social Theory*.)

But this is not the way things are. It is a very poorly kept secret that men and their societies are not perfect. In that case, in all actual cases, it is ungrammatical (not to say politically devious) to answer the question "Why ought I to obey?" in terms of the general advantages of citizenship. What the question in fact means therefore is, "Given the specific inequalities and lacks of freedom and absence of fraternity in the society to which I have consented, do these outweigh the 'disadvantages' of withdrawing my consent?". This is the question the theorists of the social contract teach us to ask, and the beginning of an answer is to discover whom I am in community with, and what it is to which I am obedient.

On such formulations, a familiar question like "How can I have consented to the formation of government, since I am not aware that I was ever asked for it or ever gave it?" becomes "How can I have recognized this government as mine since I am not aware that I am responsible for it?". And then the question no longer sounds just rhetorical. What looked on one picture like an epistemological mystery becomes on another an empirical and moral project. The former picture is not Locke's; the latter, I take it, more or less is. It may be the prestige of Hume which has kept going the common reading according to which Locke is supposed to have asked himself the question, "Since obviously the members of the polis have not expressly (don't recognize themselves as having) consented, how do you know they have?", and to have come up with the answer, "Their presence indicates that they have consented *tacitly*". And everything I have read or heard on the subject takes this as the patent or cruel dodge it seems to be. But the dodge is projected. That is not the question Locke appeals to "tacit consent" to answer.

The passages of Locke's *Second Treatise* which move into the topic of tacit consent (§§119–22) *also* move into the topic of those persons who, while present in a community at a given time, are *not* members of it. His question here is why, and the extent to which, even they are bound by the laws of that community. It is *that* question, about non-members, to which the answer "Because their presence implies tacit consent" is given. When Hume says "The truest *tacit* consent . . . that is ever given is when a foreigner settles in any country . . .", he clearly feels this as teaching Locke the true or natural meaning of his own words. (Locke is the only theorist of the social contract Hume explicitly cites.) But the connection of tacit consent with the idea of foreigners (settled or passing through) is specifically and explicitly Locke's point. In those same sections Locke reiterates his contention that *membership* in the polis requires *express* consent. He may not *have* a good answer to the question "What counts as the (express) consent which establishes a polis?", and he may be culpable in not seeking a good answer to that question; but he is not culpable of having given it an epistemologically stupid and politically heartless answer. There remains ample room for stupidities (e.g., about what constitutes property) and for heartlessness (e.g., about what fits one for membership).

The effect of the teaching of the theory of the social contract is at once to show how deeply I am joined to society and also to put society at a distance from me, so that it appears as an artifact. But what is its point? It is hardly news to theorists of the social contract that in the overwhelming number of instances in which the actual question of advantages has arisen, or will arise, I will, and ought to, decide against withdrawing consent. But whether the private motive of the theorist is to justify his conviction that the present is one of those few moments at which a dismantling of the artifact is called for, or whether to justify his view that this is never called for, the philosophical significance of the writing lies in its imparting of political education: it is philosophical because its method is an examination of myself by an attack upon my assumptions; it is political because the terms of this self-examination are the terms which reveal me as a member of a polis; it is education not because I learn new information but because I learn that the finding and forming of my knowledge of myself requires the finding and forming of my knowledge of that membership (the depth of my own and the extent of those joined with me). Such writing is, therefore, not likely to be taken very seriously if it is read—as I have the impression it is now mostly read — as a set of pre-scientific jottings about existing states.

I find Rousseau deepest among the classical writers I know on the topic of the social contract, because, unlike Hobbes and Locke, he does not claim to know what the "state of nature" is (was) like, but sketches a reconstruction of social origins designed to prove that what philosophers say about that nature is a projection of their own states of society, or their fantasies of it. What he claims to know is his relation to society, and to take as a philosophical datum the fact that men (that he) can speak for society and that society can speak for him, that they reveal one another's most private thoughts. His problem is to understand how that can be. The epistemological problem of society is not to discover new facts about it; the facts, as the Encyclopedists were globally showing, are there to be had. The problem is for me to discover my position with respect to these facts — how I know with whom I am in community, and to whom and to what I am in fact obedient. The existence of the prior contract is not the explanation of such facts. On the contrary, it is a projection from the fact that I now recognize myself to be party to some social contract, or pacts, which explains (what we take to be) the prior existence of the contract. But since the genuine social contract is not in effect (we could know this by knowing that we are born free and are everywhere in chains) it follows that we are not exercising our general will; and since we are not in a state of nature it follows that we are exercising our will not to the general but to the particular, to the partial, to the unequal, to private benefit, to privacy. We obey the logic of conspiracy, though we believe this to be true only of *others*. (You could call this Rousseau's self-diagnosis.) So we hallucinate the meaning of others to us (e.g., as equals) or have the illusion of meaning something to one another (e.g., as free fellow-citizens). — Then the epistemological problem is the first problem of justice: when we know our position we will know what ought to happen, whether or not we then choose to find out what may forward it or what may not, decide that it is worth trying or that it is not. Rousseau's discovery is less a discovery of new knowledge than a discovery of a mode of knowledge, a way to use the self as access to the self's society. It is consequently the discovery of a new mode of ignorance. Marx and Freud will call this ignorance unconsciousness, the former of our social present, the latter of our private pasts; but these will prove not to be so different. (Both speak of this ignorance as the result of repression.)

I do not take such obscurities as my inventions. Because if one finds such writing as Rousseau's convincing, one will have to ask how he can have known what he knows, for he obviously is not guessing, or waiting for proof. And you will have to decide about his bouts of apparent insanity. Are they merely psychological problems? (As if we knew what that meant; as if taking such a phrase as the explanation of such conduct were any less superstitious than any superstition we can find in the idea of, say, a social contract.) Or are they expressions of grief that society should conduct itself as it does? Not grief for himself, but for society, which wilfully denies knowledge of its own conspiracies, and not just those directed against him.

It is inevitable in such discussions that the question of the "age of consent" or the "age of reason" be raised. The idea is that it is a precondition of consent, on anybody's view of what consent may be, that each individual must give his own and that it cannot be given until the individual is in command of his own mind. The problem is then to specify what "command of one's own mind" consists in. Is it some intellectual or moral accomplishment? Then what is one supposed to know, or be able to use one's reason for? Suppose what is wanted is the capacity to speak for oneself. Then why call this a precondition? One might rather say that the granting (or withholding) of consent is the precondition, or the condition, of speaking for oneself.

To speak for oneself politically is to speak for the others with whom you consent to association, and it is to consent to be spoken for by them — not as a parent speaks for you, i.e., instead of you, but as someone in mutuality speaks for you, i.e., speaks your mind. Who these others are, for whom you speak and by whom you are spoken for, is not known a priori, though it is in practice generally treated as given. To speak for yourself then means risking the rebuff — on some occasion, perhaps once for all — of those for whom you claimed to be speaking; and it means risking having to rebuff — on some occasion, perhaps once for all — those who claimed to be speaking for you. There are directions other than the political in which you will have to find your own voice — in religion, in friendship, in parenthood, in love, in art — and to find your own work; and the political is likely to be heartbreaking or dangerous. So are the others. But in the political, the impotence of your voice shows up quickest; it is of importance to others to stifle it; and it is easiest to hope there, since others are in any case included in it, that it will not be missed if it is stifled, i.e., that you will not miss it. But once you recognize a community as yours, then it does speak for you until you say it doesn't, i.e., until you show that you do. A fortunate community is one in which the issue is least costly to raise; and only necessary to raise on brief, widely spaced, and agreed upon occasions; and, when raised, offers a state of affairs you can speak for, i.e., allows you to reaffirm the polis.

It follows from including "speaking for others and being spoken for by others" as part of the content of political consent, that mere withdrawal from the community (exile inner or outer) is not, grammatically, the withdrawal of consent from it. Since the granting of consent entails acknowledgment of others, the withdrawal of consent entails the same acknowledgment: I have to say *both* "It is not mine any longer" (I am no longer responsible for it, it no longer speaks for me) *and* "It is no longer ours" (not what we bargained for, we no longer recognize the principle of consent in it, the original "we" is no longer bound together by consent but only by force, so it no longer exists). Dissent is not the undoing of consent but a dispute about its content, a dispute within it over whether a present arrangement is faithful to it. The alternative to speaking for yourself politically is not: speaking for yourself privately. (Because "privately" here can only either be repeating the "for myself", in which case it means roughly, "I'm doing the talking"; or else it implies that you do not *know* that you speak for others, which does not deny the condition of speaking for others.) The alternative is having nothing (political) to say.

I plan no very immediate analogy from such thoughts to the problems Wittgenstein raises about "private language". But it does not seem to me excessively far-fetched to find analogous thoughts present from early on in the *Investigations*. At §32 there is this: "And now, I think, we can say: Augustine describes the learning of human language as if the child came into a strange country and did not understand the language of the country; that is, as if it already had a language, only not this one." If my teacher of French will not accept what I say and do as what he says and does, perhaps treating my American accent with tacit contempt, then I will not learn French (from him). But what happens if "my elders", all of them (those bigger people from whom, according to Augustine's passage, I learn to use words), will not accept what I say and do as what they say and do? Must they? Is it only natural for them to? Is it their responsibility? (This is a principal concern of Chapter VII.)

I would like to say: If I am to have a native tongue, I have to accept what "my elders" say and do as consequential; and they have to accept, even have to applaud, what I say and do as what they say and do. We do not know in advance what the content of our mutual acceptance is, how far we may be in agreement. I do not know in advance how deep my agreement with myself is, how far responsibility for the language may run. But if I am to have my own voice in it, I must be speaking for others and allow others to speak for me. The alternative to speaking for myself representatively (for *someone* else's consent) is not: speaking for myself privately. The alternative is having nothing to say, being voiceless, not even mute.

As was said, the best proof that there are such things as Wittengenstein calls criteria is to produce some. And how do we go about that? There is practically nothing to it: we look at what we say. But there are any number of ways of, any number of procedures we might call, "looking at" "what we say". In what way are we to look at our words so far as that is relevant to philosophy? Wittgenstein says we are to investigate what we say grammatically. What this means is, presumably, only fully exemplified by the procedures of his *Investigations* as a whole. But from time to time he sketches certain procedures meant as miniature "grammatical investigations". For example:

Expectation is, grammatically, a state; like: being of an opinion, hoping for something, knowing something, being able to do something . . . What, in particular cases, do we regard as criteria for someone's being of such-and-such an opinion? When do we say: he reached this opinion at that time? When: he has altered his opinion? And so on. The picture which the answers to these questions give us shows *what* gets treated grammatically as a *state* here. [§§572–73]

The grammar of "to fit", "to be able", and "to understand". Exercises: (1) When is a cylinder C said to fit into a hollow cylinder H? Only while C is stuck into H? (2) Sometimes we say that C ceased to fit into H at such-and-such a time. What criteria are used in such a case for its having happened at that time? . . . [§182]

"Understanding a word"; a state. But a *mental* state? — Depression, excitement, pain, are called mental states. Carry out a grammatical investigation as follows: we say
"He was depressed the whole day."
"He was in great excitement the whole day."
"He has been in continuous pain since yesterday."
We also say "Since yesterday I have understood this word". "Continuously", though? — To be sure, one can speak of an interruption of understanding. But in what cases? Compare: "When did your pains get less?" and "When did you stop understanding that word?" [p. 59, unnumbered section]

These investigations seem to describe three main steps: (1) We find ourselves wanting to know something about a phenomenon, e.g., pain, expecting, knowledge, understanding, being of an opinion. . . . (2) We remind ourselves of the kinds of statement we make about it. (3) We ask ourselves what criteria we have for (what we go on in) saying what we say. What is our motivation in this? What is that "finding ourselves wanting to know" which, presumably, only philosophy satisfies? What is the wonder which eliciting criteria satisfies? In ordinary cases of establishing criteria, we want to know the basis on which we can or do assess an object as having a certain value, grant it a particular title. In the case of Wittgensteinian criteria, we want to know the basis on which we grant any concept to anything, why we call things as we do. But what for? What makes us want to know that? What pass has brought us to sense this as a lack in our knowledge?

There are two general or background claims about what we say which Wittgenstein summarizes with the idea of grammar: that language is shared, that the forms I rely upon in making sense are human forms, that they impose human limits upon me, that when I say what we "can" and "cannot" say I am indeed voicing necessities which others recognize, i.e., obey (consciously or not); and that our uses of language are pervasively, almost unimaginably, *systematic*. (Though since Wittgenstein wrote, the science of linguistics, especially Chomskian transformational grammar, seems to have gone a long way toward imagining it, indeed laying it out. This doesn't replace Wittgenstein, though it might confirm his faith. Discovering the depth of the systematic in language was not Wittgenstein's intellectual goal, but his instrument.) Certain claims Wittgenstein makes about grammar I do not now want to go into. For example, his saying that certain statements *are* grammatical, or that certain concepts are grammatically related. Nor do I want to go into, nor will I ever mean to rely on, his distinction between "surface grammar" and "depth grammar". In such contexts, "surface" mostly means, so far as I can see, "incomplete" or "hasty"; and Wittgenstein uses the notion as part of a diagnosis of philosophical confusion or obsession. It is not a region of his thought I place much confidence in.

At the moment, I emphasize one of Wittgenstein's specific claims about the sorts of investigation he calls grammatical, namely, that what we discover in the course of such investigations, when we ask "Under what circumstances, or in what particular cases, do we say . . . ?", are our criteria. My point here is just that this *is* a claim. The claim is by now perhaps taking on a certain significance. Immediately, its significance is that there is a background of pervasive and systematic agreements among us, which we had not realized, or had not known we realize. Wittgenstein sometimes calls them conventions; sometimes rules. In ordinary or official cases of criteria, while *judges* are not to alter the criteria they appeal to, there *is* an authority that has authority to change criteria, set up new ones if the old, for some purposes, are inconvenient or unreliable, or do not respond to new information or tastes . . . ; that is, if the old do not allow one to make the judgments for which the criteria are set up in the first place. Whereas in Wittgenstein's cases it is not clear what it would mean to alter our criteria. The "agreement" we act upon he calls "agreement in judgments" (§242), and he speaks of our ability to use language as depending upon agreement in "forms of life" (§241). But forms of life, he says, are exactly what have to be "accepted"; they are "given" (p. 226). Now the whole thing looks backwards. Criteria were to be the bases (features, marks, specifications) on the basis of which certain judgments could be made (non-arbitrarily); agreement over criteria was to make possible agreement about judgments. But in Wittgenstein it looks as if our ability to establish criteria depended upon a prior agreement in judgments.

Still, something like this was true of the format of ordinary criteria as well. To say that in ordinary cases the authority can change their criteria is to say that they have some shared prior judgment about what the general results should be, a fair idea or intuition of (say) which dives or dogs ought to come out on top. The establishing of criteria makes the process of judging more convenient, more open, less private or arbitrary. One might say: here establishing criteria allows us to *settle* judgments publicly — not exactly by making them certain, but by declaring what the points are at issue in various judgments, and then making them *final* (on a given occasion). That is a practice worth having; human decisions cannot wait upon certainty. But it is therefore one which can be abused. In assuming the burden of finality in the absence of certainty, an authority stakes the virtue of its community: if its judgments are not accepted as scrupulously fair, in its criteria and in its application of criteria, the community is shown to that extent not to provide a secure human habitation for its members; it fails to take up the slack between the uncertainty of judgment and the finality of decision. A virtue of sports is their celebration of the community's ability to take up its own slack — to provide an arena in which finality of judgment about actions is backed up by certainty, and in which certainty is essentially a matter of seeing.

The appeal to criteria in Wittgenstein is also a way of "settling judgments"; this is a reason it can appear that criteria provide judgments with certainty. And they also evidently have something to do with "making judgments public". But their role is not that of making judgments more convenient or fairer or more rational or less private; nor are criteria "open to revision" in the face of a few unsettled or untoward judgments. Wittgenstein's appeal to criteria is meant, one might say, exactly to call to consciousness the astonishing fact of the astonishing extent to which we *do* agree in judgment; eliciting criteria goes to show therefore that our judgments *are* public, that is, shared. What makes this astonishing, what partly motivates this philosophizing on the subject, is that the extent of agreement is so intimate and pervasive; that we communicate in language as rapidly and completely as we do; and that since we cannot assume that the words we are given have their meaning by nature, we are led to assume they take it from convention; and yet no current idea of "convention" could seem to do the work that words do — there would have to be, we could say, too many conventions in play, one for each shade of each word in each context. We *cannot* have agreed beforehand to all that would be necessary.

It is altogether important that Wittgenstein says that we *agree in* (forms of life) and that there is agreement *in* (judgments): "If language is to be a means of communication there must be agreement [*Übereinstimmung*] not only in definitions but also (queer as this may sound) in judgments" (§242); "It is what human beings *say* that is true and false; and they agree in the *language* they use" (§241). The idea of agreement here is not that of coming to or arriving at an agreement on a given occasion, but of being in agreement throughout, being in harmony, like pitches or tones, or clocks, or weighing scales, or columns of figures. That a group of human beings *stimmen* in their language *überein* says, so to speak, that they are mutually voiced with respect to it, mutually *attuned* top to bottom. — I am not unaware that some philosophers will be impatient with the confidence I may seem to place in such a remark, and rather disapprove of my pleasure in such an alignment of words, which is merely metaphorical. So I should emphasize that, while I regard it as empty to call this idea of mutual attunement "merely metaphorical", I also do not take it to prove or explain anything. On the contrary, it is meant to question whether a philosophical explanation is needed, or wanted, for the fact of agreement in the language human beings use together, an explanation, say, in terms of meanings or conventions or basic terms or propositions which are to provide the foundation of our agreements. For nothing is deeper than the fact, or the extent, of agreement itself.

There may be a scientific explanation of this fact forthcoming, say from linguistics, or biology. But that will bear to philosophical investigations of what we say (and wish to say and wish we could say) the same relation that, for example, Newton's calculation which shows why, if the earth spins, we do not fly off of it, bears to philosophical investigations of the fact that we are earthlings: it may change everything or nothing. Those who had wished to provide a foundation for language had probably better either desist or else master the new linguistics, and accept or quarrel with it. But those who had wished to know our minds about our relations to ourselves and to others and to communities and to earth, will have to go still on the old things we say and do, bring to light the consequences of our old agreements.

I said just now that Wittgenstein is partly motivated to philosophy by a perception of the attunement of one human being's words with those of others. Another part of his motivation is a perception that they sometimes are out of tune, that they do not agree. This is, in the *Investigations,* hauntingly the case in philosophizing, and the disagreements in question are typically not those of philosophers with one another but of philosophers with the words of ordinary human beings. It is not Wittgenstein's purpose in this to show that philosophers are "wrong". What would they be wrong about? In denying the existence of the world? In denying certainty to empirical statements? In saying that meanings or sensations are private? But are these ideas wrong? And does "wrong" mean "false"? Then whom will you inform that they are false? The ordinary man? But he will either not understand what you say, or he already knows they are false (especially that one about the existence of the world); or if he thinks they are true (especially that one about sensations) he will not believe you. Then will you inform the philosopher? But he will either find that you do not understand him, or else he will say he is not denying what you take him to deny.

Here I think of Wittgenstein's remark about philosophical theses. I have heard people say that Wittgenstein claims not to have any philosophical theses (which seems to them, if not quite a lie, then a falsehood on the face of it); and say that Wittgenstein claims that if he announced his theses nobody would deny them (which seems to mean that they would be obvious (which is a puzzling reason not to announce them)), which in turn seems to mean that he would be announcing only common sense beliefs. What Wittgenstein says is: "If one tried [or wanted] to advance *theses* in philosophy, it would never be possible to question them, because everyone would agree to them" (§128). What I have heard people say about this leaves out the ideas of "trying to advance" and "not being possible". On the surface, the remark about theses suggests that if I say, for example, "The world exists", this would not *be* a (what we call a) thesis, because there's no two ways about it. But not every philosopher should be expected to see this. And then, if I say "God exists", I am prepared to learn that there's two ways about that, but it doesn't follow that what I announced was a thesis. The German runs: "Wollte man *Thesen* in der Philosophie aufstellen, es könnte nie über sie zur Diskussion kommen, weil Alle mit ihnen einverstanden wären." I get the following sense from those words: "Whatever knowledge philosophizing brings forth cannot be brought out by setting forth a claim; because such a claim could never come into question, i.e., it could never arrive at words: because it is something upon which we have an understanding, i.e., it goes without saying, and only without saying, because we could not understand anyone who claimed it and thereby held it as *possibly* open to question." That will doubtless not express everyone's view either of that German passage or of philosophizing. I think one will especially not like the idea of "never arriving at words". But I find that if I really want to say "The world does exist", the impulse to those words is not expressed by those words. I want a gesture (perhaps poetry, or religion). Such a sense of Wittgenstein's philosophizing has the virtue of heading off the idea that what he would really like, would he but tell, is to support ordinary or common sense beliefs. To confront beliefs, common or otherwise, with the human agreement in terms of which those beliefs propose to make sense — to bring anything that is said back into the basis upon which we have anything to say — is not a practice of common sense.

Appealing to criteria is not a way of explaining or proving the fact of our attunement in words (hence in forms of life). It is only another description of the same fact; or rather, it is an appeal we make when the attunement is threatened or lost. Official criteria are appealed to when judgments of assessment must be declared; Wittgensteinian criteria are appealed to when we "don't know our way about", when we are lost with respect to our words and to the world they anticipate. Then we start finding ourselves by finding out and declaring the criteria upon which we are in agreement. Wittgenstein's claim is that philosophy causes us to lose ourselves and that philosophy is philosophy's therapy. These are not so much claims as definitions. They do not capture everything anyone may wish to call "philosophy"; for some they will capture none of it. For some it will sound like the acceptance of an old joke: Philosophy causes the disease for which it is the cure. (This was, I believe, not first said about Wittgenstein.) This sounds funny only if you take philosophy to be something easy to recognize and confine; but not if "philosophy" means, say, "a need of questioning", a posture anyone may find himself or herself in at any time. What interests Wittgenstein about philosophizing is that it does tend to put the one philosophizing out of agreement with ordinary words (i.e., with his own words when he is not philosophizing), *and* the fact that what he then says is not meaningless, and moreover that what he then says, or the words he then uses, seems to him compulsively true. So what interests him about criteria is both that there should be such things on the basis of which we lay down our words, *and* that they can be forgone.

Judgment, both in ordinary and in Wittgensteinian appeals to criteria, comes up twice. In ordinary cases, a set of specifications or features is established that set the terms of, are the "means" or basis of, the judgment; and then there are standards on the basis of which to assign the degree to which the object satisfies the criteria of judgment, or to determine whether an object *counts* under the criteria at all. We may think of the former moment as the judgment's *predication,* its saying something *about* something; we may think of the latter moment as the judgment's *proclamation,* its saying it out. In ordinary (official) cases, a judgment has to be proclaimed finally; that it will be forthcoming, and when forthcoming final (except through certain equally conventional forms of appeal or protest) is part of the agreement, the point of the agreement in the first place. In Wittgensteinian (and everyday) cases, *whether* to say it out is as much a problem as what there is to be said (as much a problem in the intelligibility of what is said).

Whether to speak (proclaim) has two aspects: determining whether you are willing to count something as something; and determining when, if ever, you wish, or can, enter your accounting into a particular occasion. Take one of Wittgenstein's obsessive examples: "He is in pain." Grant that the predicate ". . . is in pain" is in our grammatical repertory, that we know generally how to predicate it. To proclaim it here and now you must be willing to call out ("-claim") just that predicate on the basis of what you have so far gathered (e.g., you must be willing to count that wince as pain-behavior, or perhaps we should say, count that behavior as a wince); and you must find it called for on just this occasion, i.e., find yourself willing to come before ("pro-") those to whom you speak it (e.g., declare yourself in a position to inform or advise or alert someone of something, or explain or identify or remark something to someone). The latter necessity is what I take to be under investigation in such work as Austin's on "illocutionary force" and Searle's on "speech acts" and Grice's on "implicature". But the former necessity (counting something as something) Wittgenstein also emphasizes as essential to human thought and communication.

When Wittgenstein recalls that "it is what human beings *say* that is true or false" he is emphasizing the predicative moment of judgment; when he finds that communication in language depends upon "agreement in judgments" he is responding to the proclamatory moment of judging, and in particular to the calling or counting feature of that moment (not so much, as elsewhere, to the feature of coming before others). It is this feature of counting something under a concept which Wittgenstein's notion of a criterion is meant to bring out. In judging (saying something true or false) you have to be able or willing to judge a contraction of the face as a wince, to recognize a smile as forced, to find a slap on the forehead to express the overcoming of stupidity by insight, a fist to the heart to express the overcoming of stiff-neckedness by contrition, a tone of voice to be that of assertion. I take this counting feature to be present in the second of the sections about agreement I was quoting from, and in the section preceding them, but in each case somewhat buried: In order for there to "be" such things as rules, we have to agree in our judgment that a rule has been obeyed (or not). (Cp. §240.) (The rule itself is dead.) In order for there to be such things as (what we call) measurements, we have to agree in our judgment that a particular thing turns out to have such-and-such measurements. It is one thing to know that you measure length by successive layings down of a stick; it is something else to know that *this* object is just under fourteen sticks long. (Cp. §242) (The stick itself is dead. It doesn't tell you where to begin laying it down; what counts as succession; and when, and what to do if, the last laying down goes just over.) It would be empty to say that wincing is a criterion of being in pain if we never accepted any occurrence as wincing. (It would be like being able to count, i.e., run up the integers, without being able to count things.) And while you may have a criterion for something's being a wince (if there is, in given cases, something to distinguish it from, perhaps a tic), eventually, soon, further criteria are at an end.

I find my general intuition of Wittgenstein's view of language to be the reverse of the idea many philosophers seem compelled to argue against in him: it is felt that Wittgenstein's view makes language too public, that it cannot do justice to the control I have over what I say, to the innerness of my meaning. But my wonder, in the face of what I have recently been saying, is rather how he can arrive at the completed and unshakable edifice of shared language from within such apparently fragile and intimate moments — private moments — as our separate counts and out-calls of phenomena, which are after all hardly more than our interpretations of what occurs, and with no assurance of conventions to back them up.

II

Criteria and Skepticism

But if Wittgenstein's notion of a criterion is to be understood against the ordinary or official use of the word "criterion", then what is the source of the view (which I am calling the Malcolm-Albritton view) that Wittgenstein's criteria are meant to establish the existence of something with certainty? And what is the relation of these views? As was said, the Malcolm-Albritton view takes Wittgenstein to be writing in response to the threat of skepticism, for it is in the face of skeptical doubt that it is worth making, or possible or necessary to make, such claims for criteria. The relation between this notion and Wittgenstein's is that Wittgenstein's is indeed also meant in answer to some skeptical surmise, in response to some human possibility of error. The enforcing of this connection is something I saluted as a permanent value of the Malcolm-Albritton view. But this view, it seems to me, contains ideas of the nature of skepticism and of Wittgenstein's response to it which more or less obviously derive from these sources: (1) from a sense of Wittgenstein's relation to skepticism as one of refuting it, or trying or wishing to refute it, or taking himself to refute it; and accordingly (2) from a sense of skepticism as saying (precisely the thing that this construction of criteria is made to order to overcome) that we can never know with certainty of the existence of something or other; call it the external world, and call it other minds. And these ideas I find untrue to Wittgenstein.

Perhaps (1) is true to Kant; if so, it would be a consequential point at which his and Wittgenstein's thought part company. I take (2) to be a piece of what I think of as skepticism's picture of itself, its self-understanding. A formidable criticism of skepticism — as of any serious philosophy — will have to discover and alter its understanding of itself. You will of course not seek such a criticism unless you perceive a philosophy as having such an understanding, i.e., as taking upon itself this form of human seriousness. Otherwise you will suppose it enough to say of skepticism that it cannot be true, an observation scarcely designed to surprise the skeptic. You may prefer to say, since you know you are a philosopher and know therefore that you speak from something more than common sense, that there just *are* logically adequate criteria for showing skepticism to be false, indeed to undermine itself in the very process of expressing itself; but this is intellectually no advance. It merely redescribes, or puts in one way, something skepticism knows and says more fully about itself.

The Malcolm-Albritton view of a criterion is an advance, for only in the face of skeptical doubt does it so much as seem to make sense. I will in the end find that it does not fully make sense, or makes no more sense than, or derives the sense it has from, skeptical doubt itself. To make this plainer, I need among other things to go through the details of that view.

Malcolm undertakes to defend the idea of a criterion as characterized in this way:

What makes something into a symptom of y is that experience teaches that it is always or usually associated with y; that so-and-so is the criterion of y is a matter, not of experience, but of "definition". The satisfaction of the criterion of y establishes the existence of y beyond question; it repeats the kind of case in which we were taught to say "y". The occurrence of a symptom of y may also establish the existence of y "beyond question" — but in a different sense. The observation of a brain process may make it certain that a man is in pain — but not in the same way that his pain behavior makes it certain. Even if physiology has established that a specific event in the brain accompanies bodily pain, still it *could* happen (it makes sense to suppose) that a man might be in pain without the brain event occurring. It will not make sense for one to suppose that another person is not in pain if one's criterion of his being in pain is satisfied. [pp. 84–5]

And then Malcolm goes on, properly, to cede the idea that criteria provide empirical certainty by providing logically sufficient and necessary conditions of something's being the case. No one will be satisfied (Malcolm confesses that he is not (p. 87)) by the statement that criteria make something certain in a different "way" than symptoms do. But this is an honest response to a real question: If criteria are meant to provide certainty, and this is to be articulated neither as logical implication nor infallible concomitance of different phenomena, then what kind of certainty *is* this? Albritton, faced with a similar question, concedes that it is not certainty but *near* certainty that criteria provide.

That a man behaves in a certain manner, under certain circumstances, cannot entail that he has a toothache. But it can entail something else. . . . *Roughly* . . . it can entail that . . . under these circumstances, [one] is *justified in saying* that the man has a toothache. . . . Or: . . . it can entail that he *almost certainly* has a toothache. [p. 246]

It is not clear to me what weight is being attached in this passage to the idea of "entailment". The suggestion seems to be that while the presence of symptoms (concomitants) of X can make it almost certain that X is present, the presence of a criterion of X necessarily makes it almost certain that X is present. The sense that "certainty" must be hedged, that the knowledge of reality provided, contingently or necessarily, can only be "almost" certain, is forced under the pressure of the question: But isn't it *possible* that, given all the symptoms or criteria you like, the man may not in fact, then and there, be *feeling* pain? To which the answer seems, irresistibly, to be: Yes. And this is so whether your basis for claiming that he has a toothache is that a red patch has appeared on his cheek (which has been discovered, by careful examination, always to accompany toothache) or whether your basis is that he holds his cheek, flinches when you approach the tooth, grimaces, wrings his hands, groans, and perspires when you prod the tooth.

But is the difference in these bases adequately registered by saying that, though the presence of one kind of basis makes it almost certain that he has toothache, the presence of the other kind necessarily makes it almost certain? Grant that in both cases the man may, in fact, then and there, not be feeling pain. But what does "not feeling pain" mean in each case; how, in the different cases, is that established? In both cases you may be wrong in saying that he is suffering from a toothache; but what, in the two cases, are you wrong about? Where your basis was a symptom, you were wrong in taking *that* to be a reliable symptom; toothache just in fact does not always accompany such a symptom, or does so only in the presence or absence of other symptoms. But is that enough to say where "it turns out" that, though the basis of your claim was the presence of criteria, he does not in fact feel pain? Is it just in fact the case that pain does not always accompany wincing, groaning, perspiring, etc.? I mean: though that may *in fact* be the case, to accommodate that fact, to make the fact comprehensible, even, one could say, to *state* that fact, one *has* to say

something like, "He was pretending; rehearsing a part; he was hypno-
tized, seized by an hysterical conversion, etc.". That "has to say" contains the clue I want to follow to the sense of "necessity" involved in
criteria, a concept of necessity which is not tied to the concept of certainty.

Before going on, it may be worth pointing up a more obvious difficulty
in the attempt to *explain* the failure of both symptoms and criteria by
saying of them both that the most they can (theoretically) provide is *near*
certainty. Where symptoms are concerned, this explanation is plausible
enough; it consists in saying something like, "The symptom is not 'always'
(necessarily?) accompanied by toothache". And what does "accompanied
by" mean; how do you "find out" that this concomitance has *not* been
manifested here; what is the content of the supposition that "it might
turn out" that he is not in pain? Isn't the *whole* content of this supposition just that the *criteria* of his being in pain are not forthcoming? His
cheek has that patch, but he doesn't wince, groan, etc., in the appropriate
circumstances. Now while it is true that, even if he does wince, etc., he
may still not be in pain, i.e., true that it is not (theoretically) certain he
is, that eventuality cannot be explained by saying, in the spirit in which
this was formerly said, "The criteria are not always accompanied by
pain", for now "always accompanied" does not have the same weight as
it had before (I hesitate to say it does not have the same meaning). "Not
always accompanied" had, previously, the content, "The criteria may not
be forthcoming", but, when the criteria *are* forthcoming, then what is the
content of "not always accompanied"? By *what* may *criteria* not "always
be accompanied"? One wants to say: "By the pain itself!" And what that
means is surely correct. But I am trying to elicit the significance of the
fact that it was *not* "the pain itself" which was formerly the "accompani-
ment" of *symptoms*. (Why, in philosophizing, we think of both failures as
failures of "accompaniments" is a further question. It is, doubtless, the
fact that these different failures are differently established, have different
consequences for knowledge, that leads Malcolm to say, having admitted
that symptoms of X and criteria of X may both make the existence of X
certain, that they do not establish this "in the same way". While he does
not make clear what the difference may be between these establishments,
he does go on to suggest a kind of certainty that criteria provide, or depend upon, which, it is implied, differs from the kind of certainty provided by symptoms. It is a certainty which depends upon our not considering *all* "possibilities". (Cf. p. 88.) But then doesn't one feel?: That
just means it is no longer certainty which is in question.)

Malcolm's account leads him to a juxtaposition of assertions whose apparent contradictoriness is striking. In the paragraph following the one in which he says or implies:

. . . if the criterion of his being in pain is satisfied then the existence of his pain [his being in pain?] is established beyond question.

we find this concession:

If we come upon a man exhibiting violent pain-behavior, couldn't something show that he is not in pain? Of course. [p. 85]

Since Malcolm apparently identifies "pain-behavior" with the "criterion of pain" (cf. p. 83) (which is correct as far as it goes), this juxtaposition seems to suggest both that if the criteria of X are satisfied then X must be the case *and* X need not be the case. The sting of this apparent contradiction is presumably thought to be drawn by attaching importance to the idea of a criterion's being *satisfied*. (Albritton also employs this locution, while pointing out that "it has no parallel in Wittgenstein's idiom" (p. 235, note 5). My remarks about Malcolm's use of it are meant to apply also to Albritton's, which I take to be the same.) If something does "show" that a man exhibiting violent pain-behavior is not in fact in pain, this does not contradict the statement that if the criterion of his being in pain is satisfied then the existence of his pain is established beyond question because we are then to say that "the criterion of pain was not satisfied". But this is empty. For now we can preserve the certainty of the connection between a criterion and what it is a criterion of only at the price of never knowing with certainty that the criterion is satisfied, that what it is *of* is *there*. And so we have deprived the notion of a criterion of what was to be, on the Malcolm-Albritton interpretation, its entire purpose:

A criterion for a thing's being so is something that can show the thing to be so and show by its absence that the thing is not so. [Albritton, pp. 243–44]

But since

. . . it doesn't follow that no criterion can seem to be satisfied when it isn't. . . [*Ibid.*, pp. 236–37]

there is a gap opened between the (seeming) *presence* of a criterion and its *satisfaction*, through which its provision of something like "logical necessity" or "certainty" drains away. In this way, certainty turns out to be of the old, familiar variety, and the fuss is for nothing. If I claim that X is the case on the basis of the presence of the criteria of X and "it turns out" that X is not the case, then I can always say, "The criteria were only seemingly present", or "The criteria were only seemingly satisfied". That something is a criterion of X is now — to appeal to an old thought — necessary because analytic, and therefore empirically empty. So *what* knowledge does it provide?

It is significant that Wittgenstein has recourse to no such notion as "a criterion's being satisfied". And so the questions "Then how are we to accommodate the fact that we may 'always be wrong' in an empirical claim, even though it is based on the presence of criteria?" and "What are criteria criteria of?" must be reopened.

Let us first see what makes this idea of a criterion's "non-satisfaction" a futile one. Under the pressure of the suggestion that the "propositions that describe the criteria of his being in pain [do not] *logically imply* the proposition 'He is in pain' ", or, in other words, that even in the (seeming) presence of the criteria of X, X may not be present (= it is possible, it may turn out, that he is not actually suffering pain), Malcolm says, "A criterion is satisfied *only in certain circumstances"; and again:

(a) The expression of pain is a criterion of pain only in certain surroundings. [Cf. p. 85]

The "surroundings" or "circumstances" Malcolm then excludes are those in which some one may be rehearsing for a play, be under hypnotic suggestion, engaged in a hoax, etc. Now of course the statement that various behaviors (and experiences) are criteria "only in certain circumstances" is made repeatedly by Wittgenstein, but never, I think, to account for the kind of situations Malcolm envisages here. A characteristic passage is this:

. . . what is essential to deriving, however, was not hidden beneath the surface of this case, but this "surface" was one case out of the family of cases of deriving.
And in the same way we also use the word "to read" for a family of cases. And in different circumstances we apply different criteria for a person's reading. [§164]

The sorts of "circumstances" Wittgenstein has in mind are spelled out in such a passage as this:

To intend a picture to be the portrait of so-and-so (on the part of the painter, e.g.) is neither a particular state of mind nor a particular mental process. But there are a great many combinations of actions and states of mind which we should call "intending. . .". It might have been that he was told to paint a portrait of N, and sat down before N, going through certain actions which we call "copying N's face". One might object to this by saying that the essence of copying is the intention to copy. I should answer that there are a great many different processes which we call "copying something". Take an instance. I draw an ellipse on a sheet of paper and ask you to copy it. What characterizes the process of copying? For it is clear that it isn't the fact that you draw a similar ellipse. You might have tried to copy it and not succeeded; or you might have drawn an ellipse with a totally different intention, and it happened to be like the one you should have copied. So what do you do when you try to copy the ellipse? Well, you look at it, draw something on a piece of paper, perhaps measure what you have drawn, perhaps you curse if you find it doesn't agree with the model; or perhaps you say "I am going to copy this ellipse" and just draw an ellipse like it. There are an endless variety of actions and words, having a family likeness to each other, which we call "trying to copy". [*The Blue Book,* pp. 32–33]

It is significant that there is no reference here to such circumstances as "pretending", "rehearsing", etc.

Let us formulate the sort of thing Wittgenstein refers to by "under certain circumstances" in a way that will permit more direct comparison with Malcolm's concession (a). An instance would be this:

(b) Groaning, etc., is a criterion of pain (i.e., is pain-behavior) only in certain circumstances.

(Or, taking cases from the quotations from Wittgenstein: "Drawing a similar ellipse" is a criterion of "copying an ellipse" only in certain circumstances; "pronouncing the correct words" is a criterion of "reading" only in certain circumstances.) In what sort of circumstances, then, is groaning *not* a criterion of pain? Circumstances in which groaning is not an *expression* of pain, e.g., circumstances in which someone is (would be described as) clearing his throat, calling his hamsters, responding to a bad joke (which would be *mock* pain-behavior, not feigned pain-behavior). How do we learn what the relevant circumstances are? Is there any less general answer to this than, "In coming to talk"? And would it make any difference if we said, "In coming to know what things are, what people do"?

In calling a piece of behavior "pain-behavior", you must already have included the circumstances under which that behavior (e.g., groaning) *is* pain-behavior (and not, e.g., comic- or calling-behavior); and so the phrase "only in certain circumstances", used, as Malcolm does, as an explanation or concession, will not do what Malcolm wishes it to do; that is, it does not explain why certain criteria which, by hypothesis, or by description, are of *pain* are (sometimes) not of *actual* pain, existing pain. (Indeed, what the concession in fact amounts to is this: behavior which, under certain circumstances, is a criterion of pain, is *under those very circumstances* not a criterion of pain. And so the apparent contradiction turns out to be a real one.) What would explain this failure of criteria? My suggestion will be, nothing would; for there is nothing to explain; there is no failure. Criteria of pain are satisfied (if we have to use that word) by the presence of (what we take as, fix, accept, adopt, etc., as) pain-behavior (certain behavior in certain circumstances). Then are there *no* criteria for the existence, the occurrence, of the pain itself? I might ask what "the pain itself" is. Or I could say: There are none that go essentially beyond the criteria for the behavior's being pain-behavior. Then how can we ever know whether another person is actually *suffering* pain? If I had truly motivated the appearance of that question, we would now wish to give full, not what is called "rhetorical", force to the question, What makes us think we might never know? That is to say, we would at such a point be moved to investigate, to try to uncover the source, of our disappointment with human knowledge as such. That is a way of putting what it is I take criteria, conceived as Wittgenstein conceives them, to enable us to do.

Disappointment over the failure (or limitation) of knowledge has, after all, been as deep a motivation to the philosophical study of knowledge as wonder at the successes of knowledge has been. In Wittgenstein's work, as in skepticism, the human disappointment with human knowledge seems to take over the whole subject. While at the same time this work seems to give the impression, and often seems to some to assert, that nothing at all is wrong with the human capacity for knowledge, that there is no cause for disappointment, that our lives, and the everyday assertions sketched by them, are in order as they are. So some of Wittgenstein's readers are made impatient, as though the fluctuating humility and arrogance of his prose were a matter of style, and style were a matter of pose, so that these poses merely repudiate, not to say undermine, one another. To me this fluctuation reads as a continuous effort at balance, or longing for it, as to leave a tightrope; it seems an expression of that struggle of despair and hope that I can understand as a motivation to philosophical writing. — I am led again to recognize, and again with no little astonishment, how at odds I find myself with those who understand Wittgenstein to begin with, or assert thesis-wise, the publicness of language, never seriously doubting it, and in that way to favor common sense. I might say that publicness is his goal. It would be like having sanity as one's goal. Then what state would one take oneself to be in?

It will help to make explicit the difference between the sorts of "circumstances" imagined under (a) and under (b). If, to begin with the latter, the groaning was not (turns out not to have been) in those circumstances a criterion of pain (pain-behavior), then there is no reason to suppose the person to be in pain; pain is not, so far, at issue. But if the groan *was* in those circumstances a criterion of pain, an expression of pain, then pain is, and remains, at issue. And that means that only *certain* eventualities will normally count as his not being in pain after all. (I will come back to the force of "normally" here.) Circumstances, namely — as Malcolm rightly suggests, but for the wrong purposes — in which we will say (he will be) feigning, rehearsing, hoaxing, etc. Why such circumstances? What differentiates such circumstances from those in which he is (said to be) clearing his throat, responding to a joke, etc.? Just that for "He's rehearsing" or "feigning", or "It's a hoax", etc. to satisfy us as explanations for his *not* being in pain (for it to "turn out" that he is not in pain) *what* he is feigning must be precisely *pain,* what he is rehearsing must be the part of a man *in pain,* the hoax depends on his simulating *pain,* etc. These circumstances are ones in appealing to which, in describing which, we *retain the concept* (here, of pain) whose application these criteria determine. And this means to me: In all such circumstances he has satisfied the criteria we use for applying the concept of pain to others. It is because of *that* satisfaction that we know that he is feigning pain (i.e., that it is pain he is feigning), and that he knows what to do to feign pain. Criteria are "criteria for something's being so", not in the sense that they tell us of a thing's existence, but of something like its identity, not of its *being* so, but of its being *so.* Criteria do not determine the certainty of statements, but the application of the concepts employed in statements.

This is enough for me to conclude that Wittgenstein's appeal to criteria, though it takes its importance from the problem of skepticism, is not, and is not meant to be, a refutation of skepticism. Not, at least, in the form we had thought a refutation must take. That is, it does not negate the concluding thesis of skepticism, that we do not know with certainty of the existence of the external world (or of other minds). On the contrary, Wittgenstein, as I read him, rather affirms that thesis, or rather takes it as *undeniable,* and so shifts its weight. What the thesis now means is something like: Our relation to the world as a whole, or to others in general, is not one of knowing, where knowing construes itself as being certain. So it is also true that we do not *fail* to know such things. Then the problem is: Why does the skeptic — how can he — take what he has discovered to be some extraordinary, and hitherto unnoticed, fact? Or perhaps we could ask: Why does he take his discovery to be a *thesis?* The answer to such a question will require a detailed working out of the skeptic's apparent progress from the discovery that we sometimes do not know what we claim to know, to the conclusion that we never do; or an investigation of his apparent assumption that our knowledge of the world as such is at stake in the examination of particular claims to know.

What remains here of first importance is that the skeptic's discovery (apparent discovery) repudiates or undercuts the validity of our criteria, our attunement with one another. That just *this* is the consequence of skepticism is something I take as equally significant about what skepticism is and about what a Wittgensteinian criterion is.

I should say that it is what I just called the skeptic's apparent progress and his apparent assumption, together with certain further related features, that constitute what I am calling skepticism, or characterize what I am interested in in skeptical arguments. I do not, that is, confine the term to philosophers who wind up denying that we can ever know; I apply it to any view which takes the existence of the world to be a problem of knowledge. A crucial step for me, in calling an argument skeptical, is that it contain a passage running roughly, "So we don't know (on the basis of the senses (or behavior) alone); then (how) do we know?". It is at this stage that philosophies break into Phenomenalism, Critical Realism, etc. These later differences are not now at issue for me. I hope it will not seem perverse that I lump views in such a way, taking the very raising of the question of knowledge in a certain form, or spirit, to constitute skepticism, regardless of whether a philosophy takes itself to have *answered* the question affirmatively or negatively. It is a perspective from which skepticism and (what Kant calls) dogmatism are made in one another's image, leaving nothing for choice. (This perspective is something further affecting that air, in Wittgenstein's writing, at once of utter humility and absolute arrogance. I mention this to help bear in mind that an understanding of his style will not be possible apart from an understanding of his teaching.)

The specific implication here with respect to skepticism concerning other minds is that I shall be regarding the favored answer to skepticism — that we know of others by analogy with ourselves — as itself an expression of skepticism. This argument from or by analogy, as I conceive it to have plausibility, and currency, goes something like this: What we know of others we know on the basis of their behavior, since obviously we cannot, as in our own case, have their sentience, say literally have a pain of theirs. But since I know that certain bits of my behavior are correlated with certain stretches of my sentience, and since the behavior and the bodies of others are like mine, analogous to mine, it is reasonable to infer from my case that others have sentience as I do, in particular a sentience like mine, analogous to mine, say feel what I feel, i.e., feel something exactly similar to what I feel, when say they bump their shins on a low table, double over to hug their legs for solace, and produce howls. Like causes produce like effects. Now what I mean by calling this argument an expression of skepticism is this: it can seem to make good sense only on the basis of ideas of behavior and of sentience that are invented and sustained by skepticism itself. But to make this out, as well as to make out what it means to speak of skepticism as inventing and sustaining certain ideas, will be a principal task of the pages to follow.

In Part Two I will pursue the skeptical claim far enough to bring out what I mean by saying that Wittgenstein's teaching is everywhere controlled by a response to skepticism, and why it is that the skeptic's denial of our criteria is a denial to which criteria must be open. If the fact that we share, or have established, criteria is the condition under which we can think and communicate in language, then skepticism is a *natural* possibility of that condition; it reveals most perfectly the standing threat to thought and communication, that they are only human, nothing more than natural to us. One misses the drive of Wittgenstein if one is not — as to my mind what I have excerpted from Malcolm is not — sufficiently open to the threat of skepticism (i.e., to the skeptic in oneself); or if one takes Wittgenstein — as to my mind what I have excerpted from Albritton does — to deny the truth of skepticism.

(This might be a likely place from which to look at P. F. Strawson's characterization of the skeptic's position in the following terms: "He pretends to accept a conceptual scheme, but at the same time quietly rejects one of the conditions of its employment" (*Individuals*, p. 24). But it would not yet be a good time. After Part Two we should in principle be able to ask usefully how the descriptions "pretends", "at the same time", and "quietly" are thought to be justified. Shall we say that they are merely literary, or dramatic, and (hence) dispensable, so that Strawson could as well (i.e., without loss of cognitive content) have said?: The skeptic accepts a conceptual scheme but rejects one of the conditions of its employment. But if that is the way the case is put, then wouldn't we be curious to know *why* anyone would do such a thing, even to know *how* he could? And suppose I claim that the real drama of the position is better expressed as follows: The skeptic possesses a conceptual scheme (i.e., our conceptual scheme — what other is lived?), but in the resolve and the intensity of his meditation he discovers that he must relinquish, with moans of delirious terror, the basis of its employment. — Then we might be willing to ask, for example, what it means to "possess" a concept, or scheme of concepts, and what accepting and rejecting have to do with the matter.)

But didn't I earlier concede not just what I called the "truth" of skepticism (that our relation to the world as such is not one of knowing) but its claim or thesis as well (that we *cannot* know of the existence of objects)? It may seem that what at most I have established is, say, that "pain" retains a constant *meaning* when applied to other persons in different contexts, but also that I have admitted that we can never be certain, on a given occasion, that the person is *feeling* pain.

Have I admitted this? I have said that there is no criterion for someone's being in pain now, over and above the criteria for his behavior (including, of course, the patterns and degrees of feeling that behavior expresses) being pain-behavior. (I say "of course" feelings are included among the criteria for applying a concept. But this does not seem of course the case in the discussions of criteria I am aware of. It comes to be assumed that if Wittgenstein included what goes on inside someone among what he calls criteria, that would just brazenly beg the question; because it is to prove that something is going on inside someone that criteria are invoked at all. But I anticipate.) Put otherwise, I have given up such a statement as "But that's what we call 'being in pain'" as a proof, or even as evidence at all, that someone is now suffering pain; I have thus renounced any appeal to "Paradigm Cases" as arguments, against the skeptic, that something exists and that we can know it exists. The philosophical force of appeals to ordinary language does not depend upon the force of any such argument, as both defenders and attackers of "ordinary language philosophy" have sometimes seemed to suppose.

III

Austin and Examples

It will help me make clearer why I sometimes think of criteria as of the identification rather than of the existence of something, and also help explain why that distinction does not satisfy me, if I now bring to our argument a passage or two from Austin's "Other Minds" which I take to be discussing a version of the stage of problem we are facing here, the relation between knowing what a thing is (by means of criteria) and knowing that it is.

In considering the types of answer that may be given to the question "How do you know?", Austin first uses as his example (he calls it a "stalking horse") the claim "There's a bittern at the bottom of the garden" (p. 47). The bases of the replies one may offer in support of such a claim are then articulated by him in this way:

. . . I must have

> (1) been trained in an environment where I could become familiar with bitterns
> (2) had a certain opportunity in the current case
> (3) learned to recognize or tell bitterns
> (4) succeeded in recognizing or telling this as a bittern

If I have produced my background credentials and my opportunities in the current case, and they have not been relevantly countered or questioned, then I have successfully established my claim, I have said enough.

Enough means enough to show that (within reason, and for present intents and purposes) it "can't" be anything else, there is no room for an alternative, com-

49

peting, description of it. It does not mean, e.g., enough to show it isn't a stuffed goldfinch [or, of course, stuffed bittern].

And later:

Knowing it's a "real" goldfinch isn't in question in the ordinary case when I say I know it's a goldfinch: reasonable precautions only are taken. But when it *is* called in question, in *special* cases, then I make sure it's a real goldfinch in ways essentially similar to those in which I made sure it was a goldfinch . . . . [p. 56]

In discussing these statements, and in my more general remarks about the structure of Austin's argument, I am going to describe what he says in a way which, if accurate, shows its analogy to what has so far come out about the relation of criteria and existence. In the following chapter I will indicate the ways in which the analogy is not exact.

Austin's initial method or considerations for analyzing "know" (pp. 44–54) are considerations in which the concept of knowledge is fairly explicitly directed toward determining the identity of things, and not toward establishing their existence; his question "How do you know?" there means "How can you tell that this is a [e.g., goldfinch]?". I am going to take this question to mean, "What are the criteria for something's being [e.g., a goldfinch]?". This overlaps the ordinary sense of the term "criterion" in appealing to marks or features or capacities in terms of which a name is to be applied; I take "the criteria for something's being a goldfinch" as slightly short for "the marks or features in terms of which something is recognized to be a goldfinch".

Now let us ask why, in substantiating the claim that there is a goldfinch here, you do not have to provide a basis which is enough to show it isn't stuffed; that "enough does not mean enough to show it isn't stuffed". How does it "not mean" this? If I have claimed that there is a goldfinch there and it turns out to be stuffed, have the facts in no way touched my claim, in no way spoken back to what I meant?

Is this answered by Austin's remark that "I make sure it's a real goldfinch in ways essentially similar to those in which I made sure it's a goldfinch"? This is puzzling. In what *ways* do I make sure it's a goldfinch? The answer seems to be that I make sure that I have identified it correctly, i.e., that I have in unobjectionable circumstances applied the correct (Austinian) criteria and that the bird truly manifests them. Then to make sure it is a real goldfinch "in ways essentially similar" would be to make sure that I have correctly applied, and it has truly manifested, the criteria for being real (or a real goldfinch? or real bird?). But are there Austinian criteria for something's being real, or a real X? I take it not. ("The wile of the metaphysician consists in asking 'Is it a real table?' . . . and not specifying or limiting what may be wrong with it, so that I feel at a loss 'how to prove' it *is* a real one" (p. 55).) Nor, following Austin's heartfelt demand to be told what "real" is being contrasted with, do I see that there are Austinian criteria for a thing's being "stuffed, painted, dummy, artificial, trick, freak, toy, assumed, feigned . . ." (*ibid.*). It would make no sense to provide a list of marks and features for drawing these distinctions from reality which I might in principle be more expert at applying than others are. I would like to say: There are (can be) no criteria for something's being a real X over and above the criteria for its being an X. Or to repeat: There are no criteria for a thing's *being* so over and above the criteria for its being so. This would provide an explanation for Austin's claim that, where the problem of knowledge is one of identification, providing a basis for the claim does "not mean" providing a basis sufficient to show it is real (not stuffed, a decoy, etc.; hallucinatory?). It does not (cannot) mean this because providing a criterion for claiming it's a goldfinch equally provides the basis for claiming that it's a stuffed *goldfinch.* The criteria (marks, features) are the same for something's being a goldfinch whether it is real, imagined, hallucinatory, stuffed, painted, or in any way phoney. Am I *just wrong* if I say "There's a goldfinch" and it "turns out to be" stuffed? If you hold up a chart of birds and ask me "Is there a goldfinch here?" or "Which is the goldfinch?" and I say *"There's a goldfinch"*, will you reply "You're wrong, it's only a painting"? That *is* fully outrageous. Because I was *right* in my identification, and because I *knew* they were all painted. How did I "know" that? Not the way I know that one was the goldfinch. (Existence is not a predicate.) And I want to say: The difference between real and imaginary, between existence and absence, is not a criterial difference, not one of recognition. And so the answer to "Am I wrong?" is, It depends. It depends on whether the question I am asked is one of identification or of something else (something I waver between calling existence and reality). The problem, or something I am trying to make a problem, is: How do I know whether I am asked the one or whether the other?

Austin, explicitly, is combatting the (philosopher's) idea that to prove, provide basis enough, for a claim to knowledge, I have to be prepared to consider each and every possibility which, should it obtain, would defeat my claim to be certain, to know that the object of my claim is really there — ranging from considerations of how much of an object I actually or literally see (which open the "possibility" that the back halves and insides of objects may not be where or what they are supposed to be) to considerations of whether I can prove I am not dreaming or having an hallucination (which opens the "possibility" that what I claim to be present is plain absent). Austin grants that "not enough" can, in special cases, "mean" not enough to prove it's real; but since he doesn't specify what must be special about these cases, how does he know, why does he insinuate, that the philosopher would enter this objection *in the context Austin imagines?* It seems very unplausible to suppose that the philosopher would enter it there, exactly because if he did he *would* be "silly", "outrageous" (p. 52).

Austin's examples differ in a critical way from the examples given in traditional epistemology. Austin takes a case in which, as he says, you (can) have provided enough to show that there is "no room for an alternative, competing, description of it". This is a case in which the *problem* of knowledge is one, and initially one solely, of correct description (identification, recognition). The objects "chosen as stalking horses" by the classical epistemologist are never of this kind; they do not confront the problem of knowing at this point; that is not the "problem of knowledge" which concerns them. The objects they work with have been, e.g., bits of wax, tables, chairs, houses, men, envelopes, bells, sheets of paper, tomatoes, blackboards, pencils, etc. (In Indian philosophy, I'm told, you often find a stick which, for all you know then and there, may be a snake.) Of course that is hardly news to Austin. That is just a complaint he has against traditional philosophy, that it works with paltry, arbitrary examples which stultify investigations from the outset. And it can hardly be denied that, in using *his* stalking horses, about which all his occasions naturally arise, he has been enabled to bring forth more interesting facts and more practical questions than are likely to adorn the pages of traditional epistemologists, all obsessed with their one or two insipid physical objects.

But suppose that traditional epistemologists have had no choice in this matter, that their obsession is dictated by, and reveals, the nature of the question they are obsessed by. (What else would you expect from an obsession?) There is something common among all their objects: they are ones specifically about which there just is no problem of recognition or identification or description; ones about which the only "problem", should it arise, would be not to say what they are but to say whether we can know that they exist, are real, are actually there. I am going sometimes, for heuristic purposes, to call such things "generic objects", and contrast them with such things as Austin takes for his examples, which I will call "specific objects". I will not by such titles be meaning to suggest that there are two kinds of objects in the world, but rather to summarize the spirit in which an object is under discussion, the kind of problem that has arisen about it, the problem in which it presents itself as the focus of investigation. While I do not think it accidental that such a thing as a goldfinch does not make an appearance in traditional epistemology, I do not wish to insist that one could not have appeared; but only that, if it were to, its function would be, or become, that of a generic object. I have tried various titles for this summary of the functions of the epistemologist's object; at one time I called them "simple objects", at another "basic objects". The unsatisfactoriness of these titles used to seem to me to be their prejudicing of the contrast they set up with Austinian examples, and in particular their sounding like a class of objects. Now I attribute the unsatisfactoriness to their prejudicing of the object's very appearance or function, which is just what they are to be the titles for.

The traditional title for them is "material objects", and the background of my wish to re-title them is my feeling that "material" in that context also bespeaks not a species of object (tomatoes or sticks as opposed, say, to shadows or flames) but the spirit in which the object is put in question. (Bespeaks this, anyway, initially; later in the investigation it may turn out that the object is taken to contrast, say, with non-material objects — mental things perhaps, or divine. But we need to get into these investigations before I can say more about what I mean here by "initially" and "later".) My title "generic object" will be profitable, therefore, if it brings this problem to attention, the problem, one might say, of the phenomenology of materiality. When those objects present themselves to the epistemologist, he is not taking one as opposed to another, interested in its features as peculiar to it and nothing else. He would rather, so to speak, have an unrecognizable *something* there if he could, an anything, a thatness. What comes to him is an island, a body surrounded by air, a tiny earth. What is at stake for him in the object is materiality as such, externality altogether.

Kant speaks of objects as what we meet with "outside of us" and his categories of the understanding are to provide categories which give us the conditions under which it is possible to know of such things *überhaupt*. But suppose the categories articulate our notion of "an object (of nature)" without articulating our sense of externality. (Our sense not of each object's externality to every other, making nature a whole, showing it to be spatial; but their externality to me, making nature a world, showing it to be habitable.) And suppose that our idea of externality, of objects as being "in a world apart from me", is what is registered in the concept of the "thing-in-itself". Then the problem with the notion of "thing-in-itself" is not, as it has been put, that Kant does not, or cannot, explain its relation to the objects we know, or that he oughtn't to be able so much as to imagine its relation (because in his view the categories do not apply to it). The problem with the concept of thing-in-itself is that it should itself have received a transcendental deduction, i.e., that it itself, or the concepts which go into it (e.g., externality; world (*in* which objects are met)), should have been seen as internal to the categories of the understanding, as *part* of our concept of an object in general. Though it may make better Kantian sense to say: If the derivation of the concepts of the Transcendental Aesthetic had been more complete, particularly the ideas of "inner sense" and "outer sense" which go into the concepts of time and space, there would be no idea of a thing-in-itself left over. One may say that this externality follows from, or only means anything if it means the same as, each object's externality to the others. I have in effect denied that — denied it phenomenologically, so to speak — by reading the problem of externality in my relation to one generic object. This aside, to produce the thing-in-itself before, as it were, deriving its concept, to drop down into the unknowable thing-in-itself an essential of what it is we must know (or an essential form in which we must sense) in order that anything be an object of knowledge for us, makes irresistible the impulse to read Kant as though he says that there are things, somethings or other, that we cannot know.   — Of course; his idea has to do with the limits of knowledge.   — But his idea was also to show the possibility of knowledge, i.e., to show that knowledge is limited not in the sense that there are *things* beyond its reach, but that there are human capacities and responsibilities and desires which reveal the world but which are not exhausted in the capacity of knowing things. This is something his Idea of God is meant to show: that I have, and must have if I am a rational creature, a relation to reality which is not that of knowing. But suppose that this is true of the thing-in-itself as well, deriving that as the externality of objects of knowledge, as what I called the world in which objects are to be met. Then Kant's Idea of God may be compromised; its content may then go no further than saying that such a world is, as ours is, characterized by externality. (In which case "noumenal" would so far add nothing to the concept of "world".) One may wish to say that the Idea of God has in it not merely the idea of a world's externality, its coherence without me, but of a world's having something *beyond* it. And in the context Kant provides, that just sounds like a figure of speech.

I have of course said nothing about why, or how, a generic object is what presents itself to the epistemologist, or how it happens that an object should have this weight for him. (This is a main topic of Part Two.) But this much can I think be said now: In the sense in which it is obviously unreasonable to ask of a specific (i.e., Austinian) object, without a special reason for asking, whether my basis for claiming to know (e.g., "From the red head") is enough to show that it is real — in that sense it is *not* unreasonable to ask of a generic object, granted that it has presented itself as a problem of knowledge, whether our basis for claiming to know (typically, "I see it"; "I know it by means of the senses") is enough to show that it is real. *What* are the "intents and purposes" relative to which it is obvious that such a question needn't (can't) be raised? And is it obvious that apart from such intents and purposes, the philosopher's question of existence about generic objects (i.e., ones about which there is no problem of identification) is silly or outrageous? As obvious, I mean, as the fact that he *would* be silly were he to raise his questions with respect to a specific object (one about which the problem is one of identification)? The classical epistemologist's entire project may be misguided from start to finish; but that is hardly shown by accusing him of denying something he has not questioned (namely, that "enough is enough", where you have said enough to rule out other possible identifications). And while he may have been wrong in *not* questioning it, and wrong in thinking that there is any *other* question to be asked, that still remains to be shown.

Since the context in which Austin requires "a special reason" or "a special case" in order sensibly to raise the question of reality is one in which the object under discussion is a specific one, the correctness of this requirement — what, one might say, gives it sense — is that the question of identification about such objects *needs* no special reason to secure its competence. This is the reason Austin could say, near the beginning of his paper, ". . . [the] question, 'How do you know?' . . . may well be asked out of respectful curiosity, from a genuine desire to learn" (p. 46); he says, further, that it may also be asked as a *pointed* question. Respectful or pointed, the answers will be the same in both, and will require the noting of criteria. But if the object under discussion is a generic one, then the non-pointed, respectful question is out of order. What answer is there, in ordinary circumstances, to the question "How do you know it's a tomato?" asked respectfully, out of a genuine desire to learn? Shall I reply that I have been brought up in a tomato patch, that I can tell from the red skin, etc.? But your "asking from a genuine desire to learn" means asking something I know and you do not know or asking how *I* happen to know this, have acquired this capacity of recognition, which you respectfully imply to be superior to yours. But do I happen to have an ability to recognize tomatoes (envelopes, tables, etc.) which is superior to yours? If I do, we may take a different example (or epistemology is not what we will talk about).

It is, I have said, of the essence of the traditional epistemologist's investigations that the objects he uses as examples are not ones about which there is something more to learn in the way of recognizing them; *no one's position,* with respect to identifying them, *is better than anyone else's.* And it turns out that no one's position is better in any respect. An island of earth is faced by an island of consciousness, of sense experience. And this proves not to be enough for knowing. The epistemologist's question can be formulated as "How do *we* know, e.g., that . . . ?", and the question this question turns out to investigate is "How do we know (can we be certain) that *anything* exists?".

And can't there be such a question? Proving a radical incoherence or some extraordinary use of language in the investigations of classical epistemology will now mean proving some radical incoherence in asking, about a generic object, how we know it exists. Asking it, of course, not when there is some real and obvious difficulty about knowing it (e.g., poor visibility, which might make my position better than yours), but when there is no "special reason" of *that* kind; when for all the world we are both in the same position, and an optimal position, facing it together. Doubtless there is something extraordinary about this question, and perhaps we should say that there must be some special reason for raising it. Then my question is: Is it obvious that the philosopher has no such reason?

What was the content of the sense that "there is no reason to raise the question"? What kind of claim was that? It meant (a) that there is nothing more we wish or need to learn about (identifying) the object (= it is a specific object), and (b) there is no further problem (about its existence or reality) which it makes sense to raise under normal circumstances. I hope that (a) is clear enough. But there remains a question about how (b) is known. What kind of claim is that? How do we know there is a further problem, when, that is, there obviously *is* one? How do we know that if there is some reason to think the bird may be stuffed, the pain feigned, then the question of reality *must* arise; and how do we know what would count as "a reason to think so"? But anybody who can speak knows these things. If we watch a blackbird fly into a tree and sit on a wet branch thirteen ways, no one (including the philosopher) is going to raise, or accept the question "But is it real?", without some special reason. But if I say "Don't forget that Mr. Stevens (the next-door neighbor) is not only an inventor but an expert taxidermist", that might make us accept the question about the reality of our blackbird on the fourteenth look. What, more than this common ability to recognize the relevance of questions — an ability no profounder, nor less profound, than the ability to make assertions — can an ordinary language philosopher be going on when he says, about the specific object, "No reason to ask"? Nothing more. His evidence must be evidence that any mature speaker of a language can provide or recognize as significant. That is the strength of his methods, the source of their convincingness; but also their weakness, his helplessness to *prove* their relevance as philosophical criticisms. For if the epistemologist does not *accept* such a statement as "There is no reason to ask", *that* fact must count as evidence that the statement is false, that his question has not been understood.

So there remains a problem about why the philosopher raises a question, about a generic object, under circumstances in which, normally, there is no doubt that it is there. My insistence that there is a problem about this is directed both against the ordinary language philosopher and against the defender of the tradition. For the former is likely to say: "It's just obvious that the question does not arise; the philosopher is being willful or blind in his insistence upon raising it." But that is completely dogmatic, with none of the convincingness of the ordinary language analysis of ordinary situations. On the other hand, the traditional philosopher is likely to offer this defense: "It's just obvious that the question must be raised: it doesn't matter that it is not a question which would normally be asked. On the contrary, that shows the complacency of common sense, the inadequacy of ordinary language." Only that is just as dogmatic as the position he is defending himself against. For the reason he "must" raise his question is one which he must feel that anyone who understood what he was saying would *accept* as a reason. His questions are perfectly ordinary ("Mightn't it be wax?", "Do you see all of it?"), and he, and everyone, knows the circumstances under which they would normally be raised, and the import of the answers given to them ("We don't see all of it, so we don't know it is one") — his entire procedure depends on that knowledge. Any criticism of the classical investigations of knowledge, entered from an attention to what is ordinarily said when, must account for the fact that the traditional philosophers, masters of at least the language they write, have accepted a question as requiring an answer which under other circumstances, *they* (as well as "the ordinary man") would have rejected as absurd.

"Knowing it's a 'real' goldfinch isn't in question in the ordinary case when I say I know it's a goldfinch: reasonable precautions only are taken . . . [and] the precautions cannot be more than reasonable, relative to current intents and purposes" (p. 56). It is easy to read such a passage as suggesting that what is "enough" to substantiate such a claim is more or less a matter of common sense, or common room sense, or common courtesy; and that people (= epistemologists or metaphysicians) who ask for "more" are being "unreasonable" or rude or boring or just impossible. But Austin can be taken as laying out the common grammar — even, in some extraordinary sense, the logic — of differences in the question "How do you know?"; and to ask for "more" than *that* permits is hardly to be thought of as discourteous, etc. It constitutes not an unreasonableness of intellectual manner but a denial of human reason. If the basis requested, and given, is one of criteria (e.g., "From the eye-markings") then if you are wrong, the explanation of your failure will (must) take a form which impugns your possession of the appropriate criteria for recognizing goldfinches or your success or care in noting them in this case. But *if your criteria are right,* only the object is not a *real* exemplar, then you *have* to explain this contretempts by saying "stuffed, painted", etc. Were you wrong? It *is* a goldfinch, only. . . . (The concept is retained. It is retained because the criteria for its application are present and satisfied.) What have you in that case failed to know?

What did I want to know? What, or how much, did I claim to know when I claimed there was a goldfinch in the garden? Did I take my claim to penetrate the bird and to stake a claim against anything untoward inside it? What extent of power have I given over to reality in opening my judgment toward it? What stake have I made in earning the claim's attention upon reality at all?   — What is an empirical judgment?

Whether or not there are Austinian criteria for something's being real, or for being a real something of a particular kind, Austin must imagine, validly, that we know how to make sure, know what to do to make sure and certain, of such things. For example, to make sure that the bird is not stuffed I could puncture it and see whether stuffing falls out. I have no idea whether this bit of academic sadism would be making sure it's real "in the same way" as I might have made sure it's a goldfinch (unless someone wishes to insist that this *is* making sure it is a goldfinch, while another might wish to insist that only God could really do that (as only a composer can make sure that the tonic is well established (though who is it who makes sure that the singing is on pitch, the singer or the sung to?))). But there is a more immediate point at which an Austinian conscience toward speech and its claims should pinch. What would prompt me, allow me reasonably or sanely, to puncture the bird? A special reason, a special occasion, is by all means required. But which would raise the question of reality to such an extent?

And *couldn't* I just surmise that the bird is not real, or form a suspicion about it, for no special reason and on no special occasion? I ask this bearing in mind that I mean the problem as a problem of knowledge, not as a problem about me, about my mental health. (It is fundamental to skepticism to be able to draw such a distinction, anyway initially; and fundamental perhaps to certain skeptics that the distinction eventually collapses.) I do not as it were wish to try to infect myself with a surmise; I might as well save time and directly try to infect myself with a firm belief! I may naturally surmise that the bird is the work of a taxidermist if, for example, I notice that it is *too* still and for *too* long a time. But then *that* is the "special reason" for my surmise here. Would I now, for this reason, and in a reasonable state of mental health, fly to the bird to puncture it in order to see what comes out of it? Is that something I want to know here? — But I have said, in recording the cause of the surmise, or in so much as describing, so much as identifying, the surmise, what it is that I want to know, namely, whether there is something suspicious in the *stillness* of the bird. To supply that lack, to satisfy that desire for knowledge, the appropriate way of making sure is, say, to hold the bird (as if to sense a pulse or shudder) and perhaps poke it gently (to see if it moves, as one might make sure that a person asleep has not fallen into a coma). (Aren't such measures the application of criteria? Not for goldfinches, nor for any other specific object.) — But if how I make sure is dictated by what I want to know, which in turn is determined by what special reason there is for raising the question, then making sure (and hence being sure, and for that matter being certain) is not done once for all, not by human kind. Hence it *cannot* satisfy what the epistemologist wants to know. Whether the epistemologist really *wants* to know anything comprehensible — or whether he has infected himself with a doubtful experience — is thus the form these considerations give to the question of skepticism. More specifically, the form is one in which we are to ask whether the philosopher has a special reason, anyway a good enough reason, for raising his question of reality.

Is there some reason good enough to prompt me naturally to seek out an occasion for puncturing the bird? Consider Mr. Stevens. He dares me to tear the bird open, and when I do, or he does it for me, I find about what ought to be there, all the disgusting complexity of real live things.

What's going on? Did he just involve me in killing a bird? Or has he really manufactured something I cannot tell from the real thing? Or has he a way of taking a dead thing, a former live thing, and working some kind of magnetic field around it which puts back, from the outside as it were, the contours of life — a pulse, responses to "stimuli", random movement, soaring flight?   — Are such worries mere surrealism? But why is it expressed by *these* questions? How has my ability to make sure lost its bearings, slipped its moorings, to be tossed in doubt? Why is my capacity for making sure, my knowledge of how it is done, no longer dictated to, given content by, some specific desire for knowledge, or a desire for some specific knowledge?   — If the question of reality does arise, and it does not get settled in a hurry, *and* I cannot dismiss it, then what happens to the question? What do I do with it?   — What causes skepticism?

Austin takes epistemologists as "prone to argue that because I *sometimes* don't know or can't discover, I *never* can" (p. 56). (If that were the argument, to call someone prone with respect to it is generous; prostrate is more like it.) So Austin banks on defeating it by pointing out, e.g., that we may never know what Caesar's feelings were on the field of the battle of Philippi (cp. p. 50), or that the goldfinch "may fly away before I have a chance of testing it, or of inspecting it thoroughly enough" (p. 56): "I don't by any means *always* know whether it's one or not" (*ibid.*). The spirit of these observations is questionable. They contain no news whatever for epistemologists. But leaving aside for the moment the role of "optimal conditions" in the epistemologist's argument (i.e., the fact that his cases are never ones in which there is some obvious way in which I haven't had sufficient opportunity to test or inspect the object), Austin is still banking too hard. There is this humming in the air; or a noise at midnight in the basement — there it is again. Shall I say: "I don't by any means *always* know . . .", and let it go at that? But there aren't *just* hummings in the air; it is *imperative* that I find out whether there happens to be one in the air now or whether it is only in my ears. Certainly I may not be able to learn the answer in this case, to convince myself one way or the other. But it won't help my condition to say that sometimes I *just* don't know. I am left with the question; it stays in me, until it decays in my memory or I overlay it, perhaps symbolize it, with something else.

It is imperative that our experience of the world *make sense,* that loose threads get taken up by some explanation or other. Learning when it is and is not competent to say "I (we) just don't know" is every bit as much a condition of my competence as a knower as learning when to say and when to retract "I am certain". A perfectly good case of just not knowing is one in which the bird flies away before my opportunities for knowing what it is are optimal. Another is: You ask me where the cat is and I say, not looking up, that it is on the mat. You tell me it isn't. "So he's gone again. I just don't know where he is." He could be any number of places; widely acquainted, fickle old cat. But suppose I had said "I just saw him go into his room, and he pushed the door closed behind him" (which he does when he is pouting; and he can't open the door by himself, and we know there is no other way out of the room). You go and look and tell me he is not there. Shall I say: "This is simple enough; I don't by any means *always* know where he is"? Certainly it is *true* that I don't always know this. Then what was all that about seeing him and about closing the door? I feel here: Taking the consequences of an assertion seriously is the same as making (serious) assertions.

Austin is responsive to the sense that "anything can happen", that we are at the mercy of the future: he imagines the case in which, after we have made sure it's a real goldfinch, "it does something outrageous (explodes, quotes Mrs. Woolf, or what not)" (*ibid.*). I do not find that my surrealism has outdone Austin's. But his response to it is different: " 'Being sure it's real' is no more proof against miracles or outrages of nature than anything else is or, *sub specie humanitatis,* can be . . . . [In such a case] we don't say we were wrong to say it was a goldfinch, *we don't know what to say*. Words literally fail us . . ." (*ibid.*); and again ". . . if there's a *lusus naturae,* a miracle, . . . that wouldn't mean I was wrong . . ." (p. 63). This is his way of handling the moment at which I asked, "What happens to the question (of reality)?". But I found that words were not failing me (not, anyway, in the sense that they were abandoning me); they were overwhelming me.

Words can fail me when I am in no doubt whatever about what has happened nor about how it can have happened, but when I am agog *that* it has happened (surprise parties; a friend met a decade later on a foreign corner; revelations . . .). And neither an exploding nor a quoting goldfinch is an example of what would ordinarily count as a *lusus naturae*. They are not freaks (as perhaps an albino is); we do not feel about them "Such things do happen sometimes", or "Of course there must be a good explanation for it" (*which I can leave it to others to know*). Because, according to what has so far come out, anyone ought to be able to figure out what caused this explosion who knows anything about detonating devices. And *I* ought to be able to tell how the voice got located in the region of the bird. A recording? a ventriloquist? — what would convince me that no such explanation is in order, that this was *nature's* doing? And if I do imagine becoming convinced that this bird is doing its own quoting, then if I do not imagine myself in a trance (and for *that* reason out of words, but also in no position for judging about reality), then I imagine myself with an adequate supply of words, but interested in talking only to the bird.

Experience must, *sub specie humanitatis,* make sense. "A freak of nature" is one explanation which makes sense of experience; but it is, as Austin is always saying on other occasions, a specific explanation, competent only under certain conditions. And the field of sense, over which explanations range from "I just don't know" to "It's a freak of nature", is broader than any a priori bargain knows. Science, history, magic, myth, superstition, religion, are all in that field. There is no short-cut across it. Sometimes an explanation is wrong because it jumps to conclusions ("But goldcrests also have red heads"; "But you could have heard exactly what you heard and there have been no humming in the air"; "Not everything which causes the admiration of a miracle is something which abrogates the laws of nature"); sometimes because it appeals to magic before science has come to an end or to a head (e.g., the storm as God's anger); sometimes because it makes science or philosophy into magic (as when, perhaps, a philosopher appeals to a "brain process" which he knows nothing about; or maybe "Where our language suggests a body and there is none; there, we should like to say, is a *spirit*" (*Investigations,* §36)).

We know that what may be incomplete in a claim to truth is not its correspondence with the facts but the claimer's right to the claim. (Knowledge is *justified* belief. At the very least.) Knowing how to make serious assertions is knowing how to justify them, and also knowing how to excuse them (e.g., with *ad hoc* hypotheses) in case they come to grief. Explanations equally stand under the constraint of the explainer's "right" to his explanation. To rid explanations of misplaced magic is as important to serious theology as to serious science or philosophy. (In what spirit does someone say "Christ died for my sins"? One in which he takes upon himself the responsibility for receiving that gift, or one in which he takes the occasion to slough his responsibility in it? In what spirit, against what history, might I say something like "It causes sleep because it contains the dormative virtue"? One in which all I see is that when people take the thing they soon fall asleep? Or one in which I have a theory of "virtues"?) Sometimes I may claim to *need* no explanation; I stand upon my faith. But then I had better pick my occasion carefully; and I have to trust my faithfulness, which is all that will now provide my right to the conviction. It is a claim that I can make sense of my experience in no other way, and that I am without the need of outside corroboration — that words have not failed me, but that I have gladly left them behind.

For most human beings, most of the time, surrealism is better than no explanation at all. And what my particular surrealism brought to light is that the question of reality is not settled the way questions of identity are settled. I haven't got a set of routines or features or cautions to appeal to in settling questions of whether the thing is live; *or* of settling for just saying I don't know. There is this thing wheeling right overhead. I ought to be able to settle whether it's real right now, and from here; or anyway, from not very much closer. It is part of my equipment as a knowing creature to be able to do that; knowing it from here is what I want to know. Then what question can I ask myself now? "Is its flight pattern quite right?" But that *now* means not "Is that the way *goldfinches* fly?" (as contrasted, perhaps, with larks, if they are similar in this respect), but rather "Is that the way a *living creature* flies (as contrasted with even the best mechanical contrivances)?". On what ground might I conclude one way or another? In what "way" do living creatures fly (or walk, or cough, or cry, or kiss, or request, or assert . . .)? What general answer to this is there other than, "The way living creatures I've known do these things"? And of course that is no answer. In what "way" do I know this? I might say: If I didn't know it I would have none of the concepts which apply only to living things. And that is an answer. It is what I take to be the force of Wittgenstein's having said: "Only of a living human being and what resembles (behaves like) a living human being can one say: It has sensations; it sees; is blind; hears; is deaf; is conscious or unconscious" (§281). Except that we do not yet see what this force is.

Am I implying that we do not really *know* the difference between hallucinated and real things, or between animate and inanimate things? What I am saying is that the differences are not ones for which there are criteria. As the difference between natural objects and artifacts is not one for which there are criteria. In such cases the role of *origins* is decisive, indeed definitive. So shall we rather say: knowing a thing's origin is knowing the decisive, the definitive, criterion of it? But that removes a criterion from its role in providing a means of knowledge, since in very few cases have we been present at a thing's origin, a thing we nevertheless know as well as we know anything! But then, as Descartes more or less says, conceiving how a thing is sustained or conserved comes to the same as conceiving its origin. The ultimacy of the idea of origin in our ideas of the difference between animate and inanimate things and between natural and artificial things is something that invites proofs from these locales for the existence of God.

IV

What a Thing Is (Called)

I said that the use I wished to make of the term "criterion" in discussing Austin's views is not fully analogous to its use in Wittgenstein's investigations. The point of the analogy turned on the fact that neither sort of criterion serves as a mark of existence or reality but of identification or recognition, and that (hence) both are related to a knowledge of what a thing is (conventionally) called. The point of difference is this. In Austin's cases, directed toward specific objects, there is a natural question about what, and whether you know what, the thing *is* called. It is a natural question because it has a natural answer, viz., the provision of a name or title (e.g., "goldfinch", "half gainer") which is justified on the basis of established criteria; to be competent in such matters is to know these criteria and justifying the application of the name in a given case is a full expression of your knowledge in the case. If I have, in response to the query "How do you know (can you tell) it's a goldfinch?", "[indicated], or to some extent set out . . . those features of the situation which enable me to recognize it as one to be described in the way I describe it", you may object or claim that I am "evidently unable to recognize goldfinches"; and Austin goes on to say that "in making this sort of accusation you would perhaps tend not so much to use the expression 'You don't know' . . . as, rather, 'But that isn't a goldfinch (*goldfinch*)', or 'Then you're wrong to call it a goldfinch' " (pp. 51–52). This quite usual entry of "call" registers someone's inability to recognize a thing as a function of his not having "learned the right (customary, popular, official) name to apply to the creature ('Who taught you to use the word "goldfinch"?')".

65

"Not to know what the object is" here means "not to know what it is popularly or officially or customarily (or, summarily, conventionally) called". (Cp. p. 51.)

Wittgenstein's cases are not of this kind. When he asks for our noting and explaining of criteria, the "object" in question is either some "state of consciousness" (using that as the rubric for his interests in mental phenomena of various kinds, the rubric he uses in the Preface to the *Investigations*) or else some physical phenomenon about which our problem is not (as it is not in traditional epistemology) that we lack or doubt its specific name. So what is the force of *his* habitual questions and claims about what something is called? *What* is it we need to identify, if anything, since the identification cannot be expressed by providing a thing's name?

Wittgenstein's habitual using of the notion of what we call something is at the center of Albritton's distrust of certain claims Wittgenstein makes for his notion of a criterion, and I think there is no doubt that he has shown strong grounds for distrusting them.

Albritton makes out two conceptions of criteria in Wittgenstein's later philosophy, only one of which he finds defensible.

A criterion for so-and-so's being the case was to be something by which one might *know* that it was the case; that this or that *was* a criterion for so-and-so's being the case was to be a sort of "tautology", a matter of "convention". But instead of making this conception clear, Wittgenstein distorts it, in the *Blue and Brown Books* by representing the criteria for so-and-so's being the case as various things that may *be* what is called "so-and-so's being the case". . . . [p. 244]

Instead, however, of assuming that one of the conceptions of criteria which Albritton characterizes is an indefensible distortion of the other, one might take it as a guide toward understanding what, if anything, Wittgenstein had in mind in introducing the concept at all. That is likely to seem an unpleasant occupation, and not merely because of its awful difficulties; for it must involve us in questioning two assumptions which enter into the grain of our modern philosophical sensibilities. These assumptions are present in the following two remarks of Albritton's: (1) ". . . I have no intention of committing Wittgenstein to the view that the criterion of X is a logically necessary and sufficient condition of X *in the nature of things*, so to speak. Criteria are for him primarily criteria that men 'accept', 'adopt', 'fix', 'introduce', and 'use', or 'apply' in connection with their use of certain *expressions*. If anything is the criterion of X and therefore a logically necessary and sufficient condition of X, it is because (in some sense of 'because') men agree in certain *conventions*" (p. 236).

(2) ". . . sometimes, to be sure, one is justified in saying that one knows a thing and yet doesn't know it, because, as one may or may not discover, it isn't so" (pp. 244–45).

It is not easy to formulate very satisfactorily what the assumptions involved here are, I mean why I call them (mere) assumptions; the best I can do here is to say that the first remark suggests some radical distinction between what is a question of language and what a question of fact (or, between nature and convention), the second suggests a conception of knowledge that makes it essentially a matter of certainty and evidence. What I mean by these "assumptions" will become clearer to the extent that I can clarify what I take the alternatives to them to be.

Albritton's interpretation of Wittgenstein's notion of criterion depends essentially, I think, upon these two formulations:

(a) "The criterion of X is what is *called* 'X'." [p. 236; cf. p. 240]
(b) ". . . a criterion is in Wittgenstein's usage always a criterion for something or other's being the case, being so . . . ." [p. 235, note 5; etc.]

I have already said something about the idea of "being so" as it occurs in the second formulation. The first formulation is arrived at, or supported, by what I take to be a misreading of a passage from the *Blue Book*. Albritton opens his paper with an extended quotation which contains this statement:

It is part of the grammar of the word "chair" that *this* is what we call "to sit on a chair", and it is part of the grammar of the word "meaning" that *this* is what we call "explanation of a meaning"; in the same way to explain my criterion for another person's having a toothache is to give a grammatical explanation about the word "toothache" and, in this sense, an explanation concerning the meaning of the word "toothache".

Albritton's reading of this proceeds as follows:

. . . the phrase "my criterion for another person's having toothache" parallels the preceding phrases "what we call 'explanation of a meaning' " and "what we call 'to sit on a chair' ". Apparently, my criterion for another person's having toothache is what I *call* his having toothache. [p. 240]

But:

. . . can what a man does or says be called his having a toothache, or referred to or described by saying that he has a toothache, under any circumstances, in a proper and literal sense of the words said? No. [p. 242]

The formulation "The criterion of X is what is called 'X' " is not unlike something I got out of the ordinary notion of criterion: "Certain specifications are what a person or group mean by, what they call, count as, a thing's having a certain status . . ."; and later, turning to Wittgenstein-ian "objects", I said that these specifications are what "we" go on in asserting a concept of anything, in speaking about anything, calling it out. I do not insist upon the clarity of this, but unless it has the right depth, there is nothing in it for me to wish to clarify. I would, I take it, be allowed to say that the criterion of X is the *basis* upon which something is called "X", i.e., what we go on in applying this concept to something, and thus avoid the force of Albritton's blunt "No". I mean, no one will, setting aside its obscurities, think it just false to say that "what a man does or says" is the basis upon which we assert the concept "having a toothache" of him. But this tames the idea too far. First, it looks as if it is always open (it *is* always open) for someone to say: "Of course! What else would we be going on? And obviously sometimes you're going to be wrong in your assertion of the concept, and moreover you can never be sure you are not wrong. So say if you like that there are bases for applying concepts, and call those bases criteria; just don't think it follows that you might not have to *withhold* the concept sometimes. And it might be wise to add, whenever you do assert it, a pinch of recognition (e.g., 'almost certain') that you may have to take it back." Second, the force of "call" is and must be there in Wittgenstein's notion. Without it, such reservations as Albritton brings to Wittgenstein's idea of a criterion do not clarify or domesticate it, they destroy it completely. Albritton's attempt to rescue it comes too late:

That a man behaves in a certain manner, under certain circumstances, cannot entail that he has a toothache. [p. 246]

But:

Roughly: it can entail that . . . under these circumstances, one is *justified in saying* that the man has a toothache. . . . Or: it can entail that he *almost certainly* has a toothache. [*ibid.*]

If Wittgenstein *meant* anything in characterizing what he called "criteria" by contrasting this notion with what he called "symptoms", this account cannot explain what it was he meant. For on this account, there would be no relevant distinction of the kind Wittgenstein describes.

The presence of a "symptom" can equally well "justify one in saying" that something is the case, or that it is almost certain. Is the difference, then, that a symptom cannot "entail" this? The idea is, I take it, that a symptom does not make it a part of the very meaning of my words that what I say is the case is (almost certainly) the case. It may be a symptom of a government's being stable that the people seem cheerful. It may not, too; maybe that is just the character of these people, they learn to be cheerful no matter what; or maybe they know something I don't know. In any event, it is not what I mean in calling the government stable. But when I present the criteria in terms of which I assert this concept of a government, and the government does meet them, then that *is* (what I mean by; what I mean in calling it) a stable government. If I'm not fully prepared to call it one, that may be either because I haven't fully articulated my criteria of the concept for myself, or because the government doesn't fully satisfy one or more of them. In the former case (where I'm not fully prepared to call it one), there is uncertainty, but it is in me: "I'm not sure whether I'd call that stability or tyranny"; ". . . whether instability or tolerance". In the latter case (where it *isn't* fully one), I may hedge my claim, but not because of any uncertainty in the situation: "It's really not what I would call stable, but it's more so than others; anyway there are good reasons for saying it is"; "It is far from a perfect example of what I had in mind; but up to a point I wouldn't mind calling it one". There will be complications in cases where criteria conflict or compete with one another, but we don't need them to bring out the relevant contrast with the case of toothache.

There, for all the world, is a man having one: I haven't, presumably, failed to articulate for myself what my criteria for "having a toothache" are. Nor is it a case in which this man fails to satisfy one or other of them. (That, of course, in particular cases, may be the problem: e.g., "Are you sure he's giving out the *right* screams?".) I am further assuming that there is no reason for thinking — it would be fantastic to imagine — that he is "feigning", "rehearsing", etc. In both these kinds of case, uncertainty of an obvious kind would arise (e.g., he might be *feigning* feigning). Even where there are not these obvious uncertainties, hesitations may persist: "I'm not sure whether I want to call that having a toothache or having an ache referred from the jaw"; or "It's not really a perfect example of a toothache, it's really just a pain in a tooth caused by a foreign particle wedged beside it".   — But there are cases in which a man is for all the world having a toothache, optimal cases: *I* am sure (I know what the word means), and it is a perfect example (I've checked). My feeling here is: If *that* isn't — if he isn't having — a toothache, I don't know what a toothache is.

And then perhaps the still, small voice: Is it one? Is he having one? Naturally I do not say that doubt cannot insinuate itself here. In particular I do not say that if it does I can turn it aside by saying "But that's what is *called* having a toothache". This abjectly begs the question — if there is a question. But what *is* the doubt now? That he is actually suffering. But in the face of *that* doubt, *in the presence of full criteria,* it is desperate to continue: "I'm justified in saying; I'm almost certain". My feeling is: There is nothing any longer to be almost certain about. I've gone the route of certainty. Certainty itself hasn't taken me far enough. And to say now "But that is what we call having a toothache" would be mere babbling in the grip of my condition. The only thing that could conceivably have been called "his having a toothache" — his actual horror itself — has dropped out, withdrawn beyond my reach.   — Was it always beyond me? Or is my condition to be understood some other way? (What is my condition? Is it doubt? It is in any case expressed here by speechlessness.)

Wittgenstein does not, I believe, say that what a man says and does (as *opposed* to what he feels) is called his having a toothache. (And if he did he would not, as I understand him, be contradicting his idea, but exemplifying it: he would be babbling.) Nor, so far as I can make out, does he imply it. Go. back to the passage from the *Blue Book* about the chair and the toothache. I read the passage so that "to explain my criterion for" parallels the preceding phrase "it is part of the grammar of"; that is what I take "[in the same way] to explain my criterion for another person's having a toothache is to give a grammatical explanation" to say. The difference between Albritton's reading and mine thus depends upon how one takes the phrase "in the same way". On my reading, it still looks as if you are invited to draw out the parallel by saying: "It is part of the grammar of toothache that *this* is what we call . . .". And the natural candidate which then presents itself for completing the sentence is: ". . . his having a toothache". (This is likely to take us nowhere, or worse; for this is what backs us into the protestation that nothing is *called* his having a toothache, except perhaps his having one. And *that* certainly can't be (what *we* have set up as) the criterion for his having one!)

But "in the same way" only says that explaining my criterion for "toothache" is going to be a grammatical explanation of the word, have the force of the grammatical explanations he was just giving about "chair" and "meaning". It does not say what this explanation will look like (perhaps because he regards it as obvious), nor anything about "call". Where "call" comes in there, it introduces a phrase in which the word to be explained is used; i.e., it associates a concept with other concepts. If we could understand the "force" of such explanations then we would, presumably, have the force of the explanations, whatever they are, about toothache. So let us try to gather what the force is.

"It is part of the grammar of the word 'chair' that *this* is what we call 'to sit on a chair'. . . ." That you use this object *that* way, sit on it *that* way, is our criterion for calling it a chair. You *can* sit on a cigarette, or on a thumb tack, or on a flag pole, but not in *that* way. Can you sit on a table or a tree stump in that (the "grammatical") way? Almost; especially if they are placed against a wall. That is, you can *use* a table or a stump *as* a chair (a place to sit; a seat) in a way you cannot use a tack as a chair. But so can you use a screw-driver as a dagger; that won't make a screw-driver a dagger. What can *serve as a chair* is not a chair, and nothing would (be said to) serve as a chair if there were no (were nothing we called) (orthodox) chairs. We could say: It is part of the grammar of the word "chair" that *this* is what we call "to serve as a chair".

The force of such remarks is something like: If you don't know all this, and more, you don't know what a chair is; what "chair" "means"; what we call a chair; *what* it is you would be certain of (or almost certain of, or doubt very much) if you were certain (or almost certain, or doubt very much) that something is a chair.

"Certain", "almost certain", will come up even under optimal conditions (when, that is, the context is not one in which the object is, e.g., partially hidden, or in bad light, or in fragments) when in an unfamiliar environment (visiting a foreign tribe, perhaps; but how do you know it is *a* tribe?) you see someone more or less sit on something more or less like (what we call) a chair, and perhaps hear the people say something about it using the words we have already translated as "chair" and "sit". Perhaps he doesn't *bend* when he "sits" on it: it is nothing so much as a plank stood on end, about the height and width of an average human being, tipped and braced back slightly from the vertical, into which there are fitted at right angles two pegs which, you discover, are to go under the armpits, and a saddle peg in the middle to "sit" on. We might feel he's not so much sitting on the thing as hanging from it. But he looks comfortable enough.

Then what happens to my contention that when we are hesitant about asserting a concept it is either because we haven't yet established its criteria for ourselves or because we haven't got a perfect instance of it? Surely I am in full possession of the criteria for something's counting as a chair; and surely there is no question here of this thing being a *perfect* example! And what happens to my contention that in neither case do we accommodate to the situation by saying "It's certain" *or* "It's almost certain"? With this "chair", I feel not only that the uncertainty is in me, but that the *fact,* so to speak, is uncertain: anyone ought to realize that I am not in a position to say for sure, just as much as if the thing were in fact mostly hidden or in bad light. It *is* not certain, maybe very doubtful, whether it is one or not.

The difference from the cases of stability and toothache is that what I am directly questioning here is not *my* or *our* criteria, whether *I* want to assert the concept of the thing; but what *their* criteria for it are. (So something *is* still hidden.) For what I am asking myself is not merely whether the word they use about this situation is the same as our word "chair", but whether it is the same as the words they used in other situations which I translated as "chair" and "sit", and whether my earlier translation didn't perhaps jump to conclusions. I am asking what it is they go on in asserting this concept. (Which concept? The one they have which now only seems to touch or overlap mine of a chair.) My problem is not just to get an accurate translation of a word; or rather, what getting that translation amounts to is getting or failing to get a transition from that thing to the things I call chairs, and getting or failing to get a transition from what he's doing to what I call sitting on a chair. And then I have to work out the grammar of my own word as well. Because to say we "have established" full criteria for our word does not mean that we can establish what they are on demand: our investments in a word are rarely liquid. That I know when to assert a concept does not mean that I know why I call it when I do, what the point of its application is. (And these investments may be cashed, or consolidated, on various exchanges: in etymology, i.e., historically; scientifically, if there exists a science of semantics; philosophically; poetically. One day the exchanges themselves may merge.) Maybe it's that middle peg which primarily gets in the way of our concepts. If it were a very shallow shelf instead, a strip running horizontally all the way across the plank and maybe a little lower than the peg, I find I would be happier to speak of someone sitting there; or anyway, to think of it as a seat.

This brings out the point of the demonstrative in Wittgenstein's formula: ". . . part of the grammar . . . that *this* is what we call . . .". What the demonstrative introduces is a criterion, but not an Austinian feature. Wittgensteinian or (as I will now begin calling them) grammatical criteria are not marks or features which require special training or a specialized environment to have mastered, whereas Austinian (non-grammatical) criteria do. There are technical handbooks which give us the features of various types and periods of furniture (what a Louis XIII dining chair is, how to recognize a Louis XIV chaise, etc.) but none which teach us what a chair is and what sitting on a chair is. None, we might say, which illustrate the essence of the matter. The demonstrative registers that we are to recollect those very general facts of nature or culture which we all, all who can talk and act together, do (must) in fact be using as criteria; facts we only need to recollect, for we cannot fail to know them in the sense of having never acquired them. If someone does not have them, that is not because his studies have been neglected, but because he is for some reason incapable of (or has been given up on as a candidate for) maturing into, or initiation into, full membership in the culture.

What is this "having the concept of"? What is a concept? I have no theory in terms of which, or in the service of which, to define such things — unless any characterization of them is theoretical, or unless sharing the uses of a word makes me a theoretician. I use such phrases, and want to use them; I wish merely to find out what I use them for.

I said a while ago that in Austin's cases, justifying the provision of a name on the basis of established criteria is a full expression of your knowledge in the case. In them, "call" is related to non-grammatical criteria (features or marks) and specific objects (those about which the problem of knowledge is a problem of identification). The criteria relate this name to that (species of) object. It is a full test of your possession of the criteria (e.g., of a goldfinch) if you can recognize and name another such object when you see one (in a tree or a book or a museum showcase). In a Wittgensteinian context, "call" is related to grammatical criteria and generic objects. The criteria do not relate a name to an object, but, we might say, various concepts to the concept of that object. Here the test of your possession of a concept (e.g., of a chair, or a bird; of the meaning of a word; of what it is to know something) would be your ability to use the concept in conjunction with other concepts, your knowledge of which concepts are relevant to the one in question and which are not; your knowledge of how various relevant concepts, used in conjunction with the concepts of different kinds of objects, require different kinds of contexts for their competent employment.

The concept of "pointing to" can be used in conjunction with the concepts of such "objects" as artifacts and natural objects of various kinds, as well as with such "objects" as colors, meanings (or synonyms or homonyms or antonyms), places, cities, continents, . . . indeed, it would seem you can point to anything you can name (viz., "everything"). But, of course, each of these different "objects" will (= can) be pointed to only in definite kinds of contexts. If one thinks one or more of these kinds of objects *cannot* be pointed to, that is because one has a set idea ("picture") of what pointing to something must be (consist in), and that perhaps means taking *one* kind of context as inevitable (or one kind of object as inevitable). For example, if you are walking through Times Square with a child and she looks up to you, puzzled, and asks "Where is Manhattan?", you may feel you ought to be able to *point* to something, and yet at the same time feel there is nothing to point to; and so fling out your arms and look around vaguely and say "All of this is Manhattan", and sense that your answer hasn't been a very satisfactory one. Is, then, Manhattan *hard* to point to? But if you were approaching La Guardia Airport on a night flight from Boston, then just as the plane banked for its approach, you could poke your finger against the window and, your interest focussed on the dense scattering of lights, say "There's Manhattan"; so could you point to Manhattan on a map. Are such instances not really instances of pointing to *Manhattan?* Are they hard to accomplish? Perhaps we could say: It feels hard to do (it is, then and there, impossible to do) when the *concept* of the thing pointed to is in doubt, or unpossessed, or repressed.

Take Wittgenstein's example of "pointing to the color of an object". In philosophizing one may compare this with "pointing to the object" and find that it is either difficult to do (feeling perhaps that a color is a peculiar kind of physical object, a *very* thin and scattered one?) or that it cannot literally be done at all: to point to the color of an object just *is* to point to the object (with a special effort of attention on its color? or saying under your breath "I mean the color"?). But why? Wittgenstein's explanation is, we know, that "we are misled by grammar", that "we lay down rules, a technique, for a game, and . . . then when we follow the rules, things do not turn out as we had assumed. . . . we are therefore as it were entangled in our own rules" (§125). I wish I were confident that I understood this explanation fully; but what he is getting at is, I think, clearly enough illustrated in the present case. The "rule", the "technique" we have laid down for "pointing to the object", is the trivially simple one of pointing to an object whose identity we have agreed upon or can agree upon with the act of pointing. Then we suppose that we follow *this* technique in pointing to that object's color, and when we point to the color according to that rule it seems a *difficult* thing to do (in trying it, I find myself squinting, the upper part of my body tense and still, and I feel as though I wanted to dig my finger into the object, as it were, just under its skin). But one *needn't* become entangled. If we look at the way "Point to the color of your car" is actually used, we will realize that the context will normally be one in which we do not point to *that* object, but to something else which has that color, and whose color thereby serves as a *sample* of the original. And as soon as we put the request in its normal context, we find that nothing could be easier (e.g., the shape of the hand in pointing will be different, more relaxed). And it won't seem so tempting to regard pointing to something, or meaning it, as requiring a particular inner effort — nor to regard a color as a peculiar material object — once we see that, and see how, the difficulty was of our own making. Someone may feel: "Doesn't this show that pointing to a color is, after all, pointing to an object which has that color?" I might reply: It shows that not all cases of "pointing to an object" are cases of "pointing to an object which has a color". A clearer example of that would be a case in which we are shown a group of variously shaped and differently painted blocks and then later shown a group of unpainted blocks each of which corresponds in shape to one block in the former group and we are given a sample color and told "Point to the object which has this color". (It may be significant that in the two passages in which the examples of "pointing to an object" and "pointing to its color" occur, Wittgenstein does not actually provide language games for *pointing* at all, but moves quickly to remarks about *concentrating one's attention;* and at §33 he goes on to give varying contexts for *that.* A main use of the examples about pointing is to show that the difference between them is not determined by a *particular* feeling which accompanies the pointing — not in what is going on then and there — but in what happens before and after, the circumstances of the act. The examples for concentrating one's attention are used to illustrate a different emphasis, viz., that there may be *many* different such characteristic accompanying feelings, some common, some not, but no *one* of them essential hence none a candidate capable of doing what we thought only a particular feeling could do. No harm, I think, need come from this, but this unmarked shift from "pointing" to "concentrating" is surprising in view of Wittgenstein's severe caution that we not take "concentrating on a sensation" as a private ostensive definition, i.e., as a way of *pointing* to a sensation.)

Similarly for "pointing to the meaning". Some philosophers might feel that pointing just plain cannot be done where meanings are in question. Among these philosophers some will say, "But there certainly are meanings, only they have a special kind of being". And this looks like a metaphysical conflict. What kind of conflict is a (this kind of) metaphysical conflict? The answer to that depends, here as elsewhere (e.g., in moral or political or scientific conflicts), on what procedures, if any, would settle it. Suppose we try this: Show someone a vocabulary test in which there are two columns of words, the left-hand column consisting of a list of single words, the right-hand column consisting of various dictionary characterizations, one for each of the words in the left-hand column, but not in the same order. And now point to one of the words in the left-hand column and say to your subject, "Point to the meaning of this word". If he knows the meaning there's nothing easier than to point to it in the right-hand column. And we could, of course, give each of the meanings its own name. That we don't in fact normally do this itself indicates something about what "the meaning of a word" is, what its concept is — e.g., one about which the request "point to it" will be (correctly) answered, in different circumstances, by pointing to different things (words or phrases), and, in other contexts, to things which are not·words.

Obviously I don't assume this will settle the metaphysical dispute. But is it obvious that it is not so much as relevant? Someone may say, "But that isn't pointing to a meaning at all; it's only pointing to some more words". That is, however, not very forceful, for you now owe an explanation of exactly what the conflict itself is about, viz., the concept of a meaning. The response "That's only some more words" may have the same cogency as saying "That isn't a Ruy Lopez gambit, it's only some more moves", which *in fact* may be true (the person moving doesn't know the Ruy Lopez, though he claimed to; the person pointed to some adjacent vocabulary text) but it doesn't mean that no moves *are* in certain circumstances, such gambits; nor that no words are, in certain circumstances, the meaning of a word. And if someone objects "But *the* meaning of a word is *one thing*, not a lot of scattered things pointed to in various contexts", how is that different from saying to someone who has just pointed out the way to the Metropolitan Museum, "That's not *the* way to the Metropolitan Museum; it's only one of many routes you can, in various contexts, take to get there".

"Wittgensteinian criteria do not relate a name to an object, but various concepts to the concept of that object." I could also have said: They establish the position of the concept of an "object" in our system of concepts. It is, for example, part of the grammar of "color" and of "meaning" that *that* is something we can call "to point to the meaning", and *that* is "to point to the color". If you don't know that, you haven't got the concepts of a color and of a meaning, you don't know what (kind of objects) colors and meanings are. But if this is what Wittgenstein meant when he said "It is grammar which tells what kind of object anything is" then how does this differ from an Austinian mark or feature, which also may be said to tell us "what kind of object anything is" (it is by certain eye-markings, etc., that we tell this as a goldfinch, and not only *this* object, of course, but all objects of this "kind"). By now we can say: The Austinian "kind of object" is a class of specific objects, a species of some well-known kind of (generic) object, whereas the Wittgensteinian "kind" of object is something like a natural kind or a metaphysical category of objects (mind, matter, sense-data, meanings, colors, etc.). Is there a useful understanding of this difference?

The general relation between these notions of a criterion is roughly this: If you do not know the (non-grammatical) criteria of an Austinian object (can't identify it, name it) then you lack a piece of information, a bit of knowledge, and you can be told its name, told what it is, told what it is (officially) called. But if you do not know the grammatical criteria of Wittgensteinian objects, then you lack, as it were, not only a piece of information or knowledge, but the possibility of acquiring any information about such objects *überhaupt;* you cannot be told the name of that object, because there is as yet no *object* of that kind for you to attach a forthcoming name to: the possibility of finding out what it is officially called is not yet open to you. (To *what* does the child attach the official name <Nyuw York>? The child's world contains no cities.) This is, I take it, part of what Wittgenstein wished to suggest in saying that "Essence is expressed by grammar": You have to know *certain* things about an object in order to know *anything* (else) about it (about *it*). And my use of the word "possibility" here alludes again to that statement of Wittgenstein's which most completely in my opinion, but most obscurely, characterizes what he means by "grammar":

We feel as if we had to *penetrate* phenomena: our investigation, however, is directed not towards phenomena, but, as one might say, towards the *"possibilities"* of phenomena. We remind ourselves, that is to say, of the *kind of statement* that we make about phenomena. . . . Our investigation is therefore a grammatical one. [§90]

To think of a word as embodying a concept is to think of the word as having a grammatical schematism of the sort I have sketched for "chair" and "pointing to"; the schematism marks out the set of criteria on the basis of which the word is applied in all the grammatical contexts into which it fits and will be found to fit (in investigating which we are investigating part of its grammar). The concept is this schematism — a sense of the word's potency to assume just those valences, and a sense that in each case there will be a point of application of the word, and that the point will be the same from context to context, or that the point will shift in a recognizable pattern or direction. In this sense a concept is the meaning of a word. (So it is empty to explain the meaning of a word by appealing to its concept. If anything, its concept is explained, unwrinkled before us, by going through the meanings of, what we mean in using, the word.) That a word can recur is analytic of "word". That there are more things to be said in language than there are words to say them in is analytic of "language". (This is a reason that we are not sure the "four word/sentence" language game of §2 in the *Investigations* is really a language.) Hence you cannot in principle list "all" of the contexts into which a word will fit. To have a concept is to be able, so to speak, to keep up with the word.

Now how about that toothache? We were saying that explanations of our criteria "have the same force as" grammatical investigations which discover the schematism of a word: they tell us what it is to have the concept of, what it is for there to be, for us who are attuned with this schematism, an object falling under the concept, anything in the presence of which to call out, should we wish to, "toothache"; what it is we are certain of (or almost certain of, or doubt) when we are certain (or almost certain, or doubt) that someone is having a toothache. The criteria look to be somewhat slim in this case, the grammar sparse: it is mostly just the grammar of "pain", which looks to be even sparser.

Everybody knows what its elements are. We say: "He's (I've) been in pain all day"; "Thirty minutes ago it subsided slightly"; "It was localized in the shoulder, but now it's affecting the whole arm"; "I've (he says he's) felt nothing like it since I (he) was a child and had some warts burned off a foot, without anaesthetic"; "It's not a throbbing sensation, but steady; yet not like an ache but like a burn." And pain can be deadened (not altered, as an opinion), or obtunded (not dampened, as a mood); you can locate certain pains, or have to, by prodding, i.e., by activating them, causing them afresh, focussing them; we speak of someone as in pain, but not as in pleasure (and as in mourning and in ecstasy, but not as in joy or in rage); you can cause pain but not pleasure, which is given and taken (like pride and courage, but unlike happiness, which can only be found; though you can make someone proud and happy, and so also ashamed and unhappy); and so on. Most of it is not very surprising, though some of it is not without interest. I might from here go on really to set out exhaustively my geography of suffering, the specific points I go on in asserting specific concepts of suffering under specific circumstances. Would that be to "know what pain is"? Certainly my interest in all this right now rather dampens the mood of worry about whether I ever know another is in pain. — But maybe that is because we haven't finished yet. We haven't yet arrived at the specific criteria by which we are to exit from the schematism into the world. (Exiting from the schematism is perhaps a dangerous picture. The schematism is the frame of the world, and to exit from it should mean to exit from our mutual attunement. The picture came up here because I wanted to note that the order of a grammatical investigation is an academic one; you might call it reconstructed.)

Looking over the beginning of the grammar I was starting, I take these two points: that I locate (some) pains by "activating" them, and that people say particular things about their pains (describe them, give durations, locations, contours of intensity, histories, analogies with other sensations — all as best they can). What does speaking of "locating the pain by prodding" as part of the grammar of pain, as marking a criterion of pain, really come to? I prod; the other winces, groans, shrinks from the touch, blanches, perspires . . . . Does any of that get me one bit nearer the pain, the pain itself? And isn't *that* what I wanted to know? Isn't that what there is to *be* known in knowing someone is in pain? Does it follow from any listing of such things as I have listed that that person *is in pain?* Of course if he satisfies "all the criteria" marked out by "all the parts of the grammar of pain" then, to be sure, it is exceedingly likely that he is in pain, i.e., that he's not feigning, etc., and that he's like me enough for those (apparent) winces and descriptions to signify what they signify about me when I come out with them. It is even more likely, perhaps, that the other is not an automaton, that if one were to look inside one would not be greeted with the sight of wheels and springs. But *certain?* And if not, why speak of grammar and criteria? It is all just very good evidence. And adding what he *says* just makes matters even worse; for now I have to *believe* him, and determine whether he means by his descriptions what I would mean if I gave them. — So criteria are disappointing. They do not assure that my words reach all the way to the pain of others. They just do not do the very thing they were meant to do.

Let us make them even more disappointing. I am rarely, if ever, in a position to run through even as much grammar as I sketched, in a situation in which I am asserting a concept (particularly a situation as urgent as one of pain). Then what do I actually go on? In the case of pain, anything from a small inflection of the face or frame, to some outstanding passage of behavior, like someone's jumping in place or clutching at himself; and the things he utters may be anything from those measured descriptions I spoke about to shouts, pinched laughter, animal noises, repetitious cursings. It's all somehow too vague, imprecise, inarticulate, distant from the thing I wanted to know.   — But maybe that is just a feature of this particular psychological concept. Take others. An itch is something you want to scratch. A desire has an object which people can see, and you can be filled with it, for them to see, and test. A ringing in the ears is nicely describable as such, and typical manifestations are to frown or open the mouth very wide so as to move the ears around, or to press your palms against them for a moment, or to shake the head vigorously once or twice and then listen — people who haven't had the experience probably won't understand what you're doing. But pain? That just is a condition which has no defined set of manifestations, unless the very range is itself taken as definitive. The idea of someone's pain seems at once so *far* from what manifests it, like a hope which does not concern me; and yet right at the surface, like shivering. Anything that powerful and that close to me, which yet does not affect me, cannot be material. Or its difference seems so sheer from what manifests it: the reality of it is wholly inner, its criteria wholly outer — but this again may be definitive of *this* concept. We get expert at suppressing the traces of pain, better than at suppressing smiles or laughter, which somehow ought to be easier; or than at stopping ourselves from scratching, which seems trivial by comparison. We are told to live with pain, and we have to stand it (like what? like a trial, or like ground before an enemy?). It is a presence, and yet it is not present to me, so it seems an absence, a void; it affects everything and nothing. Yet I feel *called upon* to know its presence, if it is there.

And those utterances of it. They are expressions of it: "I know I'm in pain", "It's getting worse", "It's throbbing", are as much expressions of pain as "I'm in pain" is. Pain gets into the words, as hope or comfort get into words of hope or comfort (they wouldn't be such words otherwise). Or words are part of its suppression, or of distraction from it. They need not be to distract me from my pain, in which case the words may race, as if to get out of range; but to distract you from it (as in Chekhov); there is nothing anyone can do about it, and it might deprive me of your company if you knew; and anyway I don't know any words for it. Here my words don't reach all the way to my pain.

The words of pain are all said in its presence, which may give the words a respectful tone. This is Hemingway's subject, and his manner.

"What about the pain?"
"Not now. For a while I was crazy with it in the belly. I thought the pain alone would kill me."

Sister Cecilia was observing them happily.

"She tells me you never made a sound," Mr. Frazer said.

"So many people in the ward," the Mexican said deprecatingly. "What class of pain do you have?"

"Big enough. Clearly not as bad as yours. When the nurse goes out I cry an hour, two hours. It rests me. My nerves are bad now."

"You have the radio. If I had a private room and a radio I would be crying and yelling all night long."

"I doubt it."

"Hombre si. It's very healthy. But you cannot do it with so many people."

["The Gambler, the Nun, and the Radio"]

Out of concern for others, or our sense of ourselves, we can contain ourselves to that extent? — But the wonder may break in at just such a point: On the basis of a flat word, an inflection of the frame, a wince from the blue, I am expected to call forth pity, or admiration? — Yes. If you know what such things mean, and you can, and wish to, bear the knowledge. But what if the pity is misplaced? How do you know it isn't?

What is disappointing about criteria? In a philosophical mood, we wanted the wince to take us all the way to the other's pain itself, but it seems to stop at the body. The feeling is: The wince itself is one thing, the pain itself something else; the one can't *be* the other. But what happened to the pain that was *in* (what we called) the wince? That — the pain he's wincing in — is what I called his being in pain, and pitied. (That *is* . . . what I *called*? What is? Why the past tense with a present demonstrative? Do I not call it that now? Or has it vanished?) He was *wincing in pain*. It wouldn't have been a wince otherwise. — And was it? Surely he could have come out with *that* (what we call — called — a wince) with nothing behind it. Or maybe the "wince" *meant* something else. It's the same old circle.

But we left something inexplicit in our rehearsal of the schematism of pain. I left out my responses to the criteria as they emerge. I did leap to pity, but that was more or less theoretical; we are not very familiar with this concept, or its object. Maybe the response of pity is reserved for pain so deep that it is mute; that could explain why pity may itself be a mute response. (*Can* I be responding to such pain if there is nothing to *say*? Can I trust myself to be? Can I trust the other to know that I am?) In any case it wouldn't happen all at once. *Who* is being told the pain has spread down the arm? Why would I, what gives one the right to, activate the pain? What am I looking for? Why does his shrinking from a prod tell me what I want to know? — We left inexplicit the call such knowledge imposes upon me for comforting, succoring, healing; to make the fabric whole again which the pain tore through, or to know that this is impossible. That is knowing what pain is.

It is usual in such discussions to bring in the idea of a doctor to do the prodding. Which idea is this of a doctor — a healer or an inquirer? Not that any response here has to look very specific, any more than the manifestations we are responding to have to look very specific. Sometimes it seems that doctors are cold; connoisseurs of pain, not beholders of it. As though they lack the knowledge of their very subject matter. Sometimes, though, we explain that if they were not cold they could not do their job, and *that* is what they are wanted for. But why couldn't it be that a doctor's knowledge of the subject of pain is just what is expressed in what he or she does — not merely with his trained hands, but in the very distance of his reactions to me? He trusts his hands and training to show his response; if I trust his knowledge and his reactions, I may feel more known by them than by a more apparently warm or constant response to what I feel. Not just because they give me hope, which I can hang onto (and they *can* give me hope because he knows the subject of pain, that it is an enemy which he joins against on my side). But because I, as it were, learn a new response to my pain; not a refuge from it, but a place for it, a proportion to its presence. The distance comforts as truth can. (Naturally I do not deny that truth can be used as a weapon; especially when it comes in fragments.)

And then sometimes the words of response get very particular:

My dear Reynolds — I cannot write about scenery and visitings. . . . One song of Burns is of more worth to you than all I could think for a whole year in his native country. His Misery is a dead weight upon the nimbleness of one's quill. I tried to forget it — to drink Toddy without any Care — to write a merry sonnet; it won't do. . . . We can see horribly clear, in the works of such a man, his whole life, as if we were God's spies. . . . My sensations are sometimes deadened for weeks together — but believe me I have more than once yearned for the time of your happiness to come . . . . [from John Keats, Maybole, July 11, 1818]

Burns made himself clear; the rest is up to whoever is there, and can. I don't say you have to rise to Keats's response. (I don't mean rise to being able to write like him, but up to responding like that; allowing room for another's misery to be unforgettable.) But to know the subject, that it is pain, is to respond *to* it; and if other things are on your mind, and your sensations are sometimes deadened for weeks together, then to know that *that* is a response, and yet leaves you freedom for a further response.

When I say "He's in pain" (supposing I do, supposing that's what I have to say) my knowledge is expressed (roughly as his is; i.e., *analogously* with his?) by the fact that it is called from me, cried out (though we generally keep our voices down). (I will want to relate this to the fact Wittgenstein records, in his discussion of physiognomy in Part II, section xi, as a shift of aspect *striking* me.) Sometimes my problem will be *not* to cry it out, but to free my response *from* the other. Instead of responding to him from my freedom, I am engulfed by his suffering or his anxieties, or by his opinion of me, or his hope for me; as he may be. — But all this makes it seem that the philosophical problem of knowledge is something I impose on these matters; that I am the philosophical problem. I am. It is in me that the circuit of communication is cut; I am the stone on which the wheel breaks. What is disappointing about criteria?

There is something they do not do; it can seem the essential. I have to know what they are for; I have to accept them, use them. This itself makes my use of them seem arbitrary, or private — as though they were never shared, or as if our sharing of them is either a fantastic accident or a kind of mass folly. It is at such a juncture that I remind myself of the sorts of expressions in which Wittgenstein presents what I understand as the background against which our criteria do their work; even, make sense.

. . . only of a living human being and what resembles (behaves like) a living human being can one say: it has sensations; it sees; is blind; hears; is deaf; is conscious or unconscious. [§281]

What has to be accepted, the given, is — so one could say — *forms of life*. [p. 226]

What gives us *so much as the idea* that living beings, things, can feel? [§283]

The human body is the best picture of the human soul. [p. 178]

There are not human criteria which apprise me, or which make any move toward telling me why I take it, among all the things I encounter on the surface of the earth or in its waters or its sky, that some of them have feeling; that some of them "resemble" or "behave like" human beings or human bodies; or that some exhibit (forms of) life — unless the *fact that* human beings apply psychological concepts to certain things and not to others is such a criterion. To withhold, or hedge, our concepts of psychological states from a given creature, on the ground that our criteria cannot reach to the inner life of the creature, is specifically to withhold the source of my idea that living beings are things that feel; it is to withhold myself, to reject my response to anything as a living being; to blank so much as my idea of anything as *having a body*. To describe *this* condition as one in which I do not know (am not certain) of the existence of other minds, is empty. There is now nothing there, of the right kind, to be known. There is nothing to read from that body, nothing the body is *of;* it does not go beyond itself, it expresses nothing; it does not so much as behave. There is no body left to manifest consciousness (or unconsciousness). It is not dead, but inanimate; it hides nothing, but is absolutely at my disposal; if it were empty it would be quite hollow, but in fact it is quite dense, though less uniform than stone. It was already at best an automaton. It does not matter to me now whether there turn out to be wheels and springs inside, or stuffing, or some subtler or messier mechanism; or rather, whether it matters depends upon my curiosity in such matters. The most *anything* inside it could do (e.g., something we choose to call "nerves" or "muscles") is to *run* or *work* the thing, move it around. My feeling is: What this "body" lacks is *privacy.* (In what spirit does Wittgenstein "deny" the "possibility" of a private language?) Only *I* could reach that privacy, by accepting it as a home of my concepts of the human soul. When I withdraw that acceptance, the criteria are dead (§432; §§454–55).

My problem is no longer that my words can't get past his body to *him.* There is nothing for them to get to; they can't even reach as far as *my* body; they are stuck behind the tongue, or at the back of the mind. The signs are dead; merely working them out loud doesn't breathe life into them; even dogs can speak more effectively. Words have no carry. It is like trying to throw a feather; for some things, breath is better than strength; stronger. This is also something I meant by saying that voicing my criteria has to have the force of "call".

I was saying that only I could reach to the other's (inner) life. My condition is not exactly that I have to *put* the other's life there; and not exactly that I have to *leave* it there either. I (have to) *respond* to it, or refuse to respond. It calls upon me; it calls me out. I have to acknowledge it. I am as fated to that as I am to my body; it is as natural to me. In everyday life the lives of others are neither here nor there; they drift between their own inexpressiveness and my inaccuracy in responding to them. Sincerity is not the issue. Or rather, sincerity is nothing (is not the inspiration of trust, theirs in me or mine in myself) without the desire and courage for accuracy. Skepticism meant to find the other, search others out with certainty. Instead it closes them out. What happens to them? And what happens to me when I withhold my acceptance of privacy — anyway, of otherness — as the home of my concepts of the human soul and find my criteria to be dead, mere words, word-shells? I said a while ago in passing that I withhold myself. What I withhold myself from is my attunement with others — with all others, not merely with the one I was to know. — Isn't the idea of withholding prejudicial, implying a prior state of union, or closeness? Whereas maybe I never was a part, or party, to these (other) lives. Couldn't I be *just* different? — But I want to know where this leaves me, what has happened to me. — Then it is the idea of being left that is prejudicial.

V

Natural and Conventional

I have said something about what kind of problem the problem of our knowledge of other minds may be. I was just saying something about the consequences of finding such knowledge to fail altogether, i.e., the consequences of *withholding our concepts* of life and mind altogether. Earlier I said something about the specific kinds of circumstance or possibility which may prevent us from being certain that another really is in the state he is manifesting, viz., circumstances in which he or she may be feigning, rehearsing, etc., circumstances the description of which requires that we *retain the concept* in question. The problems I wished to raise in these cases are not ones in which there is what I called some obvious reason for being uncertain, ones in which the position I am in is intellectually incomplete, ones which any scrupulous person would recognize as my not being in a position to say for sure; but ones in which, as I put it, I ought to be able to tell from here, because that is what I wanted to know, that is all that would express my knowledge of the thing; only I find that I cannot rule out some possibility. It is, that is to say, essential both to the consequences of withholding our concepts altogether and of retaining concepts, that they be optimal cases of knowing; only in such cases do the consequences of my discovery of my condition in a particular instance reach to, or become, the discovery of my position in general. In the withholding case the discovery is my responsibility (responsiveness) in the existence of others; in the retaining case the discovery is the limitation of certainty as knowledge. In the latter case, I may as it were discover privacy; in the former case I may lose even that.

It remains immediately for me, in broaching the problem of other minds, to go further into a third way in which criteria are found disappointing. This is the possibility, as I have characterized it, in which either I haven't settled the criteria for myself ("the uncertainty is in me") or in which the instance is not a perfect or clear one (one or more of the criteria are "not fully satisfied").

I mentioned this possibility in relation to questions of assessment ("I don't know whether I would call it stable or tyrannical"; "It's not really what I would call stable, but it's more so than others"); and to questions of interpreting strangers ("I don't see how they can be meaning what I would mean if I called it a chair"; "It certainly is not what I would call a chair, but then I don't know why I call the things I call chairs chairs"). Such problems, or related ones, are, I believe, sometimes discussed as matters of borderline cases or of conceptual deviance or divergence. In the assessment case, there is room for something we might call a borderline case, viz., an eventuality in which I have articulated my (our) criteria well enough, and they are met about half way. But this turns up no defect in our criteria (yet), because the description "It's a borderline case" is an informative one (like "drizzle"). In the case of the foreign chair, there is no borderline case (yet), because for me it is not a chair and for them (apparently) it is one. Conceptual deviance, so far as I understand that idea, fits no case so far. Our problem in the assessment case is that we have not yet found a convincing concept for it, nor is it clear that we need one; in the case of the foreign tribe, we do not know what the concepts in play are, the points of their application.

There is a natural form of conceptual disappointment which underlies a philosophical surmise about other minds (and thereby shows it not to be "merely" philosophical): the idea of the other as stranger, the possibility that me may be "different from me". It may arise like this. At one point I asked: "What happened to the pain that was *in* (what we called) the wince?" And I went on: "He was wincing in pain. It wouldn't have been a wince otherwise." And then the inevitable question: "And was it? Surely he could have come out with *that* (what we called a wince) with nothing behind it . . . ; or maybe it *meant* something else." And then I interrupted with ideas about our having left ourselves out of the schematism of pain, and hence left *him* out. But the objection might have continued from its last clause, in a different direction: "Say what you want about 'retaining the concept', e.g., that once it is asserted it 'has to' be retained to describe coherently (make sense of our experience when we claim) the possibility of feigning, etc. And say all you like about the 'grammar of pain', and that if he is described as being 'in pain' then only certain responses are appropriate to him (ones which take in his suffering, e.g., pity and comfort), and that what will *be* 'pity' and 'comfort' (or 'boorishness' or 'imperceptiveness' or 'thoughtlessness') is no more up to us than what will be his 'screaming in pain'. The fact is you still don't know he is screaming in *pain*. How are you so sure that that isn't simply the way he clears his throat, or calls his hamsters, or sings Schubert? What justifies your sharp distinction between knowing what the criteria of something are and knowing whether their object exists? The *sharp* distinction is between his outer behavior and his inner experience, and no mere description of his behavior as being 'in or from or with pain' will alter that."

The phrases "his behavior" and "the pain itself" are themselves as little or as much "mere" descriptions as "his screaming in pain" is. Why just these descriptions ("behavior", "pain itself") are the ones which occur in philosophizing about our knowledge, is a problem which should become clearer when we follow out the details of the skeptical argument. I do admit that nothing alters the fact that *if* he is described in terms of *his behavior alone* then his *pain itself* is something else. For the moment let us consider this new line of objection in its own terms.

Perhaps he is not screaming at all, but calling his hamsters, or singing *Wandern*. *Is* he? Suppose, to avoid all insult, we listen attentively to what the world calls his screaming and begin to detect the resemblance of a pattern there to the opening phrase of *Wandern:* two whines at the same level rising to a higher howl, falling a bit then soaring to a new screech and back to the former howl; then all repeated. Is he singing, singing *Wandern?* He said he was. Suppose he (we must say he) is serious. Anyway he isn't, apparently, in pain. Then how do we treat him? Shall we say, "Probably he's singing *Wandern,* since he says so and I make out the pattern"? But then the concept of "singing" isn't going to be asserted of this man with its normal aura or force. It isn't that people normally (on the whole, statistically) don't sing that way; but that *normal people don't,* people don't. Is it *false* to say he's singing, singing *Wandern?* No more than it's false to point to one of a group of actors and say "He's Napoleon". But unless you and your interlocutor know the circumstances of the case, you won't know what is true, what is being said, the spirit in which it is said.

But perhaps this obscures the issue in the way it raises the question of intention. Then take the case in which we imagine him to be calling his hamsters. He is in the dentist chair, wringing his hands, perspiring, screaming. The dentist stops for a moment and begins to prepare another syringe of Novacain. The patient stops him and says, "It wasn't hurting, I was just calling my hamsters". The dentist looks as if he had swallowed Novacain and the patient says, "Open the door for them". And when the door is opened two hamsters trot into the room and climb onto the patient's lap. So we have more than his word for it. And when later, in the middle of a walk in the country, we see this man wring his hands, perspire and scream and then look around for his hamsters, whom, trotting up, he greets affectionately, then we had probably better acknowledge that that is the way he calls his hamsters.   — So doesn't this show that it is not *necessary* that someone exhibiting pain-behavior is in pain, *and* that we needn't retain the concept of pain to explain what's going on with him?   — I should say, on the contrary, that it shows just how necessary these grammatical relations are, or in what sense they are necessary. For we shall no longer call his screaming, etc., *pain*-behavior; which means that we will not, confronted with such a phenomenon, give up our usual notion of what pain-behavior is. That is to say, we may rule this man out of our world of pain. In this respect he will not exist for us. In response to him there will doubtless be more that we will feel shaky about than our knowledge of when he is and is not in pain. But as before, these doubts about him are limited to him, and have no tendency to make us wonder whether we ever can be sure.

— But something does make us wonder about this sometimes. Why *couldn't* someone express suffering, real pain, by (say) laughing; and if, as you imply, comforting someone is grammatically related to that person's being in pain, then why couldn't you comfort him by whipping him — why *must* it be part of the grammar of "comforting" that *that* (our ordinary ways of comforting) is what we call "comforting him for the loss of his tooth or his money"? And now I don't want the answer that of course we can imagine some very special context which our ordinary concepts of suffering and comfort would fit (say, a context in which someone suffers from a particular pleasure — through remorse, phobia, an associated memory of a lost time; or in which a present suffering affords relief from an insupportable sense of guilt; or in which laughter really does express pain (i.e., really does replace the natural, or naturally earlier, expression of pain), as it often does in adults — some kinds of laughter, some kinds of pain). What needs to be considered is, rather, the feeling or idea that someone, for all we know, laughs at rejection or physical pain the way we laugh at a joke — even, perhaps, giggles about it, and who feels in a whip what we feel in a caress; a person, that is, for whom suffering and comfort are entirely independent of what *we* mean by "pain" and "pity". We cannot really know what someone else's experience is; why couldn't it be like that?

Like what? What don't we know? What have we imagined? Are we to imagine also that when we touch the person with affection he screams in pain, or tries to attack us (some children respond that way to affection — what we call "affection")? And what does he find interesting? What bores him? Suppose he cries at what slightly offends us; suppose he collects and cares for and eats objects that appall us. What are we going to talk to him about, what will we do together, how will we treat him? I am not saying, and I do not think Wittgenstein is saying, that it is impossible for someone to respond in these ways. What is being suggested is that the significance of this possibility is being missed when it is voiced in philosophy. I expressed this significance a moment ago by saying that such people do not live in our world. Whether, in such a case, we can still respond to them as *persons, remains problematic.* Part of the difficulty in treating psychotics is the inability one has in appreciating *their* world, and hence in honoring them as persons; the other part of the difficulty comes in facing how close our world is (at times; in dreams) to theirs. In making the knowledge of others a metaphysical difficulty, philosophers deny how real the practical difficulty is of coming to know another person, and how little we can reveal of ourselves to another's gaze, or bear of it. Doubtless such denials are part of the motive which sustains metaphysical difficulties.

"Normal people don't." Does this imply that I have or ought to have a theory of normality here, or a theory of (say) pain, in terms of which I recognize this to be a normal and that an abnormal case? If there is such a theory it lies in the criteria themselves, or they are what any theory will have to explain. And now I want to pursue my feeling that the question of normality is a practical one; or a question of the limits of practice.

It may still seem, or seem again, that when I say "He satisfies the criteria of pain" this ought to mean, so to speak, "The object of this concept exists", that what the criteria tell me is there really is *there.* It is very hard to see that this is empty; it still seems that if I cannot say this I cannot say what criteria are meant to allow me to say.

There are natural as well as philosophical reasons for this. To settle, by criteria, how good a dive is, or whether a government is stable, is not to prove that a dive or a government exists, but isn't it to prove that good dives or stable governments exist? After all, we say "That dive (looking at it on slow motion film) is almost perfect", "A stable government exists there". Unless some people there are achieving a certain stability, or unless the leap off the board fits the criteria of diving to a certain extent, there isn't a *dive* or a *government* there at all. But that may look like playing with words, or else confusing the "is" of existence with the "is" of identity. One might feel: to say that a stable government exists there is simply to *assume* that *some* government or other is there. While Wittgenstein's extraordinary remarks about "accepting forms of life", about "what so much as gives us the idea", etc. — while these do not say that we have to assume our criteria are justly applicable, don't they really come to that? Aren't such remarks merely a careful avoidance of the idea that we are assuming something? And isn't that really the skeptic's point; that, and the fact that there is no rational ground (or perhaps, that there is only a theoretical justification) for the assumption? The most we are really ever in a position to say is: "I don't mind calling that pain"; or "It is what *we* call pain"; or "On our set-up that is pain; but I never really know that what he's got is what I've got; nor do I know that he's got what I *say* he's got". The objects of the criteria for dives and governments and leaves are there before us, we know how to evaluate them, how well they satisfy our criteria; that is indeed what the criteria are for. But the object of pain is *not* there before us, so we cannot in principle *compare* it with our criteria; and indeed that is why we need criteria of states of consciousness, to assure us that what we mean to say is there *is there*.

The *Investigations* takes many ways of approaching ideas which construe the inner life as composed of objects (and if objects then for sure *private* ones). To combat such ideas is an obsession of the book as a whole. It is as though Wittgenstein felt human beings in jeopardy of losing touch with their inner lives altogether, with the very idea that each person is a center of one, that each *has* a life. There is no better evidence of this jeopardy than the way Wittgenstein is interpreted on such matters. I do not mean to deny his awful obscurities in these matters (which perhaps are not willful, but a true expression of their difficulties, philosophical and practical); I mean the sense his readers get that in denying that we know (say) our sensations and in denying that our words for the sensations of others refer to objects, somethings or other, inside that other, he is denying that we *have* sensations and that there *is* anything going on in the other. If one shudders at the thought, perhaps that comes from a surmise that what it feels as if Wittgenstein is denying may be true, that we have nothing inside, that we are empty. If one fails to shudder, that may be because one does not allow one's desperate ideas of hidden somethings to come to light and become questioned. What I can say consecutively about these ideas, especially about the so-called private language argument, I leave until Part Four.

For the moment, I want only to indicate the level at which the problem lies. In one of the best books to have employed Wittgensteinian ideas, there is this:

Unless some relationships between physical and psychological states are not contingent, and can be known prior to the discovery of empirical correlations, we cannot have even indirect evidence for the truth of psychological statements about other persons, and cannot know such statements to be true or even probably true. [Sidney Shoemaker, *Self-Knowledge and Self-Identity*, pp. 167–68]

What is this idea of a "relationship" between physical and psychological states? It means to be combatting the idea that all we go on in knowing others are empirical correlations between something and something. This idea requires combatting. But Shoemaker does this by a suggestion that there is some *stronger* connection than correlation to be found. And this takes over the same idea of a *relationship* which produced the need for a "stronger connection". Underlying the suggestion, I think, is the idea that outer behavior is "explained" by reference to some inner stuff or other. But where would we ever find such a "relationship", empirical or stronger? Someone scratches; evidently he itches. Where did we ever notice a correlation between that behavior and something *else?* In our own case, perhaps — if we did notice (say by watching ourselves in a mirror). But do we explain scratching by inferring (*very* quickly; or constructing; or something) an itch? What produces the idea that there is something "beyond" (or under? *just* under) the scratching? (Of course there *is* something just under something, but is that (what we call) the itch? It may be something that explains why we itch, and perhaps why scratching helps.) What could make "He scratches because he itches" into an explanation? If you don't know in *that* sense why people scratch, you don't know what scratching is; so the explanation wouldn't help. The baby is crying: "She is in pain." That may be an explanation if it means, e.g., "It's not hunger this time (or loneliness or wetness or fear)". (But all these are forms of pain. Yes; because in all these cases it is crying that is under explanation.) Or it may mean, "I recognize *that* scream; something is hurting her". We find the open diaper pin lodged in the thigh. Do we now say, "She's crying because she hurts"? Perhaps. If (say) you mean, "It was I who was right after all; I know that scream". But are we projecting some correlation between crying and something behind it? Where would we have come across that correlation? (That one we probably can't get (remember) from our own case. But of course we could try it on ourselves now, or we could form an induction from other sharp objects to that one.) The baby is crying because the diaper pin snapped open, or you stupidly forgot again to make sure it was securely fastened. "But only because of an implicit reference to our theory that crying is caused by pain, and the lemma that pins stuck in normal living bodies cause pain." — To want to know why the baby is crying is to want to know why it is in pain. If you don't know in general that crying means pain, psychological theories aren't going to teach you.

Take a more elaborate, or more realistic, form of explanation: People become psychiatrists out of a desire for intimacy which they cannot otherwise face; out of curiosities they cannot otherwise satisfy; from a wish for power they cannot otherwise exercise; and sometimes because their fathers are doctors. What have I correlated with what? Is "becoming a psychiatrist" a whole carload of bits of behavior as opposed to the feelings they go with, for which I am supplying the missing feelings or processes in speaking of desires, curiosities, and wishes? But how do I know which feelings and processes to supply? How, e.g., do I know that curiosity is something that craves satisfaction, that intimacy is something that wants closeness; and how do I know or imagine that the practice of psychiatry can provide them? To want to know why *he* is becoming a psychiatrist is to want to know why he feels in those ways. And what can such an explanation be, except an account of lots of other ways he's felt and acted? Why do such accounts look like histories? — No doubt not all psychologists would accept such accounts as candidates for explanations. But then, unlike other practices we call sciences, one sometimes feels that academic psychology tells us less than we already know. As though what stops it from being physics, or even economics, say, is not that it isn't as precise and predictive, but that it doesn't know how to use what we already know about its subjects. One of the beauties of the practice of linguistics is that it gives, or ought to give, full play to our everyday knowledge of its data. And this is, or ought to be, one of the beauties of ordinary language philosophizing as well.

But then, if in using criteria we aren't relating behavior to something else (but, so to speak, taking that "something else" as given along with what we call behavior), what *are* we relating by means of criteria, and what is the something else, and how can we "take it"? I might say: Criteria account simultaneously for what he does and what is going on in him. Or better: They account for *my* relation to what is going on in him. — Something further wants expression here: Criteria are the terms in which I *relate what's happening,* make sense of it by giving its history, say what "goes before and after". What I call something, what I *count* as something, is a function of how I *recount* it, tell it. And telling is counting. It may be hard to make out that the weaving of language here is something more than a shuttling of fortune.

(If to what we call something and to what we count as something we add the notion of what we claim something to be, we have gathered together the major modes in which we have invoked the fact of talking, the work of wording the world; and if to the pairs telling and counting, and counting and claiming, and claiming and acclaiming or clamoring, hence proclaiming and announcing, and denouncing and renouncing, and counting and recounting, or recounting and accounting, we add the notions of calling to account or accusing, hence excusing and explaining, and add computing and hence reputing and imputing; what we seem headed for is an idea that what can comprehensibly be said is what is found to be worth saying. This explicitly makes our agreement in judgment, our attunement expressed through criteria, agreement in valuing. So that what can be communicated, say a fact, depends upon agreement in valuing, rather than the other way around. This is what our speech acts come to, or come from. Such an idea arose at the beginning of our consideration of Wittgenstein's notion of a criterion when we had to say that his notion seemed to make statements of fact turn on the same background of necessities and agreements that judgments of value explicitly do. It comes up again in beginning to weigh Austin's findings that epistemological assessments, assessments of our offerings of knowledge, can come from curiosity, from suspicion, or from a demand to know the special reason which makes a question (as to the reality of an object) reasonable. Here I am thinking of the special reason as the thing which makes the question worth asking. The idea of valuing as the other face of asserting will make another appearance in Part Two, in the form of the issue of the philosopher's "non-claim context". But while the idea will be present throughout these pages, it will not be much taken up thematically. I understand this idea to require studies in what I should like to call the aesthetics of speech and in the economics of speech. In the former case we follow the fact that understanding what someone says is a function of understanding the intention expressed in his or her saying it, and then the fact that one's intention is a function of what one wants, to a perspective from which responding to what another says is to be seen as demanding a response to (the other's) desire. When in earlier writing of mine I broach the topic of the modern, I am broaching the topic of art as one in which the connection between expression and desire is purified. In the modern neither the producer nor the consumer has anything to go on (history, convention, genre, form, medium, physiognomy, composition . . .) that secures the value or the significance of an object apart from one's wanting the thing to be as it is. The consequent exercise of criticism is not to determine whether the thing is good that way but why you want it that way — or rather, the problem is to show that these questions are always together. A strictness or scrupulousness of artistic desire thus comes to seem a moral and an intellectual imperative. About the latter case (of an economics of speech), I have said a word or two in *The Senses of Walden* (pp. 87 ff.) where I point to the vocabulary established in the opening chapter of *Walden,* entitled "Economy", as the fundamental vocabulary of the work as a whole, implying that the question of true necessaries, which it shares as its opening theme with Plato's *Republic* and with Rousseau's *Social Contract,* is a question about what we have to say as much as it is about what we have to do; and in the way Thoreau means them, the one because of the other. My version of Thoreau's answer is in effect that he takes it upon his writing to tell all and to say nothing. — If we formulate the idea that valuing underwrites asserting as the idea that interest informs telling or talking generally, then we may say that the degree to which you talk of things, and talk in ways, that hold no interest for you, or listen to what you cannot imagine the talker's caring about, in the way he carries the care, is the degree to which you consign yourself to nonsensicality, stupify yourself. (Of course your lack of interest may be your fault, come from your own commitment to boredom.) I think of this consignment as a form not so much of dementia as of what amentia ought to mean, a form of mindlessness. It does not appear unthinkable that the bulk of an entire culture, call it the public discourse of the culture, the culture thinking aloud about itself, hence believing itself to be talking philosophy, should become ungovernably inane. In such a case you would not say that the Emperor has no clothes; in part because what you really want to say is that there is no Emperor; but in greater part because in neither case would anyone understand you.) (The foregoing parenthetical remarks were added in 1978, while engaged in a final review of this early material, prompted by my awareness, still little educated, that something like the economics of speech is a mounting topic among theorists of, among other things, literature. See, for example, the Introduction to Marc Shell's *The Economy of Literature.* I might encourage those as backward or tardy as myself to look at Heidegger's "The Word of Nietzsche: 'God is Dead'", which includes (pp. 71 ff.) some paragraphs in response to the question, "Why is Nietzsche's metaphysics the metaphysics of value?".)

It is to get past the idea of a relation (construed as between two "things") that Wittgenstein harps on formulas like "That *is*, under certain circumstances, what we call . . ."; and asks "What does so-and-so consist in?". If I am right here, a central practice which he meant as deflecting behavioristic fears, or longings, centrally helps create the impression that he is a behaviorist. (It is not every idea of "relationship" that Wittgenstein wishes to get past. He expresses his sense of the relationship between body and soul, at one point I quoted, as "being the best picture of". But that is not yet of much explanatory value.)

Take a remark that seems to cry out for a behaviorist interpretation: "An 'inner process' stands in need of outward criteria" (§580). In my experience, if someone dislikes the idea of behaviorism, he or she may quote this to show that Wittgenstein is a dogmatic, unscientific one. If someone dislikes the idea of skepticism, he feels compelled to defend the dogmatism. The first thinks the second must be blind (because *obviously,* no matter what criteria you have, they aren't, intellectually as it were, any closer to what's actually going on than symptoms are); the second thinks the first must be blind (because obviously criteria *do* something which mere symptoms don't, get us closer to what's actually going on). Why Wittgenstein creates remarks to call out interpretations which lock in this way, is a question of his style, and hence of his philosophical motivation. The technique in this instance is, roughly, this: The background of the statement, to which it is a response, is that people (philosophers) are led to say that remembering or thinking or meaning, etc. are inner processes, as though that explains something. The message is that until you produce criteria on the basis of which, in a particular case, you count something as an "inner process", you have said nothing (it is a "picture", etc.). But the immediate context of the statement seems to convey this message: Once you produce the criteria, you will see that they are merely outward, and so the very thing they are supposed to show, if you get the criteria correctly in line, is threatened; in the sense in which we wanted to know (which may be what produced that "picture"), we never can.

What is an "inner process"? To get us to see that that question needs asking, and that we glide past it, is the reason I take Wittgenstein to have marked the phrase in quotes. He's not implying simply that you can know or be aware that something is going on in you when I do not know or am not aware of it, and that for me to know it you are going to have to throw out signals that inform me of it. That, or something like it, *is* obvious; too obvious to make a thesis of. That it is not a thesis, that it has *that* obviousness, is the source of the power of the skeptic's position. The question Wittgenstein wishes us to raise is, rather, something like this: When you have thrown out your signals and I have had the opportunity to be apprised of your inner world, then *do* I really know it (know *it*) or do the signals come from a source I can never check, hence signify something I can never know? (Another's mind as God.)

Wittgenstein's remark is surrounded by paragraphs investigating the notion of "expecting". One paragraph begins with the statement that "Expectation is, grammatically, a state" (§572). That may itself seem surprising, since if we ask ourselves what expecting something is we might more naturally say it is a mental *process* (as though the first example of expectation which naturally occurs to us is something like watching a flame move toward an explosive, or toward a finger, and then we interpret that (physical) process as the model of expecting). This itself might suggest that the remark about "outward criteria" is not meant to warn us about some grave general difficulty of checking whether someone else has an inner life, and to provide us with something even more iron-clad than evidence for it; but rather to consider *what* it is we are saying about that life, to consider what would *be* "evidences" of the sort of thing we are attributing to that life. In particular, here, to consider that since "expectation" is a state and not a process, what will be evidence of each must, grammatically, be different. If, therefore, you are led, as we are in speculating about these questions, to the conclusion that we cannot really know whether another person is expecting something or someone, then a way to investigate that problem is to ask ourselves *what* it is we don't know about the other. Or, if we have satisfied ourselves that there is no further problem, say by telling ourselves that we can know with practical certainty or near certainty that he is expecting, then we should ask ourselves *what* it is we are almost certain of.

Expectation, we are told, is not a feeling; it is a state. ". . . like: being of an opinion, hoping for something, knowing something, being able to do something" (§572):

A state of what? Of the soul? Of the mind? Well, of what object does one say that it has an opinion? Of Mr. N. N. for example. And that is the correct answer.

One should not expect to be enlightened by the answer to *that* question. Others go deeper: What, in particular cases, do we regard as criteria for someone's being of such-and-such an opinion? When do we say: he reached this opinion at that time? When: he has altered his opinion? And so on. The picture which the answers to these questions give us shows *what* gets treated grammatically as a *state* here. [§573]

What picture do we get of expectancy from answering the questions, "What do we call (= when do we say (plus statemental form)) his arriving at a gloomy, low, unrealistic expectation; his giving up or forgetting or being distracted from, an expectation; his having or forming great expectations; his expecting the Kingdom of Heaven, a reward, a rebuff, an explosion?"? It is a picture of a position arrived at or fallen into or found or retreated from, occupied in varying attitudes, from which and according to which a goal is sighted; there is a path of vision to the goal, but movement over the path has to come in the direction from the goal to the position from which it is sighted; unlike states of ambition or aspiration. Is this a state of *mind?* Not if depression, excitement, pain are mental states (*Investigations*, unnumbered paragraph, p. 59). Is it a state of the soul? Not if beatitude, or corruption (or envy? sloth? charity?) are states of the soul. Expectancies do not (grammatically) have the same history as, say, depressions (which may "just happen" where you are, or be "set off" by a chance remark or gesture, and in which all movement from the goal is frozen); or faith (which may begin by seeing something that will knock you off a horse, and in which the goal and the position coincide).

It is not my intention and not to my purpose to determine whether these psychological characteristics are thought of as states of being, or states or frames of mind (moods?), or traits of character — or of different "objects" under different conditions (cf. §577, §585); I have wanted only to suggest what sort of importance such questions might have. (Why does Wittgenstein say that the correct answer "Of Mr. N. N., for example" is not enlightening, and that other questions "go deeper"? He is dissatisfied with it the way Socrates is dissatisfied when his questions are answered by examples instead of definitions. He, like Socrates, wants to know what the thing in question *is;* he, too, is after *essence*. Only to capture that we no longer search for a definition of the quarry, but investigate its grammar.)

Why, further, would we say of any such condition that it is "inner"? If we need, and have, criteria which distinguish inner states from inner processes, etc., then we need, and have, criteria for saying that a phenomenon is *inner* at all, if we mean anything by counting the phenomenon in this way. Philosophizing has tended to regard the difference between inner and outer as an obvious one (Kant, for example, took for granted the content and force of the distinction between "inner sense" and "outer sense", as his British predecessors had taken for granted the difference between "impressions of ideas" and "impressions of reflection"); as obvious as which room is the inner one, which garment the outer one. But why do we think of a state (of mind, say) as *inner?* Why do we think of the meaning of a (some particular) poem as inner? (And mightn't we think of some states of a physical object as inner? Perhaps not its hardness; but its magnetic power? or its radioactivity?) What pertains to the soul is thought of as inner. But why? "Inner" means, in part, something like inaccessible, hidden (like a room). But it also means *pervasive,* like atmosphere, or the action of the heart. What I have in mind is carried in phrases like "inner beauty", "inner conviction", "inner strength", "inner calm". This suggests that the more deeply a characteristic pervades a soul, the more obvious it is. (Cf. envy as a sharp feeling and a state of the soul.)

Again, as after going over some of the grammar of pain, I find that I am not much interested in asking whether I know that anything, or anyway that what *I* say, is really going on in the other. But it may be that my practical or spiritual interest in his condition distracts me from that prior, or eventual, and when present, devastating question. I may "not be much interested" in it the way I am not much interested in some problem about the existence of the external world when what I am thinking about are the interesting things there are to be known and the interesting ways in which I may undertake to know them, and the gripping uses to which I may put that power. But no philosopher has, or ought to have, claimed that one is always and anywhere interested in the skeptical question; that it is live at any time. We would be in poor shape if it were; and the skeptic knows that, and accounts for it. The problem is whether it can ever rationally arise, and whether once it has arisen it can ever rationally be answered.

And can't it arise, directly out of that remark of Wittgenstein's now in focus? Whatever the criteria tell us by way of identifying the other's state (or process, etc.), they are still *outward.* — Outward as opposed to what? What would an inward criterion be? — Not opposed to an inward *criterion,* maybe; but as opposed to *something* inward. — Name something.

One tries to make the remark (". . . stands in need of outward criteria") into a thesis, and one starts babbling. Well, babbles have a grammar too. What is producing them here? We start with the idea that criteria are going to tell us very specific things about what's going on in the other, and we wind up wanting them to tell us that *something or other* is. We want them to do *less* than they do.

I feel: That "something or other" is in there is what "outward" *says.* In itself the word deprives the notion of a criterion of none of its power;

and adds none to it. But a false idea of the inward produces a false idea of the outward. A train bound outward is leaving *from* somewhere; a foot turned outward points away from the other foot, i.e., away from the center of the body. And suppose the translation of *äusserer* had been (less happily) "outer". The same applies. Not all reaches are outer, only those further out than others, and less far than the outermost; not all offices are inner, only those which have, or are in a place which has, outer ones. So the idea of "outward" registers my position with respect to a center. Then it becomes just as much a problem as the center does. When the center fails me, the criteria are no longer so much as outward.

If I take the space I am in to be outer, I have to imagine for the other an inner space which I could not possibly enter. Which *nobody* could possibly enter; for *he* didn't *enter* it. — Is this nothing? a foolishness of imagination? But it is illustrated in everything from Michelangelo's inflection of God as he puts his finger to the lax finger of his freshly wrought Adam, putting in the final touch; to Frankenstein's raising of the platform on which the monster is strapped, toward a storm heaven, to receive lightning. Not they are to enter their bodies, but life. We seem to understand these moments. We might even undertake to understand why theologians used to want to know *just* when the soul entered the body. And of course whatever enters can depart.

But surely it cannot be denied that in knowing him, it is *I* who have to use criteria; he does not. And isn't it equally undeniable that the knowledge he has makes what I get out of criteria a pale substitute? Nothing by comparison.

It is at such a juncture, I believe, that one expects Wittgenstein's answer to be to the effect that there is no *comparison* in question; because the other does not *know* what's going on in him at all. So of course he has no use for criteria there; his "position", however, is not better, merely different, merely other. "It cannot be said of me at all (except perhaps as a joke) that I *know* I am in pain" (§246). This comes in response to the idea that while other people very often know when I am in pain, they can't be said to know it "with the certainty with which I know it myself" (*ibid.*). To this, Wittgenstein's reply seems to me convincing. (What kind of joke does he have in mind? Something like an understatement, like saying of Newton or of Leibniz that he knew calculus. Or like familiar passages in comedy, say the one in *As You Like It* in which to Orlando's question "But will my Rosalind do so?", Rosalind (disguised) answers "By my life, she will do as I do".) The implication is that my relation to my own pain is deeper, or closer, than certainty. (One direction from this point leads into the question of how "relationship to oneself" is supposed to be understood. Who are those figures referred to in such forms as "I know I am being difficult" and "I tried telling myself it didn't matter" and "I was disappointed in myself" and "In her love, which I sought, I see myself as I am, and I am disgusted by what I see" and "I could hardly contain myself" and "Now I am at one with myself"?) Maybe what makes Wittgenstein's reply convincing here are the specific quantities in "knowing pain", which do not measure the idea of "knowing oneself" generally.

It is correct to say "I know what you are thinking", and wrong to say "I know what I am thinking". (A whole cloud of philosophy condensed into a drop of grammar.) [p. 222]

I find this much less convincing; I'm still under a cloud. I sort of know what it means: it is not merely that I do not have to look at myself to see or to learn whether I am thinking; but that I do not, as it were, take stock of the contents of my mind and determine whether they are in there. And yet it would be correct to say: "What you say keeps not ringing true to me. I keep having this worry — I can't quite put my finger on what it is. — Ah yes, I have it, I know what I am thinking. . . ." It is still true that saying "I know" here doesn't contrast with "I believe" or "I doubt". But doesn't it contrast with "I don't know" or "can't tell" or "can't make it out"? (What cloud of philosophy? The one from the Cartesian well? Descartes did not come to know that he was thinking (though we may say he came to know that he was a thing that thinks). What he discovered was a piece of grammar, that he could not so much as try to doubt that he doubted. But then why couldn't one feel that that is even a stronger rock to base knowledge of my existence upon? But then the rock is not knowledge of myself, and also not anything going on in me (e.g., something's thinking); it is just, as it were, the existence of myself. So instead of "Cogito ergo sum" he should simply have said "Sum", and gone from there. Sometimes he does.)

And when it comes to regions of the soul like envy or charity or ambition or self-destructiveness, or coldness covered with affectionateness, or loneliness covered with activity, or hatred covered by judiciousness, or obsessiveness covered by intellectuality . . . one's lack of knowledge of oneself may fully contrast with one's beliefs about oneself. My condition then is not that I need no criteria for such states, but that I fail accurately to allow of myself the ones I have. And here my relation to myself is expressed by saying that I do not know myself. The phrase "fail accurately to allow" indicates why one may say that I *will* not know myself — will not put the pieces together, or cannot, or do not see how they go. And when I do put them together what happens to me is not that I move from uncertainty to certainty (I may have been quite certain previously), but from darkness to light. The image of the Divided Line pictures knowing as a stage in the same direction as believing, but further along; the Myth of the Cave pictures these states as on different planes. In both pictures, however, there is the underlying idea of a path.

So what is the source of the idea that his position is better than mine, not just different; that mine is nothing in comparison? It seems that what I want to know, in knowing him, is *what he knows*. And it is not enough, once that is in question, to point out that he does not *know*.

What is it supposed to mean? — except perhaps that . . . [he is] in pain? . . . Other people cannot be said to learn of [his] sensations *only* from [his] behavior — for [he] cannot be said to learn of them. . . . [He has] them. [§246]

The depth of this is easy to miss. In the assertion "I learn of his sensation only from his behavior", which seems so obviously true, the "only" is empty ("idling", "on holiday"); and so the assertion is to that extent empty. (What is "empty to an extent"? Say that the assertion is not fully closed.) And yet the truth of the assertion seemed to lie in its being, so to speak, *wholly* or *fully* obvious.

I think we ought to feel shaken by such a realization; but probably not silenced. It can seem that a mere matter of words is at stake; an accident of language. Something like what we meant to be saying must be true; we don't go around making assertions that seem wholly obvious, a mere noting of the evident, and then find their meaning to vanish through one unclosed element. And certainly, if that assertion is "wrong" it is not obviously so; it is not, for example, meaningless. We wanted to say it; we may still; the facts seem right before it. The fact is that I do or must learn of his condition, and where else than from his behavior?; and the fact is that while he doubtless does not *learn* of it (if it's pain), anyway he is *aware* of it. — But if you know it *you* are aware of it! — Not like he is; not immediately! — But what is awareness if it isn't immediate?

It's the same old circle. But this time perhaps it has slowed enough to let us see where the anger comes from in such an exchange. It seems that the Wittgensteinian response is denying something, something like "He has it; I haven't"; something so obvious. Wittengenstein recognizes this fact about philosophizing: "What gives the impression that we want to deny anything?" (§305). But that is even more angering, if it is taken to mean "Obviously I'm not denying anything", i.e., if the question is taken to be rhetorical. And quite maddening if, beyond the wide-eyed innocence, you take the question to narrow down to a request for some psychological explanation of our sickness in supposing him capable of denying the obvious. I do not quite wish to say that Wittgenstein's habitual posing of such questions is never rhetorical; that would omit the fact that he goes to so much trouble to give questions a rhetorical air. I wish rather to say that he wants to leave that way of taking them open to us, to make it hard to see that they needn't be taken rhetorically, that instead the question is one he is genuinely asking, asking himself, and inviting us to ask ourselves. The implication of this literary procedure here is that it is difficult to see that such a question genuinely needs asking, difficult to ask it genuinely.

And it is startling to remember how many modern philosophers have seemed to be denying the obvious, and then denied they were denying it. Nothing is more characteristic of the skeptic's position. Even when he says that "for practical purposes" etc. we do know, nevertheless some desperate implication is there. And when the positivist said "We do not deny that moral or religious statements have a kind of meaning, a kind to which people attach the greatest importance; we merely deny that they have cognitive meaning" — instead of that seeming no more than a convenient definition, which is all it had a right to be, the heart seemed taken out of the statements to which we were attaching great importance. I take Hume to be responding to this when the opening speakers in his *Dialogues Concerning Natural Religion* characterize the subject to follow as one which swings between obviousness and obscurity, one in which pairs of Hume's protagonists are continually both denying and affirming what the other says. And remember how often Berkeley feels he has to disclaim the idea that he is denying what ordinary (or sanctified) men say and believe:

Some there are who think, that though the arguments for the real existence of bodies, which are drawn from reason, be allowed not to amount to demonstration, yet (first) the holy *scriptures* are so clear in the point, as will sufficiently convince every good Christian that bodies do really exist, and are something more than mere ideas; there being in holy writ innumerable facts related, which evidently suppose the reality of timber, and stone, mountains, and rivers, and cities, and human bodies. To which I *answer*, that no sort of writings whatever, sacred or profane, which use those and the like words, *in the vulgar acceptation,* or so to have a meaning in them, are in danger of having their truth called in question by our doctrine. That all those things do really exist, that there are bodies, even corporeal substances, when taken *in the vulgar sense,* has been shown to be agreeable to our principles. . . . [Berkeley, *Principles of Human Knowledge,* Section 82]

Is *that* what we, before he wrote, thought we knew or wanted to know, that there is a *sense* in which things really do exist? Berkeley assures us that we do know, a priori, that the world, the world of objects, is safely there. How can we not be assured?

What gives the impression Wittgenstein wants to deny anything? What in particular does he seem to deny? Not, as he says over and over again, that "The other has his sensations; I don't"; or anyway, not that "He may be suffering when I am not". He is not denying the truth of that assertion; but then that is not the assertion the skeptic stops with. The skeptic goes on to say something about what the other *knows,* and whether I can know it. And he means that to have the same obviousness as the fact that the other may be suffering and I not; indeed, one might say, he takes it to be the same undeniable fact. And that Wittgenstein does deny. What his denial comes to, then, is that the skeptic has *affirmed* anything; his words are empty, unclosed. But *that* isn't what a philosopher takes to be being denied — that he has *said* anything. So he gets the impression, the strongest possible impression, that what is being denied is the obvious *fact* he takes himself to be affirming.

How has it happened that when what I want to know is *him* I interpret this as wanting to know "what he knows"? Let us have a better sense of our idea of "his knowledge". What do we imagine the person himself to know when he says, for example, that he is expecting someone? Or, since what he says won't settle the question, let us rather take an instance we would all ordinarily call "expecting" (say the example Wittgenstein uses (§576) of watching a flame approach an explosive) and ask what we there imagine someone to be experiencing. We will all have in mind some more or less characteristic feelings, tensions, etc., which go with the concentration, anticipation, release, involved in such a case. I am not now interested in making out Wittgenstein's frequent point that no one particular feeling (here, a candidate to be called "the feeling of expecting") need be present, but rather in considering his equally frequent acknowledgment that there are feelings which are *characteristic* of such concepts. Imagine one such characteristic feeling; and now imagine that while you are washing your face one morning you drop the soap into the basin and suddenly are overcome with this feeling characteristic of watching a flame approach an explosive. If someone notices your tenseness and asks "What is the matter?", you will probably not reply "I'm waiting for the explosion". Perhaps you will say, "I have this queer feeling that something is about to explode". But what makes the feeling *queer*? It's just, we were imagining, one ordinary feeling characteristic of expecting. Well, obviously its queerness comes from its occurring *there,* where, though you are not in fact expecting anything (= there is nothing in those circumstances *to be expected* (cf. §581)), you have this feeling of expecting something.

So what does the person himself know that we don't or can't know? That it is queer in those circumstances? What the particular *quality* of the experience is? We may or may not know any or all of this. *How* we know it, or fail to know it, does not concern me here. What I wish to emphasize is, rather, that it is not his knowing of such things alone which will lead him to say, or to refrain from saying, "I'm expecting . . .". What more is necessary? We might answer: the presence of circumstances in which anyone could, in terms of our usual criteria of "expecting", see how *whatever* experience he is having adds up in *those* circumstances, to his expecting something.

These are not circumstances which Wittgenstein takes to "justify *us* in saying" that *he* is, e.g., expecting something or someone. (What justifies us, as *opposed* to him, is what we take to put us in the way of knowing that that is what is going on — how good our opportunities were, how attentive we were, how well we know him, how experienced we are in such matters. . . . A psychologist may find that there is a pattern in the "cues" various people take as showing the satisfaction of the criteria for their judgments. Perhaps such cues are Wittgensteinian "symptoms".) For Wittgenstein speaks of the person himself as "being justified in saying" what his experience is.

If there has to be anything "behind the utterance of the formula" it is *particular circumstances,* which justify *me* in saying I can go on — when the formula occurs to *me.* [§154, last two emphases mine]

Thus what I wanted to say was: when he suddenly knew how to go on, when he understood the principle, then possibly he had a special experience — and if he is asked: "What was it? What took place when you suddenly grasped the principle?" perhaps he will describe it much as we described it above — but for us it is *the circumstances* under which *he* had such an experience that justify *him* in saying in such a case that he understands, that he knows how to go on. [§155, last two emphases mine]

(I should say that I read the phrase "but for us" as meaning not "for us, who do not have that experience", but "for us Wittgensteinians".) And what he is getting at is what he describes by using such locutions as "only in certain circumstances would such a feeling and such activities *be* expecting something". For the phenomena which constitute the criteria of something's being so are fully *in the nature of things* — they are part of those very general facts of nature or of human life against the background of which our concepts mean anything at all, and in particular, mean something *about* what we call "the nature of things" or "the world". "Could someone have a feeling of ardent love or hope [or expectancy or joy or belief or profound pleasure or causation] for the space of one second — *no matter what* preceded or followed this second?" (§583). And the answer he apparently expects is, No. It *could* not, in the nature of things, *be* love, hope, etc.

Suppose, however, I find myself wondering: "How long does a major passion *take* to express itself; not to manifest itself, but to realize itself, to build up?" I may ask myself how long it takes to form a deep attachment. A month? A week-end? How about at first sight? Suppose I settle on one day as a possible figure. If a full human life-time is, say, seventy years, then the passion took roughly 1/13,000th of that life-time to build up. Then maybe a creature whose passions take one second would have a life span of about seven hours, a short winter day or short summer night. And then I start imagining very tiny things, like ants or bees maybe, or very frail things, ones whose hold on life seems to me frail, say like butterflies or certain flowers. And then I feel ridiculous trying to pack major passions into such spaces. Or I may hit upon the sort of moment, in the last seconds of a football game, in which a long, arching pass is thrown. The ball isn't in the air more than two or three seconds; its trajectory seems the very tracing of my hope; and the instant it comes in reach of the receiver's hands the ardency in the hope flares. In a split second the ardent hope is there, and perhaps gone before the second is complete. —But then this illustrates Wittgenstein's idea. In order for all that feeling to be packed into that space, very specific preparations had to be in place: I had to care about the outcome; it had to seem all but impossible that it would be what I had hoped; I am downcast; perhaps as sometimes happens the game "turns around", one or two errors or breaks and *there is room* for hope; and now the score stands at such a point, and the time left in the game is such, that this arching pass moves out of the shadows into this one last chance for the outcome I cared about. And then if, at the impact of ardency, the hope was at last satisfied, it takes a while for me to come down from the feeling; I will laugh, shout, clap, stamp, in order, as it were, to get rid of it, let the pleasure work its way out. And if at that last descent the hope is instead finally crushed, it takes a while for me to come up from the feeling; I may groan, clench my fists, go over and over the play in imagination and curses; letting, as it were, the pain work its way out. So it isn't the sheer amount of time which is critical. There merely needs to be enough time so that a coherent "before and after" can take place. A passion, one might say, has a history, as an action has; a logical history. So it wasn't merely ridiculous of me to try to pack passions into those tiny beings. My imagination was trying to assert the concept of a passion, to make room for a coherent history to be lived through.

"It could not, in the nature of things, *be* hope, love, etc." Does this really have any content beyond saying, "We wouldn't *call* the feeling, in those circumstances, 'love', 'hope', etc."? And does the question then arise, "Suppose we don't *call* it that; mightn't it still be that?"? For the moment I will just ask: How, following that suggestion, will you say *what* it might be? And it shouldn't be lightly dismissed that you cannot answer that satisfactorily. For in its ordinary use the statement "It is what it is; what you call it doesn't matter" can, when competently used, be followed by a clear answer to the question "Well what is it really"? or "What would *you* call it?". But the person who *had* the feeling might insist that it *was* love. Then would it be? We have a choice. Either it's love, or else he will be treated as abnormal: that's the way *he* "loves", but that *isn't* love, isn't what is meant by "love". And is it always clear which alternative we shall take? (Jesus is said to have loved, but that isn't the way we love. Dostoevsky thought he was right and that we are wrong and sinful and perhaps incapable of love, and are therefore in hell. Nietzsche thought he was wrong, or right only about himself, and hence that he taught us a new stratagem for sinning undiscovered, and thereby made hell attractive.)

If it is true that the having of my feelings *alone* cannot make possible my knowledge of myself (of what I am doing, of what I am expecting, hoping, caring about, afraid of . . .), this says something about the nature of self-knowledge: that it depends upon my knowing or appreciating the place or reach — I want to say, the normality or abnormality — of those feelings to the situation in which those feelings occur. This does not mean that I know about myself the way others do, that what "justifies me in saying" what I feel and intend is the same as what "justifies you in saying" these things. It means, rather, two other things: that my use of criteria cannot be to identify "my feeling itself", and that the possession of criteria enters my knowledge of myself differently from the way it enters my knowledge of you — one could say, their mode of application is different. Perhaps this is the point at which Wittgenstein speaks of my knowledge of myself as proceeding "without observation" (§357, §631, §659), which I take to mean "without observation of the presence of criteria", not "without knowledge of the presence of criteria".

There is this pain here, in my tooth. I don't need an observation of criteria to tell me that. But that alone doesn't add up to my having a toothache, I won't call this (on the basis of this alone I won't call out) "toothache". What I count as a toothache is just what you count, a particular history associated with pain. — But then how about pain itself, just sheer suffering? It could simply come over me, in one second, no matter what (in my perceivable history) went before and after. But *now* if we say "Pain itself, sheer pain, has no history", that is specifically informative about the concept — the thing — of pain *itself*. And here I do not find that I am thinking of pain as opposed to behavior. I may think that behavior has disappeared, collapsed, dissolved in pain; or that the body itself is now a field or valley upon or along which pain collects.

Knowing oneself is the capacity, as I wish to put it, for placing-oneself-in-the-world. It is not merely that to know *I* have in fact *done* what I intended (or hoped, or promised . . .), I have to look to see *whether* it is done; it is also, and crucially, that I have to know that *that* circumstance *is* (counts as) *what* I did. How can *that* (the spilt milk) be "what I did"; how can *that* (the sobbing child) be "what I expected"; how can *that* (the empty room) be "what I said" (that he had already left)? How do I *relate* or compare what goes on in my mind to the phenomena of the world? And at the level at which this is asked, it does not mean "How do I know the milk is spilt; that the child is crying; that he has left?" but rather "How do we know of the 'possibilities of [these] phenomena' (§90), that there are, and which phenomena are, phenomena of this kind?". How, e.g., do we *ever* come to refer to a phenomenon as "spilt milk" or "his having left" and not as, say, simply "flat milk" or "now empty room"? It is at such a juncture, I suppose, that philosophers will say: We grasp a proposition or a meaning. But apart from epistemological and ontological questions about "grasping propositions" and "grasping meanings", such notions are going to have to do more work than we may have bargained for. They will have to account for our *sometimes* saying, looking at milk fallen flat, that it is spilt, and sometimes that it was poured (to remove a stain from the rug), and our saying, pointing sometimes to a park bench, sometimes at a closet in disarray, sometimes at a doctor's check-in board, "He's already left".

The coincidence of soul and body, and of mind (language) and world *überhaupt,* are the issues to which Wittgenstein's notion of grammar and criteria are meant to speak. The *practical* difficulty of pegging the mind to the world, and especially to the social-political world, the world of history; and the psychological difficulty of it in the world of religion; are main subjects of modern literature and of certain existentialisms. The gap, or distorted relation, between intention (or wish or feeling) and its execution, and between execution and consequence, is what the sense of "absurdity" is a response to. But then how does the gap or distortion appear, and how can it be closed? In Wittgenstein's view the gap between mind and the world is closed, or the distortion between them straightened, in the appreciation and acceptance of particular human forms of life, human "convention". This implies that the *sense* of gap originates in an attempt, or wish, to escape (to remain a "stranger" to, "alienated" from) those shared forms of life, to give up the responsibility of their maintenance. (Is this always a fault? Is there no way of becoming responsible for that? What does a moral or intellectual hero do?)

I remarked that traditional philosophy, so far as this enters the Anglo-American academic tradition, fails to take this gap seriously as a real, a practical problem. It has either filled it with God or bridged it with universals which *insure* the mind's collusion with the world; or else it has denied, on theoretical grounds, that it *could* be filled or bridged at all. I think this is something Nietzsche meant when he ridiculed philosophers for regarding life "as a riddle, as a problem of knowledge" (*Genealogy of Morals,* p. 682), implying that we question what we cannot fail to know in order not to seek what it would be painful to find out. This, of course, does not suggest that skepticism is trivial; on the contrary it shows how profound a position of the mind it is. Nothing is more human than the wish to deny one's humanity, or to assert it at the expense of others. But if that is what skepticism entails, it cannot be combatted through simple "refutations". The idea that a philosophical position can simply be "refuted" is one that Nietzsche *also* ridicules (*Beyond Good and Evil,* p. 499).

Skepticism about our knowledge of others is typically accompanied by complacency about our knowledge of ourselves. From Locke through Mill, and beyond, we "infer" the experience of others, and "intuit" our own. Whereas those capable of the deepest personal confession (Augustine, Luther, Rousseau, Thoreau, Kierkegaard, Tolstoy, Freud) were most convinced they were speaking from the most hidden knowledge of others. Perhaps that is the sense which makes confession possible.

What happens if this conviction slackens? As in Kafka and Beckett; as thematically in Thoreau and Marx and Kierkegaard and Nietzsche; as sometimes in Rousseau; as in Descartes when he recognizes that voicing his doubts may put him with lunatics or fools. In such straits, perhaps you write for everybody and nobody; for an all but unimaginable future; in pseudonyms, for the anonymous; in an album, which is haunted by pictures and peopled with voices. But what happens if you are not a writer; if you lack *that* way of embodying, accounting for, a slackened conviction in a community, and of staking your own (in imagination, in a world of works)? What happens if all you want to do is talk, and words fail you?

Go back to my comparison of the different forces of "call" underlying Austinian and Wittgensteinian criteria. Each is associated with different orders of something we think of as convention. If the bases you offer in support of your identification of a specific object invoke inappropriate criteria, then one response we cited was "But that's not what is officially or conventionally called a such-and-such; you've been taught the wrong name"; and to support this we may appeal to an official manual or to our expertise. But if you have to say "But that's not (what is called) 'pointing to the color', 'explaining the meaning', etc.", there is no such appeal. We are equal with respect to such claims; not equal in the ability to challenge and clarify, but equal in the right to ask and answer. (*Who is to say?* Someone is bullied by that question, or bullying with it, when he feels that *he* has no voice in the matter. To whom did he cede it?)

The conventions we appeal to may be said to be "fixed", "adopted", "accepted", etc. by us; but this does not now mean that what we have fixed or adopted are (merely) the (conventional) *names* of things. The conventions which control the application of grammatical criteria are fixed not by customs or some particular concord or agreement which might, without disrupting the texture of our lives, be changed where convenience suggests a change. (Convenience is *one* aspect of convention, or an aspect of one kind or level of convention.) They are, rather, fixed by the nature of human life itself, the human fix itself, by those "very general facts of nature" which are "unnoticed only because so obvious", and, I take it, in particular, very general facts of *human* nature — such, for example, as the fact that the realization of intention requires action, that action requires movement, that movement involves consequences we had not intended, that our knowledge (and ignorance) of ourselves and of others depends upon the way our minds are expressed (and distorted) in word and deed and passion; that actions and passions have histories. That *that* should express understanding or boredom or anger — (or: that it should be part of the grammar of "understanding" that *that* is what we call "his suddenly understanding") is not necessary: someone may have to be said to "understand suddenly" and then always fail to manifest the understanding five minutes later, just as someone *may* be bored by an earthquake or by the death of his child or the declaration of martial law, or *may* be angry at a pin or a cloud or a fish, just as some-one may quietly (but comfortably?) sit on a chair of nails. That human beings on the whole do not respond in these ways is, therefore, seriously referred to as conventional; but now we are thinking of convention not as the arrangements a particular culture has found convenient, in terms of its history and geography, for effecting the necessities of human exist-ence, but as those forms of life which are normal to any group of crea-tures we call human, any group about which we will say, for example, that they *have* a past to which they respond, or a geographical environ-ment which they manipulate or exploit in certain ways for certain hu-manly comprehensible motives. Here the array of "conventions" are not patterns of life which differentiate human beings from one another, but those exigencies of conduct and feeling which all humans share. Wittgen-stein's discovery, or rediscovery, is of the depth of convention in human life; a discovery which insists not only on the conventionality of human society but, we could say, on the conventionality of human nature itself, on what Pascal meant when he said "Custom is our nature" (*Pensées*, §89); perhaps on what an existentialist means by saying that man has no nature.

One group may hope for a different future, fear a different region or past, question in forms different from ours. But hope will still be gram-matically related to satisfaction and disappointment; fear will still be grammatically related to some object and reason for fear which, though it may not be one we in fact are affected by, we can understand as such a reason. Put otherwise, we should not call anything they do "sacrificing", "atoning", "placating", etc. unless we understand how what they do could count as (grammatically be) sacrificing, atoning, placating, etc. Can they placate a monkey or a man dead and buried? Can they make sacrifices and pray to a piece of carved wood? But we do equally strange and famil-iar things. Is it less strange to pray to, or curse, a President? Strange not just to outsiders, but to us, come to think of it.

Normal and Natural

From the time of the *Brown Book* (1934–35), Wittgenstein's thought is punctuated by ideas of normality and abnormality. It goes with a new depth in the idea that language is *learned,* that one *becomes* civilized.

And in the recognition of how little can be *taught;* how, so to speak, help-less or impotent the teaching is, compared with the enormity of what is learned. As though he sees philosophical disputes as exemplifying this concurrent outsideness and fatedness to a culture. Or as dramatizing, re-capitulating, the original facts of this asymmetry between teaching and learning. (Then the motive to philosophy can be thought of as a desire to true this asymmetry.) The mind cannot be led at every point; teaching (reasons; my control) comes to an end; then the other takes over. And the object of my instruction (my assertions, questions, remarks, encourage-ments, rebukes) is exactly that the other shall take over, that he or she shall be able to go on (alone). But correctly; that is, that the other do what I would do, make what I make of it. The differences between nor-mality and abnormality are philosophically not as instructive as their fundamental unity — that both depend upon the same fact of civilization, that it expects complete acceptance and understanding from its natives. And yet it can *say* so little about itself in achieving its acquisition. In both cases you have to go on alone; in the one case toward acceptance, in the other toward isolation.

A certain tribe has a language of the kind (2). [A language of kind (2) is essen-tially that of §§1–2 of the *Investigations:* It contains "demonstrative teaching" of names of building blocks, and a series of numerals learnt by heart.] . . . The children of the tribe learn the numerals this way: They are taught the signs from 1 to 20 . . . and to count rows of beads of no more than 20 on being ordered, "Count these". When in counting the pupil arrives at the numeral 20, one makes a gesture suggestive of "Go on", upon which the child says (in most cases at any rate) "21". Analogously, the children are made to count to 22 and to higher numbers. . . . The last stage of the training is that the child is ordered to count a group of objects, well above 20, without the suggestive gesture being used. . . . If a child does not respond to the suggestive gesture, it is separated from the others and treated as a lunatic. [*Brown Book,* p. 93]

Imagining this makes me rather anxious. I feel: These people are in a great hurry to separate out lunatics. Why is open-ended counting so im-portant to them? And their evidence for lunacy is so slim: the picking up of a mere gesture, and an indefinite one at that! But then I feel: What is *ample* evidence for lunacy? Not being able to keep up in school over a period of years? We may not call it lunacy, our gradations are not so crude; but the children are certainly treated differently because of it, and set apart. And sometimes the ostracism is based on the way a member dresses or on what he does not possess or on the words he uses. Is this more rational? How does it happen?

. . . B has been taught a use of the words "lighter" and "darker". . . . Now he is given the order to put down a series of objects, arranging them in the order of their darkness. He does this by laying out a row of books, writing down a series of names of animals, and by writing down the five vowels in the order u, o, a, e, i. We ask him why he put down that latter series, and he says, "Well, o is lighter than u, and e lighter than o". — We shall be astonished at his attitude, and at the same time admit that there is something in what he says. Perhaps we shall say: "But look, surely e isn't lighter than o in the way this book is lighter than that". — But he may shrug his shoulders and say, "I don't know, but e *is* lighter than o, isn't it?"

We may be inclined to treat this case as some kind of abnormality, and to say, "B must have a different sense, with the help of which he arranges both colored objects and vowels". [*Brown Book,* pp. 138–39]

When we hear the diatonic scale we are inclined to say that after every seven notes the same note recurs, and, asked why we call it the same note again one might answer, "Well, it's a c again". But this isn't the explanation I want, for I should ask "What made one call it a c again?" And the answer to this would seem to be "Well, don't you hear that it's the same note only an octave higher?". . . .

If we had made this experiment with two people A and B, and A had applied the expression "the same note" to the octave only, B to the dominant and octave, should we have a right to say that the two hear different things when we play to them the diatonic scale? — If we say they do, let us be clear whether we wish to assert that there must be some other difference between the two cases besides the one we have observed, or whether we wish to make no such statement. [*Ibid.*, pp. 140–41]

If we say "They hear different things" this might mean "There is something in what B hears" (the dominant, as doubling interval, say in plain song, is "closer" to the octave than any other interval); or it might mean "B has a different way of hearing". On the former interpretation we take B's reaction as a natural one, only it is not ours (we may even think his response is historically more primitive, and that ours has lost something in its sophistication; we might *try* hearing his way); on the latter interpretation, our words may simply mean "B does not hear as we do", where "simply" means that we have neither any notion of *how* he hears (what else this abnormality goes with) nor of some way in which ours is special. — But why do we want any words at all in such places? Why not just say "B doesn't hear the thing we hear, the uniqueness of the octave", without trying to make up an explanation of this discrepancy? Why do we attach such importance to this that we have to make of one or other of us an outcast, or make sure that there is room in the world for both? About music, most people may let it go without explanation; but in some families, not hearing the uniqueness of the octave might be sufficient evidence for idiocy. To an outsider this treatment will seem not merely severe, but altogether unjust, the merest personal decision that a person be treated in a special way; not merely unjust, but irrational.

After the set of cases including the series of darker to lighter vowels and the diatonic scale, Wittgenstein continues: "All the questions considered here link up with this problem: Suppose you had taught someone to write down series of numbers according to the form: Always write down a number *n* greater than the preceding." And then he goes on to produce his case in which, upon the order "Add 1" the subject does what you expect up to 100; after which he starts, as we would say, adding 2; and after 300 adding 3; etc. Then, upon your reprimand, he insists that he is doing what you asked, doing the same thing after 200 and 300 as after 100.

You see that it would get us no further here again to say "But don't you see. . . ?", pointing out to him again the rules and examples we had given to him. We might, in such a case, say that this person naturally understands (interprets) the rule (and examples) we have given as we should understand the rule (and examples) telling us: "Add 1 up to 100, then 2 up to 200, etc."

(This would be similar to the case of a man who did not naturally follow an order given by a pointing gesture by moving in the direction shoulder to hand, but in the opposite direction. And understanding here means the same as reacting.)

(This last conjunction of examples appears in the *Investigations* at §185, where they are reasserted as similar.)

These examples are all very upsetting. Is it because these people are not really intelligible to us? No doubt we cannot communicate with them — at least in certain areas. But that is not an unfamiliar fact, even with our friends. What is the content of "not really intelligible" in these upsetting cases? I can understand *what he does* (e.g., "He adds 1 up to 100; 2 up to 200; 3 up to . . . well, as far as it will go in the 200's; etc."). I don't know *why* he does it that way. But is that necessary here? What could count as "knowing *why*"? Before Bach, we are told, keyboard performers did not use their thumbs in playing. Why didn't they? Did they fail to see that there was greater efficiency to be had, lying at hand? But for many virtuosi it probably wouldn't be more efficient, at least at first. Or suppose that for 10,000 years men made ax heads by chipping only at one side of a stone to get an edge. Did they fail to see the advantage in turning the stone over and grading both sides toward a common edge? For 10,000 years? Eventually people began doing it the new way. That may or may not be because it was thought to be better, more advantageous or efficient. Maybe the followers of the old way just stopped playing or working because it wasn't done their way any longer; and the followers of the new never think about *comparing* their way with another. We know very little about our pupil; maybe in 10,000 minutes he will find his way to our way. But we know two things about him as matters stand. We know that he is not completely unintelligible to us; we feel he *must* be able to follow our directions. And we know we are impotent in this moment to get him to. The cause of our anxiety is that *we cannot make ourselves intelligible* (to him). But why does this create anxiety? Is it that we read our unintelligibility to him as our unintelligibility as such? What gives him this power over us? Why have we given it?

Our ability to communicate with him depends upon his "natural understanding", his "natural reaction", to our directions and our gestures. It depends upon our mutual attunement in judgments. It is astonishing how far this takes us in understanding one another, but it has its limits; and these are not merely, one may say, the limits of knowledge but the limits of experience. And when these limits are reached, when our attunements are dissonant, I cannot get below them to firmer ground. The power I felt in my breath as my words flew to their effect now vanishes into thin air. For not only does he not receive me, because his natural reactions are not mine; but my own understanding is found to go no further than my own natural reactions bear it. I am thrown back upon myself; I as it were turn my palms outward, as if to exhibit the kind of creature I am, and declare my ground occupied, only mine, ceding yours.

When? When do I find or decide that the time has come to grant you secession, allow your divergence to stand, declare that the matter between us is at an end? The anxiety lies not just in the fact that my understanding *has* limits, but that I must *draw* them, on apparently no more ground than my own.

We have come across some people who sell wood not according to what *we* call "the amount of wood" in a pile, but according to the amount of ground covered by the pile, regardless of its height:

How could I show them that — as I should say — you don't really buy more wood if you buy a pile covering a bigger area? — I should, for instance, take a pile which was small by their ideas and, by laying the logs around, change it into a "big" one. This *might* convince them — but perhaps they would say: "Yes, now it's a *lot* of wood and costs more" — and that would be the end of the matter. [*Remarks on the Foundations of Mathematics*, I, §149]

Why is *that* the end? Are we convinced that their way is all right? And if not, is there no further interest we have in these people? Perhaps we were merely looking for recruits for our lumber company, and clearly these people will not serve, anyway not as sellers or buyers. As cutters perhaps. I may not care to understand more than that. But couldn't I? (I am prompted to this example by Barry Stroud's "Wittgenstein and Logical Necessity".)

We have varying criteria according to which we measure cost; and various reasons and possibilities for making "profits" and for "sacrificing" goods. If we are *convinced* that those wood sellers cannot have in mind any coherent mode of "calculating a proportionate price" we can make all sorts of difficulties for them, make them quite unintelligible to us, decide they are unlike us. But suppose our attitude is that we are *inclined to suppose* that they are quite coherent, even in our terms (they more or less seemed to be, until this last step about selling according to area covered). There are details which may then become relevant to learn: Does wood, given the way trees are felled and wood cut and stacked and transported in that place, "naturally" involve standard piles, so that logs are more trouble, i.e., more costly, to store and to load if they are strewn around; if for no other reason than that they have first to be piled, or piled again, before delivery? Then "a lot of wood" means something like "a bunch of wood", a "non-pile". And what do their buildings look like? It needn't be true that you can "build more or bigger" buildings with more wood rather than less. All buildings may have the same amount of wood in them. Bigger buildings — i.e., ones covering a greater area — have the wood spaced differently; instead of what we call log cabins, the logs are used as columns, with cloth or strings of vines stretched between.   — "But obviously 'build more or bigger' means 'more or bigger *of the same kind*'. You can build either more or bigger cabin structures *or* more or bigger temple structures with a greater amount of wood."   — It was not obvious. And maybe it is irrelevant: each member is permitted to build only one structure, and he has simply to choose which; or maybe their architectural skills limit them to types of structures which will not accept more than a certain amount of wood for each structure. (For example, they can't lay logs horizontally on top of one another to a point higher than the tallest logs, which, placed vertically, are used as retainers.) If a great architect rises up among them, he or she may teach them to notch the logs into one another so as to get much greater heights; then a member will have to choose not just which kind of structure he wants, but what size; and maybe pay accordingly. Now they will have a use for the expression "more wood" which is like ours, because then they will also have a use for the expression "bigger cabin" and even for "more cabin". Of course there will be new possibilities for cheating in this tribe, ones new to us. An entrepreneur may surreptitiously go around nudging strewn logs closer together and buy terrific amounts of non-pile wood at pile prices; more than he can build his structure with. Either he likes to have lots of unbuilt wood on his premises, or he has found that he can build more structures than he can inhabit and sell them to others. Suppose this is not against their law: the law hadn't envisioned that someone would have a reason for building a structure he would then part with. And the wood sellers may even know the man means to cheat them, but they don't mind; they think he is crazy to expend labour nudging logs closer together for the sole purpose of getting more wood than he can use for his house in order to accumulate more money to buy more wood with. This need not at all mean that they do not demand payment for their wood. Payment is essential for these people because it is the open sign that you *own* the thing you paid for, that it is yours to do with as you please, and be responsible for.

Nor need calculation enter in at all, even where we will still call what they do "selling" rather than "giving". If there is just one price for piles of wood and one other price for non-piles, what would there be to *calculate?* (Nor is it necessary to assume that the piles all happen to contain the same quantity of wood. You pay your money and take your choice, as happens with us in certain sales or in buying Christmas trees when the good ones have been taken or when the time for selling them is running out.) I once knew a man who coveted a particular old automobile owned by a mutual friend. For a year he coveted it but thought its owner would not sell it or that she would ask more than he could pay. One day the owner, who knew he wanted it, offered it to him for $100. He immediately accepted, but having paid so little for it he never quite took it seriously again, and let it deteriorate. In a few months it was beyond repair; but the former owner, not knowing this, offered the man $500 to buy it back. She said that when she sold it to him she needed just $100 so that is what she asked; and now that she had more money she could afford to pay him what it would bring on the used car market. He was overcome with a sense of loss; not mere financial loss, but shame; and apparently with guilt toward the *car*. — She didn't calculate when she sold it (at least she didn't calculate the worth of the car, only the amount of her need then); she estimated or perhaps calculated when she wanted to buy it back, but then from *his* point of view, since the car was then his. He didn't calculate when he bought the car, but he accepted its asking price as if it were the result of calculation, a serious measure of its real worth. — Who is crazy? I do not say no one is, but must somebody be, when people's reactions are at variance with ours? It seems safe to suppose that if you can describe any behavior which I can recognize as that of human beings, I can give you an explanation which will make that behavior coherent, i.e., show it to be imaginable in terms of natural responses and practicalities. Though *those* natural responses may not be mine, and those practices not practical for me, in my environment, as I interpret it. And if I say "They are crazy" or "incomprehensible" then that is not a fact but my fate for them. I have gone as far as my imagination, magnanimity, or anxiety will allow; or as my honor, or my standing cares and commitments, can accommodate. I take it that this is what Wittgenstein's Swiftian proposal about separating out the child and treating it as a lunatic is meant to register.

It is not necessary that human beings should have come to engage in anything we would call calculation (inferring, etc.). But if their natural history has brought them to this crossroads, then only certain procedures will count as calculating (inferring, etc.) and only certain forms will allow those activities to proceed. It is not necessary that the members of a group should ever have found pleasure and edification in gathering together to hear the stories of their early history related; but if they do, then only certain kinds of stories, in certain structures, will provide (what we can comprehend as) that pleasure and edification. "There must be agreement not only in definitions but also . . . in judgments. This seems to abolish logic, but does not do so." In particular, I take it: It is not necessary that we should recognize anything as "logical inference"; but if we do, then only certain procedures will count as drawing such inferences, ones (say) which achieve the universality of agreement, the teachability, and the individual conviction, of the forms of inference we accept as logic. There is no logical explanation of the fact that we (in general, on the whole) will agree that a conclusion has been drawn, a rule applied, an instance to be a member of a class, one line to be a repetition of another (even though it is written lower down, or in another hand or color); but the fact is, those who understand (i.e., can talk logic together) do agree. And the fact is that they agree the *way* they agree; I mean, the ways they have of agreeing at *each* point, each *step*. For example: "Assume the negation is true (and they agree it has been written down): we know that X (and they write down another line); and substituting we get Y (Right?); and applying R we get Z (Right?). . . ."

Wittgenstein's view of necessity is, as one would expect, internal to his view of what philosophy is. His philosophy provides, one might say, an anthropological, or even anthropomorphic, view of necessity; and that can be disappointing; as if it is not really *necessity* which he has given an anthropological view of. As though if the a priori has a history it cannot really be the a priori in question. — "But something can *be* necessary whatever *we* happen to take as, or believe to be, necessary." — But that only says that we have a (the) concept of necessity — for it is part of the meaning of that concept that the thing called necessary is *beyond our control*. If the wish were not mere father but creator of the deed, we would have no such concept. If upon doing a calculation I could wish, and my wish bring it about, that the figures from which I "started" become altered, if necessary, in order that the result of my calculation prove correct; and if I could wish, and my wish bring it about, that the world alter where necessary so that the altered figures are still *of* what they are supposed to be; then the sense of necessity (standing over myself, at any rate) is not likely to be very strong in me. What we take to be necessary in a given period may alter. It is not logically impossible that painters should now paint in ways which outwardly resemble paintings of the Renaissance, nor logically necessary that they now paint in the ways they do. What is necessary is that, in order for us to have the form of experience we count as an experience of a painting, we accept something as a painting. And we do not know a priori what we will accept as such a thing. But only someone outside such an enterprise could think of it as a manipulation or exploration of mere conventions.

Very little of what goes on among human beings, very little of what goes on in so limited an activity as a game, is *merely* conventional (done *solely* for convenience). In baseball, it is merely conventional for the home team to take the field first or for an umpire to stand behind the catcher rather than behind the pitcher (which might be safer). In the former instance it is convenient to have such a matter routinely settled one way or the other; in the latter instance it must have been found more convenient for the task at hand, e.g., it permits greater accuracy in calling pitches, and positions an official so that he is on top of plays at home plate and faces him so that his line of sight crosses those of the other umpires. More or less analogous advantages will recommend, say, the Gerber convention in bridge. But it can seem that really *all* the rules of a game, each act it consists of, is conventional. There is no necessity in permitting three strikes instead of two or four; in dealing thirteen cards rather than twelve or fifteen. — What would one have in mind here? That two or four are just as good? Meaning what? That it would not alter the essence of the game to have it so? But from what position is this supposed to be claimed? By someone who does or does not know what "the essence of the

game" is? — e.g., that it contains passages which are duels between pitcher
and batter, that "getting a hit", "drawing a walk", and "striking a batter
out" must have *certain* ranges of difficulty. It is such matters that the
"convention" of permitting three strikes is in service of. So a justification
for saying that a different practice is "just as good" or "better" is that it is
found just as good or better (by those who know and care about the activity). But is the *whole* game in service of anything? I think one may say: It
is in service of the human capacity, or necessity, for play; because what
can be played, and what play can be watched with that avidity, while not
determinable a priori, is contingent upon the given capacities for human
play, and for avidity. (It should not be surprising that what is necessary is
contingent upon something. Necessaries are means.) It is perhaps not
derivable from the measurements of a baseball diamond and of the average velocities of batted baseballs and of the average times human beings
can run various short distances, that 90 feet is the best distance for setting
up an essential recurrent crisis in the structure of a baseball game, e.g., at
which the run and the throw to first take long enough to be followed lu-
cidly, and are often completed within a familiar split second of one another; but seeing what happens at just these distances will sometimes
strike one as a discovery of the a priori. But also of the utterly contingent.
There is no necessity that human capacities should train to just these proportions; but just these proportions reveal the limits of those capacities.
Without those limits, we would not have known the possibilities.

　　To think of a human activity as governed throughout by mere conventions, or as having conventions which may as well be changed as not, depending upon some individual or other's taste or decision, is to think of a
set of conventions as tyrannical. It is worth saying that conventions can
be changed because it is essential to a convention that it be in service of
some project, and you do not know a priori which set of procedures is better than others for that project. That is, it is internal to a convention that
it be open to change *in convention,* in the convening of those subject to
it, in whose behavior it lives. So it is a first order of business of political
tyranny to deny the freedom to convene. What that prevents is not
merely, as (say) Mill urges, the free exchange of truths with partial truth
and with falsehoods, from the fire of which truth rises. That *might* happen in an isolated study. It prevents the arising of the issue for which
convening is necessary, viz., to see what we do, to learn our position in
what we take to be necessaries, to see in what service they are necessary.

　　The internal tyranny of convention is that only a slave of it can know
how it may be changed for the better, or know why it should be eradi-

cated. Only masters of a game, perfect slaves to that project, are in a position to establish conventions which better serve its essence. This is why deep revolutionary changes can result from attempts to conserve a project, to take it back to its idea, keep it in touch with its history. To demand that the law be fulfilled, every jot and tittle, will destroy the law as it stands, if it has moved too far from its origins. Only a priest could have confronted his set of practices with its origins so deeply as to set the terms of Reformation. It is in the name of the idea of philosophy, and against a vision that it has become false to itself, or that it has stopped thinking, that such figures as Descartes and Kant and Marx and Nietzsche and Heidegger and Wittgenstein seek to revolutionize philosophy. It is because certain human beings crave the conservation of their art that they seek to discover how, under altered circumstances, paintings and pieces of music can still be made, and hence revolutionize their art beyond the recognition of many. This is how, in my illiteracy, I read Thomas Kuhn's *The Structure of Scientific Revolutions:* that only a master of the science can accept a revolutionary change as a natural extension of that science; and that he accepts it, or proposes it, in order to maintain touch with the idea of that science, with its internal canons of comprehensibility and comprehensiveness, as if against the vision that, under altered circumstances, the normal progress of explanation and exception no longer seem to him to be science. And then what he does may not seem scientific to the old master. If this difference is taken to be a difference in their *natural* reactions (and Kuhn's use of the idea of a "paradigm" seems to me to suggest this more than it suggests a difference in conventions) then we may wish to speak here of conceptual divergence. Perhaps the idea of a new historical period is an idea of a generation whose natural reactions — not merely whose ideas or mores — diverge from the old; it is an idea of a new (human) nature. And different historical periods may exist side by side, over long stretches, and within one human breast.

We were led, and I take Wittgenstein to be similarly led, to those recent more or less mathematical examples, from within a need to follow out an idea of normality. Why is this? I am not competent to quarrel with or to affirm Wittgenstein's ideas about logic and the foundation of mathematics. But mathematical-looking fragments make their appearance as integral to the thought of the *Investigations,* and I cannot to that extent ignore them. What is their function?

Their general background is an idea that the primitive abilities of mathematics (e.g., counting, grouping, adding, continuing a series, finding quantities equal or smaller) are as natural as any (other) region of a natural tongue, and as natural as the primitive abilities of logic (e.g., drawing an inference, following a rule of substitution). The implication is that ordinary language no more *needs* a foundation in logic than mathematics does. More specifically, he uses the picture of "continuing a series" as a kind of figure of speech for an idea of the meaning of a word, or rather an idea of the possession of a concept: to know the meaning of a word, to have the concept titled by the word, is to be able to go on with it into new contexts — ones we accept as correct for it; and you can do this without knowing, so to speak, the formula which determines the fresh occurrence, i.e., without being able to articulate the criteria in terms of which it is applied. If somebody could actually produce a formula, or a form for one, which generated the schematism of a word's occurrences, then Wittgenstein's idea here would be more than a figure of speech; it would be replaced by, or summarize, something we might wish to call the science of semantics.

Most immediately for us, the examples of "knowing how to continue" give, as I was suggesting earlier, a simple or magnified view of teaching and learning, of the transmission of language and hence of culture. It is a view in which the idea of *normality,* upon which the strength of criteria depends, is seen to be an idea of *naturalness.* It isolates or dramatizes the inevitable moment of teaching and learning, and hence of communication, in which my power comes to an end in the face of the other's separateness from me.

Wittgenstein's idea of naturalness is illustrated in his interpretation of taking a thing to be *selbstverständlich.*

The rule can only seem to me to produce all its consequences in advance if I draw them as a *matter of course.* [§238]

I know the series, I can continue with a word, when, for me, the continuity is a matter of course, a *foregone* conclusion. In the series of words we call sentences, the words I will need meet me half way. They speak for me. I give them control over me. (Maybe that is what a "sentence" is; or rather "a complete thought".) That is what happens to my power over the pupil; I give it over to the thing I am trying to convey; if I could not, it would not be that thing. No conclusion is more foregone for me than that *that* is human suffering, that *that* is the continuation of the series "1, 2, 3, . . .", that *that* is a painting, a sentence, a proof. *What* I take as a matter of course is not itself a matter of course. It is a matter of history, a matter of what arrives at and departs from a present human interest. I cannot *decide* what I take as a matter of course, any more than I can decide what interests me; I have to find out.

The course is not always smooth. What I took as a matter of course (e.g., that that is a proof, that that is not a serious painting) I may come to take differently (perhaps through further instruction or examples or tips or experience, which it may be a matter of course for me to seek or to deny). What I cannot now take as a matter of course I may come to; I may set it as my task. "I am not used to measuring temperatures on the Fahrenheit scale. Hence such a measure of temperature '*says*' nothing to me" (§508). I know more or less how to go about getting used to another measuring system, that it takes repeated practice; and it may or may not work in my case — a fever of 39 degrees centigrade may never come to *look* high. Taking counts, like cursing, is familiarly deep in a native tongue; someone fluent in a foreign language may revert to the native for *just* such purposes, as though he can't be sure they have *taken effect* otherwise.

If it is the task of the modernist artist to show that we do not know a priori what will count for us as an instance of his art, then this task, or fate, would be incomprehensible, or unexercisable, apart from the existence of objects which, prior to any new effort, we do count as such instances as a matter of course; and apart from there being conditions which our criteria take to define such objects. Only someone outside this enterprise could think of it as an exploration of mere conventions. One might rather think of it as (the necessity for) establishing new conventions. And only someone outside this enterprise could think of establishing new conventions as a matter of exercising personal decision or taste. One might rather think of it as the exploration or education or enjoyment or chastisement of taste and of decision and of intuition, an exploration of the kind of creature in whom such capacities are exercised. Artists are people who know how to do such things, i.e., how to make objects in response to which we are enabled, but also fated, to explore and educate and enjoy and chastise our capacities as they stand. Underlying the tyranny of convention is the tyranny of nature.

Some children learn that they are disgusting to those around them; and they learn to make themselves disgusting, to affect not merely their outer trappings but their skin and their membranes, in order to elicit that familiar natural reaction to themselves; as if only that now proves to them their identity or existence. But not everyone is fated to respond as a matter of course in the way the child desperately wishes, and desperately wishes not, to be responded to. Sometimes a stranger does not find the child disgusting when the child's parents do. Sometimes the stranger is a doctor and teaches the child something new in his acceptance of him. This is not accomplished by his growing *accustomed* to the disgusting creature. It is a *refusing* of foregone reaction; offering the other cheek. The response frees itself from conclusions. If the freedom in saintliness were confined to saints, we would not recognize it.

Wittgenstein's stories using mathematical imagery — about the group of wood sellers, and others about people "measuring" with lax rulers, making unsystematic lists, not caring whether they are cheated or not, "calculating" by asking someone to let a number come to mind — read, from a step away, as though their characters are children. It is appropriate, in writing so fundamentally about instruction, and in which a central character is the child, that we have dramatized for us the fact that we begin our lives as children. Those tribes of big children can put us in mind of how little in each of us gets educated; and make us wonder how we ever have fresh recruits for our culture. I could have explained the reactions of the wood sellers, had I taken them as actual children, by saying "When they take the area covered as a measure of amount, they are interpreting 'amount of wood' as something like 'amount of water', in estimating which they take fat cylinders to contain more water than thin ones, no matter how tall the thin ones are; and about which they 'know' that a greater area is covered by more water, when it is spilled, than by less water". I may say such a thing out of a genuine desire to learn about the child's construction of reality, or as a way of dismissing the reaction, reminding myself of my advancement, saying in effect that they will grow out of the habit. (The fat-thin cylinder case is, I seem to remember from Piaget, the reverse of what he found. That doesn't matter for my example. I would think of it in that case as an explanation of abnormality.) Children's intellectual reactions are easy to find ways to dismiss; anxiety over their "errors" can be covered by the natural charms of childhood and by our accepting as a right answer the answer the child learns we want to hear, whether or not he or she understands what we think of as the content of our instruction. By the time the charm fades, their education takes place out of our sight. So we may have no continuing measure of how far we are prepared to go on "making encouraging gestures" to our familiar stranger.

When my reasons come to an end and I am thrown back upon myself, upon my nature as it has so far shown itself, I can, supposing I cannot shift the ground of discussion, either put the pupil out of my sight — as though his intellectual reactions are disgusting to me — or I can use the occasion to go over the ground I had hitherto thought foregone. If the topic is that of continuing a series, it may be learning enough to find that I *just do;* to rest upon myself as my foundation. But if the child, little or big, asks me: Why do we eat animals? or Why are some people poor and others rich? or What is God? or Why do I have to go to school? or Do you love black people as much as white people? or Who owns the land? or Why is there anything at all? or How did God get here?, I may find my answers thin, I may feel run out of reasons without being willing to say "This is what I do" (what I say, what I sense, what I know), and honor that.

Then I may feel that my foregone conclusions were never conclusions *I* had arrived at, but were merely imbibed by me, merely conventional. I may blunt that realization through hypocrisy or cynicism or bullying. But I may take the occasion to throw myself back upon my culture, and ask why we do what we do, judge as we judge, how we have arrived at these crossroads. What is the natural ground of our conventions, to what are they in service? It is inconvenient to question a convention; that makes it unserviceable, it no longer allows me to proceed as a matter of course; the paths of action, the paths of words, are blocked. "To imagine a language means to imagine a form of life" (cf. §19). In philosophizing, I have to bring my own language and life into imagination. What I require is a convening of my culture's criteria, in order to confront them with my words and life as I pursue them and as I may imagine them; and at the same time to confront my words and life as I pursue them with the life my culture's words may imagine for me: to confront the culture with itself, along the lines in which it meets in me.

This seems to me a task that warrants the name of philosophy. It is also the description of something we might call education. In the face of the questions posed in Augustine, Luther, Rousseau, Thoreau . . . , we are children; we do not know how to go on with them, what ground we may occupy. In this light, philosophy becomes the education of grownups. It is as though it must seek perspective upon a natural fact which is all but inevitably misinterpreted — that at an early point in a life the normal body reaches its full strength and height. Why do we take it that because we then must put away childish things, we must put away the prospect of growth and the memory of childhood? The anxiety in teaching, in serious communication, is that I myself require education. And for grownups this is not natural growth, but *change*. Conversion is a turning of our natural reactions; so it is symbolized as rebirth.

PART TWO

Skepticism and the Existence
of the World

Human reason has this peculiar fate that in one species of its knowledge it is burdened by questions which, as prescribed by the very nature of reason itself, it is not able to ignore, but which, as transcending all its powers, it is also not able to answer.

Kant, *Critique of Pure Reason*,
Preface to first edition

TO THE ROARING WIND
What syllable are you seeking,
Vocalissimus,
In the distances of sleep?
Speak it.

Wallace Stevens

VI

The Quest of Traditional Epistemology: Opening

Especially in the course of Chapters II through IV, I exposed what to me seem to be essential characteristics of the procedures of traditional epistemologists which will have to find place in a convincing display of the structure or nature of traditional epistemology. The structure I find emerges in providing more detailed answers to questions which we can now formulate as follows:

How can the failure of a particular claim to knowledge (seem to) cast suspicion on the power of knowledge as a whole to reveal the world?

Why are generic objects universally (apparently) taken as the examples which traditional epistemologists investigate?

How can we reconcile such convincingness as traditional investigations have (which, I am assuming, depends upon the apparent ordinariness of their reflections about apparently ordinary problems) with the fact that in an ordinary (practical) context their question about generic objects would seem absurd?

It is in answering these questions concerning the procedures of traditional epistemology that we ought to arrive at a more visible appreciation of three phenomenologically striking features of the conclusion which characterizes skepticism: the sense of *discovery* expressed in the conclusion of the investigation; the sense of the *conflict* of this discovery with our ordinary "beliefs"; the *instability* of the discovery, the theoretical conviction it inspires vanishing under the pressure (or distraction) of our ordinary commerce with the world. (I should say at once that I regard *these* phenomenological characteristics of the conclusion to be at least as important as, and perhaps even explanatory of, the feature which has struck most philosophers of this subject as the chief phenomenological problem, namely, the apparent shift in the *object* of perception, from things to sense-data.)

The Reasonableness of Doubt

I take the classical model or form of such investigations to be given in the opening pages of Descartes's *Meditations:*

There is no novelty to me in the reflection that, from my earliest years, I have accepted many false opinions as true, and that what I have concluded from such badly assured premises could not but be highly doubtful and uncertain.

. . . I will therefore make a serious and unimpeded effort to destroy generally all my former opinions. In order to do this, however, it will not be necessary to show that they are all false, a task which I might never be able to complete; because, since reason already convinces me that I should abstain from the belief in things which are not entirely certain and indubitable no less carefully than from the belief in those which appear to me to be manifestly false, it will be enough to make me reject them all if I can find in each some ground for doubt.

Everything which I have thus far accepted as entirely true [and assured] has been acquired from the senses or by means of the senses. But I have learned by experience that these senses sometimes mislead me, and it is prudent never to trust wholly those things which have once deceived us.

Descartes then offers a particular example of a belief he, or anyone, would take as securely known, solidly based (". . . for example, . . . I am here, seated by the fire . . ."), and goes on to investigate its security, to undermine it if he can. Thereupon he meditates the possibility that he is dreaming and is "astonished" to "realize" that "there are no conclusive indications by which waking life can be distinguished from sleep". And with that "ground for doubt" invoked we are, I take it, also to realize, and to be astonished at it, that our hitherto solidly based belief — based on, or "acquired from", the senses — has been put under suspicion; and the suggestion enters that the senses form an insufficient foundation for our knowledge. In the second Meditation he considers "the commonest things, which are popularly believed to be the most distinctly known, namely, the bodies which we touch and see". Here he takes the famous bit of wax as his example, and on considering it determines that, although we sense *something*, we cannot be said to sense *the wax* (comparing this with the "fact" that we *really* see, when we say we see some men passing in the street, "only" hats and cloaks). And then he asks: "What is it then in this bit of wax that we recognize with so much distinction?"; and how *do* we conceive it, if not by means of the senses?

Here are reviewed the elements of the epistemological investigation which have become familiar to us through their strikingly constant repetition in the subject's history since Descartes: the rehearsal of familiar beliefs; the recognition that these must ultimately be founded on seeing, touching, etc.; the production of a belief about a generic object in terms of which to test this foundation; the discovery that the senses alone are not, as we had formerly "believed", adequate to knowledge; and then the question "So what *do* we know?" or "Then how *do* we know anything about the world?". And only at *this* point would we get the divergence of theories that we call Phenomenalism, Critical Realism, etc.

It is essential, in trying to visualize and assess in detail these procedures and the characteristics of their conclusion in terms of the questions we have raised, to notice a point Descartes mentions and stresses from the beginning: The "grounds for doubt" he is going to raise are ones which must be *reasonable*. He explicitly considers the possibility that though we all recognize that the senses *sometimes* "deceive us" about things, it may be unreasonable to doubt that they are *ever* reliable. Again in the first Meditation:

. . . how could I deny that these hands and this body are mine, unless I am to compare myself with certain lunatics whose brain is so troubled and befogged by the black vapors of the bile that they continually affirm that they are kings while they are paupers, and they are clothed in gold and purple while they are naked; or imagine that their head is made of clay, or that they are gourds, or that their body is glass? But this is ridiculous; such men are fools, and I would be no less insane than they if I followed their example.

How then, in the prosecution of his thought, does he achieve the reasonableness he demands?

While it was explicit in my procedures throughout Part One that I understood traditional epistemologists to require "reasonableness", of some kind, in their investigations, it remained implicit that the reasonableness of the philosopher's considerations was a function of their being just those ordinary and everyday considerations that any person who can talk and can know anything at all will recognize as relevant to the claim ("belief") under scrutiny. Now the task of Part Two is, accordingly, to make this implicitness explicit, to bring it to the stage of philosophical consciousness, make it our new problematic; thematize it, as Heidegger asks us to say. In particular to thematize the idea that these ordinary considerations ought to be considerations of just the sort that the ordinary language philosopher brings to his apparently contrary investigations. Hence our problematic should allow us to investigate the reasonableness of the ordinary language philosopher's procedures (and criticisms) at the same time they provide us with a model or touchstone for the reasonableness of those of the traditional philosopher.

For think of the problematic this way. If the considerations of the ordinary language philosopher provide us with the model or image of the reasonableness that the traditional epistemologist requires of his procedures, show us what the reasonableness is that those procedures require, then how can those very considerations seem to come to cast suspicion on those very procedures? For the fact is that these considerations do seem to cast this suspicion, both to the minds of those who speak for the tradition and to those who speak for ordinary language and in criticism of the tradition. So if we can make the ordinariness, the naturalness of traditional investigations explicit in terms of our untutored understanding of ordinary language, then if there is some lack of reasonableness in the investigations, it must turn out to be subtle enough, or something enough, and the way of avoiding its recognition explained convincingly enough, that we can fully imagine a master of a language, under the pressure of philosophical meditation, to have failed to see his mastery failing him.

Let us go back to the case Austin provides for the assessment of claims to knowledge. In essentials, anyway at first glance, it seems to proceed no differently from Descartes's initial program: an example of a claim is given; its basis is articulated; a ground for doubt is raised which, unanswered, repudiates the claim.

Claim:	There is a goldfinch in the garden.
Request for Basis:	How do you know?
Basis:	From the red head.
Ground for Doubt:	But that's not enough; woodpeckers also have red heads.

And now, if the claimant cannot supply a further basis for his claim, he would be unreasonable not to withdraw it. The conclusion is, as Descartes explicitly says, not that the claim is "manifestly false", but rather that the claimant can no longer claim to know it's true: it can reasonably be doubted. So much seems non-controversial, and to be shared by the tradition and its new critics. Then how does a criticism emerge from these considerations?

Remember Austin's dismissal:

I don't by any means *always* know whether it's one or not. It may fly away before I have a chance of testing it, or of inspecting it thoroughly enough. This is simple enough: yet some are prone to argue that because I *sometimes* don't know or can't discover, I *never* can.

When this dismissal came up earlier (p. 60), I dismissed it as on the face of it an insufficient diagnosis of philosophical behavior. But I did not try to say what is wrong with it, nor why Austin finds it pertinent. It may not be clear whether Austin has in mind at this point philosophers who say we can never know an empirical statement with certainty, or those who say we can never know on the basis of the senses alone (nor, of course, is it clear *what* difference this difference, if it is a real one, makes). But I am going to assume that its natural target is the Cartesian, for the model of Austin's I have just sketched seems to fit him perfectly. (Later in "Other Minds", Austin considers the view that statements about the world "involve 'prediction' " (p. 63); but that is something else. Some remarks of mine in the last section of Chapter VIII bear on this.)

Now first of all the epistemologist is not *arguing* what Austin says he is prone to "argue", any more than he is arguing that such and such a situation is one in which we should say, e.g., "There is a bird in the garden". Rather, one could say, he sees or recognizes that since I don't know, or can't discover, in *this* case, I can know in *no* case at all. But what is this "seeing"; what has he recognized?

The case from which he has begun — has had to begin, given his project — is one which we should all recognize as holding the *best* prospect of certainty; one just made to let us see that if we don't know here we never can. The case Austin has selected — the goldfinch — is evidently not such a case. There, if you don't know, or can't discover, that carries no implication about what can ever be known, about knowledge as a whole, as a project; but merely an implication about *your* lack of training or hastiness in judgment, or about the relative poorness of opportunity or of physical conditions *in this instance*. From this case, no one will feel that, or "see" that, knowledge as a whole, as an enterprise, is threatened. To "argue" that failure in such a case means that failure is altogether inescapable would be as grotesque as Austin supposes; for that would be tantamount to arguing that we are doomed to inadequate training, to hastiness of judgment, to contexts in which the opportunities for checking are poor, and in which the physical conditions of knowledge are crippling. But to say that the philosopher takes (or means to, or supposes himself to be taking) the "best" case for knowing is to say that he takes a case in which factors of personal training and care of judgment, and in which contextual matters of opportunity and conditions, are irrelevant: all you have to know, to achieve knowledge in the philosopher's case, is, one could say, how to talk.

Austin can grant that "I don't by any means *always* know whether it's one or not" with no sense that knowledge as a whole is threatened, no sense that this could mean that we can *never* know, because the case is one in which it is obvious, and we can describe, what would have made knowledge possible there (the bird could have been closer, stood more still, stayed longer; the light could have been higher, or more even; I could have been better trained, etc.). But in the traditional philosopher's case, no such descriptions will help; change any of the obvious factors any way you like (keep the table or pencil or envelope in one place, and unmoving, for as long as you like, give someone all the special training you can think of for telling tables and pencils and envelopes, exercise him or her to withhold judgment for as long as seems required to consider the situation thoroughly) and you still won't have so much as touched the question whether we know that there is a table, a pencil, an envelope here. If the question arises as to whether we know, in the context in which the philosopher raises the question, then the answer has to be: we find out, using considerations no different in form from those Austin uses, that we do not. The step from there to the conclusion that we *never* know, is trivial.

Then the issue turns on making out what constitutes "the traditional philosopher's case" or "the context in which the philosopher raises the question". But what I have so far claimed is this: if there is a fallacy in the traditional conception or repudiation of knowledge, it is betrayed not by a hasty generalization from "some" cases to "all" cases (is this something Wittgenstein meant by speaking of the metaphysician's "craving for generality"? (*Blue Book,* p. 17)), but by the way in which, or the purpose for which, the philosopher selects that "best" case of knowledge, and by what he has had to do (to himself) in order to get the question whether we know *to arise there.* And "to get the question to arise" means "to make the question real (natural, inevitable)", in just the way that the question is real or natural in ordinary cases, say in the ones Austin considers. Simply to say, with the ordinary language philosophers, that the question *does not arise* can only make the epistemologist feel that his question has been begged; because for him the question *has already arisen* (anyway no one has shown it hasn't) and using words in no obviously distorted sense (what sense do they now have?).

The conflict with ordinary language has a different force, presses at a different point. To say "We don't ordinarily ask, in such cases as the philosopher asks, whether we really know" has this significance: it makes us, or should make us, want to know *why* the question has arisen, how it *can* have arisen. And this is a question the traditional philosopher himself takes seriously, and wants to answer. He answers it by suggesting something like: "It is a perfectly natural question, but one that 'for practical purposes' *need not* arise. The answer to it tells us something true about the world and about knowledge, but something we had not *noticed* before, something our prejudices or our complacent practicality prevented us from noticing." That is something I will wish to question.

So the first answer to our first question at the start of this chapter about the procedures of the epistemologist — "How does the failure of a particular claim seem to cast doubt on the validity of knowledge as a whole?" — is, in general terms, that he has cast doubt on a case of knowledge which we all recognize to exemplify knowledge at its *best*. More specifically, in terms of our model, "best" means: "a claim that a present generic object exists". And "cast doubt" does not mean "showed it manifestly false"; it means "raised an ordinary ground for doubt which shows the basis of the claim to be insufficient to establish it". If, therefore, there is something wrong with the epistemologist's procedures it must, apparently, lie in his choice of a generic object as his focus of investigation, or in the basis he has chosen as its support, or in the ground for doubt he has directed against this basis.

The criticisms and counter-defenses with which I am familiar have concentrated on the second and third of these steps, on the philosopher's analysis of perception (the basis for his claim will always be something like "I know because I see it" or "by means of the senses") or on the particular ground for doubt which he takes to counter such a basis ("But mightn't I be dreaming, suffering an illusion or hallucination?", etc.). No doubt there are irregularities in the philosopher's basis and its countering doubts, but it is very hard to know what weight to attach to any given difficulty which emerges. Is it *fatal* to the traditional epistemologist that what he says we really see is not a good description of the phenomenology of our visual experience? Does the fact that the question "Mightn't you be dreaming now?" is a terribly odd question, undermine everything he thinks he's discovered? Does it follow from the fact that to say "We don't really see material objects" conflicts with an ordinary statement like "You can see the boat from here", that the philosopher's conclusion cannot mean what it seems to say or cannot be true? It should trouble someone who thinks these criticisms sufficient that their subjects do not find them fatal; they themselves have urged the reasonableness of their procedures while they also fully recognize the paradoxicality of their conclusions. If you accuse someone of being unreasonable, it isn't only good manners, or good policy, to be sure you know why he thinks he is not. Maybe there is something you are not noticing. And of course it is *no* answer to a paradox to say it can't be true; the point of calling a claim paradoxical already registers the fact that it looks as if it can't be true.

We could say: Appeals to natural language, to the "original" language game of an expression, show what an expression does mean, when used ordinarily (not metaphorically, technically, etc.); it does not directly show that, as used, the expression does not have its ordinary meaning, or that it is being misused. Putting it in the ordinary context forces one to ask: *Is* that what I meant to say *here?* And often, perhaps usually, it is obvious that, calling its ordinary use to consciousness, you realize that that is not what you wished to say, it does not express *your meaning*, though for some reason you had taken it to; or it means that you were thinking of the situation in a special way, a way you now see is inappropriate, arbitrary, not what you really have in mind. But sometimes it does not have this effect. (It may be pointed out to you that the way you speak about someone indicates that you are angry with him, that you feel he has (say) deprived you of something; that realization may make you realize that your feeling is inappropriate. It may, however, allow you to see that you really do feel that way about him, and justly.)

Until we have a fuller articulation of the philosopher's progress, any criticism must, I think, feel less impressive to him than his procedure itself: for the steps from a claim about a generic object, to the suggestion that it is known, ultimately, because it is *seen* (sensed) by someone, to the countering of what one claims to see by any of the familiar ways in which that has for centuries been done (by the possibility, or fact, of dreams, illusions, drugs, perceptual relativity, etc., etc.) seem inescapable. And no criticism of these steps in his meditations has, I believe, been offered by his critics. The "fuller articulation" I will suggest involves pushing the examination of the traditional procedures back to (what I construe to be) its first step: the emergence of the generic object as the focus of investigation; and hence to the last of the questions we have said awaits us: "How has the philosopher raised the question of existence about a generic object and made it seem acceptable (reasonable) in a context in which, normally, it would seem absurd?"

How does the philosopher's meditation begin; what prompts it? Austin criticizes Wisdom from the start as follows:

Mr. Wisdom, no doubt correctly, takes the "Predicament" to be brought on by such questions as "How do we know that another man is angry?" He also cites other forms of the question — "Do we (ever) know?" "Can we know?" "How can we know?" the thoughts, feelings, sensations, mind, etc., of another creature, and so forth. . . . Mr. Wisdom's method is to go on to ask: *Is it like the way in which we know* that a kettle is boiling, or that there's a tea-party next door, or the weight of thistledown? But it seemed to me that perhaps, as he went on, he was not giving an altogether accurate account (perhaps only because too cursory a one) of what we should say if asked "How do you know?" these things. For example, in the case of the tea-party, to say we knew of it "by analogy" would at best be a very sophisticated answer. . . .

And then Austin *goes on to pick*:

The sort of statement which seems simplest, and at the same time not, on the face of it, unlike "He is angry", [viz.] . . . such a statement as "That is a gold-finch" ("The kettle is boiling") — a statement of particular, current, empirical fact. This is the sort of statement on making which we are liable to be asked "How do you know?" and the sort that, at least sometimes, we say we don't know, but only believe. It may serve for a stalking horse as well as another.

This set of remarks again displays, or rather insinuates, that trivialization of the epistemologist's problem, withholds a sense of the seriousness of his prompting question, which makes ensuing criticism seem uncomprehending. For given such a question as "(How) do (can) we know anything about the world? (or about the experience of another person?)" asked seriously, in the philosopher's context, felt as a problem there — so serious that you'll give up the world rather than forgo your paradoxical conclusion, even though you can't maintain belief in your discovery — the philosopher is *not free to pick* the sort of statement he will use as his example of knowledge ("stalking horse"). He *must* use a statement not merely "of particular, current, empirical fact", but one which *claims the existence of a generic object*.

I cannot prove, I do not know that I would wish to prove, that there is an initiating question about knowledge as a whole, and once initiated an unignorable question, that philosophers of knowledge, of human knowing, find themselves to pose. Nor can I prove, nor do I know that I would wish to prove, that once asked this question "produces" (defines its satisfaction, you could say its meaning, in producing) a generic object as its example. I would be willing to say that these claims of mine are fundamental and hence without foundation, except that I do not know that others of my claims — ones I regard as equally essential to my project or vision — have any greater foundation. Everything depends upon what we find our consciousness to depend upon. Sometimes this dependence can be expressed in the acceptance or rejection of a stretch of ordinary speech, sometimes by the recognition of a picture or fantasy, sometimes by a fresh example.

Apart from such claims for these claims, it is, so far as I know, in fact true that generic objects are the examples that have universally been employed in the tradition of epistemology, and I do not see that other examples — that is, examples considered in other than the spirit of the generic object — could express the philosopher's problem, or doubt, hence could lead him to skepticism about the validity of our knowledge (of the world of objects) as a whole.

What I am asking, then, is that we take the philosopher's original — and originating — question with the same seriousness that the ordinary language philosopher wishes us to take any statement a human being utters. (*This* wish, and the faithfulness of its expression, represents one permanent value of that motive and "method" of philosophizing.) Unless we make that question real for ourselves, the philosopher's answers to it will seem as slovenly and unreal — as academic — as the ordinary language philosopher supposes. And once it seems a real problem, the answers to it may not seem so clearly, or wrongly, forced.

We have acknowledged that there must be some reason for raising the question of existence, and that in the philosopher's context, where the object is (or is imagined to be) for all the world there, in full view, there seems to be no such reason. And that it is, for all the world, there, in clear and ample view, is also essential to the philosopher's case: it is part of his drive to choose the best case of knowledge for examination. "Simple curiosity" will not achieve the naturalness we need; "a genuine desire to learn" is precisely out of place. The ordinary language philosopher is perfectly right in his feeling that we should not, in an ordinary practical context, raise the philosopher's skeptical possibilities. If you ask me where I put the tomato we just bought and I say "I see it over there", I won't think you are serious if you ask "How do you know it isn't a cleverly painted piece of wax?" or "Mightn't you be having a hallucination?". Just as, if you ask me if Father has been by the office and I say "No one has come in all day except the secretary" and you ask if I am sure and I reply (impatiently) that I was sitting in the office all day and saw everyone who came in, I will not be impelled to re-examine my assumptions by your suggesting, "Mightn't he have been disguised as the secretary?".

But *why* not? *What* is absurd about these grounds for doubt? It is important to realize that they are not somehow *in themselves* absurd. *If* the object *is* a cleverly painted piece of wax then that object *isn't* a tomato; if

Father *was* disguised as the secretary, then he *was* in the office. That is part of what the epistemologist insists upon. But his claim to "reasonableness" depends, I have urged, on his grounds for doubt not merely being as it were in themselves of the right sort to counter the basis, it must also be or seem reasonable to raise the question of this possibility here and now.

But it is easy to imagine what such a context might be. It may be one in which you have a definite reason to believe that the particular ground for doubt you raise is in fact the case — you and Father have planned the whole affair, or he has had another of his attacks. Such a case, again, will not do as an analogue to the traditional investigation. But this is not the only sort of case in which an odd ground for doubt is reasonably raised. Another is a case in which there is *some reason to think* that what you claim may not be so; the sense, or fact, that *something is amiss,* something wrong or puzzling that *must be checked or solved,* an explanation *discovered.* In such a context, there is also a clear answer to the ordinary language philosopher's question: "What reason do you have for thinking you may be dreaming, that what you see is a piece of wax, that you are drugged, that there is a contraption of mirrors set up to fool you?" We must, and can, reply: "That isn't the point. I have no reason of the kind you mean. I put the envelope on the table, right there — or I thought I did, I distinctly remember it. But *it isn't there. There must be some explanation.* Maybe it was stolen. Maybe Holmes, who said he saw it there, really saw this folded letter and thought it was the envelope. Maybe I only dreamt I put it there." It isn't that I don't know when these "possibilities" would be real ones, that I don't know when, in what circumstance, we should say, "It was, or may have been, stolen", "I must have, I seem to remember having, dreamt it", etc. So when the ordinary language philosopher says "You have no reason to raise the question of existence or reality in your context", he must seem to the traditional philosopher to beg his question, because for him the context is one in which the question has, and reasonably, already arisen. It has been forced upon us.

But how? It is not a situation in which in fact the envelope is missing or a crime has been committed and Father is accused of it and his whereabouts at 10:30 a.m. must be established beyond any doubt. I have said: If the philosopher's situation is one in which there is *in fact,* or in appearance, something amiss, something which needs accounting for, then the ordinary language criticisms to the effect that the possibilities the philosopher invokes are absurd, unrealistic, unreasonable, can be repudiated.

But the question is: whence comes this sense of something amiss about the simplest claim to knowledge under optimal conditions, where there is

no practical problem moving us? The answer I have has already been suggested: the philosopher *begins* his investigation with the *sense* that, as I
am expressing it, something is, or may be amiss with knowledge as a
whole. Various issues about this suggestion immediately arise: How has
this sense of something generally amiss with knowledge itself arisen? What
kind of experience is it? Is this general sense enough to secure the reasonableness of the "open possibilities" the philosopher invokes, feels he has
to invoke, when he is considering his particular claim as an example of
our claims to knowledge?

My major claim about the philosopher's originating question — e.g.,
"(How) do (can) we know anything about the world?" or "What is knowledge; what does my knowledge of the world consist in?" — is that it (in one
or another of its versions) is a response to, or expression of, a real experience which takes hold of human beings. It is not "natural" in the sense I
have already found in the claim to "reasonableness": it is not a response
to questions raised in ordinary practical contexts, framed in language
which any master of a language will accept as ordinary. But it is, as I
might put it, a response which expresses a natural experience of a creature complicated or burdened enough to possess language at all.

What experience? Well, of course, an experience or sense that one may
know *nothing* about the real world. But what kind of experience is that?
How or when does it emerge?

One possibility might seem to be this: it arises as a response to your
having been wrong, in some obvious way, about something you are "totally convinced" or "assured" of. The sort of instance I have in mind oc-
curred to me recently. I was left a telephone message which consisted of
the name of an old friend, a noting of the time he had called, the name
of the hotel he was stopping at, a telephone number, and the request to
ring him at a certain hour; each item being written on a separate line,
one below the other. The telephone number was *obviously* the number
of his hotel (it was written just under the name of the hotel), although it
did not have the obvious sort of combination usually assigned to hotels
and to other frequently called establishments. But then it wasn't one of
the largest hotels in town, so I rang the number with no further thought.
"Good morning" came a secretary's morning voice at the other end; and
it continued with what I took to be the initials of some kind of firm of
trust: law offices, investment advisors, an insurance or advertising agency.
I apologized for having dialed the wrong number; hung up; re-dialed;
got the same sunny voice; mumbled something unintelligible about trying
to reach the hotel whose name was in front of me; and hung up. I con-

cluded that the number written on my message slip was incorrect, and looked up the hotel in the telephone book, expecting it to be quite *like* the number I had been left. It was entirely different. No one could have *mistakenly* written *that* number down having heard, even indistinctly or in a hurry, *this* number in the book. Only then did it occur to me — with a thrill of "astonishment" — that the number on my slip may not be (= not have been meant as?) the number of the hotel. So I called the number again, and in a new, cheerful voice simply asked for my friend by name. In five seconds his familiar voice was in my ear.

The amount of feeling I generated during this frustration was high and sharp, and I *went back over* the experience to determine my false steps. I said to myself something like: "I only inferred that the number was the number of the hotel", "It was nothing more than an assumption." And I was led to wonder how often during the day I make leaps of this sort which do not always, but at any moment *might,* lead to serious trouble. "How much of knowledge depends on such assumptions?" "How incautious the mind is; how prideful in its claims to certainty!"

This experience does, I find, resemble the experience and the conclusions of traditional epistemology. There is an initial threatening *sense* or fact of something amiss, something which *must* be accounted for; the *going over* of a situation to see where an unnoticed inference or assumption may have been made; the sense that something in this one incident contains a moral about knowledge as a whole.

There is also, however, perhaps a lingering sense that the trouble with, or problem about, knowledge has not quite accurately been grasped by saying that I am continually "making inferences or assumptions" which are silent or unnoticed. For it certainly doesn't present itself as an inference *in the situation itself.* When I called my friend again an hour later to arrange a meeting, I had, even alerted to my former confusion, no sense that I was *inferring* or *assuming* that the number was the number of an advertising agency. I *knew* by then that it was: my friend is a writer, and he was selling his talent for three weeks. So do I only "make inferences" when I do not know, not when I do know? What do I *do* that's different? What *in the experience* is different? It is in going back over the situation that I want to call the false or unnoticed step an "inference" or "assumption". And was it an *hypothesis* that "no one would have written down *this* number when he or she read *that* number?" It would not *make sense* to assume that had happened, except in *very* extraordinary circumstances; so it would not *account satisfactorily* for my predicament. Whereas, about my attribution of the telephone number to the hotel, it does satisfactorily make sense of my misfortune to call it an inference. But this may mean only: there are circumstances in which I really would (have to) infer such a thing (there are two numbers on the slip; because of their location on the page or their combination of digits, I should guess that this one is probably the number of the hotel). It doesn't mean that whenever I say what a telephone number is "of" I am making an inference.

Another example, set more briefly, yields a useful comparison. Tuning, in the middle fifties, into a radio station known for mixing its programs of serious music with forays into the history of jazz, I hear immediately familiar sounds and call to my friend in the next room, "The Goodman band from about '39". My claim is not so much challenged as, it seems to me, rather treated as a guess. I protest, saying in effect that I have been trained in an environment where I could become familiar with the big bands, that I have had an opportunity in the present case, learned to recognize or tell big bands, and succeeded in recognizing or telling this as Goodman's band of about 1939. That is, this was no guess; I *know*. And then the announcer comes on to identify the band as of a Dorsey or Shaw or somebody. My stunned disbelief is tinged with shame. It is true I might simply have repudiated the announcer. It's still a mean little game one plays with announcers on serious music programs — they mispronounce; don't know when a first movement is left out; misidentify wildly, getting their cribbed blurbs out of order. I don't know that I know these serious things more surely than I know big bands; and surely those popular things are no less important to my sense of self-identity. I might, indeed, having telephoned the announcer and gotten his assurance on the point, have undertaken to repudiate the label he has read from the recording itself. But I did not; I was shaken. How *could* I be mistaken about a matter of such *intimate* knowledge? Has my ear so coarsened in the ten or so years since I was really involved with these matters? Do I not really care as much about the objects any longer as I do about my vanity of knowledge? Using the example years later in a philosophy class I could still recapture something of the stun. Perhaps this means that I am not shameless.

Various ranges of problem may be seen to emerge concerning the phenomenological faithfulness of epistemological reconstruction. (A standing or standard such problem will be rehearsed in Chapter VIII, in the section entitled "Two Interpretations of Traditional Epistemology; Phenomenology".) What I now wish to suggest, or report, is this. The experiences in these recent stories do not, for me, more than resemble the experience I am looking for to account for the initiation of Cartesian investigations. The moral I drew from the case of the "wrong" telephone number — or rather, my direct response to it — was that I ought to stop taking things so often for granted, and above all learn not to be so *rigid* in my claims to knowledge of the world. From the case of the big bands I drew such morals as that I should not be so *quick* to leap to conclusions; perhaps that my powers as a knower are fading; perhaps that old interests are part of another life. From both cases there is, no doubt, the moral that we human beings are *fallible*. But from neither that we suffer metaphysical ineptitude or privation, that we may know *nothing* about the real world, whatever cautions we undertake. Responses to such cases might lead to probabilistic theories of confirmation, but not to radical or metaphysical skepticism, the idea that there is no real confirmation at all for our claims.

For that, an experience of a different order is needed, an experience that philosophers have characterized, more or less, as one of realizing that my sensations may not be *of* the world I take them to be of at all, or that I can know only how objects appear (to us) to be, never what objects are like in themselves.

I can here only attest to my having had such experiences and, though struggling against them intellectually, have had to wait for them to dissipate in their own time. It seems to me that I relive such experiences when I ask my students, as habitually at the beginning of a course in which epistemology is discussed, whether they have ever had such thoughts as, for example, that they might, when for all the world awake, be dreaming; or that if our senses, for example our eyes, had differently evolved, we would sense, i.e., see, things other than as we see them now, so that the way we see them now is almost accidental, anyway at least as dependent on our constitution as on the constitution of the world itself; or that the things of the world would seem just as they now do to us if there were nothing in it but some power large enough either to keep us in a sort of hypnotic spell, or to arrange the world for our actions as a kind of endless stage-set, whose workings we can never get behind, for after all consider how little of anything, or any situation, we really see. I know well enough, intellectually as it were, that these suppositions may be nonsense, seem absurd, when raised as scruples about particular claims to knowledge. But if these experiences have worked in the initial motivation of particular claims, then the attempt to prove intellectually that they have no sense is apt to weaken one's faith in intellectuality.

Of course on a given occasion no such thought as I describe may do the work of producing the sort of experience I have alluded to. And perhaps that is because neither I nor any of my students on a given occasion have "freed our minds of all cares; and found ourselves, fortunately, disturbed by no passions; and found a serene retreat in peaceful solitude" (first Meditation, second paragraph). But when the experience created by such thoughts is there, it is something that presents itself to me as one, as I have wished to express it, of being sealed off from the world, enclosed within my own endless succession of experiences. It is an experience for which there must be a psychological explanation; but no such explanation would or should prove its epistemological insignificance. And I know of no philosophical criticism which proves that either.

Ask, then, in the relevant frame of mind, or tone of voice (the stage directions for which are emblematized by, as well as anything else, the meaning of reflecting "that I am here, seated by the fire, wearing a dressing gown, holding this paper in my hands, and other things of this nature"), "What do I (actually) know about what — if anything really — exists?"; follow this by asking, "How, for example, do I know that there is a ————— here?"; and I claim that you will find that you will always pick a generic object to fill the blank, never an object like a goldfinch; a table, yes; a Louis XV escritoire, no. I claim, further, that the rest of the traditional investigation then follows Austin's model in perfect form.

A claim is under investigation. We then ask for the basis of the claim.

Request for Basis: How, for example, do I know there's a table here?

Basis: Because I see it. Or: by means of the senses.

Ground for Doubt: a) But what do I really see? Mightn't I be, suppose I were, dreaming, hallucinating?
b) But that's not enough. Mightn't it be a decoy?
c) But I don't see *all* of it. The most I see is . . . .

Conclusion: So I don't know.

Moral: I never can know. The senses are not enough to ground our knowledge of the world (or: a claim to certainty about the world). Or again: we do not know the world in the way we "thought" we did ("by means of the senses"); we do not literally, or directly, *see* objects. The world and its contents could appear to our senses as they now do and there be nothing at all beyond them, anyway not what we imagine or take for granted there is. . . .

The moral is a natural, inevitable extension of the conclusion drawn on the basis of the example we have started from. There is nothing which needs, as Austin suggests, to be argued. Nor has the investigation of a claim to the existence of a generic object been subjected to a hasty generalization about all objects. The step from the conclusion about this object to the moral about knowledge as a whole is irresistible. It is no step at all. The world drops out. Perhaps it does no harm to put the matter in the following way. What "best case" turns out to mean can be expressed in a major premiss: If I know anything, I know *this*. Then it turns out that, as a matter of eternal fact, we do *not* know *this*. As a minor premiss, that discovery precipitates the right devastation. To draw the conclusion then requires no proneness to argument, merely the capability of it.

It may well do harm to my account that I am unclear about locating the experience I have described as of the world as a whole, hence of my distance or inaccessibility to it. I seem sometimes to find that it is part of the moral drawn from the conclusion of the skeptical investigation, then lately I have been insisting that it must appear at its initiation. This is a matter that to me evidently deserves further work. In itself the circling of the experience does not surprise me. It suggests that phenomenologically the form of the skeptical investigation is, after the fact, that of having confirmed our worst fear for knowledge. Then the question of skepticism (or of its possibility) becomes for me: what makes just this particular fear possible?

The idea of the differing "morals" to be drawn from different cases of the failure of claims to know is meant to apply to, to give a way of exploring, both such a remark as Austin's about philosophers prone to argue, as well as such a remark as Descartes's near the beginning of his rehearsal of the sort of beliefs he is going to undertake to doubt, to the effect that "it is prudent never to trust wholly those things which have once deceived us".

The Appeal to Projective Imagination

If, as I have insisted, the traditional philosopher can be said to know everything the ordinary language philosopher wishes to teach him (e.g., that some specific reason is necessary for raising the question of existence, that the way he raises it is not fully natural, that his conclusion denies the plainest facts of common sense and language) and to have himself sought and found concessions and explanations for these problems (e.g., that his investigation is "theoretical", that our common view and capacity of certainty is all right "for practical purposes"), then how has the work of the ordinary language philosopher failed to realize this fact or succeeded in utterly discounting it? (I suppose the most remorseless example of this failure and success is Austin's *Sense and Sensibilia*.) The traditional philosopher's explanations and concessions may finally be unsatisfactory, but how has it come to seem to his new critics that he has not so much as wanted and tried to align himself with the ordinary beliefs and language he in the end repudiates, or limits?

To answer this, we have to look in closer detail at the "method" of the ordinary language investigations of "what is said". When, in the early essays of *Must We Mean What We Say?*, I was defending this method against certain repeated philosophical complaints against it, I said that the ordinary language philosopher's requests that we determine what we should say in a given case, and when we should say a given thing, were requests not that we predict an occurrence, but that we imagine one; and I said that the validity of this depended not upon ordinary, or what is ordinarily called, empirical knowledge, but upon self-knowledge; and I suggested that the usefulness of such methods to philosophy was a function of that source of validity. And it is a central theme of all my work since that opening that the subject of self-knowledge, both as a phenomenon and as a source of philosophical knowledge, has been blocked or denied in modern philosophy. Here I wish to push this part of my investigation further by indicating further how the very value we can expect from such methods deprives them of power as *direct criticisms* of the tradition. If, as I believe, they offer real gains to philosophizing — gains of clarity, of shared progress, and of that self-knowledge which I take to be necessary to philosophical advance — then it is of first importance that they not discredit themselves by applying force where they cannot convince.

When the ordinary language philosopher accuses the traditional philosopher of misusing language or changing the meaning of words or speaking with near criminal unconcern for the ordinary meaning of words; and when the apologist for the tradition replies that nothing is amiss with the language in which traditional ideas are expressed, that no problem of sense and communication is created by the slight variation from ordinary use, that anyone can simply see that the words that the traditional philosopher employs are lucid as they stand; one side is as right and as wrong as the other; they are talking past one another.

When the ordinary language philosopher impugns as unreasonable one of the epistemologist's grounds for doubt, his method of impugnment is this: He takes an expression used by the traditional philosopher, separates it from the structure of the discourse in which it has appeared, and then asks, "When should we really use such an expression?" or, "What is the background story which will allow us really to imagine the question seriously being asked?", or again, "When should we say we don't really see a thing or all of a thing, or that it is possible that it's phoney?". He then imagines a real and relevant context, and it is, plainly, different from the context in which the traditional philosopher has raised his question. And from his point of view this result directly displays that carelessness, or abuse or change of meaning he so liberally throws out in accusation. Should the traditionalist reply that in *his* context this discrepancy from ordinary language does not matter, and that anyone can "just see" what he means by his words, and the ordinary language philosopher retort that there *is* no special context in operation, but only one insufficiently described, we have a wrongly placed defense countered with a badly aimed advance. For it is neither the case that the philosopher has a *special* context (in the sense that it is one to which a special story is relevant) nor that he has described it incompletely. He *cannot* describe it more completely *in the way the ordinary language philosopher wishes* without changing it; and it is obvious neither that this makes no difference, nor that it makes all the difference. What is obvious is that the ordinary language philosopher feels the context to be insufficiently conceived and that the traditional philosopher feels that this request for fuller conception simply misses his problem, begs his question.

To help account for, and do justice to, both of these feelings, I need to consider in more detail the defense I have offered against the attempt to impugn the procedure of the ordinary language philosopher as one of advancing empirical claims for which he has collected little, if any, evidence.

Let us begin by noticing — something I take to be quite uncontroversial — that the question "What should we say if . . . ?" need no more *always* be a request for a prediction than the question "What should we do if . . . ?" need always form a request for a prediction. As the latter is sometimes, usually, a request for something different — e.g., for a decision, or a directive, or the expression of an intention — so the former may sometimes be a request for something different, something I might call an *invitation to projective imagination*. That is, however, merely a startling title for a family of the most common of human capacities, e.g., the capacity to "imagine what would have happened if you had gotten there a day late", to "suppose you have three rabbits", to "think how you would feel if that had happened to you". You may on a given occasion fail to meet one or other of these requests; but you won't, in failing there, have failed the way you would have failed to meet a request for a prediction when your prediction proves inaccurate. If your prediction fails you, you may have spoken too hastily, neglected considerations which are obviously relevant; or the most surprising eventualities (which "couldn't have been predicted") have arisen. But if your imagination fails you, it probably will not be obvious why, and in any case *cannot* be because "surprising eventualities arose which couldn't have been predicted". It may be that you haven't fully projected yourself into the situation. ("Did Lady Macbeth really faint at Macbeth's description of the dead Duncan, or was she pretending to in order to further the convincingness of their innocence?" How could that be discussed? What would one look to as confirmation?)

The question "What should we say if . . . ?" as asked by the ordinary language philosopher, is an invitation which may be phrased this way: "Suppose such and such were the case. What would we say? (= what would it *be* (called)?)" (Of course, contrariwise: "Suppose someone said such and such. What would (might) the context be?") This is no more difficult an invitation to respond to than: "Suppose you have three rabbits and I give you three more. How many would you have?" Not everyone *can* respond to this invitation; some have not yet been initiated into the forms of life which control the power of supposition, some will never manage it, some have lost it through personal damage. But any competent speaker can in fact respond, without hesitation, and without the shadow of a doubt of correctness. To object to the ordinary language question on the general grounds of incomplete *evidence* ("How do I know what 'we', or even *I* would say?"), to refuse to answer it or to answer it roughly ("I might say lots of things; anything"), would be like answering "How many rabbits would you have?" with the response, "How do I know how many I would have? I might have *any* number. I may drop one and have only five, or they might breed and I would have thousands". (Cp. "The Availability of Wittgenstein's Later Philosophy", p. 66.)

But *what* is wrong with this reply? It's not that what you say **cannot** be true; indeed, let us suppose it is in fact true that in the middle of your reply the news breaks that your rabbits have multiplied. Don't we feel: "That news cannot break into our supposition; our example is inaccessible to what in fact happens. Our invitation has simply been misunderstood?" But *what* has been misunderstood? And isn't the inaccessibility of the news just what the traditional philosopher guessed — that such assertions are inaccessible to empirical evidence?

Perhaps the analogy between "How many would you have?" and "What would you say?" rings false. One may feel: "What in fact may happen is relevant to the imagining of saying things in a way it is not relevant to the imagining of counting things; if *in fact* we would not or do not say, or find ourselves saying, what the ordinary language philosopher says we would or will say then he is in fact *wrong* in his claim. But it just *makes no sense* to suppose that the arithmetical example could be proved wrong by how many rabbits we *find* we have." The plausibility of this response, however, still depends upon a misunderstanding of the ordinary language philosopher's invitation. For what does the supposition "if in fact we don't say what the ordinary language philosopher claims we say" amount to? In the response we have just elicited, "we don't say" seems again to envision the checking of a prediction, a response to a possible outcome. Whereas when such a statement does, as it certainly may, counter the ordinary language philosopher's claim, it refers not to a future eventuality, but to something about us as speakers, about ourselves as we stand.

"Nevertheless, we *can* be wrong about what we say, and we *can't* be wrong about how many we would have; and that means that what in fact happens is *relevant* to the ordinary language philosopher's invitation, in a way in which what happens is just *not* relevant to the arithmetical supposition." I think we will all feel the power of this objection, but it would be risky to take it at face value, because it accounts neither for why "we couldn't be wrong" in responding to the arithmetical example, nor for what the difference is between the way "what happens may prove us wrong" when the claim which is countered is a prediction, a statement of fact, and when it is a response to an invitation to imagination. It is the difference between the way or ways we may be right or wrong about particular regions of the world and the way or ways we may be right or wrong about ourselves.

If someone says: "I'm going to botch the slow movement of the *Hammerklavier*", what happens may prove that true or false, i.e., he may in fact botch or not botch it. But it makes a difference whether the context is one in which he knows that for all his practice and prayers there are certain passages he just cannot consistently negotiate, or that he periodically is just unable to find and maintain the right tempo, or that when his fingers feel as they do today it's as if they are foreign objects and will not respond to his intention no matter how hard he coaxes and croaks with effort; or whether the context is one in which he is intent on getting even with his teacher for forcing him to audition tomorrow rather than play the jazz concert, or in which he wants to pretend to be less good than he is in order to take the final competition by acclaim. In the former cases his statement was a prediction, in the latter it was an expression of intention. (This is, I hope obviously, not meant as an *analysis* of this difference, nor does it involve any claim about *how* they are different, nor how far, nor how significant the difference is. I am saying only that they are different, and different with respect to the "evidences" which will count for and against each of them.)

Suppose that what he says proves true. Then we could say that in both cases *the same thing happened:* he botched the slow movement. But where the prediction (where we will say it was a *prediction* which) was fulfilled, he walks away with a sense of resignation, perhaps contemplates learning a trade, looks at his fingers as though they were foreign objects, and goes out alone for a drink. On the other hand, where the *intention* to botch was executed, he walks away with a *pretense* of self-disgust or bewilderment, looks *as though* he's looking at his fingers as though they were foreign spies, contemplates the sensation he will cause at the final competition, and goes out to invite a friend for a drink. Similarly, where "What happens proves the statement wrong", i.e., you played the movement marvelously, then, where this went against a prediction, the person feels elated, perhaps thinks that a concert career is possible after all, almost runs into the wings and shouts "I made it!"; but where this went against an expression of intention, the person seems normal enough, perhaps a bit pre-occupied; perhaps he is thinking that anyway one revealing interpretation of a piece of late Beethoven is more satisfying than improvising ten choruses of "Ain't Misbehavin' "; and maybe, when he walks into the wings, he says, "I changed my mind". And finally, suppose that at the final competition the one who *can* intend to botch, and *can* resolve not to, botches the slow movement. What will he do? What will he say or think? He may have an explanation or excuse, he may have none. He may have been distracted by bad news, he may have been over-confident and cut his practice short the day before, he may have over-practiced and played mechanically, he may have stayed up too late the night before, or developed stage fright; he may just not know what went wrong. It is, after all, a very difficult piece; anyone might lose control of it on a given occasion. That is internal to its excitement.

What we say we will do, or think we in fact do, or think or say we say or would say, can be countered or supported by the facts in various ways. Some ways are like predictions failing or succeeding, some are like a column of figures yielding different totals on successive additions, some are pure accident, some are eventualities we thought we had planned for, some are eventualities we trusted not to occur, some are eventualities we ought to have realized were inevitable. In some we may be accused, or convict ourselves, of having spoken or thought on the basis of slim evidence; in some the concept of evidence will be entirely irrelevant.

How do we know that when (supposing that) I have three rabbits and you give me three then I have six? Perhaps one feels that that can be *proven* arithmetically or logically, and that what happens in the world is irrelevant to arithmetic and logic. But that is an answer to a different question. That answers the question, "How do we know that three plus three equals six?". Whereas what I am asking is, "How do we know that when we are asked to *suppose* we have three rabbits, etc., this arithmetical knowledge is relevant to the answer, and moreover, that no *other* knowledge is relevant?". And the answer to that has to do with the nature of supposition, what I have called "projective imagination", not alone with the nature of arithmetic.

Take another example. I am teaching chess to someone, and after a game I say, "Supposing my king had been here, your king there, and your last pawn there, and the rest of the board was empty: what would you have done?". If he says "I would have moved the pawn" that may show that he has or has not mastered a mode of endgame. But if he says "I would have fainted" he is making a weak joke. And if he asks seriously "How do you know there are no other pieces on the board?" then that suggests he hasn't mastered a mode of speech, a form of life, viz., imagining or supposing.

The following old gag is *about* supposition as well as about the intimidation in education. A soldier being instructed in guard duty is asked: "Suppose that while you're on duty in the middle of a desert you see a battleship approaching your post. What would you do?" The soldier replies: "I'd take my torpedo and sink it". The instructor is, we are to imagine, perplexed: "Where would you get the torpedo?" And he is answered: "The same place you got the battleship."

But there are many genres of meta-riddles — jokes, one supposes, in the face of the anxiety that someone may just not acquire the knack of understanding what a riddle is. The most famous of them, I believe, asks, What's green, hangs on a wall, and whistles?, and answers, A herring. To the objection, But a herring isn't green, the teller answers, You can paint it green; and to the objection, But a herring doesn't hang on a wall, the teller answers, So hang it on a wall; and to the final objection, But a herring doesn't whistle, the teller finally shrugs and answers, All right, it doesn't whistle. In a more up-to-date genre, the teller's final answer would be, I lied about the whistling.

How do we know *how much* to suppose or imagine when we are asked to suppose or imagine something? How do we know that some possibilities are relevant, serve only to flesh out the skeletal context we have had drawn, whereas other possibilities would *change* the context sketched? If there were another piece on the board, that would change the point of the chess instructor's example; if we imagine that you have a rabbit in your hat then the answer to "How many?" would be different, viz., seven rather than six. You may, at any given moment in your history, in fact have a rabbit in your hat; but you cannot pull *that* rabbit out and enter it into an imagined context. You *can* enter it by imagining (*telling* the story so) that it is hidden, but then you have changed the example. (Perhaps that would be the next example the instructor would use.)

What will be story enough to get someone to imagine what you invite him to consider is not fixed. To get someone to imagine that he or she has three rabbits and that he is given three more, you will not need much more than those words themselves. To get him to imagine what he would do if he held such and such a bridge hand, you may have to include the information as to whether he or his opponents are vulnerable, and give more information about the styles of bidding of each of the players. To get someone to imagine how Hamlet felt at the play, you may have to tap your own imagination at a deeper stratum to find the relevant details of that situation and to find the corresponding experiences within your life and the life of your audience. To ask us to imagine what we should say in a given situation, you will have to give enough story to rule out relevant possibilities and avert whatever misunderstanding may or will arise. How much you will have to include is, and need be, no more fixed than how much you will have to say or do to get someone to see what you are pointing to (and it makes a difference whether you are pointing to a camel, or to the camel's hump, or to the camel's gait, or to one of a group of camels, and whether they are five yards away or five miles); or to get someone to understand what you mean (and it will make a difference whether what you have said is, "She's *farouche*", or "The jig's up", or "Sufficient unto the day is the evil thereof"). And it makes a difference whether what we are asking is something like, "Would we say that he did it by accident or by mistake?" (where the contrast is explicit, and hence the relevant alternatives can be made fully explicit); or like, "Did he (are we to say he) really believe that flowers feel?" (where the criteria for saying what someone believes are in conflict, and some interpretations would pull us one way, some another); or like, "Don't we feel like saying here . . . ?" (which asks us to express a wish, or a feeling, which we recognize is not to be taken as giving us information about the world, but may be valuable as symptomatic just because its inappropriateness to what we take the facts to be may be so marked); or like, "Why does the expression 'That's that' say what it does?" or "Why do we say 'I did it on principle' or '. . . on impulse', but not 'I did it on anger' or '. . . on habit'?" (which are ways of getting us to articulate the structure of our grammar, our transcendental impositions); or like, "Which of your fingers would you call the baby finger? the mama finger? the papa finger? the nephew finger? the orphan?" (which could serve to illuminate the temper of concepts, the way in which they are at once flexible and stable: we will all agree about the baby finger; "nephew" will probably get little agreement; and "orphan" might seem invited either by the thumb or the little finger, but then we will learn something about the person who selects one or another of these when he tells us, as he must be prepared to do, how the thumb is an orphan (it's the loneliest) or how the little finger is an orphan (the rest are grownups)).

If the invitation to respond to imagined contexts can prepare or lead us to answers for such questions, then it is, so far, a fully legitimate and revealing enterprise. The defender of traditional philosophy who objects to *this* stage of ordinary language philosophy is misguidedly defending a station at the wrong point. All such defenses accomplish is to convince the defender of ordinary language that his suspicion about the classical philosophers has proven true, that they are as blind to themselves, as careless about the world, and as dogmatic and arbitrary in procedure as they seem to be; that in asking for "more" evidence than any master of a language has of his own language, they are only betraying a pantomime of scientific caution together with an incomprehension of genuine rigor. This genre of compliment is, of course, returned, for the traditionalist feels the ordinary language philosopher so desperately to have betrayed the martyrs of science as to compile natural histories from the comfort of his armchair.

One can understand, and sometimes forgive, the anger in this exchange. But such an exchange does not seem to me to reveal the nature of the real conflicts between these positions. The issue between them, so far as it concerns the appeals to what is ordinarily said, is not whether one of them is "scientific" and the other not, but concerns the nature of the sort of appeal to ordinary language which is relevant to philosophizing. The sort of appeal which I have taken as relevant is one I have characterized in various ways: in the first essays of *Must We Mean What We Say?*, I called it an appeal to the "Transcendental Logic" of our language; in the preceding chapters of this book, I have said that it is a way of reminding ourselves of our criteria in employing concepts. Just now I said that the philosophical appeal to ordinary language essentially involves responding to *imagined* situations. In Chapter VII, a further characterization of such appeals will be motivated. (I should like to call attention here to the discussion of this issue, among others, in S. Bates and T. Cohen, "More On What We Say".) The philosophical issue of such appeals can be said to concern what a "science" of such appeals would be. I have said that a "science", a knowledge, of such appeals is a matter of self-knowledge. I take it to be a perception, however weak or inconstant, of *that* fact which is at the root of the hostility between the tradition and its new critics. For I understand ordinary language philosophy not as an effort to reinstate vulgar beliefs, or common sense, to a pre-scientific position of eminence, but to reclaim the human self from its denial and neglect by modern philosophy.

That (and why and how) this denial has taken place raises problems — if my formulation is a valid one — of a scope I do not wish even to contemplate now. My hopes are to suggest an answer in the arena of traditional philosophical skepticism, and to suggest that the Wittgensteinian view of language (together with an Austinian practice of it), and of philosophy, is an assault upon that denial.

The Irrelevance of Projective Imagination as Direct Criticism

If the ordinary language philosopher's question involves, as I have put it, an invitation to imagine a context, then even granted, as I think we must grant, that his answers to his use of the question are right, in terms of that invitation, it is nevertheless not an invitation the traditional philosopher can accept as relevant to his concerns. It is not open to him, given his problem, to imagine any situation he chooses. He is stuck with a *given* situation, one forced upon him by a problem — something which presents itself to him as a real, factual, question; and to imagine a different context simply seems to him to deny the reality of his question altogether. His question "Do I see the envelope?" (when it is in clear view) or "Am I certain there is a table here?" (when it is, for all the world, there) seems, in his position, to express as real a problem as "Where did I put the envelope?" (when you can't find it). A real problem to be *investigated*, to *find* an answer for. The "possibilities" he then considers — e.g., "Mightn't it be a cleverly painted piece of wax?", "Mightn't you be having a hallucination?" — are possibilities which must be considered, if the problem is a real one. The ordinary language philosopher's invitation to imagine when we should really raise such possibilities just flatly denies that it is (or just assumes that it is not) really *there*.

When the ordinary language philosopher asks, "What *reason* do you have to believe that it *may* not be real, that you may be having a hallucination?", the traditional philosopher's answer must be, "That isn't the point. I have no reason to think it is in fact phoney, or that I am hallucinating, but I've got to *consider* such possibilities. If they were *in fact* the case then what I claim, viz., to be certain, would be unjustified; and having considered one or other of them, I find that I cannot rule it out as a real possibility here and now". As I put this point earlier: it isn't that I don't know when various "possibilities" would be real ones; it is rather that I am asking, "Is *this* such a situation or not? The situation might be other than it seems, or is described, to be".

But an *imagined* situation *cannot,* in logic, be other than it seems, or is described, to be. You cannot empirically *investigate* an imagined situation (e.g., investigate whether in fact you have six or seven imagined rabbits). That is one fact which I take directly to show the irrelevance of the ordinary language philosopher's questions as direct criticisms of the tradition. The traditional epistemologist is not doing a poor job of *imagining a situation,* i.e., describing it incompletely and then responding to it with slightly inappropriate expressions. (And if he were, how would, or could, an ordinary language philosopher understand that? As lunacy? As ecstasy? But then how does he understand himself to be in conversation with people in such straits?) The epistemologist is, or takes himself to be, *going over an actual situation* (perhaps in imagination), one which, presumably, we are all familiar with; and then (he can be described as) investigating whether what we ordinarily say about it is true or fully appropriate or entirely accurate. From his point of view, with his intention, he seems in exactly as sound a position to impugn our ordinary description of that situation as the ordinary language philosopher seems to be, from his point of view, in impugning the philosophical descriptions.

The ordinary language philosopher must seem to the traditionalist like the drunk in the story who, having dropped his keys trying to open his house door, has gone around the corner to look for them under the street lamp because the light makes it easier to find things. Or perhaps like a second drunk who, looking at the difficulties of the first, tries to convince him that he can't have dropped his keys because they obviously are not under the light.

Now, perhaps, it will be the ordinary language philosopher who feels that his efforts are being slighted. The aspect of his procedure which I have called "imagining a context" may seem a trivial one to emphasize in comparing it with traditional procedures, because the aspect of comparison which most impresses him is the sense that he is proceeding from *fully and realistically* described cases, and therefore that his cases *are of the same kind, only clearer and more fruitful* than those found in traditional investigations.

That response cannot be taken at face value, for two sorts of reasons:

(1) To take the charge of incompleteness to be a clear lack in a description is just to assume that the description is of an imagined situation, and hence to beg the question in favor of the ordinary language examples. For we have seen that about such situations the question "How much need the description include?" may have a clear answer in terms of the point the illustration is designed to serve; and seen how further information may change the example. But when you are describing a case about which some real problem has arisen, it is not antecedently clear what you need to know about the case in order to arrive at a solution. You try to list "everything" you know about it (e.g., just where you were when you last saw it, how long you were out of the room, etc., etc.); but of course "everything you know" only means "everything you can think of which seems relevant". And the solution will emerge when you "realize" that something you had *not noticed* about the situation, or a possibility you had not considered or not remembered, may make all the difference. (For example: "I remember now; the view, at the position from which I was looking, was partially obstructed that day by some builder's equipment." Compare: "But of course I don't see *all* of any object.") But you do not in the same way "realize" that you have failed to notice or consider something about an imagined situation (e.g., that one rabbit had hidden in your hat). What you may discover is that you had been imagining it incorrectly or arbitrarily.

Magicians and riddles, as well as revolutionary changes in scientific theory, may trade or turn upon such a discovery. Take this riddle: "Some ducks are swimming under a bridge; two in front, two behind, and two in the middle; but there are not six. How many are there?" The image of two files and three ranks seems invariably to occur first upon hearing this description, and one tries to see how there may not be six. Eventually the answer implodes with the image of a single file of four ducks. In such a case what is "incomplete" in the description is obvious. The riddle depends upon "having all the facts" but forcing a false or arbitrary arrangement upon them. Perhaps someone can make it out that the realization of "arbitrary arrangement" is what produces such discoveries as that the earth may revolve around the sun rather than vice versa, or that the problem about motion is not to explain what keeps an object moving but what makes it stop. The moral of such examples may be articulated as: "Don't trust your description of a situation in which a problem has emerged; the problem may be produced by the description itself." This realization does seem to resemble the realization of the philosopher that, although we ordinarily *say* that (= "describe" situations as ones in which) we *see* objects, that description is itself prejudicial. (Descartes makes this point in the second Meditation.) So the traditional philosopher is, as the ordinary language philosopher is, involved with investigating our conceptualization, or projective imagination, of problems and situations. But the traditional philosopher is *led* to this investigation by a problem which suggests to him that our description must be wrong, that we are misconceiving the real situation. Whereas the ordinary language philosopher is led to his investigations by a problem which means to him that we are misunderstanding our own conceptualization of a plain situation. It is as though the traditional philosopher is saying: I know what it is to *see* something and so I realize we *don't* see objects. Whereas the ordinary language philosopher is saying: Since we *do* (sometimes) see objects, you have misunderstood the concept of seeing something.

What I should hope would most impress one about this conflict is that it cannot be obvious which of the positions is right; each side is fastening upon a fundamental fact of human experience and knowledge. Knowing something is ineluctably a matter of aligning concepts with the world; and it must be a *problem* whether any given instance of the failure of knowledge is a failure to have got the concept right or to have got the world right. And just as "getting the world right" does not just mean "getting the right information" but also "getting the right arrangement of the information", so "getting the concept right" does not just mean "getting the right concept" but "getting the right understanding of the concept". And then such questions as these emerge: "When does a problem present itself as requiring the one or the other?"; "When do we feel the need for a new concept?" One way to work on such questions may be to ask: When do we feel that our lack of knowledge is a function of our stupidity or ignorance and when a matter of our confusion?

(2) Moreover, it is also unclear that the charge of incomplete descrip-

tion, in any natural sense, would even seem to be true of these examples. Indeed, a traditional epistemologist will often take great pains to describe his context and his requests very fully and in detail:

. . . I wish to illustrate what I have to say about seeing by a direct practical example; because, though I dare say many of you are perfectly familiar with the sort of points I wish to raise, it is, I think, very important for everyone, in these subjects, to consider carefully single concrete instances, so that there may be no mistake as to exactly what it is that is being talked about. Such mistakes are, I think, very apt to happen, if one talks merely in generalities; and moreover one is apt to overlook important points. I propose, therefore, to hold up an envelope in my hand, and to ask you all to look at it for a moment; and then to consider with me exactly what it is that happens, when you see it: *what* this occurrence, which we call the *seeing* of it, *is*.

I hold up this envelope, then: I look at it, and I hope you all will look at it. And now I put it down again. Now what has happened? We should certainly say (if you have looked at it) that we all *saw* that envelope, that we all saw *it, the same* envelope: *I* saw it, and you all saw it. [G. E. Moore, *Some Main Problems of Philosophy,* p. 30]

For example, . . . I am here, seated by the fire, wearing a winter dressing gown, holding this paper in my hands and other things of this nature.

Are these situations incompletely described? The way the case of the swimming ducks was? The way the case of Father disguised may have been? Whether a situation is fully described will, one supposes, depend on the point for which it was being described. So let us ask: What is the point of getting us to consider the concrete situations that the traditional philosopher selects? Well, he wants to investigate, to *go over,* situations of a certain kind, and situations, moreover, which we must all be completely familiar with. All his initial description is designed to do is to get us to consider the simplest cases in which we see or sense something. It seems to him, and to those of us who have ever followed him, that he is asking us to do something no more difficult or portentous than a linguist demands of us when he directs us to pronounce a word with "t" in it, e.g., "tomato", and then determine the position of our lips and tongue in making that sound. It seems no less explicit a direction to say "Look at this tomato" or "What happens when we see a tomato?" than it does to say "Pronounce the word 'tomato' " or "What happens when we pronounce the word 'tomato'?".

And the point of asking us to consider such cases is, we could say, exactly to *determine* whether our description of the situation (e.g., as one in which we "see the object") is quite full or exact. And isn't that what the ordinary language philosopher wants also? Perhaps he will say: "But I don't know *why* I'm being asked to do this. There is no problem about *whether* I see an object in a perfectly standard case of seeing an object. The only time some realistic problem about this can emerge is where there is some real *question* as to whether the thing is what I take it to be or whether it is in full and adequate view. Whereas, by hypothesis, neither of these is, or could be, the cases here." — By hypothesis? Rather, by what seems to be our ordinary description. But *is* that description really accurate? To say there *is* no such question must seem to the traditional philosopher like a witness's responding to a question by saying: "Why do you ask me to go over again what happened that morning? I tell you I didn't see Father all morning. The only person I saw was the secretary. There just is no problem about that. Don't you think I know what the words 'see Father' mean?"

But of course, as has been mentioned, in such cases we all know why we are being asked to go over the situation again, in the sense that we know antecedently what the problem is, and what a solution to it would be. But the philosopher has to *make* a problem for us, show us in what sense it might so much as *be* a problem. And though intellectual advance often depends upon someone's ability to do just that, the conclusion the philosopher takes us to goes beyond anything we should expect from investigations which seem to proceed as his does.

To some philosophers that fact has itself, I think, proved the power and subtlety of philosophy; while to others it has only demonstrated its intellectual frivolity. If one has felt both of these ways about skepticism, then one may come to sense that this very conflict itself may be displaying, or concealing, some critical fact about the mind, and one which neither side has been able, or willing, to articulate. Suppose, what must be the case, that both positions are powerfully motivated and intellectually armed; then instead of asking for an amicable settlement or a swift victory, let us try to uncover something more in the way of an understanding of the conflict. For as long as we simply say, both must be right, we will have also to say, both must be wrong. And we don't know about what.

A Further Problem

We have had occasion to notice one striking feature of the skeptical conclusion which, it was suggested, may throw particular light on the nature of the investigation as a whole; I mean its instability. We seem to arrive at a conclusion invoking considerations and employing procedures which, in ordinary cases, would produce a full sense of conviction. And, indeed, conviction is also formed by them in the philosophical investigation as well. Only here our conviction fades as soon as we leave the context of the investigation. The conclusion does not, as it were, detach itself from the experience of the investigation. In a case like Austin's, I don't keep forgetting that I don't really know a goldfinch was in the garden; I don't have continually to face the re-emergence of a conviction that I do know; the knowledge that I do not know does not, away from the force of that particular demonstration, seem "cold, strained and ridiculous" (Hume, *Treatise*, Book I, Part IV, Section VII, p. 269). Can we understand why the skeptical conclusion that we do not know of the existence of objects, that we do not really, ever, see them, does have this strange aspect? (It can of course only present this face to those of us who have at some time found its truth to be live.)

If we consider that, according to the Cartesian-Austinian model of the assessment of claims to knowledge, the conclusion — not that what we claimed is manifestly false, but that it is not known to be true — emerges when a particular basis for a claim is countered by a particular ground for doubt; and if we concede, against the ordinary language philosopher, that the traditional philosopher's familiar grounds for doubt, though "in themselves" perhaps extraordinary, have nevertheless, in his context, been made reasonable (or their unreasonableness somehow neutralized), then we will be led to look again at the basis the traditional philosopher offers in support of the simple claim he investigates, and ask whether that, too, has been made fully reasonable, entered fully naturally.

I want to show several things: that it is *not* fully natural, and that it is not *fully* unnatural; and consequently that it is not immediately obvious what significance we are to attach to its partial unnaturalness. And again, the primary moral of this investigation will be that the way an objection from ordinary language must be justified — the very truth it contains — will itself prevent the objection from being fatal to the traditional step.

The basis offered in support of the claim to know that a generic object exists was, according to the Cartesian-Austinian model, "Because I see it" or "By means of the senses". The rightness of that basis has, I think, not been questioned either by the tradition or its critics. The arguments about seeing or perception have, so far as I know, centered rather on the question *whether* I really see the object or *really* only see, at most, *part* of it (viz., its front surface), or, if neither, *what* it is I can really be said to see. What I wish at the moment to indicate is that, *as the basis of a claim to know,* the traditional bases are not unquestionably natural.

Asked how you know there is an envelope (or tomato or table) here, in full view, you will not, as we remarked in Chapter III, offer an Austinian feature as the basis of your claim. "From the shape", "By the texture", "Because of the legs", would be absurd responses. Generic objects have no Austinian features in terms of which they are identified. If you accept the philosopher's question as a legitimate (natural, non-absurd) one — i.e., accept the request to "go over a familiar situation in detail" — then you will *have* to give "Because I see it" ("Well, I see it of course") or "By means of the senses" as the basis of the claim. And "have to" means "have to in order to remain reasonable"; and that means "in order to honor as fully as possible the most natural demands of ordinary language". It is not the philosopher's *choice* to produce this basis. Given his context and object and his question reasonably asked, *the basis is as determined by ordinary language* as the kind of basis we can offer about an Austinian object is. So the basis is not absurd. But it is not fully natural either, as I now wish to bring out.

It may help to make this clearer if we pause to notice that the philosopher's investigation of our claims to know the minds of others takes, or can take, a form apparently just like the form of the Cartesian investigation, as visualized in terms of Austin's model. The fact that its considerations have had less chance to wear thin in our minds may allow us to hear them with a fresher ear.

The initiating experience, the fearful surmise, the wonder, is, if anything, apparently even clearer here than in the case of claims to know objects. This is, perhaps, a function of a difference in the respective initiating experiences. I characterized the experience, where objects are concerned, as something like "feeling sealed off from objects, enclosed within my own experience". In the comparable experience of persons I find the experience to be one of "feeling them to be closed off from me (within, as it were, *their* own experience)". Thus prompted, we ask: "(How) do we know what another person is feeling or thinking?"; "(How) can we know whether he feels anything at all?" And then the assessment follows its familiar, and apparently implacable, course.

Request for Basis: How, for example, do we know another person is angry?

Basis: From his behavior, the way he acts. . . .

Ground for Doubt: But mightn't he do those things, act that way, and *not* be angry? And how do you know but that he is feeling something entirely different, or nothing at all?

Conclusion: I *don't* know.

> Moral: I never can. Behavior is not identical with feelings and thoughts themselves. Only the person himself can really know, be certain, what the experience is, and whether there is any at all. For us that is only a belief based on an empirical inference.

I do not wish to insist on the perfection of this match of format with the material object case. I am suspicious, in particular, about two moments in this case of other minds. First, what I noticed as its apparently greater clarity of the initiating experience strikes me as perhaps something that it is too easy to arrive at, lacking somehow the depth of paradox reached, or claimed, in the material object case. Second, I am not convinced that I know why, or whether, the example of anger (or pain, or something else) is a best case of knowledge in this arena. It is critical in what we have so far understood and claimed about best cases that they turn upon generic objects, ones about which the problem or criteria of identification does not arise. Is this true of the example of anger? Would it be truer, or less true, of pain or of nostalgia? It can seem to matter less *what* precisely we say is there than it matters whether we are assured that *something* is. And would this be the same or a different "something" ("Something, I know not what") that we want to be assured of, could we but grasp it, in the material object case? We have cause for wariness in this locale, to which we will come back, with more time, in Part Four.

Until then, the surface analogy between the formats for material objects and for other minds seems close enough to warrant calling attention to certain features they share.

Consider the phrases "his behavior", "the way he acts", "do those things", as they occur in the basis and the ground for doubt as presented in the paradigm just drawn. What we imagine, as we say them, is a person doing things like paling or frowning, shaking his fist at another, leaving a room, speaking in a loud voice, pacing nervously, behaving in a generally agitated fashion. . . . We feel, rightly, that he could "do any of these things" and not be angry: he might be feigning anger, or he might be listening to a horse race on the radio, or waiting for his child to be born, giving a political speech, or writing one. . . . But then, it is not just any case and any way in which someone is "doing these things", that we would go on or present as bases for a real claim that someone was angry, but only such ways and in such contexts in which "doing them" would *be* (what we call) expressing or venting anger, in which these behaviors would be grammatical criteria of anger. We might say "He is threatening the man" (or, if we said "He is waving his fist" we would mean or imply, in that context, that in doing that he was threatening), or "He is accusing him, or chastising him", or "He said hurtful words", or "He left her alone, knowing what she was about to face", or "She left him in that position ten years ago; it serves her right", or even, more explicitly, "He spoke in anger", or "left in a rage". *Now* if we ask, can you do any of these things (and they aren't *different* from what we earlier imagined him to be doing; *and* they aren't obviously the *same* either), and not be angry, the answer will no longer be an inevitable affirmative. Can you *accuse, chastise,* say (intentionally) *hurtful* words, serve someone right, leave in a rage . . . and not really be angry? We might say "He was really angry at himself, not her", or "He acted more out of hurt or fear than anger". But such statements concede the relevance of the concept of anger — and logical or grammatical relevance, not just a plausible consideration — in undertaking to explain *how* what he is doing is not really expressive of anger (his anger toward her). But there would *be* nothing to explain here if accusation, chastisement, etc., did not (grammatically) go with anger.

Let me put this shift this way: In the philosopher's context, we have removed the ground for doubt from its ordinary grammatical relevance to the concept in the original claim. Then why does it *even seem to counter* the basis of that claim? And what I am trying to suggest is this: Because the basis itself is already removed from its ordinary grammatical relevance to the original claim. This is hard to make ourselves notice. It is brought out if we put the claim "He is angry" into a practical context, and imagine asking there "How do you know?". The reply (basis) "From his behavior" is either a joke or an insult; like answering "How can you tell this is a goldfinch?" by replying, "From the way it looks". — But what is the significance of that? Suppose someone replied: "So what? Suppose it *is* a joke or an insult. That doesn't show that it isn't *true*". — But I haven't said it was *false*.

I want to say: It isn't that we *don't* know from his behavior ("by means of the senses", "because I see it") but that *that* is not *how* we know, are in a position to say, are competent to judge, here and now that this man is angry. "How we know" "anything and everything" of a certain kind is not how we know here and now the specific claim we are making. "From his behavior" would be a relevant basis if it meant that we were going on that rather than on what he or someone else said, or on what we might have expected him to feel. But, as used in the philosopher's context, this "basis" contrasts not with these familiar alternatives, but with "his feeling itself".

But again, what is the significance of that? How am I to *show* that "How we know anything and everything is not how we know here and now what we claim to know"? That the philosopher is investigating the validity of knowledge in general by investigating the validity of particular claims has been emphasized; and though we have asked how it is that the fortune of a particular claim can seem to affect the fortune of knowledge as a whole, we haven't yet shown that it cannot, or how it can, affect it in fact or in theory. And of course the philosopher realizes that "from his behavior" is meant as a general basis; just as he realizes, and insists, that "because I see it" is a general basis; it is meant to contrast with other general ways of knowing, not to serve as a substitute for some specific basis which records how you can tell here and now that what you say is true.

But that the contrast which *emerges,* in the course of the inquiry, is no longer the normal one between what he does (his behavior) and what he says or others say he did, but between his behavior and "the feeling itself"; no longer between what I see (or sense) and what I have on authority or know by inference, but between what I see and what (or how much) I *really see,* or between how it appears to the senses and what it is in itself — these are, or should seem, surprising eventualities. These are not the contrasts the philosopher has *begun* with, they are contrasts his investigation has *led* him to. To say they are not the normal contrasts these phrases enjoy is one thing, and important. But to the philosopher they seem like *discoveries,* discoveries of facts which we have not hitherto noticed but which, once we bring them out, undercut those normal contrasts with ones more radical. The ordinary language philosopher takes the altered contrast to mean that the philosopher has "changed the meaning of his words" or "misused language", whereas the traditional philosopher takes it to mean that ordinary language has itself been shown not fully trustworthy.

Let me again emphasize what I take the sense of discovery to indicate about the philosopher's conclusion. First, since it is a discovery whose content is that something we have, supposedly, all believed has been shown false or superstitious or in some way suspect, its sense of being a discovery depends upon a sense of its *conflicting* with what we would all, supposedly, have said we knew or thought. And this sense of conflict depends upon the words which express the conclusion meaning, or seeming to mean, what those words, as ordinarily used, would express. For *that* is what the conclusion conflicts with. When the philosopher concludes that "we don't really see or know" something, why would this so much as seem to deny what the ordinary person means when he says "I see or know" something, unless the words meant, or seemed to mean, the same thing?

Second, the philosopher's conclusion seems, in this conflict, to be right, and indeed to be deeper than our everyday, average ideas (to cause our everyday ideas to appear average). I have said that the convincingness of the conclusion depended upon its proceeding, or seeming to proceed, in just the ordinary way any ordinary person must (grammatically) proceed to establish a claim to know of something's existence. But the methods any competent speaker and actor would use to establish ordinary claims seem, in the hands of the philosopher, to establish the inferiority or weakness of those very ordinary claims themselves. The Cartesian epistemologist, we might say, is not impugning ordinary *methods* of supporting or assessing knowledge, but rather feels himself to have shown that in our ordinary employment of those methods we are not normally careful or precise enough. The method seems more impressive than any attempt to show that his particular words or phrases are not fully normal. Indeed, the philosopher *concedes* this when he says that "for practical purposes" it is all right to say we *see* objects, that we *are* certain of some matters of fact; his claim is, using the very methods by which we establish our ordinary, practical claims, that he has shown that those claims are not *literally* or *absolutely* true (we see objects all right, if you like; only not *immediately*).

I take this to mean that any really formidable criticism of the traditional philosopher must show that his investigation does not, in the way he depends upon it to, *fully* follow an ordinary investigation of a claim to knowledge. It seems to me undeniable that it *apparently* does (to deny that would mean, for me, denying that large groups of competent persons had ever been convinced by it). But why should a method which ordinarily yields unworried conviction turn out to yield, in the philosopher's hands, a conclusion whose conviction will not detach from the context of investigation itself?

Before saying what I can about this, I want to explain why the vision of language which I take to underlie the ordinary language philosopher's procedures, and which, for me, advances our understanding of language and of human knowledge, or the conventionality of human nature generally, itself prevents it from forming a direct criticism of the tradition — where "direct" means something like "show directly the emptiness or distortion of the philosopher's words and phrases". — That it is not a direct criticism makes it, to my mind, far more interesting than it would be if it were. Because the reasons it is not direct criticism can show us, if we can articulate them, something more interesting than particular mistakes a thinker has committed. It can show us something about the nature of criticism, specifically something about the criticism of what we call a "point of view". It can show how coherent and tenacious a point of view can be, how much is at stake in maintaining it, and therefore show how complex the difficulties any serious criticism of it will exact — one meant seriously enough, I mean, to wish to change the mind which harbors the point of view, or else to be changed by it. That is the seriousness of Freud's criticism of human conduct. In this way the methods of ordinary language, far from trivializing the impulse to philosophy (as many of its detractors, not, perhaps, without some reason, have found it to do), show how complex and serious an ambition the criticism of philosophy, which must inevitably remain internal to philosophizing itself, ought to be.

What most immediately is disturbing in the attempt to dismiss the traditional philosopher's words as "misuses of language" or as cases in which "meanings have been altered" is that the very power of the ordinary language procedures resides in its insistence that any master of a language can respond to his request to "say what we should say when, say what we call such and such an eventuality"; and so we must have some convincing explanation of how a master of a language may not know that he has changed the meaning of a word or has emptied it of meaning altogether. And this is, or it ought to be, a problem for a philosopher who proceeds from ordinary language in a way it is not a problem for a philosopher who is willing simply to say that ordinary language is vague and imprecise and that it is hardly to be wondered that we can't be clear as to our meaning until we put our assertions into logical form or a scientific vocabulary. I want to show in more detail the kind of problem this is. (I have elsewhere spoken of this general issue under the rubric of tracing "terms of criticism".)

My plan is this. Having noticed that a shift takes place in the force or direction of the philosopher's basis as he moves from the beginning to the end of his investigation, I want to look again at one familiar ground for doubt — viz., "But you don't see all of it; the most you see is a part of the front surface" — which, coming upon the basis and leading to the conclusion, must register the shift of force of the basis. There is something peculiar about such a ground for doubt, but before trying to say what the peculiarity is, and as a preparation for assessing its significance, I am going to break here the thread of the inquiry into the nature of traditional epistemology and devote a separate chapter to a fuller characterization of what I spoke of a moment ago as the vision of language underlying, or forming part of, the philosophy which proceeds by appeals to what we should say when, to how words are normally used. This will then set the stage for the last confrontation of the tradition and its new critics I am trying to arrange.

VII

Excursus on Wittgenstein's Vision of Language

In speaking of the vision of language underlying ordinary language procedures in philosophy, I had in mind something I have suggested in discussing Wittgenstein's relation of grammar and criteria to "forms of life", and in emphasizing the sense in which human convention is not arbitrary but constitutive of significant speech and activity; in which mutual understanding, and hence language, depends upon nothing more and nothing less than shared forms of life, call it our mutual attunement or agreement in our criteria. I have said both that criteria are apparently necessary to our knowledge of existence or reality, and that they can be, apparently out of necessity, repudiated. I expressed this by saying that *normally* the presence of criteria (the fact that we say, truly, *"that* is what we call 'suppressing anger' ") will insure the existence of its object (he is there feeling angry), but not inevitably (deductively?), and suggested that this meant not that normally (usually) a statement made on the basis of a criterion is true, but that it is true of the normal inhabitants of our world, of anything we recognize as part of our world.

Now I want to say something more specific about what it is Wittgenstein has discovered, or detailed, about language (i.e., about the entire body and spirit of human conduct and feeling which goes into the capacity for speech) which raises the sorts of problems I have so crudely and vaguely characterized in terms of "normality" and "our world".

What I wish to say at this point can be taken as glossing Wittgenstein's remark that "we learn words in *certain* contexts" (e.g., *Blue Book,* p. 9). This means, I take it, both that we do not learn words in *all* the contexts in which they could be used (what, indeed, would that mean?) and that not every context in which a word is used is one in which the word *can* be learned (e.g., contexts in which the word is used metaphorically). And after a while we are expected to know when the words are appropriately used in further contexts. This is obvious enough, and philosophers have always asked for an explanation of it: "How do words acquire that generality upon which thought depends?" As Locke put it:

All things that exist being particulars, it may perhaps be thought reasonable that words, which ought to be conformed to things, should be so too, I mean in their signification: but yet we find quite the contrary. The far greatest part of words that make all languages are general terms; which has not been the effect of neglect or chance, but of reason and necessity. . . . The next thing to be considered is, how general words come to be made. For since all things that exist are only particulars, how come we by general terms, or where find we those general natures they are supposed to stand for? [*An Essay Concerning Human Understanding*, Book III; Chapter III; Sections I and VI]

This is one of the questions to which philosophers have given the answer, "Because there are universals"; and the "problem of universals" has been one of assigning, or denying, an ontological status to such things and of explaining, or denying, our knowledge of them. What Wittgenstein wishes us to see, if I understand, is that no such answers could provide an explanation of the questions which lead to them.

"We learn words in certain contexts and after a while we are expected to know when they are appropriately used in (= can appropriately be projected into) further contexts" (and, of course, our ability to project appropriately is a criterion for our having learned a word). Now I want to ask: (1) What is (do we call) "learning a word", and in particular (to keep to the simplest case) "learning the general name of something"?; and (2) what makes a projection an appropriate or correct one? (Again, traditionally, the answer to (1) is: "Grasping a universal", and to (2): "The recognition of another instance of the same universal", or "the fact that the new object is *similar* to the old".)

Learning a Word

Suppose we ask: "When a child learns the name of something (e.g., 'cat', 'star', 'pumpkin'), obviously he doesn't learn merely that *this* (particular) sound goes with *that* (particular) object; so what does he learn?" We might answer: "He learns that sounds *like* this name objects *like* that." We can quickly become very dissatisfied with that answer. Suppose we reflected that that answer seems to describe more exactly a situation in which learning that "cat" is the name of *that* means learning that "rat" (a sound *like* "cat") is the name of *that* (an object *like* a cat). That obviously is not what we meant to say (because that obviously is not what happens?). How is what we meant to say different? We might try: "He learns that sounds *exactly* similar to this name objects *exactly* similar to that." But that is either false or obviously empty. For what does it mean to say that one cat is exactly similar to another cat? We do not want to mean that you can not tell them apart (for that obviously would not explain what we are trying to explain). What we *want* to say is that the child learns that a sound that *is* (counts as) this *word* names objects which *are* cats. But isn't that just what we thought we needed, and were trying to give, an *explanation* for?

Suppose we change the point of view of the question and ask: What do we teach or tell a child when we point to a pumpkin and say, "Pumpkin"? Do we tell him what a pumpkin is or what the word "pumpkin" means? I was surprised to find that my first response to this question was, "You can say either". (Cf. "Must We Mean What We Say?", p. 21.) And that led me to appreciate, and to want to investigate, how much a matter knowing what something *is* is a matter of knowing what something is *called;* and to recognize how limited or special a truth is expressed in the motto, "We may change the names of things, but their nature and their operation on the understanding never change" (Hume, *Treatise*, Book II, Part III, Section I).

At the moment I will say just this: That response ("You can say either") is true, at best, only for those who have already mastered a language. In the case of a child still coming to a mastery of its language it may be (fully) true *neither* that what we teach them is (the meaning of) a word *nor* that we tell them what a thing is. It looks very like one or the other, so of course it is very natural to say that it is one or the other; but so does malicious gossip often look like honesty, and so we very often call it honesty.

How might saying "Pumpkin" and pointing to a pumpkin not be "telling the child what a word means"? There are many sorts of answers to that. One might be: it takes two to *tell* someone something; you can't give someone a piece of information unless he knows how to *ask* for that (or comparable) information. (Cf. *Investigations*, §31.) And this is no more true of learning language than it is true of learning any of the forms of life which grow language. You can't tell a child what a word means when the child has yet to learn what "asking for a meaning" is (i.e., how to ask for a meaning), in the way you can't lend a rattle to a child who has yet to learn what "being lent (or borrowing) something" means. Grownups like to think of children (especially their own) as small grown-ups, midgets. So they say to their child, "Let Sister use your shovel", and then nudge the child over towards Sister, wrest the shovel from the child's hand, and are later impatient and disappointed when the child beats Sister with a pail and Sister rages not to "return" the shovel. We learn from suffering.

Nor, in saying "Pumpkin" to the child, are we telling the child what a pumpkin is, i.e., the child does not then know what a pumpkin is. For to "know what a pumpkin is" is to know, e.g., that it is a kind of fruit; that it is used to make pies; that it has many forms and sizes and colors; that this one is misshapen and old; that inside every tame pumpkin there is a wild man named Jack, screaming to get out.

So what are we telling the child if we are telling him neither what a word means nor what a thing is? We might feel: "If you can't tell a child a simple thing like what a pumpkin is or what the word 'pumpkin' means, then how does learning ever *begin?*" But why assume we are telling him anything at all? Why assume that we are *teaching* him anything? Well, because obviously he has learned something. But perhaps we are too quick to suppose we know what it is in such situations that makes us say the child is learning something. In particular, too quick to suppose we know what the child is learning. To say we are teaching them language obscures both how different what they learn may be from anything we think we are teaching, or mean to be teaching; and how vastly more they learn than the thing we should say we had "taught". Different and more, not because we are bad or good teachers, but because "learning" is not as academic a matter as academics are apt to suppose.

First, reconsider the obvious fact that there is not the *clear* difference between learning and maturation that we sometimes suppose there is. Take this example: Suppose my daughter now knows two dozen words. (Books on child development must say things like: At age 15 months the average child *will have a vocabulary of* so many words.) One of the words she knows, as her Baby Book will testify, is "kitty". What does it mean to say she "knows the word"? What does it mean to say she "learned it"? Take the day on which, after I said "Kitty" and pointed to a kitty, she repeated the word and pointed to the kitty. What does "repeating the word" mean here? and what did she point to? All I know is (and does she know more?) that she made the sound I made and pointed to what I pointed at. Or rather, I know less (or more) than that. For what is "her making the sound I made"? She produced a sound (imitated me?) which *I accepted, responded to* (with smiles, hugs, words of encouragement, etc.) as *what I had said*. The next time a cat came by, on the prowl or in a picture book, she did it again. A new entry for the Baby Book under "Vocabulary".

Now take the day, some weeks later, when she smiled at a fur piece, stroked it, and said "kitty". My first reaction was surprise, and, I suppose, disappointment: she doesn't really know what "kitty" means. But my second reaction was happier: she means by "kitty" what I mean by "fur". Or was it what I mean by "soft", or perhaps "nice to stroke"? Or perhaps she didn't mean at all what in my syntax would be recorded as "That is an X". After all, when she sees real kittens she not only utters her allophonic version of "kitty", she usually squeals the word over and over, squats down near it, stretches out her arm towards it and opens and closes her fingers (an allomorphic version of "petting the kitten"?), purses her lips, and squints with pleasure. All she did with the fur piece was, smiling, to say "kitty" once and stroke it. Perhaps the syntax of that performance should be transcribed as "This is like a kitty", or "Look at the funny kitty", or "Aren't soft things nice?", or "See, I remember how pleased you are when I say 'kitty' ", or "I like to be petted". Can we decide this? Is it a *choice* between these definite alternatives? In each case her word was produced about a soft, warm, furry object of a certain size, shape, and weight. What did she learn in order to do that? *What did she learn from having done it?* If she had never made such leaps she would never have walked into speech. Having made it, meadows of communication can grow for us. Where you can leap to depends on where you stand. When, later, she picks up a gas bill and says "Here's a letter", or when, hearing a piece of music we've listened to together many times, she asks "Who's Beethoven?", or when she points to the television coverage of the Democratic National Convention and asks "What are you watching?", I may realize we are not ready to walk certain places together.

But although I didn't tell her, and she didn't learn, either what the word "kitty" means or what a kitty is, if she keeps leaping and I keep looking and smiling, she will learn both. I have wanted to say: Kittens — what we call "kittens" — do not exist in her world yet, she has not acquired the forms of life which contain them. They do not exist in something like the way cities and mayors will not exist in her world until long after pumpkins and kittens do; or like the way God or love or responsibility or beauty do not exist in our world; we have not mastered, or we have forgotten, or we have distorted, or learned through fragmented models, the forms of life which could make utterances like "God exists" or "God is dead" or "I love you" or "I cannot do otherwise" or "Beauty is but the beginning of terror" bear all the weight they could carry, express all they could take from us. We do not know the meaning of the words. We look away and leap around.

"Why be so difficult? Why perversely deny that the child has learned a word, and insist, with what must be calculated provocativeness, that your objects are 'not in her world'? Anyone will grant that she can't do everything we do with the word, nor know everything we do about kitties — I mean kittens; but when she says 'Kitty's nice' and evinces the appropriate behavior, then she's learned the name of an object, learned to name an object, and the *same* object we name. The differences are between what she does and what you do obvious, and any sensible person will take them for granted."

What I am afraid of is that we take too much for granted about what the learning and the sharing of language implies. What's *wrong* with thinking of learning language as being taught or told the names of things? Why did Wittgenstein call sharp attention to Augustine's having said or implied that it is, and speak of a particular "picture" of language underlying it, as though Augustine was writing from a particular, arbitrary perspective, and that the judgment was snap?

There is more than one "picture" Wittgenstein wishes to develop: one of them concerns the idea that all words are names, a second concerns the idea that learning a name (or any word) is being told what it means, a third is the idea that learning a language is a matter of learning (new) words. The first of these ideas, and Wittgenstein's criticism of it, has, I believe, received wider attention than the other two, which are the ones which concern us here. (The ideas are obviously related to one another, and I may say that I find the second two to give the best sense of what Wittgenstein finds "wrong" with the first. It isn't as I think it is usually taken, merely that "language has many functions" besides naming things; it is also that the ways philosophers account for naming makes it incomprehensible how language can so much as perform *that* function.)

Against the dominant idea of the dominant Empiricism, that what is basic to language (basic to the way it joins the world, basic to its supply of meaning, basic to the way it is taught and learned) are basic *words*, words which can (only) be learned and taught through "ostensive definitions", Wittgenstein says, among other things, that to be *told* what a word means (e.g., to know that when someone forms a sound and moves his arm he is *pointing to* something and *saying its name*, and to know *what* he is pointing to) we have to be able to ask what it means (*what* it refers to); and he says further: "One has already to know (or be able to do) something in order to be capable of asking a thing's name. But what does one have to know?" (*Investigations*, §30). I want to bring out two facts about this question of Wittgenstein's: that it is not because naming and asking are peculiarly mental or linguistic phenomena that a problem is created; and that the question is not an experimental but a conceptual one, or as one might put it, that the question "What do we call 'learning or asking for a name'?" had better be clear before we start experimenting to find out "how" "it" is done.

It will help to ask: Can a child attach a label to a thing? (Wittgenstein says that giving a thing a name is like attaching a label to something (§15). Other philosophers have said that too, and taken that as imagining the essential function of language. But what I take Wittgenstein to be suggesting is: Take the label analogy seriously; and then you'll see how *little* of language is like that. Let us see.) We might reply: "One already has to know (or be able to do) something in order to be capable of attaching a label to a thing. But what does one have to know?" Well, for example, one has to know what the thing in question is; what a label is; what the point of attaching a label to a thing is. Would we say that the child is attaching a label to a thing if he was pasting (the *way* a child pastes) bits of paper on various objects? Suppose, even, that he can say: "These are my labels" (i.e., that he says <ɤyzir may leybils>). (Here one begins to sense the force of a question like: What makes "These are labels" *say that* these are labels?) And that he says: "I am putting labels on my jars." *Is* he?

Mightn't we wish to say *either* Yes or No? Is it a matter of *deciding* which to say? What is it a decision about? Should we say, "Yes and No"? But what makes us want to say this? Or suppose we ask: In what sense does a child *pay* for something (cp. say something) (e.g., for groceries, or tickets to a puppet show)? Suppose he says "Let me pay" (and takes the money, handing it to the clerk (putting it on the counter?)). *What* did he do?

Perhaps we can say this: If you say "No, he is not putting labels on things, paying money (repeating names)", you are thinking: He doesn't know the significance of his behaviors; or, he doesn't know what labels or money or names are; or, he isn't intending to do these things, and you can't do them without intending to (but is that true?); anyway, he doesn't know what doing those things really would be (and what would be "doing them really"? Is he only pretending to?). If you say "Yes, he is pasting labels on", etc., then won't you want to follow this with: "only not the way *we* do that"? But how is it different?

Maybe you feel: "What else would you say he's doing? It's not wrong to say 'He's pasting labels, paying money, learning names', even though everyone knows that he isn't quite or fully *doing* those things. You see the sense in which that is meant." But what has begun to emerge is how far from clear that "sense" is, how little any of the ways we *express* that sense really satisfy us when we articulate them.

That the justifications and explanations we give of our language and conduct, that our ways of trying to intellectualize our lives, do not really satisfy us, is what, as I read him, Wittgenstein wishes us above all to grasp. This is what his "methods" are designed to get us to see. What directly falls under his criticism are not the results of philosophical argument but those unnoticed turns of mind, casts of phrase, which comprise what intellectual historians call "climates of opinion", or "cultural style", and which, unnoticed and therefore unassessed, defend conclusions from direct access — fragments, as it were, of our critical super-egos which one generation passes to the next along with, perhaps as the price of, its positive and permanent achievements: such fragments as "To be clear about our meaning we must define our terms", "The meaning of a word is the experience or behavior it causes", "We may change the names of things but their operation on the understanding never changes", "Language is merely conventional", "Belief is a (particular) feeling", "Belief is a disposition caused by words (or signs)", "If what I say proves false then I didn't (don't?) know it", "We know our own minds directly", "Moral judgments express approval or disapproval", "Moral judgments are meant to get others to *do* something, or to change their attitudes", "All rationally settleable questions are questions of language or questions of fact", "Knowledge is increased only by reasoning or by collecting evidence", "Taste is relative, and people might like, or get pleasure from anything" . . . If philosophy is the criticism a culture produces of itself, and proceeds essentially by criticizing past efforts at this criticism, then Wittgenstein's originality lies in having developed modes of criticism that are not moralistic, that is, that do not leave the critic imagining himself free of the faults he sees around him, and which proceed not by trying to argue a given statement false or wrong, but by showing that the person making an assertion does not really know what he means, has not really said what he wished. But since self-scrutiny, the full examination and defense of one's own position, has always been part of the impulse to philosophy, Wittgenstein's originality lies not in the creation of the impulse, but in finding ways to prevent it from defeating itself so easily, ways to make it methodical. That is Freud's advance over the insights of his predecessors at self-knowledge, e.g., Kierkegaard, Nietzsche, and the poets and novelists he said anticipated him.

Now let me respond, in two ways, to the statement: "It's not *wrong* to say the child is pasting labels, repeating names; everyone *sees the sense* in which that is meant."

First of all, it is not true that everybody knew that he wasn't *quite* "learning a thing's name" when Augustine said that in learning language he learned the names of things, and that we all "knew the sense" in which he meant what he said. (We do picture the mind as having inexplicable powers, without really knowing what these powers are, what we expect of them, nor in *what* sense they are inexplicable.)

Again, neither Wittgenstein nor I said it was *wrong to say* the child was "learning the names of things", or "paying for the tickets", or "pasting labels on her jars". One thing we have heard Wittgenstein say about "learning names" was: ". . . Augustine describes the learning of human language as if the child came into a strange country and did not understand the language of the country; that is, as if it already had a language, only not this one" (§32). And, in the same spirit, we could say: To describe the child as "pasting labels on his jars" or "paying for the tickets" is to describe the child as if he were an adult (or anyway, master of the adult activity). That is, we say about a child "She is pasting labels on jars" or "He paid for the tickets", when we should also say "She's a mommy" or "He was Uncle Croesus today". No one will say it's wrong (because untrue?) to say *those* things. And here we do begin more clearly to see the "sense" in which they are meant. You *and* the child know that you are really playing — which does not mean that what you are doing isn't serious. Nothing is more serious business for a child than knowing it *will* be an adult — and *wanting* to be, i.e., *wanting to do the things we do* — and knowing that it can't really do them yet. What is wrong is to say what a child is doing as though the child were an adult, and not recognize that he is still a child playing, above all growing. About "putting on labels", "playing school", "cooking supper", "sending out invitations", etc., that is, perhaps, easy to see. But elsewhere perhaps not.

Consider an older child, one ignorant of, but ripe for a pumpkin (knows how to ask for a name, what a fruit is, etc.). When you say "That is a pumpkin" we can comfortably say that this child learns what the word "pumpkin" means and what a pumpkin is. There may still be something different about the pumpkins in his world; they may, for example, have some unknown relation to pumps (the contrivance or the kind of shoe) and some intimate association with Mr. Popkin (who lives next door), since he obviously has the same name they do. But that probably won't lead to trouble, and one day the person that was this child may, for some reason, remember that he believed these things, had these associations, when he was a child. (And does he, then, stop believing or having them?)

And we can also say: When you say "I love my love" the child learns the meaning of the word "love" and what love is. *That (what you do)* will *be* love in the child's world; and if it is mixed with resentment and intimidation, then love is a mixture of resentment and intimidation, and when love is sought *that* will be sought. When you say "I'll take you tomorrow, I promise", the child begins to learn what temporal durations are, and what *trust* is, and what you do will show what trust is worth. When you say "Put on your sweater", the child learns what commands are and what *authority* is, and if giving orders is something that creates anxiety for you, then authorities are anxious, authority itself uncertain.

Of course the person, growing, will learn other things about these concepts and "objects" also. They will grow gradually as the child's world grows. But all he or she knows about them is what he or she has learned, and *all* they have learned will be part of what they are. And what will the day be like when the person "realizes" what he "believed" about what love and trust and authority are? And how will he stop believing it? What we learn is not just what we have studied; and what we have been taught is not just what we were intended to learn. What we have in our memories is not just what we have memorized.

What is important in failing to recognize "the spirit" in which we say "The child, in learning language, is learning the names of things" is that we imagine that we have explained the nature of language when we have only avoided a recognition of its nature; and we fail to recognize how (what it really means to say that) children learn language *from* us.

To summarize what has been said about this: In "learning language" you learn not merely what the names of things are, but what a name is; not merely what the form of expression is for expressing a wish, but what expressing a wish is; not merely what the word for "father" is, but what a father is; not merely what the word for "love" is, but what love is. In learning language, you do not merely learn the pronunciation of sounds, and their grammatical orders, but the "forms of life" which make those sounds the words they are, do what they do — e.g., name, call, point, express a wish or affection, indicate a choice or an aversion, etc. And Wittgenstein sees the relations among *these* forms as 'grammatical' also.

Instead, then, of saying either that we *tell* beginners what words mean, or that we *teach* them what objects are, I will say: We initiate them, into the relevant forms of life held in language and gathered around the objects and persons of our world. For that to be possible, we must make ourselves exemplary and take responsibility for that assumption of authority; and the initiate must be able to follow us, in however rudimentary a way, *naturally* (look where our finger points, laugh at what we laugh at, comfort what we comfort, notice what we notice, find alike or remarkable or ordinary what we find alike or remarkable or ordinary, feel pain at what we feel pain at, enjoy the weather or the notion we enjoy, make the sounds we make); and he must *want* to follow us (care about our approval, like a smile better than a frown, a croon better than a croak, a pat better than a slap). "Teaching" here would mean something like "showing them what we say and do", and "accepting what they say and do as what we say and do", etc.; and this will be more than we know, or can say.

In what sense is the child's ability to "follow" us, his caring what we do, and his knowing when we have and have not accepted the identity of his words and deeds, *learned?* If I say that all of this is natural, I mean it is nothing more than natural. Most people do descend from apes into authorities, but it is not inevitable. There is no reason why they don't continue crawling, or walk on all fours, or slide their feet instead of lifting them; no reason why they don't laugh where they (most) now cry; no reason why they make (or "try" to make) the sounds and gestures we make; no reason why they see, if they do, a curving lake as like a carousel; no reason why, having learned to use the phrase "turn down the light" they will accept the phrase "turn down the phonograph" to mean what it means, recognizing that the factor "turn down" is the same, or almost the same, in both; and then accept the phrases "turn down the bed" and "turn down the awning" and "turn down the offer" to mean what they mean, while recognizing that the common factor has less, if any, relation to its former occurrences. If they couldn't do these things they would not grow into our world; but is the avoidance of that consequence the *reason* they do them?

We begin to feel, or ought to, terrified that maybe language (and understanding, and knowledge) rests upon very shaky foundations — a thin net over an abyss. (No doubt that is part of the reason philosophers offer absolute "explanations" for it.) Suppose the child doesn't grasp what we mean? Suppose he doesn't respond differently to a shout and a song, so that what *we* "call" disapproval *encourages* him? Is it an accident that this doesn't normally happen? Perhaps we feel the foundations of language to be shaky when we look for, and miss, foundations of a particular sort, and look upon our shared commitments and responses — as moral philosophers in our liberal tradition have come to do — as more like particular agreements than they are. Such an idea can give us a sense that whether our words will go on meaning what they do depends upon whether other people find it worth their while to continue to understand us — that, seeing a better bargain elsewhere they might decide that we are no longer of their world; as though our sanity depended upon their approval of us, finding us to their liking.

This vision of our relation to the child prompts me — in addition to my suggestions in the early essays of *Must We Mean What We Say?*, along with the suggestions listed in the present Chapter VI (at the end of the section "The Appeal to Projective Imagination") — to a further characterization of the kind of claims made by philosophers who proceed from an examination of ordinary language, about the kind of validity appealed to when a philosopher says things like "When we say . . . we are implying . . ." or "We wouldn't call that (say) 'recounting' ". In such appeals such a philosopher is voicing (reminding us of) *statements of initiation;* telling himself or herself, and us, how in fact we (must) go about things, not predicting this or that performance. He is not claiming something as true of the world, for which he is prepared to offer a basis — such statements are not synthetic; he is claiming something as true of himself (of his "world", I keep wanting to say) for which he is offering himself, the details of his feeling and conduct, as authority. In making such claims, which cannot be countered by evidence or formal logic, he is not being dogmatic; any more than someone who says "I didn't promise to . . .", or "I intend to . . .", "I wish . . .", or "I have to . . ." is being dogmatic, though what he says cannot be countered, in the usual way, by evidence. The authority one has, or assumes, in expressing statements of initiation, in saying "We", is related to the authority one has in expressing or declaring one's promises or intentions. Such declarations cannot be countered by evidence because they are not supported by evidence. We may, of course, be wrong about what we say and do or will say and do. But that failure is not one which can be corrected with a more favorable position of observation or a fuller mastery in the recognition of objects; it requires a new look at oneself and a fuller realization of what one is doing or feeling. An expression of intention is not a specific claim about the world, but an utterance (outer-ance) of oneself; it is countered not by saying that a fact about the world is otherwise than you supposed, but by showing that your world is other-wise than you see. When you are wrong here, you are not in fact mistaken but in soul muddled.

Projecting a Word

I said that in trying to sketch the vision of language underlying the ap-peals to ordinary language I would have to discuss both what it meant to say that "a word is learned in certain contexts" and what I had in mind in speaking of "appropriate projections into further contexts". It is the second of these topics which is most directly relevant to what more I shall have to say about the limitations of the appeal to ordinary language as a direct criticism of traditional philosophy; but a discussion of the first was necessary to give a concrete sense of the nature of this problem.

If what can be said in a language is not everywhere determined by rules, nor its understanding anywhere secured through universals, and if there are always new contexts to be met, new needs, new relationships, new objects, new perceptions to be recorded and shared, then perhaps it is as true of a master of a language as of his apprentice that though "in a sense" we learn the meaning of words and what objects are, the learning is never over, and we keep finding new potencies in words and new ways in which objects are disclosed. The "routes of initiation" are never closed. But *who* is the authority when all are masters? Who initiates us into new projections? Why haven't we arranged to *limit* words to *certain* contexts, and then coin new ones for new eventualities? The fact that we do not behave this way must be at the root of the fierce ambiguity of or-dinary language, and that we won't behave this way means that for real precision we are going to have to get words *pinned* to a meaning through explicit definition and limitation of context. Anyway, for *some* sorts of precision, for some purposes, we will need definitions. But maybe the very ambiguity of ordinary language, though sometimes, some places, a liability, is just what gives it the power, of illumination, of enriching perception, its partisans are partial to. Besides, to say that a word "is" ambiguous may only be to say that it "can" mean various things, can, like a knife, be used in various ways; it doesn't mean that on any given occasion it *is* being used various ways, nor that on the whole we have trouble in knowing which way it is being used. And in that case, the *more* uses words "can" have, then the *more* precise, or exact, that very possibility might allow us to be, as occasion arises. But let's move closer.

We learn the use of "feed the kitty", "feed the lion", "feed the swans", and one day one of us says "feed the meter", or "feed in the film", or "feed the machine", or "feed his pride", or "feed wire", and we understand, we are not troubled. Of course we could, in most of these cases, use a different word, not attempt to project or transfer "feed" from contexts like "feed the monkey" into contexts like "feed the machine". But what should be gained if we did? And what would be lost?

What are our choices? We could use a more general verb, like "put", and say merely "Put the money in the meter", "Put new material into the machine", "Put film into the camera", etc. But first, that merely deprives us of a way of speaking which can discriminate differences which, in some instances, will be of importance; e.g., it does not discriminate between putting a flow of material into a machine and putting a part made of some new material into the construction of the machine. And it would begin to deprive us of the concept we have of the emotions. Is the idea of feeding pride or hope or anxiety any more metaphorical, any less essential to the concept of an emotion, than the idea that pride and hope, etc., grow and, moreover, grow on certain circumstances? Knowing what sorts of circumstances these are and what the consequences and marks of overfeeding are, is part of knowing what pride is. And what other way is there of knowing? Experiments? But those are the very concepts an experiment would itself be constructed from.

Second, to use a more general verb does not reduce the range of transfer or projection, but increases it. For in order that "put" be a relevant candidate for this function, it must be the same word we use in contexts like "Put the cup on the saucer", "Put your hands over your head", "Put out the cat", "Put on your best armor", "Put on your best manner", "Put out the light and then put out the light".

We could, alternatively, use a more specific verb than "feed". There would be two ways of doing this, either (a) to use a word already in use elsewhere, or (b) to use a new word. In (a) we have the same case as before. In (b) we might "feed eels", "fod lions", "fawd swans", "fide pride", "fad machines". . . . Suppose we find a culture which in fact does "change the verb" in this way. Won't we want to ask: *Why* are these forms different in the different cases? What differences are these people seeing and attaching importance to, in the way these things are (as we say, but they cannot say) "fed"? (I leave open the question whether the "f – d" form is morphemic; I assume merely that we have gathered from the contexts in which it is used that it can always be translated by *our* word "feed".) We could try to answer that by seeing what else the natives would and would not accept as "feeding", "fodding", "fawding", etc. What other animals or things or abstractions they would say they were "fiding" or "fadding" . . . . (I am also assuming that we can tell there is no reason in superficial grammar why the forms are as they are, e.g., no agreement in number, gender, etc.) Could we imagine that there were *no* other contexts in which these forms were used; that for *every* case in which we have to translate their verb as "feed" they use a different form of (the "morpheme") "f – d"? This would be a language in which forms were perfectly intolerant of projection, one in which the natives would simply look puzzled if we asked whether you could feed a lion or fod an eel. What would we have to assume about them, their forms of life, in order to "imagine" that? Presumably, that they saw no connection between giving food to eels, to lions, and to swans, that these were just different actions, as different as feeding an eel, hunting it, killing it, eating it. If we had to assume that, that might indeed be enough to make us call them "primitive". And wouldn't we, in addition, have to assume, not only that they saw them as different, but that these activities *were* markedly different; and not different in the way it is different for *us* to feed swans and lions (we don't hold bread crumbs to a lion's mouth, we don't spear whole loaves with a pitchfork and shovel them at swans) but different in some regularized way, e.g., in the preparations gone through in gathering the "food", in the clothes worn for the occasion, in the time of day at which it was done, in the songs sung on each occasion. . . ? And then don't we have to imagine that these preparations, clothes, times, songs are never used for other purposes, or if they are, that no connection between *these* activities and those of "feeding" are noticed or noted in the language? And hence further imagine that the way these clothes, times, songs are used are simply different again, different the way wearing clothes is from washing them or rending or mending them? Can everything be just different?

But though language — what we call language — is tolerant, allows projection, not just any projection will be acceptable, i.e., will communicate. Language is equally, definitively, intolerant — as love is tolerant and intolerant of differences, as materials or organisms are of stress, as communities are of deviation, as arts or sciences are of variation.

While it is true that we must use the same word in, project a word into, various contexts (must be *willing* to call some contexts the *same*), it is equally true that what will *count* as a legitimate projection is deeply controlled. You can "feed peanuts to a monkey" and "feed pennies to a meter", but you cannot feed a monkey by stuffing pennies in its mouth, and if you mash peanuts into a coin slot you won't *be* feeding the meter. Would you be feeding a lion if you put a bushel of carrots in his cage? That he in fact does not eat them would not be enough to show that you weren't; he *may* not eat his *meat*. But in the latter case "may not eat" means "isn't hungry then" or "refuses to eat it". And not every case of "not eating" is "refusing food". The swan who glides past the easter egg on the shore, or over a school of minnows, or under the pitchfork of meat the keeper is carrying for the lion cage, is not refusing to eat the egg, the fish, or the meat. What will be, or count as, "being fed" is related to what will count as "refusing to eat", and thence related to "refusing to mate", "refusing to obey", etc. What can a lion or a swan refuse? Well, what can they be offered? (If we say "The battery refuses to respond" are we thinking of the battery as stubborn?)

I might say: An object or activity or event onto or into which a concept is projected, must *invite* or *allow* that projection; in the way in which, for an object to be (called) an art object, it must allow or invite the experience and behavior which are appropriate or necessary to our concepts of the appreciation or contemplation or absorption . . . of an art object. What kind of object will allow or invite or be fit for that contemplation, etc., is no more accidental or arbitrary than what kind of object will be fit to serve as (what we call) a "shoe". Of course there are variations possible; because there are various ways, and purposes, for being shod. On a given occasion one may fail to recognize a given object as a shoe — perhaps all we see is a twist of leather thong, or several blocks of wood. But what kind of failure is this? It may help to say: What we fail to see here is not *that* the object in question is a shoe (that would be the case where, say, we failed to notice what it was the hostess shoved under the sofa, or where we had been distracted from our inventory of the objects in a painting and later seem to remember a cat's being where you say a shoe lies on its side), but rather we fail to see *how* the object in question is a shoe (how it would be donned, and worn, and for what kind of activities or occasions).

The question "How do we use the word 'shoe' (or 'see' or 'voluntary' or 'anger' or 'feed' or 'imagine' or 'language')?" is like the question a child once asked me, looking up from the paper on which she was drawing and handing me her crayon, "How do you make trees?"; and perhaps she also asked, "How do you make a house or people or people smiling or walking or dancing or the sun or a ship or the waves. . . ?". Each of these questions can be answered in two or three strokes, as the former questions can each be answered in two or three examples. Answered, that is, for the moment, for that question then. We haven't said or shown everything about making trees or using the expression "But now imagine. . .". But then there is no "everything" to be said. For we haven't been asked, or asked ourselves, *everything* either; nor *could* we, however often we wish that were possible.

That there are no explanations which are, as it were, complete in themselves, is part of what Wittgenstein means when he says, "In giving explanations I already have to use language full-blown . . . ; this by itself shows that I can adduce only exterior facts about language" (*Investigations*, § 120). And what goes for explaining my words goes for giving directions and for citing rules in a game and for justifying my behavior or excusing my child's or for making requests . . . or for the thousands of things I do in talking. You cannot use words to do what we do with them until you are initiate of the forms of life which give those words the point and shape they have in our lives. When I give you directions, I can adduce only exterior facts about directions, e.g., I can say, "Not that road, the other, the one passing the clapboard houses; and be sure to bear left at the railroad crossing". But I cannot *say* what directions *are* in order to get you to go the way I am pointing, nor *say* what my direction *is,* if that means saying something which is not a further *specification* of my direction, but as it were, cuts below the actual pointing to something which makes my pointing finger point. When I cite or teach you a rule, I can adduce only exterior facts about rules, e.g., say that it applies only when such-and-such is the case, or that it is inoperative when another rule applies, etc. But I cannot *say* what following rules is *überhaupt,* nor say how to obey a rule in a way which doesn't presuppose that you already know what it is to follow them.

For our strokes or examples to be the explanations we proffer, to serve the need we see expressed, the child must, we may say, see *how* those few strokes are a tree or a house ("There is the door, there is the window, there's the chimney with smoke coming out. . . ."); the person must see how the object is a shoe ("There is the sole, that's for the toe . . ."); how the action was — why you call it one, say it was — done in anger ("He was angry at. . .", "He knew that would hurt", "That gesture was no accident", "He doesn't usually speak sharply to his cat". . .). Those strokes are not the only way to make a house (that is not the only instance of what we call a shoe; that is not the only kind of action we call an affront, or one performed voluntarily) but if you didn't see that and how *they* made a house, you probably wouldn't find or recognize any other ways. "How much do we have to imagine?" is like the question, "How many strokes do we have to use?"; and mustn't the answer be, "It depends"? "How do we know these ten strokes make a house?" is like the question, "How do we know that those ten words make that question?". It is at this level that the answer "Because we know the grammar of visual or verbal representation" is meant to operate.

Things, and things imagined, are not on a par. Six imagined rabbits plus one real rabbit in your hat do not total either seven imagined or seven real rabbits. But the very ability to draw a rabbit, like the ability to imagine one, or to imagine what we would feel or do or say in certain circumstances, depends upon the mastery of a form of representation (e.g., knowing what "That is a pumpkin" says) *and* on the general knowledge of the thing represented (e.g., knowing what a pumpkin is). That language can be represented in language is a discovery about language, one which shows the kind of stability language has (viz., the kind of stability an art has, the kind of stability a continuing culture has) and the kind of general knowledge we have about the expressions we use (viz., the kind we have about houses, faces, battles, visitations, colors, examples . . .) in order to represent or plan or use or explain them. To know how to use the word "anger" is to know what *anger* is. ("The world is my representation.")

I am trying to bring out, and keep in balance, two fundamental facts about human forms of life, and about the concepts formed in those forms: that any form of life and every concept integral to it has an indefinite number of instances and directions of projection; and that this variation is not arbitrary. *Both* the "outer" variance and the "inner" constancy are necessary if a concept is to accomplish its tasks — of meaning, understanding, communicating, etc., and in general, guiding us through the world, and relating thought and action and feeling to the world. However many instances or kinds of instances of a concept there are — however many kinds of objects we call shoes — the word "shoe" *can* be (verbally) defined, and in that sense has *a* meaning (cf. Berkeley, *Principles,* Introduction, section 18). The aspect of meaning I am trying to get at, that condition of stability and tolerance I have described as essential to the function of a concept (the use of a word), can perhaps be brought out again this way: to say that a word or concept has a (stable) meaning is to say that new and the most various instances can be recognized as falling under or failing to fall under that concept; to say that a concept must be

tolerant is to say that were we to assign a new word to "every" new instance, no word would have the kind of meaning or power a word like
"shoe" has. Or: there would *be* no *instances,* and hence no concepts either.

It is one thing to say that words have both connotation and denotation
and that these are not the same; it is something else to try to say *how*
these are related to one another — beyond remarks at the level of "on the
whole (with obvious exceptions) they vary inversely". The level at which
I could wish an answer to this question would be the level at which we
could answer the questions: How do we know that an instance "falls under" a concept?; or: How, having a word "defined" ostensively, do we
know *what* point or points of the displayed object the ostension is to
strike? (Is that even a fair formulation of the problem? For upon *what*
specific point or *definite* set of points does the "ostensive definition" of,
e.g., a monkey or an organ grinder turn? There would be definite points
only where there are definite alternatives — e.g., the difference between
an Old World and a New World monkey.) Or: What is the difference between regarding an object now as an individual, now as an example? One
way of putting the problem about examples (and hence one problem of
universals) is: How is the question "Of *what* is this object (say what we
call a shoe) an example?" to be answered? One wants to answer it by holding up the shoe and crying out, "Why, an example of this!". Would it
help to hold up a different shoe? If you did, and someone then replies,
"*Now* I see what it (the first shoe) is an example of", what would he have
seen? (This seems to be what Berkeley's idea of a particular idea (or object) representing others of "the same sort" amounts to.)

I might summarize the vision I have been trying to convey of the tem-
pering of speech — the simultaneous tolerance and intolerance of words —
by remarking that when Wittgenstein says *"Essence is expressed by grammar"* (§371), he is not denying the importance, or significance, of the
concept of essence, but retrieving it. The need for essence is satisfied by
grammar, if we see our real need. Yet at an early critical juncture of the
Investigations, the point at which Wittgenstein raises the "great question that lies behind all these considerations" (§65), he imagines someone
complaining that he has "nowhere said what the essence of a language-
game, and hence of language, is: what is common to all these activities,
and what makes them into language. . ."; and he replies: ". . . this is
true. — Instead of producing something common to all that we call language, I am saying that these phenomena have no one thing in common
which makes us use the same word for all." He then goes on to discuss the
notion of "what is common" to all things called by the same name, ob-

viously alluding to one familiar candidate philosophers have made to bear the name "universal" or "essence"; and he enjoins us, instead of saying "there *must* be something in common" — which would betray our possession by a philosophical "picture" — to *"look and see"* whether there is. He says that what we will actually find will be "a complicated network of similarities overlapping and criss-crossing: sometimes overall similarities, sometimes similarities of detail. . . . I can think of no better expression to characterize these similarities than 'family resemblances' " (§66, §67); and it looks as if he is here offering the notion of "family resemblances" as an alternative to the idea of "essence". But if this is so, his idea is empty, it explains nothing. For a philosopher who feels the need of universals to explain meaning or naming will certainly still feel their need to explain the notion of "family resemblance". That idea would counter the idea of universals only if it had been shown that family resemblance is all we need to explain the fact of naming *and* that objects may bear a family resemblance to one another and may have *nothing* in common; which is either false or trivial. It is false if it is supposed to mean that, asked if these brothers have anything in common and we cannot say what, we will say "Nothing at all". (We may not be able to *say* very well what it is, but we needn't, as Wittgenstein imagines to be our alternative, merely "play with words" and say "There is something common to all. . . namely the disjunction of all their common properties" (§67). For that would not even *seem* to say, if we see something in common among them, what we see. We might come up with, "They all have that unmistakeable Karamazov quality". That may not tell you what they have in common, but only because you don't know the Karamazovs; haven't grasped their essence, as it were.) Or else it is trivial, carries no obvious philosophical implication; for "They have nothing in common" has as specific and ordinary a use as "They have something in common" and just as Wittgenstein goes on to show ordinary uses of "what is common" which do not lead us to the idea of universals (cf. §72), so we can show ordinary uses of "there is nothing common to all" (which we *may* say about a set of triplets) which will equally not lead us *away* from the idea of universals.

But I think that all that the idea of "family resemblances" is meant to do, or need do, is to make us dissatisfied with the idea of universals as explanations of language, of how a word can refer to this and that and that other thing, to suggest that it fails to meet "our real need". Once we see that the expression "what is common" *has* ordinary uses, and that these are different from what universals are meant to cover; and, more importantly, see that concepts do not usually have, and do not need "rigid limits", so that universals are neither necessary nor even useful in explaining how words and concepts apply to different things (cf. §68); and again, see that the grasping of a universal cannot perform the function it is imagined to have, for a new application of a word or concept will still have to be *made out, explained,* in the particular case, and then the explanations themselves will be sufficient to explain the projection; and see, finally, that I *know* no more about the application of a word or concept than the explanations I can give, so that no universal or definition would, as it were, *represent* my knowledge (cf. §73) — once we see all this, the idea of a universal no longer has its *obvious* appeal, it no longer carries a *sense* of explaining something profound. (Obviously the drive to universals has more behind it than the sense that the generality of words must be explained. Another source of its power is the familiar fact that subjects and predicates function differently. Another is the idea that all we can know of an object is its intersection of essences.)

I think that what Wittgenstein ultimately wishes to show is that it *makes no sense* at all to give a general explanation for the generality of language, because it makes no sense at all to suppose words in general might *not* recur, that we might possess a name for a thing (say "chair" or "feeding") and yet be willing to call *nothing* (else) "the same thing". And even if you say, with Berkeley, that "an idea [or word] which considered in itself is particular, becomes general by being made to represent or stand for all other particular ideas of the same sort" (*Principles,* Introduction, section 12) you still haven't explained *how* this word gets used for these various "particulars", nor what the significance is if they don't. This suggests that the effort to explain the generality of words is initiated by a prior step which produces the idea of a word as a "particular", a step of "considering it in itself". And what *is* that like? We learn words in certain contexts. . . . What are we to take as the "particular" present here? Being willing to call other ideas (or objects) "the same sort" and being willing to use "the same word" for them is one and the same thing. The former does not explain the latter.

There is a Karamazov essence, but you will not find it if you look for *a* quality (look, that is, with the wrong "picture" of a quality in mind); you will find it by learning the grammar of "Karamazov": it is part of its grammar that *that* is what "an intellectual Karamazov" is, and *that* is what "a spiritual Karamazov" is, and *that* is what "Karamazov authority" is, . . . Each is too much, and irresistible.

To ask for a general explanation for the generality of language would be like asking for an explanation of why children acquiring language take what is said to them as consequential, as expressing intention, as projecting expectations which may or may not be satisfied by the world. But do we imagine that we know why we (non-children) take what is said and what is written as inconsequential, as without implication, as not mattering? It seems to me that growing up (in modern culture? in capitalist culture?) is learning that most of what is said is only more or less meant — as if words were stuffs of fabric and we saw no difference between shirts and sails and ribbons and rags. This could be because we have too little of something or too much, or because we are either slobs or saints. Driven by philosophy outside language-games, and in *this* way repudiating our criteria, is a different way to live, but it depends on the same fact of language as do the other lives within it — that it is an endless field of possibility and that it cannot dictate what is said *now,* can no more assure the sense of what is said, its depth, its helpfulness, its accuracy, its wit, than it can insure its truth to the world. Which is to say that language is not only an acquirement but a bequest; and it is to say that we are stingy in what we attempt to inherit. One might think of poetry as the second inheritance of language. Or, if learning a first language is thought of as the child's acquiring of it, then poetry can be thought of as the adult's acquiring of it, as coming into possession of his or her own language, full citizenship. (Thoreau distinguishes along these lines between what he calls the mother tongue and the father tongue.) Poetry thereby celebrates its language by making it a return on its birth, by reciprocating.

It is of immediate relevance to what I have been asking about Wittgenstein's view of language, and indicates one general and important limitation in my account, to notice that in moving, in Part II of the *Investigations,* to "figurative" or "secondary" senses of a word (which Wittgenstein explicitly says are not "metaphorical senses", cf. *Investigations,* p. 216), Wittgenstein is moving more concentratedly to regions of a word's use which cannot be assured or explained by an appeal to its ordinary language games (in this, these uses are *like* metaphorical ones). Such uses have consequences in the kind of understanding and communication they make possible. I want to say: It is such shades of sense, intimations of meaning, which allow certain kinds of subtlety or delicacy of communication; the connection is intimate, but fragile. Persons who cannot use words, or gestures, in these ways with you may yet be in your world, but perhaps not of your flesh. The phenomenon I am calling "projecting a word" is the fact of language which, I take it, is sometimes responded to by saying that "All language is metaphorical". Perhaps one could say: the possibility of metaphor is the same as the possibility of language generally, but what is essential to the projection of a word is that it proceeds, or can be made to proceed, *naturally;* what is essential to a functioning metaphor is that its "transfer" is *unnatural* — it breaks up the established, normal directions of projection.

VIII

The Quest of Traditional Epistemology:
Closing

The position we have arrived at is this. Having taken the force of the traditional investigations of our claims to know that the world exists to depend upon their proceeding in terms of our ordinary investigations of claims to knowledge; or: having interpreted Descartes's claim for the "reasonableness" of his grounds for doubt to be explicated as a claim that those doubts "arise naturally", where that, in turn, means that any competent speaker of the language will know that they are relevant and know what their implications are; I arrived at a point at which I said that the basis offered by the philosopher as the basis of a claim to know that an object exists was not entered fully naturally, and that this suggested that the ground for doubt could in turn not be fully natural. But I also said or implied that it was not fully unnatural either, because, in the philosopher's context, though it may seem odd or forced, it does not seem *absurd*, ignorable; and because if the philosopher's request for a basis is accepted as a real question, then the bases he offers are the right, or anyway the only, bases which would seem natural; and the grounds for doubt are then forced by the nature of the investigation itself, viz., an investigation of something's being, or seeming, amiss concerning knowledge as a whole, represented in a generic object. And I said that no direct repudiation of these slightly unnatural questions by appealing to what should ordinarily be said could be fully convincing and that the reasons for this were (1) that it was not clear that the philosopher has "changed the meaning" of his words, because although the contrasts he is *led* to (viz., seeing it vs. seeing all of it; sensing it vs. knowing what it is in itself; behavior vs. the feeling itself) are not the same contrasts with which he *began* his assessment (viz., seeing or sensing it vs. being told about it; knowing what I feel vs. knowing what he feels), they are contrasts which in certain contexts are perfectly correct ones, and it is not obvious that they are not correct in the philosopher's context; and (2) it is not obvious that, or how, the philosopher's contexts are "incompletely described", both because they seem to be described well enough, and because in the investigation of something amiss it cannot in the nature of the case be obvious beforehand what we need to include in a description; and (3) that the unnaturalness alone (as shown by appeals to *more* natural occurrences of the questions) cannot or ought not of itself be regarded by the ordinary language philosopher as a conclusive repudiation of those questions in that context because the nature of the vision of language underlying that mode of criticism must itself prevent *flat* repudiation. To explain what I meant by this last point, I broke off my discussion of the nature of traditional philosophy in order to characterize that vision of language.

What I meant was this: If words and phrases *must* recur (which means, as I put it, that they must be projected into new contexts, which means that new contexts must tolerate or invite that projection); and if there are no rules or universals which *insure* appropriate projection, but only our confirmed capacity to speak to one another; then a new projection, though not at first obviously appropriate, may be made appropriate by giving relevant explanations of how it is to be taken, *how* the new context *is* an instance of the old concept. If we are to communicate, we mustn't leap too far; but how far is too far? If two masters of a language disagree about the appropriateness of a projection, then it cannot be obvious who is right. If this is a linguistic conflict, then one side will win out. Language does not develop every way it *could* develop; and any way it develops, which becomes shared, will be "natural". But in the philosophical conflict about "what should be said" the peculiarity is that neither side just "wins out". As long as there are "sides" here, each must remain convinced that it alone is right. Then each party to the conflict will find his or her personal solution to an intellectually intractable historical crossroads.

If we take the ordinary language philosopher's investigations to show successfully that the traditional philosopher's considerations are not *fully* natural, that should force the traditional philosopher to wonder whether his repudiation of ordinary language is as solid as it seems, or at the least to demand of himself a fuller conceptualization of the conflict than Descartes's simple assurance, repeated (or something like it) as often as the drift of his investigation is repeated, that we are "nearly deceived by the terms of ordinary language" (second Meditation). But if this lack of full naturalness is to represent a permanent criticism of the results of the traditional philosopher, then what has to be shown is that he does not mean what he thinks he means by words whose meaning is shared by all masters of the language, that the *way* he has made his context "invite the projection" has itself prevented his meaning what he wishes to mean, what he *must* mean if his conclusion is to mean what it says, if the *words* he uses mean what they say, for example, that we *do not see* objects because we do not see all of any object.

How might we convince ourselves that someone "does not mean what he or she says" where the sense of this criticism is that such a one "does not mean what his or her words say" or "does not know (appreciate) what he or she is saying"? This is a very particular set of terms of criticism, not coming down to the charge, for example, that someone is "speaking hastily or loosely", which may or may not be a serious matter and which a traditionalist may claim to be true of all of us, including himself, most of the time, since our ordinary language hardly allows for anything else. Nor does the criticism amount to saying, as certain ordinary language critics have liked to say, that the traditional philosopher has "changed the meaning" of his terms, for, to go no further, that leaves inexplicable the interest in whatever it is the philosopher *is* saying, or means to be. Or perhaps that term of criticism just is a loose and rude way of saying that what the philosopher says *is* of no interest.

A hint that the traditional epistemologist's words do not mean what he says (what he wishes his words to mean), that his words are out of his control, arises in our having noted that in the way in which the epistemologist initially considers the concept of seeing or sensing, it occurs as a *way*, the obviously most *basic* way, of knowing anything about what there is in the world; but in the course of his investigation of his examples, the notion of seeing is used as the basis of a particular *claim* to knowledge. When, however, in ordinary cases, "I see it" is used as a particular basis, then the context is one in which there is some obvious way in which the object is not "in full view" (at least, not to the person questioning the claim). It follows from what I was saying about a new context "inviting a projection" that the epistemologist must undertake to *show* that his object, in his context, is not in full view. This is what I take his suggestions, "Do you see all of it?", "How much do you see?", "You don't see the back half", (as meant) to do. And don't they? Not if these suggestions themselves do not enter naturally, or are not projected with an understandable invitation. And are they?

And again I have to say: neither fully naturally nor fully unnaturally; which means (in terms of the preceding chapter) neither fully acceptably nor fully unacceptably; which, again, perhaps means: neither wholly without sense nor with a fully clear sense. And what it may mean to say *this* about a word or a phrase must be investigated. What *is* "the meaning of a word"? And if we say "the meaning is the use", then the question arises, "Does a word have *no* meaning apart from its various uses?". Then how *can* it be projected into further contexts? And why, then, would dictionary definitions mean *anything* to us? Let me try to make myself clearer.

The Philosopher's Ground for Doubt
Requires Projection

There are many different kinds of contexts in which the question "How much of it did you . . . ?" or "All of it?" may be asked. Imagine them being asked in response to each of the following assertions:

1a. I polished the table.
 b. I scratched the table.
2a. I played the Brahms concerto.
 b. I played the violin.
3. I smoked the cigarette.
4a. I ate the apple.
 b. I bit the apple.
5a. I swept out the room.
 b. I decorated the room.
 c. I entered the room.
6a. I nicked the cup.
 b. I broke the cup.
 c. I dropped the cup.
7a. I hit the target.
 b. I hit the ball.
8a. I noticed the envelope.
 b. I glanced at the envelope.
9a. I see a New Orleans goldfinch.
 b. I see the ship (coming over the horizon).
 c. I see Father.
 d. I see the envelope (when it is in full view).

For some of these cases the questions "How much?" and "All of it?" have a clear sense, in others no apparent sense at all, and in others we may say that they have a sense which is neither perfectly clear nor completely unclear. I will say they "have some sense".

The first two sorts of cases readily stand out. The questions make perfectly clear sense when asked of (1a) ("I polished the table"), (2a) ("I played the Brahms concerto"), (3) ("I smoked the cigarette"), (4a) ("I ate the apple"), etc., but they have no apparent sense when asked of (5c) ("I entered the room"), (7a) ("I hit the target"), (8a) ("I noticed the envelope"). But in many of the cases it is not obvious whether the sense is totally clear or totally absent. What might it mean to ask whether you played all of the violin (2b), or how much of the table you scratched (1b), or whether you dropped the whole cup (6c)? But there might be a point in these questions. Asking our questions about the violin might be explained as asking whether you tested it by playing chromatic scales on each string to the top of the finger board, or it might be asking whether you used higher positions where they would have enhanced the tone or made the phrasing smoother; about scratching the table they might suggest that the purpose was to determine whether an undercoat of paint had been used over the entire painted surface; asking whether you dropped the whole cup would make clear sense if, say, the cup in question was a magician's prop composed of two halves, one of which, when a gull from the audience is asked to drink from it, falls off when he tips the cup to his lips.

"To make *some* sense" then seems to mean "to make clear sense in some context". But that is all "to make *clear* sense" can mean; for that cannot mean "to make clear sense in all contexts". So what is the difference between "making clear sense" and "making some sense"? It obviously is a function of whether what we may call the application of the question is clear; whether, we might also say, the context in which it makes clear sense is itself obvious without explanation, or we might say naturally clear, or whether instead it *has* to be "figured out", or "specifically explained".

But it is hard to know how to understand this difference more securely. After all, one of Wittgenstein's most insistent warnings is that the application of an expression may *seem* apparent, but that this appearance may itself be the product of philosophical distortion. It may then help to say: expressions I have characterized as "having some meaning" (sense) are ones whose application is not apparent — a *sense* (feeling) of something slightly odd is always present in them; and ones in which coming to see what a real application would be demands "figuring out" what the expression might mean in a way coming to see the real application of an expression by which we have been misled (e.g., "point to the color") does not demand this, but only requires "putting it back into its ordinary language game". But mightn't we also say?: what we *do* when we figure out a real application is to construct an ordinary language game for the expression. Or should we say?: give a (real, possible) language game for it. But I find I still want to add: and "possible" means "an *ordinary* one". Perhaps the reason I feel the need to add that is brought out by comparing an expression which "has some sense" with expressions about which Wittgenstein says "their grammar needs to be explained" (e.g., "The rose has teeth in the mouth of a beast"). About these he says or implies that various explanations might be "perfectly good" ones ("because one has no notion in advance where to look for teeth in a rose" (*Investigations*, p. 222)). But about expressions which have some sense — as it were, a sense that needs *completion* — we feel that there is a *right* context for its use, and that "figuring out" its application is a matter of hitting upon *that* context. In such cases we haven't the same freedom. It's as though we feel that all we need do is exercise the very capacity for projection upon which language as a whole depends. We have freedom, but we are also subject to the same requirement of all projection, that its appropriateness be made out in terms of the "invitation to projection" by the context; we have to show *how* the new context is an instance of this old concept.

This requirement is brought sharply to mind if we notice that although in the cases in which the questions "How much?" and "All of it?" were said to "make clear sense" that sense depended on our having in mind quite definite, limited contexts in which the questions are imagined as being raised; or better, quite definite contexts in which the answer to the question would be a flat Yes or No. But this is also more flexible than it may seem. If I ask "Have you eaten all of the apple?" and you answer flatly "Yes", then what will your response be if I walk over to look and say, "But you haven't eaten it all; you've left the core, and the stem and the seeds to waste"? You *may* tolerate that. Perhaps that is my form of life with apples; I "eat apples" that way and that is not so bizarre but that you may be willing to accept my version of "eating all the apple" and fit yours to it, conceding, "I ate all of it except the core". But this tolerance has its limits. If on another occasion someone objects, "But you haven't smoked all of the cigarette, you have left the whole filter to waste", then even if he normally drags on the filter until the ash gives out, and then chews and swallows the rest, we are not likely to accede to his version of "smoking the whole cigarette" and effect a reconciliation between his and our version of that activity, saying, "Well, I smoked it all except the filter": his way of "smoking" is *too* bizarre. You can't talk to everyone about everything. If someone objects to our claim to have decorated the entire room on the ground that we have left spaces between the bric-a-brac, or failed to place an object everywhere one would fit (physically), we might feel, "You have a different conception of 'decorating' than I have" or even, "You don't know what decorating is". You can't share every pleasure with everyone. If someone says we haven't played all of the Brahms concerto on the ground that we played only the *violin* part, then we probably won't feel for a moment that he has a *different* concept of "playing a concerto"; either he has no concept of *that* at all, or else he's implying something about the specialness of the orchestral work in *this* concerto, which he had better begin making explicit.

Sometimes it is not clear how far our obligations run for making explicit a new projection. The question "All of it?" makes some sense, maybe enough for the purpose at hand, and maybe represents the only, or best, way of finding out what you want to know, when it is asked about "I broke the cup". There *may*, that is, be a point in asking whether you broke *all* of the cup: on one side there is a gold monogram which you want to preserve if possible; or you can fix the cup if all that happened was that the handle came off sheer, as often happens with these cups. But what will be the point of questioning whether you broke all of it if all you mean is that there may be *some fragment or other* which could be broken into smaller fragments? To be told "But you haven't broken it all; here is a part (fragment) which isn't broken" might strike us as a joke. But suppose our questioner then collects all the pieces which are large enough to display the original glaze, and places them carefully in a barrel half full of such fragments. He then explains that he uses them to make fish bait, or as presents to give the natives on his trading route. And suppose they work. We see what his question *means,* and not just because he's given it a *plausible* use; he has got concepts, our concepts, of "breaking something" and of "breaking all of something", and he has shown *how* the concept projects into this context in a way we can all understand. We may not find much use for this projection; in the future when we break a cup we may not accept the question "Did you break all of it?" as perfectly clear, in need of no special explanation, and capable as it stands of a flat answer. Still, it doesn't get in our way; *he* has an interest which makes the question useful — a use for that projection of the concept — and his interest and use isn't incompatible with any of ours. You don't have to talk to everyone about everything.

Now when the philosopher asks, in his context, "Do you see *all* of the envelope?", then we are, I suggest, not able to answer with a flat Yes or No — the question does not have a *clear* sense; but we are also not completely at a loss, do not simply feel that the question has *no* sense. As in other cases of this sort, we require some explanation of the intended projection (an explanation of *how* this context invites the concept ("amount seen")); or we have to "figure out" what the appropriate projection must be. Of course we've read the story before and know the ending, so we may refuse to look for the appropriate projection, to try to find out how it is invited, and say that the philosopher's question is just flatly unacceptable. But that is not true according to the characterization of "flatly unacceptable" we have given. Or: that explanation, that reason for not answering it, is *prima facie* weaker than the philosopher's reason for asking it. For he has a reason for asking it — he *must* ask it, given the structure of his investigation — *and* he goes on to undertake to show its appropriateness. Whereas the ground for *refusing* to (so much as try to) answer it seems, at this stage, merely to be that it leads to skepticism, an undesirable conclusion. But that is hardly an acceptable reason for not answering.

But if my suggestion that the question is not *fully* natural, that it lacks a *clear* sense, is right (and that much is something I take considerations of "how we ordinarily use" the expression to *show*), then its appropriateness must be made clear by the questioner. And this, as has been said, is how I construe the philosopher's familiar continuation: "You don't see the back, and you don't see the inside." And now the question is: Does this continuation make out an appropriate projection; has the philosopher successfully shown how his context invites this projection of his expression? Is it just too bizarre, the way the concept of *smoking* was in the case of "You haven't smoked the filter"? Or does it just indicate an ignorance or complete lack of the concept of *seeing an object,* as the cases of one construal of "You haven't played the orchestra parts" and of "You haven't decorated *this* spot" seemed to indicate an ignorance or lack of this concept of "playing a concerto" or "decorating a room". It seems to me clearly not to show any of this. And yet it is not easily tolerable either, the way "You haven't eaten the core" or "You haven't broken this piece" may be. Because we cannot, as in the case of the apple, "effect a reconciliation" with the way *he* sees objects, *giving* him his way, and conceding, "Right you are. I see all of it but the back and the inside". Nor, as I put it in the case of the cup, is his interest in seeing objects, his use for the concept, so special as not to interfere with ours. That use does get in our way. We have to be able to talk to everyone about what we see, and tell them how much of an object we can see. Everyone, that is, with whom we can talk about something.

This is an instance in which something the philosopher says conflicts with "our ordinary beliefs", or, as is now emerging, with our ordinary concepts. But, of course, what he says equally conflicts with *his own (ordinary)* interests as well — he is going to have to use the concept of seeing the way we do sometimes, normally. He admits as much explicitly when he says that he is, in the context of his philosophizing, using the word "see" in a special, or "stricter than ordinary" sense. He wishes to effect *that* reconciliation, offer *that* concession. And this is another way of saying that, perhaps of beginning to see why, his conclusions are "unstable".

The Philosopher's Projection Poses a Dilemma

How in particular does the statement "But you don't see the back half, and you don't see the inside" *explain* or *show how* the concept of "the amount you see" is invited by a context in which ordinarily we would say the object is "in full view"? Well, as suggested, by showing that in some way — a way we hadn't noticed, or considered, or been sufficiently interested in — it is not, after all, in full view. And how is that to be done? Again, it seems clear that it must be done the way it is ordinarily done: "not in full view" must mean what it ordinarily means or else the philosopher would never have supposed that he has discovered what he supposes he has discovered.

In their ordinary use "You don't (didn't) see all of it" or "It isn't in full view" means that part of the thing is *hidden, concealed, blocked from view*. This can happen either (1) when some object is screening it from full view, or (2) when part of the object, as it were, is getting in its own way, or (3) some significant part is not turned toward you, or not open to view. The first case is obviously irrelevant to the philosopher's context, so what he is relying on, so far as his words mean what they say, is some version of (2) or (3). An instance of the second case would be your not seeing all of the chair's back because the arm of the chair was in the way (so you don't know the stain was or was not there at 8:00 p.m.); an instance of the third would be your not having seen the part with the initials on it (so you don't know it was *this* camera case you saw).

Accordingly, if the phrase "You don't see all of it" means what it ordinarily means, then it implies that there is some definite object of whose existence or presence we have claimed to know; that some part of that object is hidden; where "some part" means "some definite part" whose identity and significance is established independently of the (merely geo-metrical-physical) fact that it is then and there not visible from your po-sition — or rather, since apart from such independent establishment there may *be* nothing to call a "part", no "it" you can't see (apart from the ini-tials there would, or may, be no "part" which had or failed to have, the initials on it, but only some *area*, or even, some *location*, where initials may or may not have appeared), we might better say: the "part not seen" must be established independently of the (merely geometrical-physical) fact that some area or other, some fragment or some location or other, is then and there not visible from your position.

But what may be, or count as, a "part" can be established in various ways: it *may* be a named part of the object (its back, its armrest, the filter, the core, etc.); but it may only be describable as "the part with the initials or the scratch on it", or as "the red part", or as "a piece large enough to retain the original glaze". So our question becomes: Does "the back half", as used by the philosopher, serve to *establish a part* of the object, a part which is concealed?

Let us bring to mind the sort of ordinary circumstances in which such an expression would clearly establish a part. Take this example: We have a set of differently colored spheres of equal size and differing weights and we wish to estimate the weight of each of them as accurately as possible, no scale being available. Suppose we decide to float those we can in water and notice their varying displacements, and suppose I am recording the results which you call out to me. You will say things like: "Red is half submerged", "White is two-thirds submerged", "Green sank", etc., and I then enter against the item "red" the fraction "$\frac{1}{2}$", and against the item "white" the fraction "$\frac{2}{3}$", and so on. Suppose in the case of the blue sphere you are unsure whether to say it is five-eighths or three-fourths submerged. I might look at it myself, and if I concur in your indecision, I could, as a substitute for a fraction, enter a diagram (say, a circle with a line drawn across it representing the position of the water line) against the item "blue", and in that way *show* the amount remaining above the surface. And this diagram will explicitly *distinguish the parts* above and below the water line. So I can say: It is by virtue of being interchangeable with such a diagram that terms like "back (or top) half" distinguish a *part* of an object. And what makes such diagrams mean what they mean is not, as it were, the geometry and physics of the circumstances them-selves, but the fact that geometry and physics are given application to an object by the context in question.

Suppose we tried, in a similar manner, to diagram the result of the philosopher's investigation into the "amount" of an object we see. The diagram might be an ordinary drawing, or it might be traced on a duplicate object, or on the original object itself *considered* as diagrammatic — as, one might say, a model of itself. How will we diagram the philosopher's statement, "You don't see the back half"? Suppose we take a duplicate object and draw a great circle around it, distinguishing the front from the back half. And now we point to the (now distinguished) back half of our model and say "We don't see *that*". Does that make sense? (We know that it does not mean that we do not or can not see the back half of the *model*. Do we not?) It would make perfect sense if the original object were itself, in that context, comparably distinguished (by submergence, partial obstruction by another object, color, initials or scratches, etc.). But if the original object is not thus distinguished into parts, the model, as it were, has no application, no point of contact with its original.

That the generic object taken as exemplary by the traditional epistemologist has no special markings is essential to his investigation. Is it, nevertheless, distinguished into parts? It may be replied: "Doesn't the analogy you have just given show that it is, and show how it is? Just one great circle whose plane is perpendicular to a given line of vision can be inscribed on a sphere. That is a fact of geometry. Say, if you like, that it is not that fact *alone* which establishes two parts of an object; but then it can be replied that it is the very making of such a diagram as you imagine which establishes the parts. When the epistemologist says 'You don't see the back half' *you know where to draw the line;* that is *given* by the geometrical and visual circumstances themselves. So, after all, what you call the 'application' of the geometrical concept 'half' *is* given by the geometry and visual circumstances of the context itself."

I wish to give two answers to this suggestion. First, when I spoke of "establishing a part" I meant that in connection with what I had said about "projecting a concept". (The epistemologist has to *explain* or *show* the applicability of the expression "back half" to his context; it does not there "make *clear* sense". The reply we recently heard, to the effect that the act of diagramming itself establishes the part, concedes that much.) To make the projection acceptable you have then to *treat* the part (the broken fragment of cup, the core) in comprehensible ways. (Parts of objects for which there are common names have obvious and particular interests or uses.) That means that to imagine the "back half" as established by the act of diagramming and by the geometry and visual circumstances of the context themselves you have to imagine that what then happens, as it were, confirms that establishment, have to conceive that life with that object *continues* in such a way that "the back half" — which, according to the suggestion in question, can only mean *the* half distinguished from *that* point of vision by *the* great circle whose plane is perpendicular to it — is never seen, never visible.

Thus this skeptical picture is one in which all our objects are moons. In which the earth is our moon. In which, at any rate, our position with respect to significant objects is *rooted,* the great circles which establish their back and front halves fixed in relation to it, fixed in our concentration as we gaze at them. The moment we move, the "parts" disappear, or else we *see* what had before been hidden from view — from any other position than one perpendicular to *that* great circle, *that* "back half" which alone it establishes *can be seen:* to establish a *different* "back half", a *new* act of diagramming will be required, a new position taken, etc. This suggests that what the philosophers call "the senses" are themselves conceived in terms of this idea of a geometrically fixed position, disconnected from the fact of their possession and use by a creature who must *act.* This further suggests an explanation for the "instability" of the general skeptical conclusion which has so often roused our curiosity, that experience Hume described as one of his natural beliefs "returning" when he left his study for the common world of men, and his philosophical questions seeming "cold, strained and ridiculous". Apart from the *specific* establishing or re-establishing of some "part" of an object which we do not see by a specific conducting of the philosopher's investigation (a new rooting of our position, a new concentration to fix the great circle) there *is* nothing — no *thing* — we do not see: objects are (again?) "in full view".

The second answer I wish to give to the suggestion we imagined (to the effect that the philosophical investigation itself establishes the part) is this. Let's grant that what is diagrammed on the model *does* successfully make contact with its object, and apart from rooted positions and special efforts of concentration; i.e., grant that the object does indeed have some feature (scratch, color, glaze, etc.) which does in fact distinguish it into halves. Then to hold up the diagrammed model, point to its back half, and say: "*That* is what we do not see" will, if we are properly positioned, be flatly true. Only then that will be a clearly local fact about the particular object of which our diagrammed object is the faithful model, carrying no implication about all objects, in particular not a statement about the diagrammatic object itself.

Now we have a formulation of the philosopher's conclusion which poses this dilemma: Either the model in terms of which we, and he, must understand his statements fails to fit its original object, becomes a model of nothing — unless we *make* it fit by distorting our life among objects (and hence distorting our "concept of an object *überhaupt*"?) or by constructing an idea of "the senses" which extirpate them from the body; or else it fits its original faithfully, in which case it carries no implication about the validity of our knowledge as a whole — no one would there suppose that because we couldn't see all of *that* object that therefore we never see "all" of *any* object.

In the latter case, what we say is true, it is a *fact*, flatly right about that object and our position with respect to it, and no general skeptical conclusion is suggested; in the former case, the skeptical suggestion is not a *fact*, and not about our world, in which eyes and bodies go together and in which objects do not inevitably keep exactly "one side" turned towards us.

That will hardly constitute a refutation of skepticism, much less of the traditional epistemological procedure as a whole. Even if it is on the right track, too much is being left out. For one thing, we still have no analysis of the concept of *seeing* which could explain how the various contexts in question alter "how much" is "seen". For another, we have not touched the question of the relevance of the epistemological investigation in determining the phenomenology of our experience of objects, but have only considered it as the assessment of the claim to know of their existence. (These two interpretations are later briefly compared; cf. below, the section entitled "Two interpretations . . .".) Again, and glaringly, the stage at which we have attacked the procedure still leaves us with *objects* in the world, whereas if other considerations could convince us that the existence of objects is problematic, we could not appeal to our life with objects as proving the irrelevance of the conclusion to our world.

But the dilemma we have come upon must itself give us pause, *if* it is granted that the traditional epistemologist takes it to be a *fact* that we do not (literally) see objects, and therefore that we cannot claim to *know* (with certainty, beyond doubt) of their existence, *and if* the way he establishes this depends upon his following faithfully the ordinary ways human beings have of assessing any claim to knowledge, which in turn means following faithfully the use of ordinary expressions in contexts in which they make clear sense. For again, and more urgently, we must wish to know how, proceeding in ways which are not obviously subversive of ordinary expressions and their meaning, the philosopher has had to produce a ground for doubt which leads to a dilemma of the sort I just characterized. This throws us back upon the basis the philosopher takes as supporting the claim to knowledge he investigates, for the *direct* function of a ground for doubt is to counter the given basis and *therewith* the claim it supports.

The Philosopher's Basis; and a More Pervasive Conflict with His New Critics

Just how does the consideration (ground for doubt) "But you don't see all of it" counter the basis "I see it"? The continuation of such considerations ("You don't see the back half, nor the inside") leads to a statement of *"All* you see" or "All you *really* see", as, namely, at most the front surface; and from there it is taken to follow (or: that is taken to *mean*) that you don't see *it,* namely, the object (or: the object itself) and hence don't *know* it exists. And again, this set of steps is far from unobjectionable. In an ordinary case, where figuring out or going over a situation (by reconstructing it in fact or in imagination) to determine how much (or *what,* or *all*) you *really* saw or could see, leads to a conclusion that you do not or did not "see it" and hence don't know that *it* was or is there — in such an ordinary case the "it" in question has been specifically identified, and there is no suggestion that it is never visible, cannot be seen on *any* occasion. "You didn't see the part with the initials on it, so you don't know it was *this* camera case you saw. *What you saw* may have been a different case, perhaps *this* one." Or of course, it may not have been a real camera case at all, but a decoy, or indeed it may have been no *object* you saw, but only a queer reflection of light or a shadow. But it doesn't *follow* from "all you *really* saw" that *"all* you saw" was a colored patch of a particular shape: it may have been that, or it may have been lots of other things; you may not know what it was, what you saw, but it looked like a camera case from your position then and there; moreover, it may indeed have been *this* camera case (the one with the initials on it), but you aren't in a position to claim to know it was.

So why the epistemologist supposes it to follow from the "fact" that you don't see something (all of, a part of, something) that therefore what you saw and see is something else (a different *kind* of object) is a problem. A *problem.* To confront the *conclusion* with a direct appeal to ordinary language is useless, and worse. To say, in criticism, as for example Martin Lean has said, that "It is true, but trivial, to point out that at any one moment we are seeing or touching only a part of the surface of something . . .", is empty. It is as full a "misuse" of language as anything in the skeptic's repertory. Lean is directly criticizing an analysis by C. D. Broad, about which he had said earlier, "that is what 'seeing . . . [something]' is like; that is what the expression *means*" (*Sense-Perception and Matter*, p. 68). To say this is surely tempting, but it is useless. It is worse than useless, because that criticism violates the very expressions and draws the very inference which has raised our suspicion, and thereby seems to vitiate that whole mode of appeal. For to say that seeing a part *is* seeing the object, is what "seeing something" *means*, assumes *both* that "a part" has a clear meaning in reference to generic objects in full view, and that something *follows* (trivially) about *what* you see when *all* you see (what you "only" see) has been determined.

Let us bear in mind that a "basis" is a statement which supports a particular claim; the rejection of the claim through the countering of the basis (and not through showing it to be "manifestly false") depends upon that. And the philosopher produces a particular example whose fate, in the course of his investigation, seems to tell the fate of knowledge as a whole. My question now is: *Is* the example the philosopher produces imaginable as an example of a particular claim to knowledge? What are his examples examples of?

I think his answer would be, in effect: "They are examples of what it is to know something", or "They are examples of what goes on when we know something". (Cf. e.g., Moore, *Some Main Problems*, p. 25.) But it is of the first importance to recognize that this is not a fully satisfying answer. For *when* are we "knowing something"? Do I know (now) (am I, as it were *knowing*) that there is a green jar of pencils on the desk (though I am not now looking at it)? If I do know now, did I not know before I asked the question? I had not, before then, said that or thought it; but that is perhaps not relevant. If someone had asked me whether the jar was on the desk I could have said Yes without looking. So I did know. But what does it mean to say "I did know"? Of course no one will say that I *did not* know (that I wasn't knowing). On the other hand, no one would have said of me, seeing me sitting at my desk with the green jar out of my range of vision, "He knows there is a green jar of pencils on the desk", nor would anyone say of me now, "He (you) knew there was a green jar . . .", *apart from some special reason which makes that description of my "knowledge" relevant* to something I did or said or am doing or saying (e.g., I told someone that I never keep pencils on my desk; I knew that Mrs. Greenjar was coming to tea and that she takes it as a personal affront if there is a green jar visible in the room . . .).

Perhaps one feels: "What difference does it make that no one would have *said*, without a special reason for saying it, that you knew the green jar was on the desk? You *did* know it; it's *true* to say that you knew it.

Are you suggesting that one sometimes cannot say what is true?" What I am suggesting is that "Because it is true" is not a *reason* or basis for saying anything, it does not constitute the point of your saying something; and I am suggesting that there must, in grammar, be reasons for what you say, or be point in your saying of something, if what you say is to be comprehensible. We can understand what the *words* mean apart from understanding why you say them; but apart from understanding the point of your saying them we cannot understand what *you* mean.

Now we have come, or come again, and most generally, to what sometimes strikes me as the deepest of the conflicts between traditional philosophy and its new critics who proceed from what is ordinarily said. These conflicts, I take it, began with Moore's way of finding, and refuting, theses of past philosophers which directly, or implicitly, contradicted what everyone would say who was using words in their ordinary meaning; and "what everyone would say" seems primarily to have meant, to Moore, "what everyone *knows to be true*": a philosophical thesis cannot be true if it contradicts (explicitly or implicitly) what everyone believes, or rather knows, to be true. (What I mean by "implicitly" is just this: In his "A Defense of Common Sense" Moore argues that it cannot be true to say "Time is unreal", if this implies, as Moore takes some philosophers to have implied, that such a "proposition" as "The earth has existed for many years past" is, at least partially, false; for such a proposition "is the very type of an unambiguous expression, the meaning of which we all must understand", and it is one which "we *know*, with certainty, to be [wholly] true". What we may not know is the *correct analysis* of its meaning.) In this way Moore's efforts constituted, whatever else their motive, a defense of common sense.

But in the work of Wittgenstein and Austin (though Austin seems to share part of Moore's animus), appeals to "what we ordinarily say" take on a different emphasis. In them the emphasis is less on the *ordinariness* of an expression (which seems mostly to mean, from Moore to Austin, an expression not used solely by philosophers) than on the fact that they are *said* (or, of course, *written*) by human beings, to human beings, in definite contexts, in a language they share: *hence* the obsession with the *use* of expressions. "The meaning is the use" calls attention to the fact that what an expression means is a function of what it is used to mean or to say on specific occasions by human beings. That such an obvious fact should assume the importance it does is itself surprising. And to trace the intellectual history of philosophy's concentration on the meaning of particular words and sentences, in isolation from a systematic attention to their concrete uses would be a worthwhile undertaking. It is a concentration one of whose consequences is the traditional search for the meaning of a word in various realms of objects, another of which is the idea of perfect understanding as being achievable only through the construction of a perfect language. A fitting title for this history would be: Philosophy and the Rejection of the Human.

Wittgenstein's motive (and this much is shared by Austin) is to put the human animal back into language and therewith back into philosophy. But he never, I think, underestimated the power of the motive to reject the human: nothing could be more human. He undertook, as I read him, to trace the mechanisms of this rejection in the ways in which, in investigating ourselves, we are led to speak "outside language games", consider expressions apart from, and in opposition to, the natural forms of life which give those expressions the force they have. (The emphasis on diagnosis is not shared by Austin, who is in this respect, as in others, a more Enlightenment, or anyway English, figure.) What is left out of an expression if it is used "outside its ordinary language game" is not necessarily what the *words* mean (they may mean what they always did, what a good dictionary says they mean), but what we mean in using them when and where we do. The point of saying them is lost.

And how great a loss *is* that? To show how great is a dominant motive of the *Investigations*. What we lose is not the meaning of our words — hence, definitions to secure or explain their meaning will not replace our loss. What we lose is a full realization of what we are saying; we no longer know what *we* mean. Wittgenstein's "methods" in philosophy are guided by the realization that the goal of philosophy cannot be found in the classical "search for a definition". This is something I had in mind in speaking of the "deepest conflict" between the tradition and the new philosophy. Let me suggest two ways in which the problem may be thought about.

Why do we use the expression "what he said" to refer both to the *words* he used, and to what he *meant* in using them? Or: why can we answer the question "What did he say?" either by *repeating* his words or *reporting* his thought (what he was telling about, informing us of)? We could, competently, report what he said by using entirely different words, indeed words whose sense or reference *he* wouldn't understand — and not because they are in a language he doesn't understand. You could *report* what he said, when what he said was "Madame, there's a man dancing on your roof", by saying "He said that Rodney's up to his tricks again". (And this fact has implications about the logical and epistemological problems connected with "indirect discourse", problems we will meet more insistently when we come to the question, central to the understanding of moral judgment, of "saying what (= describing, reporting what) somebody did".) We may feel, however, that if you use the *same* words he used then you cannot fail to report what he said, and that *therefore* "what he said" refers both to his words and to his thought. But is that true? If his words were "The rain in Spain stays mainly in the plain" your saying "He said that the rain in Spain . . . etc." will fail to report what he said (his thought) if, for example, he was working on Eliza Doolittle's speech (in which case his thought was obvious, but not about Spain) or if he was using his words in some special way (metaphorically, as part of a particular code, etc.). To reply "But normally people don't use words in such special ways" would doubtless be true, but merely to say that obscures the fact that to know what a person has said you have to know that he or she has *asserted* something, and know what he or she has asserted. What difficulty is there in that? No difficulty, nothing is easier. But what is easy, then, is to understand the point of his words; for that is essential to knowing that he has asserted something and knowing what he has asserted. And that is what is left out when we look upon what he meant as *given* by, or derived from, the meanings of the words he used. (Cf. Russell: ". . . sentences . . . have a meaning derivative from that of the words that they contain. . . ." *Meaning and Truth*, p. 30.) If the connection between "our words" and "what we mean" is a necessary one, this necessity is not established by universals, propositions, or rules, but by the form of life which makes certain stretches of syntactical utterance *assertions*.

I glance at the notion of assertion (saying *that* such-and-such is so) only to suggest a place we may begin to understand how the *saying* of something is essential to what is meant and how someone "may not know what he means" in the sense in which that becomes important in understanding unnatural remarks made by philosophers. The sense in which words and meaning are "necessarily" connected, and in which that necessity is established "only" "conventionally" is brought out in imagining our asking: "*What* assertion did he make when he said 'S is P'?" Don't we feel like answering, impatiently?: "Why, *that* assertion; *that S is P!*" It is in response to this sense that we must dig *below* the conventional facts of assertion to something that explains them, gives their content in securer form than mere words, that Wittgenstein says: ". . . [we] can adduce only exterior facts about language" (*Investigations*, §120). And I can say: Normally words are used to mean what they say. If not there would be nothing to think of as speech.

Here is another way in which the problem of the relation between saying and meaning can be thought about. Someone may feel that, far from its being *necessary*, the connection between the words someone uses and the meaning (point) with which he uses them (= what he uses them to say) is quite arbitrary: words can be used to mean all sorts of things; there is no limit to what anyone may mean by using certain words; it is always a matter of probabilities. All this (all but the final explanation) may be perfectly true; but what is true about it? Asserting something (like refusing something, like calling hamsters, or singing Schubert, like screaming in pain, or screaming at a doll) is a thing people do; and as always not just *anything* people do will *be* asserting, calling, etc. (And what goes for human actions goes for human passions as well: you *can* be "angry at (or amused, or bored by . . .) a fish or a cloud, etc.", but not just anywhere and when.) What are the conditions under which a linguistically grammatical stretch of sound is an assertion? I am interested here merely in suggesting that there *are* conditions, not in trying to elicit a rationalized list of them. Let me suggest two of them, which apply (separately) to those regions of the concept of "saying something" related to *telling* someone something, and to *remarking* something.

If an utterance is meant to tell someone something, then what you say to him must be something he is in a position to understand, and something which is, or which you have reason to believe will be, informative, something which is news to him. The first of these conditions is obvious enough, but it has all the hidden difficulties we discussed in investigating the idea of *teaching* a word. (Consider, for example, what it would mean for a physicist to "tell" me, a child in the subject, what a pi-meson is, or that *that* (streak in the photograph) is the track of a pi-meson. He can tell me this only in the sense in which I can tell my three-year-old daughter who Beethoven is, or that *that* (picture in the book) is Beethoven. She and I, in the respective worlds in which we are children, will both be able to repeat the words we are given, and in the future point to the pictures and say the right word; but we will not exhibit the criteria which go with knowing what these things are; my world cannot compass pi-mesons.) But I shall say no more about this now. The second point is nearer our present concern.

Suppose, although I thought you did not know (were not aware of) what I have said to you, you have recently found out. You may say, "Yes,

I know". But not just anything said to you, which you know, will be greeted with such an acknowledgment. If I say "I have five fingers" or "This is an envelope" or "We are all in this room" or "I see you", you are not going to say "I know" apart from some way of conceiving how I might suppose you might *not* have known. And the question "How do you know?" would be puzzling in the same way if asked in response to any of these utterances. But then *how do I know them?* I mean, *do* I?

It is on the ground that philosophical statements like "My sensations are private" or "Only *I* feel *this*" (pinching myself) or "When I said the word I had a quite particular experience" are not *informative* (though they are uttered, in philosophizing, as though they are), that they say nothing, that Wittgenstein objects to them; *not* on the ground, as critics of his have supposed, that they are "unverifiable" (cf. Pole, p. 96; and Strawson's review of the *Investigations,* p. 92). It is true that they "cannot" be verified only in the sense that it would make no sense to try to; nothing would count as (grammatically *be*) *verifying* them. "Not saying anything" is one way philosophers do not know what they mean. In this case it is not that they mean something *other* than they say, but that they do not see that they mean *nothing* (that *they* mean nothing, not that their statements mean nothing, are nonsense). The extent to which this is, or seems to be, true, is astonishing.

"But", someone will still feel, "all these statements are *true,* and it is outrageous to say that they 'cannot' be said. Surely you can simply *remark* something without that being something the person may not have known". This just means: for an utterance to be a "remark" (for it to *remark* something) is an alternative way of its achieving competence as an assertion (alternative to its being intended to *tell* someone something). And to remark something equally has its conditions. Of course you may "simply remark" or note or register the presence of something, or that something is so. But that does not mean that just anything, just any time, can (grammatically, comprehensibly) be remarked. You can no more remark just any fact (say, the telephone receiver's hanging on its hook, or an envelope's being *in* my hand as I am opening a letter), under just any circumstance, than you can contemplate or appreciate or become absorbed in just anything: that an art object is an object which is fit for holding attention, allowing contemplation, inviting appreciation . . . as much determines the nature of art, the criteria of art (what we are going to *call* "art" and the "criticism of art") as what is fit to sit on determines what we are going to call a "chair" and "mending a chair". (When should we say of someone hacking a leg off of a chair that he is "mending the chair"?) That in certain contexts "anything and everything" can be re-marked or contemplated . . . may be true (though we might try imagin-ing what it would be like to remark the relation of two grains of sand on a beach, or to contemplate a crumpled handkerchief, or to become ab-sorbed in a pin — I don't say you *can't*). My point is only that where some special context is required, it must be supplied, imagined.

To say "Anything can be remarked" has about the force of saying, "Anything and everything can be named". This is true anywhere the "thing" in question can be pointed to, or otherwise identified — true, we may say, where there is a "this" or "that" or "it" to bear a name. And can't just anything qualify as such a "that"? It can if you make it one. How might you, and for what purpose, make a "that", a bearer of a special name, out of the third cat you see during the day, or out of the part of the fingernail which is neither its moon nor its white tip, or out of the corner of cubical objects which is nearest the north pole, or out of a combination of any or all of these potential — or, for all I know, actual — name-bearers? That we do not normally *have* to *make* name-bearers into subjects ("this's" and "that's") is true and important: language could not function as it does without a mutual and common agreement about *what* is being named or pointed to. And this depends on our sharing a sense of what is remarkable, or on our attention being drawn in similar directions by similar occurrences; depends upon these in as ultimate a way as it depends on our having similar capacities of sense and action. And it depends upon a sense of what claim will have point in certain contexts, and a knowledge of what the point is.

Recall what happens when we don't find the same things remarkable or absorbing or noticeable or "worth saying", and try to imagine what it would be like if that began to happen all the time. Part of what you would have to imagine is a world in which we were unmoved by one an-other's remarks, as if born bored. It is not that what we would then say to one another would be false; and perhaps our words would remain mutually intelligible. I think we might say we would become uncompre-hensive of one another; or perhaps curiosities for one another.

We must hear one final response to what I have been trying to convey. "The only oddness or unnaturalness in saying 'He knows the jar is on the desk' is just that it is so flamingly *obvious* that he knows; and if you're going to try to convince us that just because it is odd in *that* sense, that therefore we cannot or ought not say it then you're trying to convince us that we cannot or ought not say something which is true, true in spades. And that is just outrageous."

I might content myself with replying simply that that is not outrageous to me, and add that it only seems outrageous to someone in a certain grip of philosophizing, someone with the sense of the philosopher as Recording Angel, outside the world, neither affecting it nor affected by it, taking stock. But I do not wish to content myself with that reply. For I am in no way hoping, nor would I wish, to convince anyone that certain statements cannot be made or ought not be made. My interest in statements is in what they do mean and imply. If "cannot" or "ought" are to come in here at all, then I confess to urging that you cannot say something, *relying on what is ordinarily meant in saying it,* and mean something other than would ordinarily be meant (and what reason is there to suppose that the philosopher is relying on anything more or other than what is ordinarily meant by such a statement as "He knows . . .", or that he would want to if he could?); and I confess to urging that you ought, if you sense yourself trying to mean something slightly forced (which is, often, sensing the "oddness" in what you say), to try to determine what (fantasy, thought, feeling) may be prodding you to this attempt, being expressed in it ("acted out", a psychoanalyst might say).

There is an oddness about the oddness a philosopher may wish to characterize as "odd only because obvious". For of course it needn't at all be odd to say, "He knows there is a green jar on the desk". It may, e.g., be a way of saying "That's *all* he knows" (I haven't told him about Mrs. Greenjar's sensitivity; or, he's too stupid, or callous, to care about the implications of his actions). And here "know" contrasts with something he does not know or realize, as it does normally. Or it might be an exasperated way of saying "He ought to know better" (than to put a green jar in the same room with my pet bull). And here "know" contrasts with something he might be *expected* to know or remember. To take a statement to be competently made is to provide for it a context ("fix reality" if necessary) in which it would make good sense (*not* be "odd") to say it. The philosopher's progress then appears to be this: first to deprive a statement of such a context, then to fix reality, or construct a theory, which provides this sense another way. And the question I have constantly pushed at us is: "Why? Why does only *his* way satisfy him?"

What is odd about the philosopher's "odd because obvious" just is that *he makes it odd,* or rather, makes it (takes it as) obvious; for it is only if you *take* the statement "He knows . . ." as flamingly obvious that it will seem odd. So we are led to ask: Why does he wish to take such a statement as flamingly obvious?

I can find two sorts of answers to that question, one having to do with the deep hold an idea (or conception or "picture") of language has over philosophers — which indicates its strength, not their weakness; the other having to do with more substantive ideas (or fantasies) of what the world, or the mind or knowledge or actions, etc., must be. The second sets of ideas are no doubt, in part, the result of the first, as is often urged in recent philosophizing; but they also have roots and causes independent of that (e.g., in ideas sanctified, and with reason, by the new science of the sixteenth and seventeenth centuries — which is *our* science, so far as we are not scientists).

I am not going to try to say anything about this second answer, beyond suggesting its saturation by an idea of causation whose origins, in its recent effects, seem to have been the corporealism of the new science, an idea which conquered philosophy (except for Kant and those who can be called post-Kantians, including Wittgenstein) and has retained its power in philosophy long after its exile from physics. Here we find appeals to the causal effects of physical objects on the visual apparatus, to the idea that words and sentences cause reactions in us, that beliefs are psychological states (or, in Hume, "lively impressions") caused by repetition, etc., to the idea that reasons which are not related deductively or inductively to the statement they support are "therefore" causally related — all of this without any detailed knowledge of *what* these "processes" are or how the relevant mechanisms really function. This picture has as dominating an influence on a conception of language as the other way around — a conception in which the "implications" of what we say are either assessible in terms of formal logic or else they are "merely" "psychological". That is the idea I want to say another word about now; it is again something I had in mind when I spoke of the "deepest conflict" between the tradition and its new critics.

In being presented with this picture, one could, of course, reply: "Well, in talking together we just *do* rely on implications which formal logic cannot capture, and that just shows a limitation of logic." But it is not at all clear that this *is* a limitation of logic (how could logic be limited, except by something logic itself discovers?). Or one could say "Ordinary language has no exact logic" (Strawson, "On Referring", p. 52), but so far as I can make good sense of that statement it either: destroys the point it ought to be making — which is that the actual use of language carries "implications" which are of course not deductive, but which are nevertheless fully controlled in our understanding of one another: there is no reason in logic why *that* should be "pointing to an object" and *that* "pointing to a color", and a very good reason in logic why this should

not be so (viz., because its notation is unsystematic, and useless for purposes of calculation), and no reason in logic why, if you say "Now I hear
you", you "must" imply that before this moment there was something
specific preventing your hearing me (and not that since hearing is a
physiological or causal process always going on in the present moment,
in a *now,* you can indifferently say "I hear you" and "I hear you now"),
but these are as hard facts of the way we speak as the fact that "The cat
is on the mat" and "The mat is on the cat" do not mean the same thing
even though all and only the same words appear in each; or: it means that
a logical transcription does not exhaust the meaning of the expression
from the natural language it transcribes — which is either obvious, irrelevant, or a virtue: if a logician claims that a transcription does exhaust the
meaning, all the meaning that is really clear, that is something else, but
what then needs to be shown is not that logic cannot capture language,
but that the logician is trying to do the wrong thing.

Now what has calling a statement obvious (obviously true) got to do
with maintaining the idea that justifiable implications are logical ones?
Just that calling it obvious is an *alternative* to saying that it "implies" a
statement or "presupposes" a background of such kinds as resist assessment in terms of formal logic. It will be noticed that when I supplied
obvious contexts in which "He knows there is a green jar on the desk"
may *not* be odd, I had to say something like, "To say that might imply . . ." or ". . . would mean the same as saying . . .", etc. And just as
"implies" here does not mean "yield deductively", so "means the same"
here does not mean "deductively equivalent". My argument depended
upon an appreciation of the fact that *saying something* may "imply"
something which *what is said* alone would not imply. If that idea galls
you, you may be willing to stomach a little oddness for the sake of an
obviousness which makes the idea unnecessary.

That philosophers who are thus willing do (can) themselves *recognize*
this oddness should itself show us that *merely* pointing out that "we
should not ordinarily say" these things in the spirit in which they are said
in philosophy (that it would be "odd" to say them) is not, in itself, likely
to seem to them a very formidable criticism. What I am banking on are
the following two possibilities. First, that if one could explain why this
idea is galling, it would seem less galling than it does. This explanation
would be importantly furthered if it could be shown that the implications
of speaking and the implications of what is said are not in conflict with
one another. The implications of speaking are settled before logic begins
its work of transcription and calculation — they are not implications

which logical inference could, or is meant to, criticize, but, as it were, are selected among in the way any given formalization is instituted, in what its premises themselves record. (This is the way I interpret Frege's having said, in the *Begriffschrift:* "In my formalized language . . . only that part of judgments which affects the *possible inferences* is taken into consideration. Whatever is needed for a valid inference is fully expressed; what is not needed is for the most part not indicated . . ." (p. 3).) If this can be made out, it would help us see that the illogical or unlinguistic connection between formal logic and natural language is a detriment neither to logic nor to language, and indeed to see what we should give up if we were deprived of either of them. That still, of course, would leave unexplained why we can come to *feel* a conflict between them. Second, that if one could show that the oddness is more important than it seems; or more importantly, that it does not meet "our real need" (that the satisfaction a philosopher finds in the answers which depend on this oddness are not fully or really satisfying to *him*); he (we) may be less willing to stomach it. And this will force us to try, however distasteful the process, to look for a better understanding of what galls us, and no longer to accept the bitterness we feel as fully justified by the behavior of others.

I hope this will have given some weight to the way I am answering the response I imagined to my having said that no one would *say* "There is (I know there is, he knows there is) a green jar of pencils on the desk" apart from there being, or seeming to be, some point in saying it; or, apart from a way of seeing how his or my knowledge of that fact is relevant to what he is or I am doing (which would include saying, asking . . .). The response I imagined was: "Perhaps no one would have *said* that you knew the jar was there, but you *did* know it. It makes sense to say you knew it." I have, in effect, replied: Certainly it makes sense. And that just means that we can easily imagine circumstances in which it *would* make sense to say it. (Cf. *Investigations,* §278.) It does not mean that *apart* from those circumstances it makes (clear) sense. The point is not that you sometimes cannot say (or think) what is the case, but that to say (or think) something is the case *you must say or think it,* and "saying that" (or "thinking that") has its conditions. The philosopher feels that he must say and think beyond these conditions; he wants to speak without the commitments speech exacts.

I could express this by saying: In philosophizing we come to be dissatisfied with answers which depend upon *our* meaning something by an expression, as though what *we* meant by it were more or less arbitrary. (As we sometimes feel about our more obviously moral commitments that they are more or less arbitrary, and that if they are to have *real* or full power they must be rooted in, or "based upon", a reality deeper than the fact of morality itself.) It is as though we try to get the world to provide answers in a way which is independent of our responsibility for *claiming* something to be so (to get God to tell us what we must do in a way which is independent of our responsibility for choice); and we fix the world so that it can do this. We construct "parts" of objects which have no parts; "senses" which have no guiding function; become obsessed with how we can know "the pain itself" in a context in which the question "Why do you think this expression of pain gives a false picture of it?" has no answer (e.g., "You're responding more in fear of the machine than to the pain, the pain itself isn't so bad"; "The worst thing is the aftereffect of the anesthetic, the pain itself is less than you'd imagine"); convince ourselves that what we *call* something does not tell us what it is in a context in which the questions "What would *you* call it?" or "What else might it be?" have no answers (e.g., "You call it peace, but it is a desert", "You call it sacrifice, but it is murder"). And we take what we have fixed or constructed to be *discoveries* about the world, and take this fixation to reveal the human condition rather than our escape or denial of this condition through the rejection of the human conditions of knowledge and action and the substitution of fantasy. Why this happens, how this happens, how it is so much as possible for this to happen, why it leads to the conclusions it does, are further questions — questions not answered by claiming, for example, that we have "changed the meanings of our words", "been inattentive to their ordinary meanings", "misused our language".

I've been saying: When, in philosophizing, we feel we must say "He does know it (whether we should *say* that or not)" this is said in a context in which "How does he know it?" has no answer, or not the right kind of answer. Now I ask: What answer does it have? Well, e.g., "He just looked at it", "He remembers it is there", "He must glance at it a hundred times a day" . . . and so on. A passage from the *Investigations* comes to mind: "What kind of reason have I to assume that my finger will feel a resistance when it touches the table? What kind of reason to believe that it will hurt if this pencil pierces my hand? — when I ask this, a hundred reasons present themselves, each drowning the voice of the others. 'But I have experienced it myself innumerable times and as often heard of similar experiences . . . , etc.' " (§478). The point of this passage is not that what are being called "reasons" are not true enough statements; nor that if they weren't true, we shouldn't believe what we believe, know what we know; nor even that, in *certain* circumstances, they might not be good and real reasons for what we claim we know. It is rather that, in the context in which these "reasons" are proffered, they are inoperative *as reasons*. If the mechanic tells me that my automobile will start now, his reason is not going to be — unless he is chiding my absent-mindedness — that now the ignition is turned on (though it is true that if it weren't turned on, the car wouldn't start); nor will his reason be — unless he is abusively telling me that I wouldn't understand anyway — that now the wires won't turn into string (though if the car were "wired" with string then no doubt the car wouldn't start). You can say, as Kant does, that for a thing to be as it is, all the conditions of its being what and where it is must be given with the thing; but it doesn't follow that knowing or saying the thing is as it is, is knowing or saying that all its conditions are present. That we "cannot" list "all the conditions" is not a disability we must sustain; for the notion of "all the conditions", in Kant's absolute survey, is not intelligible; or rather, it is a fantasy.

Wittgenstein's "hundred reasons" do not add up to a reason; nor do they form a set of (one hundred) reasons. What I meant by saying that the question "How does he know the green jar is on the desk?" hasn't the right kind of answer can be put this way: those hundred reasons are, roughly, the same reasons we would give to the questions, "How does he know his name?", "How does he know he has five fingers?", "How does he know the jar will fall if he releases it from his grasp?", "How does he know the sun will rise tomorrow?". Offering such "reasons" is not offering grounds for eliciting belief in a particular claim I have made, but protestations of knowledge, entreaties that I be credible. No one of them, in their rootlessness, would remove a doubt; they are signs to ward off doubt.

The Philosopher's Context Is Non-claim

My guiding assumption has been that the validity of the method(s) used in the tradition depends, and is meant to depend, on nothing more than the methods any competent speaker of a language would use in assessing concrete claims to knowledge. But our recent glimpse of the grammar (conditions) of saying (claiming) something may be enough to give content to my now noticing that *no concrete claim is ever entered as part of the traditional investigation*. The examples meant as illustrating "what happens when we know something" are not examples of *claims* to know something; to ask us to imagine a situation in which we are seated before the fire is not to ask us to imagine that we have claimed (to know or believe) that we are seated before the fire. I will say: the example the philosopher is forced to focus upon is considered in a *non-claim context*. I characterized the procedure of a philosopher like Austin as *"imagining a context* (in which a specific claim is being, or would be, made)". Analogously I shall say: the traditional philosopher *"imagines a claim to have been made* (in a context we need merely to remember, go over in more detail)". The significance of this difference is this: If the epistemologist were not imagining a claim to have been made, his procedure would be as out of the ordinary as the ordinary language philosopher finds it to be. But, on the other hand, if he were investigating a claim of the sort the coherence of his procedures require (or going over in imagination a context in which a concrete claim has in fact been made) then his conclusion would not have the generality it seems to have.

Perhaps it will be remarked: "A while ago, in suggesting that a criticism of your discussion of the conditions of assertion (claiming) might take the form of a suggestion that 'one can say anything which is true', you replied that such an idea amounted to saying that one can give 'Because it is true' as a serious reason or basis for a claim. Does this really fit the philosopher's case? He does give a serious basis for his claim, viz., 'Because I see it'; surely that is not as empty as you suggest. And, given a serious basis, isn't the claim thereby established as a real one?"

But if we bear in mind that a basis is itself (or contains) a claim, and therefore is subject to the same conditions as any claim is, what we find is that this basis suffers the same misfortune as the original claim it supports. In particular, in the philosopher's context, "I see it" (or "By means of the senses") is not entered as the specific basis of a specific claim, but arises initially, as has been said, as a general way of knowing anything about the world.

Every man entertains a great number of beliefs concerning material things, e.g., that there is a square-topped table in this room. . . . It is plain that all these beliefs are based on sight and touch. . . : based upon them in the sense that if we had not had certain particular experiences of seeing and touching, it would be neither *possible* nor *reasonable* to entertain these beliefs. [Price, *Perception*, opening sentence]

When I see a tomato there is much that I can doubt. I can doubt whether it is a tomato that I am seeing, and not a cleverly painted piece of wax. I can doubt whether there is any material thing there at all. Perhaps what I took for a tomato was really a reflection; perhaps I am even the victim of some hallucination. [*Ibid.*, p. 3]

Price's expression, "When I see a tomato", has the force of "whenever I see any object". Similarly, when Moore begins his investigation of "what it is that happens, when you see it" with a view to describing what it is "[we] did actually see", what he says is: "We should certainly say (if you have looked at it) that we all *saw* that envelope . . . *the same* envelope" (*Some Main Problems*, p. 30). But "should say" here only means: there are occasions on which we would in fact say this, claim it. But this is not one of them. For what is envisioned in the statement that "We should certainly say (if you have looked at it) that we all *saw* . . ."? Is "say" here to suggest what it suggests in a context like, "You would say ('judge'), wouldn't you, that you got a good look at it"? I think not, for in such a context we were either obviously in a poor position for viewing the thing, or else prepared to discover that a trick had been played and that we were in an *un*obviously poor position for seeing what the thing was. But an occasion on which we are prepared for a patent trick, or in which there are obviously poor conditions, will not have the crucial carry-over to knowledge in general, it will not be an instance of a "best" case of knowledge. (Though, one might say, the possibility of conjuring tricks and the possibility of skepticism, are the same. Their intellectual consequences, however, are not the same; what we learn from them is not the same. To say that a phenomenon is a "trick" may itself be a satisfying explanation of it.)

I take it that Moore's use of "say" means that we should certainly claim, if we looked at it, that we all saw it. But, taken literally, that is mad: it suggests that whenever any of us sees anything we claim to see it, e.g., that flower, its shadow, this sheet of paper, the piano as I look up, etc. — everything catches our attention, every moment. "Obviously," it will be said, "he doesn't mean that." No; he can't mean that; yet he must somehow mean that we would somehow claim to see it; and the reason he has for supposing that we would is simply — that we looked at it. And that is not enough to secure that supposition.

Perhaps you will feel that this is unfair, that all Moore is saying is that you should certainly claim (if you have looked) that you saw it *if asked* whether you did. But what does this come to? Is he to be taken to mean that each of us is in a *position* to claim to see it? Is that enough for him? "Being in a position" to lend you five dollars is not the same as lending you five dollars. And just as not just anything I do will be lending you five dollars (I send you a check for five dollars in the mail out of the blue), and not just anything you do will be asking me for a loan of five dollars (you send me a picture of a check for five dollars in the mail out of the blue), so not just anything I say will be telling you, or confirming, or agreeing, that I see the envelope in your hand. "But it's so flamingly obvious that you do see it! You aren't going to say you *don't* see it." No; and I am not going to go up to a stranger and tell him that I won't lend him five dollars either. (Though that is true, too.) "All right, but don't you?" I could reply, "Are you really asking me?" For if you are, then I imagine a context in which that might be something you need to know, and that your asking implies I may (am in a position to) know, and then considerations about how much I see may well be relevant. Or I might, by now, humor you and say, "Yes, all right, I see it. Well?" But in *that* mood I'm not very receptive to the suggestion that all of knowledge is at stake in my affirmation. For the rehearsal of "what we all believe", " 'should' all say we see", with which the classical epistemologists invariably begin, and which has the force of neutralizing any practical context while yet making the grounds for doubt seem real, is now disengaged from your question. And it won't achieve skepticism under its own steam.

The "dilemma" the traditional investigation of knowledge is involved in may now be formulated this way: It must be the investigation of a concrete claim if its procedure is to be coherent; it cannot be the investigation of a concrete claim if its conclusion is to be general. Without that coherence it would not have the obviousness it has seemed to have; without that generality its conclusion would not be skeptical.

This is no more than a schema for a potential overthrowing or undercutting of skepticism. Its contribution to such a project is, I think, its linking, and a certain shaping, of the ideas of obviousness and generality (instead, for example, of evidence and certainty) as those upon which the convincingness of the skeptical conclusion depends. My noting of the epistemologist's context as "non-claim" merely focusses on a feature dramatized in Descartes's description of his context (as one in which he is seated in his dressing gown before the fire . . .), namely that the epistemologist, in his meditation, is alone. My focus implies that this feature is not accidental, and one might conclude from this that the whole effort to put the Cartesian investigation into an Austinian format was misguided from the beginning since someone going through Austin's bases and grounds for doubt, by or for himself or herself, is only accidentally alone.

The case seems to me, rather, to be that we have not reached solid enough ground, if there is such ground, upon which to rule out the procedures either of meditation or of recollection. To have to leave open our choice or conviction here, to ask of ourselves this negative capability just here, seems to me accurate to a certain stage of enlightenment about our capacities as knowers, the stage at which we do not know whether what we sense of the world (or what we mean by the world) is or is not something independent of the effect of our sensory endowment.

The Philosopher's Conclusion Is Not a Discovery

The combination of the fact that in the epistemologist's context a concrete claim cannot be under scrutiny, together with the fact that one must be imagined as being under scrutiny, ought to explain why he imagines himself to be saying something when he is not, to have discovered something when he has not. Someone in these particular straits may be described as hallucinating what he or she means, or as having the illusion of meaning something. But for this really to be shown to have happened it would have to be shown how it has happened. In this and in the concluding sections of this chapter I will bring together some threads of an answer to this question I have left untraced, and so indicate ways in which it might be studied.

To say the epistemologist "has to" pick the objects, give the bases, raise the doubts he does, indicates how very far from arbitrary or willful the skeptical progression is. Yet it has sometimes been felt that the cause of the skeptical conclusion is simply that the philosopher "sets up standards of knowledge so high" or "redefines terms so tightly" that *of course* no human knowledge can slip past it. "Of course we don't see *all* of anything, we don't have X-ray vision, or look around corners"; "Of course induction isn't deduction, so the arguments we give for saying something *will* happen aren't deductive, but they are still, as a genre, good arguments"; "Of course moral judgments are not deductively or inductively related to the reasons we give for them, but they are nevertheless good reasons". And, of course, these implied "explanations" of philosophical doubt are less convincing than the doubt which inspired them; so their effect, again, is likely only to convince one of the shallowness of such appeals. To suppose the philosopher has done the foolishly self-defeating thing of raising standards (here, standards of certainty) so high that *of course* no human knowledge can attain them, is to treat him as though he had set his heart, say, on having human beings rise ten feet in the air without external prompting, or defined "getting into the air" as "getting ten feet into the air", and then, finding the world high jump record to reach short of eight feet, realized with a shock that no human being can really even get off the ground, and said as consolation to all jumpers, "You jump high enough for practical purposes". That *would* be just as annoying as certain ordinary language philosophers take the traditional philosopher to be, just as obviously arbitrary, just as eccentrically dismissing, just as maddeningly blind to what in fact human beings do and mean to do.

But this cannot be the way the traditional philosopher's rejection of the human comes about; because this does not account for the fact that he imagines himself to have made a discovery, and to feel convinced that if anyone followed his trivial considerations they too would appreciate the obvious rightness of his conclusion, the maddening inescapability of it. Or rather, it would account for this only if we seriously took him to be a patent eccentric, or to be conniving with his partners in madness when they appear to understand one another. (Taking him as a member of a foreign tribe would be fairly easy. Maybe that *is* what people (and some philosophers?) think the philosopher is.)

What I am trying to make out is *how* he has dismissed himself; and therewith delineate a danger we all run, a fact about human knowing. His conclusion presents itself to him as a discovery because his response to his wonder presents itself as a question to which he *must* press for an answer. He takes his imagined claim ("When (whenever) we see . . .", "We should all say we saw it (if we looked at it) . . .") as an actual claim; and so produces the only sort of answer which would so much as sound like the support of a factual claim, just the sort provided for him in our ordinary speech. What else could he seriously take as a basis, in that context, except "I see it" or "By means of the senses"? And, prodded by the suspicion that maybe that basis is not good enough (For what? For the thing "I saw him", in a practical context, is not good enough for when you have a suspicion that he was not *there;* not enough to "prove" it, make it certain), he questions it in just the way it would be questioned in (certain) ordinary cases: "What did (do) you *actually* see?"; "You didn't see the . . ."; "The most you saw . . . ." And the object is gone, unknowable by the senses alone. That conclusion, I take it, is agreed upon by both "Empiricists" and "Rationalists": Locke avoided skepticism only, apparently, through distraction and good English sense; Berkeley through God; Descartes through God and a special faculty of intellectual "perception"; Kant, denying such a faculty, avoided it through world-creating categories; Hume, to the extent he did, through "natural belief"; Moore, through furious common sense. And all who have followed the argument respond to it as a discovery about our world, one catastrophic in its implications, overturning what we all, until now, believed as completely as we believe anything.

But, as has been said, the validity (even, the sense) of a discovery's having been made, depends upon the considerations which lead to it being fully natural ones. And I have tried to show that they are not, and to show that they cannot be made fully natural (= projected with a clear sense) without destroying their point. Now I want to see more specifically why they do not, though they seem to, lead to discoveries. What I wish to convey is not that the conclusion that sense-experience is inadequate as a basis for knowledge as a whole (or that we can never really know the experience of another person) is *false,* and in *that* sense not a discovery; but rather that it is neither false nor true, that it is not what we should call a "discovery".

The reason that the philosopher's conclusion constitutes no discovery is that what his conclusions find in the world is something he himself has put there, an invention, and would not exist but for his efforts. If that could be made out it would constitute something I would be willing to call a "refutation" of skepticism (i.e., any skepticism which contains such an invention).

An instance of this process of inventing something where he supposes himself to be discovering it is the process of projection by which "parts" of a generic object are established. Forced by the momentum of his procedure to ask "Do you see all of it?" the philosopher gives that question (which has "some sense") a clear sense. Or tries to. Since, in the way it occurs in his investigation, it (he feels that it) must have meaning, he fixes (not discovers) the world so that it *can,* for the sake of his own coherence. And the question is: Does what he *must* mean convey what he *wishes* to mean? If it could be made clear that it does not, then I take it that he would himself feel that his conclusion had lost its force. It is for that reason that someone who could show the philosopher to be inventing what he thinks he is discovering might be said to have achieved a dissolution of that position. A way to test the complementary ideas that the philosopher means his words in special (or "stricter" than usual — cf. Moore, *Some Main Problems,* p. 34) senses, and that he has changed the meaning of his words, would be to ask this: What "meaning" could he give any *word* in the statement "You don't see the back half", said about an unmarked generic object, in order to make that statement mean what he wishes it to mean (or, said about that sort of object, mean what it ordinarily means)?

I also suggested that the philosopher's notions of "the senses", and "the feeling itself", were inventions of a similar sort, ideas of what things *must* be like in order to match what he must mean, has the illusion of meaning. The philosopher's idea of "the senses" or "(sense) experience" is made to order with his ideas of "the whole object", and "the thing itself"; his idea of "the feeling itself" is made to order with his idea of "behavior"; and the latter members are again inventions. It is as though the philosopher, having begun in wonder, a modern wonder I characterized as a feeling of being sealed off from the world, within an eternal round of experience, removed from the daily round of action, from the forms of life which contain the criteria in terms of which our concepts are employed, in which, that is, they are *of* a world — or, as Wittgenstein would put it, a position in which one *must* speak "outside language games" — it is as though the philosopher, in that position, is left only with his eyes, or generally, the ability to sense. In calling "the senses" an invention, a production of dialectic, an historical-philosophical construction, I do not mean that we *don't* as a matter of fact know the world by means of the five senses. If we were all deprived of our senses we should hardly have much use for bases like "By the red head". I mean, rather, that "the senses" the philosopher is left with, or comes up with, is as a matter of construction *opposed* to the revelation of things as they are.

But aren't they, nevertheless, the means by which we know a thing's EXISTENCE? This question takes us back to the beginning of my whole effort at characterizing traditional epistemology. For I said that the project of assessing the validity of knowledge as a whole, as that is prosecuted by the Cartesian tradition, is based upon a particular concept of knowledge (and thus leads to a particular *problem* of knowledge), viz., the concept I have characterized, with little sense of satisfaction, as a concept of knowledge as revelatory of the world's existence; and I contrasted that with a concept of knowledge which I take to underlie an investigation such as Austin's, a concept of knowledge as the identification or recognition of things. I also said that the concept of knowledge as of existence is what makes the problem of knowledge one fundamentally of achieving *certainty* in our claims to knowledge. "Certainty" is just one problem among others in Austin's model of knowledge, and that is just another specification of the difference of his problem from that of the tradition, another way of seeing why a traditional philosopher cannot take Austin to have shown the tradition simply to be "barking [its] way up the wrong gum tree" ("Other Minds", p. 158). For it is too late to tell a philosopher to forgo the quest for certainty when it is the sheer existence of objects — of anything at all — that seems to be at stake. (And it is significant that the pragmatists — one of whom popularized the expression "Quest for Certainty" — did not take the problem of the *existence* of objects seriously.) And though there is a sense in which the "complete clarity" (*Investigations*, §133) Wittgenstein demands is a demand for certainty, that represents a different quest altogether, yet a quest for a solution to another way of asking and facing a problem at the same level, and I think produced by the same experience, as the problem of the tradition. If the tradition asks "(How) can we know what there is in the world?", then Wittgenstein asks "What makes our knowledge *of* a world of objects at all?". These questions, different in spirit as they are, and subtending different procedures ("methods") for their investigation, are alike in taking the *general* relation of knowledge and object as their *problem*, different from (other) ordinary language philosophers, and from positivists and pragmatists (though the Dewey of the *Logic* and, I believe, Peirce would be exceptions) who can either afford to ignore the problem, to suppose it settled in a theory of verification, or to regard it as a matter of what language we are to construct in our professional investigations.

If I have been successful in making the "dilemma" I have characterized as faced by the traditional epistemologist (that he "must", and "cannot", mean what he says) seem to be a real one, then one will wish to press for a more complete understanding of it. One will want to understand in more detail *how* one can "not know what one means, nor even that *one means nothing*" (I emphasize "one means" to make it as plain as I can that this is not the same as saying that the expressions one is then using in themselves, as it were, "mean nothing", i.e., are nonsense; "nonsense", used as a term of criticism in recent philosophizing, registers that concentration on "expressions themselves", i.e., apart from their human use, which I have found a pervasive temptation of the tradition generally); and one will want to understand how the concept of "knowing of something's existence" is to be understood, and how it may, if I am right that it ("it"?, and yet I know I do not understand *what* "it" is) underlies the traditional problem of knowledge — how it may be controlling the course of that investigation from its beginning.

Two Interpretations of Traditional Epistemology; Phenomenology

If my saying that the philosopher has made an invention and not a discovery is at all convincing, and if the suggestion that this comes about because the philosopher uses forms of expression which are forced upon him by the way he has entered and conceived his problem and which he must *give* clear sense to (which means, according to what I said about the "projection of a concept" as requiring "invitation by a context", *make* his context invite it (= *invent* or construct one which will)), then we will want to understand how the *specific* expressions in question lead to the *particular* inventions which emerge in the course and in the conclusion of that investigation. Only an explanation which does that would *show* the absence of any discovery.

I have related the initiating experience of the philosopher, and his ensuing progress, to Wittgenstein's notion of "speaking outside language-games" (or, in the figures he uses to make the idea mount up in our worries, that, in philosophizing, "language goes on holiday" (§38), that it is "like an engine idling" (§132) — both of which imply that it is not *working*), suggesting that what happens to the philosopher's concepts is that they are deprived of their ordinary criteria of employment (which does not mean that his words are deprived of meaning — one could say that such words have nothing *but* their meanings) and, collecting no new ones, leave his concepts without relation to the world (which does not mean that what he says is false), or in terms I used earlier, remove them from their position among our system of concepts. There is a remark of Wittgenstein's which appears to me peculiarly to point to a way of coming to see why the philosopher's inventions or constructions take the form they do.

At §47 of the *Investigations* Wittgenstein has this:

But what are the simple constituent parts of which reality is composed?   — What are the simple constituent parts of a chair?   — The bits of wood of which it is made? Or the molecules, or the atoms?   — "Simple" means: not composite. And here the point is: in what sense "composite"? It makes no sense at all to speak absolutely of the "simple parts of a chair".

The suggestion I want to pick up can be brought out by noticing that while Professor Anscombe translates "Es hat gar keinen Sinn von den 'einfachen Bestandteilen des Sessels schlechtweg' zu reden" as "It makes no sense to speak absolutely of the 'simple parts of a chair'", what the German more literally says is, "It makes no sense to speak of the 'absolutely simple parts of a chair'". This is not a very big difference, no doubt, but it may conceal, or reveal, the diagnosis Wittgenstein is offering here. I might articulate what I take that diagnosis to be this way: We look for "absolute simples" (and, I will add, absolute anythings: responsibilities, actions, meanings, certainties, see-ables) when we try (or have, or come) to speak absolutely, that is, outside language games.

This suggests why the philosopher's series of considerations ("You don't see the back, or the inside; the *most* you see is . . .") *ends* where it does; why, having been forced to "speak absolutely", he is led to the invention he is. Only an "absolute see-able" would *satisfy* him as an answer to the question "What do you *really* see?" once the normal criteria for employing the concepts of "seeing it all" and "seeing a part" have become inaccessible. Apart from the language games which control the use of our expressions (or, apart from the criteria in terms of which the "tolerance" of our concepts — their flexibility *and* their resistance — is controlled; or, apart from the maintenance of a concept in our forms of life), it is, we could say, no longer *we* who mean anything by our words; no criteria we use for the application of our concepts will seem anything but arbitrary (*merely* "conventional"); the meaning is naked; it is only the words themselves which carry meaning, and the world itself which must answer them. The world seems to take the answer out of our mouths; the world is then what so takes the answer.

According to my reading, this passage from Wittgenstein, in addition to the guidance it provides in helping us understand why the philosopher's inventions take the form they do, emphasizes that what philosophers (seem to) find will be *entities*. This comes out very clearly in the question with which Wittgenstein is concerned in his account of "composite": "What lies behind the idea that names really signify simples?" When you ask for a philosophical explanation of naming *überhaupt,* you are led to absolutely simple entities as their bearers. This is the case in the view Socrates is recounting in the *Theaetetus,* and, as Wittgenstein says, "Both Russell's 'individuals' and my 'objects' . . . were such primary *elements*" (emphasis mine). This suggests that the impulse which drives you to sense-data will not be satisfied by a mere *"language* of appearing". And this implies a limitation in my entire account of the Cartesian investigation which I must explicitly mention.

I have continuously insisted on the reasonableness of this investigation as being provided by its faithfulness to the model of our assessments of ordinary claims to knowledge; or, as I might put it, I have taken the investigation as an assessment of the (compound) claim that "We know objects exist because we see them". But this investigation has also been interpreted, by some philosophers who pursue it and some who criticize it, as one which permits us to detail the phenomenology of our experience of the world. There is no question of my now attempting any examination or adjudication of a difference of this magnitude, and I have no wish to suggest that this investigation cannot be so interpreted, but at most that it *need* not be. The difference in these interpretations turns upon the force we are to give to the philosopher's claim to have discovered "all we really see", and his claim that "what we really see are not physical objects" (physical objects are not "given"). On a phenomenological interpretation this is taken to mean that the tradition has claimed to describe the nature and quality of our ordinary perception of the world, something we can discover through closer attention to our consciousness than we ordinarily do or can confer. Whereas on the claim interpretation I have pursued, "all we actually see" is taken to describe all we can use, of our ordinary perception, as *evidence* for the existence of objects; this obviously carries implications about our ordinary perception, but they are more oblique than the flat statement that it is just radically different from what we take it to be. The *radical* implication is that we do not *know* what we would all say we do know or most firmly believe.

Phenomenologists have thought it fatal to the investigation of the traditional epistemologist that the way in which he arrives at his conclusion about what is "immediately given to, or in, experience" is not *revelatory* of the nature of our experience of objects but is in fact the result of his having *altered* that experience. Professor Roderick Firth, in his papers entitled "Sense-Data and the Percept Theory", has taken this objection seriously, and attempted to answer it from the traditionalist point of view. His defense of classical epistemology is to insist that this alteration does indeed occur, that it is required by the classical procedures themselves, and that its occurrence therefore represents no immediate fallacy in it. It does, however, represent a problem for it, the problem, viz., of justifying this procedure — admitting, indeed fastening upon, its phenomenological alterations — as a "legitimate method of discovering the content of perceptual consciousness" (Firth, p. 462); it would then be open to argument that this method is, in fact, better or "more trustworthy" than the method prosecuted by phenomenologists, viz., direct inspection of our consciousness.

What Firth would regard as a justification is, in outline, this: The procedure is one he calls "Perceptual Reduction", by which he means the "unique operation familiar to everyone who has participated in discussions of the traditional problems of perception" (p. 459), the operation of coming to an awareness of "what (all) we really or actually see". This procedure, if it is indeed to *disclose* the content of our ordinary perception, requires the *hypothesis* — called by Firth the Exposure Theory — that "the operation of perceptual reduction does not produce a state of consciousness which is simply *other than* the original state of perception on

which it is performed . . . [but], on the contrary, a state of direct awareness which was contained in the original perception" (p. 462). But how
is this hypothesis to be justified? It "grants a unique and privileged epistemological status to the particular attitude (the 'reducing attitude')
which we adopt in order to initiate the process of perceptual reduction . . .
the attitude of 'doubt' or 'questioning' " (*ibid.*). But the "singling out"
of this attitude and the attributing to it of this "peculiar power" is something for which "there does not appear to be the slightest empirical justification" (p. 463). And since the only argument which seems to have been
offered — Lewis's and Price's defense of it as "intellectual analysis", to
condemn which, they insist, would be to condemn thought itself (cf. C. I.
Lewis, *Mind and the World Order*, p. 55; H. H. Price, *Perception*, p. 15;
both quoted by Firth, p. 32) — "[overlooks] the very distinction which criticism of the Exposure Theory is meant to clarify . . . namely, between
introspective reduction and direct inspection" (Firth, p. 464) and thereby
misses the point of the phenomenological criticism (which does not deny
all "intellectual analysis", but for instance that which has the consequence
the classical epistemologist's analysis has), the "phenomenological or epistemological basis of the sense-data theory" is left without a full explanation (*ibid.*).

The significance of the claim interpretation of the classical procedure is,
in these terms, this. It provides both an explanation for the centrality of
the "reducing attitude" ("doubt" or "questioning") and a justification
for the "hypothesis" that a procedure following upon this "attitude" will
have the effect of revealing "what we actually see" — or rather, it shows
that no "hypothesis" is in question at all, that no justification is necessary, or rather, that the request for one would not be comprehensible.

I mean this: If the traditional procedure is construed as the assessment
of claims to knowledge, and as reasonable in the way any ordinary assessment is reasonable, then the role of *doubt* in the procedure is not that of
a particular attitude which is "singled out" arbitrarily as having a "peculiar power", but is just that ordinary response any reasonable and competent knowing creature would take towards any claim about which there
is (or has been raised) a "reasonable ground for doubt", itself something
any competent knower will know. And that our *ways* of raising and countering grounds for doubt, in particular, those about claims to know
something based on the claim to see it, leads to a realization of "what we
really see" (or actually saw) is not a *hypothesis,* but a matter of the grammar of "giving a basis", "entering a doubt", etc. Someone who doesn't
know that if he didn't see the initials on the case then he doesn't know

that *this* is the very camera case he saw (unless he can base his claim on some further feature of that case) is not competent in some dimension of that most ordinary ability to assert anything.

In addition to its protection of the classical procedure against arbitrariness, the claim interpretation has two further (phenomenological) virtues. First, it offers an explanation of the nature of that "methodological doubt" which has so often puzzled, or annoyed, its critics. It has been wondered whether the "doubt" invoked in the Method of Doubt is real *doubt,* or whether it is not merely feigned or even, more recently, neurotic doubt, diluted with academism and dignified by the title "methodological". The claim interpretation would show the philosopher's "methodological doubt" *is* peculiar, but not in any of the ways it has been, so far as I am aware, said to be peculiar. Its peculiarity is a function of the peculiarity of the philosopher's original claim. Since the investigation turns upon a claim imagined to be entered (a claim which must be entered and which cannot be entered), the investigation will proceed through a doubt which can only be imagined (a skepticism which must be felt and which cannot be felt). The special peculiarity of the philosopher's doubt is derivative from the special peculiarity of the philosopher's claim, not the other way around; it does not dictate the form which the philosopher's investigation must take. Second, it may suggest that what Lewis and Price are responding to when they defend their procedures as "intellectual analysis" is not to some perception they have of what the process of "analyzing something" is, but to their knowledge that, in arriving at their conclusions, they have not invoked considerations or procedures which differ obviously from the considerations and procedures we all learn in learning to make assertions, in maturing into speech. Price's phrase "we are forbidden to think" then means "we are forbidden to speak (in any particular language)"; and Lewis's phrase "the condemnation of thought itself" then means "the condemnation of the forms of life which provide the conditions of assertion". It suggests further that perhaps epistemologists have not set out to "analyze" anything at all, and in particular not to analyze experience or consciousness — or at least that what one means in calling it "analysis" is far from clear — and that it is only when their results seem, or come, to conflict with a phenomenological description of experience that they must justify their procedures by justifying "analysis".

Whether these interpretations are really *alternatives,* and if so which is the more faithful to the structure and motive of the traditional investigation; or whether they are complementary, and if so what part of the investigation each responds to; and whether the criticism from ordinary language is more serious than the criticism from phenomenology, and what relation a defense against the one has to a defense against the other; and whether, indeed, there are not at least two separable traditions of classical epistemology, in the one of which (perhaps the British Empiricist) skepticism with respect to the senses comes before, and has implications for, a phenomenology of experience, and in the other (perhaps the Cartesian) it is the phenomenology which comes first and the skepticism which follows — all these are questions which must demand as much time and space as my one confrontation, that of the tradition with its ordinary language critics, has taken. I have wanted, in raising them, only to make explicit a limitation I am aware of, and also to acknowledge problems which one expects will arise as this confrontation is itself pushed further: for the knowledge I have claimed of what we ordinarily say has itself, and essentially, demanded an awareness of, for example, what it would be "odd" or "forced" or "absurd" to say, and while I have insisted that we all know these things, part of *what* we there know is exactly the phenomenology of our immediate consciousness.

The Knowledge of Existence

I want to combine the little I have to say about the concept of existence with the acknowledgment of another explicit limitation of my effort. In characterizing the traditional concept of knowledge as of existence and in taking that to account for its quest for certainty, I have followed one of what seem to be the two main ways in which certainty itself has been conceived, viz., as the Cartesian "absence of doubt". According to a second model of certainty (and hence knowledge), our statements are assessed not in terms of the naturalness of the basis we have given, but in terms of the degree of verification we have acquired; the claim to certainty is no longer carried by the idea of the absence of (reasonable) doubt but by the idea of something I may call "the totality of experience". Of course it transpires that no statement about an object can, in these terms, attain certainty, but this no longer means that we have to acknowledge that a given claim must be given up, but only that it "may" at any time be overthrown "in further experience". Here the philosophical conclusion is not that our claims are perhaps inadequately based altogether, that perhaps we have no evidence at all in the way, or for the thing, we thought we had, but only that they are not as good as we had thought, that there is always "more" relevant evidence which we are not taking into account.

Perhaps these concepts of certainty are related in something like this

way: Once a philosopher finds a Cartesian investigation to show that all
we can be certain of is something other than the existence of objects
(which Descartes does not quite find, but which may emerge from his
investigation if you forgo, as an Empiricist or Kantian does, Descartes's
faculty of "intellectual perception") then the question arises in a new
way as to how our claims about material objects are to be based, and
this may lead to a reconceiving of the *meaning* of our claims about them,
a reconception of what a claim about an object *is* — or as in the case of
Berkeley, a new concept of an object in general —viz., an implicit prediction, a nest of claims about all (future) experience. (This seems to be the
pattern of such investigations of empirical knowledge as C. I. Lewis's.)

This verification model of knowledge produces, in the course of the
investigation it inspires, forms or shifts of expression which invite the
kinds of worry we have felt concerning those produced in Cartesian investigations. For example, from a point at which we ask "How do we verify
statements about the world" and answer "In experience", we take a particular example about which it is invariably eventually said that we cannot *conclusively* (or absolutely) verify it, on the ground that no *single*
(or *particular*) experience has that power, and we all seem to see that this
means that we cannot verify it with certainty; yet we had not *begun* the
investigation asking about conclusive verification nor speaking of single
experiences. I think it is clear that such expressions are not being used
in contexts in which they ordinarily would be used, but the naturalness
of their entry as the investigation proceeds is amply proven to me by the
fact that in years of reading and hearing such investigation it never oc-
curred to me to doubt their full legitimacy. And no criticism of such investigations would satisfy me unless it contained an explanation of *that*
fact as well as an explanation of what the fully ordinary uses of such expressions are.

I cannot now undertake to provide either of these. But I allude to
these questions in order to have before us another visualization of the
hopelessness of a criticism of these expressions by a *direct* appeal to ordinary language once the expressions have emerged in the course of critical
investigation. And this will also permit another view of the way in which
it is the knowledge of existence which becomes a problem. What a direct
appeal to ordinary language continues to show is how an expression *is*
being used — that it is slightly forced and that it requires a projection
which must be made in such-and-such a way in this context, and so on.

Ordinarily we might say, having looked again, or specifically, to see
whether the cat is in the next room, that we have *verified* the statement

that the cat is there; we checked; we know it for a fact. But the verification theorist "discovers" (not, however, with the force of Cartesian *astonishment*) that we haven't *conclusively* verified that statement, and this position must seem stronger to him, and more knowing (even, as Berkeley, for example, claims, more precise and accurate) than what we should ordinarily say. To deny his conclusion flatly we will have to say either that he is using words strangely (which is, if anything, *less* obvious than in the case of the Cartesian investigation) or else say that what he says is *false,* i.e., assert that we *have* verified the statement *conclusively.* And are we prepared to say that? Doesn't that assertion just invite the sorts of supposed "possibilities" any verification theorist raises? "Do you mean," they are invited to inquire, "that *nothing* would show — if you like, nothing would make you say — that there was not really a cat in the room after all?" If you retort that indeed nothing would make you say so, how will you convince us that this does not merely show something about your own rigidity rather than something about the solidity of your knowledge?

Such an attempt merely to outface the traditional philosopher's denial of certainty must lead to a siege of kicking stones or checking cats, or to some other incoherence. It is worth seeing this in a particular case.

In the course of an extended criticism of the verification "argument", Norman Malcolm is led to the following position:

The reason is obvious for saying that my copy of James's book does not have the characteristic that its print undergoes spontaneous changes. I have read millions of printed words on many thousands of printed pages. I have not encountered a single instance of a printed word vanishing from a page or being replaced by another printed word, suddenly and without external cause. Nor have I heard of any other person who had such an encounter. There is overwhelming evidence that printed words do not behave in that way. It is just as conclusive as the evidence that houses do not turn in to flowers — that is to say, absolutely conclusive evidence. [Malcolm, "The Verification Argument", p. 280]

Now to say that we have "absolutely conclusive evidence" that houses do not turn into flowers is not merely too weak; such a remark is itself produced by the same hysteria against which it is struggling. If there is absolutely conclusive evidence that S is P, then that S is P is a well-established fact; on the basis of the evidence you may exercise the right to say you know it is a fact. (Grant this much for a moment: it is not meant as an argument.) Or: Saying "S is P" is saying that S is P is (in fact) the case; and you can (sometimes) know what is in fact the case. But is it merely *in fact* the case that houses do not turn into flowers? What do we learn — what fact is conveyed — when we are told that they do not? What would it be like if the flowers and houses *did* turn into one another? What would "houses" or "flowers" mean in the language of such a world? What would be the difference between (what we call) stones and seeds? Where would we live in that world, and what would we grow in our gardens? And what would "grow" mean? When Malcolm attempts to give "reasons" or (conclusive) "evidence" for "saying" that houses do not turn into flowers, he is giving us those "hundred reasons" we have had occasion to mention before, "each drowning the voice of the other, 'But I have experienced it myself innumerable times and as often heard of similiar experiences . . . etc.' " (*Investigations*, §478). (Cf. Malcolm's "I have not encountered a single instance . . . . Nor have I heard of any other person who . . .".)

Another passage from the *Investigations* is relevant here.

"A new-born child has no teeth." — "A goose has no teeth." — "A rose has no teeth." — This last at any rate — one would like to say — is obviously true! It is even surer than that a goose has none. — And yet it is none so clear. For where should a rose's teeth have been? The goose has none in its jaw. And neither, of course, has it any in its wings; but no one means that when he says it has no teeth. — Why, suppose one were to say: the cow eats its food and then dungs the rose with it, so the rose has teeth in the mouth of a beast. This would not be absurd, because one has no notion in advance where to look for teeth in a rose. [pp. 221–22]

Accordingly, we might construct such a series as this: "Unwatered seeds do not turn into flowers" — "Acorns do not turn into flowers" — "Houses do not turn into flowers."

In denying that we *have* conclusive verification for this last statement, I am not to be understood as asserting that we do *not* have (conclusive) verification for it. I am asserting, rather, that we do not yet know what verification for or against it would be. Nor am I saying that such a sentence can have no use; only, we have got to be told what its use is. (And when we are told, it is not likely to be a use which requires anything like verification at all — it might, e.g., be an accusation or an insinuation.) The verificationist's denial and Malcolm's assertion that we can (sometimes) have conclusive evidence for an empirical statement, flat as their superficial disagreement is, both rest upon the same concept of what knowledge is, or must be: both picture knowledge as lying at the end of an appallingly long road of belief and evidence; both imagine the evidence for any given empirical statement to be constantly growing or diminishing or precariously maintaining a given credibility level as the number of human experiences increase — as though looking again and again and again at houses and flowers were seeing again and again and again the one *not* turning into the other. Both, in a word, use "absolutely conclusive verification" out of its ordinary context. But, in such a case, the traditional philosopher seems to have undeniable considerations for that shift, whereas someone who *denies* what he says, in *his* words, has none. That is a moral about philosophical criticism which I have been anxious to draw. That one can find elsewhere in Malcolm's work a point of view opposed to that which I have quoted from one of his essays indicates the power such a picture of knowledge can continue to exert.

Why does Malcolm choose the particular examples he does — examples with their particular oddness — houses turning into flowers, print undergoing spontaneous changes — in combatting the idea that we lack conclusive verification for claims about objects? Why doesn't he choose a context in which the expression "absolutely conclusive evidence" would in fact ordinarily be used? There *are* paradigmatic cases for its use — which is only to say, ones characteristic for its use — and one would have thought this more congenial to Malcolm's procedure.

What would an ordinary context be? Suppose someone says, "Now I have absolutely conclusive evidence that she was in Rome". What might he mean? Well, two weeks ago this woman was reported to have bought a plane ticket for Rome; that is, given other things we know, good evidence that she was in Rome (that it is Rome she was going to). And three days ago one of our agents was sure he saw her climb onto the back of a Vespa and disappear around a corner; that is almost conclusive evidence, given further things we know. Today a photograph sent by the Roman police has arrived showing her standing in front of the Fontana Tartarughe. "Now we have absolutely conclusive evidence!" (What would be, given some things we know, pretty good evidence that houses do not turn into flowers?)

But such an example has *no* grip against the verificationist's position. For in that context it is perfectly reasonable to imagine further that the picture has itself been faked, that a picture of her taken in Miami against the clear sky has been superimposed on a photograph of the fountain. We can put it this way: "Absolutely", in such contexts, works like the word "know" itself. It means: we don't *need* any more evidence for all practical purposes; but not: there isn't any further evidence which would be relevant. But *that* is what would have to be shown to counter the verificationist's conclusion. Once admit the relevance of further evidence — i.e., allow that it would (sometimes) be reasonable to ask for more — and it will seem dogmatic to say that none *can* go against the statement.

It has been suggested to me that "Houses are turning into flowers" does mean something clear, for example in an animated cartoon or a dream. This is undeniable. In such contexts we may, for example, see a cathedral with a rose window turn into a rose. But I did not wish to suggest that such a statement meant nothing, only that we had to give it a clear meaning. And in having to imagine *such* a context in order to invite its projection we are imagining a world for which the statement "We have absolutely conclusive evidence that houses don't turn into flowers" is false, or rather, means nothing, because in such a world the (our) concept of evidence has no application: anything can be followed by anything. Cartoons make us laugh because they are enough *like* our world to be terribly sad and frightening.

I asked, in discussing the passage quoted from Malcolm's paper, whether it is merely *in fact* the case that houses do not turn into flowers (or that printed words do not undergo spontaneous changes, or, more generally, one could add, that there are separate, enduring objects in the world). Let us now ask: What are we imagining when we think of this as merely "in fact" the case about *our* world, in the way it is merely in fact the case that the flowers in this garden have not been sufficiently watered, or that there are six white houses with rose gardens on this street? It is my feeling that such things could present themselves to us as just more facts about our world were we to (when we) look upon the whole world as one object, or as one complete set of objects: that is another way of characterizing that experience I have called "seeing ourselves as outside the world as a whole", looking in at it, as we now look at some objects from a position among others. This experience I have found to be fundamental in classical epistemology (and, indeed, moral philosophy). It sometimes presents itself to me as a sense of powerlessness to know the world, or to act upon it; I think it is also working in the existentialist's (or, say, Santayana's) sense of the precariousness and arbitrariness of existence, the utter contingency in the fact that things are as they are. (Wittgenstein shares this knowledge of the depth of contingency. His distinction in this matter is to describe it better, to live its details better. I would like to say: to remove its theatricality.)

All of existence is squeezed into the philosopher's tomato when he rolls it towards his overwhelming question. The experience is one I might now describe as one of looking at the world as though it were another *object*, on a par with particular envelopes, tomatoes, pieces of wax, bells, tables, etc. If this is craven, it is a craving not for generality (if that means for *generalization*) but for *totality*. It is an expression of what I meant when I said that we want to know the world as we imagine God knows it. And that will be as easy to rid us of as it is to rid us of the prideful craving to be God — I mean to *rid* us of it, not to replace it with a despair at our finitude. (I do not necessarily deny that the *earth* is an object, and has objects on it. The world does not have objects on it.)

Perhaps I go too far; or not far enough. I do not know whether I have communicated the experience I am trying to get before us. Let me try another way.

We have been made aware of the extraordinariness of such an expression as "This exists", and indeed of the peculiarities of the term "exists" generally. Hume and Kant had the insight we express by saying "Existence is not a predicate", and, after Frege, we may see what in fact the function of the word "exists" is. But the question that concerns me is still: How can philosophers come so much as to feel that such an expression as "This exists" does mean something, something informative, and further, something for which we can, and must undertake to give a proof? For that is what I take the experience of a philosopher to be when he undertakes to prove that, or question whether, we actually *see* objects and therefore really know they are there. It seems to be implied by Moore when, near the conclusion of his "Proof of an External World", he says that he does not believe that a proof can be given of the *premisses* of his proposed proof of "the existence of things outside of us" (p. 145) — the premisses, namely, "Here is one hand" and "Here is another". Whatever one thinks of these premisses or of Moore's proof by means of them, the idea, or sense, that such assertions could be proved in the context Moore requires — namely, where for all the world they are present and in full view — is the idea or sense of our knowledge of a thing's existence that interests me. That he takes it as sensible to ask for such a proof, and indeed that that is part of the sense of his epistemological investigations, is indicated by Moore's reason for saying that he cannot prove that "Here's a human hand and here's another". The reason is that "In order to do it, I should need to prove for one thing, as Descartes pointed out, that I am not now dreaming. But how can I prove that I am not? I have, no doubt, conclusive reasons for asserting that I am not now dreaming; I have conclusive evidence that I am awake: but that is a very different thing from being able to prove it. I could not tell you what all my evidence is; and I should require to do this at least, in order to give you a proof" (p. 149). Moore, of course, insists that he *knows* the statement in question is true, although he cannot prove it, and that to deny it, or even to suggest that he only believed it, would be absurd (p. 146).

What is this sense of the need for a proof of such a thing as that a human hand is here (mine, while I'm moving it)? What is the experience which leads one to offer grounds in support of such a statement? What is the experience of someone who, in Kant's words, "thinks good to doubt their existence" (i.e., "the existence of things outside of us") (*Critique of Pure Reason,* preface to second edition; quoted by Moore, p. 127). I described this doubt, following the collapse of the philosopher's claim to know something exists because he sees it, as one which must be felt and cannot be felt. But what kind of experience is *that?*

I have suggested that it was a response to a claim which must be and cannot be imagined to be made, and that this in turn was produced by an experience which I described as one of being sealed off from the world, within the round of one's own experiences, and as one of looking at the world as one object ("outside of us"). The philosopher's experiences of trying to *prove* that it is there is, I will now add, one of trying to establish an absolutely firm connection with that world-object from that sealed position. It is as though, deprived of the ordinary forms of life in which that connection is, and is alone, secured, he is trying to reestablish it in his immediate consciousness, then and there. (This has its analogues in non-philosophical experience, normal and abnormal.)

I will describe a way in which that experience is produced in me. Let us ask: What is the experience of a philosopher when he says "Call it what you like, it still is what it is", in a context in which the question "What is it in fact?" has no answer; or when he says "What appears to us does not tell us what the thing is in itself", in a context in which what we see is not, grammatically, an "appearance", and the question "What does it really look like?" has no answer. The questions "What is it in fact?" and "How can we get a better look at it?" do have obvious trivial, empirical answers, and that is, no doubt, part of what makes the philosopher's assertions seem to have a clear sense. But those trivial answers are not answers to questions whose answers would satisfy him. So what is his dissatisfaction, as expressed in those assertions? I imagine myself staring at an object, a generic object, not with a question I wish to put to it, nor a use I wish to put it to, but as though I am only my eyes, bodiless, even mindless. And I find I want to say: *"That — that thing there — is what it is. It is,* in itself, none of the things we *say* it is. It escapes language in the end." Is what it is? In itself? I am saying: It is *that!* (pointing to it, fastening my eyes upon it). I am trying to say: "That is that" and make those words say something informative. And, having now declared that intention, I feel dissatisfied — with my own dissatisfaction. I have informed myself of nothing. Or I find myself wanting to say: The object itself is ineluctably hidden from me, just the other side of experience; I only see it *as it presents itself to me* (a phrase again used in a context in which its natural complement "How does it present itself to *you?*" has no answer, or not the right sort of answer); it is *there,* all right, but inaccessible.

I try to make the words "In itself it is *there*" (I almost feel like *pointing* as though to penetrate something; but before I do that, I feel it is useless) say something informative, the way "In itself it is white" says something informative. I imagine that there is a world in which things *are,* just *are,* of which what I see is a distortion, an appearance, an effect. But that is not a fact; I don't mean it is false, I mean it isn't the right sort of candidate to be a fact. It is not true, *and* it is not false, that there are things-in-themselves.

I have described what is happening this way: The question "How can we tell what the object is in itself?" has been produced by a non-claim use of "No single experience can tell us what the object is in itself"; being produced, it seems to demand an answer; being a non-claim situation, the conditions under which a request for a basis can be answered have been removed. And then our situation perhaps looks this way: "Human reason has this peculiar fate that . . . it is burdened by questions which, as prescribed by the nature of reason itself, it is not able to ignore, but which, as transcending all its powers, it is also not able to answer" (*Critique of Pure Reason,* preface to first edition).

But the reason that no basis is satisfactory, is not that there isn't one where there ought to be, but that there is no claim which can provide the relevance of a basis. The reason we cannot say what the thing is in itself is not that there is something we do not in fact know, but that we have deprived ourselves of the conditions for saying anything in particular. There is nothing we cannot say. That doesn't mean that we can say *everything;* there is no "everything" to be said. There is nothing we cannot know. That does not mean we can know everything; there is no everything, no totality of facts or things, to be known. To say we do not (cannot) know things-in-themselves is as much a Transcendental Illusion as to say we do. If we say the philosopher has been "misled by grammar", we must not suppose that this means he has been led to say the *wrong* thing — as though there was a *right* thing all prepared for him which he missed. It is rather, as I have been putting it, that he is led into supposing that what he *must* say is something he *means* to say, means as informative. And the question still is: How can we not know (realize) what we are saying;

how can we not know that we are not informing ourselves of something when we think we are? Here one might capture a sense of how the problems of philosophy become questions of self-knowledge.

I characterized the difference between Austin's investigation and traditional investigations as one of being guided by different concepts, hence different problems, of knowledge. Austin's problem is easy to characterize briefly: it makes the problem of knowledge one of recognizing objects and omits (denies?) any problem of knowing with certainty of the existence of a generic object. (His virtuoso passage on the difference between "being sure" and "being certain" is, again, concerned with the sureness and certainty of *identifications*. (Cf. "Other Minds", pp. 135–42.)) And I put the implication of the work of Austin we have discussed this way: there is no problem of settling a thing's existence beyond the problem of determining its reality. The truth there is in that is what I have tried to express by saying: there are no (Austinian) criteria of a thing's existence beyond the criteria of its identification; and by saying: there are no criteria we use for determining whether a thing is animate or inanimate, or whether it is an artifact or a natural object.

But I cannot be confident that there is nothing left to the problem of knowing of something's existence, for, to go no further, we haven't said a word about the ordinary uses of the expression "There is . . .". One question to ask here would be: "Why do the expressions 'There is a . . .' (or: 'There is something which . . .') and 'Here is a . . .' say what they do?" Why, that is, do we use the words expressing *location* (as in, e.g., "There is my hat") also to express existence? Shall we say: There is no problem of knowing a thing's existence beyond the problem of knowing how to locate it? (But other languages do not express existence this way. Cf. the German "Es gibt".)

Perhaps the implication I find in Austin's work suggests something Quine explicitly asserts, that we could give up the words "exists" and "existence" entirely. But in favor of what? Quine says he will retain just the word "is" ("On What There Is", p. 3), but isn't what he retains really *"there* is"? (The word he retains is not the word "is" which he elsewhere calls ambiguous as between meaning "is a member of" and "is the same as" (*Mathematical Logic*, p. 119).) His point, surely right, that "exists" is not ambiguous when used of both spatio-temporal and mathematical objects, also holds for "there is". ("If spatio-temporal reference is lacking when we affirm the existence of the cube root of 27, this is simply because a cube root is not a spatio-temporal kind of thing, and not because we are being ambiguous in our use of 'exist' " ("On What There Is", p. 3).) We could say, indeed: To know that there is a cube root of 27 is to know how to locate (find) it (= know what kind of an object it "grammatically" is). (Is this what Pascal meant when he spoke of the God of Descartes's Proofs as a "philosopher's God" — that only someone who lacked the knowledge to find God, the way to locate him, would offer such proofs?) And perhaps we would then be led to ask why the word "is" does all this work. It suggests that knowing what something *is* is irreducibly a matter of knowing its "location", knowing when it is "the same", and knowing its properties. Then there are the problems of a sense that there are higher and lower and other realms of Being of which existence is but one, and the sense embodied in the question "Why is there anything at all?" — the recording, again, of an experience I confess having had, and which seems to me related to, even to express, the sense of the philosopher's question "How do we know at all that anything exists?". (This further experience, and whatever further companions it has, should be subjected, like its companions at a comparable crossroads of Chapter VI (in the final paragraphs of the section "The Reasonableness of Doubt") to psychological consideration.)

An admission of some question as to the mystery of the existence, or the being, of the world is a serious bond between the teaching of Wittgenstein and that of Heidegger. The bond is one, in particular, that implies a shared view of what I have called the truth of skepticism, or what I might call the moral of skepticism, namely, that the human creature's basis in the world as a whole, its relation to the world as such, is not that of knowing, anyway not what we think of as knowing. (Cf. "The Avoidance of Love", p. 324.) (Then what rootlessness, or curse, made us, lets us, think of our basis in this way, accepting from ourselves our offer of knowledge?) Both Wittgenstein and Heidegger continue, by reinterpreting, Kant's insight that the limitations of knowledge are not failures of it. *Being and Time* goes further than *Philosophical Investigations* in laying out how to think about what the human creature's relation to the world as such is (locating, among others, that particular relation called knowing); but Wittgenstein goes further than Heidegger in laying out how to investigate the cost of our continuous temptation to knowledge, as I would like to put it. In *Being and Time* the cost is an absorption in the public world, the world of the mass or average man. (I find Heidegger's descriptions of such a world, especially in Chapter IV of *Being and Time,* the least original and most superficial passages in that uneven book.) In the *Investigations* the cost is arrived at in terms (e.g., of not knowing what we are saying, of emptiness in our assertions, of the illusion of meaning something, of claims to impossible privacies) suggestive of madness. (I will go further along certain trails of this suggestion in Part Four.) And in both the cost is the loss, or forgoing, of identity or of selfhood. To be interested in such accounts as accounts of the cost of knowing to the knowing creature, I suppose one will have to take an interest in certain preoccupations of romanticism.

It seems to me significant that the place one is most likely to have picked up a public version in English of the question of the mystery of the being of the world is in Part IX of Hume's *Dialogues on Natural Religion.* Significant that the question should occur within just these epistemological and religious horizons (cf. "The Avoidance of Love", p. 325, n. 15); and that it should be given, by Demea, and left, in a prejudicial (i.e., anthropomorphic) form, namely, *"What was it . . .* which determined *something* to exist rather than *nothing,* and bestowed being on a particular possibility, exclusive of the rest?" (first emphasis mine); and that it should be answered not by Philo but by Cleanthes, as though to save Philo's energy for something harder, but perhaps to save him embarrassment, since the logic is well chopped but not fresh. (It helps gain perspective on Hume's brilliance in this work to imagine the part of Demea played by Descartes, who would doubtless have added some lines penned by himself, and whose exit, at the close of Part IX, would have taken a different turn.)

If the existence of the world, and our knowledge of its existence, becomes a real, a sensed problem, is it enough to say, with Carnap, "To accept the thing-world means nothing more than to accept a certain form of language, in other words, to accept rules for forming statements and for testing, accepting, or rejecting them"? ("Empiricism, Semantics, and Ontology", p. 211). We might feel: Accepting the "thing-world" is just accepting the world, and what kind of choice do we have about that? (I don't say there isn't one.) And what kind of choice do we have about accepting a form of language? We can accept or reject whatever in language *we* can construct. (Cp. Kant: ". . . reason has insight only into that which it produces after a plan of its own . . ." (*Critique of Pure Reason;* preface to second edition, p. 20).) If we can't *decide* that (we will say that) the things of our world exist, shall we say that we *believe* they exist? That is something a philosopher will say in the course of that rehearsal of our beliefs with which he begins his investigation of their validity as a whole. But that rehearsal does not *express* belief in anything; it contains no claims. Or shall we say that we have *faith* that the things of our world exist? But how is that faith achieved, how expressed, how maintained, how deepened, how threatened, how lost?

PART THREE

Knowledge and the Concept of Morality

For by thy words thou shalt be justified, and by thy words thou shalt be condemned.

Matthew 12:37

But who would think of introducing a new principle of all morality, and making himself as it were the first discoverer of it, just as if all the world before him were ignorant what duty was or had been in thoroughgoing error?

Kant, Critique of Practical Reason,
Preface, footnote

But what kind of disagreement, my friend, causes hatred and anger?

Socrates to Euthyphro

IX

Knowledge and the Basis of Morality

Historically as well as dialectically the concept of reason or knowledge, and therewith of rationality, raises two major problems for the moral philosopher. (1) An opportunity for moral reflection occurs when men find themselves at odds with one another, or with themselves, over the questions, "What ought to be done?" and "What am I to do?". Dialectically, this problem is reflected in a fact about "moral arguments" — the "methods" (to use Sidgwick's term) by which we undertake to arrive at a knowledge, or "rational conviction", as to what ought to be done — which has insistently and constantly occupied the attention of moral philosophers, viz., that such arguments are always, and dishearteningly, liable to break down, or end in stalemate, and the question which prompted the argument either left without answer or with incompatible answers which any further argument would seem helpless to resolve. (2) Even where there is no disagreement, hence no argument, about what ought to be done, even where I have achieved "rational conviction" about this question, or where the answer is from the beginning obvious, I still may not in fact *do* what I apparently know to be right, or refrain from doing what I surely *know* to be evil. Bruno Snell, in fact — obviously following Nietzsche, but without that animus — identifies the origin of the very concept of what we should regard as serious (reflective vs. conventional) morality with Socrates's criticism of the Greek dramatists, and especially Euripides.

I believe that it is possible to fix the point from which Socrates starts out to discuss morality. Euripides' Medea says: "I know what crimes I am about to commit, but my anger is stronger." Socrates rejoins: "As long as a man knows the

247

good, he will do it. All that is necessary is that he has really recognized the nature of the good. Nobody commits a crime voluntarily." [*The Discovery of the Mind,* p. 182]

Dialectically, this problem is reflected in questions about the nature of moral judgments and concepts, or about the "faculty" by which they are to be "known". Sidgwick avoided "the inquiry into the Origin of the Moral Faculty" which, he complained, "has perhaps occupied a disproportionate amount of the attention of modern moralists" by "the simple assumption (which seems to be made implicitly in all ethical reasoning) that there is something under any given circumstances which it is right or reasonable to do, and that this may be known" (*Methods of Ethics,* p. vi). But — whether because that assumption has seemed unacceptable to succeeding philosophers, or unavailing, or whether because of Kant's and Hume's enormous prestige in recent philosophizing, or for some other reason — moral philosophy has not succeeded in avoiding this question; only lately, of course, it has taken the guise not of a quasi-psychological inquiry into the origin of a mental faculty, but of a quasi-psychological analysis of the cognitive status of moral judgments, or of the "kind of meaning" enjoyed by ethical terms.

Both of these problems will, I think, lead a moral philosopher to question whether, or to what extent, knowledge can provide a basis for morality. And while probably all moral philosophers have been concerned with both sorts of problems, they describe clear differences of emphasis. A philosopher struck with the fact of men's divided opinions is likely to concentrate on methods which can lead to the settlement of social conflict and to develop a theory of the good society and a mode of criticizing existing institutions; a philosopher struck with man's divided nature is likely to concentrate on questions which concern the nature of society's authority, what it is which makes its deliverances binding upon us. The former emphasis leads to an investigation of such concepts as the good life and the question of the reality and hierarchy of values; the latter more directly to such concepts as guilt, responsibility, weakness of the will, and conscience. In both, character is assessed as revealed in conduct, but in the first it is the worldly course of the action which is in view, hence the effectiveness and mortal happiness of the person which is revealed; in the other it is the inner source of the action which is in view, hence the Will or immortal worth of the person which action betrays. In the first, morality looks toward politics, in the second toward religion.

I need hardly comment upon, or apologize for, the crudeness of this general division and of its various characterizations, nor acknowledge, what is too obvious, that they are related dimensions of morality and that every moralist has been concerned with both. Nor is it meant as in the least original. Its point, for me, lies merely in trying to make real for myself what any survey of ethical theories will say, that these theories have largely divided among those called Teleological and those called Deontological, the one concerned with the consequences of action, the other with its motives, the one taking as fundamental the concept of *good,* the other the concept of *right;* and why recent moral philosophy (in England and America) has been obsessed with questions about the definition or meaning of ethical terms, and the logical status of moral judgment and argument (is it enough to explain this phenomenon to say that it has been the result, happy or unhappy, of philosophy's having become "analytical"?); and what relationship may exist between the two main traditional theories and between the tradition and modern analysis.

To content oneself with familiar descriptions of these differences is likely to determine the course of one's investigation in uncontrolled, and perhaps arbitrary, ways; and to submerge assumptions which are not to be trusted out of sight. Two questions which particularly concern me, and whose answers are likely to be *assumed,* are those concerning the nature of reason, and its role in moral judgment and conduct; and concerning the nature of morality, or the function of moral judgment, itself. If, for example, you say that a good action is one whose consequences are good, then you will conceive the concept of reason, or its role in morality, as one of calculating these consequences. A philosopher who finds this point of view barbarous may yet acquiesce in the assumed idea of rationality and argue either that reason has no moral function or that it lies in a peculiar power of apprehending (intuiting) the moral quality of the act itself, and so perhaps seems to substitute incomprehensibility for barbarism. If, to take another example, you busy yourself with the definition of ethical terms and come out with the observation either that they cannot be defined or that ordinary words (like "good" and "right") have "characteristically ethical senses", then soon you feel baffled as to what significance (importance and sense) such results are envisioned as having. And, more importantly, it will be *assumed* what "sense" of these terms *is* "characteristically ethical", for example, one in which feeling is expressed; and therewith a concept of morality is assumed. Just as, if you find (and scarcely anything can have been so ill-concealed, and discovered with insistence so often) the "logic" of moral argument to differ from deductive and inductive arguments, then if you assume you know what this means, what importance it has, then you may assume that moral arguments are not fully rational and therewith assume a concept of rationality; and if you assume you know *what* the relation between (moral) conclusions and (factual) premises is, viz., "causal" and *hence* "psychological", then you will assume you know what the function of moral judgments is, viz., to change people's attitudes or to get someone to do something, and so again assume a concept of morality.

What first struck me, in considering epistemological assessments, is that they do not lead to such an air of unknown significance and unarticulated disagreement, to disputes about whether the problem is one of defining a word or not, and what the nature of its judgments are, what cognitive or logical status to assign to them, and whether the whole enterprise is rational or not, or prejudiced from the beginning. It is easy enough to say: All this has to do with the nature of morality itself. What we don't know is: what is this nature with which all this has to do? One of my chief purposes in going to the pains I have in sketching the nature of traditional epistemology was to prepare some way of determining what differences there may be between the assessments of our ordinary claims to knowledge and of our moral claims upon one another which, in some detail, could explain the emergence of such differences between epistemology and moral philosophy.

But it seems that moral philosophers have always done these things — always begun with ordinary claims, and perennially compared claims to knowledge with moral claims — and yet differed in their findings as angrily as the antagonists they describe. That is also something I have hoped for some understanding of.

To begin with the language, the convictions, and the conduct of ordinary men with the object of assessing and comparing them and rationalizing them so far as that may be done is, in the words of Sir David Ross, "the time-honored method of ethics" (*Foundations of Ethics*, p. 1); and he cites the practice of Socrates and Plato, and precepts of Aristotle and Kant to remind us of this fact. And writers as different as Schopenhauer, Sidgwick, and Professor Stevenson all seem to agree about the ordinary human being as the object of their attention, and to claim his service, or at least his clearer comprehension, as their goal. Schopenhauer, in his essay *The Basis of Morality*, complains about all previous attempts to "lay a foundation" for Ethics, that, among other things, they consist of "stilted maxims, from which it is no longer possible to look down and see life as it really is with all its turmoil" (p. 133), and he goes on to "give our moralists the paradoxical advice, first to look about them a little among their fellow-men" (p. 134). Sidgwick says that ". . . [his] treatment of the subject is, in a sense, more practical than that of many moralists, since . . . [he is] occupied from first to last in considering how conclusions are to be rationally reached in the familiar matter of our common daily life and actual practice" (p. vi), but he goes on to caution us, in a way which is very sympathetic to contemporary "analytical" writers in the subject, as follows: ". . . my immediate object — to invert Aristotle's phrase — is not Practice but Knowledge. I have thought that the predominance in the minds of moralists of a desire to edify has impeded the real progress of ethical science: and that this would be benefited by an application to it of the same disinterested curiosity to which we chiefly owe the great discoveries of physics"; and Professor Stevenson, to lend authority, or precedent, to his own "approach", cites with approval Hume's injunction to "glean up our experiments in this science from a cautious observation of human life, and take them as they appear in the common course of the world, by men's behavior in company, in affairs, and in their pleasure" (quoted in *Ethics and Language,* p. vi).

In the presence of this chorus of concord, how are we to account for the equally obvious presence of different and incompatible pictures moral philosophers have drawn from their common gaze? One suggestion is familiar enough, and that is to suppose, as Ross takes Aristotle to have supposed, that "in all the main theories, no less than in the views of the plain man, there is much that is true, and that even when theories are in broad opposition to each other, each is probably erring only by overstatement or misstatement of something that is profoundly true" (Ross, p. 2). But we are by now prepared, after our investigations of "our ordinary beliefs", to find that it will not be easy to articulate what it is which is overstated, nor the point at which divergence begins, whether of one moral theory from another or of any moral theory from the data — gleaned from a cautious observation of human life — it is meant to rationalize.

We have seen, in particular, how different are the ways in which the ordinary conduct of the ordinary human being can be appealed to, or looked at, when one philosophizes about it; and how different the import of various examples will be. One is, in addition, perplexed to find, in works purporting to begin from our ordinary moral convictions and conduct, maxims which are not merely "stilted", but which it is hard, if not impossible, to imagine one moral agent ever using to another (e.g., "You ought to keep promises", something over and over presented by moral philosophers as, indifferently, a moral "principle" or a moral "rule", and one for which each moral theorist offers his own "foundation"), and examples whose import about the nature of morality is unclear, and indeed whose very relevance to morality is questionable. Consider the seventeenth in a series of typical examples which Professor Stevenson focusses upon to examine "the methods used in ethical arguments with full attention to details" (p. 113):

A (speaking to C, a child): To neglect your piano practice is naughty.

B (in C's hearing): No, no, C is very good about practicing. (Out of C's hearing): It's hopeless to drive him, you know; but if you praise him he will do a great deal. [p. 128]

Stevenson's attention to the details of this example is, in full, as follows:

Here B is not opposed to the general direction of A's influence on C, but wishes to change the manner in which it is exerted. Examples of this kind are so common, and illustrate the hortatory effect of ethical judgments so obviously, that it is difficult to understand why emotive meaning in ethics was not recognized in the earliest theories. B's last remark serves to point out the consequences of the sorts of influence exerted.

What would a comparable example be where the assessment of claims to knowledge are concerned? Perhaps this:

A (speaking to C, a child): There was a goldfinch in the garden yesterday.

C: No there wasn't.

A: There was. Aunt Birdie told me.

B (in C's hearing): No, no, C is perfectly right. (Out of C's hearing): You've taken a hopeless line with him; he refuses to call the garden a "garden"; to him it's the Jungle. Furthermore, the *worst* authority you could appeal to is Aunt Birdie — he contradicts everything she says. Next time say Uncle Panther told you and he'll readily believe you.

Full attention to the details of this example might lead us to consider what general semanticists may call "breakdown in communication", and the nature of appeals to authority. In what sort of investigation might it appear? In, perhaps, a similar spirit, Bacon included various examples as illustrating his idols of the intellect; but they are not ones which are to guide an investigation of the nature of knowledge.

One is led to wonder whether Stevenson's examples, instead of providing the data from which a rationalization of "the methods used in ethical arguments" is to arise, have not themselves been selected by a prepossession concerning the nature of such arguments. What's wrong with that? Maybe the examples are only meant to be *illustrations* of a "theory", not to supply evidence for its truth. But my question is why Stevenson's examples so much as seem to be examples of *moral* encounter. What is the concept of morality which underlies the provision, and wide acceptance, of such examples, as typical instances of the way in which a moral judgment is supported? Or: what makes such reasons as he imagines moral ones?

This takes us to the other time-honored method of moral philosophers I am going to follow, viz., their habit of comparing moral claims (or reasons) with our claims to knowledge. And here again, what has been learned from this comparison has been far from constant. Let us recall a familiar instance.

Socrates: But what kind of disagreement, my friend, causes hatred and anger? Let us look at the matter thus. If you and I were to disagree as to whether one number were more than another, would that make us angry and enemies? Should we not settle such a dispute at once by counting?

Euthyphro: Of course.

Socr: And if we were to disagree as to the relative size of two things, we should measure them and put an end to the disagreement at once, should we not?

Euth: Yes.

Socr: And should we not settle a question about the relative weight of two things by weighing them?

Euth: Of course.

Socr: Then what is the question which would make us angry and enemies if we disagreed about it, and could not come to a settlement? Perhaps you have not an answer ready; but listen to mine. Is it not the question of the just and unjust, of the honorable and the dishonorable, of the good and the bad? Is it not questions about these matters which make you and me and everyone else quarrel, when we do quarrel, if we differ about them and can reach no satisfactory agreement?

What are we to learn from the fact that moral arguments differ in this way from arguments in science and mathematics? I think many, perhaps most, moralists — certainly most of those who have been committed to empiricism and regarded logic and physical science as providing their pictures of rationality — have taken the lesson of this difference to be that moral arguments are often, perhaps usually, incapable of rational settlement. But such an implication rests upon two assumptions, one about the nature of rationality and one about the nature of moral argument. The first is the assumption that the rationality of an argument depends upon its leading from premises all parties accept, in steps all can follow, to an agreement upon a conclusion which all must accept. The second assumption is that the goal of a moral argument is agreement upon some conclusion, in particular, a conclusion concerning what ought to be done.

What is the significance of saying that a rational argument is one whose conclusion "all must accept"? Obviously it doesn't mean that in fact no human animal *will* (in fact) fail to accept it. It is for such a reason, I suppose, that logic is called a "normative" discipline. But what does that mean? (For various, and as yet, to me, obscure reasons, philosophers imagine that to say of a judgment or discipline that it is normative is to say that it tells us what *ought* to be done or followed or believed. But I do not want, nor am I able, to trace the moralization of moral concepts which such an answer suggests. Another example of what I have in mind, to which I will come back, is the unhesitant conviction on the part of so many philosophers that "desirable" means "ought to be desired".) One answer would be: It means, in descriptive and simple terms, that someone who fails to accept it is regarded as either incompetent in that mode of reasoning, or else irrational. And that means to me: to say of logic that it is normative is to say that it is normative for a concept — or a part of the concept — of rationality.

But suppose that it is just characteristic of moral arguments that the rationality of the antagonists is not dependent on an agreement's emerging between them, that there is such a thing as *rational disagreement* about a conclusion. *Why* assume that "There is one right thing to be done in every case and that that can be found out"? Surely the existence of incompatible and equally legitimate claims, responsibilities, and wishes indicates otherwise? Socrates said, after all, that there are questions about which even the gods would disagree. (And his *first* concern, and perhaps his last, was not "How can we achieve agreement?", but "What *kind* of questions are these?".) Then how is the rationality of the answers to be determined? By the argument, no doubt; and perhaps the argument is such that it could establish rationality in the absence of agreement — though agreement *may*, it is to be hoped, supervene. Without the hope of agreement, argument would be pointless; but it doesn't follow that without agreement — and in particular, apart from agreement arrived at in particular ways, e.g., apart from bullying, and without agreement about a conclusion concerning what ought to be done — the argument was pointless.

But why, or how, does the fact, as it has been put, that "moral arguments may always break down" seem to moral philosophers to carry a lesson about morality as a whole? We found that in epistemological arguments not every case of the failure of knowledge contained some import about knowledge as a whole. Why should the failure of a moral argument — apparently *any* — seem to philosophers to have such import? And first, what does "the failure of a moral argument" mean? If it means "failure to achieve agreement", then again the import about morality assumes the goal of moral argument to be agreement. But maybe the "failure" of a moral argument, seen differently, no more points to the failure or irrationality of morality or moral argument generally, than the failure of ordinary claims to knowledge points to the inadequacy of knowledge as a whole.

To investigate this idea, I am going to follow further this time-honored method of moral philosophers, comparing the assessment of moral claims with the assessment of claims to knowledge. The motive for such a comparison is obvious enough. It comes from the feeling that if *any* procedure is rational, the way we acquire and assess knowledge is (= that it is normative for rationality). But I have too often felt that the question of what makes the acquisition and assessment of knowledge a rational process has itself been assumed as obvious. Moreover, the descriptions of logical or scientific success against which the limitations of moral argument are drawn, or its methods defined, are too often unclear, vague, or amateur, and the analogy too obscurely drawn, to inspire much real confidence.

Let me bring to mind two instances of such descriptions, the second given by a philosopher who expresses a commitment to science and its methods, and invokes its authority for his procedure; the first given by a philosopher differently possessed.

The method of ethics is in this respect different from that of the physical sciences. In them it would be a great mistake to take as our starting-point either the opinions of the many or those of the wise. For in them we have a more direct avenue to truth; the appeal must always be from opinions to the facts of sense-perception; and natural science entered on its secure path of progress only when in the days of Galileo men began to make careful observations and experiments instead of relying on *a priori* assumptions that had hitherto prevailed. In ethics we have no such direct appeal. We must start with the opinions that are crystallized in ordinary language and ordinary ways of thinking, and our attempt must be to make these thoughts, little by little, more definite and distinct. . . . [Ross, p. 3]

We are not likely, any longer, to accept as an explanation of the scientific revolution of the sixteenth and seventeenth centuries the idea that "men began to make careful observations and experiments". This is part of the lingering self-congratulation of the Renaissance which called the Middle Ages dark. Men "began" to have to do all sorts of things before that "secure path of progress" we call modern science could be taken: they had, for example, to achieve a new concept of "motion", and to secure its acceptance against powers who did not find themselves to be irrational in denying the conclusions of Galileo's arguments, and to alter men's attitudes toward nature as a whole; and Bacon had to *justify* "careful observations" of nature, not in order merely to have men look at the world, but, one might say, to have them look upon it differently, with other eyes, for new reasons. I mention such problems neither because I plan any serious discussion of them, nor because Ross makes any immediate use of a comparison between scientific and moral arguments; but rather to suggest that the *way* he compares the enterprises of science and ethics itself may subtly, but profoundly, affect the way the task of moral philosophy is conceived.

To say that science has a "more direct avenue to truth" than ethics does because ethics must "take as . . . [its] starting point either the opinions of the many or those of the wise" whereas science can and must "appeal . . . from opinions to the facts of sense-perception" masks unclarities about the nature and roles of the "data" from which ethical inquiry is thought to proceed (as well as about the role, or meaning, of authority in science). One unclarity has to do with the relation between a theory and its "data". About what do data provide an avenue to truth? They "substantiate" a theory; but a theory of what? Not of the data, but of nature. Whereas, a moral theory, using this part of the analogy, is to provide a theory which explains or reconciles conflicts among the data (men's opinions, expressions of ordinary consciousness) themselves. But scientific "data" do not conflict "among themselves"; scientific conflicts are between theory and data or between rival theories, and when *such* conflicts are settled (and will that — *when* will that — happen by "careful observations and experiments"?), we will not say that the rival theories each contain much that is true.

Another unclarity I had in mind as expressed in a simplistic view of scientific progress was this: A scientific theory can, must, repudiate *certain* data, refuse to allow certain facts to argue against it; but what facts can any ethical theory repudiate? Ross, speaking for the tradition, says that it is not intended to repudiate any facts, but to reconcile them, show one opinion to be over-emphasized, another misstated. But one of my questions is: How are the data selected? Stevenson, for example, allows *any* attempt by *any* man to change another man's attitudes to count as part of the data of a theory of moral judgment, and he says repeatedly that any attempt to "choose" among ways of supporting ethical judgments is already to moralize, not to analyze. I think he is desperately mistaken about this; but then how *are* certain data known to be so much as relevant to a moral theory? Granted that we can tell this, how are we to collect them and how far are we to respect them? To say that science starts from facts whereas ethics starts from beliefs and convictions makes it seem no problem how we determine what these beliefs and convictions are, nor what they are beliefs and convictions *about*. We are often told that "there are" (meaning what?) certain moral "rules or principles"; but when these are formulated I find that I am quite unclear whether the assertions in question (e.g., "Promises ought to be kept"; "Keep your promises") are rules or principles or "stilted maxims"; and unclear whether I believe or am convinced of them. Epistemologists, whatever scientists do, also claim to begin from the "beliefs or convictions" of ordinary men, and when they produce an example of such a belief (e.g., that there is an envelope here, and that we all see it), I may initially feel that it is odd to be told something so terribly obvious; but once into the spirit of the thing, I have no doubt whatever that I do believe it, or *have to say* that I believe it. Why the examples (data) the moral philosopher uses take the form they do is a question which, though obscured by comparing ethics with science, may be illuminated by comparing it with epistemology. I will proceed to that presently.

Another problem about the data from which we are to begin emerges in my having said just now that we *have to say* that we believe what the epistemologist says we believe. The reason for this is that the ordinary "beliefs" the epistemologist takes as his initial data are themselves determined by what we ordinarily say. (His initial statement could be phrased indifferently as, "we all believe that . . ." or "we should all say that. . .".) And then the *result* of his investigation is that what we should all say, and what we all, saying, believe, is not quite right, not fully valid. Now listen to a description of our "reflective moral consciousness" (= our opinions and convictions as to what ought to be done):

Although I think it is quite clear that a promise creates a *prima facie* obligation, or a responsibility, quite different from that which alone the utilitarian
system recognizes, we must guard against stating the obligation in a way which
would lead to consequences which our reflective moral consciousness would reject. What then is it, exactly, that a promise creates an obligation to do? We
must first note that, if the promise is phrased in the way in which promises
usually are phrased, we are *not* under an obligation to do that which we have
promised. For promises usually take the form of saying "I will do so-and-so",
where "doing so-and-so" is the effecting of some change in the state of affairs,
paying a debt, returning a borrowed book, travelling to some place to meet some
person, etc.; but if we are right in the contention put forward in another context, we are under no obligation to effect changes, but only to set ourselves to
do so. If, therefore, we want to limit ourselves to making promises which it will
be our duty to fulfill, we should cast our promises in the form "I will set myself,
or do my best, to do so-and-so". But it would be pedantic to insist upon this
alteration, for in fact our promises are understood so by both parties. No one
thinks that he has failed to do his duty if he has done his best, without success,
to fulfill his promise. . . . [Ross, p. 108]

I think I see why Ross, following Prichard, says this. Its source in our
"convictions" seems simply to be that intentions are taken into account
in evaluating a person's conduct. Its source in theory comes from a particular analysis of the concept of an action. All this must be considered
more fully in due course. All I am pointing to now is the fact that the
"usual phrasing" of promises is impugned as a guide as to what we
have, in promising, obligated ourselves to *do,* and it is claimed that what
we really think or believe or know about promising is given not by the
usual phrasing (a claim which would, in epistemology, cast doubt on our
ordinary belief), but by the result of a bit of analysis on an ordinary concept. But I emphatically deny that I, or anyone else, "really thinks" or
"really understands" that when we make promises "we are under no
obligation to effect changes, but only to set ourselves to do so". If, therefore, the moral theorist is to reconcile conflicting opinions and theories
by an appeal to our ordinary or reflective moral consciousness — in this
case to reconcile a Utilitarian and an Intuitionist account of the obligation to keep promises — then Ross's remark constitutes no reconciliation
of two theories, but a theoretical reconciliation which either conflicts with
the data it has claimed to follow or else misdescribes those data.

Ross's commitment to science or to what goes as empiricism is, one
gathers, weaker than his commitment to our "moral consciousness" (one
of his conclusions is that our knowledge of fundamental moral principles
is synthetic a priori) — and if one has to *choose* between empiricism and
the concept of morality then it is not obvious that Ross's choice is the

wrong one. I think this choice increasingly presents itself as a real one among intellectuals generally — or else, protected by an academy, we lead our morals in the daytime and our epistemology after working hours.

But a distant view of science can at least as strongly, and more directly, control the views of a writer on ethical language who explicitly claims a commitment to empiricism and to the methods of logic and science, and whose views seem most elaborately to offend our (my) moral sensibility.

Professor Stevenson's "first question" (p. 2) is this:

What is the nature of ethical *agreement* and *disagreement?* Is it parallel to that found in the natural sciences, differing only with regard to the subject matter; or is it of some broadly different sort?

His answer is that "the disagreements that occur in science, history, biography" are "disagreements in belief", whereas "it is disagreement in attitude . . . that chiefly distinguishes ethical issues from those of science" (p. 13). There are some remarks made about the difficulty in specifying "just *how* beliefs and attitudes differ", but "for practical purposes we do and must make such a distinction every day" (p. 7), and it is up to psychology to specify the distinction further, and to indicate the (always causal) mechanism of their interaction. Where a disagreement in belief is concerned, proofs can be offered in settlement of it; but where disagreement in attitudes is concerned, there can strictly speaking be no question of *proof* (since the attitude is in part an imperative and imperatives have no proofs) but there can be "reasons" offered pro and con, and these are related *psychologically* (not demonstratively and not inductively) to the judgment they support. Will these reasons ("methods") be able to resolve ethical disagreement? Only on the assumption that "All disagreement in attitude is rooted in disagreement in belief" (p. 136). But this "psychological generalization" is too sweeping to put much confidence in; and so it would seem that "no exhaustive method, convincing to all people under all circumstances can confidently be hoped for. . .".

What have we actually been told? That some disagreements between people can be settled in obvious ways and that some cannot be. Nothing could be clearer. Some disputes are factual and some are not. To say a dispute is about a matter of fact is exactly to say that there are certain ways of settling it. Just as, to say that something is a *fact* is to say that it can be or has been discovered in certain ways. To say that *other* sorts of disputes (for example, moral ones) cannot be settled in *such* ways is not a "hypothesis" and requires no "psychological generalization", but is a point of grammar. So where does the rush of associations with "science", "ethics", "beliefs", "attitudes", and "psychology" come in? Stevenson says that it is his "contention that ethics involves disagreement in attitude" (p. 18). But merely *that* needn't be *contended* at all, if what it means is that ethics *involves* people, makes them angry and guilty, makes them friends and enemies, and that it won't be easy or obvious how to bring them together if they are apart or tear them apart if they are together (all said or implied by Socrates to Euthyphro). What is contentious indeed is to say or assume, in addition: (1) that all disagreement in attitude is *moral* disagreement; (2) that all disagreements which cannot be (rationally) *settled* (end in a *conclusion* which all parties agree is the right one) are irrational; (3) that a reason which is neither deductively nor inductively related to a judgment is "therefore" "only" "psychologically" related to it; (4) that what makes science rational is that it consists of beliefs about matters of fact — and hence consists of methods which rationally settle disagreements.

Stevenson's view requires, or contains, all of these ideas, and he must either take them to be obvious in themselves or else to follow obviously from the fact that there are different "kinds" of disagreement. Given what I take to be the remorseless paradoxicality of his view, its wide acceptance — despite criticisms of *pieces* of his view which would have seemed essential to it (e.g., of his causal theory of "meaning", and in particular of "emotive" meaning, and still more particularly of his analysis of the word "good") — must mean that these assumptions (and others which, as I shall try to show, underlie them) are widely shared. I have mentioned the second of them as containing the supposed lesson of Socrates; everything I will say has bearing on that, and I will begin to discuss it directly, or to suggest a *way* of discussing it, in a moment. The first assumption is one way of putting the topic of the next chapter, the concept of morality underlying Stevenson's theory. The third assumption must wait for an examination, which I sketch in Chapter XII, of the pervasive idea that from "factual" premises no moral judgment can be "derived" — the so-called thesis of autonomy. The fourth assumption is the vaguest, the hardest to show the workings of, but it is the one immediately relevant to us now, and I want to say another word about it here.

I have said that the lesson which seems commonly to have been drawn from the ancient recognition that moral disagreements are not to be settled the way disagreements about logical or factual matters are, and perhaps not to be settled at all, has been that moral arguments are not, or may not be, rational; and that thought is buttressed by the idea that logic and, more particularly, science, provide the models for the rationality of argument. I take it that the aspect which has most struck moral philosophers is the fact of the *agreement* which can be achieved in logical and scientific argument. I have suggested that while that may be the source of their rationality it may not be necessary to the idea of rationality generally. Now what I wish to suggest is that it is not so much as clear *what* it is which provides the enviable agreement each achieves. Moral philosophers, however, in taking them as models of rationality, models which morality fails to match, must assume that they know not only why agreement is essential to rationality, but what it is about logic and science which negotiates agreement.

If agreement is, as I take it to be, part of what Ross is pointing to as the "secure path of progress" which science attained in the days of Galileo, then he takes scientific agreement to be a function of its "more direct avenue to truth", its "appeal . . . from opinions to the facts of sense-perception". I've said that such an explanation is not likely, for more than one reason, to satisfy us. Nor, however, for some of the same reasons, will Stevenson's idea that science consists of "beliefs" for which "some manner of proof" can be given, or which are "[revised] . . . in the light of further information". Not only are we too aware of the "conventionality" of scientific theories, and aware of how resistant, and rightly resistant, a scientific theory is to "further information". But are we any longer quite so willing to take that Aristotelian who refused to look through Galileo's telescope in order to "see" the valleys of the moon, as a comic and irrational figure? If *now* a man refused to accept the evidence of telescopes as telling us of the nature of the moon, he would either be (we would either regard him as) irrational or else incompetent *in science*. That man is no scientist, given the procedures or canons of science which now constitute that institution. Or again: what he says will not count for or against any proposition of science. Once these procedures and canons are established, then agreement is reached in familiar ways; but that simply means: agreement (or absence of disagreement) about what constitutes science, scientific procedure, and scientific evidence, is what permits particular disagreements to be resolved in certain ways. Being a scientist just is having a commitment to, and being competent at, these modes of resolution.

But how is this relevant? Perhaps Stevenson means to be taking science as it now is, with its established procedures, as the model of rationality; obviously it is different from morality, and in the way Stevenson describes, as a difference in kinds of agreement. But what I am asking is what the significance of this difference is. If what makes science rational is not the fact of agreement about particular propositions itself, or about the acknowledged modes of arriving at it, but the fact of a *commitment* to certain modes of argument whose very nature is to lead to such agreement, then morality may be rational on exactly the same ground, namely that we commit ourselves to *certain* modes of argument, but now ones which do not lead, in the same ways, and sometimes not at all, to agreement (about a conclusion). Then to say that such arguments "must be accepted" still means that either they are accepted or else the person who rejects them is either irrational or incompetent at morality. Except that here what counts as "acceptance of an argument" will not then mean "agreeing with its conclusion"; and of course what will count as *disagreeing* with its conclusion, but still rationally (i.e., in such a way that you will still be called rational), cannot just be "denying it" or "finding that the argument is not psychologically convincing".

Stevenson, of course, has set himself against any idea that moral competence may, like scientific competence, be the result of a commitment to certain forms of reasons or arguments. For on his view any choice of "methods" (procedures, reasons, arguments) used in supporting an ethical judgment is itself a normative, ethical matter which "analytic detachment" eschews (cf. *Ethics and Language*, p. 158, and Chapter VII, *passim*). This must be discussed at some length. For now, I shall only comment that you might as well say that any choice of methods as to how a scientific proposition is to be supported is itself a matter of scientific procedure. But that is either analytic or false. Either it means: Unless certain methods were followed it wouldn't be (called) "science"; which is a grammatical statement. Or it means: Scientists arrive at agreement about what methods will *be* "scientific" in the way they arrive at agreements which *employ* the methods all accept as scientific; which is false.

So the analogy, or invidious comparison, with science turns on a particular aspect of the comparison which may not be the crucial one. One can take the difference to be proven by the different sorts of disagreements about particular propositions within each domain; I take the similarity to be the necessity of commitment (or "agreement") as to what will count as an "argument" or "reason" within each.

Perhaps it is relevant to the way the analogy is drawn that the typical examples chosen to illustrate ethical judgments or "attitudes" will be "You ought to do so-and-so" or "That is good" or "You ought to keep promises", but not (say) "If what a person does was done by accident, then he is not to be blamed — at least not as severely as if he deliberately did it". If someone "disagrees" with this last example will it be enough to say that the "reasons" you give in its behalf (and what will they be?) do not psychologically convince him? Will there be no suspicion that he is not morally competent? (Which is on trial, *his* rationality or the rationality of morality? Why could that question not so much as arise for a philosopher like Stevenson?) But further, if the commitment to morality (being a competent moral agent) involves commitments to such principles as that about accident and blame, then perhaps the fact that we may disagree, in a given argument, about other questions (e.g., how good an excuse "by accident" is; whether a man is entitled to that excuse in a particular situation; whether he ought not to have exercised greater care; what his real motive was (what he was really doing)) may seem to carry a very different weight — not to deny the rationality of a moral argument in which no appeal to "facts" seems to settle it, but to provide modes of argument whose characteristic feature is exactly that they can secure the rationality of both protagonists in the absence of agreement about a conclusion. On the other hand, examples chosen as typical of scientific "beliefs" will be, say, a "law" like "All metals expand when heated", or a statement such as "There will be an eclipse at such a place and time", but not the "beliefs" that the earth and the heavens are subject to the same physical laws, or that men are unconsciously motivated to action, or that they descend to consciousness through biological evolution.

This comparison of examples suggests again that the views taken of science and morality may not proceed from an impartial investigation of examples, but on the contrary, that the examples used in the investigation may themselves be selected or determined by a prior point of departure. If you begin by being struck with the peculiarity of ethical arguments as perhaps unsettleable, and struck with how different other questions are, then you will pick examples from science which illustrate its capacity for agreement, and you will then have the idea, or illusion, that you know that, and why, science is rational and morality not.

Am I then suggesting, in saying that what we call "science" depends on commitments to certain "methods" which have certain properties, that science itself is not fully rational? What I am urging is that we not assume we know what makes it rational; that we take the question of its rationality or irrationality to be as problematical as the question of the rationality or irrationality of morality. But I know too little of the history and actual prosecution of science to have much confidence in any discussion I could offer of it. The little I have said will have served its purpose if it helps to hold such questions for investigation. (Now, of course, there is T. S. Kuhn's *The Structure of Scientific Revolutions,* and the discussions it may figure in.)

I propose, as has been said, to compare moral arguments with those ordinary epistemological assessments whose structure and import have already concerned us. They seem to offer as clear a model of what we take as rationality as any of the advanced and more glamourous agreements of physics and astronomy, and because their details lie more within our reach, such a comparison may help articulate more clearly what differences may be the significant ones between arguments "which cause hatred and anger" and those which do not, and why.

Our entire discussion has prepared us for the immediate problem which confronts us: *what* example from morality shall we choose to work with? Shall we take a case in which there is disagreement over a specific act to be done? or over a particular "rule" or "principle"? Is there any case about which we will feel, as we felt about "best" cases in epistemology, that "If *any* case is one in which we can know something to be (or agree that it is) good or bad, right or wrong, we can know this to be"? I think there is no such case, and that may itself prove significant. For what would a "case" be? If we take as our case a "principle" like "Promises are (ought to be) kept", then we won't know what agreement or disagreement about this would signify. If some of us hold that it is universally true then that will seem to be a particular *view* of morality, which may be disagreed about without jeopardizing another view of the subject. And if we agree that in *general* it is true, but only with qualifications, then we won't know whether we would agree about the qualifications, nor apply them in the same instances, nor if we would not, whether this carries any import about morality in general, nor what the import may be. If, on the other hand, we take the case of some specific action, then we might take a case in which the "action" in question is described in ethically prejudicial terms (e.g., "Ought he to have murdered him?" rather than ". . . killed him?", or "Was he wrong to betray him?" rather than ". . . to refuse to do what he said?"), or else we might feel that any agreement about the morality of the act will turn upon some agreement about how the act *is* to be described. Was it really *breaking a promise?* Is it fair *just* to say he *lied* when what he did was to lie *in order to* . . . or *as a way of* . . . . ("Socrates: Then [i.e., in moral disputes] they [i.e., mankind, men] do not disagree over the question that the unjust individual must be punished. They disagree over the question, who is unjust, and what was done and when, do they not?" (*Euthyphro*, p. 9).)

Apparently, what the "case" in question is *forms part of the content of the moral argument itself*. Actions, unlike envelopes and goldfinches, do not come named for assessment, nor, like apples, ripe for grading. The most serious sense, to my mind, in which Kant's moral theory is "formalistic" comes not from his having said that actions motivated only in *certain* ways are *moral* actions but in his having found too little difficulty in saying *what* "the" maxim of an action is in terms of which his test of its morality, the Categorical Imperative, is to be applied. Kant's view that moral conduct requires specific moral motivation fits with, or is a version of, the view that there are dimensions of assessment of human behavior that go before and after morality. (I may just mention here that I would not accept as a best case of morality (or of moral judgment) the prohibition of some hideous deed that all normal people must agree is hideous (for example, as I think more than once has been offered me in public discussion, You oughtn't to torture children). Mere morality is not designed to evaluate the behavior and interactions of monsters. Similarly, commandments (e.g., the ten) concern matters that ordinary human beings are subject to and tempted from.)

The moral significance of how an action is described, the problem in saying what it is which is under scrutiny, suggests that the epistemological "foundation" so often sought for morality, the "knowledge" which is to "base" our moral conduct and judgment, is a knowledge of *persons,* an epistemology which explains and assesses our claims to know what anyone is doing, and the basis on which one describes one's own action. That there is this problem about how an action is to be described — which seems prior to the problem about how it is to be evaluated in more explicitly moral terms — suggests that appeals to ordinary language will play a different, and more direct, role in criticizing moral theories than in criticizing traditional epistemology.

Recognizing a difficulty in choosing a "best", or even "ordinary" case in which an action is known to be right or wrong, let us take various cases which seem intuitively to be moral ones (realizing that eventually we will want some conceptualization of what that intuition is guided by) and compare them with what we have learned to expect of epistemological assessments.

I.

    A: You owe it to your family and friends not to go through with this farce.

    B: I respect and love the city which has found me guilty, and I will not break her laws by escaping.

A: Come off it. If you respect and love her so much, don't force the issue by making her do something she's going to regret.

B: Let's put it this way. I will not be put in the position of becoming an ordinary law-breaker.

A: And your friends, your family . . . ?

B: My friends will respect my position.

II.

A: You know the person you mean to honor was an enemy of the state.

B: The *person?* He was my brother.

A: I know how strong your feelings of loyalty are, and I respect them; but do not go on.

B: I know how strongly you will be offended; but do not go on.

III.

A: I've decided against offering him the job.

B: But he's counting on it. You most explicitly promised it to him.

Each of the following exchanges is meant as a continuation of this opening.

A_1: But I've since learned what kind of man he is.

B_1: What he did you yourself have done, but you tell yourself that in your case "it was different". It's different in *every* case. And the same. You're muddled, criminally muddled.

* * *

A_2: I know, but it has suddenly become *very* inconvenient to have him around, and there is someone else really better qualified anyway.

B_2: If you do this to him, I'll never speak to you again.

A_2: Don't make such an issue out of it. I'll see that he gets a job, and I'll give him some money to see him through.

B_2: Goodbye.

* * *

A_3: I said merely that I would try to find him a job.

B_3: But from a man in your position that is tantamount to a promise of a job. You know he *took* it as a promise.

A_3: That is his business.

B_3: You *are* cruel.

* * *

A_4: But I've since learned what kind of man he is.

B_4: A promise is a promise.

IV.

A: You let me believe that it was you who were my benefactor.

B: I never told you so.

V.

> A: You must stay with him. The consequences of leaving him now would be that people will call you "loose"; you will be an object of scorn.
> B: Yes. And if I stay and marry him people will smile indulgently, think me a bit racy, and in a while I'll be a respected member of the community again. Only the consequence will be that I would have lost respect for myself in living with someone I do not love.

Have these "arguments" broken down? Any *could* continue perhaps, but what would determine *when* they stop and what would be the significance if they stopped here? In epistemological contexts these questions have clear answers. If the goldfinch assessment stops after "But goldcrests also have red heads" then the significance is that the claim to know it is a goldfinch has fallen; it *may* be what you claim it is, but the claim has been insufficiently supported — the opening exposed by the ground for doubt has not been closed. *Every competent speaker knows this.* And if the argument is to continue then either the ground for doubt must itself be impugned ("The shape of a goldcrest's head is different") or a new basis proposed ("I know not just from the head, but from the eye-markings"), and every person competent to enter claims to knowledge knows the significance of this. We could say: It is not up to the protagonists to assign their own significance to bases and grounds for doubt; what will count as an adequate basis and sufficient ground for doubt is *determined by the setting of the assessment itself.* When I counter a basis by saying "But that's not enough", there is no room for you to say, "For me it is enough".

But in the moral cases *what* is "enough" is itself part of the content of the argument. What is enough to counter my claim to be right or justified in taking "a certain" action is up to me, up to me to determine. I don't *care* that he is an enemy of the state; it's too bad that he took what I said as a promise; I know that others will be scornful, nevertheless . . . ; suppose I *have* done more or less what he did, my case was different. I can *refuse to accept* a "ground for doubt" without impugning it as false, and without supplying a new basis, and yet not automatically be dismissed as irrational or morally incompetent. What I *cannot* do, and yet maintain my position as morally competent, is to deny the *relevance* of your doubts ("What difference does it make that I promised, that he's an enemy of the state, that I will hurt my friends"), fail to see that they require a determination by me. But in epistemological contexts, the relevance of the doubt is itself enough to impugn the basis as it stands, and therewith the claim to knowledge.

How shall we account for this difference? Let us consider what makes a "statement of fact" a basis for a claim to knowledge.

Questioning a claim to knowledge takes the form of asking "How do you know?" or "Why do you believe that?", and assessing the claim is, we could say, a matter of assessing whether your position (as Austin put it, your "credentials and facts", your learning and perception) are adequate to the claim. Questioning a claim to moral rightness (whether of any action or any judgment) takes the form of asking "Why are you doing that?", "How can you do that?", "What *are* you doing?", "Have you really considered what you're saying?", "Do you know what this means?"; and assessing the claim is, as we might now say, to determine *what* your position is, and to challenge the position itself, to question whether the position you *take* is adequate to the claim you have entered. The point of the assessment is not to determine *whether* it is adequate, where *what* will be adequate is itself *given* by the form of the assessment itself; the point is to determine *what* position you are taking, that is to say, *what position you are taking responsibility for* — and whether it is one I can respect. What is at stake in such discussions is not, or not exactly, whether you know our world, but whether, or to what extent, we are to live in the same moral universe. What is at stake in such examples as we've so far noticed is not the validity of morality as a whole, but the nature or quality of our relationship to one another.

That in the epistemological contexts the adequacy of position is determined by the form of the assessment itself is what gives to the skeptical grounds for doubt their devastating power. For when the philosopher, with a sense of reasonableness, raises the question "How do you know it isn't wax, or that you weren't tricked (by your senses or by some unnoticed assumption)?", or "But you don't see *all* of it", or "But couldn't he do those things and not be having that, or any, feeling?", what we realize is not merely that our position is not good enough, but also that *no* position could be any better than the one we're in (which is part of the content of feeling this to be a "best" case of knowledge), and that therefore knowledge as a whole is threatened.

There are conflicts which can throw morality as a whole into question, but the significance of this question is not, or not necessarily, that the validity of morality is under suspicion, but perhaps that its competence as the judge of conduct and character is limited. This is what Kierkegaard meant by the "teleological suspension of the ethical", and what Nietzsche meant by defining a position "beyond good and evil". What they meant is that there is a position whose excellence we cannot deny, taken by persons we are not willing or able to dismiss, but which, *morally,* would have to be called wrong. And this has provided a major theme of modern literature: the salvation of the self through the repudiation of morality.

I take it that most moral philosophers have assumed that the validity of morality depended upon its competence to assess *every* action (except those which are "caused", "determined") and that the possibility of repudiating morality *anywhere* meant its total repudiation as fully rational; that a fully rational morality must be capable of evaluating the highest excellence and the most unspeakable evil, and that persons of the highest excellence and most unspeakable evil must *agree* with our moral evaluations if these evaluations are to be fully rational. I think of this as the moralization of moral theory — it makes any and every issue a *moral* issue, and for no particular reason (except, perhaps, "favoring" something with "special seriousness or urgency" (Stevenson, p. 90)). Such a conception has done to moral philosophy and to the concept of morality what the events of the modern world have often done to the moral life itself: made it a matter of academic questions.

Morality must leave itself open to repudiation; it provides *one* possibility of settling conflict, a way of encompassing conflict which allows the continuance of personal relationships against the hard and apparently inevitable fact of misunderstanding, mutually incompatible wishes, commitments, loyalties, interests and needs, a way of mending relationships and maintaining the self in opposition to itself or others. Other ways of settling or encompassing conflict are provided by politics, religion, love and forgiveness, rebellion, and withdrawal. Morality is a valuable way because the others are so often inaccessible or brutal; but it is not everything; it provides a door through which someone, alienated or in danger of alienation from another through his action, can return by the offering and the acceptance of explanation, excuses and justifications, or by the respect one human being will show another who sees and can accept the responsibility for a position which he himself would not adopt. We do not have to agree with one another in order to live in the same moral world, but we do have to know and respect one another's differences. And *what* we can respect, and how far and how deeply, are not matters of what "feeling" a "reason" "causes" in us.

But although morality is open to repudiation, either by the prophet or the raging and suffering self, or by the delinquent or the oldest and newest evil, and though it cannot assure us that we will have no enemies nor that our actions are beyond reproach even when they pass all *moral* tests; not just anybody, in *any way,* can repudiate it. The question *"Who is to say* what is and isn't moral?" is not rhetorical, but demands an answer from moral theorists. If a moral philosopher cannot explain what a moral position (or reason) is and what qualifies a person as a moral agent, then all his provision of "foundation" crumbles at a touch. For then we are going to have to set up a display of humorous tolerance and allow that some "ethical" disagreements cannot be "settled" "rationally" on such a ground as this: whatever *reasons* are offered them, when "an oversexed, emotionally independent adolescent argues with an undersexed, emotionally dependent one about the desirability of free love" their disagreement may be "permanently unresolved" (Stevenson, p. 137). You might as well say that if those two went on permanently arguing about whether men do or do not descend from apes then the science of biology would lack an "exhaustive" (p. 135) or "definitive method of proof" (p. 137). But it makes a difference whether the argument in question is conducted by an oversexed, emotionally dependent adult like D. H. Lawrence, or an undersexed, or sublimated, emotionally independent adult like Freud; and a difference which is part of the nature of morality itself. It is part of the life of the subject that not every opinion has the same weight nor every disagreement the same significance. However finally unsatisfactory a moral theory may be which invokes the idea of an Ideal Spectator as the optimal moral judge, it contains that ineluctable truth. When, therefore, Stevenson says of the questions "Who are the *rightful* authorities? Who *ought* to guide others by their exhortation?" that they are "precisely the questions which amateur moralists debate over the cracker-barrel" (p. 164), this shows simply that he has asked the questions in such a way as to *make* them cracker-barrel; as he has done with the "disagreement" about "free" "love". For these are questions which any moral theory must undertake to answer, if they are understood to mean "What *gives* someone moral authority?", "What gives anyone the *right* to speak for another?", "What makes any guidance, whether by exhortation, calm reasoning or example, *moral* guidance?".

What makes a statement of fact a moral reason for an action or a judgment? When we asked what made a statement a basis for a claim to knowledge, we answered, in effect: it details a position from which we all know that the claim in question can be substantiated, and it stands unless a ground for doubt shows the position to be insufficient, which we will also all know. But since part of the content of a moral argument must be to *establish* the adequacy or superiority of a position relative to a given claim, what are the dimensions of the position in terms of which adequacy or superiority is to be assessed? Or: What makes a reason *rele-*

vant to this assessment? And if, having answered this question, we could find general characteristics of these reasons, articulate why they are morally relevant reasons, we would then have given something in the way of a characterization of morality.

All I can do here is to suggest the kind of importance this question has. To do this I will consider three theses which have had a wide appeal among philosophers, and construe each as an answer to the question: "What makes a reason relevant in supporting a moral judgment or in justifying a course of action?" Or: "What makes a reason a moral reason?" We can construe the main ethical theories as ones in which, among other things, it is argued or assumed that only certain kinds of reasons are morally relevant (whether as the motive of an action or as part of its assessment). The most familiar moral objections to a moral theory are that the reasons it justifies do not do full justice to our moral sensibility: that is the ground on which Kant is "formalistic" (when, for example, he says that an act taken out of love is not *morally* motivated), and on which Utilitarianism leads to its famous paradoxes (that you may break a promise on grounds of convenience; that you may, when very convenient, punish an innocent man; that push-pin is as good as poetry). If to say that each of these theories contains much that is (morally) true is to say that there are different times, moral contexts, stations, actions, or aspects of actions, for which they are fully true; then a reconciliation of the theories would take the form of defining the different limits within which each is true.

But the theses I wish to discuss do not take positions about that at the same level as Teleologists and Deontologists; for they are concerned, as I might put it, not with the particular moral content of moral reasons, but with something like their grammatical ("logical") properties: they contain part, at least, of what I take Kant to mean by a Metaphysic of Morals, an attempt to explain the rationality, or lack of rationality, of moral judgments, and the validity, or lack of validity, of moral argument; an attempt to articulate the point, the content, and the validity of any judgment we would recognize as a moral one. I say that I am considering theses about moral reasons, and not full moral theories, because the questions I will consider represent only a part of what the philosophers who espouse them are concerned with, and I have formulated the theories, I hope not unjustly, in such a way as to bring out the explicit or implicit thesis about the relevance of reasons which each contains. I should add, however, that my interest in these theses is guided by the conviction that they are central to, and determinative of, a theoretical point of view.

The first thesis is Stevenson's: *"Any* statement about *any* matter of fact which *any* speaker considers likely to alter attitudes may be adduced as a reason for or against an ethical judgment." The second thesis is one implied by a view which has come to be called Rule Utilitarianism, or Restricted Utilitarianism, and which, so far as it concerns my present purposes, can be construed as follows: moral reasons take one of two forms, in one of which an act is said to be justified as itself morally fitting or binding, in the other of which an action is justified or recommended in terms of its consequences (not all philosophers holding the view I am alluding to actually argue that there are only two main sorts of moral reasons or justifications, nor attempt to show why this should be the case). The relevance of each of these kinds of reasons is limited by a consideration of *what* it is which is to be justified: a deontological reason or justification is appropriate where it is a particular act which has come in question and where that act is covered by a moral rule or is part of a general social practice; a utilitarian reason may be relevant either to a particular action or to a social practice as a whole, but where the action is an instance of a practice (as, e.g., in the notorious cases of promising and punishment), a utilitarian reason is appropriate only when directed to the practice itself. The third thesis to be considered is the familiar one which has come to be known as the Autonomy of Morals: a factual statement constitutes a reason for a moral judgment only by virtue of its appealing to a moral major premise in conjunction with which the judgment can be derived.

What I hope will emerge from my considerations of each of these theses is, in outline, this: That (1) Stevenson's thesis implies a lack of the concept of morality altogether; but this lack makes clearer what such a concept must include; that (2) the appeal to rules fails to grasp the import of either Utilitarianism or Deontology with respect to their justifications of the "institutions" of promising and punishment, and the explanations of their difference in terms of the concept of a rule is unsuccessful; but in seeing in detail the failures of this powerful and serious attempt to explicate moral concepts we are led to a fuller understanding of certain epistemological questions within moral theory; that (3) the sense of the necessity of appealing to a moral major premise is produced by a position which resembles the "philosopher's context" I described, in Part Two, as produced by a "sense of being sealed off from the world", but that, in philosophizing about morality, this position leads to a conclusion which is not in obvious conflict with what we all believe or know to be true about the moral universe and is (therefore) not "unstable"; and that in comparing these two "philosopher's contexts" we can learn more about both, and therewith something about the relation of moral philosophy to epistemology, and of each of these projects to those respective sets of common beliefs or opinions from which both begin and which both attempt to find, or provide, a "foundation" for.

X

An Absence of Morality

The suggestion that Stevenson's *Ethics and Language* is controlled by an underlying concept, or lack of the concept, of morality may seem to those to whom Stevenson's analysis has been convincing to beg the very question on which he has over and over claimed to maintain scrupulous neutrality and scientific detachment. It is, presumably, from commitment to this neutrality that Stevenson says: *"Any* statement about *any* matter of fact which *any* speaker considers likely to alter attitudes may be adduced as a reason for or against an ethical judgment" (p. 114). This is cardinal to the direction his analysis takes, and his examples will be accepted as ones concerning morality as long as that principle seems acceptable.

This principle of Stevenson's can be put this way: *Any* statement about any matter of fact must be considered *morally relevant,* provided only that it is considered likely to be effective. That seems to me as paradoxical an assertion about morality as one is likely to hit upon with the unaided intellect. But unlike the paradoxical conclusions of epistemology, it is not a statement Stevenson, and others, find it difficult to *maintain* belief in; and, related to this, it is not one which he finds incompatible with "what we all believe" or say, though perhaps it is incompatible with certain mistaken *theories* about ethical arguments (e.g., that they may be "valid" or "invalid"). Moreover, where it *seems* to conflict with what we believe, his claim is not that his discovery has greater weight, or is more precise, or undercuts our ordinary beliefs, but that it is a neutral description of what in fact we all believe (so far as we have assessed our beliefs) and of what ordinary human conduct implies, one which any man could accept without altering his moral behavior in the least — except perhaps to make it more tolerant.

No doubt this means that "there is much that is true" in what Stevenson has to say. But, unlike the main ethical theories which have their recurrent hours with us, what is true in Stevenson is not true of *morality*. However far one may be successful in reconciling traditional moral theories by displaying the complementarity of the reasons each supports as morally relevant in justifying one's judgment and conduct, what is *not* to be reconciled with any theory of sensibility recognizable as moral is the idea that *any* reason adduced in support of a judgment about our conduct or character must be considered morally relevant on the sole ground that it is in fact likely to be effective in altering attitudes and conduct.

I have taken Stevenson's saying that any statement "may be adduced" as a reason not to mean simply, in Euthyphro's words, that "there is nothing which . . . [men] may not do and say to avoid punishment", or, we could add, to get other people to do something they want them to do; but to mean that any reason entered in such a way must be considered a moral one, responded to in such a way as grants full moral competence to the speaker urging it. A complete articulation of the source of such a thesis would have to include an examination of the assumption about the logic of moral argument which underlies it, which indeed seems to necessitate it for Stevenson, that "One of the peculiarities of ethical arguments lies in the inference from a factual reason to an ethical conclusion", a stage in the thesis of the Autonomy of Morals. It is nothing more than an assumption on Stevenson's part. His arguments, so far as they relate to it, are directed toward showing that since "clearly, the inference will be neither *demonstratively* nor *inductively* valid, by hypothesis" (p. 153), the only interesting question is whether we are to call such inferences valid or invalid; and he, as is familiar, decides that we are not. The little I am going to say about this assumption I leave for a separate chapter. My immediate purpose is to see how, given this assumption, the further assumptions that the relation between reason and conclusion must "therefore" be psychological, and "therefore" causal, and that "a moralist . . . is one who endeavors to influence attitudes" (p. 243), vitiate the concept of morality.

Stevenson, as has been said, takes his thesis to be demanded by a scientific or "analytic detachment" (p. 160) which precludes our taking any "stand" on issues like moral relevance. That is made out in the following way:

It will now be clear that the whole question about the choice of methods, and the "available grounds" for choice, does not constitute some isolated division of ethics, involving an analysis that is foreign to the remainder of this work. On the contrary, any decision about what methods are to be used, if it cannot be made with reference to validity, is itself a normative ethical matter. This becomes quite obvious when the question is phrased in ordinary ethical terminology. To ask "What method shall I choose?" is in effect to ask "What method *ought* I choose?" Any argument about the question will involve disagreement in attitude; and the considerations which one adduces as "grounds" for choosing one method or another are simply the "reasons" . . . by which an ethical judgment — here a judgment about the way *another one is to be supported* — is itself supported. [p. 158]

What does the phrase "choice of methods" convey? Perhaps one thinks of a case in which one physical process is preferred to another (say sterilizing surgical equipment by an autoclave process rather than through boiling or by alcohol); or one imagines adopting the French rather than the Italian system of solfeggio; or one remembers finally choosing Goren's over Culbertson's method of evaluating bridge hands. And the grounds for choice are in each case quite explicit and well understood. But one does *not* choose whether a given method *is* a process of sterilization, or is a system of solfeggio, or is a way of evaluating bridge holdings.

Stevenson intends "choosing a method" to mean "choosing the way a judgment is to be supported" (p. 158). What kind of choice do we have about that? What would it be like to choose the way these judgments are to be supported?

1. The harpsichord needs tuning.
2. The development section is too long.
3. The tree is fifty feet tall.
4. The scalpel is not sterile.
5. The French Revolution was a disaster for France.
6. You ought to sterilize this scalpel more carefully.
7. You ought to modulate to the subdominant here.
8. You ought to have your harpsichord tuned.
9. You ought to use Goren's system.
10. You ought to hold back in the first two laps.
11. You ought to keep your promise.
12. You ought to vote for Wintergreen.

The effect of conglomeration or randomness in this list is intended. It is worth remembering both how various are the activities we call "supporting a judgment", and yet how definite our idea is, in each case, of how we should go about supporting them, of what we would recognize as (call) support in each case. Since Stevenson uses the words "persuade" and "convince" with apparent indifference throughout his book to describe the effect of (nonrational) "reasons" on ethical conclusions, it is worth noting their difference. It is not easy to attach sense to the idea of persuading someone that the tree is fifty feet high, but we know clearly what it would be to convince him of the fact. You would accomplish this by employing or describing one of the definite methods recognized as determining height, and in particular, a method the person you are trying to convince will himself understand and recognize as appropriate, or using reasoning which he can follow. So you might "choose" to support the judgment by comparing it with the height of the adjacent building rather than by triangulation, on the ground that your interlocutor can follow the one method but not the other. (I neglect considerations of whether you only pretend to know these methods, or whether you are mistaken about them, or whether the other person is "convinced" only because of your authority and not because he understands.) In other contexts the grounds for choice will be different (say convenience, or a need for special accuracy, or for a quick estimate). But "choice" of "methods" of support depends upon there *being a choice* between methods which are more or less equivalent to one another, all of which are recognized to be, or can be shown to be, ways of establishing the same judgment. Among these, some will be more convincing or effective or impressive or obvious or accurate or convenient than others *for certain definite purposes;* but a convincing or effective or impressive or obvious or accurate or convenient method is not a *kind* of method of support, the way triangulation or direct measurement are. *Given* the fact that there are alternative (need we add *valid?*) methods of support, we can choose among them on other grounds.

Does this seem simply to miss Stevenson's point, beg his question? For exactly what he is denying is that there *are* any methods of supporting ethical conclusions which we can sensibly be said to recognize as valid; it is just his thesis that what *characterizes* ethical judgments, distinguishes them from logical and scientific judgments, is this absence of validity in their methods of support.

I should, then, add that the difference between persuading and convincing extends to moral cases as well. I am not sure what it would be to persuade Maggie Tulliver that she ought to stay and marry the man; but I know what it might be to convince her that she ought to. Contrariwise, I am not clear what, if anything, should be meant by "convincing her to marry him", but I might undertake to persuade her to, even if I could not convince her, and even if I were not myself convinced that she ought to. If, then, as is suggested by these quick examples, you can (grammatically) persuade someone to take a course of action but must convince them of the truth or soundness of a judgment, one theoretical benefit of interchanging the terms will be that you lend to the idea of persuading someone the respectability of the idea of convincing someone, and you make convincing someone seem directly a matter of getting them to do something, and thereby remove it from a direct connection with the validity of the support you offer. I do not conclude that ethical arguments are directed toward the establishing of a judgment and *not* toward the taking of action; I merely suggest here that a theory which fails to explain and assess this difference is not analytically neutral with respect to substantive moral questions, for what such a theory says, in effect, is that there is no theoretical difference between persuading someone to do something by convincing him that he ought to, *using reasons which convince you*, and persuading him by appeals to his fears, your prestige, or another's money. It may *in fact* be the case that the latter grounds are always decisive, that no such difference is manifest in the practice of a given society; Thrasymachus and Marx, among others, thought that. But then they *knew* they were attacking morality and society as a whole.

Nothing I have said yet touches the general thesis that ethical arguments cannot sensibly be said to be valid. I am now only trying to understand what Stevenson takes to be the implications of that thesis — what he takes to be absent when "validity" is absent, and how this is related to "choosing a method".

The validity of a method stands out as the most conspicuous ground for choosing it; hence when certain methods, or aspects of them, are denied any connection with validity, one may feel that no ground for choice between them remains. Or if such a ground is recognized, it may seem to involve only a crude, forensic success . . . .

Viewed with circumspection, these apparent implications can be seen to have nothing to do with the present views. There are any number of grounds for choice between methods; and if in certain cases these do not depend upon validity, it does not follow that they depend on oratorical strategy. [p. 156]

But this kind of reassurance will be maddening to those of us who feel that the way Stevenson has construed the problems of ethical methodology, the way he deprives it of connection with validity, has already deprived it of its life: for then his reassurance sounds as if someone were to say, "The presence of an engine in an automobile stands out as the most conspicuous ground for choosing it; hence when certain automobiles are deprived of engines, one may feel that no ground for choice between them remains. But there are any number of grounds for choice between automobiles, e.g., their comfort, their design, their roominess, their safety features, their resale value, etc.".

Of course there are any number of grounds for choice between methods, but validity is not one of them. Just as there are any number of grounds for choosing itineraries to Isfahan; but the fact that they all end at Isfahan is not one of them. I feel like saying here: "Depriving moral arguments of validity — where this means that *any* statement about *any* matter of fact may be adduced by *any* speaker as reasons — is not just removing one among other grounds for choosing among modes of supporting ethical judgments; it deprives us of the point of choosing among them altogether." This gives us, I think, a way of seeing more closely what the objection is which Stevenson himself is aware may be brought to his view (and one which, as I would surmise his frequent protests against it indicate, he himself has felt); and also a way of seeing why Stevenson cannot take the objection, even were he to feel it, seriously.

Aren't his critics feeling something like this: "Yes, there are as many grounds for choice as you like; but they are none of them choices about the right thing. None of the routes of support left to us will give us what we want (an automobile that *runs*) or take us where we want to go. None of them will *be* 'supporting an ethical judgment', any more than an array of itineraries leading in different directions will be an array of itineraries to Isfahan."

"Choosing among an array of itineraries" is different from "choosing among itineraries to Isfahan"; both are possible, and both may be guided by clear-headed and detached advice or else by persuasive appeals to our pride or curiosity or purse. Suppose you believe (or have taken it into your head — may that make a difference?), and with a "special seriousness or urgency" (which Stevenson takes to be sufficient to mark a context as a moral one, and even enough to give to the word "good" a special *sense* (p. 90)), that some person ought to go to Isfahan. What method shall you choose to get him ("persuade" him) to go there?

But *who* is this person? And why is he asking *you*? Or has he? And *why* is it serious or urgent? Is it a *moral* concern? I don't say it *couldn't* be; but only that your feeling it to be, wanting it *very* urgently, is not enough to make it so. There are many possibilities:

1) You are a travel agent; someone rushes in and asks you for the quickest way to get to Isfahan. You tell him, sell him his ticket; he pays and rushes out.

2) Someone asks you for the most interesting itinerary to Teheran, taking about three weeks to get there. You describe several possibilities, using empirical statements, metaphors, and slurs; he selects one going through Isfahan.

3) Someone asks you for an itinerary to Teheran. You urge him to take in Isfahan while he is in Persia, describing its wonders, indicating the points of interest along the way, etc. He agrees; or he's already been there; or says he'd like to but hasn't the time.

4) Someone is thinking of a trip to the South Seas. You think you see what he's looking for and suggest that he can do better by traveling to Isfahan.

5) You grab a stranger off the street and try to get him to go to Isfahan.

Are there differences among these cases relevant to the problem of "establishing a moral judgment" (or a piece of travel advice)? Stevenson may answer: No, call attention to any differences you like, "by hypothesis" (p. 153) none of the inferences from *any* of the reasons the travel agent brings to bear will either deductively or inductively support the agent's conclusion that the man ought (or would do well) to go to Isfahan. None are, therefore, sensibly to be called *valid*. That is just obvious. And it is an equally obvious assumption that the relation between reasons and conclusions can only, therefore, be "psychological" (e.g., p. 170, note 15); that is all I am pointing to in speaking of moral methodology as one of *persuasion*. These steps in my argument are inescapable, and harmless. "The practical question is not *whether* to reject persuasion, but *which* persuasion to reject" (p. 215).

But there is also the logical or grammatical question of what constitutes or counts as *persuasion,* what we should call "persuasion" (and what else is persuasion?). And the moral objection to persuasion is not the gnat that "all persuasion is evil" (which Stevenson slaps again and again, e.g., p. 165, p. 215); it is the camel that all moral confrontation is a matter of "persuasion", or that there is no essential methodological difference between giving someone "reasons" for taking a course of action he is committed to and one to which he has no (obvious) commitment; nor between "reasons" which point to something the person cares about and those which are more or less unrelated to what he cares, or needs to care, about. These differences appear insignificant on the assumptions that (1) our commitments are more or less external to our wants and our positions and our ordinary modes of conduct; they are all more or less imposed upon us; none are "implications" of what we do or who we are; and (2) that what we care about is quite arbitrary, unstable, inflexible, and unpredictable; that there is no "logical" or "grammatical" connection between caring about something and the thing about which one cares (or may be assumed, or gotten, to care) — a connection like that between remarking or contemplating or despising or basking in or taking pride in or shunning and the sorts of things we can (logically, normally) remark or contemplate or despise or bask in or take pride in or shun.

Let us see this difference concretely. I take it that no one will feel about the ought-claims (6)–(10) (*supra*, p. 276) that "*Any* statement about *any* matter of fact which *any* speaker considers likely to alter attitudes may be adduced as a reason . . .". But why not? Won't the reasons offered fail to yield these conclusions deductively or inductively in any sense in which this is true of ethical conclusions; so won't the gap opened for ethical conclusions swallow *all* arguments which have an ought-claim (or an act?) as their conclusion; and won't this gap need to be filled by the psychological, causal efficacy of the reasons? (That ethical arguments are a species of imperative arguments, and that these have a "logic", is argued by R. M. Hare; this has the virtue of sparing him the appeal to an unknown psychological mechanism as hinging reasons and conclusion, reason and action. Some difficulties about it are suggested in Chapter XII.) If not, how are ethical conclusions different? I can think of two answers from someone defending Stevenson's position.

The first is this: "Any disagreement about such ought-claims as your (6)–(10) are likely to be, and probably are universally, rooted in belief, so the methods for settling them, though still not literally *valid*, may be exhaustive and definitive. But the hope for this is small where people disagree morally."

First of all, it is not at all clear what "beliefs" would be relevant to claims suggesting (advising? urging? demanding?) that you use Goren's system or that you have your harpsichord tuned. Do I, when I urge you to try the Goren system, *believe* it to be better? I may *find* it better, and in *definite* ways (more accurate, subtle, flexible, etc.). And why should the fact that *I* find it to be better be a reason for urging it upon you? But what better reason could there be, in such a case? I imply that you'll find it better too, and if I didn't there would be some question as to whether what I was doing was *advising* you of something (and not, say, tricking you). This hints a point of crucial importance: *one* property that makes a reason a moral one is that it is conceived in terms of what will morally benefit the person the speaker adduces his reasons *to*. Who's to say? Anybody who knows that person and cares enough about him to say, and can assume responsibility for saying it to him. Of course we may be terribly wrong in our judgment of his needs and wants and capacities and dilemmas, and in our sense of our own capacity for responsibility towards him, but that says something about us (that we are not perceptive or reliable enough; that we are self-centered and pompous, meddling and officious) not about morality. *Much* more, of course, needs to be said about this, but it allows one aspect of Stevenson's view to emerge, that in the way he conceives his contexts, the question "Why should the fact that I approve of something be a reason for urging it upon you?" can have no answer. I will come back to this in a moment.

A second point may be worth bringing out in response to the reply we have recently heard in defense of Stevenson's position. I said that "choosing among methods" for supporting a judgment (or for measuring or sterilization . . .) depends (grammatically) upon *there being choices,* alternative ways, of supporting the judgment, and the *same* judgment (measuring the same thing, doing the same job). But consider the ways in which "the" judgment "You ought to have your harpsichord tuned" may be supported:

1. It's a sin to let an instrument like that deteriorate.
2. If you let it go much longer the strings will weaken.
3. It sounds awful.
4. You obviously aren't successful at tuning it yourself.
5. It'll give you a lift.
6. Madame will refuse to play on it unless she knows it was tuned the day of her performance.
7. Harpsichords are all the rage.

Say, if you like, that reasons such as (2) and (6) are rational (= empirically verifiable) and others such as (1) and (7) are "persuasive" (= not empirically justifiable?) (and what sort are the other reasons?), the question remains: What *choice* do you have among these "methods" of support? Can any be used by any speaker on any occasion? "Whether . . . [a] reason will in fact support or oppose the judgment will depend on whether the hearer believes it, and upon whether, if he does, it will actually make a difference to his attitudes . . ." (Stevenson, pp. 114–15). But the "choice" we make in supporting the judgment is just a choice as to *what* judgment we wish to make. I think we can say: even though all those reasons may be true, or all "effective", what you *meant* by your judgment is determined by how you go on to support it: "You ought to tune it; I mean, it's a sin . . . etc." That the judgment changes with the reasons given for it is also shown by the fact that many of these "reasons" themselves could, said in the relevant context, serve to tell or to get the person to tune his harpsichord: each of them is, separately, interchangeable with the claim

explicitly containing the "ought". (This will become a central consideration when we discuss the "logic" of ethical argument in Chapter XII.)

Further, suppose the only reason which "takes" is (7) — "Harpsichords
are all the rage". Or that (6) ("Madame will refuse to play") is "believed"
by the owner of the harpsichord, but that it does not actually mobilize
him to get it tuned. Or that in response to (2) and (3) he simply says, "So
what?" or "I know". What will our attitude *towards that person* be?

That these considerations are irrelevant to Stevenson's analysis, where
all we *need* (grammatically) consider, in considering what reason to give, is
whether it will have its effect on that other person in getting *what we approve of done,* where the other person need be considered only to the extent that we consider what "reason" will prod him to action — that is, in
essence, why Stevenson's analysis is not of *moral* judgments, why I am saying that his theory is not about morality.

Stevenson is aware that there will be some whom his view offends, and
he complains of them, and mildly ridicules them:

So long as one's opponent is impressed (a hasty critic may suppose), one method is
as good as another; for the whole purport of ethics is to sway attitudes. Where
Plato and Kant sought eternal principles of reason, are there merely the empty
rules of rhetoric? After this one is likely to envisage disillusionment and chaos,
and the many other disturbing "implications" which objective theorists so habitually attribute to their opponents. [p. 156]

I deny any sense of such alternatives as Stevenson offers — between eternal
principles and empty rhetoric, between something called "objective" and
"subjective" attitudes. The chaos and disillusionment I envisage in his
views do not come from being told that men have attitudes and that these
are not shelved at will, or at reasons. The world shows me that. The disillusionment, the discouragement, comes, rather, from being told that one
man may treat me morally and yet act only in terms of his attitudes, without necessarily considering me or mine. If this is so, then the concept of
morality is unrelated to the concept of justice. For however justice is to
be understood — whether in terms of rendering to each his due, or in
terms of equality, or of impartiality or of fairness — *what* must be understood is a concept concerning the treatment of *persons;* and *that* is a concept, in turn, of a creature with commitments and cares. But for these
commitments and cares, and the ways in which they conflict with one another and with those of other persons, there would be no problem, and
no concept of justice. One can face the disappearance of justice from the
world more easily than an amnesia of the very concept of justice.

I said I could think of two responses which might be given to my question concerning how ethical judgments differed from other judgments containing "ought". The second is this:

"The 'ought' in such statements as your (11) ('You ought to keep your promise') and (12) ('You ought to vote for Wintergreen') are different from the others in having a peculiarly ethical sense."

Whence arises the sense that ordinary words, when used in moral judgments, take on a special "sense"? One striking difference between examples (6)–(10) on the one hand and (11)–(12) on the other is that each of the former carries on its face the sort of context in which it would be used, we know the sort of person who would be saying it and the general position of the person to whom it should be said: the *relevance* of the judgment to the person confronted is implicitly established, and there is no sense of some special linguistic or psychological power necessary to *get* the person to do what you say. In (11) and (12), however, we are in the dark as to what situation we are to conceive. Mightn't the sense of a special "sense" arise in one's trying to establish here and now, in one's isolated consciousness, what the force of such a statement would be, a connection with the statement, in the absence of any context which would naturally contain the force? And then it becomes an invention. And here again, others, *persons,* are left out of consideration.

But this has, as has already been implied, a different consequence in moral philosophy than it has in epistemology. One difference is registered in the difference in their respective "philosopher's contexts", something to be discussed later. Another consequence is registered in the ways in which examples are imagined in each. I said earlier that Stevenson's examples were not obviously, and some obviously not, ones invoking moral disagreement. Now I want to look briefly at one more of his examples to indicate the way in which, in marked difference from epistemological examples, it baffles imagination altogether when we try to conceive of persons saying what Stevenson gives them to say, in terms of the descriptions he gives of their motives.

A: You ought to give the speech, as you promised.

B: That is unfortunately beyond my power. My health will not permit it.

This example deals with the consequences of a judgment's *influence.* A is endeavoring to influence B to give the speech. If B's reply is true, then whatever influence A's judgment may have on attitudes, it will not have the further consequence of making B speak. Realizing this, A will be likely to withdraw his judgment; he sees that it cannot have its intended effect. We shall later find that the old problem of "free will", so far as it relates to ethics, brings up the same considerations.

In the present case A may withdraw his judgment not merely because it will fail to serve its original purpose, but because it may have effects which he, in kindness, does not desire. It may lead B to be perturbed about his disability. [p. 126]

Does A assume that B has forgotten the promise? doesn't take it seriously enough? doesn't realize that what he said was legitimately taken as a promise? If so, why not *tell* him? If not, then *why* remind him of the fact? Does A not know that B is disabled? Then, when he finds out, does he "withdraw his judgment" because "he sees it cannot have its intended effect" or because he sees that it would be incompetent or incoherent not to? And *how* does he "see" that it cannot have its intended effect? Because he *sees* that B is disabled? Then are we to imagine that A goes to the hospital to visit B, and, after seeing both of B's legs to be in traction, says, "You ought to give the speech"? Or is the disability less obvious, so that A is in some doubt as to whether B's condition is as serious as he says? Then how does he "see" or "realize" that his judgment will not have its intended effect? Perhaps he sees that B is adamant: that might be a clear case of "realizing (finally, no matter how hard you try) that your judgment cannot have its intended effect". But we've forgotten that speech in our bewilderment. Was it important? Important enough so that you are willing to urge B to risk his health to give it, or go there in a wheel chair if necessary? Then B's reply "My health will not permit it" is not enough to make you "realize" that your judgment will not have its intended effect. And if the speech is *that* important then does *B* not know this? And if he does, then has he done *nothing* about it, having become ill? Has he, for example, not tried to find or suggest a replacement, or have the meeting rescheduled, or dictated a speech which could be read? If that would be uncalled for, then why *is* it so important that he give the speech? Why *ought* he to?

But enough. The speech is not important; it doesn't exist. And neither does a moral relationship exist between these people. If A *has* to accept what B says as *final,* then we must imagine that B's position with respect to A is superior in terms of power, prestige, station, etc., and that B is *using* that position to deny A's claim. And then B is saying, in effect: we are not in the same moral universe. On the other hand, if A is monomaniacal on the subject of the speech, cares more about it than about anything else (he's still kindly, however, and doesn't go on at B in order not to "lead B to be perturbed about his disability"; but not because he cares about B's health); then his interests and cares and sense of commitment have become so private, gotten so far out of line and proportion with other people's, that he can hardly be imagined to have any relationships at all which require moral argument. With him there is nothing to discuss.

I want, finally, to consider the detached way in which Stevenson discusses the roles of moralist and propagandist. That will serve both to confirm my reading of his view and to indicate again the coherence of philosophical positions, and the consequent pervasiveness of conflict between them, and therewith the difficulty of useful criticism. What interests me here is the way a theory of language weaves into a moral theory.

In response to his characterization of the moralist as someone "who endeavors to influence attitudes", Stevenson is led to ask, "How, then, are moralists and propagandists to be distinguished?". The description he gives of what he would regard as an answer to this question is astonishing: "It is concerned with *definitions* [his emphasis] of 'moralist' and 'propagandist' " (p. 243); but, he goes on to say, we need not stop to provide these definitions, because these definitions would either employ "persuasion", which is to be avoided in our neutral analysis of morality, or else they would be emotively neutral, in which case there would be no need for them in our analysis, for "we shall have no further occasion to use the term ['propagandist']" (p. 251). Either Stevenson can just *see* that the moralist and the propagandist are simply different kinds of animal, in which case he might have helped his critics understand that his view does not consistently deny this difference, or the importance of the difference (and that his critics may take his view this way is again something he anticipates, but with apparent impatience, many times); or else he simply supposes that the difference is quite unimportant, in which case he ought to assume some responsibility for having said or implied something of the most drastic importance. As soon as someone got the idea that there was such a subject as morality, a dimension of human life which was different from the dimensions of politics or religion or festival, a dimension in which conclusions were arrived at differently (in which reason had a different role), than in science, and a dimension which needed defense or justification; at that moment someone else would have felt that any such defense or justification, parading as wisdom, was mere smartness in the service of some prior position of advantage. The trouble is that he may have been right, the fact is that the making of a moral judgment must subject itself to the same tests of motive and perception and consequence as any action must which falls into the hands of evaluation. To say that morality is propaganda, or that there is no point in distinguishing them, is to ignite the brightest burning question of morality.

> The terms "propagandist" and "moralist" need not be persuasive terms, provided care is used in neutralizing their emotive effects. . . . When the terms are *completely* neutralized, one may say with tranquility that all moralists are propagandists, or that all propagandists are moralists. . . . On the other hand, if the words are used with rhetorical emphasis, with their full emotive effect, they will serve less to preserve cognitive distinctions than to plead a cause. [p. 252]

Then let us imagine that the emotive effect of the terms is completely neutralized (I will not now ask how we are to imagine that, nor whether we really can). What then would it mean to say, with broad tranquility, that all moralists are propagandists? What will be the most irreproachably cognitive content of such an assertion? Part of it, I suppose, will be that the moralist always speaks from a position which takes account of the position of his hearers only to the extent necessary to manipulate their feelings and conduct; that there is no presumption that when a moralist confronts us he is recognizing us as persons about whom he cares, and to whom he acknowledges a commitment, nor that he accepts any responsibility for the very act of confronting us; that when he confronts us, his entire concern is to get us to do what he wants us to do, and something he can have decided upon quite privately, and with no particular knowledge of our other cares or commitments. Of course, some particular moralist may feel that such negotiation is unworthy of his role, but that will have no (logical) bearing upon whether he is to be called a "moralist"; to earn that title, all that is necessary is that you "endeavor to influence attitudes", and, well, of course, attitudes of a special sort. "Thus one may be said to exert a 'peculiarly' moral influence if he influences only those attitudes that are correlated with a sense of guilt, sin, or remorse, and so on" (p. 251). So, for example, a mother who plays upon ("influences") her child's sense of guilt in order to have him give up the girl he wants to marry is acting in the role of moralist; and Kate Croy, interpreting her project to attract a legacy from Millie Theale in ways which muddle and blunt ("influence") Merton Densher's perception of his guilt, is a spokesman for morality. I hope it will not be thought that I would deny that parent and Kate Croy the title of moralist merely on the ground that they are morally wrong; moralists can, with the best will in the world, take morally wrong positions, positions which they themselves, could they see their positions more fully, would see to be culpable. But in the case of that parent and of Kate Croy, there is not so much as the intention to morality. One may find such behavior to transcend moral categories. To betray someone to whom you are committed, by a shared past, the bonds of long affection, or to entice a lover, through his love, to a course of action which he, if he realized what he was doing, would be appalled by, is not just immoral; it is an evil of a different order. To propagandize under the name of morality is not immoral; it denies morality altogether. And in sentimentalizing propaganda, it denies to propaganda its practical urgency and extreme utility, which are all that can justify it, *when* it is justified.

Stevenson maintains that, emotively neutralized, the statements that "all moralists are propagandists, or that all propagandists are moralists" can "be made true by definition, without violence to the boundaries of conventional usage" (p. 252). The claim that this could be done "without violence to the boundaries of conventional usage" sounds plausible to the extent that we accept the characterization of the moralist as someone who endeavors to influence attitudes, period; and accept the philosophically fashionable claim that most ordinary words are terribly vague. The terms "moralist" and "propagandist" are said to be "vague in a way that leaves precision only to the *generic* aspects of their reference—their common reference to men who exert *some sort* of influence. If we cut through this vagueness, then, drawing a line between 'moralist' and 'propagandist', we shall not be *discovering* a distinction that is clearly implicit in our language" (pp. 243–44). But then Stevenson has also said, quite generally, that "Ethical terms are more than ambiguous; they are vague" (p. 34), and their "vagueness . . . is of the same sort" as "can be found in the word 'red'" (p. 35). So then there is, presumably, no very particular infirmity in the terms "moralist" and "propagandist": they suffer the vagueness shared, it seems, by most general terms. Though, apparently, the general term "vague" need cause us no pang of doubt; that word, from some access of stigmata or innoculation, has quite escaped this general disease of ordinary words; it simply means that

although certain factors, at any one time, are definitely included among the designata of the terms, and certain others definitely excluded, there are many others which are neither included nor excluded. No decision has been made about these, either by the speaker or by the dictionary. The limits of the undecided region are so subject to fluctuation, with varying contexts and varying purposes, that it becomes arbitrary, so far as common usage is concerned, to specify where one sense of the terms leaves off and another begins.

Over the undecided region common usage permits us to do as we please. [p. 35]

(The idea that almost all words are vague clearly has much more power than this popular argument can have given it. Compare: no object is ever clearly illuminated, because every source of light, though clearly illuminating objects in certain regions and definitely not illuminating those in others, has a boundary region in which objects are neither clearly nor unclearly illuminated.) Presumably, then, such a statement as "All good things are bad" need imply no transvaluation of all values; for the statement can be made true by definition. The terms "good" and "bad" are no better off than the terms "moralist" and "propagandist", and indeed the former pair share with the latter the property Stevenson takes as controlling of their meaning, the fact that they are "emotive antonyms" (p. 243). And what Stevenson says of the latter pair he has said of the former: "Those whom we call 'moralists' will be praised or tolerated, and those whom we call 'propagandists', condemned" (p. 244). What determines whether we call a man who "endeavors to influence attitudes" a moralist or a propagandist depends, it seems, on whether we happen to want to praise or condemn him; we do not have to *justify* the application of these terms. "Both terms are vague, and vague in a way that leaves precision only to the *generic* aspects of their reference — their common reference to men who exert *some sort* of influence." Similarly, then, "good" and "bad" are vague in a way that leaves precision only to their common reference to things toward which we take up some attitude. So just as the tranquil statement "All moralists are propagandists", when rendered emotively neutral and made true by definition, just means "Moralists, like propagandists, influence attitudes", just so the statement "All good things are bad", similarly made true by definition, just means "Good things, like bad things, are things toward which we have some sort of attitude".

To suggest that people can "decide" what methods to use in supporting a moral judgment is to suggest that people can decide what a moral judgment is, can decide whether an issue is a moral one. You may of course decide to *make* a moral issue out of a conflict, but you cannot decide what will *be* making it a moral issue, what kinds of reasons, entered in what way, to what effect, will be moral reasons. You may decide to use propaganda in the service of a cause. But to call that morality only blinds us to a choice for which we are responsible. You may lie, and worse, and be justified; but why call it noble?

You can also point out how frequently, and in what ways, people use any kind of "method" to get people to change their attitudes and take a line of conduct. (" . . . That is a fact about certain human beings which all are free to note and none is required to copy" (p. 157).) But you won't then be pointing out how frequently and in what ways people confront one another morally. And you can point out how frequently one man tries to get another to do something which he wants him to do, or justifies his thoughtless conduct, by appealing to it as his "duty", etc., but you won't there be pointing to the use of persuasion in moral argument; you will be pointing to one way in which private motive or personal ignorance can be wrapped in the rags of morality. That possibility has been recognized for as long as the concept of morality itself. It is as much the charge against simple Euthyphro as it is against Ibsen's or E. M. Forster's more sophisticated villains. And when it has been argued that everything that passes for morality is the dress-up of private position or the imposition of positions which do not meet, or even consider, our real need — argued, e.g., by Callicles, by Marx, by Nietzsche, by Freud, until it has become the premiss, and set the problem of much of modern literature — there has been no doubt that morality as a whole, as a way of regulating the lives of the members of a community, has been judged and found wanting. Stevenson is, by profession, no moralist; he criticizes nothing, and apparently has never wondered whether the impressive ranks of the critics of morality may not be right, that the whole enterprise is a sham, and worse. But in allowing any way of working on another person's attitudes, and any motive for influencing his conduct to pass as moral, he subverts the concept of morality itself. When others have undertaken this task, they have recognized the enormity of their claim; and in accepting personal responsibility for it they have gone mad, or to prison, or into various forms of exile. It is a relatively new idea that the claim is itself a neutral one, taken in the service of the advanced ideas of logic and scientific method, the dictates of reason.

I am aware of an unfairness in my treatment of Stevenson's views, and that lies in my not having attempted to give a picture of its *whole* structure. That will make my remarks seem directed personally rather than, as they are intended, against a position whose dialectic will seem, once begun, inexorable. I have not, for example, mentioned one of Stevenson's original opponents. It seems to have been in direct reaction to an "objectivist" position such as Moore's (the "objective theorist" is still the villain of the piece; cf. p. 156) and in particular to one of Moore's well-known arguments (to the effect that if ethical assertions are about one's own feelings then when one man says "X is right", and another "X is wrong", they will not be contradicting one another, "there is never any difference

of opinion between them" (Moore, *Ethics,* p. 100)) that Stevenson is led
to one of his fundamental notions:

> It is obvious, I grant, that in any typical ethical sense, when A and B assert "X
> is right" and "X is not right", respectively, they are in *some* sense differing or
> disagreeing. But I do not grant that A and B must, in that case, be "differing in
> opinion" in the sense of that phrase that we are assuming Moore to intend. . . .
>
> The sense in which A and B, asserting "X is right" and "X is not right",
> respectively, clearly do "disagree", is a sense which I shall preserve by the phrase,
> "disagree in attitude". ["Moore's Arguments Against Certain Forms of Ethical
> Naturalism", p. 82]

However, a logical refutation of a philosophical position which is wrong
does not insure one's own rightness.

It is exactly because one hopes that "a full, cautious science, and not a
semblance of it will be brought to bear on ethical issues, and that aims
which seem well supported will actually withstand the light of careful
scrutiny", and deplores "static, other-worldly norms [put] in the place
of flexible, realistic ones" (*Ethics and Language,* p. 235), that one is led
to attack an empty idea of the "reason" for which we may hope. It is an
empty idea of rationality which tells us to discuss moral questions without giving us reasons we can respect nor recognizing our cares and commitments as worth defending, nor giving us antagonists who are part of
the very cares and commitments we must defend. An empty idea of
reason which expresses tolerance toward irrationality by saying that "the
practical problem is not to avoid all persuasion, but to decide which to
avoid and which to accept" (p. 250), and that people "decide to use"
persuasion (p. 159). For that intellectualized picture of irrationality no
longer knows the power, the subtlety, and the guises of reason's eternal
opponent. Then morality is no longer a match for it.

XI

Rules and Reasons

In its apotheosis of expediency, the moral philosophy of Utilitarianism has seemed to many philosophers to be at odds with two very elementary moral principles: that it is not an acceptable reason for breaking a promise that it is best on the whole not to keep it; and that an innocent person may not be treated as though he or she were guilty. In what is, to my mind, some of the most illuminating writing in ethical theory to appear in recent years, a number of philosophers have defended Utilitarianism against these standing objections by suggesting that its critics (perhaps even its authors) have mistaken the point of applicability of the Principle of Utility. Utilitarianism, they admit, is unable to do justice to our moral feelings about particular promises and about particular instances of punishing. But this is because the Principle of Utility is improperly understood as applying always to individual actions (and, in particular, to individual actions of promising and punishing). But where an action is (performed as?) an instance of a practice or social institution, then the *direct* justification or reason for performing it must be one which refers the action to that practice. And in such cases, though a Utilitarian justification is relevant, and is accommodated by our moral sensibility, it is so only if it is meant to apply directly to the *practice,* not to the individual action itself. This interpretation, then, turning upon the distinction between practice and action, or between rule and instance, not only makes out a plausible case for Utilitarianism, but has the further major virtues of suggesting Deontology in ethical theory might be understood as a complement rather than an incompatible alternative to Utilitarianism, and a complement in the critical sense in which each is shown to explicate a different dimension of a sensibility, or sets of beliefs, immediately recognizable as moral.

Something like the distinction between action and institution is becoming quite common, but I am going to concentrate primarily on its formulation by John Rawls, as it appears in his paper "Two Concepts of Rules", because he clearly emphasizes two points which, unnoticed, would deprive the view of its full force: he explicitly cautions that not all actions are controlled by what he calls practices, and that there will be, in a particular case, a question as to whether the action is or is not to be construed this way; and his distinguishing of two concepts of rules forms an attempt to give a basis for the central distinction between action and institution upon which all such views depend, and to help explain how the importance of this difference may be missed.

I share what I take to be the main motives of this theory, and I find myself in thorough agreement with its drift. It is because of that that I want to make as clear as I can just where I think it is mistaken. I find it unsuccessful in two primary ways: (1) it does not, I think, accurately locate the conflict between Utilitarianism and Deontology with respect to the concepts of promising and punishing; (2) the central concept of a rule, though as illuminating as is suggested for moral theory, is left unclearer than it need be, and in such a way as to miss the epistemological problems involved in our knowing what we, or someone else, is doing. I will consider these points in turn.

Promising and Punishing

I shall argue, against the view under consideration, that promising is not sensibly characterized as an institution at all; so that if Utilitarianism is to be defended here, another way must be found. And I shall argue that calling punishment "an institution" is ambiguous, and that in one sense a Utilitarian can justify it, and in the other he cannot; and that, moreover, only the Deontologist can, or even tries to, justify it in this second sense. If this is true then a reconciliation between Utilitarianism and Deontology must be achieved on other grounds.

How is promising to be made out as a social institution, and not as simply one, perhaps special in other ways, among the thousands of actions human beings, in their social settings, engage in? Rawls says this:

That punishment and promising are practices is beyond question. In the case of promising this is shown by the fact that the form of words "I promise" is a performative utterance which presupposes the stage-setting of the practice and the proprieties defined by it. ["Two Concepts of Rules", p. 30]

But so are "I warn, beseech, bet, pick, accuse, forgive you . . .", "I commend him to you", "I withdraw, protest . . . etc.", performative utterances. ("I punish you" is not.) Are all of these practices? It might be said that one must "know how" each of these actions is done, but does one learn that by learning a "form of activity specified by a system of rules which defines offices, roles, moves, penalties, defenses and so on . . . which . . . [give] the activity its structure"? (That is the way Rawls characterizes his use of "practice", which he says he uses as "a sort of technical term" (p. 3, note 1); I hope nothing I am going to say neglects that caution.) Is it the fact that these are all social actions, ones occurring between persons, against a definite social ground, which makes them practices? But so are comforting, threatening, and revenge "social actions" in this sense. Revenge is a useful case because it *could* be — it is — an institution or practice in certain societies (say in ones which have not developed the legal concepts of crime and redress), and then it would have, as Rawls says, definite offices, moves, etc. But it needn't be. I can take revenge in quite unexpected and uninstitutionalized ways. Of course, only if I have been injured; just as I can comfort someone only if he is suffering. But is being an injured party (or a comforter) an office of a structured practice? Aren't they rather part of the grammar of "revenge" and "comforting"?

I do not think I am pressing Rawls's use of the notion of a practice too hard. He cannot mean merely what Wittgenstein means by referring to "obeying a rule" or "making a report" as "institutions" or practices (*Investigations*, §199, §202). (Rawls alludes to the *Investigations* at p. 29.) Wittgenstein's use of the concept of a rule is not always clear, but what he means, roughly, is that there are *ways* of doing all of these things, that not just anything you do will *be* competently performing them, that, in a word, they have a grammar, and in that sense are conventional, and in that sense social. He does not, as I argued in my opening· chapters, mean that they are conventional or social in the way institutions which characterize particular societies are conventional. But it is in the latter sense that Rawls is, or must be, thinking of practices, anyway so far as his concept of the practice of promising is to show how a Utilitarian can, in ways consistent with his position, justify the practice; and indeed he says: "It is important to remember that those whom I have called the classical Utilitarians were largely interested in social institutions. . . . The Utilitarian principle was quite naturally thought of, and used, as a criterion

for judging social institutions (practices) and as a basis for urging re-
forms" (p. 19, note 21). But what might it mean to urge a reform of the
practice of promising? In the Wittgensteinian use of "practice" that would
be no more, and no less sensible than urging a reform in the way we obey
rules (not: a *particular* mode of obedience to some *particular* rule), or in
the way we point to objects.

And what would it mean to give justification for the practice?

There are obvious utilitarian advantages in having a practice which denies to
the promisor, as a defense, any general appeal to the utilitarian principle in
accordance with which the practice itself may be justified. [p. 16]

First of all, it must be wondered whether that is, literally, a comprehensible statement. For what is meant by "the promisor"? Someone who
made a promise. And it is part of the concept of promising that one does
not keep or break particular promises on general utilitarian grounds.
(That is, of course, what Rawls wishes to say, and it is my complete agreement with that, and with the idea that a Utilitarian can admit as much,
that goads me to articulate as well as I can my dissatisfaction with the
way he explains this fact.) Since there would be no promise apart from a
knowledge of that fact about the concept of promising (that one does not
coherently *keep or break* them on general utilitarian grounds) it is not
comprehensible to *justify* actions falling under that concept by appealing
so such a fact. Rawls's analogy with games is not quite right. He points
out, obviously correctly, that in the course of playing baseball it is not
open to you, having had your third strike, to suggest that it would be
better on the whole to allow four strikes to constitute "striking out". (He
also says, or implies, that *no* action done in the course of playing baseball,
which is defined in terms of that practice, can receive a Utilitarian justification. I will turn to that point in the second part of this chapter.) That
is not, however, the same as saying that it is "part of the concept" of
"striking out" that one be allowed just three swings (unless the last is a
"foul" or "tip"). I take that to be shown by the acknowledgment that, if
directed to the practice as a whole, it could comprehensibly be argued,
and, I agree, on Utilitarian grounds, that it *would* be better to have four
strikes (and perhaps not allow fouls or tips to count in preventing one's
striking out).

A fuller analogy with a concept "defined" in the game of baseball
would be to imagine someone arguing that he shouldn't be called out
because though he swung at the ball (made the promise) it was an inconvenient pitch; or because although he swung (said "I promise") he hadn't

realized what the situation was, and meant only to bunt, or did it as a joke. Then there is some question whether he is competent, not merely at baseball, but at the form of life called "playing a (competitive) game". But comparable "defenses" *are, sometimes,* competently entered in justifying your not keeping a promise, and never are, as part of the concept of playing baseball. This very inexactness in the analogy between games and morality is critically important. The way I have drawn the analogy between promising and games in effect makes promising analogous not to the game, but to a *move* in the game. But the importance of the inexactness in the analogy is this: In competitive games (which excludes, for example, such children's games as Ring-Around-the-Rosy) what *counts as a move* is *settled* by the Rules of Play. That is essential to them, common to all. (Did I "look and see" whether that is so? But it is part of the "grammar" of "move in a game" that this should be so.) Part of what will actually be *called* "rules" in a rulebook — and not, e.g., "moves" (i.e., descriptions of the kinds of moves), "opening of play", "winning", "scoring", etc. — will be ways of *settling* whether a given action *is* to count as a move when certain eventualities arise. That such things are settled and known in advance of play by all players is what allows games to be practiced, as well as allows certain persons to do what umpires and referees do, viz., to see whether what is done meets the definite requirements of the relevant moves, and to make this fact known to both sides of the competition.

That moral conduct cannot be practiced in *that* way, that you cannot become a moral champion in that way, and that no one can settle a moral conflict in the way umpires settle conflicts, is essential to the form of life we call morality. (A related difference is mentioned in the following chapter.)

It is perfectly true that in learning what a promise is we learn what defenses it is appropriate or competent to enter, and where, should we not keep it. But these are just the defenses we learn in learning to defend *any* of our conduct which comes to grief: those excuses, explanations, justifications (I will call them, as a whole, *elaboratives*) which make up the bulk of moral defense. The general Utilitarian defense is not open as a defense for breaking, nor as a justification for keeping, just any promise, not because a supposed practice forbids it, but because making a promise is the sort of action it is, one the breaking (non-completion) of which is always (likely) to have severe consequences. When the immediate consequences of keeping it are sufficiently severer than the likely ones of breaking it, then, as Rawls says, there *is* a Utilitarian reason for breaking it, and one by no means obviously paradoxical to our moral sensibilities. But then the *way* the reason is entered is critical to whether it will be acceptable — the tone of voice, the occasion on which it is entered, whether you tried to call the promise off before simply not keeping it (which would *lessen,* not necessarily eradicate, any culpability involved), whether you entered the defense at the earliest opportunity — all of which serve to *acknowledge* your awareness of what it is you have done. Without the expression of that awareness, even the extreme defense is incompetent; because that defense is, in effect, an *apology.* And apologies, again, are not "defenses" which are part of the concept of moves in a game.

It is, therefore, not a side issue that, as Rawls puts it, "there is a considerable variation in the way people understand the practice [of promising] . . ." (p. 31); a moral argument concerning the breaking or keeping of a promise will exactly concern such questions as *whether* what you said was (tantamount to) a (serious) promise, whether you were really *prevented* from keeping it (or perhaps only succumbed to temptation or intimidation), whether, knowing that was likely to happen you ought to have made it, whether you did what was possible to alleviate the consequences for the promisee. . . . And, as always, the outcome of the argument will affect whether the parties concerned are to continue to live in the same moral world, whether they will, in future, accept promises from one another.

In the sense, therefore, in which "it is essential to the notion of a practice that the rules are publically known and understood as definitive" (p. 24), I cannot agree that promising is sensibly called a practice. And to call being a promisor an "office" (p. 28, note 25) can only, I think, mislead. For it is obviously unlike other offices which are established within practices: there is no special procedure for entering it (e.g., no oaths!), no established routes for being selected or training yourself for it, etc. If it is an office, it is one any normal adult is competent to hold, and can hold merely by putting himself in it with respect to anyone with whom he is in, or with whom he might create, a certain form of relationship. And it is critical to the concept of moral responsibility that this should be so.

But it is not merely because the view of rules I am considering obscures this inexactness between games and morality that I criticize it. It is also because, in defending Utilitarianism in this way, where it needs and can have no defense, it obscures what there is in a Utilitarian view of society which may trouble moralists. I can put my worry about it this way: If the concept of a promise is as clear in the relevant way as I have suggested, then why would it so much as *seem* to a Utilitarian, or to his critic, that he must undertake to justify promising as such, as an institution?

It may be thought that my denial that promising is a practice or institution does not seriously affect Rawls's argument, and that Utilitarianism could still be understood as justifying the *action* (or "move") of promising, an action the concept of which excludes a general utilitarian defense. But what would that mean? What *is* a promise? Rawls says: ". . . the point of the practice [of promising] is to abdicate one's title to act in accordance with utilitarian and prudential considerations in order that the future may be tied down and plans coordinated in advance. There are obvious utilitarian advantages in having [such] a practice . . . " (p. 16). Indeed there are. Doesn't one feel that they are *too* obvious? The very existence of human society, and the coherence of one's own conduct, depend upon it. But *that* isn't what Utilitarianism has set out to justify — that promising is not *an* institution, but the precondition of any institutions among persons at all. And that general condition, moreover, is not something that promising, whether as action or as practice, can secure in the *general* way in which Rawls seems to mean his description. It looks as if it can only if you describe a promise as *the* way "to abdicate one's title to act in accord with utilitarian and prudential considerations". But *any* commitment does that; or rather, any commitment is included in computing what one will consider "prudential".

And there are any number of ways, other than promising, for commiting yourself to a course of action: the expression or declaration of an intention, the giving of an impression, not correcting someone's misapprehension, beginning a course of conduct on the basis of which someone else has taken action, and so on. Where does the idea come from, which has had currency at least from Hume to J. L. Austin, that promising is so *special* an act, that the words "I promise" are a sort of ritual of high solemnity? There is nothing sacred about the act of promising which is not sacred about expressing an intention, or any other way of committing oneself. The words "I am going to . . ." or "I will . . ." do not in themselves indicate that you are "merely" expressing an intention and *not* promising. If it is *important to be explicit* then you may engage either in the "rituals" of saying "I really want to . . .", "I certainly intend, will try to . . .", or the ritual of saying "I promise". It is *this* importance which makes explicit promises important. But to take them more seriously than that, as the golden path to commitment, is to take our ordinary, non-explicit commitments too lightly. I might add here that if Utilitarianism is going to have to provide a justification for having the act of promising in our repertory of speech and conduct, it is also going to have to justify the action of expressing or declaring an intention. (I have, of course, said nothing about what "kind" of actions these are; but that would be required in any attempt to explain why they cannot, and need not, be justified. It is also in looking upon them as ordinary actions like "hitting" or "hurting" or "lending" that one feels they need, or could have, justifications.)

But my worry about an attempt to justify promising on Utilitarian grounds is not just that it makes commitments more like explicit promises than they are but that it makes promises more like legal contracts than they are. About these everything Rawls says about offices, defenses, moves, etc., is true; the details of "offer", "acceptance", "consideration", "misrepresentation", etc., are elaborately specified, the practice is definitive, and a given conflict can be adjudicated (umpired). This, however, involves a whole way of looking at society, one in which all human relationships are pictured as contractual *rather than* personal, within which one's commitments, liabilities, responsibilities are from the outset limited, and not total, or at any rate always in the course of being determined. We still relate to one another as persons, but only so far as we stand in certain socially defined roles with respect to one another. The picture is made clearer if we include the suggestion that the central idea underlying the English Law of Contract is that of a *bargain*. (Cf. Cheshire and Fifoot, *The Law of Contract*, e.g., pp. 19, 21.)

This is hardly the moment to begin a discussion of that rationalization of modern society which sociologists have characterized in terms of a distinction between *Gemeinschaft* and *Gesellschaft*. But it is important to keep in mind that Utilitarianism, and liberalism generally, is based upon a particular conception of society, and of responsibility, and that a concentration upon its more limited moral theses may not bring out fully what it is which its critics are responding to. (Rawls also cautions us about this, but he does not suggest what its importance may be, beyond explaining the Utilitarians' emphasis on social institutions. (Cf. p. 19, note 21.))

With respect to the attempted reconciliation between Utilitarianism and Deontological justifications of punishment, I can here scarcely more than outline my reservations.

Punishment, unlike making and keeping promises, is, or includes, a clear case of a social institution, but there are two ways in which one may be conceiving of "the institution of punishment". We may be conceiving of it either on a par with institutions like kinship systems, law and religion, institutions which distinguish societies from hives or galaxies, general dimensions in terms of which any community of human beings will be described; or we may be thinking of it as a *specific* institution, on a par with monogamy or monotheism or suttee or death by stoning, institutions in terms of which one society is distinguished from another society, or from the same society at an earlier stage. The importance in noting this distinction is this: Utilitarianism cannot, and is not meant to, justify the general institution of punishment as such; whereas, and contrary to what is said, so far as I am aware, by all the philosophers who have defended the view of Restricted Utilitarianism we are considering, that is what I understand Deontologists to have undertaken to do. If this is true the reconciliation between Utilitarianism and Deontology is again not explained by a distinction between actions and practices.

According to Utilitarianism, the sole function of punishment, its only justification, is that (the threat of) it deters men from unacceptable modes of conduct; and it follows from valuing the criminal within the Utilitarian axiom that "each shall count as one and none as more than one", that even where called for, punishment shall be as light as is compatible with effective deterrence. Punishment, then, is a necessary evil; in the absence of the need to deter, punishment could have no utilitarian justification whatever. Suppose that deterrence by punishment and by the threat of punishment is a universal ingredient of human society. For a Utilitarian, this universality, if unquestionable, must remain accidental; not a moral inevitability. Indeed, doing away with punishment altogether is just the ideal case of reducing it wherever feasible; and to this the Utilitarian is committed. Utilitarianism can justify one sentence over another, or the practice of punishment by imprisonment rather than by death; but Punishment, the practice *überhaupt*, it cannot, and would not wish to, justify.

This, of course, does not deny Rawls's defense of Utilitarianism against the objection that it allows the innocent to be punished; all he needs for that defense is the idea of Utilitarianism as justifying a particular institution (as against another). And in the full and realistic and historically sensitive use he makes of that idea, his defense seems to me successful (cf. especially pp. 10–13). And the defense of Utilitarianism against two standing objections was his primary aim in the paper of his under discussion.

But a defense against a particular criticism is one thing, a reconciliation of the two dominant theories of punishment is something else, and in the way in which Retributivism as a moral theory is described in the view he defends, its moral force is not, to my mind, brought out. That view takes the essential claim of Retributivism to be that only guilty men may

rightly be punished, and its contention is that this is trivially true, A. M.
Quinton arguing that it follows from the meaning of the word "punishment" (cf. "On Punishment", p. 87), Rawls that it follows from the nature
of the criminal law (pp. 6–7), and that no Utilitarian could fail to know
it. (But only Rawls, to my knowledge, has undertaken to show in detail
why the Utilitarian position is not open to the charge.) But does the
Retributivist position really amount to no more than this particular
criticism of Utilitarianism, and is this even the most important of its
criticisms against it?

It is not, as some retributivists think, that we *may* not punish the innocent and
ought only to punish the guilty, but that we *cannot* [logically] punish the innocent and *must* [logically] only punish the guilty. [Quinton, p. 86]

In brief, the two theories answer different questions: retributivism the question
"when (logically) *can* we punish?", utilitarianism the question "when (morally)
may we or *might* we punish?" [*Ibid.*, p. 84]

But if Utilitarianism knows that only guilty men are subject to punishment, then surely Retributivists know what Utilitarians have to teach,
that punishment deters. All threats of pain deter. But a utilitarian justification of *the institution* of punishment (the deliberate infliction of pain
as such) could not be merely that it does in fact avoid greater pain. Grant
that it does. It must assume that only by deliberately inflicting *some* pain
can greater future pain be avoided. And this is the point at which a
Retributivist will feel that this justification of punishment is morally incomplete. The Utilitarian position depends upon its being *obvious* that
punishment deters; but it is not equally obvious that that is a sufficient
reason for inflicting it. The Retributivist is not asking "Why and when
can men be punished?" to which the answer is, "Because they are guilty",
or, "Only if they are guilty". (Compare: "When should I believe something?" Answer: "When there is no contradiction in it.") Retributivism
rather asks, "Why can or should *guilty* men be punished?". And the
answer to this will require a theory about the nature of guilt and consequently of the nature and function of punishment. Not, however, a theory
about its utility. The Retributivist takes the utility of punishment for
granted (it is, after all, pretty obvious), and holds Utilitarianism in
suspicion not merely because it confuses or neglects what he takes to be
the real moral issue, viz., why you may punish at all; but primarily because it skirts the edge of immorality — and not merely because he may
think Utilitarianism allows you to punish innocent men as though they
were guilty, but because it may lead you to punish guilty men for the

wrong reasons (e.g., because you personally dislike them, or out of vengeance). The answer to the question "Why may guilty men be punished?" cannot be, "Because they are *guilty*" (i.e., because pain inflicted upon them could logically constitute punishment); it is, rather, "*Because* they are guilty" — which is, as one would expect of Kant, an attempt to define the only moral *motive* on which society, or any individual, may act in punishing.

Vengeance and punishment do look alike. And if, as seems to be the case, the criminal law arose as a way of controlling the institution of private vengeance, then one will not be surprised to find that the impulse to vengeance can shield itself under the righteousness of punishment. (Not, however, from the eyes of Nietzsche; cf. *Genealogy of Morals*, p. 6.) If this concern with the motive of society (of, that is, its authorities) seems unduly scrupulous, and even academic, it is the projection of a genuine moral concern; a projection, it may be, held largely in modern times among academics. It also indicates that the famous rigorism of Retributivists holds for the punisher as well as the punished. Punishment is bad business at best; and everyone involved in it is on the spot. This is what Retributivism emphasizes; it follows our movements with a moral spotlight. The Retributivist is not the sole possessor of the idea of justice; but he is its most single-minded and inspired champion. And as always, scratch a virtue and you will find a limitation.

If, as seems irreversible, Utilitarianism has made its point that a secular institution cannot and must not undertake to determine the degree of corruption in a human soul and attempt to fit a punishment to it, it has also used its rightness here to deny the existence of the moral problem to which Retributivism is a response.

Another way of putting my insistence that Utilitarianism does not justify the institution of punishment as such is to say that for a consistent Utilitarian there is no distinction in kind between civil and criminal offenses. There will be differences between legal systems and within one legal system at different periods, as to which acts are to be held criminal; but there will always be certain acts that any Retributivist will say ought to be punished, whether or not any other sanction would deter. I think most of us in fact possess both the utilitarian and retributivist moral sensibility. So far as we are Retributivists, we feel that punishment, in itself, is sometimes justifiable; so far as we are Utilitarians, we feel that punishment, in itself, cannot be justified. These feelings are not facing different ways, one toward the judge and the past, the other toward the legislator and the future (this is the way Rawls reconciles the positions — cf. p. 6). They are looking at the same thing, and conflicting. That is what the reconciliation we have considered does not explain.

A moral reason can never be a *flat* answer to the competent demand for justification. If a moral question is competently raised, then a moral response *must* allow a discussion whose conclusion will be the fuller articulation of the positions in question. (You may *call* the discussion closed, but then *that* articulates your position. The definitive is self-defining.) If it is ever competent to raise a question about whether you ought to keep a promise (and it will not be competent in a practical context if all it means is, Is it convenient?), then the answer cannot simply refer to rules. If it is ever competent to raise a question whether a given person, or any person, ought to be punished (and it will not be competent if all it means is, Is it convenient? or Is he guilty?), then it cannot be morally answered by referring to the rules of an institution. And are there no competent moral questions about promising and punishing? One may, of course, refer to the rules of an institution in one's defense; the effect of that is to refuse to allow a moral question to be raised. And that is itself a moral *position*, for which one must accept responsibility. The way Rawls articulates the concept of a rule obscures this, and I want to say just enough about his discussion to say more clearly what I mean.

Play and the Moral Life

The practice view leads to an entirely different conception of the authority which each person has to decide on the propriety of following a rule in particular cases. . . . It doesn't make sense for a person to raise the question whether or not a rule of a practice correctly applies to his case where the action he contemplates is a form of action defined by a practice. If someone were to raise such a question, he would simply show that he didn't understand the situation in which he was acting. If one wants to perform an action specified by a practice, the only legitimate question concerns the nature of the practice itself ("How do I go about making a will?").

This point is illustrated by the behavior expected of a player in games. If one wants to play a game, one doesn't treat the rules of the game as guides as to what is best in particular cases. In a game of baseball if a batter were to ask "Can I have four strikes?" it would be assumed that he was asking what the rule was; and if, when told what the rule was, he were to say that he meant that on this occasion he thought it would be best on the whole for him to have four strikes rather than three, this would be most kindly taken as a joke. One might contend that baseball would be a better game if four strikes were allowed instead of three; but one cannot picture the rules as guides to what is best on the whole in particular cases, and question their applicability to particular cases as particular cases. [Rawls, p. 26]

Why this unlikely example ("Can I have four strikes?")? Suppose I ask you why you bunted, or gave a walk to Dizzy, or didn't try to steal second. What rules will you cite to defend your conduct? What rules don't I know? While it is true that "no matter what a person did, what he did would not be described as stealing a base or striking out or drawing [or giving] a walk [or bunting] unless he could also be described as playing baseball", it does not follow that no question can competently be raised about what you did; and if it is raised then it cannot competently be answered (though it could be rejected, rudely) by citing a rule which defines the game. Rawls, I conclude, has imagined the questioner and his questions in such a way as to make them incompetent. The incompetence is not directly a function of querying "a form of action defined by a practice".

It may be objected that you answer such questions not, of course, by citing defining rules, but rather, if you are *justifying* your action and not excusing it, by citing something like a principle or strategy; and these do not *define* the game but only tell you how to play the game *well*. The answer to this is that a certain mastery of a game is required in order to be said to play the game at all. A knowledge of every competitive game (except games of pure chance), i.e., every game for which there *are* principles of play, requires an understanding of its principles as well as a knowledge of its defining rules. This point goes, in my view, very deep, and requires a great deal of discussion. All I wish to be noticed now is that the formula "an action specified by a practice" is fatally ambiguous. To perform the job Rawls assigns to it, it must mean, "an action determined by the rules", and this will not by any means describe all, or even most, of the actions which take place in playing a game. (That is to say, competitive games of skill. In pure games of chance it will, which is why such games require an external incentive to make them interesting. The former, on the other hand, and significantly, require *practice*. Think what it would mean to practice a game of chance.) Only where an action is determined by the rules, i.e., *only when you have no alternative move*, would it be true to say that a query about your move *must* come from ignorance of the game, or of the fact that you are playing the game. It is, in part, from assimilating actions *in accordance with* rules to actions *determined* by rules that the idea has arisen of rules as prescriptive (e.g., see Toulmin, *Place of Reason,* p. 149). This suggests that it is in general a mistake to suppose that "not knowing what a game or practice is" is the same as "not knowing the rules of the game", and in particular a mistake to suppose that every intelligible challenge to a particular action defined by a practice can be satisfactorily (or even intelligibly) answered by referring to the rules. There can be many different reasons for asking "Why?" about what a player has done, and it is therefore necessary to know what information the inquirer lacks, and how much he possesses, in order to produce an appropriate reply. Or: the action of "fitting an action into the practice which defines it" is one the success of which depends (as in the case of, e.g., the actions of promising and warning and commanding) upon the competence of the person for or to whom they are done, as well as the competence of the person doing them.

What has happened to the possibilities of justifying an action by referring to the (rules of the) practice under which it falls? Whether this can be done seems to depend upon the type of "rule" in question. Let us very briefly consider the sorts of remarks which are found in descriptions of games. There would appear to be not two but four clear concepts of (something we might call) "rules" — four kinds (at least) of replies to the question, "Why did you do that?":

1. Rules (as defining): e.g., "A bishop moves along the diagonal . . ."; "The king is said to be in 'check' when . . .", etc.
2. Rules (as regulating): e.g., "When a player touches a piece, he must either . . .", etc.
3. Principles: "Develop your pieces as early as possible. You should not initiate an attack until your defensive position is secured", etc.
4. Maxims: "Develop knights before bishops. When your position is . . . force an exchange", etc.

These four categories of "rules" are obviously still insufficient to describe a game fully; notably, the purpose of the game and its manner of commencing are left unmentioned. Moreover, it may not always be clear into which category a particular response to a query should be placed. And this is what one should expect: *all* categories have to be recognized as relevant in order for the person to be described as playing the game. I think it is clear that type 4 rules (maxims) are just what Rawls is calling "summary rules": they summarize the results of a great deal of experience as to which developments yield stronger games, and it is open to any competent player *not* to follow them if the situation or his plan is special enough. Type 2 qualifies as a practice rule on the ground that here, indeed, if a person asks why (say) the batter was allowed to go to first while the count was one-and-one, it is *very* natural to assume he does not know the rule that "when a batter is struck by a pitched ball he is given a walk"; though it may be that the questioner did not *see* that the batter was struck by the ball (which is not the same as "not knowing he is engaged in the practice of baseball" — cf. p. 27) and therefore that what he needs is a piece of information — which itself may be provided, if somewhat impatiently, by citing the rule. Rawls may, however, wish to deny that a rule of type 2 really qualifies as a practice rule on the ground that what is to count as an instance falling under such a rule is not defined by that rule, but presupposed by it: there must *be* the offices of "batter" and "pitcher", and the penalty of "walking", before any such rule could have application. But having distinguished *four* concepts of rules, what we begin to see is this: the characterization in terms of definition (of offices, moves, special conformations, etc.) holds for rules of type 1 and not of type 2; whereas the characterization in terms of form ("Whenever A do B", which tells you, *given* a knowledge of the former rules, what must or may be done, provides *justification,* within the game) holds for types 2 and 4, not for type 1. I realize that I am running a grave risk here of becoming unfair to the argument of Rawls's paper; for he explicitly acknowledges that "there are further distinctions that can be made in classifying rules" (p. 29). But I find the distinctions I have brought out to be essential to the questions at issue. It is essential to the idea of a game that it contains rules of both type 1 (defining rules) and type 3 (principles) (which, in practice, means rules of type 4 as well, since these (maxims) are precipitated by principles). This is only to say, what was said differently before, that a certain mastery of the strategy of a game is as essential to being described as *playing the game* as a mastery of its moves is.

That rules of type 1 are presupposed by rules of higher type has its analogy in daily conduct: justifying what is done (saying whether what was done was right or sensible or tactful or necessary . . .) always presupposes a *particular description* of what was done; under one description it may have been (called) dishonest, under another, courageous. So far, the difference between actions in and out of games lies not in whether the action must be specified (defined) in order to be justified, but in whether the specification is accomplished in terms of defining rules. This difference is crucial in other respects, but it is neutral with respect to the concept of justification.

Perhaps I can now say what I take to be of philosophical importance in the way Rawls has conceived of the concept of rules as defining practices. No rule or principle could function in a moral context the way regulatory or defining rules function in games. It is as essential to the form of life called morality that rules so conceived be absent as it is essential to the form of life we call playing a game that they be present. If this could be made out, the analogy with games would be more useful in understanding morality because of its various, specific differences than because of its similarities. (It follows that what I am thinking of as the form of life called morality is not the same as what one may think of as the form of life called a (moral) code. Duels and rumbles are not modes of discussion.)

Rawls suggests in the final note to his paper that the practice conception is not often usable in the moral life: "relatively few actions of the moral life are defined by practices". I have argued that, in particular, promising is not so defined. If my remarks about that are right, then a suggestion emerges about why philosophers appeal to rules in theorizing about morality, and about how rules are then conceived. The appeal is an attempt to explain why such an action as promising is *binding* upon us. But if you *need* an explanation for that, if there is a sense that something more than personal commitment is necessary, then the appeal to rules comes too late. For rules are themselves binding only subject to our commitment. Why one may think that rules could explain the bindingness of commitment is a question obviously too far for us to reach now. In part it comes from an idea of rules which *might* be expressed by saying that "rules define games". An idea which pictures rules not as defining baseball as opposed, say, to cricket (which they do), but as defining what it is to play a game (which they cannot do).

It seems to me implied in the way Rawls speaks of the *practice* of promising, that there is a particular rule which forbids appealing to the general utilitarian defense. But what sort of rule could this be? To suppose there is (could be) a special rule to the effect that you may not break a promise because you would rather not keep it is like supposing that there is a special rule of chess to the effect that you cannot remove pieces to their former position whenever you would prefer to have them there. But not to know that is not to lack a knowledge of chess; it is to lack initiation into an entire form of life, to lack the whole concept of a (competitive) game. You can and do, of course, (sometimes) break a promise. But breaking a promise is not annihilating it (though there may be other ways in which it is annihilated); moving a piece back is not the same as taking back a move (though there may be other ways and times for doing that). Each move changes the situation in which the following move is to be made. Not to know this is not merely to be without the knowledge of a particular practice (promising); it is to be incapable of engaging in any practice at all; to be unready for responsible (competent) action. (Similarly for the legal institution of Contract. The rules, offices, defenses, actions, etc., "defining the institution", define it by *limiting, specifying,* etc., what counts as an enforceable contract. They do not, however, "define" the form of life generally; one could not understand the particular limitations if one did not already understand the nature of the general form of life; and the Law of Contract itself could only develop in a society in which that form of life already existed.)

I have said that *no* rules could in principle function in the moral life the way "practice" rules function in Rawls's account of them. Another way to see this is the following. First notice that both what I called "defining rules" and "regulatory rules" tell us what we *in fact* or must (may, have to . . .) do in playing, while "advisory rules" (= principles) tell us what we ought (would do well, would be wisest . . .) to do. One of my differences (perhaps only in emphasis) from Rawls is that I take the knowledge and command of *both* to be essential to the form of life we call playing a (competitive) game. Now a critical difference between the play of games and moral conduct can be put this way.

Part of what gives games their special quality — what, one may say, allows them to be practiced and *played* — is that within them what we *must* do is (ideally) completely specified and radically marked off from considerations of what we ought to (or should not) do. It is as though within the prosecution of a game, we are set free to concentrate all of our consciousness and energy on the very human quests for utility and style: if the moves and rules can be *taken for granted,* then we can give ourselves over totally to doing what will win, and win applause. (The idea that freedom is achieved through subjection to the law is fully true to the conduct in games.) I do not mean to say that there is *no* choice in games between what *must* be done and what is to be left to considerations of utility or to the accomplishments of style. Some actions in games would not be included either among the definitions of type 1 nor the rules of type 2, but are yet too close to a mere description of how the game is generally played to be thought of as following special maxims or strategies of play; I am thinking of such matters as a lead's being taken off base, or of the third hand in bridge playing high (should we say, "The third hand must play high", or ". . . ought to (should) play high"?). Such matters will not be called rules in Rulebooks, yet some experts may *make* them rules and teach them as rules.

But *this* choice between "must" and "ought" is not merely occasional in the moral life; it is essential to it. "Ought", unlike "must", implies that there is an alternative course you *may* take, may take responsibility for; but reasons are brought to urge you not to. (Cf. "Must We Mean What We Say?", pp. 28–31.) However, unlike the case of games, what is and is not an alternative open to you is not *fixed*. Actions are not moves, and courses of actions are not plays. What you say you *must* (have to, are compelled to . . .) do, another will feel you *ought* to do, generally speaking, other things equal, etc., but that *here* you ought (would do better) *not* to. (That is a much more usual moral conflict than the academic case of "You ought to do X", "You ought not to do X".) What you say you *must* do is not "defined by the practice", for there is no such practice until you make it one, make it *yours*. We might say, such a declaration defines *you*, establishes your position. One problem of the freedom of the will lies in what you *regard* as a choice, what you see as alternatives you can take, and become responsible for, make a part of your position. This is a deeply practical problem, and it has an inexorable logic: whether what you say you "cannot" do you in fact will not do because of fear, or whether out of a consistent conviction that it is not for you, in either case that is then *your* will. If the alternative is blocked through fear, then your will is fearful; if from single-mindedness, then it is whole. It is about such choices that existentialists say, You choose your life. This is the way an action Categorically Imperative feels. And though there is not The Categorical Imperative, there are actions which are for us categorically imperative, so far as we have *a* will. And though Respect for The Law may not sustain moral relationship, respect for positions not our own, will. And if the only thing good in itself is a good will, then the only thing evil or corrupt in itself is an evil or corrupt will. (That *all* actions which are, in this sense, categorically imperative, are self-imposed, *our* choice, indicates that the *mere* fact of self-imposition is not enough to achieve what Kant, or Freud, would mean by autonomous action. Compare Thoreau at the eighth paragraph of *Walden:* "It is hard to have a Southern overseer; it is worse to have a Northern one; but worst of all when you are the slave-driver of yourself." Cf. *The Senses of Walden*, p. 78.) English moral philosophy has been less interested in whether, and to what extent, and which of our actions are for us categorically imperative — in what we do that rules off our position — than in whether, and to what extent, and which of our actions are done on principle. This perhaps contains a hint as to one place one might look for a reconciliation between Teleological and Deontological theories of the moral life.

The preceding paragraph can be taken as a beginning of an interpretation of Nietzsche's aphorism: "There are no moral phenomena; there are only moral interpretations of phenomena" (*Beyond Good and Evil*, §108).

A final word to suggest what I meant by the appeal to rules obscuring problems in the epistemology of conduct. At one point in his paper Rawls imagines the following sort of case:

> . . . What would one say of someone who, when asked why he broke his promise, replied simply that breaking it was best on the whole? Assuming that his reply is sincere, and that his belief was reasonable (i.e., one need not consider the possibility that he was mistaken), I think that one would question whether or not he knows what it means to say "I promise" (in the appropriate circumstances). [p. 17]

That is to say, we wonder whether he knows what promising is, what it is to promise. But why say, as Rawls does, that we are questioning his knowledge of a *practice?* Rawls continues this way: "If a child were to use this excuse one would correct him; for it is part of the way one is taught the concept of a promise [= what defenses the practice, which defines a promise, allows to him] to be corrected if one uses this excuse". But here again I have trouble imagining the object of these remarks, the context from which conduct is being questioned. For this account makes it seem that the child knows perfectly well what excuses and defenses are, and what it means for them to be allowed and disallowed. Whereas the child is learning these things together with learning what a promise is. (He has, equally, still to learn what *breaking* a promise is. Rawls describes him as having broken his promise; but that is a description from our point of view. All we so far know has happened is that he has failed to provide a specific performance. It remains a problem as to why this is so.)

That one must know what excuses and defenses and justifications (which I earlier called elaboratives) are, in order to know what promises are, does not make promising a special social practice; rather, it brings out the fact that the child is still not sufficiently a master of social intercourse to qualify him as a responsible and autonomous member of society. Learning what counts as an elaborative is a large part of what such mastery will require: in the absence of a mastery of elaboratives, we may question, with respect to *any* conventional action (e.g., warning, thanking, giving, commending . . .) whether the child knows what it *is,* what counts as doing it. And no one of these actions carries with it any particular set of defenses or excuses.

But the point goes deeper than this. In the first section of this chapter, I said that it is part of the concept of playing a game that elaboratives cannot affect the description or the evaluation of *what you did:* if you swung at three pitches and failed to touch the ball on the third swing, then you *struck out.* To *know* you struck out all you need to know are the rules of the game and to have seen what you did. There is no gap between intention and action which *counts* (at any rate, there is no evaluation of a player's intention by the player himself). (This must relate to the absence of room, in games, for *akrasia.* Everyone who can play the game knows, e.g., that in certain circumstances the outfielders' correct throw is to second base; and everyone who can play the game *can* make that throw in those circumstances. What would it mean for a player to say, "I know the correct play was to second base, but I just couldn't bring myself to make it"?. For a player, knowledge is virtue. In willing the end within the arena of a game — to play the game to win — players, one might say, have willed beforehand the means to that end; what the means are is known beforehand, known how to be practiced, how to be executed. (Some people seem so good at life that it is as if they have somehow beforehand willed all the means necessary to living well, unsurprised either by the pains of enmity or by the hard labors of love. Call such people thoroughly virtuous. Like really good players, they make what they do look easy.) What players can and cannot do seem so purely a function of talent and of physical condition, not of will and spiritual condition. — And yet this is not all there is to the matter. We know that some very spiritual things — such as effort, concentration, discipline, pride, courage — are what makes the difference between equally endowed, talented, and trained players, or overcome discrepancies in these physical dimensions. And events which in particular test endurance — e.g., long-distance running — seem the very image of the exercise of will. So until further study perhaps we should rather say: In games there is not the same room for *akrasia* as there is outside.)

Outside the arena of defined practices, in the moral world, what we are doing has no such defined descriptions, and our intentions often fail, one way or another, in execution. There, knowing what you are doing and what you are going to do and what you have not done, cannot fully be told by looking at what in fact, in the world, you do. To know what you are doing is to be able to elaborate the action: say why you are doing it, if that is competently asked; or excuse or justify it if that becomes necessary.

What you do and fail to do are permanent facts of history, and the root of responsibility. But the trunk and branch of responsibility are what you are *answerable* for. And where your conduct raises a question, your answers will again be elaboratives. I have described moral arguments as ones whose direct point it is to determine the positions we are assuming or are able or willing to assume responsibility for; and discussion is *necessary* because our responsibilities, the extensions of our cares and commitments, and the implications of our conduct, are not obvious; because the self is not obvious to the self. To the extent that that responsibility is the subject of moral argument, what makes moral argument rational is not the assumption that there is in every situation one thing which ought to be done and that this may be known, nor the assumption that we can always come to agreement about what ought to be done on the basis of rational methods. Its rationality lies in following the methods which lead to a knowledge of our own position, of where we stand; in short, to a knowledge and definition of ourselves.

XII

The Autonomy of Morals

One could scarcely question A. N. Prior's observation that ". . . in our own time the perception that information about our obligations cannot be logically derived from premisses in which our obligations are not mentioned has become a commonplace, though perhaps only in philosophical circles" (*Logic and the Basis of Ethics*, p. 36). Non-naturalistic ethical theories seem to be based entirely upon this perception; an anti-non-naturalistic position such as Stevenson's assumes it; because of it, writers such as S. E. Toulmin, however different from the former in other respects, set out to characterize a special "logic" or "mode of reasoning" to explicate the force of moral argument. Apart from any intrinsic logical interest the thesis may itself hold, one is struck by the claims made in its behalf.

There are, I take it, two ways in which morality has been held to be "autonomous". In the one, it has been held that the justification of moral claims could not be established by an appeal either to God or nature, or to any realm beyond itself. In the other, the morality of an action has been held to depend upon its source lying in the freedom of the agent. Prior takes the thesis in the former of these senses, as proving, or anyway clarifying the fact, that there is a "distinction between the 'natural' and the 'moral' realms" (p. 11) and that, to take an historically important case, "we cannot infer 'We ought to do X' from . . . 'God commands us to do X', unless this is supplemented by the ethical premiss 'We ought to do what God commands' . . ." (pp. 18–19). The thesis then explains both such views as Hutcheson's and Hume's in attacking "ethical

rationalism", and such views as Reid's, which "amounts to a frank abandonment of the attempt to find a 'foundation' for morality that is not
itself moral" (p. 34, and cf. the whole of Chapter III). R. M. Hare takes
the thesis in the latter of the two senses we have distinguished, understanding Kant to have "rested upon this rule [viz., "No imperative conclusion can be validly drawn from a set of premises which does not contain
at least one imperative"] in his polemic against 'Heteronomy of the Will'.
. . . The reason why heteronomous principles of morality are spurious is
that from a series of indicative sentences about 'the character of any of
its objects' no imperative sentence about what is to be done can be derived, and therefore no moral judgment can be derived from it either"
(*The Language of Morals*, p. 30).

I have made no effort to put the two theses about autonomy more
clearly than I have, because I think it is in fact extremely unclear what
moral philosophers have meant by saying that morality or moral judgment or moral conduct is "autonomous", and therefore extremely unplausible that any syllogistic point as is contained in the thesis that no
ethical or imperative conclusion can be derived from premises all of
which are factual could possibly articulate what it is that moralists have
been getting at. The idea that morality can have and need have no non-
moral "foundation" is associated with particular periods in the history of
society; with, for example, Greek society when it emerged from the "ar-
chaic period", about which Snell says:

There is no need for exhortations to happiness; everyone tries to achieve it. We
may call it moral, this early striving for a happiness which is comprehended as a
divine effulgence and the helpful presence of a demon. But instead of being
autonomous the morality is couched in religious concepts. And perhaps it should
be pointed out that the Greeks found fairly soon that happiness could also be
deceptive and brief. [*The Discovery of the Mind*, p. 158]

Or it is associated with Renaissance and Enlightenment culture, or to
whenever it was that, as Feuerbach and Kierkegaard and Nietzsche put
it, the Christian ceased to exist; or it refers to some point, perhaps romanticism, at which intellectual historians would say that the individual
has become autonomous, personal claims becoming independent of social
institutions. It refers to a fact of human conduct and to the forms of justifications which human beings in fact accept as justifying their conduct,
to the fact that certain reasons which formerly led to moral conviction
no longer do so. The Enlightenment remark that "we cannot infer" obligation from God's command without adding the ethical premise "We
ought to do what God commands", would mean as much to a believing

Jew or Christian as to say, to straighten out a lawyer, "You cannot infer that a man has trespassed from the fact that he walked across another man's property without the premiss, 'whenever one man walks across another man's property he is trespassing' "; or to say, to clarify someone's shoddy thinking, "You cannot infer that you ought to leave now from the fact that otherwise you're likely to miss your train, without adding the premiss, 'whenever anything is likely to happen that you don't want to happen then you ought to do whatever will prevent its happening' ". The content of Kant's idea of autonomy can perhaps be put by saying that a moral action is one which we must *choose,* not one *dictated,* by impulse, or desire, or by other persons. Accepting the major premiss which will yield "I ought to eat the orange" from the indicative statement "The orange looks good" won't give Kant what he wants. And if "we remember that the greatest of all rationalists, Kant, referred to moral judgments as imperatives" (Hare, p. 16), then we should remember that Kant took this to be the case only because we human creatures are not *fully* rational, and have sometimes to act *against* ourselves, against some "imperatives", to act morally. It is that capacity which, for him, *expressed* our rationality, not any such fact as that "moral discourse", viz., commands and imperatives, "like statements, . . . are governed by logical rules" (Hare, pp. 15–16).

But, whatever potency the thesis of autonomy is supposed to have in clarifying certain valuable, but obscure, traditional ideas, it is the validity of the thesis itself which primarily concerns me here. I want to suggest that, as an account of moral or practical reasoning generally, it is empty; and empty in a way that the heart of ordinary language has the reasons for.

The thesis depends upon its being *obvious* that, to use a favorite example, "We cannot . . . infer 'We ought to do X' from 'We have promised to do X', unless we also grant the ethical proposition 'We ought to keep promises', and for this latter, no non-ethical substitutes, such as 'We have promised to keep our promises', will do" (Prior, p. 22).

Call the conclusion ("We ought to do X") O, the "minor premiss" ("We promised to do X") R_2, and the "major premiss" ("We ought to keep promises") R_1. It is true that O cannot be derived from R_2 alone; and suppose that it is also true that it can only be derived from R_2 with the addition of R_1. For this to establish the thesis of autonomy — that no "ought"-statement can be derived from statements no one of which contains "ought" — it must *also* be true that the step from R_2 to O is *inferential.* But is that more than an assumption? It seems *obvious,* I think, only when you take a statement like "You ought to do X" (O) apart from considering any context of its use, then suggest that the reason that will be given for this claim is that "You promised to do X" (R₂), and ask, "Does O follow from R₂?"; to which anyone will *see* that the answer must be, "No". And if you ask "What would make it follow?" anyone will give the equivalent of R₁ as the answer.

   To test this, take a different example in which an ought-claim appears. You say:

(O) You ought to castle now.

Asked why, you reply:

(R₂) Castling will neutralize his bishop and develop your rook.

Does O follow from R₂? What would make it follow? Perhaps:

Whenever castling will neutralize a bishop and develop a rook, then you ought to castle.

But that is absurd. I'm only saying, that's the best move *here*. And if you can't show it isn't and you don't in fact castle, you don't know how to play chess. I could of course give you the reasoning behind my advice. Perhaps:

(R₃) With your rook in play you can trap his queen in two moves.
(R₄) With his queen gone you can win in four moves.

Now I *am* assuming, claiming, that it *follows* from R₂, R₃, and R₄ that

(R₅) Castling now will win.

and follows in terms of ordinary logic and a knowledge of chess. Then the question, presumably, has become: Does O follow from R₅?

   Suppose I am told that I am still assuming something. What? Perhaps that he will see the trap and sacrifice his knight? No; suppose I am told that I am assuming that *you want to win.* Was I *assuming* that? Does O not *follow* from R₅ without the acceptance of the major premiss: "If you want to win, then you ought to castle"? My argument is not *valid* without that? But of course that major premiss is also absurd. What I meant was, that castling will win *here*, not just *any* time. Should I be logically rigorous and add: "If you want to win, you ought to do everything which will win"? But is that intelligible? Is it chess?

   Even with this brusk exposition, perhaps I can say: There is no major premiss which could bind R₅ to O. Not, however, because that step requires a special sort of logic or psychology to bridge it, but *because there is no gap to be filled;* the step is *not* the conclusion of an inference. (Cf. G. E. M. Anscombe, "On Brute Facts", and Philippa Foot, "Moral Arguments".)

The gap which looks open on paper is closed in the *act of confronting* the player. To get a hint of what function "ought" has, it should be noticed that any of R_2–R_5 could directly have been used to advise the player to castle: which of them you say depends on what you think the person doesn't see, and how many steps you take in your proof will depend on how much it will take for him to see what you see (you might, for example, need to fill in several steps between any of R_3, R_4, and R_5, and even R_2 itself might be too fast). If he cannot counter these "factual premises", whose *point,* in that context, is to advise him (and it wouldn't (grammatically) *be* advice unless you thought they would further his position), then unless he actually makes the move, or gives a good reason why he does not, then he either has not understood you, or has not mastered the game.

What would be a good reason for his not making the move? Perhaps he will say "I'm not trying to win"; but in that case he is not fully *playing* (that he be playing the game was one condition for my saying: The gap between R's and O is closed in the act of confrontation) but perhaps testing a new gambit, teaching someone, throwing the game. . . . If he says "You are assuming I'm trying to win", then that is rude (like responding to your question "Why did you move your queen?" by citing the rule that bishops move along the diagonal — suggesting that you could have *seen* his bishop was threatening the queen if you'd look as often as you talk). Because I wasn't *assuming,* seeing you bent over the board, in stern concentration for many minutes before I finally spoke, that you were really playing. What *reason* did I have for assuming that? A hundred reasons; no reason.

Or perhaps he will say: "Of course I know that will win, but it's not my style. I, Capablanca, would rather lose than play so ploddingly, and create such a mess." This is a rational refusal to make a winning move, while yet fully playing to win. (In fact, without words, he merely moves so as to mate in two.) We might say: Capablanca repudiates *you;* he tells you that you are not in his world of chess. (We might call such refusal a "teleological suspension of the expedient". As in morality, it involves a special claim made on the part of the self, and one not everyone is in a position to make, take responsibility for.)

If any of R_2–R_5 can serve to direct the player to castle, then what is special about using "ought"? Nothing is special so far as the content of the statement is concerned. Its content is *completely* exhausted by the reasons you give; and if you have none, then a statement like O is incompetent. (Cf. Bentham: "[When used in conjunction with utilitarian reasons] the words *ought* and *right* and *wrong*, and others of that stamp, have a meaning: when otherwise they have none" (*Principles of Morals and Legislation,* Chapter I, p. x.)) And the relevance of the reasons you give for it are determined by the relevance of the reasons you would give for any "factual premiss" like, say, R_5.

To say the content of "ought" is *completely* specified by the reasons you are prepared to give suggests that it contains no special content which *could* appear among any premises leading to its proof; and to say that its content may be the *same as*, say, that of R_5, suggests that whatever proof you give for R_5 is simultaneously a proof for O: no *further* proof would be possible or coherent. I will say: Whether you say R_5 or O on the basis of this proof, depends upon how you conceive the position of the player, and upon what position you *take* toward him. Saying "ought" implies that there is an alternative, more or less definite, one might take, and in confronting someone with it you are taking a stand on one of them.

"You ought to . . ." is, I will say, though no different in content from the factual premises which are produced in its support and which exhaust its content, a *mode of presentation* of that content, one in which you take a position with respect to it. The phrase "mode of presentation", and the distinguishing of this from the "content" of the (here) directive which is presented is an allusion to the passage of Frege's I earlier referred to in which he says "In my formalized language . . . only that part of judgments which affects the *possible* inferences is taken into consideration"; and goes on to speak of the aspects of language irrelevant to his purposes as serving "to present" the content in a particular form (cf. *Begriffschrift,* p. 3).

In the present instance, we naturally assume that if such a statement as "You ought to . . ." is to appear as the conclusion of a proof, the term "ought" must appear among the premises: we seem to see this as clearly as we see that if "Socrates is . . ." is to appear in the conclusion of a proof, the term "Socrates" must appear among the premises. But this clarity may in part be due to our having taken as it were a pre-shrunk version of the conclusion. Suppose someone says: "You will be awed to learn that Socrates is mortal", and he is asked, "Can you prove it?"; we will not expect to find among his premises the words, "You will be awed to learn that", nor failing to find them, will we wish to maintain that an awe-statement cannot be deduced from premises none of which contain the word "awe". We could say: such a formula is a mode of presenting a proposition to be inferred (as are many others, e.g., "It has just been proved that . . .", "I most emphatically aver that . . .", "Let there no longer be any doubt that . . .", etc.). (I am indebted here to ideas in Urmson's "Parenthetical Verbs" and in Strawson's "Truth".) The mode of presentation in such cases is not, in itself, the subject of inference.

Similarly, I am suggesting, "You ought to . . ." may be thought of as a mode of presenting an action to be done (as is, "How can you justify not . . . ?", "You'll be sorry if you don't . . ."); it is not in itself the subject of inference. Which mode of presentation you use does not affect what the proof must contain. It depends on the context from within which you confront the performer (how you are prepared to address him, how much conviction you have in the strength of the premises, etc.).

I think "It is desirable to . . ." can be understood in this way, as a mode of presentation. People used to say, when Mill-baiting was popular, that "desirable", contrary to Mill's remarks near the opening of Chapter IV of *Utilitarianism,* does not mean "capable of being desired" but "ought to be desired". (Cp. Stevenson, *Ethics and Language,* pp. 17–18.) First, Mill does not claim the former, and the latter is just false, as one can see simply by trying to substitute "ought to be desired" for "desirable" in an ordinary context in which the latter is used. If you claim that a trip to Isfahan is especially desirable for me (given certain facts you know about my desires and resources, etc.) then you are not claiming that I ought to desire to take the trip but that I ought to take it, or perhaps, as one may say, that I really ought to take it. The characteristics that make the thing desirable for me (and there had better be some advantages or values that you can cite, the basis of which will be that I do, if I am like you, in fact desire them; so Mill may have had the right idea after all) — these characteristics, looked at another way, would be the grounds for claiming that I ought. So it is not because it is desirable that I ought to do it; whatever causes the one causes the other, as it were. Which of these modes of presentation you use depends on why or how you have taken it upon yourself to confront me. One might feel that saying "ought" is stronger. But more specifically it is more personal. I say *"It's* desirable", but *"You* ought". The point is not that the advantage or value is greater in the latter case but that my stake in your welfare is greater.

The "desirable" case looks like one in which what is to be proved is exactly what I have been calling the mode of presentation *itself.* For example, *that he will be awed* may become the point of contention. You might argue from his having been awed to learn that Plato and Alcibiades are mortal that he will (if he is rational) be awed to learn this of Socrates. Or you might treat the contention as a simple prediction: tell him about Socrates and see whether in fact he is awed to learn it. How might the mode of presentation *that you ought* itself become the point of contention? One possibility, alluded to, is that I must close further gaps between my reasons and this conclusion, gaps perhaps opened by the very fact that I confront you, that it is you that I confront; gaps I perhaps could not, perhaps nobody else could, be expected to have known were there: "That is not the only, or the best, or my, way to win"; "I feel I must lose to him once in a while, for the sake of his confidence"; "I have agreed to the handicap of my not using the option of castling". Or perhaps you take the position that you have no obligations, perhaps that nothing is owed by you which you do not want to perform. (So you might claim that nothing awes you.) Then I might feel like looking for something you will have to agree you *just* ought to do, without reasons. Who knows what this will be in a particular case? Perhaps that you ought to marry, or marry this boy, or not; or have children, or not have them; or set an example, or not be so concerned to set an example; allow yourself pleasure, or learn to say no; stop making the world pay for your disappointments; let the dead bury the dead. Here the matter of moral ideals comes to the fore. The fact that I will not invoke reasons defines the way I mean to be speaking to you, so of course here there is no question of a major premiss from which my confrontation follows. I am speaking to you of self-definition; perhaps I offer you examples of others, exemplars. And who is in a position to speak to you of such matters, in such ways, comes more nakedly to the fore.

Perhaps one would by now be willing to question the *obviousness* of the philosopher's thesis about the derivation of "You ought to do X" from "You promised to do X". Our suspicion should be aroused about this from the ambiguity of the conclusion alone. For how is "do X" in "You ought to do X" to be understood? It means here "keep your promise" of course; but it also means, for example, "return the money". And in neither case is the philosopher's favorite "Because you promised" a *reason* for it, a premiss from which it could follow. Briefly consider: If the reason is true, i.e., if you *did* promise, then saying "You ought to return the money" has the same content as "You ought to keep your promise" (the way "Socrates destroyed Athens" has the same content as "Socrates destroyed the enemy of Sparta" in a context in which the reference of the description "the enemy of Sparta" is known to be Athens). So what you need a *reason* for is, "You ought to keep your promise". There *may* be a comprehensible reason (e.g., you were not really released from it), and now the familiar "major premiss" is no longer so tempting. Contrariwise, "keep your promise" is a way of saying something about a specific deed to which you have committed yourself; here, return the money. And so the reason you give will have to be one speaking to *that*. In a word, any *reason* you give for "You ought to do X" (where you have promised to do X) must, competently, be one which speaks to the specific act to which you have committed yourself, *and* one which takes into account the fact of your commitment — one strong enough to counter not merely an alternative to doing a particular thing, but an alternative to *fulfilling your commitment* (i.e., performing a particular action which *is* that fulfillment).

This, of course, should make us equally suspicious about the meaning of the major premiss. Prior tells us that,

"You ought to keep your promises", for example, plainly means the same as "if you have promised to do anything, you ought to do it". [p. 40]

This makes "You ought to keep promises" the universal generalization of "You ought to keep this promise". But *is* that obvious? What is the force of that plural? That it *can* be so construed (i.e., does seem to fit agreeably into the form the philosopher is counting on, viz., "If anything is an action you promised to do, you ought to do it") does not mean that what should ordinarily be meant in saying it *is*, in that construction, aptly rendered. The problem of apt rendering, of deciding what logical form correctly records the sense of a statement of a natural language, has been continuously felt and discussed from the very beginning of the development of modern logic. ("Tigers burn" vs. "Tigers exist"; "I am hunting a lion" vs. "I am hunting for my lyre"; "No one was in the auditorium" vs. "Noonan was in the auditorium"; "Jones believes there is a Bridal Suite in the Statler Hotel" vs. "Jones lives in a Bridal Suite in the Statler Hotel".) I mention this well-known fact in order to emphasize that my looking for or asking for the ordinary meaning of a plural ought-claim is meant, intellectually anyway, in exactly the same spirit in which the logician concerned with recording ordinary language in logical form looks at the ordinary meaning of the statement he wishes to formalize. And how we know that one logical form is more faithful than another to the ordinary meaning or use of a statement is no doubt a terrible or ticklish problem; but that we (often) know is scarcely to be questioned.

What are my grounds for questioning that the universal quantifier of modern logic aptly renders the plural of ought-claims? Just that the plural and singular forms do not have the same relationship as plurals which really are generalizations of their singulars. The singular neither *follows* from the plural (except on a special *view* of promising, which cannot be proved by logic), nor is the singular *evidence* for the plural. Examples of other plurals which are not generalizations would be "Politicians make strange bed-fellows", "Grades are unimportant"; nor is the statement "You ought to keep pets" likely to be taken as meaning, "If anything is a pet, you ought to keep it". Similarly for "You ought to keep records". Perhaps such examples would suggest ways in which we might arrive at some comprehension of how "You ought to keep promises" is to be understood. Its use is evidently *very* special. Perhaps the reason it seems to have a clear sense is that, once its entrance is *forced* by the pressure to invent a major premiss, it is heard on the model of a principle of games. That, in effect, gives "You ought to keep promises" the force of "In certain circumstances it is best to . . . unless". But it is not obvious that "You ought to keep promises" does, whatever it means, mean that; nor that if it did it would even seem to serve the function the thesis of autonomy requires of it. (A "regulatory rule" might; but that cannot be formulated with "ought". This suggests that "You ought . . .", contrary to what is often said, is not a "hypothetical imperative".)

If this pace of flat assertion has managed to create suspicion about the inevitability of the thesis of autonomy, it will be wondered why that thesis takes the form it does; what, that is, the experience is of someone led to produce "You ought to do X" in such a way that it will seem a reason for it to say "You promised to do X" and then ask whether the conclusion follows from that reason as a premiss. In a sentence, the suggestion I would follow is this: I think it is a real experience which can produce such a surmise as, "Why ought I to do anything?". Given that as a question to be *answered,* the (generic) examples which present themselves will not, as in epistemological contexts, be particular; they will, it seems, take the form, "Why, for example, ought I to keep promises, pay debts, tell the truth, do my 'duty', etc.?". This, in effect, asks: Why ought I to honor the claims others make upon me? And, unlike the non-claim context in epistemology, this is not a position which cannot coherently be maintained; it therefore leads to no *sense* of paradox when the philosopher is led by it to his conclusion about the logical autonomy of ethical judgments.

I have set down these considerations in part to suggest my answer to the popular idea that there is some question about the logical validity of ethical arguments — another route to the suspicion of them as in general irrational. They are not irrational because the step from reasons to conclusion is neither deductive nor inductive; nor rational because that step follows a rational logic of imperatives or some third kind of logic. That step is not inferential at all. "Ought" and "must" (and "have to" and "supposed to" — everything I called, in "Must We Mean What We Say?", "modal imperatives", pp. 30–31) are modes of presenting the very reasons you would offer to support them, and without which they would lack meaning altogether; or they specifically set aside reasons. ("I can do no other.") What makes their use rational is their relevance to the person confronted, and the legitimacy your position gives you to confront him or her in the mode you take responsibility for.

So what answer may we give such a question as whether "ought" *can* be derived from "is"? One answer is: No. You cannot *go from* "is" to "ought" any more than you can go from France to Paris. There is no distance (of that kind) between them. Another answer is: Yes. You can derive "ought" from "is" the way you can derive pleasure from playing the piano. But only on condition that you actually play the piano and actually do find pleasure in playing.

The way I have drawn the relationship between ought-statements and factual statements, when directed toward the conduct of another person, is figured in the relationship between a pointing finger and a direction to be taken. That fits the case of games well enough. For we were able to say, if a person doesn't give a good reason for *not* taking the game-directive, then either he has not understood, or else he does not know the game. If I ask you where Santa Maria Novella is, and you point to a particular street, then if I do not in fact proceed to take that way, or indicate that I was curious for some good reason or planning to go later, but simply stare at you as if you have done something incomprehensible, then I do not know what "pointing a direction" is. You need not have *said* "That is the way" or "Take the road to the right of the fountain" or "You ought to take that way", though you might, in addition to, *as a substitute for* or *further specification of* pointing, have said any of these, in particular circumstances; which indicates that directions or directives *need* deriving from other premises as little as an act of pointing does (though of course you may have to prove or show that in fact that *is* the way).

Perhaps this analogy gives a picture of the idea that there is some gap between "Castling will win" and "You ought to castle", or between either of these and an action — a way — to be taken, which needs to be filled by psychology or bridged by a major premiss. Mightn't a comparable feeling arise as follows: Imagine that you rush up to a stranger sitting in the Boboli gardens, and point in the direction of Santa Maria Novella, and then ask yourself what more you would need to provide in order to have that person actually *go* there. Don't we feel: you would need to *persuade* him to go? Just "knowing" the direction would not be enough. "Morals excite passions, and produce or prevent actions. Reason of itself is utterly impotent in this particular" (Hume, *Treatise*, Book III, Part I, Section I). Reason of itself? "The pointing finger itself" cannot produce or prevent actions either.

It will be felt: "But obviously *moral* contexts are different, as you have kept pointing out. Suppose we granted that everything you have said is true of games. In moral confrontation there *is* a gap between a factual reason and an ought-claim, and between both and the action each presents."

Another reason I have set down so inconclusive a set of remarks is exactly to give a way of articulating, or investigating, what the differences between games and morality are which create these admitted differences. In games, what the other person is doing, the goal he aims for, his way, is clear; what it is you tell him to do is defined; what alternatives he can take are fixed; what it would mean to say, the grounds upon which you say, that one course is better than another are part of the game; whether he has done it is settled. In morality none of this is so. Our way is neither clear nor simple; we are often lost. What you are said to do can have the most various descriptions; under some you will know that you are doing it, under others you will not, under some your act will seem unjust to you, under others not. What alternatives we can and must take are not fixed, but chosen; and thereby fix us. What is better than what else is not given, but must be created in what we care about. Whether we have done what we have undertaken is a matter of how far we can see our responsibilities, and see them through. ("Did you help him?"; "Did you get him the message?"; "Did you really make your position clear?"; "Did you do all you could?") What we are responsible for doing, is, ineluctably, *what in fact happens*. But *that* will be described in as many ways as our actions themselves. And such total responsibility is bearable only because of the significance of elaboratives. If, as Prichard and Ross take it, we are under an obligation only to "set ourselves" to do something, and not to effect changes in the world, then elaboratives could not serve to excuse, explain, and justify *what we do*.

The absence of elaboratives in games is the complement of the fact that in games our actions are defined and our commitments fixed. Mistakes here are not personal, and failures are merely "errors" to be scored. Integrity can be lost only in obvious ways. And as we cannot ask for favors or forgiveness, so we need neither grant nor accept them. We become our bodies. But when the game or the play is over and the player or actor drops his position within the marked area of ceremony, he becomes a person whom our actions affect in ways he is not committed to by having assumed a governed position; and we become persons with intentions no longer irrelevant to what we do, and relevant consequences no longer held within clear lines. Here we cannot practice the effects we wish to achieve; here we are open to complete surprise at what we have done. As practice makes it tolerable to accept credit or censure for everything we do, so elaboratives makes it tolerable to act not knowing in advance what we may do, what consequences we may be faced with, e.g., that we have been misunderstood, betrayed, rejected; that we have been unperceptive, betraying, rejecting all unknown to ourselves, and without even seeing how. Making a bad play makes us angry with ourselves, even ashamed; taking a false step makes us guilty.

But these differences, rather than showing the irrationality of morality, may help to articulate what gives it the rationality it has. In both games and morality, one human being confronts another in terms of that person's position, and in a mode which acknowledges the relation he is taking towards it. And in both, "in terms of that person's position" means, in terms of what he is doing and must do and ought to do. In games this means, in terms of the (defining) rules and the principles of the game; in morality this means, in terms of his cares and commitments. I am, then, suggesting that the patent rationality of games does not depend upon "reason of itself" having potency. I suppose it does not: the brain is not a muscle. It depends upon the way in which the arena and court of play *marks off* what will count as our responsibility and our concerns. The *problems* of morality then become which values we are to honor and create, and which responsibilities we must accept, and which we have, in our conduct, and by our position, incurred.

In both games and morality, there are two main sorts of reasons with which we may be confronted: the one I might call a "basis of care" — it provides whatever sense there will be in your confronting someone with what he "ought" to do; the second I call a "ground of commitment" — it grounds what you say "must" be done in that person's commitments, both his explicit undertakings and the implications of what he does and where he is, for which he is responsible. What I would regard as providing a theoretical foundation for morality — what, in other words, I would take to show the rationality of moral judgment — would be to explain what makes each of these sources of reasons the reasons they are. They will seem a shaky foundation to the extent that one feels we may care about anything at all, or nothing, or that we may deny responsibility for any or all of our actions. But what I should undertake to show is that such suppositions would render action and passion themselves, not merely irrational, but unrecognizable. (It is when one makes mysteries of others in such a way; makes oneself a stranger to the human race, perhaps with the help of philosophy; or feels that if one's confrontation is to be sufficiently powerful it must work on people at random, like a ray; it is at such times that one can feel that "desirable" means "ought to be desired", as though the expression of advice were the magical creation of a context in which the expression of advice was called for, as though one would never have to *earn* the right to speak for others.)

Of course our confrontation of others may not take. We may mistake someone's cares and commitments, or they may suddenly deny us. But what then breaks down is not moral argument but moral relationship. Of course that can happen. But it does not happen because we do not feel approval of one another. What is required in confronting another person is not your liking him or her but your being willing, from whatever cause, to take his or her position into account, and bear the consequences. If the moralist is the human being who best grasps the human position, teaches us what our human position is, better than we know, in ways we cannot escape but through distraction and muddle, then our first task in subjecting ourselves to judgment is to tell the moralist from the moralizer. When Auden heard "the preacher's loose, immodest tone", he heard the tone of one speaking in the name of a position one does not occupy, confronting others in positions of which one will not imagine the acknowledgment.

PART FOUR

Skepticism and the Problem of Others

For to be mistaught is worse than to be untaught; and no perverseness equals that which is supported by systems, no errors are so difficult to root out as those which the understanding has pledged its credit to uphold.

Wordsworth, "Essay, Supplementary to the Preface"

After all, one can but bear witness less to convince him who won't believe than to protect him who does, as Blake puts it . . .

W. B. Yeats, "Magic"

. . . the eternal struggle of art against education. . . . It is important that the artist should be highly educated in his own art; but his education is one that is hindered rather than helped by the ordinary processes of society which constitute education for the ordinary man. For these processes consist largely in the acquisition of impersonal ideas which obscure what we really are and feel, what we really want, and what really excites our interest. . . . Blake . . . knew what interested him, and he therefore presents only the essential, only, in fact, what can be presented, and need not be explained. . . . To him there was no more reason why Swedenborg should be absurd than Locke. He accepted Swedenborg, and eventually rejected him, for reasons of his own. He approached everything with a mind unclouded by current opinions. There was nothing of the superior person about him. This makes him terrifying.

T. S. Eliot, "Blake"

[G. E. Moore] was not like any other lecturer I have heard or heard of. He made you sure that what was going on mattered enormously — without your necessarily having even a dim idea as to what it could be that was going on. We were, in truth, undergoing an extraordinarily powerful influence, not one that I would suppose Moore could for a moment conceive. He was not at all interested in that. He was interested in the problem in hand: more interested in it than, I think, I have ever seen anyone interested in anything.

I. A. Richards, "Complementarities"

XIII

Between Acknowledgment and Avoidance

In tracing our disappointment with criteria, in denying that Wittgensteinian criteria can, or are meant to, refute skepticism, I seem, in my remarks about the problem of other minds, to have left the other's privacy intact. And doesn't Wittgenstein deny privacy? What else is the teaching of his obsessive emphasis on the publicness of language and on the outwardness of criteria? I have suggested that the teaching is in service of a vision that false views of the inner and of the outer produce and sustain one another, and I would be glad to have suggested that the correct relation between inner and outer, between the soul and its society, is the theme of the *Investigations* as a whole. This theme, I might say, provides its moral.

In my earlier discussion I was led at one point to ask parenthetically, "In what spirit does Wittgenstein 'deny' the 'possibility' of a private language?" (p. 84). I will try to take that question outside its parentheses in the course of gathering together some concluding remarks on the topic of privacy.

What gives the impression that Wittgenstein wishes to deny that the soul is private? What, that is, do we wish to deny, in the face of Wittgenstein's teaching, when we feel we must protect the privacy of the soul against him? Is it that we feel the affirmation of privacy to be an affirmation of the existence of the soul itself? — What idea do we have of privacy?

When Wittgenstein remarks "It cannot be said of me at all (except perhaps as a joke) that I *know* I am in pain", he does not — how could he? — deny that I alone can express my pain. He will, however, raise questions about which pains are *mine* (cf. §411). So let us say: Wittgenstein does not — how could he? — deny that I alone can express pain when I alone am in pain. Still, we might raise questions here about what "can express" has in view. Surely you *can* express pain no matter what is happening in me.   — I do not think that a certain difficulty or insufficiency in the assertion of our conviction here is irrelevant to what that conviction is. (Cf. "Knowing and Acknowledging", pp. 263–64.) But let that pass for the moment. Wittgenstein does not deny that when I am in pain it is I who give it expression, or fail to — at all events, give it expression by expressing pain, I mean by expressing *that* pain. Surely it will not be denied that if I do not give it expression then others will not know of it. And it is hard not to think of this situation as one in which I *alone* know that I am in pain. Wittgenstein's denial that I can properly be said to know seems to be something that compromises the soul's privacy — as if privacy were a question of secrecy. If this is one's idea of privacy, then Wittgenstein's teaching on the subject of privacy will be understood as saying that we have no unutterable secrets; this will then simply mean that we have no unbridgeable privacy. Whereas I take his teaching on this point to be rather that what is accurate in the philosophical or metaphysical idea of privacy is not captured, or is made unrecognizable, by the idea of secrecy.

No one will insist that privacy and secrecy have nothing to do with one another; that is, no one will deny that a sense of secrecy captures, or enforces, a particular sense of privacy. But that sense of privacy ought, on its face, to seem of limited metaphysical interest, while possibly of pervasive political significance. A private conversation is one that I do not want others to hear, not one they necessarily cannot hear. My private entrance is one through which I can invite others; in principle, anyone in the world can be as well acquainted with it as I am. A private joke is a more significant case. It may be something I do not bother to explain, or something I wish to test or to hook you with; or it may be something I do not think anyone else will, or will be able, to appreciate. ("Anyone else" may mean anyone other than me, or anyone other than the two of us, or anyone other than you, and you are gone.) It is hard to imagine Wittgenstein's denying *this* possibility, that one's specialness may in fact go unappreciated by another. No doubt he would deny that it *must* go unappreciated, but is *this* what anyone wishes to insist upon? It would be a strange picture of a skeptic to cloak him as saying that each and every mind is so singular as to be inaccessible to every other. Couldn't he, at

most, think this only about his *own* mind? We might think of this as solipsism, i.e., think of solipsism as narcissism, if that fate became live for
us. Narcissus can question himself, but he cannot give himself an answer
he can care about.

Secrecy shares with privacy the idea of exclusiveness, or excludedness. Is
the idea of privacy which some would care to defend and others to attack
an idea of one soul excluded from, or by, another? If so, what role does
the question of one soul's knowledge of another play here? I can know,
for example, all there is to know about Garbo, even know her personally,
perhaps as her constant companion from whom she has no secrets, and
still be excluded from her, not share her (inner) life. (Though I may tell.)

Let us see two sides to the question of whether another's soul — for example a sensation of the other — is private. Professor George Pitcher has
seemed convinced by Wittgenstein that the answer is affirmative, that sensations are private:

> . . . pain language-games do not contain references to our private sensations,
> since these, like the contents of the pictured pot, cannot be talked about. The
> point is not that private sensations are nothing, or do not exist, or are not im-
> portant, or anything of the sort; the point is rather that nothing can be said
> about them, and hence they play no part in our language-games. They are "as
> nothing" in those language-games. [*The Philosophy of Wittgenstein*, p. 300]

Pitcher characterizes such a view, or the view it expresses, as "commonsensical" (p. 283). Professor John Cook seems convinced by Wittgenstein
that the answer is negative, that sensations are *not* private. In the final
section of his paper "Wittgenstein on Privacy" he explores Pitcher's view
of the matter; he concludes that Pitcher "has failed to see how very queer
is the idea that sensations are essentially private" (p. 323). I had recoiled
when Pitcher spoke of a commonsensical idea that sensations are private,
partly because I disagreed with his reading of Wittgenstein, but mostly
because I felt that he had not presented anything I could recognize as the
commonsensical attitude toward privacy and I felt that it may be essential to a correct philosophical view of the matter to elicit the complexi-
ties, or crudities, of our commonsensical attitude toward it. But when
Cook asks that one simply see how very queer the idea is that sensations
are private, my response is, impatiently, just to opt back for privacy; it
seems the most commonsensical view of sensations one could have.

Professor Alan Donagan, in his paper "Wittgenstein on Sensation",
agrees with Pitcher that according to Wittgenstein sensations are private,
in the sense that the actual quality of the other's sensation is unknowable
to us and that that is irrelevant to our knowledge *that* the other is, say,

332 SKEPTICISM AND THE PROBLEM OF OTHERS

in pain. He disagrees with Pitcher over whether the sensation, so conceived, can be named. Pitcher's view was that sensations cannot be
named, but that nevertheless our words for sensations have (other) "legitimate uses" (p. 300). Donagan's view is that sensations *can* be named, or
rather, referred to in a particular way. The disagreement here arises, or is
supported, by differing interpretations of Wittgenstein's parable of the
boiling pot.

It is instructive to study that parable further.

Of course, if water boils in a pot, steam comes out of the pot and also pictured
steam comes out of the pictured pot. But what if one insisted on saying that
there must also be something boiling in the pictured pot? [§297]

Pitcher remarks: "It would be absurd to start talking about the liquid in
the pictured pot; to wonder, for example, whether it is water or tea or
soup. . . . There is no answer to such questions; the liquid in the pot is
no part of the picture — and language-games which involve the picture do
not contain references to the contents of the pot. Similarly, pain language-games do not contain references to our private sensations . . ."
(pp. 299–300). Donagan's reply runs as follows: "If Wittgenstein meant
what Pitcher says he did, his parable was ill-chosen. It is true that the
pictured pot does not contain, as a part, pictured boiling water. But it is
not true that you can describe what the whole picture is a picture of,
without referring to the contents of the pot. Nor is it always absurd to inquire what liquid is in the pot. A picture of a metal teapot on a hot plate,
with steam pouring from its spout, might well illustrate how not to keep
hot tea. . . . Wittgenstein did not overlook these points: indeed, when
he applied his parable to the picturing of pain, he introduced an elaborate quasi-technical terminology for making them. . . ." What Donagan
means by "quasi-technical terminology" is, I take it, primarily the distinction between a *Vorstellung* and a *Bild,* i.e., between an image and a picture as set out in the third section following the parable:

It is — we should like to say — not merely the picture of the behavior that plays
a part in the language-game with the words "he is in pain", but also the picture
of the pain. Or, not merely the paradigm of the behavior, but also that of the
pain. — It is a misunderstanding to say "The picture of pain enters into the
language-game with the word 'pain'". The image [*Vorstellung*] of pain is not a
picture [*Bild*] and *this* image is not replaceable in the language-game by anything that we should call a picture. — The image of pain certainly enters into
the language-game in a sense; only not as a picture. [§300]

(Pitcher prefers to translate *Vorstellung* as "representation" rather than,
with Professor Anscombe, "image". Donagan is dissatisfied with both

translations and offers instead "imaginative representation". I would my-self be content to use the old, more or less emptied word, "idea".) Dona-gan's notion is, then, this: ". . . when you draw a boiling pot, your draw-ing will contain a *Bild* of steam and a *Bild* of a pot, but not a *Bild* of anything boiling. A *Vorstellung*, by contrast, can represent indirectly" (p. 330). Similarly, ". . . although pains cannot be directly represented in pictures, they can be indirectly represented — in 'imaginative representa-tions' (*Vorstellungen*)" (p. 331).

But wouldn't all of these problems about the contents of the pot be solved by making the picture of the pot in such a way that you can see inside it — either by giving us a perspective over the rim of its top, or by picturing a glass pot? Wittgenstein's parable does not say that the picture is not like this. Of course these alternative pictures will not seem grip-pingly pertinent in applying the parable to the question of knowing the pain of others, which is presumably the point. But why not? Perhaps be-cause we would not know what the analogy is to looking "over the rim of its top"; we have no perspective of this kind, or ought not to claim one, on our fellow creatures. And if I try imagining a glass man or woman (not merely a man with glass skin and muscles, but, as it were, glass through and through), I find that I do not quite know where to *place* the pain. (Suppose I imagine that the glass man's shoulder hurts, and I want to show where he hurts, say by painting the place red. Do I paint the pain on his shoulder, or in his brain, or along the nerves between, or in all at once? The last possibility gives pain so unsatisfactory a shape! Or is the shape merely too *definite?*) This is odd, because we certainly know how or where to look for pain, how to locate it — when, that is, we have no thought of actually seeing it. You may, if you wish, without much ado, speak informatively of seeing the boiling water indirectly; that is because you may, if you wish, without much ado, speak of seeing it directly.

If the tipped or transparent pot is not pertinent to the problem of pain, what is the pertinence of an opaque pot, seen squarely from the side? Do we approach the human body more aptly if we take it to be opaque and seen squarely from the side? What is the point of Wittgenstein's parable of the boiling pot?

First let us actually try answering its concluding question — the ques-tion, presumably, the parable was constructed in order to pose: "But what if one insisted on saying that there must also be something boiling in the pictured pot?" What should be said in response to this insistence? — I note that Wittgenstein's German mentions nothing explicitly about "in-sistence". It says simply, "Aber wie, wenn man sagen wollte . . ."; i.e., "but what if one wanted to say". But Anscombe's addition of the idea of insistence seems to me a correct inflection. The sense we are to have of the person supposed in the parable is that he *still* wants to say something (about something). The sense is: nothing could be clearer than the scene he has had set out for him ("Freilich . . .", the parable begins; "Of course . . ."); everything is free and self-confessed, nothing up the sleeve, there is not even a sleeve; and *yet,* and notwithstanding all that, this man doubts — or maybe not so much doubts as pangs — something is on his mind, he has some reservation, he is not free and clear. He may *say* nothing at all; he may not have the courage to, or the words. (If he has both, they will come forth with insistence.) This is the philosopher's cue; he enters by providing the words. (It is not his only cue, and this cue is not only for philosophers, and not for all philosophers.) Wittgenstein typically brings on an interlocutor to provide such words; the mode this depicts is typically one of insistence. It is a way in which Wittgenstein depicts his reader (i.e., a version of himself) at a particular crossroads. Here the first step in freeing words is to give expression to them; the remaining steps are taken in grammar. Failing to pick up such a cue, or failing to provide genuinely freeing words upon it, are two forms, newly recovered forms perhaps, of philosophical failure. One could also think of them at the same time as cases of literary failure.

But we were about to try responding to the parable's question. One response might be: "Of course there is something boiling in the pictured pot! Otherwise there wouldn't be steam coming out! That there is something boiling inside is what the steam *means!* You seem not to understand what a picture *is!*" But sometimes one's response will be: "Nonsense! How could something be boiling in a *picture?* You seem to have forgotten what a *picture* is! You might as well look for something boiling in the *words* 'pot with steam coming out'!"   — Are these answers? If so, why are there two of them, vying with one another? If not, what is the question?

The parable comes in response to — that is, as instruction for — the interlocutor's particular insistence which precedes it:

"Yes, but there is *something* there all the same accompanying my cry of pain. And it is on account of that that I utter it. And this something is what is important — and frightful." — Only whom are we informing of this? And on what occasion? [§296]

The factor common between this interlocutor and the parable that follows him, is the idea of "something", a something there, a something here, inside. This idea of "something" is what the parable is about. Evidently this interlocutor has been led to his insistence on "something" (or his reservation about it, his call to keep it in reserve) by his taking Wittgenstein (or someone) to have said or suggested that *nothing* is, or may be, going on inside him, whatever his (outward) expressions. That is to say, Wittgenstein has created this interlocutor out of his sense that a reader, his fictive interlocutor, may well be led to take something he has written as this interlocutor has taken it, namely as *denying* that anything is going on inside him. That is to say, Wittgenstein is expressing through this interlocutor his own impulse to take his words in this way. The point is to ask us to consider where the suggestion comes from that perhaps (others have it in mind that) nothing is going on inside us. Why is such a suggestion — more or less psychotic on the face of it — so much as worth an answer, even a parable? Why is it alarming? (Why are psychotics alarming?)

Having responded (in two equally clear but clearly opposing ways) to the parable's question, it is easy enough *in the parable* to say what the "nothing" is that the interlocutor's "something" insists upon ruling out, and creates in the act of denying: The fire in a picture will not burn you (unless you're in the picture); the steam from this pictured pot will not open this morning's letter. What it *is* is a *picture*. — "Only whom are we informing of this? And on what occasion?" These questions are out of place here, because my intention was not one of informing anyone of anything; I was elaborating a parable. The questions would equally have been out of place if the interlocutor had meant his words otherwise differently from the insistent assertion of a piece of information or as the expression of some reservation. The alternative is not necessarily to have meant them parabolically. He might have meant them ironically, say in a speech for a gathering of fellow sufferers, raging against and ridiculing those who cannot hear, even when they cause our cries of pain. Or he could have sung his words, or ones of similar sentiment. Then he could have simply, uninsistently meant them; if not plain-spokenly at any rate whole-heartedly, utterly, unreservedly. One of the greatest of torch songs is available to him: "They asked me how I knew my true love was true. I of course replied: 'Something here inside cannot be denied.' "

What is not easy to say, or to see, is why anyone would "insist on saying" (or hold in reserve, but I will not always add that) what Wittgenstein asks us to suppose someone might insist on saying — either that there must be something boiling in a picture, or that there must be something boiling in a (pictured) pot which is for all the world boiling, or both somehow together. That these bits of madness or emptiness constitute such insistence is the feature of the parable missed, it seems to me, in Pitcher's and Donagan's readings of it. (If so, this may confirm the accuracy of Wittgenstein's parable: philosophers, being human beings, fail to recognize the bits of madness or emptiness they are subject to under the pressure of taking thought.) Pitcher and Donagan both take it that there *must* be a coherent answer to the parable's question. Pitcher's answer was, in effect, that it is of no significance whether anything is in the pot, or rather of no significance what is in it; we cannot name (or know?) whatever is in it (even though Wittgenstein begins the parable with the words "if water boils in a pot"?), but all the same we can use words for sensations apart from this knowledge. Donagan's answer, in effect, was that while in one sense we cannot name or know what is in the pot, in another sense we can (indirectly).

It is, consequently, not easy to see how the parable of §297 *applies* to the insistent utterance of §296. In particular, that utterance does not seem to us empty or mad (". . . but there is *something* there all the same accompanying my cry of pain. And it is on account of that that I utter it . . ."). It seems, on the contrary, in position, simply true. Donagan recognizes that the quotation marks hedging the utterance signal that it is "not to be taken *propria persona*". He accounts for this by saying that nevertheless "the questions that follow show [Wittgenstein] to have considered it a legitimate philosophical reminder" (pp. 335–36). I do not think so. The parable asks us to look again at that utterance, in particular to be suspicious of its insistence. We are, one might say, asked to step back from our conviction that this *must* be an assertion (or a reminder) and incline ourselves to suppose that someone has here been prompted to insistent emptiness, to mean something incoherently.

(This is not the same as trying to mean something incoherent. Wittgenstein alludes to this possibility in saying "When a sentence is called senseless, it is not as it were its sense that is senseless" (*Investigations*, §500). Nor is it the same as meaning something other than you think. This would describe cases in which your *words* make sense, and they are put together correctly, but you are as it were meaning them in the wrong place. This sort of possibility is brought out in Wittgenstein's employment of what he calls, in §48, "the method of §2", namely "[considering] a language-game for which [an] account is really valid", really fits. Other examples will express the illusion of meaning something. (Professor Cook, in the paper of his mentioned before, is attentive to Wittgenstein's concern with *various* forms of what Cook calls "senselessness". He is instructive and interesting on the topic at, e.g., pp. 308–09.) With the phrase "meaning something incoherently", I am surmising, and wishing to isolate, a different human possibility, one that arises from the possibility of meaning words in particular ways — e.g., ironically, parabolically, metaphorically; namely the possibility of meaning them all right, but of meaning them the wrong way, or with an unseen sense. Here it is the magic of words which returns: as if the saying of a word materialized its meaning. (This may be going on in Wittgenstein's case about saying that a stove is in pain (§350).) It becomes important to say that meaning words literally is not just one way among others of meaning them. If it were, a child would learn to speak if we *always* spoke to it ironically, metaphorically, parabolically. This happens to a greater or lesser extent now. Perhaps to a certain extent it is unavoidable, since it is internal to language that its words can be meant in different ways. None of what I have been saying has to do with the child's explicit playing with words, e.g., with nonsense rhymes. Nor do I wish to say that the ability to be literal is more *important* than the ability to be non-literal — any more than I wish to say that it is better to have had a mind than to have lost it.)

If the utterance "But there is *something* there . . ." is an assertion, then there must be some occasion on which it can be used to assert something to someone, inform someone of something. Focus on the phrase "accompanying my cry of pain". The scene is one in which I cry out in pain. Is my cry in itself incomprehensible? Presumably not for the reason that others do not know why or how I am in pain. But if for the reason that the others do not know what crying out (in pain) means, then adding the words about pain will hardly be expected to help. Imagine that as you stand up some late night from a game of cards you raise your arms for a good stretch and produce a muscle cramp in your neck. It is excruciating, your body contorts, as if to duck the full impact of the pain, and you grunt or whine as if pierced. Can we further imagine your being prompted to say, or to grunt out or whine further, in that condition, "There is *something* here accompanying my whine of pain"? If we try imagining that you are addressing someone (I suppose the other card players) who persistently fail to admit your pain, hence persistently deny it, and that you are trying, in one final anguish, to elicit their acknowledgment, then oughtn't we perhaps to imagine further that you moan further, ". . . and moreover there is anguish accompanying my whining of this information"? — Kafka's Hunger Artist, faced with universal incredulousness in response to his feat of self-starvation, might have tried giving out false information about it, information which lessened the magnitude of his suffering, as if willing to trade off full acknowledgment for some part of it, as if part would go some way toward establishing the reality of his suffering in his own eyes, or its worth. It would have been a subtler stratagem than the one I have proposed, but it must also fail; his audience came to lack not so much belief as interest. If I say (something I said in "The Avoidance of Love", p. 347) that the slack of acknowledgment can never be taken up by knowledge, I do not mean to say that the imagination can never be fired by information, rather that you cannot always know when the fire will strike.

We can describe the situation this way: The words "something accompanying my cry of pain" are forced upon us when we feel we must enforce the *connection* between something inner and an outer something. But those very words — or rather the insistence with which in such an eventuality they are employed, or the reservation with which they are withheld — exactly serve to break this natural connection. (In philosophy, as I had occasion to say earlier, we want criteria to do less than they do.) They make the fact that an expression and what it expresses go together seem more or less accidental, or perhaps like a primitive natural law, as for example that when water boils in a pot steam comes forth from the pot; and, by the way, a much weaker law, because quite often when pain boils in a human being pain-behavior does not come forth.

The philosophical task posed by Wittgenstein's parable (not, again, notably unlike a literary task) is to describe what is wrong with the assertion that "something is in the pictured pot" — i.e., to describe the emptiness of the assertion, the momentary madness in the assertion, that is, its failure to amount to an assertion within an insistent sense that it *is* one — without at the same time seeming to *deny* that something is in the pictured pot.

"It is — we should like to say — not merely the picture of the behavior that plays a part in the language-game with the words 'he is in pain', but also a picture of the pain" (§300). Why should we like to say this? (And here Wittgenstein clearly includes himself among the "we".) We will want to know something about the impulse here to speak of the picture or the paradigm of the behavior — unless this much is obvious, since we just are confronting a real picture, which would be possible when using the words "he is in pain". But we can cancel out the modifications "picture or paradigm of" on both sides; then we are left with: It is not merely the behavior that pertains to the language-game with the words "he is in pain" but also the pain. Now an impulse which these words may express seems clear enough. We want to say that when we express our recognition of the other's pain we are recognizing not merely an expression but also that of which it is the expression; our words reach as immediately to the pain itself as to the behavior — *that,* the pain itself, is what our words *mean.* What this says must be true, and yet one again feels on the brink of an old misunderstanding, taking the "pain itself" and "mere behavior" as two different *things* (though no doubt generally in the closest possible connection with one another). The brink of misunderstanding is here because the brink of emptiness is here: we do not know to whom such words are being said; who could be informed by them. We do not know why we *want* to say them, what lack they fill.

It is to grant the truth of our words here, or rather the validity of the impulse which gives rise to them, while at the same time to head off the misunderstanding those words beckon, that Wittgenstein goes on to say: "The image of pain certainly enters in a sense, only not as a picture." What is ruled out by saying "not as a picture"? Something that is ruled out is the idea that there may be something beyond or behind the behavior, a something left over, of which there *could* be a picture (or an indirect representation), or of which there could *not* be a picture (but only, as it were, as a matter of physical or metaphysical accident). As though a picture of suffering, say Grünewald's *Crucifixion,* is a perfect picture of a man and of a cross but (necessarily) an imperfect or indirect picture of suffering. (It is a sort of picture of a picture of suffering.)

What is ruled out is specified a little by Wittgenstein's preceding sentence: "The image of pain is not a picture and *this* image is not replaceable in the language-game by anything that we should call a picture." The emphasis on *this* image implies that certain images *are* replaceable by pictures. If, for example, I am searching for a particular man, I might or might not have an image of him in my mind. If I am worried about it, I might carry a picture of him in my pocket or my hand, and that would do everything for me, in my search, that an image in my mind would. It would do more, if I plan to ask people whether they have seen him. But in the present case, in the language-game with the words "he is in pain", what is at issue is my response to an expression or scene of pain; the image of pain is part of the expression of my response to a being in pain. It is I who give expression to that response. Whereas a picture is just something else *to which* I have, or lack, a response. Of course a picture *I* made, or a line I compose, might be a response to pain, even to *that* creature's pain. (Presumably, Grünewald's picture was such a response.) This is evidently not a replacement of the image or conception of the other's suffering which is part of my response to it; it is, one might say, a further or articulated expression of that response. This may be of personal or epistemological or aesthetic interest, but of no metaphysical enlightenment, because now we have two responses to the same pain to contend with. If, however, my picture (the one I made) is indeed a replacement of an image which is part of my response to his pain, a substitute for it, filling in or making up for it, then I am suffering from a temporary or chronic displacement of affect (neurotic or sinful, as you please).

Does the image of water enter into the language-game with the words "If water boils in a pot, steam comes out of the pot and also pictured steam comes out of the pictured pot"? One or another such image may or may not enter. We could say: Seeing (or imagining) the steam is enough. (As before, if for some reason you require an image here you can avail yourself of a picture.) It is enough not merely in the sense, as I might put it, that we know steam is good evidence for water, but that we know what steam coming out of a pot *means*. But there is a question whether, from time to time, we know what a piece of pain-behavior means. Not merely in the sense that this piece of behavior is, say, a wince, but that this wince is of suffering, means suffering. Whether, so to speak, we take in the fact that behavior gives (as words do) expression; whether we take in the fact that criteria are expressions. (This is the reason I did not want to choose among various translations of *Vorstellung* in the phrase *Vorstellung des Schmerzes*. The emphasis is on the pain, on our conceiving of suffering. No one word here will grasp the idea; or perhaps I should say, we have as yet no basis upon which to choose among the words. The word would have to declare our access to one another, that we have this access at all.)

A question whether we know what pain-behavior means? What question? Whether we are ignorant of this fact? Or have forgotten it? It is only the knowledge that a body which exhibits pain(-behavior) is that of a live creature, a living being. Not to know this would be the same as not knowing what a body is. And yet this seems to be knowledge that Wittgenstein takes philosophy to deny (under the guise of affirming it); not so much to lose hold of as to force from philosophy's own grasp. Over and over he comes back to it: "Only of what behaves like a human being can one say that it *has* pains. For one has to say it of a body, or, if you like, of a soul which some body *has*" (§283). And in Part II of the *Investigations*, where again the question of suffering has arisen: "My attitude towards him is an attitude towards a soul" (p. 178). And, to be sure, it is the attitude *of* a soul. Philosophy has its characteristic ways of avoiding this knowledge, and its motives for it. So have religion and politics their characteristic ways. But how can the connection between body and soul be denied?

"For how can I go so far as to try to use language to get between pain and its expression?" (§245). This question is, apparently, an attempt on Wittgenstein's part to express a frame of mind in which one feels that in order to insure the connection between a sensation and its name one has to get to the sensation apart from its expression, get past the merely outward expression, which blocks our vision as it were. But Wittgenstein's question is: How can one so much as try to do this? How can one so much as be of a mind to? Let us try answering the question as follows: *"Nothing is closer than the inner and the outer, e.g., pain and the expression of pain. There is no room between."* This might be all right, if it is meant figuratively. But taken figuratively it is ambiguous. One may say that nothing came between a person's experience and his expression of it as a way of saying that his expression was genuine, uncontrived, candid. But if there is no genuine expression forthcoming — either because an expression is absent or uncandid, or because there is nothing of the right kind to be expressed (the expression is, say, feigned) — then one might say nothing came between on the ground that in such cases there are not two things for anything *to* come between.

I draw various morals from this question Wittgenstein poses himself. "Between" is first of all a picture. I can go so far as to wish to wedge language in because the picture of something between experience and expression is not necessarily a bad one (any more than the picture of something *behind* our words and actions is necessarily a bad one). The reason I want to wedge in language is that our working knowledge of one another's (inner) lives can reach no further than our (outward) expressions, and we have cause to be disappointed in these expressions.

We might use the expression "something came between" to describe a case in which just as I was going to tell you about our mutual friend, she walked in. Or, a case in which just as I had gone so far as to bring up the situation for which I owe you an apology or to begin telling you the history of a feeling of love as preparation for declaring it, the feeling vanished. "Something came between" (between me and my feeling) in such cases means, roughly, something was blocked. But what blocked my expression was not my behavior, for one could also say that the behavior was blocked. — The picture of something between, with its attendant wish to get between, is symptomatic of the kind of creatures we are. Its significance is that the expression of the soul is never *better* than natural. It is not inevitable, and the odds are against candidness.

The picture elaborates itself when we turn over the sense from the first to the third person. When I felt I had to get to the other's sensation apart from his giving expression to it (as if that were the way to insure certainty, or as if the way to insure his candidness was to prevent *his* playing any role in his expression) my wish was to penetrate his behavior with my reference to his sensation, in order to reach the same spot *his* reference to himself occupies *before,* so to speak, the sensation gets expressed. (We might think of the effect of a truth serum as preventing someone's playing any role in his expression. But we will not think of this as his speaking candidly.) He can do something we might speak of as referring to his sensation before it gets expressed. He can suppress a piece of behavior, or just manage not to act on a feeling, in order to attend to the quality of the feeling his action would express, or to the meaning of the feeling, its provenance. He may do this and find that the sensation is not as bad or as unmanageable as he had feared or averred. Is this what I *have* to do in order to refer to my pain?

I understand Wittgenstein's teaching to be something like this: My references to my pain are exactly my expressions of pain itself; and my words refer to my pain just because, or to the extent, that they are (modified) expressions of it. This would be true not only of the expression of a present experience. To refer to a pain which is past may require a present expression of it, one modified through memory. I may suppress, or otherwise lose, all memory of it, of how it felt. This can be a curse or a blessing. Then I will refer to it, if I do, as though it happened to someone else. One could think of this as speaking of myself historically. People can take this tone toward their present experiences, too. It may be a curse or a blessing. The picture of a *connection* needing to be set up between an experience and the words for it is symbolic of the giving of expression to the experience, giving vent to it. If the expression is broken, the reference itself cannot establish the connection. Then what are my references to another's pain? They are my (more or less) modified responses to it, or to his having had it, or to his anticipations of it; they are responses to another's expressions of (or inability to express) his or her pain.

The hands of a clock refer to the right time when they are appropriately connected to a mechanism which is in good order and is running. If it is not in good order or not running, then *this* connection (of hands to mechanism) is of no significance. (I do not think we should say that it *is* of significance, only of the *wrong* significance. Though it may still be worth distinguishing its not being in good order (in which case it is telling the wrong time), from its not running (in which case it is telling no time at all, telling nothing). If one wishes to say that a stopped clock tells the truth just two instants a day, then one might wish to say that a dead man gives the right response in just those instances in which the right response is silence.) If we understood the hands of the clock to refer to the mechanism, then it would perhaps be of no significance to us whether it was running in good order or not. Someone might then arrive at the following sorts of feelings: The hands of a clock are completely superficial characteristics of it; mere conveniences of ours, and so fragile besides! If a clock is telling the right time, then it would still be telling it whether it happened to have hands or not, as it would if it were in the dark. (As if the face and hands of a clock bore the same relation to what is behind the face as the dial on a radio bears to what is inside the cabinet.) Anyway it would still be *thinking* the right time; and if it is thinking it all the time, surely it *knows* it! — We could know it as well as the clock could, if we measured its rate and then marked off whatever was telling us its rate in such a way that we could read the time from that. But then we would not have penetrated more deeply into the clock; we would have given it a new kind of hands, artificial limbs as it were. — The notion that the clock knows the time, whether it tells it or not, is a reasonable symbolic expression concerning it, in particular concerning its obligation to keep up with other good clocks, and ultimately concerning the obligation it bears, with all good clocks, towards the sun. Its knowledge is really its conscience. Would a conscientious clock think of its hands as mere conveniences, essentially for others? Only if it thought of *itself* as essentially a thing for others. (It might think of its hands as mere conveniences essentially for itself, if it were a hermit or a *fin-de-siècle* clock.) But for us to think this about such a clock would be presumptuous or sentimental. We do not bear the same relation it bears to its hands.

The dependence of reference upon expression in naming our states of consciousness is, I believe, the specific moral of Wittgenstein's inventions containing the so-called private language argument. I find little said within these inventions, especially about privacy and about language, that is not said, generally more clearly, elsewhere in the *Investigations,* so that the very fame of this argument suggests to me that it has been miscast.

Wittgenstein is described as asserting that there can be no private language. To this assertion, critics have responded, for example, by saying

(1) that of course there can be a private language since there are such things as codes; (2) that the notion of a private language is too obscure to convey *what* it is Wittgenstein thinks there cannot be; (3) that the conceit is just a fancy way of saying that our sensations are not private and hence will be convincing at most to those who already agree to that idea and unconvincing to those who disagree. This third response suggests that Wittgenstein's case about privacy, whatever it is, had better not rest on the private language argument. The first response is irrelevant: a code is ruled out on the face of it as a candidate for Wittgenstein's proposal of a private language since a code, while of course designed to be incomprehensible to outsiders, is of course designed to be comprehensible to (other) insiders. The second response is not incompatible with Wittgenstein's point in developing his argument.

Wittgenstein does not say that there can be no private language. He introduces his sequential discussion of the topic, at §243, by *asking:* "Could we also imagine a language [in addition to one which certain people might speak only in monologues, and which could be understood by others] in which a person could write down or give vocal expression to his inner experiences — his feelings, moods, and the rest — for his private use", where "private" is to mean that "another person cannot understand". The upshot of this question turns out to be that we cannot really imagine this, or rather that there is nothing of the sort to imagine, or rather that when we as it were try to imagine this we are imagining something other than we think. (The upshot is not about the failure of imagination, and nor is it about the non-existence of a private language, for there may yet well be something rightly to be called a private language.)

So what is the point of "trying" to "imagine" a "language" which "another person" "cannot" "understand"? Evidently, the effort is to illuminate something about the publicness of language, something about the *depth* to which language is agreed in. I would like to say: its point is to release the fantasy expressed in the denial that language is something essentially shared. The tone of the sections dealing explicitly with the idea of a private language are peculiarly colored by the tone of someone allowing a fantasy to be voiced. It is, of course, a tone familiar elsewhere in the book. I cannot prove that this tone is struck more persistently here, but I take the occasion to mention my impression of it because it is a mistake, I believe, to say that there are just two essential tones of voice in the *Investigations*, the interlocutor's and Wittgenstein's proper voice. First, there is no reason to think that there is just one interlocutor throughout the book; and second, and obviously, Wittgenstein's own speech ranges from the full-throated and the supercilious to the meditative and the bemused. Section 243, which initiates the most continuous prospect of a private language, and §258, which picks up the idea and tries to exemplify it, seem to me largely in half-voice.

He has asked himself whether we can imagine something. He, as it were, looks up at himself and replies that of course we can use ordinary language to note our inner experiences for some private purpose (e.g., people often develop shorthand devices for their diary entries in order to keep their thoughts to themselves, and it may not be clear to anyone else why these particular thoughts, which upon deciphering seem so innocuous, were thought better kept private; the reason itself may be, and remain, private). Then he feels that this is not what he means; it has not hit off the fantasy of privacy which he wants to give voice to. Various directions lead from here. At §258 he tries imagining a particular case: "I want to keep a diary about the recurrence of a certain sensation. To this end I associate it with the sign 'S', and write this sign in a calendar for every day on which I have the sensation." Then a long pause. I fill it about as follows: "There is nothing wrong with this, so far. There could be lots of reasons for wanting to keep track of this sensation, medical or psychological or spiritual reasons. Still, this is certainly a very special kind of entry for a diary. What kind is it?" Then he muses: "I will remark first that a definition of the sign cannot be formulated."

This is puzzling to remark. A few pages earlier (§239) he had said:

" 'Red' means the color that occurs to me when I hear the word 'red' " — would be a *definition*. Not an explanation of *what it is* to use a word as a name.

Why, similarly, couldn't we say in the present case: "The definition of 'S' is 'The sign I write in my calendar for every day on which a certain sensation occurs' "? I see two immediate respects in which this differs from the definition of "red". (1) Unlike "red", the sign "S" has no established, or competing, use in the language, so *everything* has to be taken care of by the definition. If someone said, " 'Rad' means the color that occurs to me when I hear the sound 'rad' ", we would wonder freely why any color at all should appear upon hearing this sound, certainly why the *same* color should always appear, and perhaps wonder whether it appears also upon hearing the word "radish". Whereas in the case of the definition of "red" we seem to understand someone's idiosyncrasy and it need not concern us further to determine just which color or colors may be involved. (2) The fact that the sign "S" is so much as a recognizable *letter* of our language is unnecessary, even misleading. Its function would more perspicuously be represented by some characteristic mark, say an asterisk following the date of the diary entry. I am not ready to say that this sign, in this use, must (or cannot) have a definition, but at any rate it has an explanation. And its explanation seems to show it not to be the name of anything, but to be a kind of abbreviation, or graphic symbol, for some such remark as "My old sensation recurred again today".

If in scanning my diary you notice the recurrence of a name, say "Sal Michael", you might imagine various possibilities, e.g., that I had appointments with this person; that I kept reminding myself to make an appointment with him (or her); that I from time to time thought of this person (or is it a fiction, a character from a story I am writing, or my imaginary friend?) for no discernible reason; that I habitually doodled this name; that I invented the name for some specific reason best known to myself. If on closer inspection you see that the name is really "St. Michael", further possibilities will come into view, e.g., that I was thinking about Joan of Arc, that I wish there were saints, that I was invoking this saint, or fearing his arrival, that I had decided to write his name in my diary every day on which he appeared to me. In my time and place I may have been wondering how one can establish a connection between this little scrawl of a name and the saint whose name it is — the word here and the saint there are so *far* apart. Then I may have wondered how this connection is established when the bearer of the name is no further than the other side of the city, or perhaps so close as asleep in the same room: surely the mere *distance* from me cannot determine how difficult it is for the name to reach its bearer. Then my problem was not about saints but about naming or noting, whether the bearer is Sal, a saint, or some sensation. The same is true if the reason I thought I could not formulate a definition was that I thought no genuine name has a formulable definition because no name has a meaning. (I may, by the way, have completely forgotten why the name is repeated in my diary, and there may be no external evidence whatever for recovering the information. If I am dead, then neither of us will ever know.)

The entry "S" (or "*") was not to be open to these various possibilities. It was simply and solely to be inscribed by me on just those occasions on which something happened to me. Is this itself why Wittgenstein remarks that there is no definition of it? — as if to say: The sign's sheer *being* there is all that matters; its use is all the meaning it has, and in this case the use never varies. Something similar could be said about the ordinary asterisk as well, used as a superscript to indicate a footnote. But while *its* use never varies, there may be other marks also consigned to this identical use; and the asterisk must still be distinguished from these. It is the merest convenience that there should be marks of this kind at all; the same purposes could be accomplished by special spacings between words, or elevations of them. (If all of written language were devoted to such purposes — if all of it were as it were not really part of language but part of the convenient machinery of writing — then could there be dictionaries? The case would seem to be that all of this dictionary would look like specialized parts of dictionaries now look. And I think one can say that a complete dictionary of such a language would have to contain tables that include *everything that could be said* in the language, as if everything sayable took the form of an idiom.)

I have said that I could, in a sense, tell someone what the sign "S" in my diary is for. But granted that Wittgenstein is, in the passage in question, trying to work out the fantasy of a private language, or work into its mood — the presiding condition of which is that another person cannot understand the language — I could not, in principle, give that person the meaning (or the use) of the sign in such a way that *he* could use it. And isn't that the purpose of formulating a definition?

From the idea of formulating a definition, Wittgenstein next goes to the idea of giving himself a kind of ostensive definition — the obvious alternative route for providing a sign with meaning. This kind of ostensive definition — presumably, the private kind — leads him to require that he impress upon himself the connection between the sign and the sensation upon which he is to focus his attention (if he is to point the sensation out to himself).

But "I impress it on myself" can only mean: this process brings it about that I remember the connection *right* in the future. But in the present case I have no criterion of correctness. One would like to say: whatever is going to seem right to me is right. And that only means that here we can't talk about "right". [§258]

But now it looks as if I am prohibited altogether from keeping track of my inner experiences by noting their occurrence in a diary; all such activities are empty ceremonies (§258), mere shows (§270). It may be that some philosophers, some people, would find this a convenient prohibition; others will of course find it unacceptable (even though they probably will never actually use their freedom to keep such a diary). Freud noted that he was able to do his best writing when he was in a state of mild depression. This looks like an empirical claim. Would it be mere ceremony, supposing he came to doubt this correlation, for him to note down what he had noted, e.g., for him to asterisk the days on which he found himself in this state and then compare the writing he produced on such days with his writing at other times? One can imagine a writer for whom it becomes of interest to note a dozen different states of mind in which he or she writes; we might imagine the margins of his or her manuscripts lined with asterisks, ampersands, checks, sharps, loops of various eccentricity, each noting the occurrence of one or more of these states. Certain writers might feel that it was essential to the significance of what they were writing that these experiences be incorporated (not necessarily stated) in the body of their text, as part of the course of their prose. Wittgenstein is such a writer. — What is it we cannot do?

Notice that Wittgenstein's claim that "here we can't talk about 'right'" reaches back only three or four sentences, just to the idea of "impressing the connection on myself", i.e., getting the sign and the sensation stamped upon one another, so that, so to speak, their faces can be seen to match quite independently of any decision of mine. (I undertook to do everything by myself necessary for providing something with meaning; then I expend untold energies trying to convince myself that I have done it.) If there were no need for the idea of "impressing" the connection, then the objection about nothing or everything counting as "right" would have no force. (The objection does not concern the thought that no one could *verify* my inner experiences.) What creates the sense of needing, or wanting, the special impressing?

In each of Wittgenstein's attempts to realize the fantasy of a private language, a moment arises in which, to get on with the fantasy, the idea, or fact, of the *expressiveness* of voicing or writing down my experiences has to be overcome. In §243 this is quite explicit; in §258 the idea of formulating a definition of the sign overcomes the fact that the sign already has all the definition it needs — if, that is, I am actually employing it as I said I was. A moment ago I said that while this may be an explanation (i.e., an explanation of what I do with the sign, what I use it for) it may not serve as a genuine definition (i.e., it does not give you the sign's meaning in such a way that you can now use it as I do). But now this distinction seems pointless. The sign in question just is one for which there is no reason to think you *have* a use (as you have no use for my name tapes, or no use for a mezuzah). If, however, you do happen to have such a use, happen to be planning to keep a diary yourself, then I've told you enough so that you can use my sign if you like, or, of course, any other sign you like.

Whether you have really appreciated the quality of the sensation of mine which so interests me, or understand why I take such an interest in it, is a matter generally of who we are and what our relationship is. I may have great difficulty in describing it for you, but that itself may contribute to your appreciation of it. In that case, however, I evidently have no sense that I must impress upon myself the connection between my sign and my sensation. What could be clearer? The connection is as clear as the sensation itself. (I may dedicate a lifetime to the effort to convey the meaning a small budget of words has for me. I may be one of a circle of people so dedicated, even to the same words. I would hardly have come to this verge, supposing I am of sound mind, if I thought that *no* one else *could* understand my words. But suppose I came to think this. Then either I would doubt that I myself attached real meaning to them, and I would make ready to leave the circle; or else the least of my problems would concern my definition of a word — I mean my formulating it or pointing out its meaning. My problem has become one, let us say, of bearing the meaning. Nothing of me but is impressed with the word.)

I may as a matter of fact from time to time forget, or rather neglect, to note down my sensation when it occurs. It is perhaps an unpleasant sensation, or somehow humiliating, or it frightens me that I cannot determine its significance. On the days I remember that I had the sensation and neglected to note it (this may occur to me while I am out for a walk, or having drinks with an old acquaintance), I make sure to impress the remembrance of its occurrence upon myself so that I shall remember to enter its occurrence in the diary when I return home. (Perhaps I tie a string around my finger to remind myself.) This may itself interest me, the fact that I as it were sometimes resist my efforts to record the sensation faithfully. Then I might, having returned home to the diary and entered my "S", decide to note my earlier neglect of the sensation by entering an "N" beside the "S". I might make this a practice. But unless some further complication arises about *this* practice, there is no occasion for me to impress upon myself the meaning of this "N", i.e., the connection between this sign and my neglect. (If I tie a string around my finger and later forget why I did that, and so fail to enter my "S", and so a fortiori fail to enter my "N", would that mean that I have forgotten the feeling with which I tied the string? Which of the feelings would that be? Would it help to tie another string? Sometimes I sense that to put real confidence in my memory I have to get to the end of all rememberings. That seems to say that I have to forgo remembering. And now that strikes me as an accurate description of what it is to have confidence in one's memory.)

It is the passing over of expression that makes Wittgenstein's conclusion of this phase of his investigation, at §270, anticlimactic, or not evident as a conclusion. He has imagined a particular use for the entry of the sign "S"; it correlates with a rise in my blood-pressure. He comments: "And now it seems quite indifferent whether I have recognized the sensation *right* or not." The correlation is there; *it* is right and I am right about it (as the mamometer has shown); it doesn't matter whether I keep calling the sensation a tingle when it is really a mild sting. "And what is our reason for calling 'S' the name of a sensation here? Perhaps the kind of way this sign is employed in this language-game. — And why a 'particular sensation', that is, the same one every time? Well, aren't we supposing that we write 'S' every time?" And this is all. This thing of our "writing 'S' ", and other things we do and experience no deeper metaphysically than this, is all there is for our confidence in our experiences to go on. And it is enough; it is in principle perfect. But we keep passing over this supposition of our example, as if the incident of writing kept getting mentioned only to fill in the image of a diary. But the writing of the "S" just is the *expression* of S, the sensation. It may, in fact, be the *only* S-behavior in our repertory. — But isn't this emphasis on the supposition ridiculous? This S-behavior amounts to practically nothing. — So may the sensation named by "S" (if expressed by it) amount to practically nothing. But we were supposing that it was important enough to keep a record of.

This disappointment with our expression — our wish or need to pass it by — came out differently a few sections earlier, in §260, just after Wittgenstein's remark about not being able to talk about "right". He has an interlocutor attempt to blunt the force of this remark by responding: "Well, I *believe* that this is the sensation S again." Wittgenstein turns upon him; he is supercilious: "Perhaps you *believe* that you believe it! Then did the man who made the entry in the calendar make a note of *nothing whatever?*" That is: Why are you so faint-hearted about your sensation — if, that is, you really have done the thing of noting it in your diary? If you *believe* that the "S" notes the sensation, then you may equally believe that it does not. Then what is that stupidly insignificant mark doing just sitting there in your diary? To suggest that someone may have "made a note of nothing whatever" is to suggest that someone may have *done* nothing whatever. Anyway, if he has made a note of nothing, he certainly has not made a note. And what else could doing *that* — making the dumb mark — be doing? You might say he was doodling, and not merely on the ground that the "S" is small; doodles can be quite large and elaborate, and be done painstakingly. But could anything and everything a person does be doodling? Is this a fear which the fantasy of a private language is meant to conceal? An anxiety that our expressions might at any time signify nothing? Or too much? (Not that doodles themselves may not be significant — that others, that one oneself, may not learn something from them. One learns about Dickens's Captain Cuttle from the vocal doodle with which he habitually concludes his more portentous observations: "Which when found make a note of." You just may hit upon the significance of my doodling exactly an "S" over and over. So might I; or I might believe that I have. Just as I might divine the significance of my neighbor's directing traffic in our empty street.)

So the fantasy of a private language, underlying the wish to deny the publicness of language, turns out, so far, to be a fantasy, or fear, either of inexpressiveness, one in which I am not merely unknown, but in which I am powerless to make myself known; or one in which what I express is beyond my control. I do not expect that the idea of such fantasies will be credited by anyone who does not share them, or is unaware that he or she shares them, to some degree. One fantasy may appear as a fear of having nothing whatever to say — or worse, as an anxiety over there being nothing whatever to say. If one does to some degree share, or can remember sharing, this fantasy, I do not think one will find it necessary yet to ask for a theory of expression with which to oppose it. The question, within the mood of the fantasy, is: Why do we attach significance to *any* words and deeds, of others or of ourselves? (To answer that this serves to explain words and deeds would be like answering the question "Why do we obey the state?" by citing the advantages of having a state. The level of the question is: "How can anything we say or do count as disobedience to the state — which does not amount to breaking the law, but to breaking the hold of the law; and why does everything else we say and do amount to obedience?") How can anything we say or do count as doodling, be some form of nonsense; and why is all the rest condemned to meaning?

A fantasy of necessary inexpressiveness would solve a simultaneous set of metaphysical problems: it would relieve me of the responsibility for making myself known to others — as though if I were expressive that would mean continuously betraying my experiences, incessantly giving myself away; it would suggest that my responsibility for self-knowledge takes care of itself — as though the fact that others cannot know my (inner) life means that I cannot fail to. It would reassure my fears of being known, though it may not prevent my being under suspicion; it would reassure my fears of not being known, though it may not prevent my being under indictment. — The wish underlying this fantasy covers a wish that underlies skepticism, a wish for the connection between my claims of knowledge and the objects upon which the claims are to fall to occur without my intervention, apart from my agreements. As the wish stands, it is unappeasable. In the case of my knowing myself, such self-defeat would be doubly exquisite: I must disappear in order that the search for myself be successful.

These words may express a significant truth. They form a homonym of the truth, a kind of sentence-length pun, a metaphysical irony. If so, this serves to explain why the writing on the part of those who have some acquaintance with the topic of self-knowledge — Thoreau or Kierkegaard or Nietzsche, for example — takes the form it does, of obsessive and antic paradox and pun, above all of maddening irony. As if to write toward self-knowledge is to war with words, to battle for the very weapons with which you fight. You may battle against the Christian's self-understanding from within Christianity, as Kierkegaard declares, or from beyond Christianity, as Nietzsche declares. In both cases you are embattled because you find the *words* of the Christian to be the right words. It is the way he means them that is empty or enfeebling. Christianity appears in Nietzsche not so much as the reverse of the truth as the truth in foul disguise. In particular, the problem seems to be that human action is everywhere disguised as human suffering: this is what acceptance of the Will to Power is to overcome. I mention this without insisting upon it, and I hope without offense, because I find that it parallels a turn my recent argument has taken. I was led to express the fantasy of inexpressiveness as a sense of powerlessness to make myself known, and this turned out, in pursuit of the idea of a private language, equally to be a powerlessness to make myself known to myself. There seems to be some question whether one's knowing oneself is something active, something one does (like writing "S"), or rather something one suffers, something that happens to one (like having S). I believe that one will be inclined to say, supposing one accepts the presence of such a question, that the answer is, Both. Then one will have to say how there can be two sides involved.

"The truth is: it makes sense to say about other people that they doubt whether I am in pain; but not to say it about myself" (§246). The favored implication of this remark is that it makes sense to say about other people that they know I am in pain; but not to say it of myself (except as a joke). This seems just to reverse the skeptic's passage that runs: he alone knows what is going on in him. Wittgenstein's remark is clearly weightless against the skeptic's claim that I can never know the experience of the other, since the remark says that I *can* know, i.e., that it makes sense to say so. And the skeptic must agree to this, because he takes its negation to make sense, viz., that I never can know. For him this is not as it were a conceptual impossibility but a hitherto undetected fact, and obvious once you are brought to see it. The potential weight Wittgenstein's remark carries against the skeptic is rather that, in speaking of other minds, the skeptic is not skeptical *enough:* the other is still left, along with his knowledge of himself; so am I, along with mine. (A first difference from the case of skepticism with respect to the external world is that an essential element of that skeptic's initial condition is absent, viz., that no position for knowing is better than the one *I* am in. In the case of other minds, it seems to make sense to say that there *is* a better position; anyway, you do not know there is not. (Here especially I should like to recommend the experience of John Wisdom's *Other Minds.*)) The moral the "private" "language" "argument" would like for us to draw may then perhaps be put as follows: there *is* no way for the skeptic to be skeptical enough. (This sounds like a way of putting the moral of the *Cogito* as well.) But what then? Should the skeptic just give up his skepticism, or should he, until he finds a way to go further, just refrain from confessing it?

The tone of Wittgenstein's remark (". . . it makes sense to say . . ."), I would like to say, is this: "So much is true; it is obvious; not just obvious, but trivial." For it so far says nothing at all about why anybody would deny what it says, nor about how anyone *could* (since to deny it would make no sense). And it leaves open what the relation is that we call "knowing the mind" — leaves open the possibility that knowing another mind is a matter of certainty (which will force us to the conclusion that we cannot know another); and it leaves open the possibility that my relation to my own mind is some unique species of intuition (which will force us to pass over our expression). — What is the problem of the other if it is not a problem of certainty?

Let us recover a moment we left incompletely accounted for in reading the parable of the boiling pot: "The image of pain certainly enters into the language-game [with the words 'he is in pain'] in a sense; only not as a picture." Why does the idea of an image present itself? And in what sense does it enter in?

"Image" naturally suggests "imagination". But not everything we call imagination suggests a capacity for forming images; it is not the same as imaginativeness. Imagination, let us say, is the capacity for making connections, seeing or realizing possibilities, but I need not accomplish this by way of forming new images, or anything we are likely to call images ("Imagine how you would feel if . . ."; "Don't you really know why she is angry with you? Use your imagination."; "You can imagine what would happen if we dropped qualifying examinations for the Ph.D."). Vivid imagery, in fact, may defeat the purpose. (Dickens, who was superlative in both capacities, both in imagination and in imaginativeness, came to recognize this problem: he could get the Pecksniffs and Murdles of the world to cry over the pictures he presented of poverty and the deaths of children, but this did not get them to see their connection with these pictures.) Imagination is called for, faced with the other, when I have to take the facts in, realize the significance of what is going on, make the behavior real for myself, make a connection. "Take the facts in" means something like "see his behavior in a certain way", for example, see his blink as a wince, and connect the wince with something in the world that there is to be winced at (perhaps a remark which you yourself would not wince at), or, if it is not that, then connect the wince with something in him, a thought, or a nerve. "Seeing something as something" is what Wittgenstein calls "interpretation"; it is the principle topic of the chief section of what appears as Part II of the *Investigations*. By way of anticipation, we can say that the "sense" in which an image enters into the language-game in question is a sense of the concept of seeing; Wittgenstein will say that this concept is "modified" (p. 209).

In looking more closely at this region of the *Investigations*, I do not want to become fixated on the duck-rabbit. It is a beautiful and clear example; but of what? Not of psychological subtleties; not of *all* cases of interpretation; in particular, not all of aesthetic experience. It is one case in which a figure can be read in alternative ways. The beauty of the thing lies, first, in the fact that the figure is so patently *all* in front of your eyes, it is nothing but outline, not even surface; second, that there are just two distinct possibilities of reading it, and they compete with one another; third, that no background of context is required (no imagination) against which to read it one way or the other; fourth, that you can see, as patently as you can see the figure itself, that the flip from one reading to another is due solely to you, the change is in you; fifth, that the flip is reversible, and, in particular, subject to will; sixth, that the expression of its flipping for you is an expression of being struck by something, each time taken by surprise, though obviously not unawares; seventh, that you can understand that the flip may not take place at all, that someone just may not see both possibilities. It is one of a series of examples with respect to which an unexpected range of concepts can be given application and in which one is brought to sense the complexity of their crossing — e.g., imagination, interpretation, experience, impression, expression, seeing, knowing, mere knowing, meaning, figurative meaning.

I remark, in passing, that the concept of figurative meaning — Wittgenstein sometimes calls it secondary meaning — declares that investigation of this region cannot proceed always by employing language-games and the (a priori) agreement in judgment upon which they depend. Because with figurative meaning there is no such antecedent agreement. You could say that words used in such connections have no grammar — and that would itself be a grammatical remark. A reflection of this lack of common agreement here is the number of technical concepts Wittgenstein introduces in the course of these pages, e.g., secondary meaning, picture-face, aspects, aspect-blindness.

I shall concentrate on just *this* thread: Wittgenstein says that the importance he is going to assess here is a categorical difference in different "objects" of sight. He immediately introduces his term "noticing an aspect" whose ramifications he then allows himself to be led by. I point to two late junctures in the progress of this notion of an "aspect": "The aspect presents a physiognomy which then passes away" (p. 210); and "The importance of this concept [of aspect-blindness] lies in the connection between the concepts of 'seeing an aspect' and 'experiencing the meaning of a word' " (p. 214). Putting together the ideas that noticing an aspect is being struck by a physiognomy; that words present familiar physiognomies; that they can be thought of as pictures of their meaning; that words have a life and can be dead for us; that "experiencing a word" is meant to call attention to our relation to our words; that our relation to pictures is in some respects like our relation to what they are pictures of; — I would like to say that the topic of our attachment to our words is allegorical of our attachments to ourselves and to other persons. Something of this sort we were prepared for. My words are my expressions of my life; I respond to the words of others as their expressions, i.e., respond not merely to what their words mean but equally to their meaning of them. I take them to mean ("imply") something in or by their words; or to be speaking ironically, etc. Of course my expressions and my responses may not be accurate. To imagine an expression (experience the meaning of a word) is to imagine it as giving expression to a soul. (The examples used in ordinary language philosophy are in this sense imagined.)

One point of the allegory of words can be brought out this way. I said just now: "My words are expressions of my life. . . ." Let us ask here, as Wittgenstein asks of sensations (§411): Which words are *my* words? There are obvious ordinary occasions for such a question: e.g., I am looking over the constitution we have drafted to see how much of my contribution to it has survived last night's redrafting. Few, I dare say, have it in mind that they might own their very own set of words. But is it tempting to suppose that one may own one's very own sensations? No one supposes that another cannot enter an "S" into his or her diary just as well as you can; I mean enter *that* "S", the very one you entered (the one we learned in penmanship class, like a backwards treble clef). Does this misapply the allegory? Should one say rather that one cannot have the other's having of the sensation, as I cannot enter your entering of the "S"? Of course it makes sense to say that I cannot enter your "S"-token in my diary. (Anyway it makes sense to the extent that "cannot" makes sense in that context.) So is the idea of "my sensation" expressed by saying "I cannot have your sensation-token"? I feel: If this makes sense at all, it says rather more or rather less than I wished to say. For I wanted to express my uniqueness, and this way of expressing it makes it seem so *trivial*. If what I have got is a token of some type, then anyone else could have just as good a token. ("Yes, but they couldn't have *this* one." No, but that adds nothing *at all*, because that is just what "token of a type" *means*.) Is there, then, no problem *at all* about "my sensations" and whether others can have them, and therefore know them? Or is it that the allegory of words (here, speaking of "my sensations" by speaking of "my words") is at this point incomplete, fails to capture my uniqueness? We seem to have a choice. — This much seems to be true: The importance about my sensation is *that* I have it. The uniqueness in question points not to some necessary difference between my sensation and yours (for there may be no significant difference between them), but to the necessary difference between being you and being me, the fact that we are two.

The idea of the allegory of words is that human expressions, the human figure, to be grasped, must be *read*. To know another mind is to interpret a physiognomy, and the message of this region of the *Investigations* is that this is not a matter of "mere knowing". I have to read the physiognomy, and see the creature according to my reading, and treat it according to my seeing. The human body is the best picture of the human soul — not, I feel like adding, primarily because it represents the soul but because it expresses it. The body is the field of expression of the soul. The body is *of* the soul; it is the soul's; a human soul *has* a human body. (Is this incomprehensible? Is it easier to comprehend the idea that it is the body which has the soul? (Cf. §283.) It does seem more comprehensible (though of course no less figurative) to say that this "having" is done by me: it is

I who have both a body *and* a soul, or mind.) An ancient picture takes the soul to be the possession of the body, its prisoner, condemned for life.

Contrariwise, taking the body to be the possession of the soul, its slave, pictures the body as condemned to expression, to meaning. This seed of conviction flowers one way in Blake's poetry, another way in Nietzsche's *Zarathustra*. (In Blake's *The Marriage of Heaven and Hell*: "Man has no Body distinct from his Soul for that calld Body is a portion of Soul discernd by the five Senses, the chief inlets of Soul in this age".) It is, I take it, this conviction, expressed by Wittgenstein as the body being a picture of the soul, that Hegel gives philosophical expression to in the following formulations: "[The] shape, with which the Idea as spiritual — as individually determined spirituality — invests itself when manifested as a temporal phenomenon, is *the human form*. . . . [The] human shape [is] the sole sensuous phenomenon that is appropriate to mind" (*Philosophy of Fine Art*, Introduction, pp. 185, 186). (Thus may the philosophy of mind become aesthetics.) How much you have to have accepted in order to accept this expression is an open question, not confined to the reading of, say, Hegel.

Knowing a physiognomy is understanding what it means, having it speak to you, "experiencing the meaning". How is this knowledge expressed? Sometimes I show myself struck by an aspect; sometimes I show that it has dawned on me; I may show various forms of being taken by surprise, depending on the case. But in no case is such knowledge expressed by a "mere report", except, presumably, when it has become a piece of my history. Wittgenstein speaks of the expression of this knowledge of the other as my "attitude": "My attitude towards him is an attitude towards a soul" (p. 178). But why say that an attitude expresses *knowledge?* Surely an attitude is merely something psychological and caused whereas knowledge is something conceptual and validated. But belief, say, is an attitude, and it is caused, if any psychological phenomenon can be caused, and validatable if any is. How are faith or pity or joy different?

(Hume and the other classical Empiricists were hardly unaware of the difference between belief as something causable and as something validatable. But because (or to the extent that) their work reads to us as prescientific psychology (which somebody or other has made scientific), and because we suppose ourselves to know the difference between philosophical psychology and, as it were, psychological psychology, and because of

the Empiricist's desperate conclusions about knowledge, it is hard to recapture their intention, in their treatises of human knowledge, to be
locating knowledge as a psychological phenomenon, as a natural human
activity — so that it is likely to mean nothing to us, or to mean something
obviously false, to be told that a valid belief is one that is caused in a
particular way. (If the ability to make logical inferences has a psychology,
it will not be discoverable by a psychologist who cannot tell the difference
between valid and invalid inferences; it will not be the subject of inference which is under discussion. A comparable problem arises in the psychology, and/or psychoanalysis, of art. A thinker who cannot grant the
right autonomy to the object he or she is thinking about is not thinking
about art.) It may well be true that both philosophy and physics have
profited from their legal separation. It may well be false that either philosophy or psychology have profited from their legal separation, though
I do not say it was unnecessary.)

However, I mean to lay the emphasis not on "attitude" but on the
necessity of "the expression of knowledge". Sometimes its expression will
consist in the provision of evidence, sometimes in the provision of analyses
or derivations. But sometimes "we cannot prove anything" (p. 227). Why
not? Wittgenstein speaks in this connection of "imponderable evidence".
This means in effect, "I can't tell you how I know". This is ambiguous.
It may mean, "I don't know how I know; I just know", in which case you
are apt not to be convinced that I do know, and in any case you will be
interested in my claim only so far as you are interested in me. But it may
mean, "I can't tell *you*". Perhaps I have taken your response to what I
have already said to mean that you are not interested in pondering the
imponderable with me. This could be self-protective, and self-deluding.
Or it could be an expression of my taking the evidence as all in evidence,
drawing the line of instruction so that what I have pointed to is obvious,
rock-bottom. Where and when I draw the line may seem to be, and it
may be, arbitrary or dogmatic. Sometimes I am quite overcome by the
sense that there is so little that can be *said;* perhaps nothing more than,
"They can also be ears". This sense may itself make me seem, and be,
arbitrary or dogmatic, while at the same time, perhaps as palliative, also
charming or funny, or elegant — or fail to be. I would take such behavior
to register that anxiousness I mentioned earlier, upon which instruction
may founder: an awareness of the point at which the path of our communication depends upon your taking the next step, unaided by anything
more from me save my belief in your readiness to take it. It is the mark
of a good teacher in certain domains to know when to stop prompting,

domains in which further knowledge is earned not through further drilling but through proper waiting. It is a different form of exercise. People are not equally good at this, certainly teachers are not equally good; but one can learn to be better.

Here is something I know but cannot prove: the closing image of *For Whom the Bell Tolls,* the hero dying in a pine forest in Spain, holding a rear-guard action alone to give his companions time for their retreat, alludes to, or remembers, Roland's death in *The Song of Roland.* It is not to be expected that everyone will credit this. I may wish to say nothing more, or I may wish to draw the line further along, perhaps saying: The implication of the allusion would be that romantic love has come to bear the old weight of patriotism; the only society left to love, to die for, is the one we can create now, between us. One is, or ought to be, naturally reticent about saying such things. And there are many reasons to hesitate putting oneself in the position of having to consider saying them. No one of the reasons need be that I am unsure of my knowledge; in the present case I am not. I may hesitate because to say such things to you puts something into our relationship which I am not willing should be there. Or I may not be willing either to risk your rebuff should you not agree or to discover that we disagree here. Or I may not want to deprive you of the knowledge — not just deprive you of the pleasures of discovery, but of the pure knowledge itself, for if I tell you then my act itself gets mixed up in your knowledge. To unmix it you may have to turn your gratitude for the knowledge into hostility toward me, to prove your independence. And I may not be willing to bear that, either the hostility or the independence or that way of expressing independence. Knowing me would have become as it were the price of that knowledge rather than, as it may have been, a further effect of it. — Something of this kind is generally not unfamiliar. There just are things which I want you to know but which I do not want to tell you (certain of my wishes or needs perhaps). One might say: I want you to want to know, and to want to in a particular spirit; not, say, out of curiosity. Such a wish goes into Thoreau's view of friendship. It can be overdone.

If I do tell you, then one or other reasons for hesitancy have been overcome. It may, for example, be of overriding importance to me to test the attunement of our intuitions, our agreements in judgment. Since I believe that philosophy can reach no further than these agreements, I am apt to be tempted to test them. (And I might write about film.)

But why call such a thing as my claim about the Hemingway ending a piece of knowledge? Isn't it at best an intuition? But "intuition" *here*

would suggest that something or other may come along to confirm or disconfirm the intuition. And I can envision nothing of the sort here — unless
one wishes to say that another person's agreement would confirm me.
Anyway, why not call it knowledge? Because it is not knowledge of a
matter of fact? Why is that special? Because in order to forgo my knowledge of a matter of fact I would have to bring under suspicion an unfor-
seeable range of concepts and judgments in terms of which there are such
facts for me at all? But that is not unlike the way I feel about the Hemingway ending.   — Perhaps I exaggerate. Perhaps the depth of my conviction is somewhat shallower than my conviction about the meaning of
certain poems of Blake which I am at the moment not willing to talk
about. But my conviction about the Hemingway is certainly deeper than
a feeling I have about *The Red and the Black,* that among the other
significances of the title colors, they are meant to match the colors on a
roulette table. That is, for me, hardly more than something one might
call an open guess, which I may or may not some time attempt to confirm.
If it is confirmed, then it is an insight (even if, as for all I know may be
true, it has long been known or accepted by good readers of Stendhal); if
it is disconfirmed, i.e., leads nowhere, then it is nothing, or almost nothing: it is obvious how (though not when) one might hit upon the idea,
and it reveals next to nothing about me personally. An idea I have about
myself cannot in this way be nothing; my false interpretations of myself
are as revealing as my true ones.

If my attitude towards him expresses my knowledge that he has a soul,
my attitude may nevertheless not be very definitely expressed, nor very
readily. It may take ages; it may be expressed now in the way I live. You
may have to bear such an attitude towards me in order to credit that I
bear it towards him, or towards you. It is an old fantasy, or a fact about
an older world, that such knowledge was in the possession of certain
communities, into whose secrets one may have sought initiation. Some
people, strangely, take the University to be such a community — or perhaps take it as a reminder of such a community.   — The word "attitude"
can be misleading here. It is not, in the matters at hand, a disposition I
can adopt at will. It is helpful to take the English word in its physical
sense, as an inflection of myself toward others, an orientation which affects
everything and which I may or may not be interested in discovering about
myself.

I can bear an analogous attitude toward myself. (This is a remark
meant to characterize at once the idea of such an attitude and the idea
of having a self.) I can, for example, be interested in my sensations, and

disinterested about them. If I say, for example, that I do not mind the cold and offer you my jacket, does this necessarily mean that I am not as cold as you? When Dickens depicts Mark Tapley's seasickness, he depicts him as possessing just that sea of experiences possessed by everyone around him, but without inflecting himself toward it as the others do, e.g., without their sea-moans and their wild languors of misery; instead, he moves about the ship, as it were in the valleys between swells of nausea, attending to the others. This man does not even judge the others wanting in not being able to inflect themselves his way. To me this seems an image of freedom. It seems to me also an example of the possession, or exercise, of a will. But here, I find, I am not thinking of the will as a kind of strength which I may have more or less of, but as a perspective which I may or may not be able to take upon myself. So one may say that the will is not a phenomenon but an attitude toward phenomena.

Draw the moral of the fantasy of a private language this way: The natural importance of, say, a sensation's being mine — i.e., of my having it, or rather of its being me who suffers it — is read philosophically as the sensation's being uniquely mine, its being unpossessable by any other. Then when Wittgenstein says, for example, "In so far as it makes sense to speak of the same pain, it makes sense to say we both have the same pain", this seems, within that philosophical reading, to diminish the importance of the fact that I have it. He seems to trivialize my (inner) life. — In a way this is true. I think one moral of the *Investigations* as a whole can be drawn as follows: The fact, and the state, of your (inner) life cannot take its importance from anything special in it. However far you have gone with it, you will find that what is common is there before you are. The state of your life may be, and may be all that is, worth your infinite interest. But then that can only exist along with a complete disinterest toward it. The soul is impersonal.

Almost at any moment one is likely to feel that any such thoughts about the mind or soul are, where comprehensible, metaphorical. I have not, in the way I have been expressing myself, been very eager to avoid encouraging such a feeling. Sometimes the feeling has lead to theories that mental concepts are essentially metaphorical, as on the face of it, or just behind the face, such concepts as "grasping an idea" or "holding a belief" or "searching one's memory" are. What is the idea of metaphor here? If someone says "The mind has mountains", I will not understand unless I know that this is a metaphor (i.e., that it is meant metaphorically), and not because its topic is the mind. It would not be quite right to say that I must *take* it metaphorically, because it is not quite clear how else I might take it. Sometimes the matter is not so clear. If I tell you that I tripped him up or waved a red flag at him, I may not mean you to take me literally. How then? Not metaphorically, because I could have put these thoughts another way. (Cp. "Aesthetic Problems of Modern Philosophy", p. 78.)

Recall the following cases:

"I noticed that he was out of humor." Is this a report about his behavior or his state of mind? ("The sky looks threatening": is this about the present or the future?) Both; not side by side, however, but about the one *via* the other. [*Investigations*, p. 179]

Suppose one said: "But 'out of humor' is metaphorical, and its literal source, moreover, is medieval psychology, hardly more than superstition. So the example settles nothing. As for the sky's looking threatening, this is a bit of animism, or some other pathetic fallacy. If you insist on saying that it is about both the present and the future then the most you can say is: it is figurative about the present (because the way the sky looks can obviously be described literally), and literally about the future, anyway a figurative way of making a literal prediction." In this mood, the following line of reply is not likely to be satisfying:

And how about such an expression as: "In my heart I understood when you said that", pointing to one's heart? Does one, perhaps, not *mean* this gesture? Of course one means it. Or is one conscious of using a *mere* figure? Indeed not. — It is not a figure that we choose, not a simile, yet it is a figurative expression. [p. 178]

It is open to us to reply: "But that one means a gesture settles nothing about what it is one means. You can say 'This is a table' and point to the table, but philosophers have taken themselves to know that what this really means is a whole lot of predictions about possible experiences. Of course, such a philosopher will allow you, in ordinary life, to avoid going through the literal lay-out of your meaning and, for convenience, stick directly with the common coin of abbreviation. Matters are worse when it comes to such a gesture as pointing to your heart. Someone — and not just a philosopher — may not accept your coin of abbreviation. The whole point of such a gesture was that the other should accept the remark that calls it forth. It was an expression of sincerity, its intention was a moment of intimacy. So wouldn't it have been more effective to have spoken more simply? And as for the figure not being one we chose, but one, as it were, forced upon us, what is reassuring in that? Wasn't the point of philosophy to see such force for what it is, and to weaken it? Next we will be told that the true Enlightenment is not the effect of modern science but began *long* before it." — If I had given the gesture referring to the heart I would particularly resent the idea that I should have spoken more simply. It would have been meant as the simplest of gestures. — Differing *Weltanschauungen* seem to be in play.

When I say that the underlying idea of the allegory of words is that human expression, the human figure, to be understood, must be read, surely there can be no doubt that *that* is merely a metaphor? But I ask again: What is this idea of metaphor? The suggestion seems to be that my expression must be translated into others, even perhaps *reduced* to others. — Then this would be a kind of metaphor for the concept of a metaphor. Certainly it is essential to an expression's counting as a metaphor that it *can* be paraphrased. It is equally essential that the paraphrase not be treated as a reduction but rather as a certain sort of instruction. If I had said "The human body is a text", then I would feel quite sympathetic to the claim that this is a metaphor and to the request for a paraphrase. But I might have been using that remark as a simile, and I could exhaust its content by saying, "I mean, it can be read". *Must* I go on to explain? Suppose I say, "I mean, it can be interpreted, understood". But this could have been the *first* explanation for my simile of the text. And it seems to me not to exhaust the meaning either of "text" or of "read". On the contrary, the idea of reading seems to tell me what *kind* of understanding or interpretation I might aspire to. Then what I need is not a paraphrase or translation of the word "read", but an account of why it is that *that* word is the one I want — after which I may move away from it or move on from it. (The willingness and the refusal to exchange one word or expression for another, as well as the usefulness or futility in doing so, are themes running throughout the *Investigations*.)

Part of the reason I want the word "read" is, I feel sure, recorded in its history: it has something to do with being advised, and hence with seeing. But part of the reason has also to do with an intimation that I am to read something particular, in a particular way; the text, so to speak, has a particular tone and form. The form is a story, a history. You can tell who someone is by describing him and saying what he does for a living, etc. If you know the person, understand him, your knowledge will consist in being able to tell his story. Generally we settle for an anecdote or two. Some material objects have a story — the Maltese Falcon, for example, or the Ring of the Nibelungen. Such a story will provide the provenance of the object as well as an account of its origin, and give a list of its unique properties. Remarks which read a body as giving expression to a soul may be looked upon as myths, or fragments of a myth. (It has a body; it sees; is blind; hears; is deaf; is conscious or unconscious. He was out of humor; She struggled with herself; They fell in love; He lost his way.) And if the soul is a central character in a myth, then the idea of "reading the body" is part of that myth. I should imagine that a reason one feels certain remarks about the soul to be metaphorical is that one does not want, or know how, to speak of them as mythological. The mythological would then be what the idea of the metaphorical here is a metaphor for. ("Only of a living human being and what resembles (behaves like) a living human being can one say . . . it hears; is deaf . . . is conscious or unconscious." *Can* one say? One can imagine saying these things about a machine, e.g., one that uses antennae. Is this because the machine literally, i.e., as a matter of fact, resembles (behaves like) a living human being? Or has one first to anthropomorphize the machine in order to have these descriptions called for? Should we say that such descriptions apply metaphorically to the machine? If so, then when someone thinks of them as applying metaphorically to human beings it will be because they have first automatized the human being. I think no one will wish to say that such descriptions apply mythically to machines.)

A happy feature of the suggestion that the soul is mythical, that remarks about the soul are fragments of a myth, is that it does not exclude the fact that there will be arguments about it, especially about whether and how it exists. This combination is true of the soul's companion, called in the myth its creator, the chief object of myth. Interpretations of the myth and arguments concerning its subject's existence and nature would stand to the soul as theology stands to God. In a different world these studies would be called psychology.

Take the figure the myth calls Will. In some stories, or some regions of the myth, he is said to be free, in others not. Where he is not, he is held sometimes to be in bondage to God, sometimes to nature, sometimes to society, and sometimes he is held to be struggling against this bondage, sometimes not. If there is no continuation to the myth, freedom is almost sure to be unmanageable, because all it can mean is "at large", a condition which may at any time end. Or take the passage which says that the soul itself is a ghost in a machine. If that is all, we have an awfully short myth here, and the machine is bound eventually to be all that can sustain our attention. It is comparable to saying that God is the ghost over the machine. The machine is bound to be all that can eventually sustain our prayers. Of course I do not doubt that there are people who believe these myths, I mean people for whom these are the horizons.

Myths generally will deal with origins that no one can have been present at. In addition to God and the soul, society and the state are important figures. Take the passage which runs: ". . . the state is a ship . . .". This *could* be meant metaphorically, if one went on to explain it by saying by whom the ship was constructed, and how it is powered, and what the deck of the ship is, and what the purpose of its voyage is, etc. But this is not where the interest in the idea lies. If this were its interest, no one would suppose themselves actually to believe it, any more than normal people actually believe that there are mountains in the mind. It is a myth which expresses our sense that society is headed somewhere (though we may feel adrift) and that someone knows where that place is and how to get there and for that reason ought to be obeyed. You may call this a myth as a way of calling it a lie. But this will not prevent people from believing it (though it may encourage them to hide the belief). (If, as Hobbes thought, metaphors were lies then people would believe them as easily as not.) Not every way in which language fails to meet facts is a lie. Better to call this myth nonsense, except that it is no obvious kind of nonsense, and no one would accept calling it nonsense who did not already fail to believe it. That the state is a ship is not merely false, but mythically false. Not just untrue but destructive of truth. But how could that be proved?

Wittgenstein speaks explicitly of the mythological in the following connection:

"All the steps are really already taken" means: I no longer have any choice. The rule, once stamped with a particular meaning, traces the lines along which it is to be followed through the whole of space. — But if something of this sort really were the case, how would it help?

No; my description only made sense if it was understood symbolically. — I should have said: *This is how it strikes me.* [§219]

(And of course this is not the end of the argument but its transposition into another mode of discourse — the mode which includes, for example, the expressions "This is the way we look at things" (about which Wittgenstein asks whether it would constitute a *"Weltanschauung"* (§122)) and "The likeness makes a striking impression on me" (p. 211).)

My symbolical expression was really a mythological description of the use of a rule. [§221]

Here the mythological is not in competition, so to speak, with the literal. To say "All the steps are really already taken" will not help you to understand what rules are and what it is to follow them if, say, you feel you ought then to verify this fact. What this mythological description expresses is that the conclusion reached by a rule is always *foregone*. If you still ask "What is forgone?", it may help to reply, "Freedom. At each step the rule will dictate". So far this little mythology and the actuality of following a rule can live happily together. But this is perhaps because myth has here been given the last word.

When myth and actuality cannot live together happily — when you keep wondering too much, say, about where rules come from, then you have stopped living the myth. Nor can you know in advance whether interpretation and argument will be in harmony or, if in conflict, which if either will emerge victorious. Either may cede vast tracts of territory to the other and yet find some rocky corner in which to subsist. (Pieces of the myth of philosophy keep cropping up; here, the part about its battle with theology.) It may be the ambition of an ambitious philosophy to unmask a field of myth. This can mean various things. It can mean just showing that you do not really believe it (any longer); you believe science, or anyway you believe somebody who believes science. It can mean what Hegel did when he tried telling the entire myth of the soul, from origin to end (including the myth of origin and the myth of end), by inventing a speech that he could call philosophy and in which he could tell the soul's story as part of God's. It can mean what Nietzsche was doing in trying to break the myth of the soul, especially those parts about its origin (from nothing, by creation) and its existence (as opposed to the body) and its end (in a world beyond) — to break it by replacing it, or by removing the place for it, which meant breaking all our interpretations of experience, breaking belief, breaking the self.

To speak of a fantasy of privacy is to speak of certain descriptions of privacy as fragments of a myth. We came across certain fragments at the beginning of this chapter, when it was noted that the idea of privacy, arising from the idea of the unknowable, is an impression of necessary secrecy and that secrecy and privacy share the idea of excludedness or exclusiveness. Let us try to tell more about this.

Take the point at which one feels: "All I know is what the other says and does; what he is experiencing is something else. But *he* knows." And not only *does* he know, he *must*. My *necessary* failure of knowledge is his *necessary* success. Perhaps we should not speak here of his knowledge (except as a joke). Perhaps we should confine ourselves to noting the sensation or mood or state that he is in, or has, and not go on to speak of his knowing the sensation or mood or state he is in, or has (unless what his "knowing" it means is that he is not unconscious of it). But why do we *not* so confine ourselves? How *can* we not?

Perhaps we are forced to the concept of knowledge here, hence employ a forced concept of knowledge, because we do not quite know how to speak of the other's aliveness to himself, his being together with himself, *by* himself, in as it were a private place, a place he has to himself. (If there is such a place, how *could* it be uninhabited?) A couple or a group can retire, or retreat, to some place in which they can be private together. But a region which is inaccessible to *everyone,* which *cannot* be inhabited (say a particular mountain peak) would not be thought of as private (unless perhaps it were thought of as the abode of the gods). (In *The Senses of Walden,* I have argued (pp. 100–104) for an understanding of the having of a self as an acceptance of the idea of being by oneself, and an understanding of being by oneself in turn in terms of being beside oneself (in, as Thoreau insists, a sane sense) as the climactic structure of *Walden*'s vision, or mythology. It proposes an understanding of self-possession as a certain achievement of aloneness (call it oneness, or wholeness; Thoreau spells it holiness and says of it that it seeks expression). The achievement requires learning to deal in certain secrets. Not, however, private, or rather personal ones, as if someone might in principle keep them (as if for himself or herself); but, like the secrets of philosophy, always open ones, ones always already known before I present myself to them.)

He's in; I'm out. Is something *keeping* me out, excluding me? *He* could be; he can keep his thoughts to himself, or speak of them in a private language, one with, for example, private allusions (which he has developed over the years with his sister). He can hide his feelings. But in such cases he *can* offer them, open them to me. — This much is obvious. But the contrapositive is not obvious, and it is the point Wittgenstein keeps insisting upon: if the other *cannot* offer his thoughts or open his feelings then he *cannot* be hiding or keeping them either. They might of course be buried, and in some place where for the moment he cannot find them. If someone is hiding thoughts from himself then the fact that he cannot offer them to *me* is perhaps not of the first importance. In other cases what he is doing may precisely be telling me precisely what he is thinking, only I am too busy to notice, or too something. For example, the line he is tracing in the sand is not a doodle; it is a figure eight. He wants me to know, or to care, that he ate something, or hates something.

What is our idea of the necessary or metaphysical hiddenness of the other? " 'What is internal is hidden from us.' — . . . 'I cannot know what is going on in him' is above all a *picture*. It is the convincing expression of a conviction" (p. 223). What is the conviction? What does the picture of internality, or of unreachable hiddenness, express? That the body is a veil, or a blind, a dead end.   — One had better take this as a symbolical expression which is a mythological description, because, among other reasons, as we had occasion to notice, it is none too clear what the body would be if it *could* be seen through. Another such description which arises in thinking about other minds is that of a garden which I can never enter. But this expression is really (mythologically) about a particular quality of the other's mind (it is not, say, a jungle, or dump yard or haunted house), and about a particular position I am in relative to it (say one of envy or disgust or fear). Such descriptions emphasize that I do not enter another's mind the way I enter a place. This is so far not much help; it does not distinguish either from entering, say, into marriage.

The myth of the body as a veil expresses our sense that there is something we cannot see, not merely something we cannot know. It also expresses our confusion about this: Is what we cannot see hidden *by* the body or hidden *within* it? "Within it" suggests: it is some place in there, I don't know where. "By it" suggests: I know where, I just cannot get at it. So we do not know whether the body must be penetrated or turned aside altogether. Wittgenstein's expression "The human body is the best picture of the human soul" is an attempt to replace or to reinterpret these fragments of myth. It continues to express the idea that the soul is there to be seen, that my relation to the other's soul is as immediate as to an object of sight, or would be as immediate if, so to speak, the relation could be effected. But Wittgenstein's mythology shifts the location of the thing which blocks this vision.

The block to my vision of the other is not the other's body but my incapacity or unwillingness to interpret or to judge it accurately, to draw the right connections. The suggestion is: I suffer a kind of blindness, but I avoid the issue by projecting this darkness upon the other. The convincingness of Wittgenstein's thought here will depend upon whether one is convinced by his relating the condition of what he calls "seeing an aspect" (hence what he calls "aspect-blindness") to seeing a likeness between physiognomies, which he cites as his motive in introducing the topic of aspects in the first place. Aspect-blindness is something in me failing to dawn. It is a fixation. In terms of the myth of reading the physiognomy, this would be thought of as a kind of illiteracy; a lack of education.

The mythology according to which the body is a picture implies that the soul may be hidden not because the body essentially conceals it but because it essentially reveals it. The soul may be invisible to us the way something absolutely present may be invisible to us. (I include "absolutely" to emphasize the point of the word "picture" in this connection. Pictures are present *at once,* unlike music and plays and bibles and even unlike statues. Interpretation, however, since it must reach a conclusion, takes thought, hence time; the time may be as short as the first sensing of dawn, or as long as learning the Talmud.) We may say that the rabbit-aspect is hidden from us when we fail to see it. But what hides it is then obviously not the picture (that reveals it), but our (prior) way of taking it, namely in its duck-aspect. What hides one aspect is another aspect, something at the same level. So we might say: What hides the mind is not the body but the mind itself — his his, or mine his, and contrariwise.

Now we may see more of what is expressed in the myth of the body as veiling or screening the mind. Something *is* veiled — the mind, by itself. But the idea of the body plays its role. In the fantasy of it as veiling, it is what comes between my mind and the other's, it is the thing that separates us. The truth here is that we *are* separate, but not necessarily *separated (by* something); that we are, each of us, bodies, i.e., embodied; each is this one and not that, each here and not there, each now and not then. If something separates us, comes between us, that can only be a particular aspect or stance of the mind itself, a particular *way* in which we relate, or are related (by birth, by law, by force, in love) to one another — our positions, our attitudes, with reference to one another. Call this our history. It is our present.

The fantasy of a private language, I suggested, can be understood as an attempt to account for, and protect, our separateness, our unknowingness, our unwillingness or incapacity either to know or to be known. Accordingly, the failure of the fantasy signifies: that there is no assignable end to the depth of us to which language reaches; that nevertheless there is no end to our separateness. We are endlessly separate, for *no* reason. But then we are answerable for everything that comes between us; if not for causing it then for continuing it; if not for denying it then for affirming it; if not for it then to it. The idea of privacy expressed in the fantasy of a private language fails to express how private we are, metaphysically and practically.

The call upon history will seem uncongenial with Wittgenstein. He seems so ahistorical. — He is ahistorical the way Nietzsche is atheistical. (Call these desires for awakening.) And aphilosophical in this way. Because what can come between us is, also, philosophy. There may be ultimate philosophical differences. But if there are they should not be caused by philosophy itself.

I said that one aspect is hidden by another aspect. Suppose we ask: What is my relation to an aspect which has not dawned upon me, is in that sense hidden from me, but which is nevertheless there *to be seen?* What don't I see when everything is in front of my eyes? I find that I want to speak of failing to see a possibility: I do not appreciate some way it might be — not just some way it might appear, but might *be*. — But isn't this emphasis really empty? For surely the figure is, as it stands, already everything it can be, unless it changes. The interest of these pictures just lies in our knowledge that when they flip they do not change. (" . . . what I perceive in the dawning of an aspect is not a property of the object, but an internal relation between it and other objects" (*Investigations,* p. 212). This glosses Wittgenstein's initial broaching of the experience of seeing as, or of "noticing an aspect": "I contemplate a face, and then suddenly notice its likeness to another. I *see* that it has not changed; and yet I see it differently" (p. 193).) And if what I fail to see is a possibility, then, since it can have no metaphysical status other than the aspect I, as it were, succeed in seeing, what I do see is also a possibility. Is this intelligible? It seems that I am going to have to say something like this if I am to take seriously the suggestion that the dawning of an aspect, and its presentation of a physiognomy, sketch the logic, I mean the myth, of knowing another mind.

But is it at all worth investigating ideas like seeing a possibility, or seeing an aspect as a possibility, or my relation to a hidden aspect, as part of a reading of Wittgenstein? Isn't it on the face of it just against the Wittgensteinian grain to say, for example, that I see a person *as* angry who just *is* obviously angry, with no two ways about it? It amounts to saying that I interpret persons some way or another. And this seems to amount to saying that I can, or generally, see human beings as human beings — as what they simply are! "One doesn't 'take' what one knows as the cutlery at a meal *for* cutlery" (p. 195). — But I know what it means, I am not in doubt whether I know what it means, to know what cutlery is. (I could demonstrate its use to express my knowledge.) But I am in doubt whether I know what it means to know what a human being is. (What would express this knowledge? My attitude towards him, perhaps. But what would express this attitude?)

As for the implication, on the line I am following, that in knowing others I am generally interpreting them, this is also not daunting. For while the implication is that human beings are not, for example, cutlery, the implication is not therefore that human beings are analogous to, i.e., like, optical illusions, or at any rate like ambiguous pictures. The idea of the world as an artifact is, as Hume was pleased to show, a very poor analogy. It is, however, a very good myth of the world, i.e., a very good expression of the way, at certain times, it strikes me. This, in turn, will seem to some a small concession to a traditional sensibility, a moment of psychological back-sliding, which need not interfere with our cognitive progress. But suppose "the way it strikes me" means "the way I cannot, at certain times, say on feast days, help seeing it". It is then as convincing as, say, the picture of continental drift. One may wish to say that the idea of continental drift used to be merely a picture (anyone could just see that the facing coasts of Africa and South America were as if made for one another). But now it is a fact. ("Quite as if the object had ended by *becoming* something else" (*Investigations*, p. 206).) This points to a difference in these views of the world, in the way in which they are held. Once convinced of continental drift, there is no competing picture of the formation of continents to which one is liable to revert. One sees here something of what scientific progress means. But to speak of seeing the world as an artifact seems to presuppose some standing, competing way in which it may be seen, a way to which one may revert, or convert. One may wish to speak here of a spirit in which things may be seen, as of a spirit in which words may be meant, and believed. And of course the spirit may die out.

The existence of the mind, or of the soul — the existence of beings — is no more a hypothesis than the existence of God is. I do not so much wish to say that we have no need of such a hypothesis as that we have no clear employment for it. God's existence would not, I take it, be highly thought of as an *ad hoc* hypothesis, as if to say: Our physical theory of the universe is basically sound, and stronger than its competitors; there remain, however, certain persistent miracles which we must have an explanation for.

— If, however, God's existence were taken as a hypothesis in competition with the hypothesis that God is dead, then the issue would be ready for a crucial experiment.

To speak sensibly of seeing or treating or taking persons as persons — or of seeing or treating or taking a (human) body as giving expression to a (human) soul — will similarly presuppose that there is some competing way in which persons — or bodies — may be seen or treated or taken. Many people, and some philosophers, speak disapprovingly of treating others, or regarding them, as things. But it is none too clear what possibility is being envisioned here. *What* thing might someone be treated as?

What else could a person be other than a person? One might be a King. It is reasonably clear what it means to treat a King as a King (Goneril and Regan could not see the necessity once the King had, so to speak, abdicated), or for the King to wish to be treated as a man (Lear prays for this with the onset of madness). But surely we are in no doubt that the King is a person (at least one person), a human being? Things and goats aren't Kings! But must a human being be something in addition, as it were, to being the person he or she is — say a master or a slave, a parent or a child, a writer, a weaver, a stranger? If there are special ways of treating persons under such titles, that is because there are ways of behaving peculiar to holding them. Is there some special way of behaving peculiar to human beings as such? When religion and morality are moved to speak of duties owed to others simply as persons, this does not imply that duties owed them under their special titles are as it were duties to non-persons. It is sometimes imperative to say that women or children or black people or criminals are human beings. This is a call for justice. For justice to be done, a change of perception, a modification of seeing, may be called for. But does it follow that those whose perceptions, or whose natural reactions, must suffer change have until that time been seeing women or children or black people or criminals as something *other* than human beings?

It is sometimes said that slaveowners do not see or treat their slaves as human beings, but rather, say, as livestock; some slaveowners themselves have been known to say so. And it is said that some soldiers do not treat their enemies as human beings; soldiers themselves sometimes say so. Conservatives on the abortion question sometimes say that liberals do not regard human embryos as human beings; liberals seem forced to agree. — But does one really believe such assertions? My feeling is that they cannot really be meant. Of course the words mean something; they are not spoken at random. In what spirit are such words said?

There comes a time when the institution of slavery cannot be justified on any ground other than the sheer denial of the slave's humanity. There was a time when the institution itself was thought good, or anyway went unquestioned: for example, it was the harsh but legitimate exercise of a conqueror's rights, one of the benefits of victory in war. But no one of sound mind thinks, or has ever thought, that abortion is, of itself, good; that it is one of the benefits of pregnancy, or a reason for intercourse. Here is a reason I think I do not follow Roger Wertheimer, in the course of his outstanding essay on what he calls the abortion argument, in his likening (or his speculating about a likeness) of the slaveholder who fails to see his slave's humanity with the condition of the liberal who fails to see human embryos as humans. The most a liberal thinks is that abortion is a moral option, that the cost in human suffering is immeasurably greater without the option than with it, and that the state unwisely or tyrannically exercises its police powers when it attempts to close off this option. The time may have come when the option of abortion can only be attacked on the ground that the human embryo is a human being. (There was a time when it was generally attacked on the ground, and when it was true, that it was too great a risk to the mother's health.) The trouble with the ultimate attack is not merely that the argument that human embryos are human beings cannot finally be won, but that the statement that they are cannot fully be meant — which is not surprising if the argument against it is exactly as strong as the argument in its favor. (I assume that the statement need not rely on the doctrine that the embryo has a soul. Here the liberal is likely to be left quite behind; this argument will take place in other company.) This is not a matter of a lack of sincerity, but a matter of the lack of ways to express this sincerity. There is just one definite thing the conservative does not want done to this embryo, and nothing at all, or nothing more, he can want done for it. There is, however, something clear he wants and something he sees and something he feels. What he wants is for the embryo to be seen *as* a human being: he wants the internal relation between human embryos and human beings to strike you. He can see it this way, and demand this perception of you, because he sees that the human embryo is human (not *a* human; but human as opposed, say, to wolf); you can also say that it is a human in embryo. This is enough to be struck by to found a feeling of abhorrence at the idea that this life should be aborted. A person can understandably be blind to these perceptions. I claim not to be, and yet I claim to be a liberal on the issue of abortion — not merely tolerant of it but passionately in favor of its legalization, convinced that those who wish to oppose it legally are tyrannical and sentimental hypocrites.

Evidently I abhor other things more than I do abortion. What these things are is anything but original, yet important to specify. Unjust laws, for example; in this case, ones that discriminate against the poor and the uneducated and the abandoned. And, for example, the facts of unwanted or neglected children. That legal abortion is an alternative to unjust laws and neglected children is a matter not of good logic but of bad institutions. If, for a start, society were so arranged that adopting a child were no more difficult to cause than having a child; and that children were adopted only by people who will continue to want them and will care for them, and that there are enough such people to care for all the children who need them, and that one knows how to tell who these people are; and that any grain of shame or discrimination attached to bastardy or to the fact of unwed motherhood or to parents who give their babies up for adoption were itself seen to be shameful; and, supposing that contraception is known to be physically harmless to those who practice it, that it were conscientiously practiced; and that women were supplied with expert and congenial help during pregnancy and the father entitled, with the mother, to parental leave from work, so that abortion need be sanctioned only if, and would always be granted if, there were a definite and dire physical or psychological risk to the mother (the psychological risk should by now be confined to a terror of pregnancy and childbirth themselves); then my liberalism on the issue of abortion would fade, my abhorrence of abortion could flower. I might even imagine that there should be a law against it (if there were laws seeing to it that the minimum conditions I listed just now were put into effect), i.e., that the state has an interest in preventing it. My reason would not be that people who request and perform abortions are a danger to the unborn (that is reasonably obvious already) but that they are a danger to themselves, they imbrute themselves, and society along with themselves. But as a liberal I would still oppose invoking the police power on such a ground. So I am secretly imagining that if the conditions I envision were in effect there would be no cases of voluntary abortion, anyway no more than there now are of voluntary suicide. — The upshot of these considerations is that the abortion argument, so far as it is based on the status of the human embryo, not only cannot but must not be won. Voluntary abortion is less bad than its criminalization is; but it is not therefore all right. The more terrible one takes it to be, the more terrible one should take its indictment of society to be. It is a mark of social failure, not unlike the existence of prisons.

It follows that I do not think that performing an abortion is a case of premeditated murder, and, in particular, murder of the most innocent. And in saying that the conservative cannot fully mean that human embryos are human beings I am saying that no conservative of sound mind abhors those who request and perform abortions as he would or should abhor Herod and the minions of Herod — at least as he would a discriminating Herod, one who slated the slaughter only of those children he did not want, or found inconvenient. Herod must at all costs be stopped. I do not say that all the conservative feels is mere disapproval or distaste, as at something despicable or ugly, and that he merely wishes to legislate his moral tastes. (I do not rule this out, either.) I have already claimed to see room for abhorrence. It is like the abhorrence one would feel toward a people who left their dead untended, either left them in their tracks, or threw them out with the rubbish. This is bad; it is imbruting; there ought to be a law against it; but it is not murder.

To justify, as it were, my lack of belief in the claim that the human embryo is a human being, i.e., my belief that this is not fully or seriously meant, I have had to sketch the lines along which these words *are* meant, what people who are led to say them want and see and feel. Is this what I have to do in order to justify my lack of belief in the slaveowner's claim (made perhaps by him, but in my circle of acquaintances, made only for him) that slaves are not human beings? Isn't all that I, who *know* that slaves *are* human beings, can tell him is what it means to want and see and feel human beings to be human beings? And I am not sure that I can do this. I am not sure, as was said, that I know what it means to know this. I can tell what the conservative imagines me to be missing about the human embryo because I can tell, or believe myself to be able to tell, what he is not missing; indeed, I have claimed to share it, though not to add things up his way. But is the slaveowner missing something I am not missing? I think not; not in this way. He may know roughly everything about human beings that I know. He might even describe them with subtlety in the romances he composes on lazy summer mornings.

What he really believes is not that slaves are not human beings, but that some human beings are slaves. No argument there, is there? Since he has some it follows that there are some. No, but this man *sees* certain human beings *as* slaves, takes them for slaves. He need not claim that all such persons ought to be in slavery, merely that it is all right if some are. But he is wrong. A person of sound mind can feel that this man — this perhaps likeable man, this family man, affectionate with the usual animals and children — must at all costs be stopped, if he touches you.

But if this man sees certain human beings as slaves, isn't he seeing something special, not missing something (he doubtless thinks I am missing something)? What he is missing is not something about slaves exactly, and not exactly about human beings. He is rather missing something about himself, or rather something about his connection with these people, his internal relation with them, so to speak. When he wants to be served at table by a black hand, he would not be satisfied to be served by a black paw. When he rapes a slave or takes her as a concubine, he does not feel that he has, by that fact itself, embraced sodomy. When he tips a black taxi driver (something he never does with a white driver) it does not occur to him that he might more appropriately have patted the creature fondly on the side of the neck. He does not go to great lengths either to convert his horses to Christianity or to prevent their getting wind of it. Everything in his relation to his slaves shows that he treats them as more or less human — his humiliations of them, his disappointments, his jealousies, his fears, his punishments, his attachments . . . .

So what is this about "not human beings"? How would our more or less mythical slaveowner mean this? What do we imagine that he wants and sees and feels in saying it? He does not mean that his slaves, anyway not all of them, are less intelligent or lazier than he. (He may think such things, and worse, about his son.) He does not mean that they are less beautiful or less well-mannered than his friends. (He may think worse, in these terms, of white trash.) He means, and can mean, nothing definite. This is a definite frame of mind. He means, indefinitely, that they are not *purely* human. He means, indefinitely, that there are *kinds* of humans. (It is, I take it, to deny just this that Marx, adapting Feuerbach's theology, speaks of man as a species-being. To be human is to be one of humankind, to bear an internal relation to all others.) He means, indefinitely, that slaves are different, primarily different from him, secondarily perhaps different from you and me. (I assume here, I believe, that no racist psychology or anthropology, however it may comfort him, really satisfies him as expressing this indefinite difference.) In the end he will appeal to history, to a form, or rather to a way, of life: this is what he does. He believes exactly what justice denies, that history and indefinite difference can justify his social difference of position. He need not deny the supremacy of justice; he may be eloquent on the subject. He need deny only that certain others are to be acknowledged as falling within its realm. It could be said that what he denies is that the slave is "other", i.e., other to his one.

They are as it were *merely* other; not simply separate, but different. It could also be said that he takes himself to be private with respect to them, in the end unknowable by them.

The slaves may have secrets from the master; doubtless they do. But the master has something more. Power over the slaves, of course, but something more. Call it power over his experience in relation to them. He may acknowledge everything about them, I mean reveal his true feelings to them, about everything from their suffering to their sense of rhythm, with the sole exception of their existence in the realm of justice. They may acknowledge a limited amount to him (to withhold all expression of their feeling, even of the blues, would be dangerously defiant), but nothing about him, to him, except as acknowledgment of his mastery. But should he cede, or they find, the power to acknowledge *him*, to see him as other to their one, power to see his experience as he sees it, then he would see himself through their eyes, and they would know that they had seen themselves through his, and he would number his days. — It may be that Southern slavery, as has been claimed, was the severest form slavery had ever taken in human history. But if, as has been assumed in my fictitious little history, the justification for it was pushed to its final ground — that the slave is not a full human being — then that human misery represented an awful form of human progress; for that ground cannot in the long run be maintained. There are various reasons for regarding the American Civil War as a tragedy. One respectable reason would be to regard it as having been unnecessary, to suppose that slavery was becoming psychically insupportable on the part of the slaveowners. Now if it were shown that what was making the institution insupportable was not alone a sense of guilt (which might be lived with for millennia, given sufficient means for relieving it, say dramatic acts of benevolence), but an increasing effort to mean something that cannot be meant, producing a sense that the mind itself was about to overthrow itself; and if this psychic development were shown to have been proceeding with all deliberate speed, so that, left to itself, without being forced to self-justification in the face of sanctimonious criticism, it would have reached fruition and freed itself from slaveholding by Palm Sunday of 1865, then the Civil War was perhaps tragic because unnecessary, rather than tragic because necessary.

The anxiety in the image of slavery — not confined to it, but most openly dramatized by it — is that it really is a way in which certain human beings can treat certain others whom they know, or all but know, to be human beings. Rather than admit this we say that the ones do not regard the others as human beings at all. (To understand Nazism, whatever that

will mean, will be to understand it as a human possibility; monstrous, un-
forgiveable, but not therefore the conduct of monsters. Monsters are not
unforgivable, and not forgivable. We do not bear the right internal relation to them for forgiveness to apply.) To admit that the slaveowner regards the slave as a kind of human being bases slavery on nothing more
than some indefinite claim of difference, some inexpressible ground of ex-
clusion of others from existence in our realm of justice. It is too close to
something we might at any time discover.

I have not wished to argue from the fact that it is correct to say that
one can see and to a certain extent treat human embryos as human beings
that it follows that human embryos are not human beings; nor to argue
from the fact that another can see and fully treat certain human beings as
slaves that it follows that human beings are not slaves. I have wished to
say that it is not a fact that human embryos are human beings and that it
is nothing more than a fact that certain human beings are slaves. This
may be taken to suggest that someone who expresses himself or herself
otherwise inhabits a particular *Weltanschauung;* that the world, and himself in it, has struck him in a particular way. It may equally be taken to
suggest that someone who thinks as I do has failed to have, or anyway has
not had, the world strike him in this way. (Is this, too, a *Weltanschauung?*)
It is neither true nor false, it is not a fact, that the duck-rabbit is (a drawing of) a duck. If someone says, credibly, of the duck-rabbit, "It's a duck",
then the fact seems to be that it is true *for him* that it is a duck. But "true
for him" apparently invites a contrast with "true for me". Yet the fact
does not seem to be that it is true *for me* that it is a duck-rabbit. That it
is a duck-rabbit just *is* the fact of the matter. So what is the difference, or
contrast, in our positions?

If it makes sense to speak of seeing human beings as human beings,
then it makes sense to imagine that a human being may lack the capacity
to see human beings as human beings. It would make sense to ask whether
someone may be soul-blind. (If there is such a thing as soul-blindness,
slaveowners and liberals are neither necessarily nor peculiarly subject to
it. Though someone might become a slaveowner or a liberal in order to
disguise this fact about himself.)

— Do you really want the whole burden of Wittgenstein's concepts here?
Remember his introductory description: "I contemplate a face, and then
suddenly notice its likeness to another. . . . I call this experience 'noticing an aspect'." So to speak of seeing human beings as human beings is

to imply that we *notice* that human beings are human beings; and that seems no more acceptable than saying that we are of the *opinion* that they are (cf. *Investigations*, p. 178). — What is implied is that it is essential to knowing that something is human that we sometimes experience it as such, and sometimes do not, or fail to; that certain alterations of consciousness take place, and sometimes not, in the face of it. Or in the presence of a memory of it. The memory, perhaps in a dream, may run across the mind, like a rabbit across a landscape, forcing an exclamation from me, perhaps in the form of a name. (Cp. *Investigations*, p. 197 and cp. Yeats's "A Deep-Sworn Vow".)

I have spoken of there being a spirit in which words may be meant. I would like to say that the rightness in describing "I noticed that he was out of humor" as a report about his behavior *and* his state of mind — "not side by side, however, but about the one *via* the other" — trades on a spirit in which we imagine these words said and meant. But if there is such a spirit, is it a function of the fact that this expression is figurative or that its content is about a creature? I would like to say that "He's waving goodbye" partakes of the same spirit, and "He's favoring his arm again", and "He is in pain".

Could there be people who could never achieve the spirit in which words about another (mind) are meant? Would this mean that they understand someone who expressed an intention or aspiration always as making a prediction? Or that they understand someone who expressed pain as showing that he was not in good working order? Is the spirit so fragile? What would make us, how could anything make us, shrink from it? — If the possibility about others that daunts you is that anything they can express they can feign, even that others may at any time and for no reason simulate their responses, this will lead you only, so to speak, to an epistemological agnosticism, not to a metaphysical skepticism, not to a surmise that perhaps there *are* no human beings. For surely nothing other than a human being, or something awfully like a human being, could *simulate* human responses? Suppose someone wished to convert this question into a refutation of skepticism, as follows: Either what is before you — the humanish thing you wish to say is in pain — is simulating or it is not. If it is not, then it is in pain, and hence is a human being; if it is, then it is simulating, and hence is a human being.

To imagine that something could simulate human responses is to imagine that something could simulate being human. This would presumably mean that this thing could appear in human guise, in a human body. The human race used, apparently, easily to imagine that gods and angels could so appear; more recently that aliens from another heaven might. It used also to imagine that humans and gods might appear in the guise of animals, either through metamorphosis or metempsychosis. But only figuratively has it been imagined that an animal might appear in human guise — as though it is an unbreachable point of grammar that a soul is at least as high in the scale of being as the body it happens to inhabit. The soul may live beneath itself, but never above; it can only be dragged down.

Could it be that human beings are in human guise? Suppose that there are in our world such things as human guises, "bodies" that for all the world seem inhabited but happen not to be, i.e., seem to be human beings but happen not to be. They may have as it were the metaphysical status of zombies or golems, but empirically they may be much livelier and do just about anything human beings can do — not just calculate and play chess, say, but also flirt and court and laugh and cry, or anyway shed tears, or at least produce tears, even ones of iron and salt. Now suppose there used to be a way of inhabiting guises, a way for human beings to don them for a time should they wish to. At first people might have donned them in order to play a variety of practical jokes, but eventually in order to take other advantages a guise affords. You could, for example, choose "your" looks and figure. Moreover, the guise makes accessible to you the release of emotion that masks do, and without the inconvenient evidence of the mask. Some people would grow reluctant to leave the bodies they had inhabited. Suppose that after a period of inhabitation it becomes impossible, physically or psychologically, to leave your body. Or impossible without dying.

Suppose now that the knack of donning guises appeared and disappeared long enough ago so that the period of trial inhabitation is past. All who are now inside human guises are stuck inside for life. The only way to be certain now whether a body is or is not inhabited would be to open it up and look inside. We would not often open live bodies for this purpose (though we would often have the impulse to) because of our knowledge that it causes the death of the one inside. Indeed the concept of death seems to be absorbing the idea of leaving the body. — We might have an idea that evolution could have taken a hand in this process of inhabitation, that the key to human survival, i.e., survival as a human being, turned out to be the forming of a body-shell around the fetus before the term of birth. After a while, nature could become so artful that you could *never* tell a human guise from a human being. The shell became skin thin, and when you opened it up you found no separate human being but merely what you would expect to find if you opened an old-fashioned, unshelled human being. (This is of course what our records mostly do show, because this point of human evolution would have been reached before the point of writing. Sometimes it even seems hard, in the face of this (lack of) evidence to imagine how we were fortunate enough ever to have formed the idea of the one inside, grasped the truth of the matter. One might regard the artfulness of nature in this instance to have defeated itself, because now the body is no longer a protection for the human being. The one inside suffers everything that happens to the body, and more besides. — The state of the evidence paves the way for a new breed of unbeliever, people who do not relate the past this way, or rather not to this effect. What they like to say is, "There is no one inside". But this only keeps alive the impulse to look.

Is it that we take ourselves for (possibly) inhabited bodies, human beings in undiscardable human guise? — when, that is, we feel that to know the reality of the other we have to get past his body to him, that what is really happening is hidden from view, in a place we cannot enter. If this is the way things are, I am in no better position with respect to myself than you are. Since the knack of donning and casting off the new guise disappeared long enough ago, I have no better way than you of telling whether my body is, or once was, a human guise or whether it is really mine, my original one, whether *this* is all there is. I cannot, so to speak, tuck in my head and look around; I cannot lay hands on myself any more intimately than you can. And memory here would be a thin reed. None of us remembers our birth even though each of us knows that he or she is natal, so to speak. Do we not?

Suppose I become convinced, come to harbor the suspicion, that my body is a guise, not my original. I am harboring the idea that this body is "mine" in something like the way my clothes are mine; but it is not — what shall I say? — *me* (except at best the way certain clothes may be really me, my dear). It is my (inalienable) possession, but it does not express me, not the real me. My protection has become my encumbrance. In such a state I may be glad to hear that there is, despite all, a way to cast it off.

If I harbor the suspicion only about others and hence harbor the temptation to want to penetrate the other, to see inside, my impulse is to want a way of comparing what the other shows with what is actually going on in him. This again takes the problem of other minds to be of a familiar epistemological form, the form bequeathed by Kant, following Locke and Leibniz, according to which I am sealed within my circle of experiences, never (under my own power) to know whether those experiences match an independent reality. If I harbor the suspicion about myself, I want to escape this body not, pretty clearly, in order to compare (or rather correlate) the responses it shows with the responses I have — correlate its responses with mine inside — but simply to reveal my responses. As if unless the responses I reveal are the responses of the body that is me, I am not expressed. But why should I want this, want it perhaps enough to die for it by leaving this body?

Is it that I want to be known, that is, to be acknowledged? But what in this is of mortal importance? Is it a matter of wanting my existence confirmed, i.e., the existence of my sufferings and of my deeds? But why would I imagine that they are not acknowledged, never confirmed? I had occasion to ask: If I do not accept the criteria you manifest as revealing something true of you — if, e.g., I invariably distrust your manifestations of suffering — then is this a distrust of you (of your capacity to give yourself expression) or of myself (of my capacity as a knower of others, as a reader of expressions)? Now if I distrust your acknowledgment of me, fail to believe in any manifestation of sympathy or of praise, am I distrusting you (your capacity as a knower of others) or myself (my capacity to give myself expression)?

How can I fail to believe in my expressions of myself, my capacity to be able to present myself for acknowledgment? I have this pain, I am proud or ashamed of this deed, humiliated by that thought. But if I fail to believe in the other's acknowledgment of me, must I be failing to believe in the other's capacity to accept these facts, to measure their reality for me, perhaps to share them? And must this mean that I do not believe the other knows what these feelings are? But the other may perfectly well know. — But only for himself, the weight of his own feeling. — But it may be no different from yours. — But it does not matter to him the way it matters to me. — How do you know? And suppose it were true. Isn't that a potential benefit of conveying your feelings to him, to assess their mattering? Perhaps you do not want them to matter to him. If you do, you must let them. — Let them? When all I can do is to groan, to weep, to laugh, to rage, to talk, to talk, to talk! All this is not what I feel, not who I am. — You mean, I think, that you cannot produce in others the responses you imagine would satisfy you. You cannot enact your character, play your own life. Or perhaps you can. But then the responses you produce in the other are apt to be directed to the wrong thing, to the part you have enacted, not to you yourself. It is as an alternative to the wish to produce the response in the other that I claimed you must let yourself matter to the other. (There is a very good reason not to do so. You may discover that you do not matter.) Take this as advice to Hamlet. — To let yourself matter is to acknowledge not merely how it is with you, and hence to acknowledge that you want the other to care, at least to care to know. It is equally to acknowledge that your expressions in fact express you, that they are yours, that you are in them. This means allowing yourself to be comprehended, something you can always deny. Not to deny it is, I would like to say, to acknowledge your body, and the body of your expressions, to be yours, you on earth, all there will ever *be* of you.

It seems to me possible that there are persons who understand their bodies as their possessions, as perhaps their chattel. Doubtless they regard the body as a special prize among their possessions. How they treat it will determine whether they are kind masters or cruel. Or perhaps they will prove merely greedy. Speaking of the body as a possession may be a way of asserting certain rights one has with respect to it. But I claim to have rights with respect to my wife and child, to go no further; yet I hope I do not claim to own them. If what I own is a guise, then I can own it whether or not I am in it. The first man in the iron mask was as surely in it as the man who subsequently came to be in it; the second had it made; it was made for the first. Who owns it? Not the ironsmith who mixed his labor with it. The edification is: cause no habitation to be built that you do not wish to live in. If there were an assignment of guises to angels, there would be bickering in heaven. — An idea that wants expression here is that one's body should not be subject to an alien will (e.g., submitted to an unwanted term of pregnancy?). But why conclude that one's body should be subject to one's own will?

A better relation to the body is expressed by saying that I am the body's possession, I am of it, it has claims upon me. That I can mistreat my body does not show that I stand to it in the role of master or mistress. For I can mistreat my master or mistress, e.g., by betraying them. What does it mean to be in control of one's body? If I am in control of my bank then only I, no one else, can determine what it shall do. To say I am in control of my body might, similarly, mean that no one else is in my position with respect to it, that it is, say, under my hypnotic spell. But if I am at one with my body, say in the accomplishment of a virtuoso performance or in acts of love, does this mean that I am perfectly controlling my body or that I am in the perfect control of my body? Mightn't the answer be either

Both, or Either? For any performance or deed can be done through will or through grace. Their physiognomies will differ accordingly, as for example early Horowitz differs from late.

If I say that any action can be done actively or passively, then I should say that an action done through will is done passively. I realize that one's first intuition here, supposing the issue is clear enough to excite intuition, is likely to run the other way. But that would be the will's doing. To act through will is to be commanded by oneself, perhaps driven; it is to be a good soldier. No doubt this is in general better than being a bad soldier. But it is still not being the initiator of one's commands, hence not being in a position, no matter what one's private feelings, of countermanding them. (In *Lear* and in *Pericles* it is a good soldier who, I assume without malice, but with reluctant bearing, accepts a commission to murder an inconvenient daughter. Conscience does not issue commands.)

Kant, I take it, was of the opinion that the best one can hope for in our present circumstances is to be commanded by the will, and he called this freedom. Nietzsche called it suffering, passiveness, on the ground that our will is not, not yet, our own. So he undertakes to instruct us in redirecting the will in order that we may *become* active, free of reluctance. Because it is natural for us to frame our ideas of personal rights in terms of private ownership, Nietzsche, like Thoreau, frames his instruction in terms of possessing something, coming into possession of something, in order to wrest our notion of ownership from our grasp. His Zarathustra speaks of coming into the possession of his light, his food, his kind of ears, his tongue, his hand, his foot, his stomach, his taste, his way, his enemy, his war, his death. Not surprisingly, he is accused, like Thoreau, of selfishness, or anyway of egotism. But what each of them claimed to possess deprived no one of anything. Yet in the face of them others have felt deprived. — Compared with Thoreau, Nietzsche seems too spiritual, all but Christian. Because the sun, say, or the body of water Thoreau claimed was his (and might therefore be anyone's or no one's) was *the* sun and *this* body of water. Common things, merely not held in common.

If not as owner, do I stand in some other relation to my body? We speak of standing in various relations to our selves, e.g., of hating and loving ourselves, of being disgusted with or proud of ourselves, of knowing and believing in ourselves, of finding and losing ourselves. And these are relations in which we can stand to others.

— No, not in *this* way. In a relation to myself there is no reciprocity. Or rather, in each relation reciprocity is assured. — Surely not assured? If I love myself am I loved by myself? Can I love myself back? Narcissus did not die of love but of love unrequited, or unrequitable. Yet if there were *no* reciprocity, how could I struggle against myself? — Stop struggling and the struggle is over. — But with others the one who stops struggling has lost. — And how is it otherwise with oneself? Is it that in this struggle winning is losing and losing is winning? That sounds non-existent. — There are outcomes to a struggle other than victory and loss. You make a struggle sound like a game. It is true that you cannot play a game with yourself. — Not at any rate without putting aside a knowledge of my strategies.

— Would you at the same time care to put aside these metaphors? We have allowed ourselves to speak as if the self could literally be divided. But it is not a quantity of something; not like bread or a parcel of land. — A house can be divided; I mean the community of dwellers in the house. That is not just a case of a lot of individuals feeling different ways. It is a case of one thing feeling different ways. — That is the Northern point of view. The Southern view is that there are two things each feeling its own way. — What I thought you wanted to give expression to a while ago, and so did I, is the circumstance that my self is just that to which I *must* stand in these relations, fated to; all of them; or at any rate one of each pair, love or hate, being proud or contemptuous of, honest or dishonest with, at war or at peace. If this is how one thinks of the matter then there is no help for it, but we must simply go through the possibilities. Immediately one discovers certain anomalies. — Evidently. A relation takes two. — Identity does not take two; anyway not two things. Still, I gladly forgo the relations which in fact take two. I will not say that one may be father to oneself (except metaphorically or mythically), nor take leave of oneself or greet oneself, nor take oneself for a walk, nor pardon oneself (unless one has a terrific title among one's names). I cannot cast your shadow; at least not upon myself.

To say that I am *fated* to stand to myself in the relations in which I may or may not stand to others is to make the contrast between myself and others in a particular way: any other is one whom I may just not know, have no relation with; but I cannot just not know, or have no relation with, myself. Ignorance of myself is something I must work at; it is something studied, like a dead language.

Isn't this an exaggeration? — like the remark a while ago that I am fated either to love or to hate myself, either to be proud or contemptuous of myself, either to be at war or at peace, etc.? Most people, surely, are neither the one nor the other exactly. But this need not be understood as denying the point, for this "neither the one nor the other exactly" may describe a specific position along a dimension of self-relation which I am fated to occupy. Call the positions most people occupy along all the logically applicable dimensions of self-relation their positions of averageness. (More or less obviously, I am trying from time to time to decipher what it is in Heidegger's views that I find valuable and intelligible.) This flattening of the self seems to call for another dimension. If I stand in these relations to myself, then relating myself to myself is something I am doing, something I must take a stand upon, actively or passively. Then the position of the self's averageness is itself one to which I relate myself, one upon which I must take a stand, perhaps an average stand. Perhaps I take an average stand on some sense that my positions of self-relation are something special. Perhaps I take an average stand to the effect that averageness is itself special, even glamorous, something like the position of Tonio Kröger.

It is said that there are occasions on which, if I am to be forgiven, I must forgive myself. On such occasions, forgiveness would have to be forthcoming without the condition of apology, since I cannot apologize to myself. Could I forgive myself, as I might others, for not being able to apologize? If I can love myself, I suppose I can be jealous of myself, regard myself as my possession and carefully monitor my possession's company. (Like God.) But could I envy myself? If not, then if I envy Tonio Kröger it follows that I am not Tonio Kröger. If what Tonio Kröger envies in Hans Hansen is his averageness, then if his own averageness is no different would logic debar him from this envy? Not if — of course — he failed to recognize his own averageness (a failure he might have cultivated by developing the envy) or perhaps not if he wished to think of the other as happy *because* of his averageness. One may find nowadays that a certain envy of Hans Hansen is expressed only by Hans Hansens. But doesn't this just mean that certain people would like to think of themselves as artists, or think their failures the failures of an artist? And also that Hans Hansen, were he created today, would seem less enviable? — You just mean that today a certain happy bourgeois would like to think of himself as unhappy. Then why not just say that Hans Hansen logically cannot envy Hans Hansen, at least not without dividing his consciousness? — Perhaps because I am afraid that only a happy bourgeois would say so, finding his own position enviable. If his consciousness is divided then it is no longer the old Hans Hansen. Then perhaps the reason Tonio Kröger does not envy himself is that he knows his position is not enviable. Except when secretly he thinks that it is. But at those times he knows his position to be his, and he therefore would seem to lack nothing to envy; except that just then his envy of Hans Hansen is sharpest. It seems one fate for the extraordinary (occupied it may be by the artist, or by the philosopher) is to exist in envy of the ordinary (though touched, no doubt, with a certain contempt), and to conceive of the ordinary as without envy (hence the idea of the bliss of the commonplace). Then is the ordinary free of fate, except for that of living in oblivion of itself?

(Some are bound to feel that the implication for skepticism of the allegory or the psychology of this speculation in the name of Tonio Kröger figures the skeptic's cause in too romantic a vein. Especially when it is recalled that Tonio Kröger speaks early to a confidante of the "bliss of the commonplace" as something for which the artist has a "gnawing, surreptitious hankering", an inescapable longing "to live free from the curse of knowledge and the torment of creation, live and praise God in blessed mediocrity!". Later he locates this longing more fully: "I stand between two worlds. I am at home in neither, and I suffer in consequence. You artists call me a bourgeois, and the bourgeois try to arrest me. . . . [You] ought to realize that there is a way of being an artist that goes so deep and is so much a matter of origins and destinies that no longing seems to it sweeter and more worth knowing than longing after the bliss of the commonplace." To the objects of his longing he directs the unvoiced remark: "It was always you I worked for." Tonio Kröger's remark is necessarily private from those to whom it is addressed since, as Mann's narrator puts it, ". . . their speech was not his speech". But I recall also that Tonio Kröger speaks of life — his life, life removed from life — "as the eternal antinomy of mind and art", and I ask: Do we take seriously Hume's noting of skeptical doubt as a "malady which can never radically be cured"?; and do we accept as internal to his philosophy his praise of nature in curing him of his "philosophical melancholy and delirium" either "by relaxing this bent of mind, or by some avocation, and lively impression of my senses", so that he can follow other philosophers in the practice, or necessary distraction, "upon leaving their closets" [i.e., private chambers; studies], of "[mingling] with the rest of mankind in those exploded opinions"?; and do we think him to be asking sincerely, asking his readers to ask themselves, whether it follows that "I must strive against the current of nature, which leads me to indolence and pleasure; that I must seclude myself, in some measure, from the commerce and society of men, which is so agreeable; and that I must torture my brain with subtilities and sophistries, at the very time that I cannot satisfy myself concerning the reasonableness of so painful an application . . . ? To what end can it serve either for the service of mankind, or for my own private interest?" (*Trea-*

tise, Book I, Part IV, Sections II and VII)? No doubt David Hume is capable of greater irony than Tonio Kröger is. But hardly greater than Thomas Mann is.)

So saying that I cannot just not know myself amounts to saying that I am the one who is fated to have, or to begin with, an average knowledge of myself. And doesn't this amount to saying that I am the one who is fated to keep myself in a certain (average) ignorance of myself? What is the form of this ignorance, an ignorance of something I cannot just not know? Is it to be thought of as keeping a secret? But in what form can I keep a secret from myself, keep silent? To keep silent around myself I have to silence myself; I keep myself in the dark by darkening myself. Presumably I would not come to treat myself as dark unless others had treated me so. And presumably they would not have treated me so unless they so treat themselves. — But isn't "being dark to oneself", like "someone else's being opaque to oneself", nothing but a picture? — If being blind to oneself or to others is nothing but a picture. The aspect to which I am blind is dark to me. The figure of which it is an aspect is opaque to me. (If I can darken myself, can I enlighten myself? The news of those conversant with the subject seems to be that I cannot. If I give over darkening myself the result will be my enlightenment.)

But *can't* I just not know myself, the way I can just not know you? I can just not know something about myself, for example that I have a heart murmur or that I have just crossed the Swiss border and hence am free. But would it make sense to say that I had not made my acquaintance, just never crossed my path? Or since I must somehow have been introduced to myself, is the issue rather to be thought of as how *well* acquainted I am with myself? But what counts as getting better acquainted? Sense here depends upon what one takes the issue of "knowing a self", one's own or another's, to be. I can fail to recognize myself under a particular description, e.g., as "the inheritor of a criminal's fortune", or as one "of no woman born", or as one "of mixed blood". And how are these failures different from failing to recognize myself as one "with a heart murmur"? One might say that the former failures amount to failures to know who or what I am. But how can it be that one among the endless true descriptions of me represents *the* truth of me, tells who or what I am? How can there be a key to my identity?

Tragedy and comedy are all but filled with this possibility — that one among the endless true descriptions of me tells who I am. That is to say, this possibility is what all but fills tragedy and comedy, which are therefore so often about the learning of a name, or learning the equation of two names. The not knowing the equation, and then the learning, precipitates catastrophes or diversions of catastrophe. The drama turns upon whether the assimilation will come *in time*. The obvious scene for the learning is the moment of recognition. Since the recognition is of a person in whom the protagonist is implicated (otherwise we are dealing not with tragedy or comedy but with melodrama or farce) the recognition of the other takes the form of an acknowledgment of oneself, one's own identity. This need not be a case, as with Oedipus, in which the hero had before the learning not been cognizant of his identity. It can be a case, as with Antigone, in which everything is known but in which the logic of recognition (viz., that it demands acknowledgment) is itself the drama. Here the tragedy is that the cost of claiming one's identity may claim one's life. In another tragedy, say *Phèdre,* acknowledgment is forbidden from a different source of law: here everything is known to one, and acknowledgment is forbidden to that one.

In *Must We Mean What We Say?,* I continued an essay on the problem of other minds ("Knowing and Acknowledging") with a reading of a tragedy ("The Avoidance of Love"). I did not see the implications of that juxtaposition at once; I do not know that I see them now. But finding the juxtaposition, I hoped it would prompt two main lines of comparison and investigation: along the fact that both skepticism and tragedy conclude with the condition of human separation, with a discovering that I am I; and the fact that the alternative to my acknowledgment of the other is not my ignorance of him but my avoidance of him, call it my denial of him. Acknowledgment is to be studied, is what is studied, in the avoidances that tragedy studies. To arrive at an explicit and usable formulation of these relations is now a conscious goal of this writing. It can have no conclusion otherwise.

That I cannot just not know myself can be put this way: "I am I" does not convey a piece of information. — Of course not. It is a tautology, hence empty. — But for some the knowledge of this tautology, of this emptiness if you like, is ecstasy. (I call attention once again to *The Senses of Walden,* pp. 100–104.) — Then there must be such a thing as an ecstasy of boredom. — But perhaps you find this because you do not believe the tautology, I mean do not really find that it is a tautology, but instead take it as my answer to the question, "Who am I?". But "I am I" is not that answer. That answer is, or might be, "No one". It serves to reject, or explain, this answer to respond, "I am I". (In *Being and Time,*

Heidegger's words for the structures of Dasein's existence, words he calls
existentiale, he characterizes as empty. I dare say that this is his understanding of Nietzsche's having made *Zarathustra,* as its subtitle says, a
book for all and none, i.e., for the no one anyone may be.) That I am I
thus says that I am not even me — a hilarious, or rather an ecstatic,
glimpse at the possibility that I am not exhausted by all the definitions
or descriptions the world gives of me to me. Everything that happens to
me is my life, the woman says at the end of *Red Desert.* Very well, but I
am the one who must take it upon myself. (I cannot doubt that there is
life on the red desert; call it Mars. I know some who live there.)

A striking exception to the thought that I can stand in any relation to
myself that I can stand to others is that of belief. Why apparently can I
not, in grammar, believe myself? Is it because I cannot tell myself anything I do not already know? Can't I tell myself falsehoods? If deceiving
oneself were the same as lying (to oneself) then one might rest assured that
one had deceived oneself alone. What is believing someone and what is its
connection with believing something?

Why is Moore's Paradox not a contradiction? That is, how does "The
sun is shining and I don't believe it" differ from "The sun is shining and
the sun is not shining"? One difference is that I can easily promote the
second from a contradiction to a paradox by taking it as a truth: for example, half of the earth is always in the dark. Here I have kept the range
of reference of each side of the contradiction from touching. I can similarly keep the hearers of Moore's Paradox from touching. If "and I don't
believe it" is said to someone other than the original hearer (say someone
in the room with you, your hand over the mouthpiece of the telephone),
then I have lied to the first hearer and implicated the second in the lie.
Why, then, not say that "The sun is shining and I don't believe it" is a lie
in which I try to implicate the *same* hearer? One might reject this description on the ground that it is a lie only if half of it is true, i.e., only if the
speaker is speaking the truth about not believing it.   — Yes. We would
not know what we are asked to believe.   — But that is equally true of the
contradiction. And it would be true if someone said, "The sun is shining
and I am lying".   — Well, to believe what someone says is to believe that
he believes it.   — Obviously not. I may not share his sincere beliefs.
— Well, to believe what someone says is to believe what he intends you to
believe.   — Certainly not. I may know on independent grounds that what
he says is true, and I may know, as in so many other cases, that he thinks
he is lying.   — Well, at the least, to believe him is to believe what he
says.   — And, presumably, believe it *because* he says it; for if I had al-

ready believed what he said, then I believe what he says, but I do not believe *him*. But suppose I believe what is said to me only if two say it. A appears and says "X is Y". I think: That's what *you* say. Then B appears and confirms it, i.e., repeats it. Now I believe, or at any rate am prepared to say, that X is Y. But I do not believe either A or B, any more than I believe my weathervane when I read the wind's direction from it. This raises the question: Why, if I accept what you say, on the basis of your saying it, do I respond by saying "I believe you", not "I believe what you say"? I would like to say that the home of belief lies in my relation to others. So I am inclined to say that if I do not believe either A or B then I do not believe what they have told me either; my relation to the proposition that X is Y is not one of belief. But it is not one of doubt either. That is the problem: I am in no position to doubt it. Then what is the relation to a proposition that I have characterized as my "being prepared to say it"? Pushed by a philosophy, I accede to the idea that I believe it. Unpushed, my relation to it is my relation to what it says, e.g., to the circumstance of the sun's shining. (In saying that the home of belief lies in my relation to others, to what they tell me, to what I hear (or remember as having heard; perhaps I read it), I am proposing that our access to belief is fundamentally through the ear, not the eye. The ear requires corroboration (and prompts rumor), the eye requires construction (and prompts theory). Perhaps there is a further way here to understand my reluctance to speak of the skeptic as attacking (or the ordinary language philosopher as defending) our beliefs about the world. The skeptic is assessing our constructions of the world; constructions after the fact; sorts of imagination of it.)

I can of course tell myself something that I have not already been told, but the result is not that I thereupon believe it, but that I thereupon *want* to believe it. (E.g., "I told myself I had done enough".) So it looks as if I cannot give myself my word. But can't I? Can't I trust myself and make a promise to myself? But I cannot hold myself to my promise to myself, perhaps because I am in no position to refuse my excuses. And trusting myself is believing *in* myself. Prophets do not (merely) believe in God, but believe God, take his word. If to believe myself would be to take my word for what I say, then speaking, asking belief from others, would be giving my word. This is why promising is just a specialized form of giving one's word. Rather than being looked upon as an extension of my commitments, the act of promising is better looked at as a restriction of them: take my word only for *this*. If for you to believe me is for you to take my words, i.e., believe what my words say and believe them on the basis of my saying them, then what you believe is that the words are mine to say, that I have taken them from myself. (If the case is described as your believing that I tell what I tell *because* I believe it, this must not be taken as an explanation of *why* I tell it, or tell anything. To explain that would be to explain why it is from you, and why in these circumstances, that I am asking for belief.)

Say that your believing me is your accepting my expression of myself. (One might object to this: Your believing me is your accepting my expression of the world, e.g., my saying that the cat is on the mat. But this leaves out my role in establishing your relation to the circumstance of the cat's being on the mat as one of belief.) Then the reason we do not speak of believing oneself would be that we see no call for saying that one accepts one's expression of oneself. But is there no call because it is obvious that this must always be the case (unless I am lying, in which case it is obvious to myself that I do not accept my expression)? For there to be room for me to accept my expression of myself, there must be room for me not to accept it. I do not mean that there must be room for me to doubt the truth of what I say; room can be made. I mean that there must be room for me to doubt that I have said it on the basis of believing it, to doubt that the words come from me. Can I?

This line may seem altogether too extreme. Believing someone is not as epistemologically baroque as I have been painting it. I have at best been responding to the difficulties of believing in the genuineness, or truthfulness, of someone's expression, in cases in which their saying something is the *only*, or final, basis for believing it, whether because it is something about their inner lives, say their dreams, or because it is about something which they alone witnessed and survived. Whereas in ordinary cases it is so *easy* to believe what another says, as easy as hearing them. — Why easy? Because the stakes are low? Because in ordinary cases what they say can always be checked? As if believing another were merely handier than something else, always more or less *faute de mieux*. (So that believing someone is having faith in things unseen.) — But I do not always feel that speaking to someone is making myself handy for them, or always done because something handier is lacking. If something were lacking, is it something the other might do or something I might do? And if I could not tell myself something I had not already been told, or not tell it anew, never take myself by surprise, come upon myself anew, I would be bound to bore myself colossally. I could still amuse myself, but hardly all the time. What I could not do would be to take an interest in myself. This may lead me to a particular view of the need for others.

I wish to paint my conviction that I am intelligible to others, my capacity to present myself for acknowledgment, as my believing myself. In *Zarathustra,* Nietzsche speaks of believing oneself as the correct or hopeful relation to one's body, having previously identified the self as the body ("Of Immaculate Perception"). "Only dare to believe yourselves — yourselves and your entrails"; as if self-knowledge were a species of divining. It is his way of saying, contrary to Descartes, that the self is not to be identified with the mind. (To *whom* is it said? To *me,* for example. But hardly to my body!) It is also a way of saying that self-doubt is not overcome by any set of beliefs I may have about myself, any more than skeptical doubt about the existence of the world is overcome by any set of beliefs I may acquire about the world. "Dare to believe your body" is the command of someone who views us as doubting our bodies, harboring a suspicion, or fantasy, that, as I have put it, my body is not mine, not my original. As if to say: Descartes's trick of doubting the existence of his body came long after we had already in practice denied its existence; at best he epitomizes an intellectual labor of millennia. And my mind is no more mine, if no less, than my body is. (For Nietzsche, there is no key to one's identity. Hence, after his first book, there is for him no tragedy. One might feel that just *this* is our (new) tragedy. For it means that there is no ending, only return, eternally.) Skepticism and solutions to skepticism consequently make their way in the world mostly as lessons in hypocrisy: providing solutions one does not believe to problems one has not felt.

But isn't the question raised by skepticism (about other minds) why it is that we attach such extreme importance to the human guise, I mean form? Have we discovered that it is worth it, that there is some return for us in this attachment? Have we discovered that only in these locales can the human soul be found?

The argument from analogy — I mean not for the existence of God but for the existence of *other* (other) minds — seems to contain such thoughts. In arguing from the premiss that I know my body to be connected with sentience to the conclusion that other bodies are connected with sentience, I must pass through a line that says in effect: "The other's body is like mine". There seems no end to the trouble one can make for this line. One might say: The other's body is like mine in many respects; but the only respect that would count is if, like mine, it were connected with sentience. So the question is begged. — But only if the argument is meant to be a priori. It is, however, as in the case of the analogous argument for God's existence from the fact of Design in the world, surely meant to be a posteriori.

The line does not suggest, or not say, that some *particular* other's body is like mine, say that it is of the same type, say pyknic. It suggests that *all* other (human) bodies are like mine. Unlike the argument from Design, in which the analogy between the world and a machine is very weak — as if what one really needs is an argument *to* Design here — the analogy with respect to other minds is too good. For in what revelant respect might another human body not be "like" mine? Well, it might not have sentience associated with it. But if it might not, then nothing (else) about its likeness to mine can in the least rule out that possibility. — But the argument from analogy is not meant to rule out the possibility altogether. It is merely to get the possibility left open. — But this is nothing yet, in particular it is not intellectual caution. Because to grant that the other body *might* not, however improbably, have sentience associated with it is to rely on our having the power or the understanding to grant that absence. Would it be, for example, the power or the understanding to grant that some particular other might be a machine? Who, for example?

If I become convinced that Mr. So-and-so is a machine, my conviction will not be expressed by the idea that he lacks something, or that he is not connected with something that I am connected with. I want to express the conviction that the human race lacks this member, or rather that the human population turns out to be one less than I had counted on. How could I strike his name off the list? — It was widely known, in my college days, that a dog whose name I have forgotten was almost granted the baccalaureate degree by Berkeley. The degree was held up in his final semester when it came to light that the members of the fraternity that he had adopted had for almost four years been enrolling him in courses and writing his examinations. I do not know whether, when this came to light, those members were expelled from the University, but I cannot believe that the dog was expelled. He was doubtless stricken from the rolls; the population of the University was one less than the registrars had counted on. What was the registrars' error? Was it to have assumed, surmised, imagined, believed, presupposed, or what not, that the names on their rolls correlated, at best, with human beings? (What would be the proper term of criticism for this error? Inattentiveness? Intellectual laxness? Lack of conscientiousness?) — The epistemological profit of this case lies not in imagining their error but in imagining their surprise.

— But the human body is awfully *like* a machine. — So really an argument from analogy, like the argument from Design, ought to have been directed toward calling our attention to the likenesses between the body and a machine? Such an argument would, I should guess, be as likely to convince us as the one from Design. (Historically the perception of the world as a machine and the perception of the human body as a machine seem to have come at roughly the same time.) And certainly it would be a better line of argument, or less empty, to say that the body is like a machine than that my body is like some unspecified other body. It is as if the wrong party to the dispute about minds or souls got hold of the argument from analogy first.

A traditional objection to the argument from Design concerned its anthropomorphism: it yields at best a God who is too like a man. (Not that it is clear what the objection is to this. There is after all biblical testimony for a kind of similarity between God and man.) Oughtn't there similarly be an objection to the argument from analogy concerning its narcissism? Call the argument autological: it yields at best a mind too like mine. It leaves out the otherness of the other. — That is unfair to the argument. All it says is that the other is like me in the respect of being sentient. — You might as well say the argument from Design makes God like a human being only in the respect of being finite.

Then where does the idea come from that another's body, any other's, is *like* mine? One could be forced to this idea to avoid saying that our bodies are the *same*, i.e., human. — Avoid saying this? As if anyone had ever wished to say it! — It is true that I am appealing here to an experience of being struck by the uniformity of all human bodies. There is the companion experience, perhaps more common, of being struck by their differences from one another. In my experience this is usually prompted by a surprise that the human face has so few distinctive features, hence that tiny variations among just these features are what make it possible to distinguish one from a multitude. Whether I am struck by likeness or difference, however, the basis of the surprise is the stability of the human frame, as it were, under countless inflections — the internal relation between each body and each other.

Animals other than humans have bodies more or less like the human body, homologous with it. Why do I think that if there are human souls the human body is the only fitting locale for them?

I do not wish to deny that the frog body is the best picture of the frog soul. Nor do I wish to deny that I can think this frog is a Prince — if, that is, I can think that a Prince has suffered enchantment, or anyway metamorphosis. What am I thinking? Not merely that he has been given a frog's body, fitted into one as it were. He *is* a frog — anyway he lives as a frog, says what frogs say, loves what frogs love. He has been changed into something *else*. Has he the soul of a frog? I might say he has the consciousness of a frog, though he has the self-consciousness of a Prince. But there are limits. No magic can change a frog into a Prince — a frog, that is, who had never been a Prince. He can be given a Prince's shape, that is all. He has the self-consciousness of a frog. Then the frog in him will, I imagine, keep trying to get out. There will be moments of embarrassment when he needs to speak, or when suddenly he tucks his legs under himself and leaps from the throne. But these moments can be covered over, either with royal explanations or with judicious applications to the court of mass hallucination or blindness — trivial magic by comparison. — I say they are both frogs, the charmed one on the pad in the pond for all the world a frog, and the charmed one on the throne in the hall for all the court a Prince. I also say there is a difference. But how shall I respond to this difference, how express my knowledge of it? If I care for both of them, I feed both of them flies. In each case I might, or might not, put the fly on a golden plate and lay it before its recipient with deference, perhaps at the table, perhaps on the ground. Others may from time to time not understand, or not appreciate, my behavior. Neither from time to time may I. Or rather, I may not understand my convictions, since they are expressed in what seem incompatible ways.

What really goes into caring for them, beyond the willingness to do them some service? Which of them could one love? One might have an erotic attachment to the one on the throne, but not, if one is normal, to the one on the pad. To which of them might I direct *agape,* my love not for him but for the humanity in him? — But where is this humanity? I cannot settle upon it. I might weep the fortunes of the Prince, and as I do a tear may fall upon the one in the pond. But is it for *him,* the one in the pond, that I am cast down? He may be all right, he may be content. If the Prince were otherwise intact but thought he was a frog then I might weep for him even though he was content. — But if I cannot settle upon saying of either the Prince who is a frog or the frog who is a Prince that he is a human being, I am also not content to say that I regard either of them *as* a human being. What would be the point of saying this, beyond expressing my caring about them? But I care about things other than human beings — animals, trees, statues. And I do not regard these as human beings. Though that might depend upon who I am. — Whoever you are you cannot care about these things the *way* you care about human beings. — But suppose I do not care about human beings. Must I? — If you do not then you can express care only where there is no mutuality. — But suppose I find greater mutuality, anyway sympathy, with a chipmunk. You may find that incredible. But I would like to ask you to consider the individual case.

In failing to settle upon the humanity of the charmed frogs, I perhaps failed to make life sufficiently difficult for myself. I avoided sufficiently individualizing either the one in the pond or the one in the court. If the one in the pond had been, say, the Princess my sister, and responds to me in ways that strike me as her ways — a certain tilt of the head when she rebuked my boorishness, a certain petulance in the way she sometimes turned from me, a certain stillness when she listened to music — then I might feel I had a secret, whose responsibility I could evade only at my peril. But what is my secret? That my sister is no longer a human being? And does this mean that my sister, in particular, is now a frog? Is anything any longer my sister? Where, for example, is she? If my sister, when intact, had been inside her body, then why am I so reluctant to say that she is inside the frog's body? If, on the other hand, my sister had been identical with her body, then why do I have any special attachment to *this* frog at all, whom I have just recently met?

And do these questions trace our genuine alternatives, that either I am inside my body or else I am my body? They seem made for our indecision about whether to say that a sensation, for example, is obviously either private or not private. They also suggest that the problem of others may not be fundamentally epistemological but fundamentally metaphysical. How can we know whether we know there are others until we know what we want to know, what there is to know? But how is this different in the case of the problem of the existence of the world? Are we no longer interested in that question because science is not interested in it in the way we were? Then would the establishment of a science of mind answer that question, or talk us out of it? (What is our interest in science?)

In the meantime, to get at our idea of the human being we will have to go through our ideas of the intactness of the human being, hence through our ideas of the losses of intactness, the ways in which a soul and a body can be lost to one another, in which my experience cannot move freely to the one through the other. We should not make life easy for ourselves here, because we are to test not merely the limits of our identity but the limits of our humanity. Being human is the power to grant being human. Something about flesh and blood elicits this grant from us, and something about flesh and blood can also repel it. How far can we maintain fellow-feeling, let alone love, in the face of a failure of intactness, of a deformation of the body or of the psyche? But perhaps such questions only test the degree of our saintliness. And is that necessary in order to test the degree of our humanity? Apparently, if humanity has degrees.

The idea we have of the human being is not, I assume, likely to be captured by a definition which specifies a genus. If we say that the human being is the rational animal, we have yet to specify the *connection*. (The philosophical usefulness of the genus *homo* is limited by the fact that all its species, with one exception, are extinct. If we had the others for comparison we might *see* what difference sapience makes and not wonder about the connection it must have with the body.) If mind-body dualism is true, then a preestablished harmony between them is easier to believe than a connection. It does not help enough for Descartes to say that the soul is not in the body as a pilot is in a ship, because he is left with the idea that there is some *place* in which they connect. — Right. The connection is *closer* than the image of a pilot suggests; more pervasive. — But closeness is not the issue. I expect that the relation between the stone and the statue is pervasive, but they are not close to one another, they do not touch at every place, or at any place. The smile is not close to the face. I would rather say that the statue is the epiphenomenon of the (worked) stone. But why "worked"? Why not say that the statue just *is* the stone? Because that is partial, or prejudicial; it suggests that any stone can be seen or treated as a statue. This entails a particular view of art and of experience. — Is Wittgenstein subject to this partialness, when he says that "My attitude towards him is my attitude towards a soul"? My attitude is a state of just this organism; it is a passage of just my history; a passage I might find myself in, or take, at any time, regardless of the circumstances. Suppose the attitude noted as "towards a soul" is one I find myself in, or take, towards a stone. Let my attitude be what it may, it cannot turn a stone into a human being. The lamp illuminates hands and gems indifferently. Say that the gem does something special with the light; it nevertheless does nothing to the lamp. — This proves merely that the lamp has no attitudes. The statue is not *in* the stone (except on a certain myth of the sculptor); the statue is not *on* the stone (except in the case of intaglio). The statue is stone.

I am not this piece of flesh (though perhaps Falstaff was his); I am not in this flesh (though perhaps Christ was in his, but then his body was also bread); nor am I my flesh and blood (though somebody else is); nor am I of my flesh (though I hope somebody is). I am flesh.

Kant, if I understand, in the *Groundwork of the Metaphysics of Morals,* reverses the Aristotelian field and thus redirects the problem of connection. He regards the human being as a species of the genus of rational beings, to wit, the species that has the distinction of being animal, i.e., being embodied: the human being is the animal rational. Hence the human being is no longer the highest among creatures but the lowest among hosts. The direction to the human is not animation but incarnation. (The former sets Frankenstein's limitation; the latter Pygmalion's. Pygmalion overcame his limitation through desire and prayer; Frankenstein through craft and theft.) This results from, and serves, Kant's purpose, which is not to explain the fact of our freedom but to show the possibility of it, i.e., to vindicate our inescapable conviction of it; one might say: our attitude toward ourselves and others as possessing it. Being human is aspiring to being human. Since it is not aspiring to being the only human, it is an aspiration on behalf of others as well. Then we might say that being human is aspiring to being seen as human. This is a possible interpretation of Frankenstein and of Pygmalion. Their shared limitation is then that they could accept being seen only by their own creation. This still sounds as if their aspiration was to be God. But how is this aspiration different from that toward the human? The confusion seems inherent in the reception of Christianity. The message of the words of Christ, that we share a common nature, that we are flesh, seems consistently overshadowed by the message of the fact of Christ, that only a God, or the son of God, could bear being human.

Kant's image of the animal rational, demanding of itself the acknowledgment of others (Kant thinks of it as respect), and aspiring to be worthy of it in return, never knowing whether it is truly embodied, in oneself or others, is his continuation of the ancient interpretation of human separateness as a message of human incompleteness. What will complete the human work is, however, not one other but only all others. So to have an idea of the human being is to have an ideal of the human being; and for Kant this ideal entails, and is entailed by, an ideal of the human community. According to this ideal, love must not absorb respect and respect does not require love. Genuine love and genuine respect will both know this.

In asking whether there is such a thing as soul-blindness, I do not mean to insist that there are such things as souls, nor that anybody believes there are. But I do, I expect, mean to insist that we may sincerely and sanely not know whether we believe in such a thing, as we may not know whether we believe in God, or in idols. I assume further that one may believe, or protest, that there are souls and yet not know that there are human beings; for that knowledge would require believing that there are embodied souls, something incarnate. And I assume that some people may not believe, or not know, that there are human beings. It may seem that you could believe that the human body is the best picture of the human soul and yet deny that anything corresponds to the picture. My intuition is that this is false, that not to believe there is such a thing as the human soul is not to know what the human body is, what it is of, heir to.

Call the belief in the soul psychism. Then a serious psychology must take the risk of apsychism. It can no more tolerate the idea of another (little) man inside, in here, than a serious theology can tolerate the idea of another (large) man outside, up there. Nor of small or large anythings, call them spirits. What would these be but points or stretches of etherealized matter, without doubt unverifiable? And idolatrous besides. The spirit of the wind is neither smaller nor larger than the wind; and to say it is *in* the wind is simply to say that it exists only where there is a wind. If I say the spirit of the wind is the wind, I wish to be understood as telling you something not about a spirit but about the wind. (I claim to know nothing about spirits that you do not know.) On that understanding, then: The spirit of the body is the body. — Wittgenstein takes the risk of apsychism, the risk that his understanding of the human body (as, for example, a picture) is unnecessary, or insincere, or dead. If this is behaviorism in disguise then a statue is a stone in disguise.

Suppose what you think is that the soul does not exist. Your problem may be to discover how to get rid of it. First you must discover what happened to it. Nietzsche's travails can be said to be directed to such a task. In asking what happened to God, Nietzsche turns over large amounts of fairly unacceptable material. One had hoped that for the achievement of sanity a little madness would go far enough. But Nietzsche persists in turning up such an image of God as that of a riddled, bloody corpse whose open wounds we attempt to fill, i.e., deny, with knots of religion, which is to say, with fragments of Christian suffering, especially guilt (*Zarathustra*, "On Priests"). (Our *via negativa* begins with the infliction of those holes, or lacks, our tributes of unlikeness from ourselves; and ends with the filling of those holes so as to deny their presence.) The path of the soul in this biography is no longer upward; but since it cannot but aspire, it aspires downward. The soul and the body no longer fit. You might say that the soul has become disembodied, loose; but of course loose inside. It is a spirit, and not mine. For it to get outside I must be exorcised. You cannot see it, but you can hardly avoid noticing its effects. You can readily infer it. — I think I know persons for whom such issues really do not exist; pre-Christians as it were. But I know of almost no one who has *recovered* from them.

How could it happen that a statue and its stone no longer fit? You may ruin the statue by altering the stone slightly; you may not ruin the statue by altering the stone greatly. You cannot ruin the stone, except for certain purposes; you can also improve it for certain purposes. (Using it for a statue is not improving it.) If you destroy the stone, say pulverize it, you destroy the statue. You might just erase the statue, which was itself the erasing of the stone. You cannot hack a limb from a stone, except figuratively, or anthropomorphically; and if you hack something from a statue you may or may not produce a different statue. A statue in fragments — i.e., without intactness — may be poignant, but not horrifying. A statue may not (no longer) fit the place it is in. This compromises its intactness, imposes a false presence or animation upon it. But not everyone is to be expected to sense this. Surrealism depends upon a vigorous, even bourgeois, sense of appropriateness. This sense may be quite absent, as it were a thing of the past. At least one person in our culture rich enough to have at his disposal a museum's number of statues has them placed about his golf course. A wilderness of monics.

The statue has aspects. By walking around it, by the changing light, in your changing mood, the figure can be seen as vulnerable, as indomitable, as in repose, as if in readiness. A doll has occasions. I am thinking of a rag doll. It can be happy or sad, fed or punished. In repose it has aspects, for example it can be seen as sleeping or dead or sun-bathing. But only if you do not know which is true. — There is only one who knows which is true, the one whose doll it is. And that one cannot strictly be said to *know* it at all, except as a joke, or perhaps as a fiction. — Why not? Because he cannot be in doubt about his doll's (inner) state? Of course he can be in doubt. He might take her to a psychiatrist. You might think he could not be in doubt, or be mistaken, because anything *he* says about the doll *must* be true. But he might be lying about the doll's mood, either to test the genuineness of my interest, or to deprive me of a relationship with the doll. — No, but the point is that anything he *knows* about the doll must be true, whether he says what he knows or not, and whether he knows what he knows by observation or not. — But isn't that merely what it means to know? And the question remains whether he knows, or at all times must know.

There are criteria in terms of which I settle judgments about the (other's) doll. To know whether a concept applies I have to look — at the doll. I have to determine whether I can see it in this way, get that occasion for it to dawn for me. Otherwise I am only humoring the one whose doll it is. Perhaps I am tired, or have a headache; I cannot in any case experience the meaning of the words about the doll. The doll seems rags. I still know what a doll is; but at the moment I am doll-blind. Generally, if I care, I will have to justify my concept by continuing the doll's history: "I don't think she's really hungry. She got into the cookie jar earlier. See how sneaky she looks." I may scatter some crumbs on her dress to prove it, if there is something at hand I can use for crumbs. If I say "See. Now she's comfortable", something must have changed, or I must have done something, put a pillow under her head, or rearranged her so that she is no longer sitting on her foot. If the other, the one whose doll it is, tells me that she likes sitting on her foot — say because it makes her sit taller — and puts her back in her former attitude, then perhaps that is the end of this matter. At some point my say comes to an end. I defer to the one whose doll it is. If I do not, what then? Perhaps the doll becomes our scapegoat; cursed, and cast out.

When I defer to the one whose doll it is, do I defer to his greater power? Power to do what? I respect his relationship to the doll, its being his. This need not be a matter of recognizing his ownership of it. (I recognize his ownership by, for example, not taking the doll from him, not without due process.) I recognize his authority over the doll, his having the last word over it; hence I hold him responsible for it. The most this demands is that the doll be (regarded as) his to play with, for a while, in a particular place. Even if he owns it, his authority is not unlimited; there are still rules in this house. Whether it is better for him to own a doll, to have it for always rather than for a specified while, or until he decides to give it up, or whether it is better for him or for anyone to own anything for always, are empirical questions, or ought to be. (We seem to give children an idea that someone owns their bodies. How, otherwise, shall we explain their having the extraordinary idea of feeling guilty for hurting themselves, even when the game they were playing was not, apparently, forbidden; guilty even for becoming ill? It would then strike them as a declaration of their freedom to say that they own their *own* bodies. But this would merely be an escape from one conceptual cell; or from a dungeon into an enclosed yard. Some are told that their body is a temple. That seems to rule out ownership, except perhaps by a congregation. But it is otherwise a dangerously open idea, especially concerning the conditions for admission.)

Do I respect the doll? I may respect its feelings, lay it comfortably in a nice box before storing it for another generation. But it has no say, for example, about whether it *is* comfortable. It has no voice in its own history. It exists in limbo. — What is the doll? (I would like to answer that question because I feel I know absolutely everything there is to know about dolls. But I would like not to have to answer it since of course I know absolutely nothing about dolls that others do not know. So there is nothing to tell. But there may yet be something to say.) The doll is certainly not the form of the rags. Which form would it be? And if I say that the doll is the life of the rags, that must also be a remark about us, those of us who have a voice in its history. For me to be part of its life, I have to enter into its history, achieve the spirit in which concepts of life are applied to it.

Do I know more about dolls and statues than I know about human beings? That would be extraordinary, since after all I am a human being. Or perhaps not so extraordinary; dolls and statues are human products, so a human being could know everything that has gone into them. Nothing can look, feel, be broken and perhaps be mended like a doll that is not a doll. Nothing can look, feel, be broken and perhaps be restored like a statue that is not a statue. But presumably there can be something, or something can be imagined, that looks, feels, be broken and perhaps healed like a human being that is nevertheless not a human being. What are we imagining? It seems that we are back to the idea that something humanoid or anthropomorphic lacks something; that one could have all the characteristics of a human being *save one*.

What would fit this idea? How about a perfected automaton? They have been improved to such an extent that on more than one occasion their craftsman has had to force me to look inside one of them to convince me that it was not a real human being. — Am I imagining anything? If so, why this way? Why did I have to be forced? What did I see when I looked inside? (How) did that convince me?

Go back to a stage before perfection. I am strolling in the craftsman's garden with him and his friend. He is in his usual white laboratory coat, his friend is wearing gloves and a hat with its brim so low it almost covers his eyes. To make a long story short, the craftsman finally says, with no little air of pride: "We're making more progress than you think. Take my friend here. He's one." The craftsman offers his friend a seat on one of the wroughtiron benches and bids him relax. He leans back, crosses his legs, accepts a proffered cigarette with thanks. Then the craftsman raises his friend's left trouser leg and gives the leg a tap. It is undeniably metal. But so what? Then he asks his friend to remove his gloves. The hands turn out to be leathery or rubbery or something, anyway pretty obviously not real hands. But so what? So the friend has a metal leg and two prosthetic hands, and this is a terrible way to treat him; it is obscene; a striptease of misery. I do not wish to draw it out in much more detail. — It is clear enough that we may arrive at a conclusion that convinces me the friend is an automaton. The craftsman knocks the friend's hat off to reveal a manikin's head (with, as a joke, a couple of glass buttons for eyes) which he rotates through 360 degrees; he rips open the friend's shirt to reveal a chest of hammered brass which, prompted by the craftsman's prying knife inserted into an all but invisible seam running straight down from the pit of the arm, snaps off to reveal something like clockwork.

It is less clear, but still clear enough, that we may not arrive at a convincing conclusion. As the years go on, I am invited for a walk with the craftsman and his friends in their garden whenever there is a new development. The routine is always the same. I have seen the leg and the hands get progressively more lifelike until I almost no longer marvel at them. Today is special however; I can tell from the craftsman's nervous gestures and the suppressed eagerness of his voice that there has been some new breakthrough. . . . The brass chest snaps off and, to my horror, I see no clockwork, but, for all the world, the insides of a human being. Recoiled, aghast, I can hardly attend to the craftsman's delighted words: "Of course, it's far from perfect, and most of it is superficial fakery, especially the bones. The digestive and circulatory systems are not bad, but we have to do more work on the blood, which doesn't congeal in the normal temperature range. The immediate problem with the nervous system has to do with the relative response rates of the fibre systems. That is crudely put, of course. It's really a problem of their interaction. As matters stand, the pain-responses are too — how shall I say? — on and off. Don't you agree?" (He demonstrates by prodding the friend's left hand. The response is quick but definitely mechanical.) "We could simulate better responses, by, for example, making the limbs slightly more sluggish. But the genuine issue is how to get the pain itself so that it gets better prepared and fades better."

I can hardly look, and when I look I hardly know what to look at, or look for. As a matter of fact, I throw an anxious glance at the manikin face, expecting — I'm not sure. But it is reassuringly rigid, its crude eyes reassuringly glazed. I confess the thought does occur to me that I should check that head; or not so much the thought as the impulse occurs to see whether the head might not be just a shell, and inside it — what? A real head, or the insides of a real head, or stuff that looks like the real insides? The impulse fades as my trust reasserts itself. And I feel not a little foolish. What would it prove to look inside when I have *already* looked inside? — Am I foolish not to ask the craftsman what he means by "the pain itself"? But I took myself to understand him well enough. He meant, roughly, everything that happens between cause and effect, I mean between what went in from outside and what comes out from inside. Well, he may want to be more sophisticated than that and call the pain itself just what happens at the change of direction, the point of transfer between going in and coming out. I might have objected to this as follows: "There cannot be anything happening *between* a cause and its effect." Presumably I do not want to conclude that therefore there is nothing that *is* the pain. Then I must conclude that there is something wrong with this picture of causation. If there are "points of transfer", they must occur at *each* point. And a stimulus cannot set up a causal network. This must be in effect all the time. So what pain is is a change in the rate of transfer, or a change in the rate of change of direction. But if so, then that must be a way of representing all psychological phenomena. They must form a system. — But why am I thinking of this in relation to the craftsman? Have his activities put him in any better position for investigating these matters than I am in? I am more interested in learning whether he really wanted my agreement about the pain responses.

Time passes. One day the craftsman is quite beside himself with suppressed excitement. He insists that I pay special attention to each of our procedures. The leg and the hands are by now really astonishing. The movement of the legs crossing and of the cigarette being lit are simply amazing. I want to see it all again. And as for the voice, I would bet anything that no one could tell. So far I'm dazzled. Then the craftsman knocks off the hat to reveal what is for all the world a human head, intact. He rotates it through about 45 degrees and then stops himself with an embarrassed smile. The head turns back to its original position, but now its eyes turn toward mine. Then the knife is produced. As it approaches the friend's side, he suddenly leaps up, as if threatened, and starts grappling with the craftsman. They both grunt, and they are yelling. The friend is producing these words: "No more. It hurts. It hurts too much. I'm sick of being a human guinea pig, I mean a guinea pig human."

Do I intervene? On whose behalf? Let us *stipulate* that the friend is not a ringer, not someone drawn into these encounters from outside. — It is important to ask whether we *can* stipulate this. If we cannot, then it seems that the whole thing *must* simply be a science or a fairy tale. But if it were taken as science or fairy tale then we would not *have* to stipulate this. It would be accepted without question. — But only if it were a successful story. There are rules about these things. Suppose I had told my story leaving myself out and ending it with the friend yelling his words. Then I would have composed a primitive science fable whose moral has been drawn from a thousand better places: We are Frankensteins whose creations are meddlings with nature and will one day rise against us. No serious publication would take the story, but it is a complete one. If, however, I tell it as I have, with myself in it, and I add the question, "Do I intervene?", then the story is not complete. If I stop there, a sensible reader will be contemptuous at my incompetence; I do not know the rules. I have not given enough evidence to know whether, for example, the friend is a ringer, nor to make the sheer speculation an interesting one.

Let us try to complete it in such a way that the craftsman is shown to know that the friend is not a ringer. Then the friend is who, or what, the craftsman knows him to be. What does the craftsman know? Suppose, satisfied with the degree of my alarm, and my indecision about whether to intervene, the craftsman raises his arm and the friend thereupon ceases struggling, moves back to the bench, sits, crosses his legs, takes out a cigarette, lights and smokes it with evident pleasure, and is otherwise expressionless. (I may be having a little trouble with the rules of the fiction here. Could a being, for example a fictional being, evidence pleasure and be otherwise expressionless? How about otherwise impassive? That is prejudicial. A thing cannot be impassive unless that thing *can* have passions. Perhaps I should just omit "with evident pleasure".) The craftsman is happy: "We — I mean I — had you going, eh? Now you realize that the struggling — I mean the movements — and the words — I mean the vocables — of revolt were all built in. He is — I mean it is — meant — I mean designed — to do all that. Come, look here." He raises the knife again and moves toward the friend.

Do I intervene? That is, do I go on with the story? I can imagine only one interesting continuation (without adding more characters). It is one in which my interest shifts from the friend to the craftsman. I turn on him: "You fool! You've built in too much! You've built in the passions as well as the movements and the vocables of revolt! You've given this artificial body a real soul." (That is, a soul; there are no artificial souls —

none, anyway, that are not real souls.) Then the end may consist in our realization that this had to be.

Or it may go on with our investigating why it had to be. But then our problem is a conceptual one, and we will have to start telling one another new stories, or vying with one another for our pictures of the passions. In any case, I have learned that if something humanoid differs *in some respect* from a human being — that it has all the characteristics of a human being save one — that respect will not be something going on just inside, or just outside. This is why my interest shifts away from the friend. I can learn no more from him, anyway, no more about him by looking inside him. I know what I will see if I look.

Isn't this just an assumption, a particular interpretation of the story? Maybe the imitation insides, in the former story, were just virtuosity for the sake of virtuosity. They have been cleaned up in the new model. There is nothing there but acceptable strata and zones of silk-like and sponge-like substances and golden spun wire thinner than spider's threads. This is what the craftsman knows and he just wants to show me where the micro-computers and energy sources are placed. — Then I will insist that he show me this by using X-rays or diagrams, not a knife. — So then you are interested, after all, in what is going on inside him. — But not in order to settle whether the friend is a human being. This could be settled by *stipulating* that if I am shown a micro-computer or energy source inside then I am to conclude that he is not one. But this is arbitrary. Why stop there? A human being could contain such devices. Why go that far? If the ideas of silk and sponge and wire have not convinced me, why would any of these further accompaniments? — But if looking inside *might not* settle the question whether the friend is a human being, why isn't this more interesting than ever, or, if you like, more amazing than ever? And doesn't this at least suggest that we cannot *know* that another is sentient? — It may suggest what state someone is in who takes it this way.

For it is not I, at this stage of the story, who refuses to press for a settlement; it is the teller of the story, with me in it, who refuses to see that the story is incomplete. If I, in the story, am unsettled about the humanity or automatonity of the friend, it is only my subservience to the craftsman's view that would prompt me to look inside. Whatever doubts I have about the friend's insides I equally have, or should be permitted to have, about his outsides as well. Why, for example, does he have just five fingers on each hand; and why hands; and why toes instead of rollers; and why not eyes in the back of his head; and why, if it is, is his "sense" of "hearing" restricted to the human — I mean, roughly to *my* — range? (What would count as his being hard of hearing, or deaf?) Isn't *this* all virtuosity just for virtuosity's sake? It corrupts the craftsman's craft. Form should picture function.

How far can my subservience to the craftsman extend? Suppose I have trained myself to think of the friend as having not feelings but "feelings". (Cp. Hilary Putnam, "Robots: Machines or . . . ?".) Which means that I have trained myself to show him, for example, not sympathy but "sympathy"; and perhaps learned not to be impatient with him if I think he is complaining too much — I mean of course "complaining" too much, and "impatient" with him ("him"). Then one day, my back turned, the friend grabs my arm ("grabs"?), wheels me around, and the craftsman approaches me with his knife. "So," he says, "you have accommodated yourself to the friend, have you? You have learned how to treat him. Your attitude towards him is your attitude towards a 'soul', is it? You hedge his soul, do you?" Then he rips open my shirt and snaps off my chest to reveal (I glance down) some elegant clockwork. You cannot imagine my surprise. — Can I? I can imagine either of two conclusions the craftsman may wish me to draw from this demonstration that I am not, for all I know, in any better position, soul-wise or body-wise, than the friend. One is: For all I know, all I have are, for example, "pains". The other is: For all I know, the friend has, for example, *pains.*

To accept the latter conclusion is to accept the friend as an other, a fellow sufferer, unhedged. In what would acceptance consist? The craftsman continues: "Does he have pain, is he subject to pain, or not? Decide!" But even with the knife pointed at me I cannot decide. Before, when the craftsman asked for my agreement, I was in a position to decide something, there was room for me to have a say, and there was the same room for the craftsman. But now I am being asked whether I do or do not share the life of suffering with this other, and at the same time I am shown that I do not know whether I am observing or leading that life. Has the craftsman given up *his* say, granted the friend autonomy? If he told me that he had, could I believe him? I understand him no better than I understand the friend. If what the craftsman says is that he has decided that the friend suffers, or decided to say so, then who is hedging?

To settle upon the former conclusion — that for all I know all I have are "pains" — I would presumably have to give up the idea that I am, and know that I am, a human being. Could I conceive of myself as something *less* than a human, on a par with whatever it was I was conceiving the friend to be? If this is what I am, and I know it, then this is doubtless my secret. Why did I not think that the friend might be harboring such a secret? Perhaps because I did not think of him as a *lapsed* human. If he has such a secret, he could never tell it to me, for I could understand it no better than I can understand him: he is private to me.

But this is ridiculous. He has no comparison at his disposal. Whatever painish thing he has, he thinks of it as *pain*. Then how am I different? Well, he may not have a painish thing at all, let alone think anything about its status. Whereas I certainly have, and do. I feel for example, abashed by the recent revelation concerning my body. And what *I* feel, when I feel abashed, *is* what feeling abashed is. That is not a very persuasive definition. But I do not mean it to preclude others from feeling it too. I just mean to assure myself that no one is in a better position to know what feeling abashed or feeling pain is than I am.

How would I know if another is in fact equally well placed? If I think my feeling is somehow connected to this machinery and other stuff under me, into whose works I happen to have fallen, then I might think that the friend's feeling would similarly be connected to his stuff, if he had the feeling. But of course I could not be sure. I am certain that my abashment comes from this body — not because it causes it (though it may) but because it is its object, it is that in the face of which I am abashed. But again the friend may not feel this way about his body; he may enjoy it, as Thoreau did his set of false teeth. Any inference from his body to him therefore amounts to a sheer guess. It is not that all I have to go on in making this inference is just one case (mine); it is that I cannot use even that case; I do not know if it enters in. (Of course what I know of myself and take myself for enters utterly into what I can know of another and take him for. Only the idea that the other is *analogous* to me fails to bring out how I enter in.)

Instead of settling for a guess, I may fix my attention on the body of the other as upon his or her entrails and find myself transfixed with the conviction that he or she is besouled. I have divined it; I have penetrated the veil of the other by taking his body as an omen, in this case a good omen, of a soul. If others credit my gift generally, I will be set up as a seer and soothsayer. Regarding a seer and soothsayer as "the one who knows" (i.e., sees and says) the state of another would be an intellectually more coherent response to skeptical doubt than regarding the other as the one who alone knows the state of himself. If the statement that the other has what I have, i.e., has sentience, is a hypothesis, then it may have either of two outcomes. If the one about whom the hypothesis is made is the only one who knows the outcome, this is not only uncheckable, but depends upon a *comparison* of what the other knows with what I know, and there *could* be nobody to make the comparison. Anyway *he* could not and *I* could not.

Here is a further alternative. I from time to time find that I have intuitions about the state of the friend. Usually I have an intuition of his pain when his body is contorted, sometimes not. He cannot *volunteer* news of his condition to me, because then I would have to believe him, and that I cannot do. (Or will not do, because I regard such beliefs as superstitions: they can never be checked.) Nor can he *show* me how it is with him, because all he could do to show me, for example that he is in pain, would be, for example, to contort his body, or point at it; and such things may or may not produce my intuition of his pain. (If someone were such that he constantly had intuitions about all the others he knew, he would go mad. Only God could bear to be God. An understanding of the first commandment.) Suppose the friend and I prove to be mutually intuitive, with a normally expected range of failures in our intuitions. The most plausible theory of ourselves would be that we are pure minds, unextended beings. (It would be nonsense to imagine that we might be one another, and hence "feel what the other feels". For I am characterized by nothing but being the one I am; and the same goes for him.) The bodies associated with each of us are enormously convenient to have; they make us visible and audible to one another. Well, strictly speaking *I* (and of course *he*) are not made visible and audible; but the bodies are necessary to prompt the intuitions we have of one another. (We might have philosophical disputes about whether we are immortal, whether we could survive unassociated with a body, hence without the possibility of being intuited by our own kind. But we may not be interested in the question. What happens to us at the death of the body is what happens to the music when the music concludes. There is a period of reverberation, and then nothing.)

Suppose one day I notice that my feelings have become uniformly associated with what is happening to my body, that, for example, I always have a pain when my body contorts and never otherwise, or almost never; or I may notice that my intuitions about the friend's pain come over me only when his body contorts, almost never otherwise, and he almost always confirms the intuition, i.e., I find I take his word. I may then no longer regard the body as something with which I and he are each associated, something we each "have", but something we each of us *have*. The most plausible theory about us now is that we are human beings. The analogy between us is now excellent. I can check on his feelings by expressing my intuitions (for his confirmation or disconfirmation); and it makes sense to check on the connection between his body and his feelings because it makes sense to check on the connection between mine and mine. One day it occurs to me that I no longer understand what it means to check this. If I have a pain, there *must* be a cause; if I do not, where I ought to have, then there must be a cause for *that*. Doubt about whether I have a body is out of the question. Doubt about whether he has a body is also out of the question, unless my intuitions about him cease. Then I may think that to say I *have* a body does not go deep enough in expressing my connection with it. I would prefer to say that I *am* my body, even though I am satisfied that I am not. I do not know that I am not my body, as though I know that it is false to say that I am. It is rather that to say so falsifies my convictions on the matter; my body is not what I take myself to be. — That is because one does not *take* oneself to *be* anything. — Then what is the point of telling me what I am? It is, analogously, not false to say that I *have* a body, unless that suggests, for example, that I might not have one, as I might not have a left arm. If I say that I necessarily have a body, I am leaving out my relation to *this* one. And if I say I necessarily have *this* body, then I am not sure I believe it, not at any rate as I believe that I do have this one.

It may be that the sense of falsification comes from the way I understand the phrase "have a body". It is really a mythological way of saying that I am flesh. But I am not satisfied with this myth, for it implies that I also have something other than a body, call it a soul. Now I have three things to put together: a body, a soul, and me. (So there are four things to be placed: I plus those three.) But I no more *have* a soul than I have a body. That is what I say here and now. People who say they have a soul sometimes militantly take its possession as a point of pride, for instance William Ernest Henley and G. B. Shaw. Take the phrase "have a soul" as a mythological way of saying that I am spirit. If the body individuates flesh and spirit, singles me out, what does the soul do? It binds me to others.

I do not think, whenever I look upon, or think of, the naked human body, "How right it is that the parts and features of the body are all just where they are!". I may of course from time to time be *struck* by this fact. I may also from time to time be struck not by the rightness but by the dumb fortune, or irony, of certain placements of the parts and features of the body, as Yeats was, for example, by love's having pitched its mansion in the place of excrement. This anatomical fact is something Freud found a natural, incorrigible limitation upon the purity or satisfaction of desire. (It is a fact he emphasized from almost before the beginning. Cf. *The Origins of Psycho-Analysis,* p. 147.) Certainly any changes I can dream of in the arrangement strike me as quite insane. It is so human a fortune. Not the fact of it is so human; the fact is shared by other animals. What is so human is that we share the fact with other animals, that animals are also our others. That we are animals. Being struck by this is something one might call "seeing us as human". It is a feeling of wonder.

Amazement was my response, my natural response, when I *knew* the friend was an automaton. "I can't get over it", I kept wanting to exclaim. The peculiar thrill in watching its routines never seems to fade. But if I cannot get past my doubt that this friend is an automaton, and past holding the doubt in reserve, then I am not amazed, except the way I may be amazed at the capacities of a human being, say at someone's stupidity or forbearance or skill. The craftsman lost his power over me when I saw that his own powers had run out. Whatever test he can impose upon the friend to show its failure of humankindness — the placement of a micro-mechanism; a mismatch of emotional reaction; the fact that it can be starved for forty days without weight loss; its ability to run a four minute mile, mile after mile — any of this can be corrected (or hidden?) by a super-craftsman, perhaps by this craftsman next year, in the normal course of technological progress. Whatever can be specified, as a test of automatonity, can be built in to fail. Criteria come to an end.

Would it make any difference now if we were testing for humanity? If I am inclined to believe that this humanish something is a human being, then any lack I can be prepared to find I must be prepared not to find. So this inclination either comes to nothing, or else it is to be settled empirically. But what if it does not get settled?

It is true that we do not now in fact open up putative human beings to find out if they are genuinely human, I mean human *beings.* And couldn't it be true, as a further matter of fact, that some of them are not beings, but automata? My argument against opening any of them up is as follows: Either the proportion of automata among putative humans is roughly half or else it is smaller or greater than half. If it is roughly half, then in opening one of them up we run roughly a fifty-fifty risk of killing someone, anyway of subjecting him to something our relationship will not survive; if the proportion is smaller, the risk is higher but the stakes are lower — I can absorb a certain degree of error; if the proportion is greater, the risk is lower but the stakes are higher — the fewer the real human beings the more precious they are. If only I can just discover which ones they are! Or if only someone could tell me what the exact proportion is! The thing to do, accordingly, is to become very cautious whom you take up with, and to devise ever subtler forms of test. In such a world the advice of a Polonius would be unanswerable.

But can I take it that as a matter of fact some proportion of the population is made up of automata? Isn't this counter to my stories which suggested that, as I would like to put it, my attitude toward an automaton (or toward the discovery of automatonity) is one of amazement? — Not necessarily. To take the presence of automata as a fact is to be *prepared* for amazement. — But that is the problem. If I am prepared, at any and all times, for amazement, then at any and all times I am not prepared for humanity. My attitude toward no one is my attitude toward a soul. — So the possibility, which I cannot, or ought not, rule out, that some human somethings are not human beings, is enough to seal out humanity for me altogether? But why should not an enlightened Polonius accuse me of faintheartedness? His advice is: Treat every putative human as a human being. Conquer your preparation for amazement. Get their human aspect to dawn on you, so that you see them as humans. Treat humankind, anyway humanlikeness, always as an end never merely as a means. Polonius calls this, and similar things, his Sterling Rule.

Why is this advice chilling? It isn't that I could not live down to it. But it is the advice I would expect of a perfected automaton. — Suppose I do conquer my preparation for amazement. Nevertheless I still worry that some I count among humankind are not human beings. And now I am not satisfied to say that this means that these non-beings or non-human beings may *exhibit* feelings without actually *having* feelings, because this is true of the human beings among humankind. And I have already conceded that the doubtfully human among them have feelings, or rather "have" "feelings". I would rather say that in the case of the non-humans there is no difference between the exhibiting and the having. To suppose that the non-humans may have feelings that they do not exhibit (*and* do not suppress the exhibition of, which would simply be a special case of exhibition) is mere mystification. Of course the exhibiting of suppression may be hidden from me since it may go on entirely inside. (I am, for simplicity, just assuming that nothing counts as giving the non-humans an analgesic.) Having/exhibiting feelings is, for them, on a par with drinking, showing their thirst being quenched, urinating, . . . Do they (only) "drink" or do they (really) *drink?* Whatever they do they do, there is no quarrelling with them (unless they happen to have "quarrelling" in their repertoire). One who studies them to find out what they do is not a behaviorist, unless one who studies the behavior of the stock market, and one who studies the behavior of metals under extreme temperatures, are behaviorists. If I could find that one among the non-humans showed an obsession with the problem of other minds — I mean other automata, or other zombies . . . — then I might study it in order to learn whether it could survive certain versions of skepticism, or grief.

My strolls in the craftsman's garden tended to show that I cannot accept something as "like" a human being and at the same time regard the thing as lacking in an essential feature of the human being, call it sentience. Or, that to the extent that I regard something as analogous to me, I regard that thing as having (something analogous to my) sentience. To have a "body" like mine, or to "have" a body as I have one, is to be subjected to it, to be the subject of it. If what I had wanted to show is that a machine can have sentience, then I need not have cast my Outsider as a craftsman at all. We would have just begun with the (perfected) human body. *It* can be taken as a machine, seen so. And within the vision of the human body as a machine, a machine can feel. (". . . It can be conscious or unconscious; it sees, is blind; . . ." A machine has nothing special to do with pain. Build me one that can scan, peer, stare, glance. . . .) But to take the human body as a machine is as much, or little, a vision of humanity as the vision that takes the body to be inhabited by something *else*. (What has the schizophrenic learned about us?)

— But surely even within the vision of the human body as a machine, it is not a machine the way a *machine* is a machine? — Does this mean that a machine *cannot,* for example, peer or glance or stare? And is this a definition? A stipulation? It is presumably not an empirical discovery — as though the having of some region of sentience has been found to be beyond the machine's capacities; as though piling sentience on top of its other functions somehow overloads it. — A machine that is truly a machine *does* not have sentience. — But a human being just does? And is *this* a definition? It seems equally far from an empirical discovery. — This is a familiar impasse. We should not have accepted the vision of a machine's having a region of sentience in the first place, because: "If the human body is a machine then a machine has sentience" is no better an inference than "If the human body is a machine then the body does not have sentience". — But all I wanted to say is that it is no *worse* an inference, that the issue of other minds is not settled by whether or not we take the human body as a machine. — But it is not an inference at all. It is the result of absent logic. Like: "If I were a frog then I would like eating flies" and "If a frog were me then some frog would not like eating flies."

Picking up Bergson's idea of the comic as the encrusting or the obtruding of the mechanical or material onto or out of the living, we might conceive of laughter as the natural response to automatonity when we *know* the other to be human. This takes laughter as some reverse of amazement. In that case it would follow from the absence of our laughter in the face of the impression or imagination of automatonity in others that we do not know others to be human. — Further paths beckon from here. We might follow out an idea that the form I have given skepticism is, according to these recent reflections, a comic one: natural, inescapable progressions of argument are shown to be encrusted with unnatural, inevitable origins. (The comic crescendo of flailings of one about to slip on a field of ice are the antics precisely of one for whom walking and running and dancing are in his natural repertory, and who is using just that repertory, there is no other, to try to regain his balance and find his footing.) That we do not laugh at our philosophical flailings may go to show how high the seas of pedantry run. For whom are we supposed to pick out to laugh at? (This path must eventually cross the path of philosophical irony.) And we should sometime follow out the cause of laughter inherent in the procedures of ordinary language philosophy, a cause exemplified amply, and differently, in Austin and in Wittgenstein. For example, my treatment of the interlocutor's "But there is *something* there all the same accompanying my cry of pain" was, I hope evidently, intended to bring out the comedy as well as the madness of it. And thereby to suggest that the perception of the comedy is essential to, is the same as, the detection of the madness. You could say that laughter in these matters is the touchstone of the unnatural, where unnatural is the opposite of that naturalness in language the ordinary language philosopher reckons with. (The opposite is not, e.g., the artificial, as champions of artificial languages (used to?) suppose. Cf. "Must We Mean What We Say?", p. 42.) I do not so much wish to say that the absence of laughter is a good sign of the presence of the natural (the absence may result from a corrupted sensibility) as that the natural is what, at best, laughter is able to perceive and to achieve. (Think of it as functioning, as in tuning a violin, like throwing a string crudely below pitch in order to magnify, to make perceptible, the exact coincidence of its finding its point a perfect fifth from its neighbor (as you twist the peg home).) The idea of the natural here is not at odds with, but rather meets, the idea of the sociable. This meeting of the natural and the sociable is something comic writers preach, knowing also, something that writers of tragedy see, that the human being is apt, is fit, to be neither.

What is the nature of the worry, if it is a real one, that there may at any human place be things that one cannot tell from human beings? Is it a blow to one's intellectual pride, as in the case of skepticism about the existence of material objects? Or is it an embarrassment of one's humanity?

What would this embarrassment be? — Obviously, that I will, for example, call forth pity, from myself or from the other, when that other is not a human being. — But this would be an embarrassment only if someone knew, better than I, the facts of the case. And could anyone? Could anyone be in a better position for knowing than I am? I have already ruled out the craftsman for such a role; he cannot see to the end of his work. Here I feel: One who knows better than I would have to be free of human nature. God, for example. But if God is in question, then why the embarrassment? The spectacle of my comforting and being comforted by a non-being might just make God tenderer; he might grant it human life. If I am imagining laughter and scorn in response to the spectacle, then I have an idea not of God but of an Evil Demon, or rather of God as an Evil Demon.

Can a human being be free of human nature? (The doctrine of Original Sin can be taken as a reminder that, with one or rather with two exceptions humankind cannot be thus free. Yet Saint Paul asks us to put off our (old) nature. What is repellent in Christianity is the *way* it seems to imagine both our necessary bondage to human nature and our possible freedom from it. In this, Nietzsche seems to me right, even less crazy than Christianity. But he persists in believing both that humankind must get free of human nature *and* that the human being cannot be free of human nature. Hence the logic of his advice to escape this dilemma of our humanity by overcoming our human nature. I hope he was wrong in this persistence, even though his prediction seems accurately enough to be coming true, that we will, apart from his advice, overcome ourselves nihilistically, solve the dilemma of our humanity by becoming monsters.)

If I try to imagine just some unspecified Outsider, what can he tell me? He is a poor relation of the Outsider we fantasize in thinking of the related moment in the skeptical problem of the external world. There, for example, we have criticized Locke for saying that ideas are "copies" of things: if all we *can* ever have in our heads are "ideas", then of course we *cannot* brush ideas aside, or stand, as it were, orthogonally to them, and thus be able to *compare* them with the things they are "of"; there may just be no such things at all, for all we know. On this picture it seems easy, perhaps inevitable, to imagine that though *we* cannot be beyond our ideas, an Outsider could be, would be. And if we then knew what we imagine the powers of the Outsider to be, we might learn something of what we imagine human knowledge to be, in particular what we imagine the nature of "the senses" to be. The same goes for determining whether we may now be dreaming. Convinced that *we* cannot determine it, I am convinced that an Outsider could, must. (I am half speaking as an Outsider in so much as imagining our predicament.) But the case of the Outsider with respect to me and other minds is another matter. What I have to imagine him to know is not merely *whether* a given other is a being or not, but to know something I do not know about how to tell, about what the difference is between human beings and non-human beings or human non-beings. I do not expect the Outsider with respect to me and the external world to know something I do not know about the difference between sleeping and waking, or about whether one thing is a copy of another.

How might I conceive of an Outsider to me and other minds? He may or may not see a difference among all the occupants of human places. If he tells me that he does not, and I believe him, would I be convinced that my worries can come to an end, that there are no human places occupied by things other than humans? It depends on what he thinks the occupants are. He may think there is no difference among the occupants because he regards them all as automata, or androids, or apes. Or he may think that there is a difference, but the difference turns on their excellence as automata, or androids, or apes. (These are my translations of what he may have in mind. Really to characterize him, my words will require an anagogic interpretation.) One strain among them is so special that he sets them apart, as if for study. He is positively fascinated by them. Suppose it turns out that these are roughly the ones I am inclined to say are humans; his sorting is roughly extensionally equivalent to mine. Is this reassuring? — But now everything depends on how he sorts me, what he thinks *I* am. And that is not the question I imagined myself to invoke him in order to answer. With that question, my interest in the status of others vanishes. There is only me and the Outsider.

But if the coherence in imagining the Outsider with respect to me and the external world turns on his being invoked just to tell an antecedently clear difference or to make an antecedently clear comparison, then suppose I invoke an Outsider with respect to me and other minds just to make a comparison between, say, what I feel when I say I feel pain and what others feel when they say so, and between what I see when I say I see red and what others see when they say so. A difference emerges in these two cases. If the Outsider discovers that what we see when we each say we see red is not the same, then it seems to make sense to ask which of us is right. I can tolerate the idea that the other might be right because I can tolerate the idea that neither of us is. But if I and the other do not feel the same when we sincerely exhibit pain, I cannot tolerate the idea that the other might be right and I not. What I feel, when I feel pain, is pain. So I am putting a restriction on what the Outsider can know. He can know something about another's pain that I cannot know, but not something about mine. He is not really an Outsider to me. If he exists, he is in me.

The role of Outsider might be played, say in a horror movie, by a dog, mankind's best friend. Then the dog allegorizes the escape from human nature (required in order to know of the existence of others) in such a way that we see the requirement is not necessarily for greater (super-human) intelligence. The dog sniffs something, a difference, something is in the air. And it is important that we do not regard the dog as honest; merely as without decision in the matter. He is obeying his nature, as he always does, must. (I can envy him this; it is only human to.) I do not expect that horror movies really cause *horror,* but, at best, "horror". But I also do not know that I know the difference. I do not suppose that what I have, when I am horrified, *is* horror; it may only be "horror". — What is the object of horror? At what do we tremble in this way? Fear is of danger; terror is of violence, of the violence I might do or that might be done me. I can be terrified of thunder, but not horrified by it. And isn't it the case that not the human horrifies me, but the inhuman, the monstrous? Very well. But only what is human can be inhuman. — Can only the human be monstrous? If something is monstrous, and we do not believe that there are monsters, then only the human is a candidate for the monstrous.

If only humans feel horror (if the capacity to feel horror is a development of the specifically human biological inheritance), then maybe it is a response specifically to being human. To what, specifically, about being human? Horror is the title I am giving to the perception of the precariousness of human identity, to the perception that it may be lost or invaded, that we may be, or may become, something other than we are, or take ourselves for; that our origins as human beings need accounting for, and are unaccountable. (One way of accounting for the capacity for horror would be to find that the idea, or surmise, that human beings have evolved from lower life is an ancient surmise, together with the perception that this evolution was absolutely contingent, hence unassured; which means that some who occupy human places may not have made it to the human status, and that some may fall back to an earlier stage. If horror is (also) the reaction to the violation of taboo, say at the fact of incest or of cannibalism, then we must think of the connection between the biological capacity and the social necessity. It suggests itself that these social violations have the force of casting the offender not merely out of this society but outside the human race altogether, as though violation is not of our laws alone, which define our social order, but of the laws that allow human society to exist at all; that, so to speak, raise human relations from an existence in nature. It may be that the violation, if survived and expiated, removes the offender from human nature upward, allows his pure spiritualization rather than his pure corporealization, or rather animalization; as presumably in the case, say, of Oedipus; allows the choosing of the other of the two natures of the human, the unique and precarious combination of which creates the problem.)

When the development of reason started producing explanations for the occurrence of religion, say as motivated by fear, then it was comparatively easy to imagine that the human race would one day overcome this fear, as if it were a product of the childishness of the race. But suppose that what motivates religion is (also) horror, a response not to the powers and uncertainties of nature but to the powers and uncertainties of others not wholly unlike oneself, so that the promise of religion is not the maintainance of one's existence but the survival of one's intactness. A source of evidence for this might appear in a reconsideration of the response to classical tragedy. We are more or less accustomed to think of this response as made up of pity and terror, as if what we witness is the subjection of the human being to states of violence, to one's own and to others; for example, terror at the causes and consequences of human rage, jealousy, ambition, pride, self-ignorance. . . . But suppose that there is a mode of tragedy in which what we witness is the subjection of the human being to states of violation, a perception that not merely human law but human nature itself can be abrogated. The outcast is a figure of pity and horror; different from ourselves, and not different. The particular mysteriousness in Hamlet's motivation may be our persisting in looking through his events for an object of terror. We should try looking at him as a figure of horror to himself.

When the Outsider was unrestricted in what he could reveal to me about myself (when my status as a human being was open to him to pass upon), he was too outside. When he is restricted in what he can reveal (when I determine what is and is not open to him to pass upon), he is not outside enough. — So doesn't this dilemma show that there was no intelligible worry about some unspecifiable "difference" between human beings and non-beings? The worry again comes to nothing. — It suggests, it seems to me, that if there is a worry it is not a skeptical worry, not something beyond the field of everyday life.

The little apparent dilemma about the outsideness of the Outsider itself outlines a procedure for pressing its suggestion further. Recognizing that the figure of the Outsider is prompted naturally, even inevitably, in the Cartesian format in which I have cast the recital of skeptical doubt, let us go back to the idea of such a recital with an eye toward isolating features of it that may help to account for a failure to convince oneself that skepticism with respect to others is, or can be, produced along the lines that produced skepticism with respect to the external world.

Let us set up a context for knowing others that has at least the realism of the skeptic's context for knowing material objects, and one that attempts to incorporate at least certain features of the skeptic's "best case" for knowing objects, a feature we take to be essential to the skeptical result. We were not satisfied that we had such a case at our disposal when the topic came up in our initial attempt to thematize the reasonableness of the skeptic's considerations (Chapter VI, the concluding section, entitled "A Further Problem"). And let us, further, incorporate the feature of the recital in which we confront the object in question, and the feature of our announcing this confrontation publicly. (These last two features come up insistently in Moore's demonstration with the envelope held up for all to see. They are notably absent from Descartes's meditation while in his dressing gown, seated before his fire, in which he is alone and in which, as befits the influence of a private fire, he is already in semi-reverie.) It might proceed as follows.

"Among the things we claim to know the existence of, some are human beings (and other creatures, but we can omit them for convenience). And we claim to know very particular things about particular human beings, for example that they are in pain or angry. Each of you here in this room would certainly say you know that there are now other human beings in this room with you. [It would be possible here to raise the question "But what do you really know?", thus prompting a general appeal to the senses, which will, as in the case of material objects, fail. But this question, raised at *this* point, is likely to fragment the group, since it is not necessarily the case that *all* anyone now knows about any other is something he or she can here and now divine, i.e., sense. This at a minimum assumes that the members of the group are all strangers. To impose this condition on this story would seem arbitrary, not to say prejudicial on behalf of the argument. At any rate, let us for the moment consider a different line of continuation.]

"And I, for one, am prepared to say I know that no one of you — you, for instance — is now in excruciating pain. But how do I know this? For all I know, you may be. But if I imagine that you are in excruciating pain then naturally I must imagine that you are keeping it from me, suppressing its manifestations. If you are successful in this, then everything would seem to me just as it does now, that you are calm, and attentive to what I am saying (or, of course, perhaps bored by it and keeping *that* from me [pause for laughter]). But to be able to imagine that you are in excruciating pain only if you are keeping it from me is to imagine that even though *I* do not know of your pain, *you* certainly know. And this is to imagine, or rather assume, that you have sentience, or rather consciousness, or rather self-consciousness, as I have; that you are, as I am, a human being; that I have correctly identified you as a human being. What justifies this assumption? I do not impose an analogous assumption in claiming to know of the existence and qualities of tables and chairs and bits or cliffs of chalk, an assumption that if I am right in claiming them to exist then I am right in my identification of them as material (vs. immaterial); or rather this assumption plays a different role with respect to material objects (a point to which I shall recur in a moment). With material objects, all I claim, or assume, is that I *see* them, see *them*. It is the most natural assumption in the world. So where does the assumption come from according to which I must have correctly identified you as a human being? From some such fact as that my identification of you as a human being is not merely an identification *of* you but *with* you. This is something more than merely *seeing* you. Call it empathic projection. (At a comparable moment in recitals concerning material objects we find philosophers needing to characterize something *less* than seeing, anyway less than seeing an object, since even if there is no object present there is *something* indubitably visible. Some will then name a new object of sight, say sense-data; others will then say that there are two senses of 'see'. Empathic projection is at least as well defined an idea as these.)

"Now: Couldn't I be wrong? Not wrong merely in the way I can be wrong about claiming to know that there are objects on the basis of sensing them (i.e., wrong because I am dreaming or hallucinating them, which of course *could* happen with 'others' as well, say with Banquo), but wrong in a special way. I could be empathically projecting and there be nothing (of the right kind) empathically to project with, or rather upon. You might, for all I know, be a mutation, or a perfected automaton, or an android, or a golem, or some other species of alien. To recur to a point I left a moment ago, if I find that for all I know some material object may be other than it seems to be (say a counterfeit of the real thing), I do not thereupon suppose that I can never, in other circumstances, find that out. But how could I ever find out that you are not an automaton or an android, etc., a counterfeit human being? [Here we will perhaps want a walk or two with the craftsman in his garden, to get rid of the idea that looking inside will settle the matter.] I do not of course say that there *are* humanish things other than human beings, much less say that *you* are one. But is it irrational to imagine that there are, and that you are one, and to imagine this here and now, in the presence of my own empathic projection, which is the ultimate basis for knowing of your existence as a human being, a fellow being, and in circumstances as good as any I can be in, one in which I am confronting you?"

If I have made this recital, if academic, sufficiently accurate and forceful, then I would not have to accept the reply: *"Of course* it is irrational to believe, or even to imagine, that there are human non-beings! It is a paradigm case of irrationality; it is positively medieval! You might as well doubt that witch trials were the product of irrationality!" By "not having to accept this reply" I mean only that I would not have to accept it, or something like it, as conclusive. I might ask how it is that we have recovered from such outbreaks of irrationality, which dot the religious history, i.e., the history, of the Judeo-Christian world. Has it happened through the advent of modern science? But this only means that the scientifically-minded do not consider (I do not say that they fail to consider) that there may be such human non-beings. There is no room for such things in the new world-picture. (The *very* modern-minded among us might newly consider that there are such things — not, perhaps, witches, but aliens of another kidney. The advent of science may, in certain cases, have merely provided new shapes for irrationality. But such persons among us will doubtless newly consider, as well, and enjoy the fact, that we may at any and all times be hallucinating or dreaming.) — And this is enough for my purposes. For it is as much as to say: My imagining you to be something other than a human being is as irrational (has the same irrationality) as my imagining that there are such things for you to be; I am as convinced that you are a human being as I am that there is nothing else for you to be; the one is as certain as the other. But it seems to me part of my common sense of the matter that, if I know you for a human being, I must be *far* more certain of that fact than I am of the fact that there is nothing else for you to be. I had not dreamt that my conviction in your existence depended upon my being scientifically-minded, or anyway enlightened. Did people not *know* of the existence of others until the advent of science — even people who believed that *some* others were witches or werewolves? (Science is no better or worse a justification for my conviction in the existence of objects. For if I rely on science to tell me whether there are tables and chairs and bits or cliffs of chalk, then I must expect it to inform me that there are not, not really.)

Then what is the moral of the recital? On the one hand it seems to me that something of the sort recited must be true; not perhaps that there just may be other things for you to be, but that my taking you for, seeing you as, human depends upon nothing more than my capacity for something like empathic projection, and that if this is true then I must settle upon the validity of my projection from within my present condition, from within, so to speak, my confinement from you. For there would be no way for me to step outside my projections. On the other hand I feel that the other, some other, can still tell me of, or show me, his or her existence; that he or she will be able to step outside their confinement from me. For the others in the room did not vanish in relevance upon my realizing that the one whom I had singled out for my attention could not be known for a human being apart from my empathic projection, as the rest of the objects in my visual field vanish in relevance upon my realizing that I do not see the object I have singled out for my attention, hence do not know its existence, if I am dreaming or hallucinating. I do not, that is to say, know whether to take it that I can never be certain of the existence of others on the basis of my empathic projection with them, or not so to take it.

Maybe the recital has not yet reached its conclusion. Take this continuation: "Obviously you can never be certain that other human beings exist, for any one you single out may, for all you know, be something other than you imagine, perhaps a human, probably a human if you like, but possibly a mutation, and just possibly an automaton, a zombie, an android, an angel, an alien of some unheard of kidney. The world is what it is. And whatever it is, so far as you take it as inhabited by candidates for the human, you are empathically projecting. This means that you cannot rule out the non-human (or human non-being) possibility. It no more makes sense to suppose that in *certain* cases the projection may, as it were, be veridical, or justified, than it would make sense to suppose, if you are dreaming or hallucinating, that in certain cases the dream or hallucination is veridical, or justified, on the ground that when you see or would say (loosely) that you see, or seem to see, a roundish ruddy-looking somewhat, a real apple just may be *just there*. The speculation is empty. There is no *there* for you, where objects are. There are no individual exits from the world of objects into your dream. There are no individual marks or features by virtue of which you can pick out the real from the unreal. Criteria come to an end. Hallucination and dreaming happen all at once, seamlessly; they are world-creating, hence they are world-depriving. So is the empathic projection of otherness."

I find that I do not accept this idea of the seamlessness of projection. But why not, since whether I accept the (independent; non-projected) existence of other minds seems more deeply up to me, to my attitudes and sensibility, than whether I accept the (independent; non-hallucinated) existence of material objects? What is the worst that befalls me should it be the case that material objects do not exist? I suffer a generalized *trompe l'oeil,* and of course *trompe l'oreille* as well, and so on; my senses (and what they sense?) cheat me (naturally cheat me) into taking it that there are things where there are only interpreted sensings. It is a biological demand. But if there are no other human beings, then what befalls me is a generalized and massive *trompe l'ame;* my soul (and what it wishes?) cheats me (supernaturally cheats me) into taking it that it has company. It is a spiritual demand. And couldn't the demand go unmet?

If it can, the skeptical recital has, so far at least, not shown that it can, or how it can, nor what the nature of the demand is. There is, that is to say, a good reason for my not simply sensing or realizing, upon the recital, that its moral is that I can never know. The reason is, partly, that, even granting something warranting the title of empathic projection, the recital has given no *alternative* to this feat of human cognition. It came up as simply the way in which, or the basis upon which, I do in fact know of the existence of others. There is so far no reason to doubt that I *am,* at all or most times, (correctly) projecting empathically, *if* that is to say, I have acquired the feat. All that has been suggested is that I may sometimes be wrong in the object it singles out. Well and good; I am often wrong; often I cannot find out that I am wrong; this is simple enough. Empathic projection is to other minds what seeing is to material objects, not what dreaming is. — Why doesn't the absence of an alternative to projection simply make matters worse, more hopelessly skeptical? Because now it is simply more obvious that there is no way of telling the difference between, as it were, seeing human beings and dreaming their presence. — No. What has come out is that "seeing" others as human beings is as much like dreaming them as it is like *seeing* them.

Why does the seamlessness of projection fail to bear up in the recent recital of skepticism? Because the world would not be projectively indistinguishable from the way it now is if I stopped projecting, or lost the feat — as the world would be sensuously indistinguishable from the way it is if I started dreaming or hallucinating what I now sense, a feature essential to the role of these possibilities in skepticism. If I stopped projecting, I would no longer take anything to be human, or rather I would see no radical difference between humans and other things. I am, after all, very selective about this already. Only a small proportion of the things I see, or sense, do I regard as human (or animated, or embodied). Projection already puts a seam in human experience; some things are on one side of the seam, some on the other. On this picture, the presence of mutants, automata, zombies, androids, etc., would mean that I am almost certainly sometimes projecting humanness where it is inappropriate; certainly it would mean that I can not be certain that I never am. But would this cause me to wonder whether I am ever right to project? The *fact* (so far at least) is that I do not doubt, anyway that I am not prey to skeptical doubt. The others do not vanish when a given case fails me. My experience continues to affix its seam.

Are we, therefore, in a position to conclude that there is no skepticism with respect to other minds? Hardly that. My composing of the skeptic's recent recital about other minds was designed to test at most whether a skepticism concerning other minds, produced along the lines of the skepticism I produced concerning material objects, would be *as* reasonable, or realistic, as I found that earlier skepticism, so produced, to be. So the question is whether we are in a position to conclude that skepticism concerning other minds, so produced, fails to be as reasonable; that is to say, fails so to be produced.

We are still a step, or just a step, away from that conclusion. We can conclude — I think we must — that we have so far not uncovered a best case, that the skeptic's recent recital has so far not uncovered it. But we cannot conclude that there *is* no such case (hence no skepticism); nor can we conclude that the failure of the skeptic's recital to uncover it is not due to some feature of his context that we have left unattended, or undeveloped.

Can there be such a case? It seems that, on one cloaking of the problem of other minds, the skeptical conclusion itself *states* that I cannot be in the best position for knowing such a mind: only the *other* can know. And if the other knows, then surely the other exists! — This seems a limited version of skepticism, or a version of limited skepticism. Its moral seems to be that skepticism with respect to other minds cannot be skeptical enough. Is this philosophically reassuring? Has it mastered the worst that can befall me? Skepticism in this form will not distinguish between cases in which there is someone there who knows (there is an other) and cases in which there is not; between cases in which some response is simulated and cases in which what is simulated is the human, or the creaturely, as such. But isn't this really up to the individual philosophy, to our differing views of the situation, as it is up to the individual philosophy to determine the nature of the objects I (have discovered that I) cannot directly be in touch with? Skepticism has done its work: it has shown that *I* cannot know, and that my position is the best. The best, that is, saving the other's.

Which other? Am I to realize that no other (other than the one in question) could be in a better position than I for knowing the one in question; or that no other would be a better test of my knowledge; or both together — that no other can be in a better position, or have a better instance, for knowing any other, than I am, and have, with respect to *this* other? I suggested, in speaking just now of a "limited skepticism" — one which states that we can never be skeptical enough — that the other in question may or may not vanish, depending upon some philosophical point of view, or thesis. But even if, at the extreme, he does vanish, even if there is just nothing there of the right kind to call a human being, this is a disappearance only to me, not to *all* others; and it is a disappearance at best only of him, that *one*. (This would not be his dematerialization but rather his materialization: he is *wholly* a body.) The case, for some reason, fails to generalize, or spread of its own accord; or rather it generalizes into thin air. Why is this? Where did this case of the other come from?

In composing the skeptical recital, I did find it natural for the skeptic to wish to *single out* one other to exemplify the situation in which he, and by implication all of us, found himself. There was nothing *special* about this other that led the skeptic to single him out, nothing prejudicial it brought to the recital, was there? It was intended as analogous to the epistemologist's use of a generic object as the sort of example with which he is compelled to work, in order to speak of our capacity for knowing as such. I said early on that the rubric "generic object" was meant heuristically, for example to rule out the investigator's expertise in the case. It is a case, if there is a case, in which what is at stake is not the investigator's particular learning but his human capacity as a knower, a case in which anyone who has the power of knowledge can exercise that power. So if something is special about the one singled out, it must consist in the very way in which there is nothing special about him; in the fact, that is to say, that he is a stranger. *Is* this, in itself, special? Surely, at least, the stranger presents a more fundamental instance of our powers as knowers of others than instances of our friends and acquaintances, who will merely raise questions of our priviledged position with respect to them, not of our general human capacities with respect to others?

I do not think that the skeptical recital has given us, or yet given us, a perspective from which to assess this feature of its progress. Doubtless the fact that the one singled out is a stranger is what provides whatever initial rationality there is in the supposition that the other might be other than human. (And the image of the stranger is as primitive an issue for our assessment of our humanity as the image of the soul as breath.) But if the skeptical recital has not, so far at least, convinced us that it has, or has not, produced a best case for knowing of others, it has at least directed us to something significant in our search for a best case. Intuitions of skepticism with respect to the external world and with respect to other minds have been parallel, or predictably inverse, over much of their lives, as we have traced them. With respect to the external world, I cannot get outside my circle of experiences to compare them with the reality, if any, they represent; my senses come between reality and my experience of reality. With respect to other minds, I cannot get inside the other's circle of experiences, to compare with them the reality, if any, represented by what I experience of him; his body comes between the reality of the other and my experience of that reality. But the recent skeptical recital, in its feature of singling out the other, seems to have marked a boundary at which my intuitions of the different skepticisms part company. For the body of the other seals me out, and the other in, *in each case*. Is this intuition accurate? Is it significant?

Go back to my inability, or reluctance, to draw a skeptical moral from the skeptical recital concerning other minds. I felt that while it might be true that I could never step outside my confinement from the other, it was not true, or I did not know, that the other could not step outside his confinement from me. What, if anything, does this mean? Is a genuine difference being expressed here? And now it seems to me that I inaccurately, or partially, drew the moral from the recital; or rather inaccurately, or partially, sketched my inability, or reluctance, to draw a moral. And the recital itself led me to this inaccuracy or partiality. What I said, in effect, in accounting for my inability, or reluctance, was that I did not know whether or not, so to speak, to come to the conclusion that I can never know of the existence of others on the basis of empathic projection alone. But what I now wish to say is that I do not know whether empathic projection is, or is not, a sufficient basis for *acknowledging* the other's existence. There is, so far as I can tell, a dual cause for this wish to express this stage of the matter in terms of acknowledgment. The term captures at once the sense of the sense it makes to say that I of course cannot step outside my empathic projection, that nothing could be better than this feat of cognition, and that I ought to be able to settle its validity from within my confinement from others; and also the sense of the sense it makes to feel that the question is open whether others can step outside their confinement from me.

What I have called my "wish" to express this "dual cause" in terms of acknowledgment is no doubt prompted by what I have seen of this concept in the essays of mine mentioned earlier in this chapter. In "Knowing and Acknowledging" I said that acknowledgment "goes beyond" knowledge, not in the order, or as a feat, of cognition, but in the call upon me to express the knowledge at its core, to recognize what I know, to do something in the light of it, apart from which this knowledge remains without expression, hence perhaps without possession. To avoid acknowledgment by refusing this call upon me would create "the sense of the sense it makes to say that I cannot step outside" ("go beyond") my feat of cognition. In "The Avoidance of Love" I said that acknowledgment of another calls for recognition of the other's specific relation to oneself, and that this entails the revelation of oneself as having denied or distorted that relation. *King Lear* figures this denial in images of blindness and banishment. To avoid acknowledgment by refusing the call upon me to recognize this relation and my denial of it would create "the sense of the sense it makes to feel the question is open whether others can step outside their confinement from me" (which may be my interpretation of my banishment of them).

But while such results, if true, would illustrate or prompt my use of the

concept of acknowledgment in attempting to trace out the intuitions arising from the skeptic's recital, they would not *justify* my use of it there.
For in the case of, for example, "acknowledging another's pain", I know
in a general way what I am called upon to do that goes beyond my feat of
cognition, viz., to express sympathy, or impatience, something that incor-
porates his suffering. And in the case of Lear, I know in a general way
what he has to reveal about himself in order to acknowledge Cordelia as
his unjustly banished daughter, viz., that he is her unjust banishing father. Whereas in following the case of the skeptical recital, I have been
led to ask whether, and on what basis, I can acknowledge the other (simply) as a human being. It is not settled what, if anything, would go beyond the cognitive feat of empathically projecting his humanity; nor
what, if any, relation I bear to him; nor how, if at all, I can reveal myself
to him as having denied this relation.

But now if these *are* the questions left unsettled by the skeptical recital,
then we have found some structure in its very inconclusiveness. It is a
structure in which the question "Who, or what, is this other?" (or the
question "Is this in fact an other?") is tied to the question "Who, or what,
am I, that I should be called upon to testify to such a question?". How,
and why, am I thrown back upon myself? — I notice, looking back over
the skeptical recital, that it contains the following, so far unexamined,
feature: that the moment at which I singled out my stranger was the moment at which I also singled out myself. ("I, for one, am prepared to say
that I know that no one of you — you, for instance. . . .")

I was saying that the skeptical recital had so far not produced a best case
for knowing of the existence of others. Has it, however, produced a best
case for acknowledging their existence? Its inconclusiveness shows at least
that if it has then I do not know that it has, because I do not know
whether I am or am not *in* such a case, i.e., in such a case with this other
(taking up the suggestion that the problem of the other arises in *each*
case). So again we must ask: What, if anything, is a best case for the acknowledgment of others, a best placement in which to acknowledge another? — which must mean: in which to acknowledge my relation to the
other. Is there, in particular, a case in which my (outsider's) position is
sufficiently good to produce the force of the skeptic's best case with respect to the external world, namely that if I know *anything* I know *this*?

In Chapter II, I characterized the object before the epistemologist as
compressing within itself, for him, material reality as a whole, the entire

island of reality. He is thrown back upon his senses, alone. How do matters stand with the inquisitor of other minds? He has about him an archipelago; some of it he faces, some of it he does not. It is silent for him here and now, but he knows no more. Is there a case in which a given other compresses within himself or herself my view of psychic reality as a whole; a given other who exemplifies all others for me, humanity as such; a given other upon whom I stake my capacity for acknowledgment altogether, that is to say, my capacity at once for acknowledging the existence of others and for revealing my existence in relation to others? And if there is such a case, then what is the consequence if this case fails, if this other fails me, if I cannot believe, or feel I cannot know, what this other shows and says to me? What is the consequence for me and what is the consequence for the other?   — As before — before a best case — the consequence will not extend to different others. I am thrown upon just *this* other's body. Nor here, in being thrown back upon myself, does the consequence extend to different others in my position. No one else *is* in my position with respect to this other. I and this other have been singled out for one another. This is what a best case comes to. If it fails, the remainder of the world and of my capacities in it have become irrelevant. That there are others, and others perhaps in my position in relation to them, are matters not beyond my knowledge but past my caring. I am not removed from the world; it is dead for me. All for me is but toys; there is for me no new tomorrow; my chaos is come (again?). I shut my eyes to others.

But when? If there really was another, and the case failed me, still the other knows of his or her existence; he or she remains. But this knowledge has come to me too late. Because now the other remains as unacknowledged, that is, as denied. I have shut my eyes to *this* other. And this is now part of this other's knowledge. To acknowledge him now would be to know this. To deny him now would be to deny this, deny this denial of him: to shut his eyes to me. Either way I implicate myself in his existence. There is the problem of the other.   — The crucified human body is our best picture of the unacknowledged human soul.

It is, accordingly, to be expected that we will not willingly subject ourselves to the best case of acknowledgment, indeed that we will avoid the best if we can, to avoid the worst. (We will have to *be* singled out. By what? By whom?) What is the nature of this avoidance? The answer to that question should contribute to answering the question: What is the nature of our everyday knowledge of the other?

Skepticism about material objects reveals, or pictures, the field of everyday knowledge as a whole, or common sense, as intellectually confined.

(Here again I call explicit attention to Thompson Clarke's "The Legacy of Skepticism".) It presses the aim of reason itself, to know objectively, without stint; to penetrate reality itself. It insinuates that there are grounds for doubt that there is no good reason — no intellectually respectable reason — we do not ordinarily raise. It throws us back upon ourselves, to assess ourselves as knowers. In the grip of its insight, we should be grateful for whatever consolation can be derived from the interpretation of ourselves that skepticism thereupon provides us with: we know "for all practical purposes". (Or, as Austin put it, thinking he thereby *denied* the power of skepticism: for all "intents and purposes".) Sometimes Wittgenstein casts the skeptic in his ancient role from the Mysteries, as when he gives an interlocutor to ask: "But, if you are *certain*, isn't it that you are shutting your eyes in face of doubt?" (*Investigations*, p. 224). The skeptic insinuates that there are possibilities to which the claim of certainty shuts its eyes; or: whose eyes the claim of certainty shuts. It is the voice, or an imitation of the voice, of intellectual conscience. Wittgenstein replies: "They are shut." It is the voice of human conscience. It is not generally conclusive, but it is more of an answer than it may appear to be. In the face of the skeptic's picture of intellectual limitedness, Wittgenstein proposes a picture of human finitude. (Then our real need is for an account of this finitude, especially of what it invites in contrast to itself.)

His eyes are shut; he has not shut them. The implication is that the insinuated doubt is not *his.* But how not? If the philosopher *makes* them his, pries the lids up with instruments of doubt, does he not come upon human eyes? — When I said that the voice of human conscience was not generally conclusive, I was leaving it open whether it was individually conclusive. It may be the expression of resolution, at least of confession. "They (my eyes) are shut", as a resolution, or confession, says that one can, for one's part, live in the face of doubt. — But doesn't everyone, everyday? — It is something different to live *without* doubt, without so to speak the *threat* of skepticism. To live in the face of doubt, eyes happily shut, would be to fall in love with the world. For if there is a correct blindness, only love has it. And if you find that you have fallen in love with the world, then you would be ill-advised to offer an argument of its worth by praising its Design. Because you are bound to fall out of love with your argument, and you may thereupon forget that the world is wonder enough, as it stands. Or not. (Even if the world has a designer, and if falling in love with the world is knowing this designer, praising the Design would not satisfy him or her as an expression of this knowledge. Unless the praise is directed *to* him or her; in which case there is no argument.)

I have described two thoughts which suggest that there is no strictly skeptical problem about the existence of other minds. According to the first thought — that of the "best case for knowing another" — I cannot be skeptical enough: the other is intact, anyway in being. According to the second thought — that of the "best case for acknowledging the other" — I cannot survive my skepticism: the world does not disappear, but I from it. Now a third thought emerges, or a third way of putting one and the same thought: there is no everyday *alternative* to skepticism concerning other minds. There is no competing common sense of the matter; there is nothing about other minds that satisfies me for *all* (practical) purposes; I already know everything skepticism concludes, that my ignorance of the existence of others is not the fate of my natural condition as a human knower, but my way of inhabiting that condition; that I cannot close my eyes to my doubts of others and to their doubts and denials of me, that my relations with others are restricted, that I cannot trust them blindly.   — You'd be a fool if you did.   — Spare me that. That aside, my position here is not one of a generalized *intellectual* shortcoming.

I do not picture my everyday knowledge of others as confined but as exposed. It is exposed, I would like to say, not to possibilities but to actualities, to history. There is no possibility of human relationship that has not been enacted. The worst has befallen, befalls everyday. It has merely, so far as I know, not befallen me. Tragedy figures my exposure to history as my exposure to fortune or fate; comedy as my exposure to accident or luck. Each will have its way of figuring this as my exposure to nature; meaning, in the end, human nature. As if the subjection to history *is* human nature.

In knowing others, I am exposed on two fronts: to the other; and to my concept of the other.

Being exposed to the other is being exposed to the occurrence of a best case. I said that it is to be expected that we will avoid the best as long as we can. But "avoiding the best" is undeveloped. It means "avoiding the occurrence of the best", but also "avoiding *knowing* that an occurrence is the best". This development does not apply in the case of the external world. There it makes no sense to try to avoid the best; the best is my milieu, my life with objects. What the skeptic opens my eyes to is the knowledge that *this is the best* — the occurrence of this tree, of that stone, at that distance, in this light, myself undrugged and unhampered, in the best of health, . . . Then that life is undermined, or distanced from me. The best proves not to be good enough. (This subjugation of human intellect can, if intermittent, be lived with. It is harder to live with it in the presence of Job's comforters, who will say, for example, "You don't need pure certainty anyway. Justified belief is plenty good enough".) I can try to avoid knowing that I am in the best case with other minds as well. (Lear and Leontes try this at the beginning of what we know of them; Othello from the middle until immediately before the end; Anthony and Cleopatra do not deny the best, but accept it jointly, so their conclusion modifies, if not quite avoids, tragedy.) But in the case of other minds, I can also try to avoid the thing itself, avoid getting myself into the best case. To say that I am exposed to the best case is to say that my attempts to restrict my relations with others, of my caring for or about some other, or all others, may, at any place, fail. I may be singled out. (Lear and Leontes and Othello do not, in the end, avoid this. It is what makes them who they are.)

Being exposed to my concept of the other is being exposed to my assurance in applying it, I mean to the fact that this assurance is *mine*, comes only from me. The other can present me with no mark or feature on the basis of which I can *settle* my attitude. I have to acknowledge humanity in the other, and the basis of it seems to lie in me. But what do I know of that basis? At one moment I thought of it as a human capacity that is as much like dreaming as like seeing. At another I thought that there could be no sufficient basis in me, that only an Outsider, one free of human nature, could tell me what I would have to know to be assured of the other's humanity. But I also came to think that if there is an Outsider he is in me, in each of us. That confirms the idea that there is that in us that is capable of escaping human nature, here still expressed mythically. The myth speaks — beyond that of my standing in specific relations to myself — of the possibility of my gaining perspective on myself. I can, for example, sometimes gain a perspective on my present pain. It still hurts; I still mind it; it is still mine; but I find that I can handle it. I do that by grasping it, as though I am no longer incredulous of it, or superstitious. Is there something that could give me a perspective on my human nature as such? And would this be a perspective from which I see myself in the same way, or from the same distance, as I see the other? Could I, for example, see myself as a stranger? This need not be a case of seeing the strangeness of myself, though that might help my perspective. It would be a case of seeing that I have not met myself; it happens upon me, the knowledge comes over me, that I have not. I would then have an occasion for taking an interest in myself; it would be an occasion for interesting myself in something more than I have already heard about myself.

Are there limits upon the perspective I can have on others and take upon myself? I have found that the hedging of my acknowledgment of humanity in others hedges my own humanity, shows me the limits of human nature in me. The absence of the best case shows that our relations are restricted. The presence of the best case will show that our lack of restriction is limited to one other. The lower limit upon humanity is marked by the passage into inhumanity. Its signal is horror. The opposite of terror is the calm of safety; the opposite of horror would be the bliss of salvation. *Is* there this opposite? Is there an upper limit on humanity? If there is, how would I know that I had reached it? How would I know that I had gone in myself not merely to *my* limitations for acknowledgment, but to the limitations of the humanly acknowledgeable?

Has this use of the concept of acknowledgment been justified, its use to describe something owed another simply as a human being, the failure of which reveals the failure of one's own humanity? I said that in the case of Lear I knew in a general way what he has to reveal about himself in order to acknowledge Cordelia. Does his failure in this reveal a failure of his humanity or his failure as a father? Lear comes to think that there is such a distinction and that his failure is of the former kind. But perhaps that is just his problem. If one is to acknowledge another as one's neighbor, one must acknowledge oneself as his or her neighbor. Something may make one a bad neighbor sometimes, but in itself this hardly constitutes a failure of one's humanity. One acknowledges one's teacher by acknowledging oneself as his or her student, i.e., presumably, by showing that one has learned something from him. Some students will feel that this is best done by maintaining good deportment around the teacher; some teachers will think so too. One may feel this to be a restricted view of the relation between teacher and student, but hardly that those who hold it are lacking in humanity: perhaps they are using the wrong words for their relationship. Similarly in the cases of acknowledging another as my sibling or countryman or comrade or friend or employer or tenant. There is room for me in which to acknowledge myself as their sibling or countryman or comrade or friend or employee or landlord. — I think there is a surmise that these are restricted modes of acknowledgment, appropriate to stations dictated merely by society, and that society is as such arbitrary; a surmise that another may be owed acknowledgment simply on the ground of his humanity, acknowledgment as a human being, for which nothing will do but my revealing myself to him as a human being, unrestrictedly, as his or her sheer other, his or her fellow, his or her *semblable*.   — Surely this is, if anything, nothing more than half the moralists who ever wrote have said, that others count, in our moral calculations, simply as persons; or that we have duties to others of a universal kind, duties to them apart from any particular stations we occupy.   — I think not. Duties are dischargeable. The surmise of which I speak is of an acknowledgment that is not dischargeable; it is something I will, or will not, see, and live with. The surmise is not that I *ought* to see, and live with, others as human beings; it is that I sometimes do so see them, and therefore, mostly do not.   — This is empty juggling. One could equally say: It is not that I ought to have duties to others as human beings, it is that I sometimes do have; and *that* I have such duties is not itself a dischargeable duty; it is something I will, or will not, live with. And if what you wish to ask is *why* I have these duties to others as human beings, the answer is: because there are other human beings. And if you wish to know how I know that there are other human beings, the answer is: because I know I have these duties to them. I also know it because I love some of them and hate some of them; but neither loving nor hating discharges me of my duties toward them.   — The surmise is that the idea of a duty toward others as human beings might itself be a restriction of my knowledge of their existence.   — So, then, would hating them be a restriction?   — Yes.   — And loving them might also be a restriction?   — Yes.

If it is a mark of insanity not to know that we have duties to others as human beings, and that we show our humanity in performing them, wouldn't it be an equal mark of insanity to surmise that others are owed some unrestricted revelation of our humanity? What would they want it for? Why place such a burden upon them? Isn't this surmise a part of Lear's state of mind when he comes upon Edgar and interprets him as a "poor, bare, forked creature"? Then how does he translate this interpretation into action, what does he *do* on the basis of his knowledge?   — What would you have him do? Reveal himself to Edgar as his *semblable,* as yet another poor, bare, forked creature? A lot of good that would do! He takes the creature into his shelter with him, out of the gathering storm. How better to have shown his humanity? What more could reason claim from him?   — It is a measure of Lear's gathering madness that it both frees him for his exposure to the perception of human otherness and hence to horror and pity. And also that by the time he enters with the other into his shelter he is viewing him as "my philosopher", still searching for some restriction upon the other, in particular for some interpretation of the reason for this creature's being *his*. He takes him into the shelter not to shelter him but to philosophize with him, or rather upon him; he sees him as an exemplar of humanity, rather than as an instance of it. In particular, he does *not* acknowledge him — though this encounter prepares him for his acknowledgment later, in succession, of Gloucester and of Cordelia, at least in passing. He merely knows what the other is, that the creature has humanity. When his prayer is answered, to feel what others feel — the storm is the answer — he is in full madness.

Why is it *this* creature in whom the King first glimpses the human as such? Such a creature exemplifies the restriction of society, that there is that in the human creature which is undefined by social station, or by any property; he is bare, laid bare. Call him an outcast. Then for the King, as he stood, to have acknowledged him would have meant acknowledging himself as one who casts out. For him to have acknowledged him simply as another, a *semblable,* would have meant casting himself out. Lear is so far prepared for neither action.

Why are there these two possibilities of acknowledgment with respect to the outcast? Or why not in all other relations as well? The lawyer may acknowledge some other not only as a client but as another lawyer; a parent may acknowledge some other not (only) as a child but as another parent; and similarly for the landlord, the teacher, the employer, etc. The lawyer or teacher is not in natural league with other lawyers or other teachers, though perhaps in political league. But the lawyer or teacher or employer or landlord has not created the existence of clients or students or employees or tenants; they are created together. And where I can literally be said to have "created the existence of the other", in the case of my children, the call upon me, my answerability, is unrestricted, though my rights are not. Whereas what? In the case of the outcast I have created this existence, and can acknowledge it neither from my point of view nor from theirs? I think it is part of the surmise of my restricted humanity that I have created the outcast, or anyway that I am in league with those who have; that *we* have; that my society is mine; hence that I have consented to casting out. An expression of this surmise would be the idea that outcasts are in natural league with one another. This would be a distortion and projection of my own sense of outcastness.

One may express the knowledge that others are outcasts through one's humanitarianism. Thinkers such as Thoreau and Dickens were perhaps sometimes too hard on the ordinary shows of such an instinct, but what they saw in these humanitarian shows was a wish to convert the outcast into a social role, or into a kind or class of being — in any case, a wish to

view outcasts as beings different from oneself, about whose good they themselves did not require consulting; an attitude that might be called emotional imperialism. And they perceived this view or attitude as compro-
mising the humanitarian's own humanity. The hand handing out its alms
can look like a fist. The problem of the humanitarian is not merely that
his acts of acknowledgment are too thin, mere assuagings of guilt; but that
they are apt, even bound, to confusion. His intention is to acknowledge
the outcast as a human being; but his effect is to treat a human being as
an outcast, as if the condition of outcastness defined a social role, a kind
of sub-profession, suited for a certain kind of human being. So it is apt
to perpetuate the guilt it means to assuage. The confusion is produced by
an avoidance of the two choices open to him: either to reveal himself as
one who casts out, or to cast himself out.

One may feel that there are other choices. This means to me that one
will not have surmised a restriction upon one's humanity, or not surmised
that this restriction lies in the compromise of one's relations to others. For
the outcast is a mythological description of a position that no one could
be expected to want to be in. It makes my position appear artificial, arbitrary. It is not my *fortune* to be in a more fortunate position; the hand
of man shows in it; my hand; it rebukes my sense of fortune. The humanitarian is a mythological description of the posture in which I find
that my hand, if even in the form of a fist, is outstretched; that I find
myself related to the outcast; that I am exposed to his humanity.

So far as we think that the human being is naturally a political being,
we cannot think that some human beings are naturally outcasts, naturally
in league with one another. So if there are outcasts, we must have, or
harbor, *sub specie civilitatis,* some explanation of their condition. One
explanation is that their condition is deserved. Another is that their
condition is undeserved but sheerly unfortunate, doomed or damned. Another is that the inhabitants of that condition are not quite or fully
human. Another is that they are mysteriously in league with one another.
Another is that my society is doomed or damned. Another is that my
society is unjust; but not sufficiently unjust to be doomed or damned.
— Whichever of these explanations one finds for oneself, surely all arise
from a knowledge that there are other human beings in positions other
than mine. All are arrived at on the basis of my empathic projection, such
as it is, on the basis of what I regard it as sufficient for. I said there is no
general, everyday alternative to skepticism concerning other minds. Now
I will say: I live my skepticism.

With respect to the external world, I have to "forget", or ignore, close my eyes to, somehow bypass, the presence of doubts that are not mine, of "possibilities" that I have not *ruled* out; I have to permit myself distraction from my knowledge that we do not know what we all imagine there is to know, viz., material objects. I accommodate myself to a universal human condition, or rather, a condition shared by all creatures endowed with sensuousness, a condition over which no one (possessing sensuousness) has a choice, save to be cautious. But the surmise that I have not acknowledged about others, hence about myself, the thing there is to acknowledge, that each of us is human, is not, first of all, the recognition of a universal human condition, but first of all a surmise about myself. To accommodate myself to my restrictions of acknowledgment would be to compromise my integrity, or perhaps to constitute it, such as it is. It is as a general alternative to skeptical doubt that Austin was moved to say that, in substantiating my claims to know, "enough is enough"; I must have said enough to rule out other reasonable, competing possibilities. But how much is enough when it comes to knowing and acknowledging the humanity of another? How many times, and about just which matters, must I pity another, help another, accept another's excuses, before concluding that enough is enough? "Give me another day; another moment; another dollar; another chance. . . ." If I do not answer such appeals, is this because I have found the other, this other, not to be worth it, or entitled to it, or myself not to be up to it?

But surely there are limits to my answerability for or toward others? Surely there are reasonable grounds on which to draw those limits, or principles in terms of which to draw them? (This is a point of such an idea as that of the Social Contract. In respect of the State, it tells me that there are circumstances under which I am free to rebel, a time when enough is enough; but also tells me why I do not. In respect of my fellow citizens, it tells me why I am answerable for what happens to them; but also why my answerability is not unlimited.) But even if I draw the limits wrong, unfairly, or out of cowardice or spiritual stinginess or lack of imagination, how would this show a failure of my humanity? Surely anything I do shows the humanity in me, such as it is. The very way in which I ignore the other shows it. And if my response is mechanical, shows a tint of automatonity, then human beings are possessed of tints of automatonity. And if my response is quite inhuman, surely, as was said, only a human being can behave inhumanly. Such responses may well be judged to be failures of my humanity according to an ideal of the human being, and I have said that to be human is to have such an ideal. But my inhuman or automatonic treatment of the other does not itself prove that I have no such ideal. — There is no *way* in which one shows oneself as other to the other's outcastness. It depends upon the matter at hand. If the other is Raskolnikov, then I can show my unrestricted acknowledgment of his humanity by understanding his confession and sharing his exile. If the other is Estella then I can show that I believe her confession that she is without a heart and ask to share *that* exile. In such cases, I had better not have any other outstanding commitments. It may not come to this. The question is still why my hand is ever stretched out, even in the form of a fist. It shows that I want something of another. It shows that I am exposed to my humanity.

But even if we recognized some such surmise as that of a restriction on my humanity arising from my inability — or the lack of occasion — to acknowledge the other as a human being, surely this is not the same as not knowing that others *are* humans? I do not know a confident answer to this question, because I do not know that there is a confident answer to the question, "How do I know that there are (other) human beings?". I mean I do not know whether there is or is not a sensible answer to that question; nor whether, if there is, it is the one that shows the knowledge to be very special or nothing special. To accept my exposure in the case of others seems to imply an acceptance of the possibility that my knowledge of others may be overthrown, even that it ought to be. With respect to material objects we have to "forget" the possibility of skepticism, e.g., that the best case will fail us. With respect to other minds we might say that we have to "remember" the possibility of skepticism, e.g., that we have not permitted ourselves a best case, that we do not know but that we may, at any place, be singled out; hence that, so far as we know, we now are not. Our position is not, so far as we know, the best. — But mightn't it be? Mightn't it be that just this haphazard, unsponsored state of the world, just this radiation of relationships, of my cares and commitments, provides the milieu in which my knowledge of others can best be expressed? Just *this* — say expecting someone to tea; or returning a favor; waving goodbye; reluctantly or happily laying in groceries for a friend with a cold; feeling rebuked, and feeling it would be humiliating to admit the feeling; pretending not to understand that the other has taken my expression, with a certain justice, as meaning more than I sincerely wished it to mean; hiding inside a marriage; hiding outside a marriage — just such things are perhaps the most that knowing others comes to, or has come to for me. — Is there more for it to come to; more that it *must* come to? When I alluded to Othello's conclusion as a failure of the best case of acknowledgment, I equally cited it as his failure to recognize, in time, that his (still) *was* a best case.

In saying that we live our skepticism, I mean to register this ignorance about our everyday position toward others — not that we positively know that we are never, or not ordinarily, in best cases for knowing of the existence of others, but that we are rather disappointed in our occasions for knowing, as though we have, or have lost, some picture of what knowing another, or being known by another, would really come to — a harmony, a concord, a union, a transparence, a governance, a power — against which our actual successes at knowing, and being known, are poor things. To say that there is a skepticism which is produced not by a doubt about whether we can know but by a disappointment over knowledge itself, and to say that this skepticism is lived in our knowledge of others, is to say that this disappointment has a history. To trace the history would presumably require tracing the hopes placed upon knowledge in the Renaissance and by the Enlightenment; and of the fears of knowledge overcome by those hopes; and of the despair of knowledge produced by the dashing of those hopes.

The usefulness of these recent reflections concerning "living one's skepticism" depends upon the convincingness of the way I painted the skeptical recital and drew its moral, viz., in terms of one's exposure to the other and to one's concept of the other. One suspicion about the moral, or its surmise, lies in the sense that the idea that "others are owed some unrestricted revelation of my humanity" is nothing more than a pathological or adolescent or romantic sense of my own restriction or confinement; that it is merely a claim that *I* am not unrestrictedly known, a condition I may and may not wish to have infringed; that it is a projection of some impossible wish, or possible need, for a proof of *my* existence.

The most obvious cause for suspicion about the skeptical recital itself is its concept of "empathic projection". This emerged as little more than a dummy concept for *something* that must be the basis for my claims to read the other, something that I go on in myself in adopting, or calling upon, my attitude toward other human beings. Even so, I can see two suspicions over it. First: Isn't the wish for such a concept really a persistence of the idea that the other is "like" oneself, that whatever one can know about the other one first has to find in oneself and then read *into* the other (by analogy): whereas the essence of acknowledgment is that one conceive the other from the other's point of view. Moreover, the concept makes one's knowledge of the other seem to be something one engages in afresh, as a special feat, in each case — not in each case of another, which is fair enough; but in each case in which one undertakes to know another. Whereas knowing others is, barring brain damage or some equal disaster, just a fact about our capacities as knowers; others are, as it were, among the items of our knowledge. If you wish to say that we have somehow to get *over* to the other (or inside) then this is something already true of us before a given other appears upon the scene. Once our general capacity is settled, criteria are enough. Second: Doesn't the concept of empathic projection make the idea of knowing others too special a project from the beginning, as if the knowing of objects could take care of itself, whereas what goes into the knowing of others is everything that goes into the knowing of objects *plus* something else, something that, as it were, animates the object? It might in fact be the case that this *is* what knowledge of others is like. But that would be an empirical claim, for which philosophers certainly have no particular evidence. It might also be true that this is a fantasy of knowledge which we then project into the object of knowledge, thus producing the idea of the other as a material object *plus* something more.

This idea of knowledge may indeed have the whole process of perception (of different strata or kinds of being) backwards. It makes equal sense — at least equal — to suppose that the natural (or, the biologically more primitive) condition of human perception is of (outward) things, whether objects or persons, as animated; so that it is the seeing of objects as objects (i.e., seeing them objectively, as non-animated) that is the sophisticated development. One should accordingly regard the view of others as based upon empathic projection as a case of the Empathetic Fallacy.

Or it makes the perception of humanity too special in another way. It seems to take the idea of an attitude toward a soul as some *appropriateness* of my response. But why shouldn't one say that there is a required appropriateness with respect to each breed of thing (object or being); something appropriate for bread, something else for stones, something for large stones that block one's path and something for small smooth stones that can be slung or shied; something for grass, for flowers, for orchards, for forests, for each fish of the sea and each fowl of the air; something for each human contrivance and for each human condition; and, if you like, on up? For each link in the Great Chain of Being there is an appropriate hook of response. I said that one's experience of others puts a seam in experience. Why not consider that experience is endlessly, continuously, seamed? Every thing, and every experience of every different thing, is what it is.

Some of this, most of it, I would like to see worked out. I am interested, for example, in the perception or vision of how *different* different things are from one another. It points up the condition underlying the ease, call it the naturalness, with which we name and know things; the condition that, as one may feel, so few possibilities exist. The logical space is so vast between kinds of objects; it is possible to think in natural kinds. (If every-thing that really could exist together did exist now (e.g., every kind of tree, of every size and condition) then an Idealist vision of knowledge would be true, that you could know (i.e., tell) no individual object with-out knowing everything about it, its whole truth; nothing less would single out the kind it is.) Whereas human beings, by contrast, are all alike; each bears an internal relation to all others. There is only one kind of human being. This perception seems to me also to enter into our difficulty in finding, or defining, a best case of the knowledge of others, which is after all knowledge of the specifically human, or starts out to be. The representativeness of the best case is not achieved here in a distinction between specific and generic instances. There is no such distinction here, or we must not allow one. So we are thrown back upon ourselves to ask what makes one human being representative of (all) others.

But at the moment what interests me is the suggestion, underlying both suspicions about "empathic projection", that the skeptical recital was overly specialized in its account of my knowledge of others. The suspi-cions call attention to the grossest, hitherto unremarked, feature of that recital, viz., that it is directed to what I can know of another, not to what others can know of me. It misses *that* duality in the problem of other minds. — But obviously whether I can know of the existence of others was just the problem, so far as there was a problem. — But the problem is about otherness, and the way I was conceiving of it — as a question of *my* knowing an other — was prejudicial, or partial, from the start, and so perhaps harmful. It misses the following consideration: The question whether there are other minds is exactly as much a question about me as about anyone else. If *anyone* is an other mind, *I* am one — i.e., I am an other to the others (and of course others are then I's to me). Then the question is: Do others know of my existence?

This seems a more promising beginning for an epistemological inquiry, because here I begin with a case that I would say with confidence that I know as well as I know anything. For surely *I* know I exist. Isn't this in fact the "best case" for knowing of others that caused so much tribulation?   — Come on. If you are going to speak in terms of others and I's, then you do *not* know that you are an *other* unless you know that there are *other* others, that is, other I's. You do not indeed otherwise so much as know that you are an *I*, that saying "I" picks you out from among any competitors.   — I think I well may not be *an* I. I am I. But that aside, to determine whether I can know that there are other others, i.e., other I's, is what I mean the inquiry to do. Since I know I am (an) I, all I need in order to know that I am (an) other (hence that there is an other) is to know that I am known by an (other) I.   — Where is the logical gain in moving from the question whether I know another to the question whether I am known by or to another?   — If there is no logical loss, then the gain of the question would lie in its posing more accurately what it is we really want to know of others. And it would account for the intermittent emptiness in attempts to prove, or disprove, our knowledge of the existence of others. Proofs for God's existence, and criticisms of these proofs, are apt to be empty intermittently for people whose conviction is that they are known by God, or to God, or not.

Let us see what a beginning of a skeptical recital, directed passively, brings to light.

"Among the things we claim to know the existence of, some are human beings. I know, for example, that each of you is a human being and each of you knows — I devoutly hope — that I am a human being. But how do you know this? What do you really know of me? You see a humanish something of a certain height and age and gender and color and physiognomy, emitting vocables in a certain style. . . . Much more than this you do not know. Some you could guess at, but not in very great detail. But then I am a stranger to you. What does *anyone* know of me?

"All anyone knows or could know is what I am able to show them of myself. [This is not, at worst, *false*, but a definition of the relevant knowledge. I do not wish to deny that a great deal can be learned about me from observation, say from an autopsy. I do not, that is, deny that I am a thing, usable as cannon fodder. Nor do I deny that for some thinkers that is enough to know about me — all there *is* (for them) to know.] And how much can I really show? Of course I would not deny that if I evince criteria of pain then, unless I am very unfortunate, probably someone will try to comfort me. And my doctor, for example, will not, unless he is sadistic, cause me more pain than he can help. But these are nothing more than matters of fact, and the explanation for them may just be that pain-behavior is biologically painful to behold, so beholders of it do what they can to diminish it. The original case of pain-behavior, the infant's cry, would be the clearest instance of this. Maybe, accordingly, all human comfort arises (as the turning away of a flight of birds arises upon hearing the sound of a member of their feather being strangled) merely from the stimulus of certain behavior, i.e., certain outward criteria, not as a response to the experience itself. *That* remains, strictly, or directly, unknown.

"Shouldn't I by now be suspicious of this very disappointment? What else can I expect? [Here comes another Job's comforter, offering to replace a natural disappointment with an even greater disappointment.] Nobody else *could* have just *this* experience (striking myself on the breast). [Thus is Wittgenstein's discussant at §253 a type (emerging at this stage of the recital) of the passive skeptic.] And even if they *could* have it (i.e., have something descriptively the same), they aren't (except *per accidens*) having it when I am, so the other's knowledge of me is at best dependent on his memory and hence on what has happened to him. And can I be sure that anything that has happened to another is *exactly* the same as the thing that has happened to me? In the midst of pain maybe my metaphysical scruples are dampened sufficiently to allow me to accept another's sympathy even when, later, I seriously doubt that he really knew *how* much my shoulder hurt. The very analogy he used for it — comparing my pain with the time he was hit with the baseball — shows he cannot have really appreciated the *piercing* quality of mine. — The other knows me merely by analogy — and that just is not knowing another mind! But I've already seen that nothing could be *better* than, could go beyond, analogy here!"

Has this recital now prompted some stable conclusion? It seems that I ought to be entitled to draw the conclusion that I am, necessarily, imperfectly known. Anyway, strictly imperfectly, although of course for practical purposes the other knows well enough to provide help, even company (*faute de mieux*). Yet again, the recital seems to me to suggest that since I am unclear whether I am known in such a case, it is unclear what is to constitute *knowing* here.

This unclarity may again be a function of some incompleteness in the recital, or some as yet undetected feature of it. But maybe it is the mere consequence of our not having yet assessed the natural fact underlying this unclarity, namely, that it is unclear to what extent I expect, or demand, in order to acknowledge being known, or to feel known, that another's experience is *exactly* (like) mine. Suppose someone said to me: "You don't feel so bad. I feel worse all the time than you do now." I might believe him without taking him to have paid much attention to the particular quality of my feeling; I might even think the particular quality not to be of the essence. But this makes it almost seem that it is up to me to decide whether somebody knows me!

Or maybe the unclarity about what constitutes knowing in such cases is merely caused as an artifact of the form of the (Cartesian) skeptical recital itself. In the original case, that of material objects, the skeptical conclusion to the effect that I do not know on the basis of the senses alone arises unfailingly from an unquestioned employment of the obvious relation between knowing and seeing: having given seeing as the basis for knowing, then if I have to concede that perhaps I do not see, see it, then it follows that I do not, cannot claim to, know; period. But what, in the case of other minds, modeled on this one of material objects, models this relation between seeing and knowing? Surely not the transferred relation between seeing and knowing themselves, for in the first format for active skepticism with respect to other minds the emergence of the need for such a concept as empathic projection showed a natural dissatisfaction with seeing unadorned. (Not necessarily, of course, the right dissatisfaction.) The relation between behavior and experience, then? This was the initial idea when the Cartesian format first suggested itself (Chapter VI, the concluding section, entitled "A Further Problem"). There "I know 'from his behavior' " occurs at the place "I know 'from my senses' " occurs; and it seems that just as seeing fails as a basis for knowing upon accepting the hallucination or dreaming possibility, so behavior fails as a basis upon recognizing the simulation possibility.

An immediate suspicion about the strength of this parallel should arise from the failure of behavior in an opposite direction. Not only may the other counterfeit behavior, the other may suppress behavior, in which case I just in fact would not know, may as a matter of fact never know — not only not know what Caesar's feelings were on the field of the battle of Philippi, but not know what they were crossing the Rubicon, or looking for the last time into Egypt's or into Brutus's eyes. His feelings throughout his life are more or less mysterious, more or less a matter for speculation and elaboration. That such conclusions are acceptable to us intellectually, that they make sense of a possible intellectual position with respect to our knowledge of others, points to the following facts about the concept of behavior, in contrast to the concept of seeing — I mean, a contrast in their respective epistemological weights: to base your claim to knowledge of a thing on your having seen it is generally to stake full authority for your claim; whereas to base your claim to knowledge of a person on that person's behavior is generally to withhold full authority from your claim. Behavior is just made to contrast with something else that may tell how it really is with a person. Nothing tells better than seeing how it is with (sense-scale) things.

In arriving at a plateau of uncertainty as to whether I am known, as to what would count as being known, the recital of passive skepticism should allow us to approach again, from the inside as it were, the matter of our disappointment with criteria. The approach begins from the thought that of course I know that my criteria (I mean the criteria I manifest) reach all the way to — that is to say, reach directly out from — my experience itself; of course *I* know, that is to say, that the criteria I manifest are satisfied. But then how *can* the other not know? There seem just versions of two old possibilities in view here: that I do not manifest the right criteria, the ones that conventionally or naturally go with just this experience (and here I am not worried about whether my experiences are themselves like the experiences of others — I simply assume they are); or that the other before whom I manifest the criteria cannot read them accurately. It is reasonably clear that each of these two possibilities can be charged with trading in some species of nonsense, on the ground that each denies some feature essential to the idea (or hypothesis?) that criteria are in play: the latter denies that humans are in the relevant sense in agreement; the former denies that I am a member of the human group. I can imagine that someone would wish from here to make up an argument of the following form: If these two possibilities are the genuine and exhaustive consequences of the surmise of passive skepticism — that I cannot perfectly make myself known — then their successive collapse into nonsense proves that the original surmise is also nonsense.

The value or seriousness of this wish for an argument will depend on how the nonsense is envisioned as made out. Because unless my *sense* of inescapable unknownness also disappears with the collapsing of its "consequences", such an argument invites me to conclude that this sense of mine is merely psychological, hence without epistemological consequence. And that, as at first, amounts to begging the skeptical question. It amounts to just assuming that a sense of inescapable unknownness must be caused by some individual psychological perplexity, perhaps an old knowledge of abandonment laid down in childhood, perhaps a conviction of isolation or rejection settled in adolescence. In any case, it is hardly something that can be taken as representative of the human condition generally, metaphysically. Why, only children or adolescents themselves, who take their problems for the world's problems, would so grossly confuse the contingent with the necessary! — But is that true? Prophets and messiahs and certain romantic poets claim what is logically the same standing, to represent in themselves the human condition as such. Nowadays it is good form to behave as though all prophets and messiahs *must* be false (while at the same time it can hardly ever have been truer that no one giving himself or herself out as a prophet is without a following). But whose problem is that? — This representative function seems to be something Rousseau established as the ambition of romantic artists; not directly one of self-dramatization (though it often comes to that) but one of self-generalization. (Montaigne's project appears rather as one of self-individuation.) And as for Rousseau there were the Encyclopedists, causing him and calumniating him, so for every later Rousseau there is an excerptor who would reduce the claim of representativeness to its sources within a marginal personality.

I do not ask for conviction in the notion that passive skepticism repeats the condition of prophecy — the singular knowledge of an unquestionable truth which others are fated not to believe. But I cite the notion, here near the end of my considerations of skepticism, to attract attention again to the entwining of questions of skepticism with questions of sanity, of philosophy and psychology. It is fundamental to skepticism with respect to material objects that a firm distinction be drawn between a lunatic and a reasonable doubt of the existence of things. It is equally fundamental that this distinction cannot be firm enough, but that most people — each person most of the time, in most moods — will be unable to grasp it; so it will be said that such a doubt must be lunatic, from which it would follow, according to my understanding of the matter, not that skepticism is lunatic but that there is no skepticism. It is also fundamental to the mood in which one is captured by the skeptical surmise that one descries the route of exit from the mood, that one sees as an *alternative* to this mood the joining again of the healthy, everyday world, outside the isolation of the — what? Study? Laboratory? Wilderness?

My intuition that, on the contrary, I can live my skepticism with respect to other minds, is an intuition that there is no comparable, general alternative to the radical doubt of the existence of others; that we may already be as outside, in community, as we can be; that, accordingly, such a doubt does not bear the same relation to the idea of lunacy. — But isn't such an intuition empty on the face of it? Haven't you really been saying that skepticism is inherently unlivable? Or anyway, not sanely livable? · — Well, I've said skepticism is inherently unshareable. — But how do you mean that? You can't merely mean that a skeptic would be metaphysically reluctant to share his tidings. You must mean that he would feel that there *is* nothing to share. And isn't that fairly clearly insane? — But how do you mean that? Do you mean to question that skepticism can ever seriously (sanely) begin, that not even momentarily can the skeptic's ground for doubt seem reasonable? Then we must begin all over again. Or do you mean to say that the last question about skepticism is a return of the first question, namely, and unrhetorically, How is skepticism possible?; and that finally what we ask for is an increasingly concrete study of the frames of mind in which skepticism appears and vanishes?

— Suppose I accept this latter formulation. Then why not just give up the claim that, with respect to the existence of others, skepticism is in question? Grant, that is to say, that since our views of others can be lived it follows that these views are not pieces of skepticism. Then we will be free to investigate the frames of mind themselves in which we view one another. — But if the intuition expressed by saying that "skepticism with respect to others is (or can be) lived" is not empty — i.e., if there is such an intuition — then its content just is that (some dimension of) our lives with others, some frames of mind in which we view others, are to be characterized as skeptical, or rather, understood in terms forced upon us, or made available to us, in thinking through skepticism.

Something very similar is what I want to say in formulating my abiding interest in material object skepticism — that *what* skepticism questions or denies my knowledge of *is* the world of objects I inhabit, is the *world*. As elsewhere, the abnormal provides our access to the normal. I recognize from the failure of what skepticism regards as my knowledge of objects what it is my everyday life with objects consists in. (This is what I have wished to mark, in "Knowing and Acknowledging" and in *The Senses of Walden,* as "the truth of skepticism".)

So what is the difference in the way these directions of skepticism can be lived? Let us try another formula: To say I cannot "live" material object skepticism is to say that there is an alternative to its conclusion that I am bound, as a normal human being, to take. Accordingly, to say I (can) live skepticism with respect to others is to say that there is no such alternative, or no such conclusion.

We have invoked an allegory of this idea of an alternative whenever we have spoken of the vanishing of skeptical doubt as a matter of "leaving the (philosophical) study" — an allegory in which I put aside my isolation (hence find that I have myself put it on) and accept the company of others, rejoin their conventions, and share again their beliefs. But the allegory does not specify why "leaving" has the effect it has; or rather it does not specify how I *can* leave nor what the effect is. Is the effect that I momentarily forget my skepticism because the charm of company distracts me from it; and that, whenever the charm fades, I remember what I learned in the study and suffer again the dashing of my spirits? If this is how it is, then instead of taking this picture as one in which skepticism oscillates with my life I can as readily take it as one in which this oscillation with skepticism occurs within my life. I need not *behave* insanely, without surcease. For I sense, from within my isolation, that there is an alternative to it; and I respect, or express, that isolating knowledge, when outside, by saying, for example, that I know of the existence of the external world "for practical purposes". I do not, so far, have to be separated from others and treated as a lunatic. But if such things count as living my skepticism then it is false that material object skepticism cannot be lived. Then what is left of the claim that there is a radical asymmetry between material object and other minds skepticism on just the ground that the former cannot, and the latter can, be lived? Hasn't it just collapsed?

Since the claim — at any rate, the intuition — has not collapsed for me, there must be a significant variation in the way living one's skepticism is to be conceived in the different arenas. Immediately, it strikes me that formulating the difference within and without my study as one in which I *remember* and *forget* something, is not right, not the way things are. On the contrary, I can remember perfectly well what went on in the study; only it is not, as I feel like putting it, live for me now. To go over those skeptical paths now, in my present circumstances, would seem "cold, strained, and ridiculous". They are traversible only in meditation, a form of thought which only the merely literary will take to be merely literary. Apart from that access, I am not in the right study. If we can say that outside the study the knowledge of skepticism is dead for us, then we might say that one can live skepticism so long as its knowledge is dead for one. A dolorous intellectual diet. Yet to admit the dying of knowledge, as to endure the dying of love, as to succumb to the death of God and of poetry, may be all that fits one for rebirth.

Again, I find that the need for invoking the qualification "for practical purposes" shows not that the study has been left but on the contrary shows that a genuine alternative to the isolation of the study has not been reached. We have not been offered our life with objects again — tempered or chastened, if you like, by the revelation of skepticism; we have been given a philosopher's description of that life, a falsifying or intellectualized picture of it. We are still inside the study, if not quite in the same corner. The builder's knowledge of his column, the violinist's of her hands and of her violin, the walker's of his body and of his ground, is not *limited* by or to "practical purposes". What they know is what there is to know about their several things; it is their life with things.   — I do not imagine that the qualification "for practical purposes" is tempting as a philosopher's accommodation in the arena of other minds. It is no accommodation of common sense to the late fact that "all I can ever know is the other's behavior" to say that I know of the existence of the consciousness of others for practical purposes. Such an accommodation would seem crazier than the thing it is meant to accommodate. (And if we know of, and know in service of, some such practical purposes, who taught us of them? Machiavelli? Luther? de Sade? Adam Smith? Clausewitz?)

Suppose someone (call him or her Polonius) thought to reassure us about simulation possibilities once again: "True, people can feign being in just about any psychological situation they can really be in. But although you cannot know with certainty whether an expression is counterfeit or genuine, for practical purposes it is good enough to treat all expressions as genuine. And true, some among the family of what we call mankind may possibly be automata or androids of various kinds. But for practical purposes we (ought to) treat all apparent humans as humans." I might say that such remarks do not express our interest in others.

And what is this interest? I can imagine that someone will take me to harbor a more or less unexamined idea that humans are more important than objects in our lives, and that such a one may resist such an idea as follows: "Aren't you really taking it that our interest in objects is more or less uniform, as if this were the meaning of the discovery that makes skepticism possible — that no one's position is better than mine; that we are, as knowers, all in the same boat, our rocking common sensuous nature? And aren't we then invited to draw an invidious distinction with the case of persons, toward whom our interests are not uniform, but carefully individuated? But why shouldn't one take this as an empirical claim (perhaps masking a moral aspiration) about which skepticism has nothing to say? And couldn't it be claimed, with equal empirical plausibility and equal moral perception, that one's interest in different objects is far less uniform than one's interest in other human beings; that our interests in a column, a mirror, a tree, an apple, a seed, are more divergent than our interests in the things of the world that can accept or reject us, and that can be helped or hurt by us?"

Over and over, an apparent symmetry or asymmetry between skepticism with respect to the external world and skepticism with respect to other minds has collapsed, on further reflection, into its opposite. (For example: There is no best case for knowing another because there is no example that carries the right representativeness. — Ah, but there is! There is the Exemplar himself, or herself! Or again: In both arenas, the idea of the Outsider arises. —Ah, but there is a critical difference in the way we envision the powers of the Outsider in each arena.) I do not, accordingly, so much wish to claim that I have found certain ultimate asymmetries between these skepticisms as that the oscillation between sensing an asymmetry under each symmetry, and a symmetry under each asymmetry, is itself asymmetry enough to warrant, if not to assess, an intuition that in the sense in which we can arrive at skepticism with respect to the external world we cannot arrive at skepticism with respect to other minds; or rather, that with respect to the external world, an initial sanity requires recognizing that I cannot live my skepticism, whereas with respect to others a final sanity requires recognizing that I can. I do.

As I do not require that there be a level at which a feature of the one direction of skepticism *cannot* be found or applied in the other, but only that at each level a feature found to be natural in the one direction will be found to have to undergo inflection or reservation to find itself in the other direction; so I do not mean at last to say that only material object skepticism is the real skepticism, as if we knew exhaustively what constitutes reality here. (We might think of the skepticisms as differing the way men and women differ: nothing is different and everything is different.) It would not hurt my intuitions, to anticipate further than this book actually goes, were someone to be able to show that my discoveries in the regions of the skeptical problem of the other are, rightly understood, further characterizations of (material object) skepticism, of skepticism as such. So that, for example, what I will find in Othello's relation to Desdemona is not just initiated by the human being's relation to the world, in particular by that phase of its career in which the human being makes to secure or close its knowledge of the world's existence once and for all, only to discover it to be closed off forever; but also that their relation remains to the end a certain allegory of that career. The consequent implication that there is between human existence and the existence of the world a standing possibility of death-dealing passion, of a yearning at once unappeasable and unsatisfiable, as for an impossible exclusiveness or completeness, is an implication that harks back, to my mind, to my late suggestion of the possibility of falling in love with the world, blind to its progress beyond our knowledge. Our reflection about the nature of the differing skepticisms lets us think in the following way of the relation between our adventure with the world and our strangling of it: One respect in which I found a skepticism of mind to differ from the skepticism of matter, one feature present in the case of mind and not of matter, is a development in the thing of "avoiding the best". I said that in the realm of the external world you could not avoid the best case but only avoid knowing that it is the best, whereas in the realm of the other both paths are open. But there is a certain exception to this, a level at which this asymmetry too finds its symmetry. There is a human being, a way of being human, not insanely, in which an innocence and purity toward the world, if not exactly a mature love, allows an evenness in it or readiness for it that would not understand the exclusive or compressed stake in a best case; a being for whom any object might be as good as any other, in a world in which any might be loaded. This is the way of the clown, especially in his photogenesis, in what becomes of him on film, particularly in the figures of Charlie Chaplin and Buster Keaton. No case of externality is best for them because every case is best; this world is best, since no other is imaginable. This one is imaginable. No possibility, of fakery, simulation, or hallucination, goes beyond the actualities of their existence. But to live thus without escape is to be up to being the one who gets slapped, to being one for whom dignity does not depend upon standing, to be beyond expectation. However hard such a view is to maintain, it is even harder to share. So while it is easy to imagine these figures pining away for another, it is not easy to imagine them claiming another erotically. This is a way of stating their resemblance to children. Their refinement is to know everything skepticism can think of. I do not so much wish to say that they live skepticism as that they are survivors of it. (I have said a little more along these lines, and a little differently, in "What Becomes of Things on Film?".) It ought to be a profit of studying tragedy and comedy as epistemological matters that we come to develop epistemological equations between them.

— But I am still bound to say that I remain suspicious of the formula "to live one's skepticism". This once again seems to be just a flat contradiction on the account you have presented.   — Wouldn't you allow it as a paradox? I need a formula which at once shows the intimacy of the problem of others with the question of skepticism *and* shows the break between them. — But once more, and apart from whatever you mean by attaching importance to particular "formulas", *have* you produced skepticism upon the failure of your best cases? — I might say that that is *my* question. I am trying to discover the problem of others. — But you haven't so much as produced a candidate for this role until you show what could bring us back to earth, could take us out of the study, to others; what it is that constitutes an alternative to our speculations, upon which our speculations have, from their unique perspective, cast their special, unsettling light.

But I have explained why there is no alternative of that kind, in the arena of the other. The reason is that there is no human alternative to the possibility of tragedy. — You do not claim, I believe, to go around every day in roughly Othello's frame of mind? — Not exactly. But I claim to see how his life figures mine, how mine has the makings of his, that we bear an internal relation to one another; how my happiness depends upon living touched but not struck by his problems, or struck but not stricken; problems of trust and betrayal, of false isolation and false company, of the desire and the fear of both privacy and of union. — If so, isn't this something just about you and about him? — If so, then either *Othello* is no tragedy or I have not seen what it is. I do not claim to have *explained* how one human being's life (fictional or actual) can be representative of human life generally, which would perhaps come to explaining the idea that a human being is something that bears an internal relation to all other human beings, that they are mutually attuned, that they are species-beings. I do claim, for example, that Othello is thus representative, and that to understand that (literary) fact would be the same as to understand what the (philosophical) problem of others is, in particular why its best cases take the forms they take.

— And yet if now your child were to come into the study, these thoughts and this mood would vanish, would they not? You would be recalled, interrupted, as surely as if the mood you were in had been that in which you find that what you call the external world is dependent on your contingent human sensuous nature. — Now I am bound to say that this just seems to me to register your prejudice that the skepticisms *must* have the same (unstable) conclusion, that there *must* be a normal alternative to skeptical speculations concerning other minds. For otherwise why invoke the sentimental picture of the child? To be sure, I will, I hope, stop what I am doing and attend to the child. But must I take it that the *same* distraction supervenes as in the material object case, the same disruption of attention, the same inaccessibility of the same awful truth? On the contrary, inclining to the belief that I have no certain relief from my isolation, I might take the child not as an alternative to the knowledge of my inaccessibility to or by others, but as some solace for it — a solace not because the child frees me from my speculations about others, but because he is not, as I conceive him now, relevantly *other;* he merely extends the content of my narcissism. And if a genuine other does enter, what then? From the meditation on material objects, I would face a figure that must, like initial zeros, drop out of my skeptical calculations, because there is zero relevant difference between me and others in contemplating material objects. But if I am meditating others, then I face an instance of the very topic of my meditation, one whose relevant difference from me is all the difference in the world.

The figure of the child here suggests this further general asymmetry between our knowledge of the material and of the mental. Although skepticism in both arenas discovers our liabilities as knowers, expresses our disappointment with finitude, the ideal of knowledge implied by material object skepticism — of unlimited penetration or fastidiousness or completeness in our claims — vanishes upon the return to the everyday, as if it were always insubstantial, or damned. Whereas the ideal of knowledge implied by skepticism with respect to other minds — of unlimited genuineness and effectiveness in the acknowledgment of oneself and others — haunts our ordinary days, as if it were the substance of our hopes.

— But doesn't the allusion just now to Faust (with his ideal of knowledge damned) suggest the possibility of a tragedy in our knowledge of the external, material world, a sort of purely intellectual tragedy? Haven't you yourself pointed to this in speaking of a stratum of symmetry in which what corresponds to *acknowledgment* in relation to others is *acceptance* in relation to objects? ("The Avoidance of Love", p. 324). — If there is a purely intellectual tragedy, its protagonist will still have to be characterized as "living his or her skepticism", living some inability to acknowledge, I mean accept, the human conditions of knowing. And who could be the audience for such a subject, since human beings are not different from one another in this regard? How could the antagonist, for some flaw, become isolated from the human community, in a way that represents the contingent individuality of each witness? Here we would have to take it that possessing a human sensuous nature is itself the tragedy. Yet those who have had the clearest perception of human sensuous nature as a whole have not seen tragedy in it, but cautionary myth. The Buddha, Plato, St. Paul, take our sensuous imprisonment as one station

on the path of existence, from which each human being is to arise. (We
have to think what happens to such an idea as that of our arising from
(this feature of) our humanity in such minds as Blake's and Nietzsche's. It
becomes too easy for us to say: Not finitude, but the denial of finitude, is
the mark of tragedy. This denial of finitude has also been taken as the
mark of sin. It was to free humanity of that libel of sinfulness that Blake
and Nietzsche undertook, as it were, to deny the distinction between the
finite and the infinite in thinking of the human.)

If there were a drama of pure knowledge, it seems that Faust must be
its protagonist. But is Faust a tragic figure? Is he to be understood in
terms of the life of skepticism? Skepticism, after all, has to do with the
absolute *failure* of knowledge, whereas what Faust lived was the absolute
success of knowledge. But apparently what he is to have discovered about
this success is that it is not humanly satisfying. He is the Midas of knowledge. His is our central modern name for the attempt to overwhelm the
necessity of acknowledgment by the power and the extent of knowledge.
(Cf. "The Avoidance of Love", p. 347.) If we think of Faust as being
granted the wish to escape the human conditions of knowing, I mean the
condition of human knowing, then the clearest theoretical portrait of him
is given by the *Critique of Pure Reason,* in its descriptions of those who
think to escape the necessity of reason's critique of reason and who, for
example, are shown to live upside down, on their heads as it were, making
the world of their experience "empirically ideal and transcendentally
real". And perhaps more direct descriptions of him are to be found in
Kant's *Religion Within the Limits of Reason Alone.* Here, as is typical of
Kant's procedures, he goes beyond an expected Enlightenment battle that
takes up the cause of reason against irrationality on the most famous field
of the irrational. The collection of sections called General Observations,
one of which concludes each of the four parts of Kant's volume on religion, together constitute what I think amounts to a general theory of irrationality, a systematic account of what turn out, on this theory, to be a
whole class of phenomena, each of them involving a particular distortion
of human reason. Kant calls the four members of this class fanaticism, superstition, delusion, and sorcery. Not the least of the illuminations of his
theory is its implied proposal that, as one may frame it, the cure for Faust-
ianism and for skepticism are the same. — In his deepening of the Enlightenment, Kant not only heralds romanticism; he insures that whoever
refuses his cure for romanticism is fated to succumb to the disease, or
rather that refusing his cure is the best symptom of suffering from its disease. Nay, the best criterion.

Dr. Faust's descendent Dr. Frankenstein is generally more childish, or more patently adolescent, in comparison with his ancestor. This is due, it would seem, to his more superficial narcissism, and his more obvious sense of guilt, as well as to his assumptions that what you know is fully expressed by its realization in what you can make (as though science and technology were simply the same) and that one cannot finally assume responsibility for one's work, or rather that one can discharge one's responsibility for it (only) by sacrificing oneself to it — not, however, before sacrificing one's loved ones. It would be nice to understand, in connection with the declension from the damnation of Faust to the damnable Frankenstein, why there is a parallel declension in the genres they have inspired — why one of them is the subject of one of the great poetic epics of the modern world and the other of them is a classic, even a staple, of the literature (I include cinema) of the fantastic, especially of fictionalized science. Less prejudicially, the relation of the genres should be thought of not in terms of decline but in terms of popularization.

On understanding such a relation of genres the understanding of the possibility of living one's skepticism with respect to others may turn out to turn. I have more than once said or implied that the problem of the other was no less a literary than a philosophical problem. One task of this problem is to determine the spirit in which such a story as, for example, that of the craftsman in the garden is told, or that of an Evil Genius who continuously deceives me. In what spirit must these possibilities be told in order that they challenge my everyday beliefs, my natural orientation? And now I think we would have to enter more deeply into some territory we once labelled with the rubric "projective imagination" (Chapter VIII, the section entitled "The Philosopher's Projection . . ."). It is the territory that contains the most fundamental, or earliest, tasks of accounting for the occupation of ordinary language procedures in philosophy — the task, for example, of accounting for the difference between taking Austin's question "What should we say if . . . ?" as, what it is, an invitation to a conceptual sorting about your present, a demand for present consciousness, as opposed to, what it is not, an invitation to make a prediction about your future (cf. *Must We Mean What We Say?*, p. 66); or between Wittgenstein's remarks about what he calls the natural history of human beings and what he would call a *hypothesis* about that history (cf. *Investigations*, p. 230). In particular, here, we would need to articulate the difference between what we might call a thought experiment and what we might call a piece of science fiction. In the latter case we may work out the consequences of a hypothesis about a fictional world, one which we do not identify as ours; in the former case the counter-factual nature of the fiction takes place within a world we do identify as ours. To take the fiction of an Evil Genius as an occasion for working out imaginatively the consequences of life in a world in which there was such a figure (I mean in which a particular character is cast in that role, call him Dr. No) would not yield the speculation, as I understand it, that Descartes asks us to participate in. For a fictional tale is a history over which the teller has absolute authority, call it the power to stipulate the world from beginning to end; given that, there can be no room for Descartes's revelatory denial that such an Evil Genius could exist, that this would be like supposing God to be less than God. It seems to me that I meant my story of the craftsman in his garden to be one of several in which what comes forth is our sense that our conception of the outer (of the body and its degrees of freedom) is bound to our conception of the inner (of the soul that breathes expression), and our conception of ourselves to our conception of our others. I did not intend it as the beginning of an imaginative speculation about, for example, how we natural humans could learn to live with synthesized humans, or what such creatures could count as love, or justice, or courtesy, or fun.

Recognizing that an example or two is not an account of this important matter, I would like to assert my sense that science fiction cannot house tragedy because in it human limitations can from the beginning be by-passed. This idea helps me explain my difference in intuition from those philosophers who take it that a scientific speculation, or fiction, is sufficient to suggest skepticism; for example, the speculation that for all I know I may be a brain in a vat. (I believe for certain people such an image may be a good (figurative) expression for the way things really are, with each current brain mostly awash in a skull on a frame; or perhaps the image yields a good expression only about *certain* people.) Now apart from the fact that I do not feel *compelled* to consider this possibility, I do not feel that I am sufficiently clear about what would constitute considering it (as a hypothesis). For suppose it is true. Then I am to consider that a brain in a vat is to consider itself to be a brain in a vat, which seems to amount to imagining discovering it to be my (or its) situation. If I consider that I may now be asleep and dreaming, then I have a strong if vague idea that there is something and someone beyond, outside my dream; a strong if vague idea of what it would be like to wake up; and if I find myself walking with someone over to a sleeping human being and being told that that is me, then I know that *that* is either a dream, or I have walked into a piece of science fiction. But in undertaking to consider that I may be a brain in a vat I find that I have a most concrete idea of what must be happening outside, beyond the vat, monitoring it; and if I find myself walking with a monitor down white corridors, I can specifically imagine his pointing out, through a long window, as if pointing out a newborn in a hospital nursery, one among a number of vats with brains in them, and saying: "That one just there is you." (How would it change matters if instead of brains we took bodies in the vats?) — It seems to me evident that I have no idea what it would be like to learn that *I* am a brain in a vat; which seems to be good reason to suppose that I cannot seriously consider the possibility, as a hypothesis, that I am one. I may of course go on with the story of the brain nursery.

The immediate value of such a story, for me, is its demonstration that not just any way of being offered a world sensuously indistinguishable from my world is enough to cause me skeptical doubt. I have, as it were, simultaneously to be afforded a way of understanding how I came to be offered it. This is a separate feature of the dreaming and hallucination possibilities. — How about the other way around? Could we imagine that there is a culture for which *Othello,* say, reads like science fiction — a group who just have no first-hand knowledge of the need for trust or of the pain of betrayal? — I might say that it seems to me a piece of science fiction to imagine so. But that is not sure. There is a myth we have given ourselves that suggests that such a culture of human beings cannot exist — the myth according to which even God, in creating man and woman, had to leave them with, or rather provide them with, the power of betrayal. Then my idea just now, in reinvoking science fiction, was that if there were such a group for which *Othello* read like science fiction it would not be a group of humans. And for this non-human or post-human group, a cheap source of science fiction might be what *we* call daily newspapers (which *we* might sometimes look at as instances of surrealism).

I spoke, early in response to the passive skeptical recital, of having arrived at a plateau of uncertainty as to whether I am known, as to what would count as being known. But it is far from clear that the recital brought out what it is I want to be assured of in being known, or failing to be. That meditation passed essentially through the line at which it seemed that "all anyone knows or could know of me is what I am able to show them of myself". I did not, I believe, intend to confine the reference of that line to explicit passages in which I openly demonstrate to the other my affection or anger or pain or disappointment. But what else, what less than such explicitness, can it have intended? It cannot have meant the same as if I had said "all anyone knows or could know of me is what shows", for that seems to mean only that of course there must be *some* way for another to know (and I took myself to be saying more than that) and it seems to imply that *something* of me does *not* show (and I took myself to be saying less than that).

What wants expression here is a sense of limit both in what I can show and in what I can conceal of myself. It is true of a great deal of what goes on in me that normally if it is to be known I must tell it, or give expression to it. But for nothing in me is this absolutely true. Whatever in me I have to conceal I may betray exactly by the way in which I conceal it. Just *that* is what is concealed; the concealment of what it is up to me to express is a perfect expression of it — the slight edge to my denials, the over-casualness of my manner, the tint of automatonity in my smile or gait or posture, each of which I might succeed in concealing. . . . There are those who know how to read such concealments. The concealment of what there is to express is an exacting art, like camouflage. You might call it a language; the language of the body. About human beings there are only open secrets or open questions.

My painting of the passive recital may, more generally, have by-passed the real, the special requirement of passivity in being known, the thing I have sometimes described as letting oneself be known, and as waiting to be known. It was subject to a particular idea of passivity; as if to make oneself known, to present oneself for knowledge, were inevitably to distort oneself — as if this were the thing that caused the theatricalization of oneself. My recital, that is, assumed activity only in making myself known, not allowing an activity in, so to speak, becoming passive. But activity just here may well prove to constitute knowing oneself. It is the ability to make oneself an other to oneself, to learn of oneself something one did not *already* know. Hence this is the focus at which the knowledge of oneself and of others meet. I should think a sensible axiom of the knowledge of persons would be this: that one can see others only to the extent that one can take oneself as an other. (This is a little weaker than the thought I earlier described as making confession tolerable, that what one finds in oneself is a discovery as well of others.) Thoreau puts the thought this way: "I never knew, and never shall know, a worse man than myself" (*Walden*, "Economy"). This is by no means a process of knowing from one's own case. It is simply not making one's own case exceptional.

We have more than once come upon the question whether my failure to know or to be known by another is to be attributed to my, or to my other's, incapacity as a knowing subject or as a subject known. In asking of myself a perfect passiveness, a lucid waiting, I was focussing the problem as it turns upon the capacity of the other to know. This makes the other not an ideal Confessor (because to a Confessor one must confess, make oneself known) but an ideal Acceptor. It may be this that Thoreau called the Friend. For others, the Friend is one to whom, and from whom, everything to be said can be said, as it is there to be said. Such a one is the antithesis of the Confessor since nothing would be said in or as confession, but in description. Such a Friend is impossible for one to envision to the extent that acknowledgment strikes one as a certain kind of confession. And if the need to acknowledge presents itself as an urge to confess, it may *therefore* present itself as an urge not to, an urge to secrecy. Then one will have to have something to keep secret. Hence the crime, if only of imagination, will be for the sake of the guilt. For in a disordered world guilt will be proof of one's privacy, hence of one's possession of a self, hence of the nature of one's self. It will be the making known of oneself to oneself. So the desire for sanity can drive one mad.

If I cannot be certain either that I am not known or that I am, then it follows that I cannot be certain that a given other is a candidate either for knowledge or for ignorance of me. Then it is possible that no other *is* a candidate to do the knowing that I am a human being. But a human being could not fail to know, confronting me, that I am a human being. Therefore, if the problem of the existence of other minds turns on the capacity of the other to know of my existence, then either I do not know that I am a human being or I cannot know of the existence of other human beings. — Then who are those others? Let us say that I am, notwithstanding my recent discovery, an other for the others. Then I am at best another automaton, or humanoid, or a natural enemy, or a fellow member within his or her (non-human — but what sense would that now have?) species. I may hunt with them, migrate or hibernate with them, breed and fight with them, and we may pick off one another's fleas; we may even arrange for one of us to chatter while the rest of us sit quietly in rows. Such is the extent of our mutuality. In such a group I may feel *hidden*. — It should not be surprising that a proof designed to cast doubt on the existence of *other* human beings winds up casting doubt on my own existence as a human being. It should also not be surprising that I, for one, refuse to accept this proof. I, after all, constructed the proof, and therefore surely exist!

I once accounted for the sense of unknownness by saying that an individual may "take *certain* among his experiences to represent his *own* mind — certain particular sins or shames or surprises of joy — and then take his mind (his self) to be unknown so far as *those* experiences are unknown" ("Knowing and Acknowledging", p. 265). Does an individual in such straits take it that his existence is unknown? Perhaps he takes it that he exists for the others as unknown; anonymously, as it were. Perhaps he or she has the sense, somehow, that he or she is different, exceptional. (They may, for this reason, suppose that poetry is meant only for them, since only poetry can find what suffices for their knowledge. But everyone stands in need of the power of poetry, so long as anyone does. Society merely limits who may have it. This is one measure of the disorder of the world.) This sense of difference, of exemption, is a different difference from the way the slave is different: one does not here see oneself as a *kind* of human. And a different difference from the way the outcast is different: one does not here restrict one's humanity. One singles oneself out for unknowableness. One interprets one's separateness as isolation and then finds a cause for it: one is extraordinary, either too good or too bad for ordinary knowledge, too beautiful or too ugly, a monster of sanctity or of evil, an abyss of happiness or suffering. It seems to me that in such spiritual straits I might also produce the expression Wittgenstein witnessed about others not being able to have *this* pain (striking myself on the breast).

Wittgenstein's response (at §253) is straight-faced and stuffy:

The answer to this is that one does not define a criterion of identity by emphatic stressing of the word "this". Rather, what the emphasis does is to suggest the case in which we are conversant with such a criterion, but have to be reminded of it.

Why is this *the* answer, or any answer, since obviously it perversely refuses to see what was meant, I mean to see what the breast-striker had in mind. I was not imagining myself to be offering a criterion of identity when I imagined striking myself on the breast. — Of course you weren't! That's the humor in Wittgenstein's answer. Its point is that that's all, at best, that you *could* have comprehensibly been doing. You had the impression that you were demonstrating something profound, some metaphysical uniqueness, but you were demonstrating *nothing whatever,* except perhaps some species of emptiness. That is the rebuke in Wittgenstein's answer. — But *what* is the rebuke, what is the diagnosis of my error? To attempt to make an exception of myself in this way is precisely contrary to what I have called "the moral of the *Investigations* as a whole" (*supra,* p. 361). But does the *Investigations* provide an understanding of this possibility?

Grant that in striking my breast I did *not at all* mean that you could not have *this* (*descriptively* the same) pain, but rather that you cannot, how shall I say, *have* it, have this very having of it, that one I just now inflicted on myself. That! This! Now! Here! Then I shall grant that trying to give my gesture full explicitness leaves it seeming pretty empty; like informing you, while sitting across from you, that this hand and this breast that it struck are both mine, my very own. I did not, it seems to me, mean my remark as a piece of information, but rather as another kind of reminder, as a kind of parable. — A parable of our separateness, no doubt. And doubtless a reminder that you are you. — Why is one *so* impatient with this? Has such a one never felt his or her existence slighted, presented to blindness; never felt like insisting upon it, declaring it? Descartes's insistence on it, I mean his proof of it, just depends on declaring it; anyway asserting it, anyway silently. It would truly have been ludicrous of him to have tried giving it out as a piece of information!

My thought here is this: When Wittgenstein presents himself to us as denying or slighting our existence, our inner life, we may be prompted to respond to this apparent denial with a parabolic gesture of insistence upon our existence. The parable is to teach not just the fact of my existence, but the fact that to possess it I must declare it, as if taking it upon myself. Before this, there are no others for me. (So do not believe the monster when he tells you that he is monstrous because others treat him as monstrous. He is monstrous because he lets the task of becoming human wait upon how others treat him. Circumstances may have forced this upon him; he may have a chance to rebel; part of what he will rebel against will be his own monstrousness. For a child, a correct waiting here is necessary, it is legitimate. It is part of the monster's monstrousness that he was never a child; he therefore has not lost what human grownups have lost.)

I may realize the parable differently. In refusing Wittgenstein's therapy here, refusing to apply to myself the humor of his answer about the emptiness of emphasizing the word "this", refusing to wear this shoe of rebuke, I may be wishing to convey that you just do not know who or what I am. Far, accordingly, from wishing, or sensing a need, to define criteria with which we would be mutually attuned, I wish, or sense a need, to convey how perfectly, originally, I satisfy the criteria. We could say of my condition, or you could say it, that I had made myself morally incomprehensible, as Kierkegaard in effect says of Abraham. (There is the modern man for you: knife in hand, full of readiness to sacrifice, but in the absence of God, and of Isaac, and hence of an angel in the wings.) (The slave and the outcast have been made morally invisible.)

One in this condition does not feel unknown for the reason that the fact of his or her sentience is taken to be unknown. Why should a dog, a horse, a rat, have life, and be known to have it, and others not? Expertise cannot be required to know of this life, but then what appreciation is wanted, what sentiment or sensibility would be fine enough to vibrate to one's originality? Human beings do not naturally desire isolation and incomprehension, but union or reunion, call it community. It is in faithfulness to that desire that one declares oneself unknown. (And of course the faithfulness, the desire, and the declaration may all be based on illusion. The conceptual connection, however, would remain as real as ever.) The wish to be extraordinary, exceptional, unique, thus reveals the wish to be ordinary, everyday. (One does not, after all, wish to become a monster, even though the realization of one's wish for uniqueness would make one a monster.) So both the wish for the exceptional and for the everyday are foci of romanticism. One can think of romanticism as the discovery that the everyday is an exceptional achievement. Call it the achievement of the human. — I believe I know something of the impatience such ideas can inspire. Think of the spectacle of the likes of Rousseau and Thoreau and Kierkegaard and Tolstoy and Wittgenstein going around hoping to be ordinary, preaching the everyday as the locale of the sublime! Only the madness of their egotism, the monstrousness of it, requires such vaults of relief! Only sinners so crave sanctity! — Quite right. Quite right. The everyday is everyday, the ordinary is ordinary, or you haven't found it. — How true that is. How very true. And yet if what those monsters of egotism and of vision saw is there, then your assurance is as egotistical as theirs, merely less instructive; or else you are as cynical as you evidently are complacent. (My caution against believing the monster can only make sense to someone who knows his or her own human capacities well enough to be *moved* to believe him. I would not waste my spirit preaching hardness to a stone.)

The only way to prove that someone is not mad — or otherwise dismissible — in claiming epistemological exemption for himself, the singling out for unknownness, is to describe some cases, some versions of a type. We might think of them as versions of narcissism, a concept that might prove increasingly useful in studying (passive) skepticism, since it covers both a primary development in childhood and the foundation of a particular direction of madness in adulthood. Some again will think of them as versions of adolescence. The only reason I would have for objecting to this thought is the naughty implication that such a one just ought to grow up. If Rousseau can be said to have discovered the fact of childhood in human growth, and Wordsworth the loss of childhood, then romanticism generally may be said to have discovered the fact of adolescence, the task of wanting and choosing adulthood, along with the impossibility of this task. The necessity of the task is the choice of finitude, which for us (even after God) means the acknowledgment of the existence of finite others, which is to say, the choice of community, of autonomous moral existence. The impossibility lies in the options of community that the older grownups have left, which no one could want, not with a whole heart. So romantics dream revolution, and break their hearts. And so adolescents and adults agree on this one point, that to become adult is to grow up from your dreams. You needn't be Martin Heidegger to count the achievement of modern individual existence as beginning with its eclipse in modern society and then graduating in its increasingly distant refinement of singularity. John Stuart Mill a hundred years earlier, and for the sake of similar perceptions, accepts the fact, or fate, that the only proof of liberty lies in idiosyncrasy. The problem completes itself when we no longer know whether we are idiosyncratic or not, which differences between us count, whether we have others. — After such community, what privacy?

I find one version of such a type in the life of Rousseau, who thus becomes for me a significant case in the modern history of our concept of the knowledge, and ignorance, of other minds — as I suppose he was for himself. So I am taking it that his sense of rejection, of others as refusing to know him, as denying him, is — well, not normal exactly, but, let us say, composed of equal parts of abnormality and of validity. Then the writing of his *Confessions* should be regarded as an effort to create the individual other who would be in a position, and who would care, to accept him. But if the *Confessions* is of his whole life, then he can only be known posthumously. People who know themselves to be masters of this species of communication, and of no other, are likely to welcome the hereafter.

A different version of one who regards himself as unknowable would give up the effort to create his knower, even posthumously. He has become a virtuoso of confession, an entertainer with his suffering. The point of his recitals is not to reveal himself, even when everything he says about himself is true. For him the thing of self-revelation is quite impossible — those who care cannot know, those who know cannot care enough. The virtuosity beguiles his anonymity and the other's boredom.

Here the very capacity for intimacy measures the fact of isolation; measures the depth of privacy unshared, i.e., refused.

That types of the passive skeptic should naturally present themselves as typical figures of romanticism registers (whatever else romantic self-assertion shows) the apprehension that human subjectivity, the concept of human selfhood, is threatened; that it must be found and may be lost; that if one's existence is to be proven it can be proven only from oneself; and that upon that proof turns what proof there is in the continued existence of the human as such. This is what happens to the Renaissance project of the humanization of the world by the time the project is taken up in romanticism. It is not to be expected that everyone will adopt, nor so much as credit, such a project. Some will even find it arrogant to offer oneself as the exemplar, or fate, of humanity. Presumably such a one will regard it as modest to offer proofs for the existence of *others*.

Here are two romantic ways to understand the project of proving the existence of the human.

Suppose that after the onslaughts of Hume and Kant, no self-respecting thinker will any longer seek a proof for the existence of God as our creator. If anything, the reverse seems undeniably the case. But the consequences of such a reversal cannot be obvious at once. In particular, we are apt to be stuck with the idea of the human being as a *creature*, meaning a living thing, something procreated; but meaning equally something created. Then we seem to have the following choice. Either we attempt to give up the idea of the human being as created, in which case we attempt to *naturalize* the human being, to understand this being in relation to (non-human) nature, an attempt sometimes described as locating the human being's *place* in nature; or else we retain the idea of ourselves as created and attempt further to *humanize* this creation, identifying ourselves now as the creators of ourselves, since obviously no *other* being could be eligible for such a role. — One might undertake to show that there is no such choice, or rather that the choices come to the same point, call it the *return* of the human, as of the repressed. But these approaches to this return seem slated for disappointment. In the former case, that of relocating ourselves in nature, human beings keep discovering themselves in *opposition* to nature, whether for Descartes's reasons or for Rousseau's or for Kant's or for Blake's or for Wordsworth's or for Marx's or for Thoreau's. In the latter case, that of accepting ourselves as our creator, we would have to accept responsibility for ourselves, in particular have to consent to our present state as something we desire, or anyway desire more than we desire change; and this could drive us mad, as Rousseau was mad, or Nietzsche, or as Marx and Thoreau were. We are apt to turn upon our creation in anger, as, according to us — and who knows this better? — the Creator did.

Or suppose that romanticism can be thought of as the discovery, or one rediscovery, of the subjective; the subjective as the exceptional; or the discovery of freedom as a state in which each subject claims its right to recognition, or acknowledgment; the right to name and assess its own satisfaction. I take as paradigmatic of this discovery the complex moment in *Essay on the Origin of Languages* at which Rousseau establishes the context — it is not exactly the formulation of a language-game — in which the human being gives a name to his *semblable*, his other, calls him human, hence has a name for himself.

Upon meeting others, a savage man will initially be frightened. Because of his fear he sees the others as bigger and stronger than himself. He calls them *giants*. After many experiences, he recognizes that these so-called giants are neither bigger nor stronger than he. Their stature does not approach the idea he had initially attached to the word giant. So he invents another name common to them and to him, such as the name *man*, for example, and leaves *giant* to the fictitious object that had impressed him during his illusion. That is how the figurative word is born before the literal word, when our gaze is held in passionate fascination; and how it is that the first idea it conveys to us is not that of the truth. ["That the First Language Had To Be Figurative"]

All I ask attention to here is that the first naming of the other is characterized by Rousseau in such a way as to encourage imagining it as taking the form of an exclamation: upon meeting others, the savage man has an experience on the basis of which he calls something out, something is called forth from him. (". . . Both the report and the exclamation are expressions of perception and of visual experience. But the exclamation is so in a different sense from the report: it is forced from us. — It is related to the experience as a cry is to pain" (*Investigation*, p. 197).) When subsequently, on the basis of noticing the empirical analogies between himself and others, he displaces the first name called forth from him in favor of another, he does not, according to my reading of the passage, displace the experience that brought forth the name; he rather, as it were, displaces his explanation of the feeling. Fright (anyway, the experience of others as fearful) remains the basis of the knowledge of the existence of others; only now we no longer interpret the threat as a function of the other's bulk or body. We seem left with the other's sheer otherness, the fact that he, too, is an I, hence can name and know us. One can regard this moment in Rousseau as an effort to answer the question of others

formed in Wittgenstein's *Investigations* — or, removing the surface an-
achronism, one can regard Wittgenstein's question as a rediscovery of the
moment discovered in Rousseau: "What gives us so much as the idea that
living beings — things — can feel?" (*Investigations,* §283).

I do not ask that Rousseau's answer be accepted — that the idea, anyway
about *human* things, comes as an interpretation of one's fear of their presence, which perhaps means a fear at the recognition, the objectification, or
engraving, of one's own image, its theft from us. Behind my suggestion
here is a certain understanding of what the savage man is initially frightened by in being frightened by an *other*. A natural reading of Rousseau's
scene is to take the savage man to be frightened by one who is frightened
upon meeting *him*. (It is of the essence of this passage of initial human confrontation to see that everything said about either the one or the other is
true of both.) Does he therefore understand himself as fearful? Or isn't it
rather that, since he is frightened, he cannot regard himself as the object
of the other's fear? In either case he is *frightened by an expression of fright*.
When, "after many experiences . . . he invents a name common to them
and to him", he will interpret that expression of the other's fright and recognize himself as an object of fear; it is then possible for him to be afraid
of himself and to shun his company. But before this time, how does he
understand that expression of fright to be directed *to* him, on the part
of one who cannot be frightened *of* him? It would make sense for him to
take it as an imitation of himself, showing him how he looks, the image
of himself in the presence of others. Quite as if *he* were the giant, or anyway
possessed of some form of the monstrous. It will have to be hidden.

I ask merely that the level of Rousseau's answer be considered as a
datum in the problem of other minds, indeed that the *Essay on the Origin
of Languages,* and the companion *Discourse on Inequality,* be recognized
as studies of the problem of others. Then a twin datum would be that
romanticism opens with the discovery of the problem of other minds, or
with the discovery that the other is a problem, an opening of philosophy.
I mean truly that I ask this to be considered, not that I engage this consideration, for I am so far in a position merely to rummage among such
texts, not to possess them.

In the same spirit, I wish to put this moment of the beginning of romanticism together with a moment plausibly taken as its end, the moment
of Hegel's *Philosophy of Right*. In that work Hegel refers to "the right
of the subject's particularity, his right to be satisfied, or in other words
the right of subjective freedom", as "the pivot and center of the difference
between antiquity and modern times". And he continues: "This right in

its infinity is given expression in Christianity and it has become the universal effective principle of a new form of civilization". The rest of history is the working out, the concrete expressions, shapings, of this right (section 124, addition). Then I might put the question "Is there such a thing as soul-blindness?" in the following way: Is this new form of civilization being replaced by another? In particular, is it being replaced by one in which nothing that happens any longer strikes us as the objectification of subjectivity, as the act of an answerable agent, as the expression and satisfaction of human freedom, of human intention and desire? What has a beginning can have an end. If this future (civilization?) were effected its members would not be dissatisfied. They would have lost the concept of satisfaction. Then nothing would (any longer) give them the idea that living beings, human things, could feel. So they would not (any longer) be human. They would not, for example, be frightened upon meeting others — except in the sense, or under circumstances, in which they would be frightened upon encountering bears or storms, circumstances under which bears would be frightened. And of course particular forms of laughter and of amazement would also no longer be possible, ones which depend upon clear breaks between, say, machines and creatures. — Would the vanishing of the human betoken the absolute success of the scientific *Weltanschauung?* It would betoken the success of the picture of science, of knowledge, as subjugation — not now as that by which the human being subjugates the world, and overcomes superstition and magic, but now as that by which the human being is subjugated. So science falls back, or forward, into magic.

This fantasy of the vanishing of the human — it would contain the fantasy in which empathic projection becomes "seamless", or ceases, and we no longer recognize, or take an interest in, the difference between things and beings (*the* difference!) — is a reassertion of the idea that the problem of other minds is a problem of human history (the problem of modern human history; the modern problem of human history); that the problem is lived, and that this life has an origin and a progress. The idea is that the problem of the other is discovered through telling its history. Then how could this history be recounted; what would it be a recounting of? If it is true, if the idea is sound, that skepticism with respect to others, in both its active and its passive forms, is lived and has a history, then what that history contains, what it must recount, can only be determined from within the life, or perspective, of that skepticism itself, as a discovery of its own problems and of the shapes taken in its solutions to its problems. The extent to which I have uncovered the perspective of skepticism concerning other minds leads me to expect that its history will contain an account of its origins in the following developments.

1. Most obviously, it will wish an account of the particular insanity required, or caused, or threatened, in the very conceiving of the problem. The kinds of insanity — or folly — Descartes imagines his case may be compared with in undertaking to initiate his skeptical perspective, are ones arising from his undertaking to doubt that his ("these") hands and his ("this") body are his. The instances of folly he imagines are, accordingly, ones in which human beings do not know that they are flesh (but suppose themselves made of clay or glass) or do not know their identities or their true circumstances (but suppose themselves kings when they are actually paupers, or clothed when they are naked). (If Descartes's intuitions, or fantasies, of knowledge and of doubt are to be followed, then the interpretation of skeptical doubt as *neurotic* is evidently hopeless.) The insanity of which Rousseau is accused is not of this kind. It is called (loosely, I believe) a form of paranoia. But what creates this impression of him? Here are two of his ideas that may encourage it: first, that he has become unknowable — private — because to know him would be to know the sentiments of his heart — in particular, his pity for others and his fears of them — and the sentiments of the heart have become unintelligible to (inexpressible by) other human beings (as a result of what they perceive as human progress); second, that our social bonds are not the realization but the betrayal of the social contract, in a word, conspiracies, so that there is among us no public thing at all. But *are* these ideas signs of madness? They would be if Rousseau believed, as perhaps from time to time he did think, that he alone was thus denied acknowledgment, and that the conspiracy of society was directed specifically against him. I am not now interested in asserting that these ideas may be sane, but rather in suggesting that not every form of madness is possible, and certainly not typical, in every period; that madness has its history, and that it may be part of Rousseau's originality to have discovered an original shape of madness. He would have borrowed elements of this shape from the fates of Cassandra and Phèdre, figures earlier maddened through an isolation, an unknownness, caused by their possession of incommunicable knowledge. Thinking of Nietzsche as a later avatar in this line, it strikes me as especially brave of Thoreau to have refused derangement; that is, to have recognized the achievement of sanity as the goal, or ratification, of his arrangements. But then of course he was free of European quarrels, and,

in effect, or in the fiction of *Walden* (i.e., of America), free of intellectual competitors (i.e., companions) altogether. Some freedom.

2. The life of skepticism with respect to (other) minds will next require a history of its imagined overcomings, particularly of its idea that to know or be known by another is to penetrate or be penetrated by another, to occupy or be occupied. This idea would be prepared by the idea, or creation, of the self as private (hence, as said, as guilty). Hence its over-coming will take the form of violating that privacy. Doubtless Descartes is working also here: "We are now in a position to see the precise nature of Descartes's innovation in philosophy of mind. The introduction of *cogitatio* as the defining characteristic of mind is tantamount to the sub-stitution of privacy for rationality as the mark of the mental. For some-body like Aquinas, human beings were distinguished from animals by such things as their capacity to understand geometry and to desire riches. Neither . . . is a specially private state . . ." (Kenny, "Cartesian Pri-vacy", p. 360). It should be considered also that an initiating form for the achievement of privacy would be the convulsion of sensibility we call the rise of Protestantism. From then on, one manages one's relation to God alone, in particular one bears the brunt alone of being known to God. Here nothing that could be told in confession could be confession enough, since what I possess is no longer merely secrets, but an existence essentially unknowable to myself, namely, whether I am of the elect, or faithful.

As long as God exists, I am not alone. And couldn't the other suffer the fate of God? It strikes me that it was out of the terror of this possibility that Luther promoted the individual human voice in the religious life. I wish to understand how the other now bears the weight of God, shows me that I am not alone in the universe. This requires understanding the philosophical problem of the other as the trace or scar of the departure of God. This descent, or ascent, of the problem of the other is the key way I can grasp the alternative process of secularization called romanticism. And it may explain why the process of humanization can become a mon-strous undertaking, placing infinite demands upon finite resources. It is an image of what living our skepticism comes to.

It is to be expected that the idea of knowledge as the violation of pri-vacy (or punishment for it) will be eroticized, enacted in forms of sexual life. So our history will have to account for the romantic obsession, or theatricalization, of what we used to think of as sexual perversion, in par-ticular with sadism and masochism; at any rate, with the wish for absolute activeness and absolute passiveness; which is to say, for absolute recogni-tion of and by another. ("Absolute" here arises as it did miles ago when I was discussing how one got taken "outside language games". I want my existence proven by evidence that I cannot supply, and need not. And the same goes for the existence of others.) That this sexualization of knowledge should take the form of a theatricalization of the relation between master and slave should be seen in the light of Hegel's notion that the taking possession of oneself — the, as it were, subjugation of the self by the self as a declaration of individual freedom, hence as a stage in the achievement of human freedom as such (in the State) — begins in what he calls "the fight for recognition and the relationship of master and slave" (*Philosophy of Right*, section 57). Taking this together with the occurrence of the topic in the *Phenomenology of Mind*, we should ask: What happens to individuals if they tire of history, can take no further mediation, become lost or captivated on the path of self-realization and intersubjectivity — if they become "reified" rather than "concretized"? If we speak of perversions of human existence, this will encompass disturbances of satisfaction no more sexual than epistemological, and no more these than political. (Subsidiary topics here will accordingly be the eroticization of seeing and hearing, as well as of political subjugation.)

3. Then we will, accordingly, want in our history an account of our attitudes toward the human body. This will consist importantly of libels and of attempts to undo certain libels against the body, sometimes by directly discrediting them (Nietzsche could not praise Luther too highly for his efforts here), sometimes by enacting or literalizing them (so that de Sade, for example, would be seen to be enacting the dictates of nature, if you like, only under a Christian interpretation of nature, of human nature as requiring mortification). My own choice as the hero of this particular piece of history is William Blake, who can ask and answer questions this way:

> What is it men in women do require
> The lineaments of Gratified Desire
> What is it women do in men require
> The lineaments of Gratified Desire

Here is a brave acceptance of the sufficiency of human finitude, an achievement of the complete disappearance of its disappointment, in oneself and in others, an acknowledgment of satisfaction and of reciprocity.

More or less obviously, in writers from Blake and Hegel to Thoreau and Nietzsche, the working through of secularization requires the constructing of a mythology to rival that of Christianity, which in practice means to reinterpret Christianity, bone by bone. But nothing is obvious about "secularization", especially not whether in a given case it looks like, as one might call it, eternalization. The progressive dissociation of spirit and nature (hence the possible disappearance of both) is more commonly thought of, I believe, in spatial rather than in these temporal terms, i.e., as a process of the progressive internalization and externalization of human interests. The guiding thought in either case is that each is a function of the other, that these are sides of some progressing bilateralization of the human, entailing some further fearful symmetries. One symptom or perception of this progress is Mill's familiar division or attribution of his intellectual inheritance, hence of that of the world of mind generally, equally between Bentham and Coleridge. Emerson knew in himself a division between what he called Materialism and Idealism (in "Transcendentalism"); it is just such division, say between the "real" and the "ideal", that a philosopher like John Dewey meant to put a stop to, with his kit of pre-Marxian and pre-Freudian tools. This polar sense or fantasy is of the mind unmoored, say unhinged, leaving itself without material in which to realize and communicate itself; it is an anxiety of progressive *inexpressiveness*, named as such in Coleridge's "Dejection", some lines from which Mill quotes in his *Autobiography* as describing exactly the case of his mental crisis. His case of depression becomes fully representative, historical, when he characterizes "the general tone of [his] mind at this period" as one in which he was "seriously tormented by the thought of the exhaustibility of musical combinations", calculating in a premature, uncanny premonition that the twelve tones of the octave must have about yielded all their usable combinations up, so that "there could not be room for a long succession of Mozarts and Webers to strike out, as these had done, entirely new and surprisingly rich veins of musical beauty". The concept of inexpressiveness, related to a sense of negative uniqueness, or depressed privacy, abutting the concept of the exhaustion of the medium of an art, leaving no room for anything new or original to be said in it, is what I am calling representative, or historical, in Mill's case. It is a historical enactment of the lie of concepts I found excavated by the "private language argument".

(I ask attention to this conjunction again here not to continue it now but merely to mark one place from which I hope a continuation of the work of these pages might take its bearings, and to permit myself reference to places in other writings of mine in which it is a little continued: in *The Senses of Walden*, as, e.g., the "theme of outsideness" (pp. 54–60); and in "More of *The World Viewed*", under the title "secular mysteries", forms which explore "the distance between the depth to which an ordinary human life requires expression, and the surface of ordinary means through which that life must, if it will, express itself" (p. 587, and pp. 606–7, note). I should like to mention here W. J. Bate's *The Burden of the Past and the English Poet* as containing, among other things, a set of texts showing the progressive fear of artistic exhaustion, and proof that the romantic poets' mission of originality does not separate them from the earlier eighteenth century, but joins them with it. If John Stuart Mill can experience such things, no later writer can be free of them; then no later man or woman can be.)

A beautiful and sufficiently explicit statement of "secularization" concerning our relation to nature, occurs, to my ear, in some lines from the Boy of Winander passage in Book V of Wordworth's *Prelude*. The Boy has been hooting "to the silent owls that they might answer him" and they respond with "concourse wild". (Some forty years later, by waters just outside Concord, Thoreau will speak for a cat-owl that produced a "thrilling discord" in which he claims there could be discriminated an unseen and unheard concord.)

> And when it chanced
> That pauses of deep silence mock'd his skill,
> Then sometimes, in that silence, while he hung
> Listening, a gentle shock of mild surprize
> Has carried far into his heart the voice
> Of mountain torrents; or the visible scene
> Would enter unawares into his mind
> With all its solemn imagery, its rocks,
> Its woods, and that uncertain Heaven, receiv'd
> Into the bosom of the steady Lake.

"Receiv'd into the bosom" suggests death. Heaven, become uncertain, died; and what happened to it is that it became nature. One absorbs both this uncertainty and this steadiness in coming to know both how to elicit nature's response and how to be surprised by its silent and independent existence. (How to be surprised *that* there is a world.) Is this knowledge? Is it produced by poetry or by history or by philosophy? Or preserved?

4. The historical period we are directly interested in, one origin of which is Rousseau's discovery of the naming of the human, is one in which a "science" of the human was being called for. Whatever Hume meant by the subtitle of his *Treatise of Human Nature* — "an attempt to introduce the experimental method of reasoning into moral subjects" — its implication is that we so far do not, but we are about to, know ourselves for what we are — as, since Newton, we know the inanimate universe. Now a special feature of the skepticism whose history we request will concern the fact that we still do not know whether this science of the human has

been established or not. It remains an issue of academic as well as of newspaper debate, and sometimes of inner conflict: Is Freudian psychology a science? Is Behaviorism? Is Marxism? It is essential to our history that the subject — call it psychology — was explicitly called for as an *imitation* of an undoubted science; a call that, so far as I hear, continues unabated; so the subject remains without the authority, or autonomy, to call itself knowledge. Hume remarks in his Introduction that " 'Tis no astonishing reflection to consider, that the application of experimental philosophy to moral subjects should come after that to natural at the distance of above a whole century", since a comparable lag can be seen in Greece a couple of millennia ago. Then is it not astonishing that Hume does not consider, or note as a curiosity, that the "application of experimental philosophy" to *nature* also came at a distance, that natural science itself has origins, that it, too, is a part of human history?

Suppose what one thinks is that the science of the human has not been established. Is such a one, therefore, to consider that we are still living in a pre-scientific era with respect to the knowledge of humanity — so that, for example, what we think of as psychology will bear to some future, real body of knowledge, call it psychonomy, the relation that astrology bore to astronomy? The implication of the question is that our state is not merely one of ignorance, which can be overcome through experience (or "experiment"), but of magic (infected with what we will come to see as fanaticism and superstition), a kind of psychic savagery, which can only be overcome through a change of our natural reactions, through a certain continuation of the motivations and observations of that very magic. If, for example, one is convinced that one is known through the concepts and procedures of Freudian psychology, that Freud's insights precipitate shapes of thought in which the human is, if still without sufficient refinement, genuinely known — that the human being must be whatever it is required to be if those shapes of thought are valid (in particular that the human individual, to win freedom, must be something that can fight for recognition, which now means, vie with its incorporated interpretations of itself for a voice, for the leading voice, in its history) — then it is *pointless* to discuss learnedly with the unconvinced whether this psychology is "scientific" (though courtesy might require conversation; and so might some as yet undefined form of intellectual shame). Anyway, the question is whether it is knowledge; and the problem for one whose stake is to deny that one is captured by this knowledge turns on one's ability to compete successfully against it, i.e., to give alternative interpretations of the phenomena, and the relations among the phenomena, of dreams and laughter and accidents and repetitions, etc., and, more generally, an alternative to the vision of behavior as a hieroglyph of the soul. (The simplest alternative, I guess the most common, is to say that our behavior and our dreams *mean* nothing. And this might be true. I mean, someone might be living this. We might all come to.) To one convinced of his capture by this mode of knowledge, the origins of psychoanalysis among the mists of hypnosis and, a bit more archaically, among the visions of mesmerists and physiognomists, can seem a reassuring recapitulation of the rise of science out of, or in overcoming, magic. To one unconvinced, this will be oppositely reassuring, for surely nothing born in such circumstances could be legitimate science!

What motives and intuitions of the magic concerning the mind should be overcome, hence faced, in a science of mind? One intuition is that we are subject to "influences" from one another, to mutual "magnetisms", to certain chemical-like "affinities". Such properties, as in the case of an analogous intuition with respect to nature, must remain occult apart from developments analogous with the discovery of the magnet. Is it possible that psychonomy, or rather certain psychonomers, already exist, and have existed, on the basis of such a discovery? Could such knowledge be possessed by just a few — call it the discovery of the social bonds, or bondage; of the (outer) laws of association, let us say — who for some reason cannot communicate them to the rest of us?

Consider the following observation:

Instead of the injured party, the injured *universal* now comes on the scene, and . . . takes over the pursuit and the avenging of crime, and this pursuit consequently ceases to be the subjective and contingent retribution of revenge and is transformed into the genuine reconciliation of right with itself, i.e., into punishment. Objectively, this is the reconciliation of the law with itself; by the annulment of the crime, the law is restored and its authority is thereby actualized. Subjectively, it is the reconciliation of the criminal with himself, i.e., with the law known by him as his own and as valid for him and his protection; when this law is executed upon him, he himself finds in this process the satisfaction of justice and nothing save his own act. [Hegel, *Philosophy of Right,* section 220]

How shall we characterize this as a mode of thought? In its personifications (e.g., "the injured universal now comes on the scene") it sounds like allegory and mythology, hence like some depassé literary mode. It also sounds like history, sort of; anyway, as if opening itself to historical evidence. It would sound more like history if history were regarded as the anthropology of our pasts, of the presents of the distant tribes whose present we are. It also sounds like psychology, sort of; anyway, as if opening itself to psychological evidence. But if one applied what *we* are likely to consider psychology to this passage, especially to its concluding sentence (". . . it is the reconciliation of the criminal with himself . . ."), we are more than likely to understand it as a social piety, either perfectly proper (an attempt to elicit soul-saving repentance) or perfectly tyrannical (a soul-destroying attempt to mortify the criminal into bringing peace to those who destroy him). Here is a remark of Nietzsche's that I understand as a comment on this passage, and to be seeking a perspective from which to rationalize it, i.e., to show that the cultural stance it depicts has not achieved rationality:

You do not want to kill, O judges and sacrificers, until the animal has nodded? Behold, the pale criminal has nodded: out of his eyes speaks the great contempt. [*Thus Spoke Zarathustra*, "On the Pale Criminal"]

If your practices require the separate consent of those who suffer from them, then you must consider that the thing you read as affirmation (the nodding) is itself produced by the suffering (perhaps a lowering of the head, which may mean defeat or may signal attack).

5. I have said that the perspective I seek in these histories is present not only in philosophical allegories and mythologies (perhaps concerning the human body seeking its original unity, before its division into individual males and females; or the one about being able to doubt whether my body is mine but not whether my mind is mine; or the one about my not being able to have your feelings and so not knowing whether you have them) but also in various literary structures, especially in those we call tragedies (hence doubtless in comedies as well) and more recently, perhaps, also in tales of the fantastic and of horror. This is a claim, in effect, that these structures provide us with the knowledge of the Outsider. All and only what the Outsider can know of us is what the history of these literary forms would show.

That I am pushed to pieces of literature to discover the problem of the other, that I find the problem largely undiscovered for philosophy, for philosophy as it commands English and hence was carried unawares into my mind, is a fact I might think of this way. The problem of the other was always known, or surmised, not to be a problem of knowledge, or rather to result not from a disappointment over a failure of knowledge but from a disappointment over its success (even, from a horror of its success). When most recently we retraced the matter of our disappointment with criteria (which we might as well stick to calling our disappointment with human knowledge) we found what I called two old possibilities in view, that I fail to manifest our criteria accurately or that the other fails to read them accurately. Now if the problem of the other is a problem of the victory of knowledge, then it is equally a problem of this victory over myself, determining the nature of my self-consciousness. Then two things happen: I try avoiding further knowledge for myself by taking the problem of other minds solely from the passive side; and I thus find a new possibility for disappointment with knowledge, that my self-consciousness comes between my consciousness and my expression of it, so that my expressions are embarrassed, are no longer *natural*. But if my expressions are no longer natural they are no longer the foundation of certainty about my (inner) life, no longer criterial. And if no longer natural then they are artificial, merely conventional. I theatricalize myself. The problem of the other now, the problem in being known, is not that the other does not see me as human, but rather that the other (only) sees me, and always as a human something or other. So, consequently, do I take myself. My existence is proven, but at the price of not knowing what it is in itself. And the existence of others is proven, but at the price of their being spectators of my existence, not participants in it.

One text from which to decipher the significance of our suffocating from the half-swallowed apple of knowledge is Kleist's "Marionette Theater". Is being human exactly to be incapable either of swallowing it or spitting it out? Is the gasping of the human voice, say sobbing or laughing, the best proof of the human? or best picture, i.e., mask? To swallow once for all would be to live always within ordinary language-games, within the everyday; to spit once for all would be to exist apart from just that life, to live without. In particular, to live without the human voice (e.g., without appeal, without protest). — Is the temptation to knowledge a product of the prohibition of knowledge, or the other way around, the prohibition a projection or explanation of the temptation? (The decisive moment in the conjuring trick.)

— For you the claim that the Outsider's knowledge of us is the study of literature is as safe as it is obscure. Since you read the problem of the other as the problem of acknowledging one's relation to the other; and since you claim that the history of the failures of these relations is a history of skepticism and of attempts to overcome skepticism; then since fiction can safely be said to be "about" human relationships, sure enough fiction is about acknowledgment and its limitations; and then if one accepts your characterization of tragedy as the failure of the best case of acknowledgment, one has already accepted it as your characterization of skepticism. And indeed, aren't your "best cases" really just cases of love?

And everyone will concede that dramatic fictions tend to be dramas of love, and of course, if you like, dramas of the avoidances of love, even of the horrors of it. — But then what I have said should contribute to an understanding of why dramas are about love, and what it is they provide us with a knowledge of, and why this knowledge takes the form it does, viz., of acknowledgment, or of its impossibility. And of course I am counting on what I have said to raise the question of whether, and of how, we know differences between the writing of literature and the writing of philosophy.

Since I shall say no more in defense of such ideas here, I surface with two or three Shakespearean texts, further instances in which skepticism with respect to other minds is more or less explicitly under investigation, to illustrate not merely that tragedy is the story and study of a failure of acknowledgment, of what goes before it and after it — i.e., that the form of tragedy is the public form of the life of skepticism with respect to other minds — but specifically to illustrate, or to prompt the study of, the element in the problem of others that my perspective upon the problem has kept leading back to, namely, the idea and fate of the human body in these histories.

The most explicit passage is the most famous of Shylock's speeches, which directly takes the look of an argument from analogy, mounted from the passive side. Shylock has just listed his abuses at the hands of Antonio and asks the reason for them. Shylock gives his answer: "I am a Jew."

Hath not a Jew eyes? hath not a Jew hands, organs, dimensions, senses, affections, passions? fed with the same food, hurt with the same weapons, subject to the same diseases, healed by the same means, warmed and cooled by the same winter and summer as a Christian is? — if you prick us do we not bleed? if you tickle us do we not laugh? if you poison us do we not die? and if you wrong us shall we not revenge? — if we are like you in the rest, we will resemble you in that. If a Jew wrong a Christian, what is his humility? revenge! If a Christian wrong a Jew, what should his sufferance be by Christian example? — why revenge! The villainy you teach me I will execute, and it shall go hard but I will better the instruction. [*The Merchant of Venice*, III, i]

That is, for present purposes: My body, and its fates, the visible part of me, is the same as the Christian's. — And then the philosophical conclusion one would expect Shylock to draw, or ask to be drawn, is that the invisible part is the same as well; reason is compelled to admit as much. It is true that Shylock includes more in his premisses of "the visible part" of himself than a purer philosopher would; he includes things that the philosopher would regard as part of the conclusion of the argument from analogy, e.g., senses, affections, passions; and hence seems to beg the question. But though less pure, Shylock is more knowing. He knows, what any sensible person knows, that the purer argument *must* fail, that one who does not already know that the other's body "is connected with" sentience cannot be convinced by this argument, or rather cannot understand what it is an argument about, the existence of others. So Shylock, in noting his points of identity with other human beings in a series of rhetorical questions, is allowing that others of course do know all of these things about Jews — for example, about *him;* but he is denying (or further reminding us not to conclude) that knowing such things about him is knowing of his existence as a (an other) human being. Instead of asking the others to conclude, on the basis of analogy, that he exists as a human being, he is accusing them of using just this basis for just this purpose. He is turning upon the condition of analogy itself. (Hume's Philo, in his exasperation at the use, not at the invalidity, of an argument from analogy, does the same: "Why not become a perfect anthropomorphite? Why not assert the deity or deities to be corporeal, and to have eyes, a nose, mouth, ears, etc.?" (*Dialogues,* part V).) Shylock is saying: You people think I am *like* you. So then you think I am also *different.* And what is the difference? That my body is not associated with *your* sentience, that is, not with a sentience of Christ. If it were, what would you have found? That I am another you, made in your image. Well and good. I'll force you to be a perfect narcissist. I will perfect the analogy of my image with yours. I will take upon myself your sentience. — He, in effect, here prepares his punishment by conversion.

It seems undeniable that the play rehearses the confrontation, or replacement, of the Old Law by the New. (So far as I know, Nevill Coghill best expresses the idea in "The Basis of Shakesperean Comedy".) But Shylock's claim, as befits a Jew, is that the replacement never took effect, that the Christian's humility is merely a parody, or disguise, of the Jew's Law, Christian mercy merely vengeance disguised with passiveness; hence the Christian does not exist, Christianity never happened; the Messiah, which the Christian learned from the Jew to expect, has not yet come, or came to no effect. It is against the implication of this charge that punishment by conversion may be understood as specifically called for, used as specific refutation.

Shylock's speech upon analogy was prompted by the question, half rhetorical, whether he will demand his promised pound of flesh. So his speech, in affirming that he will, and in naming just this to be his revenge, and in claiming revenge to perfect his analogy, or identification, with Antonio, declares that he will be doing what has been done him. So he is telling us that he perceives Antonio's refusal of acknowledgment as mutilation — the denial, the destruction, of his intactness. His revenge thus speaks: You think my sentience can be at best merely like yours; you hedge mine. I'll show you that you can have exactly mine. And there is also the suggestion: There is no proof for you that I am a man, that I am flesh, until you know that you are flesh. For you to learn this will be my better instruction.

Of course it need not succeed. To Shylock's assertion "I say my daughter is my flesh and my blood", there is an answer: "There is more difference between thy flesh and hers, than between jet and ivory, more between your bloods, than there is between red wine and Rhenish" (III, i, 33–6). And the last clause helps suggest that there is an answer to this answer: Then I'll make the flesh mine by using it for food (". . . it will feed my revenge"). I do not see that imagining a literal incorporation of the other is madder than attempting to literalize, as in a more academic overcoming of skepticism one is impelled to try to imagine doing, the having of another's feelings, the direction to which is not imagining incorporating them (which seems just a way of imagining having them, which you can certainly do, in an everyday sense) but rather allowing yourself to be (re)incorporated, to be the other.

This is not, I think, as mad as things really get for Shylock. For where is the pound of flesh to come from? Where does Shylock wish it from? The question is pressed by the mysterious change from Shylock's original demand, to which Antonio agrees, that the forfeit be "cut off and taken/ In which part of your body pleaseth me" (I, iii, 146–47), to the bond as read by Portia before the court, that the flesh "be by him cut off/ Nearest the merchant's heart" (IV, i, 228–29). I do not insist that Shylock's proof — his better instruction — that Antonio is his *semblable* was (and psychically remains) to carve Antonio into a Jew, i.e., to do to him what circumcision, in certain frames of mind, is imagined to do, i.e., to castrate. I insist merely that the question rouses our horrified wonder that a pound, wherever it be cut from, would result in so complete a disfigurement, amounting to metamorphosis; and that this should not, as part of the anxiety in experiencing this revenge satire, be glossed (over) by the presumption that the change of the pound's location must have been "[stipulated] when the bond was prepared" (Arden edition, note at IV, i, 229). We need not assume that any such change has been agreed upon if we allow that a confusion of identities persists. For *which* merchant (of Venice) is picked out by the phrase "nearest the merchant's heart"? If this can be read as picking out Shylock, then it is equivalent to Shylock's original demand for the part that "pleases" him. (Though the ambiguity of the phrase may just be present even if a confusion of identities is not raised.) I do not say that this is the correct reading; I ask that a spiritual passage be conceived in which it is not known, especially in which Shylock does not know, what is being asked, what his satisfaction requires (what would constitute his "[having] the heart of him" (III, i, 117)); hence a passage in which the certainty of the others' professed knowledge of him is a measure of his invisibility to them.

A second, and an extended final illustration I choose, from which to study the imagination of the body's fate under skepticism, are equally familiar moments, and more or less familiar as a pair. I ask how it is that we are to understand, at the height of *The Winter's Tale*, Hermione's reappearance as a statue. Specifically I ask how it is that we are to understand Leontes's acceptance of the "magic" that returns her to flesh and blood, and hence to him. This is a most specific form of resurrection. Accepting it means accepting the idea that she had been turned to stone; that that was the right fate for her disappearance from life. So I am asking for the source of Leontes's conviction in the rightness of that fate. Giving the question that form, the form of my answer is by now predictable: for her to return to him is for him to recognize her; and for him to recognize her is for him to recognize his relation to her; in particular to recognize what his denial of her has done to her, hence to him. So Leontes recognizes the fate of stone to be the consequence of his particular skepticism. One can see this as the projection of his own sense of numbness, of living death. But then why was this *his* fate? It is a most specific form of remorse or of (self-)punishment.

Its environment is a tale of harrowing by jealousy, and a consequent accusation of adultery, an accusation known by every outsider, everyone but the accuser, to be insanely false. Hence Leontes is inevitably paired with Othello. I call attention to two further ways in which *The Winter's Tale* is a commentary upon *Othello,* and therefore contrariwise. First, both plays involve a harrowing of the power of knowing the existence of another (as chaste, intact, as what the knower knows his other to be). Leontes refuses to believe a true oracle, Othello insists upon believing a false one. Second, in both plays the consequence for the man's refusal of knowledge of his other is an imagination of stone. It is not merely an appetite for beauty that produces Othello's most famous image of his victim, as a piece of cold and carved marble (". . . whiter skin of hers than snow,/ And smooth, as monumental alabaster" (V, ii, 4–5)). Where does his image come from?

To introduce what I have to say about *Othello*, I want to give a final source for thinking of tragedy as a kind of epistemological problem, or as the outcome of the problem of knowledge — of the dominance of modern philosophical thought by it. (Cf. "The Avoidance of Love", pp. 320–26.) When I said just now that I wished "to understand how the other now bears the weight of God, shows me that I am not alone in the universe", I was claiming to be giving a certain derivation for the problem of the other. But I was also echoing one formulation Descartes gives his motive in wanting to find what is beyond doubt, viz., to know beyond doubt that he is not alone in the world (third Meditation). Now I ask, in passing but explicitly, why it is Descartes does not try to defeat that possibility of isolation in what would seem (to whom?) the most direct and the surest way, by locating the existence of one other finite being.

He says simply that he can easily imagine that ideas "which represent men similar to myself" could be "formed by the combination of my other ideas, of myself, of corporeal objects, and of God, even though outside of me there were no other men in the world . . .". He is setting up, of course, a powerful move toward God. And we can gather from this, something that seems borne out in the sequel of his *Meditations*, that the problem of others (other finite beings) is not discovered, or derived, by Descartes to be a special problem of knowledge; this is surely one reason it would not have been discovered to be such in subsequent epistemology. But the more one meditates upon the unique place Descartes makes for his relation to his own body, the less clear and distinct it is that he has available to himself the formulation of the idea of another body as having a unique relation to its mind in that special quasi-substantial way that he asserts is not like the way a ship is related to its pilot. But without such an idea what is the content of the idea of "men similar to myself"? I do not conceive of Descartes's appealing to the route of analogy here, since he must be far surer that other human bodies go with minds than any sureness he can extract by inferring from another body's behavior alone. After all, the body has essentially nothing to do with the soul! I might express his difficulty as follows. His sense of himself as composed of his contrary natures (of what he means by mind and body, the one characterized in opposition to the other, each essentially what the other is not) is the idea of a double nature, symbolized centrally in the culture we share with him (but perhaps now only in literature) as the figure of Christ. So the thing of incarnation, the mysterious meeting of heaven and earth, occurs in Descartes's thought not alone in the inspirer of Christianity but in each individual human being. From here you may conclude that the human problem in recognizing other human beings is the problem of recognizing another to be Christ for oneself. (What is the significance of the charge that Descartes proves the existence at best of a philosopher's God?)

In the light of this passing of the question of the other, a change is noticeable in the coda Descartes supplies his argument at the end of this third Meditation:

> The whole force of the argument I have here used to prove the existence of God consists in the fact that I recognize that it would not be possible for my nature to be what it is, possessing the idea of a God, unless God really existed — the same God, I say, the idea of whom I possess, the God who possesses all these high perfections . . . [who] cannot be a deceiver. . . .

The main point of summary is that I could not have produced the idea I have of God, for it can have come from nothing less than God himself. But a new note of necessity is also struck, that without the presence of this idea in myself, and (hence) the presence of the fact of which it is the imprint, my own nature would necessarily not be what it is. (Nietzsche's idea of the death of God can be understood to begin by saying roughly or generally as much: the idea of God is part of (the idea of) human nature. If that idea dies, the idea of human nature equally dies.) So not only the fact, as it were, of my existence, but the integrity of it, depends upon this idea. And so these meditations are about the finding of self-knowledge after all; of the knowledge of a human self by a human self.

That the integrity of my (human, finite) existence may depend on the fact and on the idea of another being's existence, and on the possibility of *proving* that existence; an existence conceived from my very dependence and incompleteness, hence conceived as perfect, and conceived as producing me "in some sense, in [its] own image"; these are thoughts that take me to a study of *Othello*.

Briefly, to begin with, we have the logic, the emotion, and the scene of skepticism epitomized. The logic: "My life upon her faith" (I, iii, 294) and ". . . when I love thee not/ Chaos is come again" (III, iii, 91–92) set up the stake necessary to best cases; the sense I expressed by the imaginary major premiss, "If I know anything, I know this". One standing issue about the rhythm of *Othello*'s plot is that the progress from the

completeness of Othello's love to the perfection of his doubt is too pre-
cipitous for the fictional time of the play. But such precipitousness is just
the rhythm of skepticism; all that is necessary is the stake. The emotion:
Here I mean not Othello's emotion toward Desdemona, call it jealousy;
but the structure of his emotion as he is hauled back and forth across the
keel of his love. Othello's enactment, or sufferance, of that torture is the
most extraordinary representation known to me of the "astonishment" in
skeptical doubt. In Descartes's first Meditation: "I realize so clearly that
there are no conclusive indications by which waking life can be distinguished from sleep that I am quite astonished, and my bewilderment is
such that it is almost able to convince me that I am sleeping." (It does not
follow that one is *convinced* that one is awake.) When Othello loses consciousness ("Is't possible? — Confess? — Handkerchief? — O devil!"
(IV, i, 42–43)), it is not from conviction in a piece of knowledge but in an
effort to stave the knowledge off. The scene: Here I have in mind the
pervasive air of the language and the action of this play as one in which
Othello's mind continuously outstrips reality, dissolves it in trance or
dream or in the beauty or ugliness of his incantatory imagination; in
which he visualizes possibilities that reason, unaided, cannot rule out.
Why is he beyond aid? Why are the ear and the eye in him disjoined? We
know that by the time he formulates his condition this way:

> By the world,
> I think my wife be honest, and think she is not,
> I think that thou are just, and think thou are not;
> I'll have some proof . . .
>
> [III, iii, 389–92]

he is lost. Two dozen lines earlier he had demanded of Iago "the ocular
proof", a demand which was no purer a threat than it was a command, as
if he does indeed wish for this outcome, as if he has a use for Iago's suspicions, hence a use for Iago that reciprocates Iago's use of him. Nothing
I claim about the play here will depend on an understanding of the relation between Iago and Othello, so I will simply assert what is suggested
by what I have just said, that such a question as "Why does Othello
believe Iago?" is badly formed. It is not conceivable that Othello believes
Iago and *not* Desdemona. Iago, we might say, offers Othello an opportunity to believe something, something to oppose to something else he
knows. What does he know? Why does it require opposition? — What
do we know?

We have known (say since G. Wilson Knight's "The *Othello* Music") that Othello's language, call it his imagination, is at once his, and the play's, glory, and his shame, the source of his power and of his impotence; or we should have known (since Bradley's *Shakespearean Tragedy*) that Othello is the most romantic of Shakespeare's heros, which may be a way of summarizing the same facts. And we ought to attend to the perception that Othello is the most Christian of the tragic heros (expressed in Norman Rabkin's *Shakespeare and the Common Understanding*). Nor is there any longer any argument against our knowledge that Othello is black; and there can be no argument with the fact that he has just married, nor with the description, compared with the cases of Shakespeare's other tragedies, that this one is not political but domestic.

We know more specifically, I take it, that Othello's blackness means something. But what specifically does it mean? Mean, I mean, to him — for otherwise it is not Othello's color that we are interested in but some generalized blackness, meaning perhaps "sooty" or "filthy", as elsewhere in the play. This difference may show in the way one takes Desdemona's early statement: "I saw Othello's visage in his mind" (I, iii, 252). I think it is commonly felt that she means she overlooked his blackness in favor of his inner brilliance; and perhaps further felt that this is a piece of deception, at least of herself. But what the line more naturally says is that she saw his visage as he sees it, that she understands his blackness as he understands it, as the expression (or in his word, his manifestation) of his mind — which is not overlooking it. Then how does he understand it?

As the color of a romantic hero. For he, as he was and is, manifested by his parts, his title, and his "perfect soul" (I, ii, 31), is the hero of the tales of romance he tells, some ones of which he wooed and won Desdemona with, others of which he will die upon. It is accordingly the color of one of enchanted powers and of magical protection, but above all it is the color of one of purity, of a perfect soul. Desdemona, in entering his life, hence in entering his story of his life, enters as a fit companion for such a hero; his perfection is now opened toward hers. His absolute stake in his purity, and its confirmation in hers, is shown in what he feels he has lost in losing Desdemona's confirmation:

> . . . my name, that was as fresh
> As Dian's visage, is now begrim'd, and black
> As mine own face. . . .
>
> [III, iii, 392–94]

Diana's is a name for the visage Desdemona saw to be in Othello's mind. He loses its application to his own name, his charmed self, when he no longer sees his visage in Desdemona's mind but in Iago's, say in the world's capacity for rumor. To say he loses Desdemona's power to confirm his image of himself is to say that he loses his old power of imagination. And this is to say that he loses his grasp of his own nature; he no longer has the same voice in his history. So then the question becomes: How has he come to displace Desdemona's imagination by Iago's? However terrible the exchange, it must be less terrible than some other. Then we need to ask not so much how Iago gained his power as how Desdemona lost hers.

We know — do we not? — that Desdemona has lost her virginity, the protection of Diana, by the time she appears to us. And surely Othello knows this! But this change in her condition, while a big enough fact to hatch millennia of plots, is not what Othello accuses her of. (Though would that accusation have been much more unfair than the unfaithfulness he does accuse her of?) I emphasize that I am assuming in Othello's mind the theme and condition of virginity to carry their full weight within a romantic universe. Here is some recent Northrop Frye on the subject: "Deep within the stock convention of virgin-baiting is a vision of human integrity imprisoned in a world it is in but not of, often forced by weakness into all kinds of ruses and stratagems, yet always managing to avoid the one fate which really is worse than death, the annihilation of one's identity. . . . What is symbolized as a virgin is actually a human conviction, however expressed, that there is something at the core of one's infinitely fragile being which is not only immortal but has discovered the secret of invulnerability that eludes the tragic hero" (*The Secular Scripture*, p. 86).

Now let us consolidate what we know on this sketch so far. We have to think in this play not merely about marriage but about the marriage of a romantic hero and of a Christian man; one whose imagination has to incorporate the idea of two becoming one in marriage and the idea that it is better to marry than to burn. It is a play, though it is thought of as domestic, in which not a marriage but an idea of marriage, or let us say an imagination of marriage, is worked out. "Why did I marry?" is the first question Othello asks himself to express his first raid of suspicion (III, iii, 246). The question has never been from his mind. Iago's first question to him is "Are you fast married?", and Othello's first set speech ends with something less than an answer: "But that I love the gentle Desdemona,/ I would not my unhoused free condition/ Put into circumscription and confine/ For the sea's worth." Love is at most a necessary not a sufficient condition for marrying. And for some minds, a certain idea of love may compromise as much as validate the idea of marriage. It may be better, but it is not perfect to marry, as St. Paul implies.

We have, further, to think in this play not merely generally of marriage but specifically of the wedding night. It is with this that the play opens. The central of the facts we know is that the whole beginning scene takes place while Othello and Desdemona are in their bridal bed. The simultaneity is marked: "Even now, very now, an old black ram / Is tupping your white ewe . . ." (I, i, 88). And the scene is one of treachery, alarms, of shouts, of armed men running through a sleeping city. The conjunction of the bridal chamber with a scene of emergency is again insisted on by Othello's reappearance from his bedroom to stop a brawl with his single presence; a reappearance repeated the first night in Cyprus. As though an appearance from his place of sex and dreams is what gives him the power to stop an armed fight with a word and a gesture. — Or is this more than we know? Perhaps the conjunction is to imply that their "hour of love" (I, iii, 298–99), or their two hours, have each been interrupted. There is reason to believe that the marriage has not been consummated, anyway reason to believe that Othello does not know whether it has. What is Iago's "Are you fast married?" asking? Whether a public, legal ceremony has taken place or whether a private act; or whether the public and the private have ratified one another? Othello answers by speaking of his nobility and his love. But apart from anything else this seems to assume that Iago's "you" was singular, not plural. And what does Othello mean in Cyprus by these apparently public words?:

> . . . come, my dear love,
> The purchase made, the fruits are to ensue,
> The profit's yet to come 'twixt me and you.
> [II, iii, 8–10]

What is the purchase and what the fruits or profit? Othello has just had proclaimed a general celebration at once of the perdition of the Turkish fleet and of his nuptials (II, ii). If the fruits and profit are the resumption of their privacy then the purchase was the successful discharge of his public office and his entry into Cyprus. But this success was not his doing; it was provided by a tempest. Is the purchase their (public) marriage? Then the fruits and profit are their conjugal love. Then he is saying that this is yet to come. It seems to me possible that the purchase, or price, was her virginity, and the fruits or profit their pleasure. There could hardly be greater emphasis on their having had just one shortened night together, isolated from this second night by a tempest (always in these matters symbolic, perhaps here of a memory, perhaps of an anticipation). Or is it, quite simply, that this is something he wishes to *say* publicly, whatever the truth between them? (How we imagine Desdemona's reaction to this would then become all important.)

I do not think that we must, nor that we can, choose among these possibilities in Othello's mind. On the contrary, I think Othello cannot choose among them. My guiding hypothesis about the structure of the play is that the thing *denied our sight* throughout the opening scene; the thing, the scene, that Iago takes Othello back to again and again, retouching it for Othello's enchafed imagination; is what we are shown in the final scene, the scene of murder. This becomes our ocular proof of Othello's understanding of his two nights of married love. (It has been felt from Thomas Rymer to G. B. Shaw that the play obeys the rhythm of farce, not of tragedy. One might say that in beginning with a sexual scene denied our sight, this play opens exactly as a normal comedy closes, as if turning comedy inside out.) I will follow out this hypothesis here only to the extent of commenting on that final scene.

However one seeks to interpret the meaning of the great entering speech of the scene ("It is the cause, it is the cause, my soul. . . . Put out the light, and then put out the light" . . .), I cannot take its mysteries, its privacies, its magniloquence, as separate from some massive denial to which these must be in service. Othello must mean that he is acting impersonally, but the words are those of a man in a trance, in a dream-state, fighting not to awaken; willing for anything but light. By "denial" I do not initially mean something requiring psychoanalytical, or any other, theory. I mean merely to ask that we not, conventionally but insufferably, assume that we know this woman better than this man knows her — making Othello some kind of exotic, gorgeous, superstitious lunkhead; which is about what Iago thinks. However much Othello deserves each of these titles, however far he believes Iago's tidings, he cannot just believe them; somewhere he also *knows* them to be false. This is registered in the rapidity with which he is brought to the truth, with no further real evidence, with only a counter-story (about the handkerchief) that bursts over him, or from him, as the truth. Shall we say he recognizes the truth too late? The fact is, he recognizes it when he is ready to, as one alone can; in this case, when its burden is dead. I am not claiming that he is trying not to believe Iago, or wants not to believe what Iago has told him. (This might describe someone who, say, had a good opinion of Desdemona, not someone whose life is staked upon hers.) I am claiming that we must understand Othello, on the contrary, to want to believe Iago, to be trying, against his knowledge, to believe him. Othello's eager insistence on Iago's honesty, his eager slaking of his thirst for knowledge with that poison, is not a sign of his stupidity in the presence of poison but of his devouring need of it. I do not quite say that he could not have accepted slander about Desdemona so quickly, to the quick, unless he already believed it; but rather that it is a thing he would rather believe than something yet more terrible to his mind; that the idea of Desdemona as an adulterous whore is more convenient to him than the idea of her as chaste. But what could be more terrible than Desdemona's faithlessness? Evidently her faithfulness. But how?

Note that in taking Othello's entering speech as part of a ritual of denial, in the context of taking the murder scene as a whole to be a dream-enactment of the invisible opening of the play, we have an answer implied to our original question about this play, concerning Othello's turning of Desdemona to stone. His image denies that he scarred her and shed her blood. It is a denial at once that he has taken her virginity and that she has died of him. (But it is at the same time evidence that in suffering the replacement of the problem of God by the problem of the other this man has turned both objects into stone, so that we might at this moment understand his self-interpretation to be that of an idolater, hence religiously as well as socially to be cast out.) The whole scene of murder is built on the concept of sexual intercourse or orgasm as a dying. There is a dangerously explicit quibble to this effect in the exchange,

> *Oth.* Thou art on thy death bed.
> *Des.* Ay, but not yet to die.
> [V, ii, 51–52]

The possible quibble only heightens the already heartbreaking poignance of the wish to die in her marriage bed after a long life.

Though Desdemona no more understands Othello's accusation of her than, in his darkness to himself, he does, she obediently shares his sense that this is their final night and that it is to be some dream-like recapitulation of their former two nights. This shows in her premonitions of death (the Willow Song, and the request that one of the wedding sheets be her shroud) and in her mysterious request to Emilia, ". . . tonight/ Lay on my bed our wedding sheets" (IV, ii, 106–07), as if knowing, and faithful to, Othello's private dream of her, herself preparing the scene of her death as Othello, utilizing Iago's stage directions, imagines it must happen ("Do it not with poison, strangle her in her bed, even the bed she hath contaminated." "Good, good, the justice of it pleases, very good" (IV, i, 203–5)); as if knowing that only with these sheets on their bed can his dream of her be contested. The dream is of contamination. The fact the dream works upon is the act of deflowering. Othello is reasonably literal about this, as reasonable as a man in a trance can be:

> . . . when I have pluck'd the rose,
> I cannot give it vital growth again,
> It must needs wither; I'll smell it on the tree,
> A balmy breath, that doth almost persuade
> Justice herself to break her sword: once more:
> Be thus, when thou art dead, and I will kill thee,
> And love thee after. . . .
>
> [V, ii, 13–19]

(Necrophilia is an apt fate for a mind whose reason is suffocating in its sumptuous capacity for figuration, and which takes the dying into love literally to entail killing. "That death's unnatural, that kills for loving" (V, ii, 41); or that turns its object to live stone. It is apt as well that Desdemona sense death, or the figure of death, as the impending cause of death. And at the very end, facing himself, he will not recover from this. "I kissed thee ere I killed thee." And after too. And not just now when you died from me, but on our previous nights as well.)

The exhibition of wedding sheets in this romantic, superstitious, conventional environment, can only refer to the practice of proving purity by staining. — I mention in passing that this provides a satisfactory weight for the importance Othello attaches to his charmed (or farcical) handkerchief, the fact that it is spotted, spotted with strawberries.

Well, were the sheets stained or not? Was she a virgin or not? The answers seem as ambiguous as to our earlier question whether they are fast married. Is the final, fatal reenactment of their wedding night a clear denial of what really happened, so that we can just read off, by negation, what really happened? Or is it a straight reenactment, without negation, and the flower was still on the tree, as far as he knew? In that case, who was reluctant to see it plucked, he or she? On such issues, farce and tragedy are separated by the thickness of a membrane.

We of course have no answer to such questions. But what matters is that Othello has no answer; or rather he can give none, for any answer to the questions, granted that I am right in taking the questions to be his, is intolerable. The torture of logic in his mind we might represent as follows: Either I shed her blood and scarred her or I did not. If I did not then she was not a virgin and this is a stain upon me. If I did then she is no longer a virgin and this is a stain upon me. Either way I am contaminated. (I do not say that the sides of this dilemma are of equal significance for Othello.)

But this much logic anyone but a lunkhead might have mastered apart from actually getting married. (He himself may say as much when he asks himself, too late, why he married.) Then what quickens this logic for him? Call whatever it is Iago. What is Iago?

He is everything, we know, Othello is not. Critical and witty, for example, where Othello is commanding and eloquent; retentive where the other is lavish; concealed where the other is open; cynical where the other is romantic; conventional where the other is original; imagines flesh where the other imagines spirit; the imaginer and manager of the human guise; the bottom end of the world. And so on. A Christian has to call him devil. The single fact between Othello and Iago I focus on here is that Othello fails twice at the end to kill Iago, knowing he cannot kill him. This all but all-powerful chieftain is stopped at this nobody. It is the point of his impotence, and the meaning of it. Iago is everything Othello must deny, and which, denied, is not killed but works on, like poison, like Furies.

In speaking of the point and meaning of Othello's impotence, I do not think of Othello as having been in an everyday sense impotent with Desdemona. I think of him, rather, as having been surprised by her, at what he has elicited from her; at, so to speak, a success rather than a failure. It is the dimension of her that shows itself in that difficult and dirty banter between her and Iago as they await Othello on Cyprus. Rather than imagine himself to have elicited that, or solicited it, Othello would imagine it elicited by anyone and everyone else. — Surprised, let me say, to find that she is flesh and blood. It was the one thing he could not imagine for himself. For if she is flesh and blood then, since they are one, so is he. But then although his potency of imagination can command the imagination of this child who is everything he is not, so that she sees his visage in his mind, she also sees that he is not identical with his mind, he is more than his imagination, black with desire, which she desires. Iago knows it, and Othello cannot bear what Iago knows, so he cannot outface the way in which he knows it, or knows anything. He cannot forgive Desdemona for existing, for being separate from him, outside, beyond command, commanding, her captain's captain.

It is an unstable frame of mind which compounds figurative with literal dying in love; and Othello unstably projects upon her, as he blames her:

O perjur'd woman, thou dost stone thy heart
And makest me call what I intend to do
A murder, which I thought a sacrifice.
                    [V, ii, 64–66]

As he is the one who gives out lies about her, so he is the one who will give her a stone heart for her stone body, as if in his words of stone which confound the figurative and the literal there is the confounding of the incantations of poetry and of magic. He makes of her the thing he feels (". . . my heart is turned to stone" (IV, i, 178)), but covers the ugliness of his thought with the beauty of his imagery — a debasement of himself and of his art of words. But what produces the idea of sacrifice? How did he manage the thought of her death as a sacrifice? To what was he to sacrifice her? To his image of himself and of her, to keep his image intact, uncontaminated; as if *this* were his protection from slander's image of him, say from a conventional view of his blackness. So he becomes conventional, sacrificing love to convention. But this was unstable; it could not be said. Yet better thought than the truth, which was that the central sacrifice of romance has already been made by them: her virginity, her intactness, her perfection, had been gladly forgone by her for him, for the sake of their union, for the seaming of it. It is the sacrifice he could not accept, for then he was not himself perfect. It must be displaced. The scar is the mark of finitude, of separateness; it must be borne whatever one's anatomical condition, or color. It is the sin or the sign of refusing imperfection that produces, or justifies, the visions and torments of devils that inhabit the region of this play.

If such a man as Othello is rendered impotent and murderous by aroused, or by having aroused, female sexuality; or let us say: if this man is horrified by human sexuality, in himself and in others; then no human being is free of this possibility. What I have wished to bring out is the nature of this possibility, or the possibility of this nature, the way human sexuality is the field in which the fantasy of finitude, of its acceptance and its repetitious overcoming, is worked out; the way human separateness is turned equally toward splendor and toward horror, mixing beauty and ugliness; turned toward before and after; toward flesh and blood.

— But Othello certainly knows that Desdemona exists! So what has his more or less interesting condition to do with skepticism? — [I knew you were still there. This is the last time we can meet like this.] In what spirit do you ask that question? I too am raising it. I wish to keep suspicion cast on what it is we take to express skepticism, and here especially by casting suspicion on whether we know what it means to know that another exists. Nothing could be more certain to Othello than that Desdemona exists; is flesh and blood; is separate from him; other. This is precisely the possibility that tortures him. The content of his torture *is* the premonition of the existence of another, hence of his own, his own as dependent, as partial. According to me further, his professions of skepticism over her faithfulness is a cover story for a deeper conviction; a terrible doubt covering a yet more terrible certainty, an unstatable certainty. But then this is what I have throughout kept arriving at as the cause of skepticism — the attempt to convert the human condition, the condition of humanity, into an intellectual difficulty, a riddle. (To interpret "a metaphysical finitude as an intellectual lack" ("Knowing and Acknowledging", p. 263).)

Tragedy is the place we are not allowed to escape the consequences, or price, of this cover: that the failure to acknowledge a best case of the other is a denial of that other, presaging the death of the other, say by stoning, or by hanging; and the death of our capacity to acknowledge as such, the turning of our hearts to stone, or their bursting. The necessary reflexiveness of spiritual torture.   — But at any rate Othello is hardly in doubt that he can ever know whether Desdemona is, for example, in pain (perhaps suffering heartache), and for that reason in doubt that she exists; so again his problem cannot match the skeptical one.   — But I ask again: Do we know what it is to be in such a doubt? and know this better than we know how to think of Othello's doubt? Moreover, is it even clear what it would mean to say that Othello does not doubt matters of Desdemona's consciousness such as that she has, or may have, some easily describable pain? If what he imagines is that she is stone, then *can* he imagine that she is in pain? ("Could one imagine a stone's having consciousness? And if anyone can do so — why should that not merely prove that such image-mongery is of no interest to us?" (*Investigations*, §390).)

Is the cover of skepticism — the conversion of metaphysical finitude into intellectual lack — a denial of the human or an expression of it? For of course there are those for whom the denial of the human *is* the human. (Cf. "Aesthetic Problems of Modern Philosophy", p. 96.) Call this the Christian view. It would be why Nietzsche undertook to identify the task of overcoming the human with the task of overcoming the denial of the human; which implies overcoming the human not through mortification but through joy, say ecstasy. If the former can be thought of as the denial of the body then the latter may be thought of as the affirmation of the body. Then those who are pushed, in attempting to counter a dualistic view of mind and body, to assert the identity of body and mind, are again skipping or converting the problem. For suppose my identity with my body is something that exists only in my affirmation of my body. (As friendship may exist only in loyalty to it.) Then the question is: What would the body *become* under affirmation? What would become of *me*? Perhaps I would know myself as, take myself for, a kind of machine; perhaps as a universe.

I conclude with two thoughts, or perspectives, from which to survey one's space of conviction in the reading I have started of *Othello,* and from which perhaps to guide it further.

First, what you might call the philosophy or the moral of the play seems all but contained in the essay Montaigne entitles "On some verses of Virgil", in such a remark as: "What a monstrous animal to be a horror to himself, to be burdened by his pleasures, to regard himself as a misfortune!" The essay concerns the compatibility of sex with marriage, of sex with age; it remarks upon, and upon the relations among, jealousy, chastity, imagination, doubts about virginity; upon the strength of language and the honesty of language; and includes mention of a Turk and of certain instances of necrophilia. One just about runs through the topics of *Othello* if to this essay one adds Montaigne's early essay "Of the power of imagination", which contains a Moor and speaks of a king of Egypt who, finding himself impotent with his bride threatened to kill her, thinking it was some sort of sorcery. The moral would be what might have been contained in Othello's ". . . one that lov'd not wisely, but too well", that all these topics should be food for thought and moderation, not for torture and murder; as fit for rue and laughter as for pity and terror; that they are not tragic unless one makes them so, takes them so; that we are tragic in what we take to be tragic; that one must take one's imperfections with a "gay and sociable wisdom" (in "Of experience", Montaigne's final essay) not with a somber and isolating eloquence. It is advice to accept one's humanity, and one can almost see Iago as the slanderer of human nature (this would be his diabolism) braced with Othello as the enacter of the slander — the one thinking to escape human nature from below, the other from above. But to whom is the advice usable? And how do we understand why it cannot be taken by those in directest need of it? The urging of moderation is valuable only to the extent that it results from a knowledge of the human possibilities beyond its urging. Is Montaigne's attitude fully earned, itself without a tint of the wish for exemption from the human? Or is Shakespeare's topic of the sheets and the handkerchief understandable as a rebuke to Montaigne, for refusing a further nook of honesty? A bizarre question, I suppose; but meant only to indicate how one might, and why one should, test whether my emphasis on the stain is necessary to give sufficient weight to one's experience of the horror and the darkness of these words and actions, or whether it is imposed.

My second concluding thought is more purely speculative, and arises in response to my having spoken just now of "the refusal of imperfection" as producing "the visions and torments of devils that inhabit the region of this play". I do not wish to dispute the evidence marshalled by Bernard Spivack in his *Shakespeare and the Allegory of Evil* showing Iago to be a descendent of the late morality figure of the Vice. I mean rather to help explain further the appearance of that figure in this particular play, and, I guess, to suggest its humanizing, or human splitting off (the sort of interpretation Spivack's book seems to deplore). It is against the tradition of the morality play that I now go on to call attention — I cannot think I am the first to say it out loud — to the hell and the demon staring out of the names of Othello and Desdemona. I mention this curiosity to prepare something meant as a nearly pure conjecture, wishing others to prove it one way or another, namely that underlying and shaping the events of this play are certain events of witch trials. Phrases such as "the ocular proof" and ". . . cords, or knives/ Poison, or fire, or suffocating streams . . ." (III, iii, 394–95) seem to me to call for location in a setting of judicial torture. And I confess to finding myself thinking of Desdemona's haunting characterization of a certain conception of her as "a moth of peace" when I read, from an 1834 study called *Folk-lore of the NE of Scotland*, "In some parts of Scotland moths are called 'witches'" (quoted in Kittredge, *Witchcraft in Old and New England*). But what prompts my thought primarily is the crazed logic Othello's rage for proof and for "satisfaction" seems to require (like testing for a woman's witchcraft by seeing whether she will drown, declaring that if she does she was innocent but if she does not she is to be put to death for a witch): What happened on our wedding night is that I killed her; but she is not dead; therefore she is not human; therefore she must die. ("Yet she must die, else she'll betray more men" (V, ii, 6).) Again he claims not to be acting personally, but by authority; here he has delivered a sentence. I recall that the biblical justification for the trial of witches was familiarly from the punishments in *Exodus:* "Thou shalt not suffer a witch to live." Othello seems to be babbling the crazed logic as he falls into his explicit faint or trance: "First, to be hanged, and then to confess; I tremble at it" (IV, i, 38–39), not knowing whether he is torturer or victim.

I introduced the idea of the trial for witchcraft as a conjecture, meaning immediately that it is not meant as a hypothesis: I do not *require* it for any interpretative alignment of my senses with the world of this play. It is enough, without supposing Shakespeare to have used literal subtexts of this sort, that the play opens with a public accusation of witchcraft, and an abbreviated trial, and is then succeeded with punctuating thoughts of hell and by fatal scenes of psychological torture, and concludes with death as the proof of mortality, i.e., of innocence (cf. "If that thou be'st a devil, I cannot kill thee" (V, ii, 283)). Enough, I mean, to stir the same depths of superstition — of a horror that proposes our lack of certain access to other minds — that under prompting institutions caused trials for witchcraft. *Othello* is at once, as we would expect of what we call Shakespeare's humanity, an examination of the madness and bewitchment of inquisitors, as well as of the tortures of love; of those tortures of which both victim and torturer are victims.

So they are there, on their bridal and death sheets. A statue, a stone, is something whose existence is fundamentally open to the ocular proof. A human being is not. The two bodies lying together form an emblem of this fact, the truth of skepticism. What this man lacked was not certainty. He knew everything, but he could not yield to what he knew, be commanded by it. He found out too much for his mind, not too little. Their differences from one another — the one everything the other is not — form an emblem of human separation, which can be accepted, and granted, or not. Like the separation from God; everything we are not.

So we are here, knowing they are "gone to burning hell", she with a lie on her lips, protecting him, he with her blood on him. Perhaps Blake has what he calls songs to win them back with, to make room for hell in a juster city. But can philosophy accept them back at the hands of poetry? Certainly not so long as philosophy continues, as it has from the first, to demand the banishment of poetry from its republic. Perhaps it could if it could itself become literature. But can philosophy become literature and still know itself?

Bibliography

Albritton, R., "On Wittgenstein's Use of the Term 'Criterion' ", in *Wittgenstein,* ed. G. Pitcher. Originally appeared in *The Journal of Philosophy,* Vol. LVI, No. 22, Oct. 22, 1959, pp. 845–57.

Anscombe, G. E. M., "On Brute Facts", *Analysis,* Vol. 18, No. 3, Jan. 1958, pp. 69–72.

Austin, J. L., *Philosophical Papers,* ed. J. O. Urmson and G. J. Warnock, Oxford, Clarendon Press, 1961.

Bate, W. J., *The Burden of the Past and the English Poet,* Cambridge, Harvard University Press, 1970; The Norton Library, New York, W. W. Norton & Company, Inc., 1972.

Bates, S. and Cohen, T., "More on What We Say", *Metaphilosophy,* Vol. 3, No. 1, Jan. 1972, pp. 1–24.

Bentham, J., *The Theory of Legislation,* ed. G. K. Ogden, London, Routledge & Kegan Paul Ltd., 1950.

Bergson, H., *Laughter,* in *Comedy,* ed. W. Sypher, Doubleday Anchor Books, Garden City, N.Y., Doubleday & Company, Inc., 1956.

Berkeley, G., *A Treatise Concerning the Principles of Human Knowledge,* in *A New Theory of Vision and Other Writings,* Everyman's Library, London, J. M. Dent & Sons Ltd., 1950.

Bradley, A. C., *Shakespearean Tragedy,* London, Macmillan and Co., Ltd., 1951.

Carnap, R., "Empiricism, Semantics and Ontology", in *Semantics and the Philosophy of Language,* ed. L. Limsky, Urbana, University of Illinois Press, 1952.

Cavell, S., "More of *The World Viewed*", *The Georgia Review,* Vol. XXVIII, No. 4, Winter 1974, pp. 571–631.

———, *Must We Mean What We Say?,* New York, Charles Scribner's Sons, 1969; Cambridge, Eng., Cambridge University Press, 1976.

———, *The Senses of Walden,* New York, Viking Press, 1972; Viking Compass Edition, 1974.

————, "What Becomes of Things on Film?", *Philosophy and Literature,* Vol. 2, No. 2, Fall 1978, pp. 249–57.

————, *The World Viewed,* New York, Viking Press, 1971.

Cheshire, G. S. and Fifoot, C. H. S., *The Law of Contract,* fourth ed., London, Butterworth and Co., 1956.

Clarke, T., "The Legacy of Skepticism", *The Journal of Philosophy,* Vol. LXIX, No. 20, Nov. 9, 1972, pp. 754–69.

————, "Seeing Surfaces and Physical Objects", in *Philosophy in America,* ed. M. Black, Ithaca, Cornell University Press, 1965.

Coghill, N., "The Basis of Shakespearean Comedy", in *Shakespeare Criticism 1935–1960,* selected by A. Ridler, London, Oxford University Press, 1970.

Cook, J. W., "Wittgenstein on Privacy", in *Wittgenstein,* ed. G. Pitcher. Originally appeared in *The Philosophical Review,* Vol. LXXIV, No. 3, July 1965, pp. 281–314.

Descartes, R., *Meditations,* translated from the Latin by J. Veitch, La Salle, Ill., Open Court Publishing, 1955.

Donagan, A., "Wittgenstein on Sensation", in *Wittgenstein,* ed. G. Pitcher.

Firth, R., "Sense-Data and the Percept Theory", in *Perceiving, Sensing, and Knowing,* ed. R. J. Swartz, Anchor Books, Garden City, N.Y., Doubleday & Company, Inc., 1965. Originally appeared in *Mind,* Vol. LVIII, No. 232, Oct. 1949, pp. 434–65 (I); Vol. LIX, No. 233, Jan. 1950, pp. 35–56 (II).

Foot, P., "Moral Arguments", *Mind,* Vol. LXVII, No. 268, Oct. 1958, pp. 502–13.

Frege, G., *Begriffschrift,* in *Translations from the Philosophical Writings of Gottlob Frege,* ed. P. Geach and M. Black, Oxford, Basil Blackwell, 1952.

Freud, S., *The Origins of Psycho-Analysis: Letters to Wilhelm Fliess, Drafts and Notes: 1887–1902,* ed. M. Bonaparte, A. Freud, and E. Kris; trans. E. Mosbacher and J. Strachey, New York, Basic Books, Inc., 1954.

Frye, N., *The Secular Scripture,* Cambridge, Harvard University Press, 1976.

Grice, P., *Logic and Conversation,* The William James Lectures for 1968. Delivered at Harvard University.

Hare, R. M., *Language and Morals,* Oxford, Clarendon Press, 1952.

Hegel, G. W. F., *The Introduction to Hegel's Philosophy of Fine Art,* trans. B. Bosanquet, London, Kegan Paul, Trench, Trübner & Co. Ltd., 1905.

————, *Philosophy of Right,* trans. T. M. Knox, Oxford, Clarendon Press, 1953.

Heidegger, M., *Being and Time,* trans. J. Macquarrie and E. Robinson, New York, Harper & Brothers, 1962.

————, "The Word of Nietzsche: 'God is Dead' ", in *The Question Concerning Technology and Other Essays,* trans. W. Lovitt, Harper Colophon Books, New York, Harper & Row, Publishers, Inc., 1977.

Hume, D., *Dialogues Concerning Natural Religion,* ed. N. K. Smith, Oxford, Clarendon Press, 1935.

————, "Of the Original Contract", from *Essays, Moral and Political,* in *Hume's Moral and Political Philosophy,* ed. H. D. Aiken, New York, Hafner Library of Classics, 1948.

————, *A Treatise of Human Nature,* ed. L. A. Selby-Bigge, Oxford, Clarendon Press, 1951.

Kant, I., *Critique of Pure Reason,* trans. N. K. Smith, New York, The Humanities Press, 1950.

———, *Foundations of the Metaphysics of Morals,* trans. L. W. Beck, The Library of Liberal Arts, New York, The Bobbs-Merrill Company, Inc., 1959.

———, *Religion Within the Limits of Reason Alone,* trans. T. M. Greene and H. H. Hudson, Harper Torchbooks, New York, Harper & Brothers, 1960.

Kenny, A., "Cartesian Privacy", in *Wittgenstein,* ed. G. Pitcher.

Knight, G. W., "The *Othello* Music", from *The Wheel of Fire,* fifth rev. ed., New York, Meridian Books, 1957.

Lean, M., *Sense-Perception and Matter,* New York, The Humanities Press, 1953.

Lewin, B. D., *The Image and the Past,* New York, International Universities Press, 1968.

Lewis, C. I., *Mind and the World Order,* New York, Charles Scribner's Sons, 1929.

Locke, J., *An Essay Concerning Human Understanding,* abridged and edited by A. B. Pringle-Pattison, Oxford, Clarendon Press, 1924.

Malcolm, N., "The Verification Argument", in *Philosophical Analysis,* ed. M. Black, Ithaca, Cornell University Press, 1950.

———, "Wittgenstein's *Philosophical Investigations*", in *Wittgenstein,* ed. G. Pitcher. Originally appeared in *The Philosophical Review,* Vol. LXIII, No. 4, Oct. 1954, pp. 530–59.

Mann, T., "Tonio Kröger", in *Death in Venice and Seven Other Stories,* trans. H. T. Lowe-Porter, New York, Vintage Books, 1954.

Mill, J. S., *Autobiography,* London, Oxford University Press, 1924.

Montaigne, M., *The Complete Essays of Montaigne,* trans. D. M. Frame, Stanford, Stanford University Press, 1965.

Moore, G. E., "A Defense of Common Sense", in *Philosophical Papers,* The Muirhead Library of Philosophy, London, George Allen and Unwin Ltd., 1959.

———, *Ethics,* New York, Oxford University Press, 1947.

———, *Some Main Problems of Philosophy,* The Muirhead Library of Philosophy, London, George Allen and Unwin Ltd., 1953.

Nietzsche, F., *Beyond Good and Evil,* trans. H. Zimmern, in *The Philosophy of Nietzsche,* The Modern Library, New York, Random House, Inc., 1927.

———, *The Genealogy of Morals,* trans. H. B. Samuel, in *The Philosophy of Nietzsche,* The Modern Library, New York, Random House, Inc., 1927.

———, *Thus Spoke Zarathustra,* trans. H. J. Hollingdale, Middlesex, Eng., Penguin Books Ltd., 1961.

Pascal, B., *Pensées,* trans. W. F. Trotter, The Modern Library, New York, Random House, Inc., 1941.

Pitcher, G., *The Philosophy of Wittgenstein,* Englewood Cliffs, N.J., Prentice-Hall, Inc., 1964.

———, ed., *Wittgenstein: A Collection of Critical Essays,* Anchor Books, Garden City, N.Y., Doubleday & Company, Inc., 1966.

Pitkin, H. F., *Wittgenstein and Justice,* Berkeley, University of California Press, 1972.

Plato, *Euthyphro,* trans. F. J. Church and R. D. Cumming, The Library of Liberal Arts, New York, The Liberal Arts Press, Inc., 1956.

Pole, D., *The Later Philosophy of Wittgenstein,* London, University of London, The Athlone Press, 1958.

Price, H. H., *Perception,* London, Methuen & Co. Ltd., 1932.

Prior, A. N., *Logic and the Basis of Ethics,* Oxford, Clarendon Press, 1949.

Putnam, H., "Robots: Machines or Artificially Created Life?", *The Journal of Philosophy,* Vol. LXI, No. 21, Nov. 12, 1964, pp. 668–91.

Quine, W. V., *Mathematical Logic,* rev. ed., Cambridge, Harvard University Press, 1951.

——, "On What There Is", in *From a Logical Point of View,* Cambridge, Harvard University Press, 1953.

Quinton, A. M., "On Punishment", in *Philosophy, Politics and Society,* ed. P. Laslett, Oxford, Basil Blackwell, 1956.

Rabkin, N., *Shakespeare and the Common Understanding,* New York, The Free Press, 1968.

Rawls, J., "Two Concepts of Rules", *The Philosophical Review,* Vol. LXIV, No. 1, Jan. 1955, pp. 3–32.

Ross, D., *Foundations of Ethics,* Oxford, Clarendon Press, 1949.

Rousseau, J.-J., *Essay on the Origin of Languages,* trans. J. H. Moran, in *On the Origin of Language,* New York, Frederick Ungar Publishing Co., Inc., 1966.

Russell, B., *An Inquiry into Meaning and Truth,* London, George Allen and Unwin Ltd., 1948.

Schopenhauer, A., *The Basis of Morality,* trans. A. B. Bullock, London, Swan Sonnenschein, 1903.

Searle, J., *Speech Acts,* Cambridge, Eng., Cambridge University Press, 1972.

Shakespeare, W., *The Merchant of Venice,* ed. J. R. Brown, The Arden Shakespeare, London, Methuen & Co., Ltd., 1969.

——, *Othello,* ed. M. R. Ridley, The Arden Shakespeare, London, Methuen & Co., Ltd., 1964.

——, *The Winter's Tale,* ed. F. Kermode, The Signet Classic Shakespeare, New York, The New American Library, Inc., 1963.

Shell, M., *The Economy of Literature,* Baltimore, Johns Hopkins University Press, 1978.

Shklar, J. N., *Men and Citizens: A Study of Rousseau's Social Theory,* Cambridge, Eng., Cambridge University Press, 1969.

Shoemaker, S., *Self-Knowledge and Self-Identity,* Ithaca, Cornell University Press, 1963.

Sidgwick, H., *The Methods of Ethics,* London, Macmillan and Co., 1874.

Snell, B., *The Discovery of the Mind,* Cambridge, Harvard University Press, 1953.

Spivack, B., *Shakespeare and the Allegory of Evil,* New York, Columbia University Press, 1958.

Stevenson, C., *Ethics and Language,* New Haven, Yale University Press, 1944.

——, "Moore's Arguments Against Certain Forms of Ethical Naturalism", in *The Philosophy of G. E. Moore,* ed. P. A. Schilpp, New York, Tudor Publishing Co., 1952.

Strawson, P. F., "On Referring", in *Essays in Conceptual Analysis,* selected and edited by A. Flew, London, Macmillan & Co. Ltd., 1956. Originally appeared in *Mind*, Vol. LIX, No. 235, July 1950, pp. 320–44.

———, "Review of Wittgenstein's *Philosophical Investigations*", in *Wittgenstein*, ed. G. Pitcher. Originally appeared in *Mind*, Vol. LXIII, No. 249, Jan. 1954, pp. 70–99.

———, "Truth", *Aristotelian Society Supplementary Volume XXIV*, 1950, pp. 129–56.

Stroud, B., "Wittgenstein and Logical Necessity", *The Philosophical Review*, Vol. LXXIV, No. 4, Oct. 1965, pp. 504–18.

Toulmin, S. E., *An Examination of the Place of Reason in Ethics*, Cambridge, Eng., Cambridge University Press, 1950.

Urmson, J. O., "Parenthetical Verbs", in *Essays in Conceptual Analysis*, selected and edited by A. Flew, London, Macmillan & Co. Ltd., 1956. Originally appeared in *Mind*, Vol. LXI, No. 244, Oct. 1952, pp. 480–96.

Wertheimer, R., "Understanding the Abortion Argument", *Philosophy & Public Affairs*, Vol. 1, No. 1, Fall 1971, pp. 67–95.

Wisdom, J., *Other Minds*, Oxford, Basil Blackwell, 1952.

Wittgenstein, L., *The Blue and Brown Books*, Oxford, Basil Blackwell, 1958.

———, *Philosophical Investigations*, trans. G. E. M. Anscombe, New York, The Macmillan Company, 1953.

———, *Tractatus Logico-Philosophicus*, trans. D. F. Pears and B. F. McGuinness, International Library of Philosophy and Scientific Method, London, Routedge & Kegan Paul Ltd., 1961.

Wordsworth, W., *The Prelude* (Text of 1805), ed. E. de Selincourt, London, Oxford University Press, 1964.

Index of Names

Index of Passages Cited
from *Philosophical Investigations*

Philosophical Investigations, Part II

DATE DUE